PRAISE FOR *SEPHER YOSIPPON*

"Bowman's work is a wonderful achievement of producing an English version of David Flusser's pioneering critical edition of the medieval anonymous *Sepher Yosippon*, merged with new breathtaking notes. This is an absolutely innovative and challenging accomplishment of a great connoisseur of medieval Hebrew Literature."

—Robert Bonfil, Emeritus Professor of Jewish History,
The Hebrew University of Jerusalem

"*Sepher Yosippon* is the major Hebrew source for Jewish Second Temple history. The translation by Steven Bowman enables everybody interested to delve into this highly important work that shaped Jewish self-understanding from the Middle Ages until the modern time."

—Saskia Dönitz, author of *Überlieferung und Rezeption des Sefer Yosippon*

"The book known as *Sepher Yosippon* is probably the very first book written in Hebrew on the continent of Europe, and it soon became one of the most popular and widely read Hebrew books. Surprisingly, it has never before been made available to English readers. Steven Bowman has done a great service to the wider public, as well as to students interested in Jewish history and literature, by producing this fluent and readable translation."

—Nicholas de Lange, University of Cambridge

"Steven Bowman has given us a readable and erudite annotated translation of the tenth-century Hebrew classic, *Sepher Yosippon*. Popular among Jews all over the world into the nineteenth century, *Sepher Yosippon* relates a consecutive narrative of Jewish history in the Persian and Greco-Roman periods, especially the Great Jewish Revolt against Rome. Bowman traces the variety of classical and early medieval sources; versions of the first-century Jewish historian, Josephus Flavius, and the Latin Apocrypha; and the ambiance of Byzantine Southern Italy, where this pseudonymous work was composed. It is a welcome contribution to our knowledge of this foundational text of Jewish historiography."

—Rivkah Fishman-Duker, lecturer emerita, Rothberg International School, The Hebrew University of Jerusalem

Sepher Yosippon

SEPHER YOSIPPON

A TENTH-CENTURY HISTORY OF ANCIENT ISRAEL

TRANSLATED AND INTRODUCED BY
Steven Bowman

Wayne State University Press

Detroit

ISBN 978-0-8143-4943-4 (paperback)
ISBN 978-0-8143-4944-1 (case)
ISBN 978-0-8143-4945-8 (e-book)

Library of Congress Cataloging Number: 2021951020

Published with support from the fund for the Raphael Patai Series in Jewish Folklore and
Anthropology.

Volume 1 of *The Josippon* [*Josephus Gorionides*], edited with introduction, commentary, and
notes, 2 vols. (Jerusalem: Bialik Institute, 1980–81), by David Flusser. First published in
Hebrew by the Bialik Institute, Jerusalem. English translation published by arrangement with
The Bialik Institute.

On cover: Page from Leiden 1 Maccabees manuscript / Codex PER F 17. Wikimedia
Commons. Cover design by Genna Blackburn.

Wayne State University Press rests on Waawiyaataanong, also referred to as Detroit, the
ancestral and contemporary homeland of the Three Fires Confederacy. These sovereign lands
were granted by the Ojibwe, Odawa, Potawatomi, and Wyandot Nations, in 1807, through
the Treaty of Detroit. Wayne State University Press affirms Indigenous sovereignty and
honors all tribes with a connection to Detroit. With our Native neighbors, the press works to
advance educational equity and promote a better future for the earth and all people.

Wayne State University Press
Leonard N. Simons Building
4809 Woodward Avenue
Detroit, Michigan 48201-1309

Visit us online at wsupress.wayne.edu.

CONTENTS

APPENDIX

ADDITIONS TO *YOSIPPON*

SELECTIONS FROM THE NORMATIVE VERSION OF *YOSIPPON*

GESTA ALEXANDROS

ACKNOWLEDGMENTS

I first met David Flusser as a Lady Davis Fellow at the Hebrew University of Jerusalem in 1978–79. In our telephone conversation, I congratulated him on his forty-year effort to present a scholarly edition of *Sepher Yosippon*, thus superseding the fourteenth-century edition of the text by Yehudah ibn Mosqoni, which I was then researching. He immediately invited me to his home along with my dissertation. We continued to discuss my work for the next twenty years, during which I enjoyed an intellectual feast of his vast knowledge. *Rav todot* to my companion and counterpart *ezer kenegdi* Yael Feldman, whose control of Hebrew language and literature as well as editorial experience has made many of my projects and this particular text more comprehensible. My thanks too to Aviad Kleinberg, who read through the entire text, applying his medieval expertise. Special thanks to Dan Ben Amos for his comments and mostly for shepherding the text through the press as part of his Raphael Patai Series. Many thanks to the many scholars with whom I have discussed the text, as mentioned in the notes. I am grateful to the libraries, institutions, and staffs whose hospitality and support over the decades have facilitated my research and study: the Hebrew University of Jerusalem, the Ben Zvi Institute, Hebrew Union College, the John Miller Burnam Classics Library of the University of Cincinnati, Indiana University, New York University, the University of California at Berkeley, the Jewish Museum of Greece, the Oxford Centre for Hebrew and Jewish Studies and the Bodleian Library at Oxford University, the Taylor-Schechter Cairo Genizah Collection at Cambridge University, and Wolfson College. Special thanks to the Judaic Studies Department at the University of Cincinnati, which succored me for over three decades, and to the Charles Philip Taft Memorial Fund at UC, which graciously supported much of my research and publications. Finally, I am most grateful to the Fulbright Foundation for its continued support of my career.

Steven Bowman
Cincinnati, New York, Jerusalem

INTRODUCTION

SEPHER YOSIPPON: AN ORPHAN CLASSIC

Sepher Yosippon (*The Book of Yosippon*, alt. Josippon, Yosifun) has been for over a millennium one of the most popular and influential books for Jews and non-Jews alike who consider it the lost work of Josephus Flavius on the Roman-Jewish war, a work that he claimed to have written for his own people in their language. The earliest date we have for this Hebrew masterpiece, 953 CE, is in an internal colophon by a copyist in a fifteenth-century manuscript of *Yosippon*, read over a millennium after Josephus's *Bellum Iudaicum* appeared at the court of Domitian, son of the emperor Vespasian, and his brother Titus, the conquerors of Jerusalem who destroyed the Temple in 70 CE (or 68, as medieval Jews calculated it).

The anonymous author of *Sepher Yosippon* had access, perhaps in Naples and other Italian locales, to a decent library of ancient and medieval material that he and his later editors gathered and translated and cobbled together in this first history of the Second Temple period since Josephus Flavius. The author's main sources were 1 and 2 Maccabees, found in Jerome's Latin Apocrypha to the Bible, Josephus's *Bellum Iudaicum* and books 1–16 of his *Archaeologies* (or *Antiquities*) of the Jews, and the fourth-century Pseudo-Hegesippus's Latin theological/historiographical polemic *De excidio urbis Hierosolynitano* (*DEH*; On the Destruction of Jerusalem), which was itself based on Josephus's *Jewish War*. He supplemented these basic sources with numerous Latin chronicles such as Jerome's translation of Eusebius, as well as Latin classics such as Virgil's *Aeneid*, Macrobius, Orosius, and later epitomes of Livy as well as midrashic allusions. For style he relied on Jerome's Vulgate Latin and the Hebrew TaNaKH. All this material and more, including Apocrypha, Late Antique (classical) and later medieval rabbinical midrash, and the new literature of the South Italian

Hebrew renaissance, was reworked into a first-class history in an elegant Hebrew style. This history, in its many secularized and translated versions, remained for centuries a most important national and religious source for Jews, as well as a key complement to Josephus for Christians and even Muslims.

Sepher Yosippon contains a history of Jews during the Second Temple period (sixth century BCE to the finale at Masada). The author begins his story with the family of nations (cf. Gen. 10) he compiled from the various travelers, diplomatic accounts, and other local sources that described the peoples of the tenth century CE. His second chapter introduces the theme of Rome and Jerusalem that he learned from Josephus and Livy and identifies Rome with the ancient rival of Edom through his biography of Zepho ben Eliphaz ben Esau, a Hebrew version of Herakles. He summarizes Rome's rivalry with Carthage, the career of Hannibal until his defeat by Scipio, and Rome's emergence as the conqueror of the western Mediterranean, which led to its victorious turn to the East. There the Roman Republic emerges first as the protector and ally of the Maccabees and Herod and later as the imperial conqueror and destroyer of Jerusalem and Masada. The author's treatment of the Maccabees is heroic, while that of Herod combines the panegyric of Nicholas of Damascus, Herod's prolific secretary, with the critique of Josephus to produce a picture that echoes the glorious but flawed careers of David and Solomon, the latter derived perhaps partly from Nicholas of Damascus and Josephus. The author's brilliant rhetoric captures the style of Pseudo-Hegesippus in the tale of the woman who ate her son and introduces a large corpus of Neo-Platonic themes that influenced his Jewish readers and interpolators. Among other additions, the interpolations to *Sepher Yosippon* include Pseudo-Kallisthenes's fabulous account of Alexander and reflections of early Christian fabulae of Jesus.

Abraham Conat summarized the contents of *Sepher Yosippon* in his introduction, which may interest readers today as it has for some five centuries:

> How all the families on earth dispersed by name according to their fathers, the wars of the Babylonians and the Romans, the wars of the Persian kings with the Babylonian king and how Belshazzar was killed, the story of Daniel's valor in the eyes of the Persian kings and the reason for his greatness and its consequences; twice he was lowered into the lions' den and how he was fed by the prophet Habakkuk; and how he destroyed the temple of Bel the major errant in Babylon and killed his priests and also how he killed the great dragon in the cave. Also the reason for the greatness of Zerubavel ben Shealtiel in the eyes of Darius king of Persia; the prayer to God of Ezra the scribe and Nehemiah ben Hakhaliah and Mordecai and Yeshua and the rest of the leaders of the Exile

for the strange fire, and how it was found since there was no priestly direction to offer up the strange fire. It also includes Queen Esther's story and her prayer, a most pleasant story, along with a lengthy history of Alexander the Great and his heroic deeds, beginning with Nektanibur the great magician, king of Egypt. It mentions by name and describes the grandeur of all the kings and caesars that were in Rome at the time of the Second Temple, as well as their love and their hate for the kings of Judah during the Second Temple. Included too are the great and terrible wars that began to break out among the people of Judah in the days of Antiochus, and the signs that were seen in Jerusalem and their consequences, and the holiness and fear of the Lord that Ḥannah sanctified with her seven saintly sons, along with the tale of Hasmonean bravery and the story of Ḥanukkah, and the record of all the kings who ruled during the Second Temple. He also tells the pleasant story about Herod's building and the gold vine that he set in our Lord's Sanctuary as well as all his exploits including the murder of his wife the queen and his three sons. This is followed by the affair of his son Antipater and his end, and many other pleasant stories, so numerous that I am wearied to recall them here. Finally, the valor of Joseph ben Gurion for God's people and His Sanctuary, and how he saved his life through his wisdom. Also his dirge over Jerusalem and the Temple of God and His people, as well as his rebukes of the men of Jerusalem in the days of Vespasian and Titus his son and his prayer to God, Lord of all the earth, and all that followed until the destruction of our Temple—let it be built and established quickly in our days, amen. Blessed be the living and awesome Lord on high who assisted me, Abraham, in completing the book, today, 49 of the reckoning [1489].

A tenth-century copy of *Sepher Yosippon* was made for the Sephardi Jewish leader Ḥasdai (ibn Shaprut). In southern Italy, Yeraḥme'el ben Shlomo included a copy of *Sepher Yosippon* in his late eleventh–twelfth century manuscript preserved in Eleazar ben Asher's *Sepher Ha-Zikhronoth* (Book of Records)—a major anthology of the early fourteenth century. A partial edition of *Yosippon* was excerpted by Abraham ibn Daud in twelfth-century Spain (critical edition by Gershon Cohen, *The Book of Tradition: (Sefer ha-Qabbalah) by Abraham ibn Da'ud* [Philadelphia, 1967]; and Katja Vehlow, *Dorot Olam: A Critical Edition and Translation of Abraham Ibn Daud's Universal History* [New York, 2013]); an expanded version of *Sepher Yosippon* was made by Yehudah ibn Mosqoni in mid-fourteenth-century Byzantium and later published by Tam ibn Yahya at the beginning of the sixteenth century in Ottoman Constantinople (1510). Abraham Conat published the first edition of *Sepher Yosippon* in Mantua 1475–77 based on Ibn Daud's excerpts.

The first modern edition was published by Baron David Guenzburg (*Yosifun: Kefi defus Mantovah . . .* [Berdichev, 1896–1913]) based on Ibn Yahya's edition. In 1978, two scholarly editions appeared in Jerusalem: Ḥayyim Hominer's fourth edition of a traditional version also based on the 1510 publication, with rabbinic annotation and an introduction by Rabbi Avraham Yosef Wertheimer (Jerusalem, 1978); and David Flusser's two volumes (Jerusalem, 1978 and 1980), the first scholarly edition to be based on manuscripts. An important critical review by Reuven Bonfil of Flusser's edition appeared in the major daily *Davar* (September 28, 1981, 12–14).

Translations of *Yosippon* were already available in the eleventh century, if not earlier, in Arabic (by Zakaria ibn Sa'id), in Old Russian, and in Slavonic. The Ethiopic version (ca. 1300)[1] was added to the Scriptures of that church. Ibn Khaldun provided a lengthy Arabic version of a Coptic text he found in Egypt in the fourteenth century; he commented that it was the only text available on the ancient history of the Jews after the Torah.[2] Sebastian Muenster published a partial Latin version of Conat's edition in 1541 (*Josephus Hebraicus* [Basle]), and an English précis of it by Peter Morvyn appeared in 1558 (*A Compendious and Moste Marveylous History of the Latter Times of the Jewes Commune Weale* [London]), often reprinted (Boston, 1718; Worcester, MA, 1805; Vermont, 1819); it became popular through its Boston publication in 1718 and was reprinted several times in New England during the early nineteenth century. A Yiddish translation by Michael Adam appeared in 1546. A revised Yiddish version by Menaḥem Amelander appeared in 1743, followed by a sequel covering the next millennium and a half since Josephus. A complete annotated version in Latin by Johannes Gagnier appeared in 1706, text by Johan Friedrich Breithaupt, *Josephus Hebraicus . . . Libri VI. Juxta editonem Venetam* (Gotha and Leipzig, 1710), and numerous modern language translations and excerpts subsequently. A Judeo-Arabic version appeared in the late nineteenth century. A scholarly Hebrew edition of the Arabic *Yosippon* appeared by Shulamit Sela (Jerusalem, 2009).

An English translation of the first section on the Maccabees of Yeraḥme'els eleventh-century recension of *Sepher Yosippon* was translated by Moses Gaster in *The Chronicles of Jerahmeel* (Oxford, 1899).[3] A recent German translation by

---

1. Murad Kamil, *Zēnā Aihūd (Geschichte der Juden) von Josef ben Gorion (Josippon) nach dem Handschriften herausgegeben* (Gluekstadt, 1937).

2. Ibn Khaldun, *Abir*, vol. 2 (translation in progress). See Ronnie Vollandt, "Ancient Jewish Historiography in Arabic Garb: Sepher Josippon between Southern Italy and Coptic Cairo," *Zutot* 11 (2014): 70–80.

3. For analysis of Yeraḥme'el, see Jacob Reiner, "The Original Hebrew Yosippon in The Chronicles of Jerahmeel," *Jewish Quarterly Review* 60 (1969): 128–46.

Dagmar Börner-Klein and Beat Zuber is interfaced with Flusser's Hebrew text: *Josippon* (Wiesbaden, 2010).

The pre-Flusser bibliography on *Sepher Yosippon* was compiled by Louis H. Feldman in his bibliographic volume on Josephus: *Josephus and Modern Scholarship (1937–1980)* (New York, 1984); this bibliography updates the entry in *The Jewish Encyclopedia* (New York, 1905), s.v. "Josippon." An extensive scholarly prolegomenon by Haim Schwarzbaum was prefaced to Gaster's *Chronicles of Jerahmeel*.[4] An update on more recent scholarship by Feldman appears in *Josephus, the Bible, and History*, edited by Feldman and Gohei Hata, 334–39 (Detroit, 1989). Subsequent basic studies include Albert Bell, "Josephus and Pseudo-Hegesippus," in Feldman and Hata, *Josephus, the Bible, and History*; and Steven Bowman, "Josephus in Byzantium," and Flusser, "Josippon, a Medieval Version of Josephus," in Feldman and Hata, *Josephus, Judaism, and Christianity* (Detroit, 1987); also see Bowman, "A Tenth-Century Byzantine Jewish Historian? A Review of David Flusser's Studies on the Josippon," *Byzantine Studies / Etudes Byzantines* 10 (1983): 133–36; Bowman, "Yosippon and Jewish Nationalism," *PAAJR* 61 (1995): 23–51. Scholarship by Saskia Dönitz includes *Überlieferung und Rezeption des Sefer Yosippon* (Tübingen, 2013); "Historiography among Byzantine Jews: The Case of Sefer Yosippon," in *Jews in Byzantium: Dialectics of Minority and Majority Cultures*, edited by Robert Bonfil, Oded Irshai, Guy G. Stroumsa, and Rina Talgam, 951–68 (Leiden, 2012); and her English summary "Sefer Yosippon (Josippon)," in *A Companion to Josephus*, edited by Honora Howell Chapman and Zuleika Rodgers, 382–89 (Oxford, 2016). An important update on Hegesippus in medieval scholarship is by Richard Matthew Pollard, "The De Excidio of 'Hegesippus' and the Reception of Josephus in the Early Middle Ages," *Viator* 46 (2015): 65–100, along with the ongoing publications of Carson Bay on the relationhip of *DEH* to *Sepher Yosippon* and his forthcoming translation of *DEH*.

The author of *Sepher Yosippon* is unique in his historical methodology, which helped him arrive at conclusions that anticipated the Jewish historians of the nineteenth and early twentieth centuries. The work of these historians—part of the Wissenschaft des Judenthums, the scholarly movement that represents the influence of German scholarship in the nineteenth century—offers an interesting modern parallel to the philosophizing influence of the Hellenistic period and the Christian influence of the Middle Ages. Yosippon was faithful to his sources—some of which are no longer extant—that represented sound medieval scholarship (as Flusser was able to test). His reliance on

---

4. For discussion and summary of pre-1960 scholarship, see Reiner.

Pseudo-Hegesippus's abstruse Latin and the faulty manuscripts he read resulted in a number of errors that have been preserved in this translation. The specialist is referred to Flusser's extensive Hebrew and Latin annotations in volume 1 and to his historical commentary in volume 2 of his Hebrew edition. A representative selection of Flusser's annotations appears in this volume's notes. For further reading, Flusser's essay "The Author of *Sepher Josippon* as Historian" (1973), reprinted in *Sefer Yosippon*, ed. Flusser, *Hanusaḥ Hamekori* (Jerusalem, 1979), 28–51, summarizes the major points of Flusser's enchantment with the author of *Sepher Yosippon*. His volume 2 of the scholarly edition contains a summary of his historiographical research; that volume's table of contents is annotated following this introduction.

Sepher Yosippon is a good read, which is probably one of the main reasons for its popularity over the ages, as attested by the plethora of translations into numerous languages throughout the medieval and modern periods. Its lively Hebrew language anticipates, in a way, Modern Hebrew and has provided numerous words and phrases to later Hebrew. Eliezer ben Yehudah plumbed the text for his *Thesaurus of Modern Hebrew*; see Yosippon's two statements by Matityahu the Hasmonean in chapter 16, for example, "Live and prosper," and *anshei shlomeinu* in chapter 42. Moreover, Abba Kovner quotes (with subtle adjustment) Matityahu's rallying cry for revolt (chapter 16). The book became a major influence on subsequent historical style and content for Jewish scholars for centuries. In sum, *Sepher Yosippon*'s author, as his modern editor David Flusser argued, may have been the only true "historian," in the modern sense of the term, during the medieval period. He devoted his story completely to the distant past, critically read his sources, and examined a wide range of materials that he adjusted to enliven his story (e.g., Virgil's *Aeneid* and the author's imaginary biography of Zepho in chapter 2).

The text chosen for this translation is the critical edition prepared by David Flusser based on the first scholarly comparison of the extant manuscripts, including Genizah fragments, and his extensive philological analysis of *Sepher Yosippon*'s sources. Whatever challenges have been raised regarding Flusser's dating and the interpretations he offered in his annotated commentary, his edition opened a new chapter in the study of this unique Hebrew text. It is also a monument to his philological and historical expertise and to his broad learning in Second Temple and medieval sources as well as modern scholarship. In addition, many of his notes include explanatory background and references to Josephus for his Hebrew audience.

Sepher Yosippon is part of a rich midrashic literature that runs the gamut from the historical and chronological commentaries of the Hellenistic period to the legal, ethical, and folkloristic material that saturates rabbinic literature. Midrash, a new term that appears first in 2 Chronicles (13:22 and 24:27), was translated in the Septuagint as "book" (*biblos*) and "writing" (*graphe*) (compare Herodotus's *istoria* as an investigation and a "history," and the Greek version of Ecclesiastes [51:23] *paideia*). Along with the two Talmuds, this postbiblical literature expanded and rewrote the biblical corpus as a tool to assist Jews to adopt and adapt to contemporary gentile challenges to the expansion of their own identity and cultural development. As the classic Roman statement of Terence put it, "nothing human is alien to me." So Jews studied everything as a potential source to expand their understanding of the Bible, the core of their national and religious history, using the panoply of intellectual tools of the period in which they wrote (classics, philosophy, mathematics, physics, and a host of nineteenth- and twentieth-century disciplines). Since God had created everything for the good by the word, so everything in our reality had to be examined and Judaized to the greater glory and holiness of that Creator and creation itself. Among Jews, the newly acquired Greek *sophia* merged with Hebrew *ḥokhmah* in a double helix of (holy) wisdom that continually redefines Western civilization.

Midrash became an ongoing project in tandem with contemporary developments of Jewish legal and moral precepts later codified in the Mishnah and Talmud and their ongoing commentaries. New materials too were translated and interpolated into older literature, just as the Apocrypha were added to the biblical corpus (see Yosippon's use of Apocryphal additions to the Scroll of Esther and the Book of Daniel, including Esther's prayer based on Asenath's conversionary prayer). Also we find the new literature generated by Jewish Messianists in the New Testament and the latter's own Apocrypha. So too the Greek and Latin popular literature of Late Antiquity was translated and interpolated into *Sepher Yosippon*, viz. the *Alexander Romance* of Pseudo-Kallisthenes and other interpolations such as Jerome's *Illustrious Men* and the coronation of the Holy Roman Emperor in 962, which was applied to Vespasian. These interpolations by later copyists from the tenth to the eleventh centuries have been isolated and translated in the appendices at the end of this volume.

The choice in this translation to transliterate the names rather than render them in modern English reflects one of Flusser's responses to his critics that the names are derived from the Latin of his sources and the Italian of the author's environment. The first mention of a name is accompanied by its more familiar form; thus, Kleopatrah (Cleopatra).

NOTE ON TRANSLITERATION

| ח | ḥ |
| צ | ẓ (occasionally ts) |

Sepher Yosippon and its derivative versions represent an ongoing exercise in the Jewish encounter with non-Jews, whose manifestation in all facets of intellectual endeavor has fructified and advanced our common striving to develop the mind and soul of the animated clump of clay that is our common ancestor, the first golem. And the tortuous path toward maturity of Adam's descendants during the period between the destruction of the two ancient Temples of Jerusalem was deemed a necessary addition to Jewish lore by an anonymous author toward the end of the first millennium of the Common Era. It is fitting that a new English version appears at the bridging of the second and third millennia. May it harbor better prospects for our common family of nations as they work through the vicissitudes of the present historical transitional period.

S.B. Rosh Hashanah 5783 / 25 September 2022

FLUSSER'S HISTORIOGRAPHICAL RESEARCH

Volume 2 of Flusser's magisterial edition of *Sepher Yosippon* summarizes forty years of his research on the text in its millennial eclectic versions and the scholarship to date of publication. Flusser's was the first comprehensive study of *Yosippon* based on the manuscripts and its influence on medieval scholars, and it remains the basis for all future research on the book. It summarizes his edition of the fantastic biography of Alexander derived from Pseudo-Kallisthenes with special attention to an unknown Byzantine Chronicle that he subjects to a full analysis of its sources and parallels. He also analyzes the later interpolations to the text of *Yosippon*, which are appended in volume 1. Volume 2 is, in essence, a well-ordered summary of Flusser's life's work on *Yosippon* and reflects his continued concern with the text even while he was drawn into the excitement of the newly discovered Dead Sea Scrolls. He devoted an additional distinguished career to the Scrolls and to their relationship to the texts of early (and later) Christianity that related to the themes and citations reflected in the Scrolls as well as the life and career of Jesus of Nazareth. This division of his research and publications necessitated a broad familiarity with Greek, Latin, and Aramaic as well as Hebrew sources including the literatures of the Talmud and midrashim along with all the polyglot commentaries of modern scholarship and its medieval predecessors. Flusser was well equipped with the medieval sources utilized in his notes to the text, as is evident in the translation.

A comprehensive survey of his attitude to Yosippon appears in his lengthy essay published in 1973 based on his lecture delivered before the Israeli Historical Society, titled "Josippon as Historian." But for now, it is the structure of volume 2 of his edition that I wish to outline here along with a brief survey of subsequent scholarship.

The volume 2 table of contents outlines Flusser's conclusions based on his earlier publications, two of which preface his publication of the Jerusalem manuscript of *Yosippon* dated 1282, one of the three main manuscripts of the Yosippon saga. Volume 2 is appropriately designated introduction.

Chapter 1: Versions of *Sepher Yosippon*: Section 1 relates the various editions beginning with the tenth-century version of Rabbenu Gershom, the Light of the Exile, the first and major scholar of Ashkenazi Jewry. Gershom's hand copy was copied by Rashi and supplemented in his classic commentary with the Byzantine midrashim he found in Ashkenazi yeshivoth where he studied. Indeed, *Yosippon* itself is a Byzantine product written by a South Italian Latin-proficient scholar, the first such Hebrew author who so used Latin sources. Ashkenazi Jews are descendants of Byzantine Jewish forebears who migrated from Italy to Ashkenaz (an early fourth-century Christian designation for the migrating Germanic tribes). He then details the three medieval versions: Version A, the Arabic translation of *Yosippon* (prior to Sela's work with Professor Moshe Gil, the necessity for which he had already called for in his publications), and the development of its Spanish background, specifically Samuel HaNagid and Ibn Hazm—Version B and Version C; the version of Judah ibn Mosqoni, its summary, and their relationship to the printed version of the sixteenth century. His argument is that *Yosippon* has been misunderstood due to reliance on corrupted printed versions that identified the book as authored by Josephus, when the early manuscripts (in particular Yeraḥme'els) clearly indicate that the author cites Josephus as well as the author. It was later copyists who perpetrated the error, which lasted for centuries. Such vicissitudes are not lacking in the history of scholarship.

Flusser's schema of redactions and their sources has been challenged and updated. A full survey of the arguments and their difficulties is available in chapter 2 of Yonatan Binyam's 2017 dissertation. To date, no one has dealt with the Syriac versions of Yosippon, which Flusser called for.[1]

Chapter 2: Circulation of *Sepher Yosippon*: *Yosippon* on the origins of Christianity in the interpolations; scholarly research for references to Jesus in *Yosippon*; translations of *Yosippon*; the *Yosippon* diaspora.

Chapter 3: Author's identification, his time and birthplace, based on Flusser's 1953 introductory article in *Zion*. There, in Flusser's initial presentation of his findings since first announcing his project in 1940, he proves *Yosippon*'s Byzantine South Italian background (already suggested by nineteenth-century Jewish scholars); the date of *Yosippon*—uniquely mentioned in a colophon of a fifteenth-century manuscript—and his times, the latter based on newly published Genizah material by Jacob Mann and other recent scholarship which he

---

1. See S. Ballaban, "The Enigma of the Lost Second Temple Literature: Routes of Discovery" (PhD diss., Hebrew Union College-Jewish Institute of Religion, December 1994).

had already published in Czech in 1948, his birthplace, and geographical data in *Yosippon*; the Jewish and non-Jewish background of *Yosippon*; the author's profession, already argued in Flusser's essay "Josephus as Historian" . . . was he in fact a physician or merely well read?

The 953 date has been challenged by a number of scholars (Bonfil, Golb, Sela, Dönitz, Binyam), who prefer a date in the first half of the tenth century on the basis of arguments regarding the Arabic precursors and additional Genizah manuscripts of *Yosippon*, which Flusser did not include in his edition.[2] One challenge, which I published in a review, raises a new question about the colophon that gives the date of 953.[3] In it, the translator uses the word *he'etakti*, which is usually rendered "I wrote"; however, the usage in that text, where it appears three times, has three different meanings: "I wrote," "I interpreted," "I copied." That raises the question of its usage by the French translator of the *Alexander Romance*: Did the copyist of the *Yosippon* in the Rothschild manuscript whose stemma Flusser traced back to the tenth century preserve in the colophon's *he'etakti* a clue to an original copyist of the tenth century and not to the author of the *Yosippon* before him? We know that a copy of the *Yosippon* was made in the tenth century by an agent of Ḥasdai (ibn Shaprut), which copy was stolen from him by robbers in Italy, as discussed by Golb,[4] although the site (Melphi or Amalphi) of the theft is difficult to decipher in the manuscript of his report.

Chapter 4: Author's literary output: the relationship of *Yosippon* to Josephus and the former's source in Pseudo-Hegesippus's *De excidio urbis Hierosolynitano*; other sources (most long known) used in *Yosippon* and his new discovery that Esther's prayer reflects the prayer of Asenath, the Egyptian wife of Joseph; the author as researcher; how the text was put together—seriatim (and most likely following his travels).

Chapter 5: Author's Weltanschauung: *Yosippon's* place in Hebrew literature; *Yosippon's* place in foreign literature, primarily Renaissance, and early Muslim scholarship (Ibn Khaldun's rendition of a Coptic version manuscript of *Yosippon* in his *Abir*); was Yosippon a "historiographer"—Yosippon as historian (Pseudo-Hegesippus was also designated as *historiographus*); author's political views;

---

2. See S. Bowman, "Dates in *Sepher Yosippon*," in *Pursuing the Text: Studies in Honor of Ben Zion Wacholder on the Occasion of His Seventieth Birthday*, ed. John C. Reeves and John Kampen, 349–59 (Sheffield, UK, 1994).

3. S. Bowman, review of *A Hebrew Alexander Romance*, by Wout J. Van Bekkum, *Journal of Jewish Studies* 48 (1997): 166–67.

4. Review of *Kazarian Hebrew Documents of the Tenth Century*, ed. and trans. Norman Golb and Omeljan Pritsak, *Speculum* 59 (1984): 474–45. See Bowman, "Dates in *Sepher Yosippon*."

war and faith in *Yosippon* based on papal exhortations of martyrdom in the wars against the Muslims invading southern Italy; religiosity of Yosippon—did he advocate *kiddush hashem* or merely copy his sources?

Chapter 6: *Sepher Yosippon* as a work of art: style and language of Yosippon; composition according to Yosippon; his sublime prose (the latter already noted by medieval professors at the Hebrew University in Jerusalem who taught specific passages, notably the description of the famous vine gifted to the Roman Senate and Pompey's awed praise of Jerusalem).

Chapter 7: The Alexander novel: Yosippon's version of the Alexander novel; the source of the first interpolation in *Yosippon*, Paladius on the Brahmans; the Parma version which Flusser published from his HUJ dissertation; the Hebrew Alexander novel and its tenth-century Greek source; the Byzantine Chronicle (a Genizah fragment is in the British Library in London, Flusser's בק). The two leaves indicate a Byzantine origin with interesting differences noted by Flusser in his "Variant Readings": the most interesting is the addition to the word "Armenians"—*they are Amalekites*. The tenth-century emperors of the Byzantine Empire were indeed of Armenian stock, which a Byzantine Jew would probably identify with the archenemy of the Jews, a tradition going back to the Book of Exodus. Here, then, we have a possible reference to the persecution of Romanos Lekapenos, if not Basil I (867–886). Also, many of the names are spelled differently from Flusser's version—the contribution of South Italian Jewry to Jewish culture.

Flusser's volume 2 ends with "Variant Manuscript Readings" and various indices to names (Hebrew and foreign) and places (Hebrew and foreign).

During the publication process of the two volumes, Flusser would frequently rush off from his home or office to the Bialik Institute for addenda and corrigenda to the manuscript and proofs, a tribute to his scholarly diligence, patience, and energy during his declining health. Flusser often mentioned that he looked forward to meeting the author of Yosippon and Jesus in the next world.

SEPHER YOSIPPON

I. TABLE OF NATIONS

Adam Shet Enosh Kenan Mehallael Yered Ḥanokh Metushelaḥ Lamekh Noah [1 Chron 1:1].[1] Noah sired Shem, Ham, and Yaphet. Sons of Yaphet: Gomer, Magog, Madai, Yavan, Tubal, Meshekh, and Tiras; and the sons of Gomer: Ashkenaz, Riphat, and Togarmah; and the sons of Yavan: Elisha, Tarshish, Kittim, and Dodanim.[2] Now the whole earth was of one language and one speech. As they traveled from the East, they found a plain, and they said one to another: "Come let us build ourselves a city." The Lord descended to see the city and the tower, and the Lord said: "Behold [they are] one people. Let Us go down and there confuse[3] their language." So, the Lord scattered them from there over the face of all the earth. Therefore, its name was called Babel.

These are the families of the sons of Yaphet and the lands to which they were dispersed according to their language in their lands among their peoples: the children of Gomer are the Frankos (Franks), who inhabit the land of Franẓa (France) on the river Signa (Seigne). Riphat are the Britanos, who inhabit the land of Britania[4] on the river Lira (Loire). The rivers Signa and Lira flow into the sea Okianus, which is the great sea. Togarmah are ten families[5] including

---

1. The chapters are titled using the modern names. For additional philological and historical comments, see D. Flusser, *The Josippon* [*Josephus Gorionides*], 2 vols. (Jerusalem, 1980–81), *ad locum*. In the notes, "[SB]" designates notes by the translator.

2. A general feature of medieval chronographers and of Jewish historians from Josephus to Joseph ha-Cohen (sixteenth century) was to begin with a Table of Nations based on Genesis 10, which introduced the idea of the family of humankind. [SB]

3. The Hebrew root is traditionally translated as "confuse," but the pun is on the name Bavel, which reflects the Hebrew root *bll*. Hence, I would prefer "babble" to "confuse." [SB]

4. Unclear why Rifat is identified with Bretagne.

5. For the following peoples, cf. entries s.v. in *The Oxford Dictionary of Byzantium*, vols. 1–3 (Oxford University Press, 1991). Shulamit Sela, *The Arabic Josippon* (in Hebrew), 2 vols.

Khuzar, Petsenek, Alan, Bulgar (Volga Turks), KhanBYNA,[6] Turk (TWRK), Boz (Ghuzz, Alghaz), ZiKhUKh,[7] Ugar (Ungar = Hungarians), and Tolmats.[8]

All these encamp in the north, and their lands are called after their names, and they camp on the rivers of HaTaL (Itil); while Ugar, Bulgar, and Petsenek camp on the great river called Danubi, which is Dunay. The children of Yavan are Yevanim (Greeks), who inhabit the lands of Ionia and Makedonia. Madai are Aldilam, who inhabit the land of Khurasan.[9] Tubal are the Toskani, who inhabit the land of Toskana[10] on the river Pisa (Arno). Meshekh are Saxani. Tiras are Russi. Saxani and Inglisi (Angles) dwell on the great sea; Russi[11] camp on the river KhYVA (Kiev)[12] that flows into the Gorgan (Caspian) Sea.[13] Elisha are Alamania, who dwell between the mountains of Yov and Septimo,[14] and they include the Langobardi, who came from beyond the mountains of Yov and Septimo and conquered Italia and dwell there unto this day on the rivers Pao (Po) and Tizio (Ticino). And among these [are the] Burgonia, who live on the river Rodano (Rhone); and of these BYORIA,[15] who live on the river Rheinus, which

---

(Jerusalem, 2009), notes to chap. 1, has a detailed commentary that argues an Arabic origin for many of the names. Flusser argues Italian origin. [SB]

6. Unidentified; variants KiNaBINA, KINNIA, RaNaBINA, KaTZaBINA. Sela reads the last as Kaspina, Byzantine Kaspion.

7. Unidentified; variants ZBDON, ZBUKH. My thanks to Dr. Michael Chlenov, who suggested the name may refer to the Zikh (Zukh), a clan name among the people living on the northeastern shore of the Black Sea between Sochi and Sukhumi. Sela suggests a tribe of the Cherkasim (*Arabic Josippon*, 130n31). [SB]

8. Turkic tribe in tenth-century Byzantine imperial guard.

9. Cf. *EI*, s.v. "Dailam" (Leiden, 2009). Khurasan is east of the Caspian Sea.

10. Cf. Jerome, *Commentary on Isa* 65.19; and *Quaestiones in Genesim*. Medieval legend has Tubal found Ravenna and Subria.

11. This is independent tenth-century support for the tradition that the Rus are Scandinavian in origin. Author's source knew that Scandinavian Teutons founded Kiev.

12. Ariel Toaff argues that this reference is to an earlier Kiev on the Volga. Toaff, *Cronaca Ebraica del Sepher Yosephon* (Rome, 1969), 6n. Kiev was the most important city of the Russians at the time. Benjamin of Tudela (1160s), who knew *Yosippon*, spells it KIV (Kiev?): Hebrew author consistently transliterates the Slavic *v* by a Hebrew *waw*; Arabic *kujabe*, Greek *kiova* or *kioáva*, Latin *Cuiewa* (or *Kitawa*), *Chiva, Chue, Kywe*. See "KYYOB" in Norman Golb and Omeljan Pritsak, *Khazarian Hebrew Documents of the Tenth Century* (Ithaca, NY, 1982), 12; see Sela, *Arabic Josippon*, 102n18. [SB]

13. Sela, *Arabic Josippon*, 102n18, notes the error of tenth-century Arab geographers (the river actually debauches into the Black Sea) who interchange the Black and Caspian Seas and argues a latest date of 945 for this *Yosippon* chapter. [SB]

14. Both are Alpine passes: Yov, medieval Mons Jovis (Grand St. Bernard); and Septimo, medieval Mons Septimus (Septimer, Passo di Sett).

15. Baioria (Byzantine Baiuria), Bairan in southern Germany, an important duchy mainly on the Danube.

flows into the great sea. Tiẓio (Ticino) and Pao (Po) flow into the Venetikia Sea. Tarshish united with Makedonia in one religion,[16] and from them came Tarsus. When the Ishmaelites captured the land of Tarsus,[17] its inhabitants fled to the border of the children of Yavan (Byzantium), and they fight against the Ishmaelites of Tarsus. Kittim [Gen 10:4; Dan 11:30] are [the] Romani, who camp on the plain Canpania on the river Tiberio.[18] Dodanim are the Danisci (Danes),[19] who live on peninsulas in the Okianus sea in the land of Danmarka and in Indania [i.e., in Dania, Denmark] in the great sea, who swore not to serve the Romans. And they hid among the waves of the Okianus Sea, but they could not [resist the Romans] for the Roman government reached unto the ultimate islands of the sea. And also, Morawa (Moravians),[20] Charwati (Czech Croats), Corbin (Lausitz?), Luẓanim (Lučané),[21] Laichin (Poles), Krakar (Krakow), and Boymin[22] are considered children of Dodanim; and they camp on the seashore from the border of Bulgar as far as Venetikia on the sea and extend unto the border of Saxani (Saxons) unto the great sea. They are called Sklavi (Latin Sclavi), and others say that they are the sons of Canaan [Gen 9:25],[23] yet they are descendants of the sons of Dodanim.[24]

---

16. Greek Orthodox Christianity.

17. Cf. *EI*, s.v. "Tarsus"; in 965, Emperor Nicephoras Phocas reconquered this frontier city, Muslim since the mid-ninth century.

18. Campania is not on the Tiber.

19. Early Germanic form *danisc* and not from *danskr*, *pace* the Danes. [Sela, *Arabic Josippon*, 104n45, reads this as a later addition to chap. 1 from Agripas's speech in chap. 60. SB]

20. On the following Slavic names, see D. Flusser, "Zpráva o Slovanech v hebrejské knonice z X. století," *Český časopis historický* 48–49 (1947–48): 238–41 (Russian summary, 594–96; and English summary, 611–13); also Zdenk Váa, *The World of Ancient Slavs* (Detroit, 1983), for archaeology. On the author's source as Slavic-speaking, cf. Flusser's note (*Josippon, ad locum*) and note 12 above to Kiev. Morawa: the Hungarians shattered the Great Moravian Empire in 904. Flusser refers to the Czech author's assumption that Yosippon's data for the Slavs was a ninth-century Slavic speaker. [SB]

21. Flusser suggests the Lučané from northwestern Bohemia near Žatec (Saaz) on the river Ohro. *Yosippon* is the earliest source to mention this tribe.

22. Bojmin; see Flusser's article in note 20 above.

23. *Yosippon* is the earliest Hebrew source to identify Slav with Canaan (meaning "slave"), later in Benjamin of Tudela.

24. Flusser suggests some Slavs were perhaps still under Danish control. The Russian chronicle *Povest let Vremennych* lists the Slavs as descendants of Yaphet. From text to note 9 until here, the genealogy of the sons of Yaphet is reprinted with variations in *The Chronicles of Jerahmeel*, trans. Moses Gaster (repr., New York, 1971, with Prolegomenon by Haim Schwarzbaum), 66–68. This section was added to *Jerahmeel* by the fourteenth-century compiler Eleazer ben Asher ha-Levi. [SB]

2. ANTIQUITIES OF ITALIA

When God had dispersed the sons of Adam over the earth, they divided into groups.[1] The descendants of Kittim united and camped on the plain of Canpania (Campania) and dwelt there on the river Tiberio (Tiber). The descendants of Tubal camped in Toscana, and their border was the Tiber. They built a city for themselves and called it Sabini[2] after the name of its founders. The Kittimites built a city for themselves and called it Foẓimagna.[3]

The Children of Tubal[4] boast over the children of Kittim, saying: "You shall not intermarry with us." When the Tubalites went to their fields during the harvest, the young men of the Kittim gathered and went to Sabini; they carried off their daughters and climbed up to Capo d'oglio.[5] When the Tubalites heard of this, they went to fight against them but were unsuccessful for the mountain was too high for them, and all the young men had assembled on the mountain. The following year, the Tubalites came again to fight against them, and the Kittimite youth raised the children [that] their daughters [of the Tubalites] had borne them above the wall they had built and said: "Have you come to fight

---

1. Cf. Gen 11:8–9. Author follows some unhistorical and lost medieval sources. The following notes are selective and do not correct here the historical errors of his sources.
2. No such city of Sabini; cf. contemporary Sabino.
3. Variant: Fochomagna and Fichimina. Hebrew Foẓimagna unidentified by Flusser. Cesare Colafemina kindly commented on my reading as follows: "If you read Foce Magna, this reading preserves also the letters of the text. Now, Foce Magna is the same as Fiumara Grande, the name of the Tiber at Ostia; the other arm of the river is called Fiumara Piccola. This identification, it seems to me, agrees with the succession of the story. Moreover, the Kittim, whose king was Usi, the father of Yania, lived nearby the Tiber." [SB]
4. The rape of the Sabine women is in Livy 1.9–13. [Compare Judg 19 end. SB] *Yosippon* places the story *before* the founding of the city.
5. Italian for the Capitolium in Rome: Capo d'oglio (top of oil) and preferably Campidoglio (fields of oil).

with your sons and daughters? Are we not henceforth of your bones and flesh?"
And they ceased from war.

The Kittimites further increased and built a city on the sea and called its
name Porto;[6] they built another city and called its name Albano,[7] and yet
another and called its name Aritsa.[8]

In those days[9] Zepho ben Eliphaz,[10] son of Esau, fled from Miẓrayim (Egypt).
It is he whom Joseph had captured when he went to bury his father, Israel, in
Hebron. The sons of Esau[11] had tried to stop him. But Joseph defeated them and
captured Zepho along with their best men [of the sons of Esau] and brought
them to Egypt. After Joseph's death,[12] Zepho fled from Egypt and came to Africa
to Agneas (Aeneas), king of Kartagini (Carthage).[13] Agneas received him with
great honor and appointed him chief of his army.

---

6. Porto (Latin Portus) is northwest of Ostia.

7. Albano is southeast of Rome.

8. Lat. Aricia; Ital. Ariccia is south of Albano.

9. Author merges two different traditions: Italy's first kings (Janus, Saturnus, Picus, Faunus,
   Latinus) with the three Italian-African wars: Aeneas's invasion to marry Lavinia, King Latinus's daughter (*pace* Virgil), the Punic wars (Asdrubel), and the wars of the Vandals (Guandali). These are telescoped in the family history of Aeneas (Agneas), his son (H)Asdrubal,
   and Zepho ben Eliphaz, who provides the link to biblical traditions.

10. Mentioned in Gen 36:11 and 16; also 1 Chron 1:37. All Hebrew MSS use the biblical Zepho
    except MS Jerusalem 8°41280, which was read as Zepher in the first mention of his name (56,
    middle). Subsequently Zepho in that MS conforms to the normative spelling Zepho (see
    56, two lines below). Hence Flusser suggests a *lapsus calami* (the published photograph of the
    MS indeed shows a smudge nearby) despite his continued comment that it is *not* just a *lapsus
    calami* since the Septuagint and the Vetus Latina use the name Sophar, which is well known
    from Job 1:11. [See Sh. Sela, "The Genealogy of Sefo ben Elifaz . . . ," in *Genizah Research after
    Ninety Years: The Case of Judaeo-Arabic*, ed. Joshua Blau and Stefan C. Reif (Cambridge, UK,
    1992), 138–43. My examination of the MS itself, however, shows clearly a *waw* with a small
    worm hole that could suggest a *resh* to an inattentive reader. The important point to emphasize
    is the reading ZPhR does not appear in any early MS and hence the name is always ZPhO. SB]

11. Cf. Y. Baer, "The Hebrew Sepher Yosifun," in *Sepher Dinaburg*, ed. Y. Baer, Y. Gutman,
    and M. Schwabe (Jerusalem, 1960), 181–82n1.4; and summary of story in L. Ginzberg,
    Legends of the Jews, 2.155–66; 5.37nn1–3. [Zepho has a major biography in *Sepher Haya-
    shar* (recently identified as eleventh-century southern Italy) based in part on *Yosippon*. SB]

12. Zepho's tale elucidates the Jewish tradition that connects Rome with Esau (= Edom in later
    rabbinic literature). Zepho as ancestor of Roman kings is mentioned by the Arab author
    Hamza al-Isphahani (d. ca. 970); see G. Levi della Vida, "The Bronze Age in Moslem Spain,"
    Journal of the American Oriental Society 63 (1943): 183–91. Since Sophar appears in the LXX
    and the Vulgate, the tale derives from Christian sources, and whereas Yosippon also uses
    Sophar, it is likely that his source was also Christian close to Hamza's. [See previous note. SB]

13. Aeneas's invasion of Rome from his kingdom in Carthage is quite different from ancient
    tradition that he sojourned in Carthage before becoming ancestor of the Romans. Flusser

In those days, there was in the land of Kittim in the city Foẓimagna a man called Uẓi;[14] he had become a false god for the Kittimites. Uẓi died without a son, but he left one daughter, whose name was Yaniah,[15] beautiful and very wise; her beauty was unmatched throughout the land. Agneas, king of Africa, asked for her in marriage. Turnus, king of Benevento,[16] also asked for her. But the inhabitants of Foẓimagna told Turnus: "We cannot give her to you because Agneas king of Africa seeks her, and should he wage war against us, you could not save us from him." They sent a letter to Agneas saying this, and he mustered his armies and came to the island of Sardinia,[17] for his brother Lukhus[18] was there. Pallas, his brother's son, went out to greet him and said to him: "When you ask my father for an army to assist you, ask him to appoint me head of the army." Agneas did so, he came by ship to the port of Astura,[19] and Turnus went out to confront him. A very great battle was waged in the valley of Canpania, in which his nephew Pallas fell. Agneas, his uncle, embalmed him and made him a golden *golem* [sarcophagus] and placed him inside. He [Agneas] waged another battle, captured Turnus, king of Benevento, and killed him. He made him a copper *golem*, put him inside, and built over it a tower at the crossroads. Also, for Pallas, his nephew, he built a tall tower over [his grave] on the crossroads and called it Tor(re) Pallas. Both are on the crossroads between Albano and Roma with the [via Appia] pavement between them, Tor(re) Pallas on one side and Loco Turnus on the other unto this day. Then Agneas took Yaniah to wife and returned to his land.

From that day hence, the Guandali (Vandals),[20] the African king's troops, began to invade the land of Kittim to plunder and rob, and Zepho always came with them. Zepho ben Eliphaz fled from Africa and entered the land of Kittim.

---

argues that the form "Agneas" derives from confusion of the letter *e* with *g*, which resemble each other in uncials. [Sela argues it is an Arabism where the letter *ayin* is transposed by the Hebrew *gimel*. SB].

14. Uẓi represents Aeneas's son-in-law Latinus, the father of the Latins and Romans; Uẓi is based on Utz = Edom (Gen 30:30; Lam 4:21) and by extension Uẓi = Roman, and Utz is also used for Romi in medieval *piyyutim* as Y. Baer found in L. Zunz's classic *Die Synagogale Poesie des Mittelalters* (Frankfurt a M., 1920), 455.

15. Yaniah is Lavinia, Latinus's daughter and Aeneas's wife; cf. Yanus (= Janus).

16. Yosippon or his source substitutes the better-known Beneventum (in Campania) for Virgil's unknown Laurentum.

17. Virgil writes Sicily. Flusser suggests a possible Vandal invasion of Sardinia in 455.

18. Misreading of *in luco* (*Aeneid* 8.104) as a proper name; see Euander (*Aeneid* 8.134–42).

19. Hebrew *maḥoẓ* is standard in *Yosippon*, also *Megillat Aḥimaaẓ*. Astura is south of Antium.

20. "Guandali" is Italian form. These tribes appeared in the fifth and sixth centuries, eventually in Africa in their capital of Carthage.

The Kittimites received him with great honor and gave him great gifts, which made him exceedingly rich. When the African hosts invaded the land of Kittim, the Kittimites assembled on Mount Capitolio out of fear of the Vandal hordes.

One day[21] a bull of Zepho's herd went astray. Seeking the bull, he heard its bellowing in the vicinity near the mountain. Zepho went, and, behold, at the base of the mountain was a cave with a large rock at the mouth of the cave. He smashed the rock into pieces, and, behold, a huge creature was eating the bull. Its lower half was the image of a man and the upper half the image of a he-goat.[22] Zepho leaped upon it and cut off its head. The Kittimites said: "What shall we do for this man who killed the creature that ate our cattle?" They agreed to make a festival for him one day each year and call that day after his name.[23] They would pour libations before him on that day and bring him offerings. And it was so done. They called that day the Janus festival, and they called Zepho "Janus" from the name of the creature that he killed.

The Vandal hordes continued to invade the land of Kittim to plunder as ever. Janus went out to confront them; he smote them, causing them to flee, and saved the land from their oppression. The Kittimites assembled and made Zepho king over them. The Kittimites went forth to conquer the Tubalites and the nations around them, and Janus, their king, led them in conquest. They called Zepho by the name Janus after the creature and also Saturnus from the star that they worshiped in those days, that is, the star Shabbtai. He reigned first in the plain of Canpania in the land of Kittim and built a very large palace and reigned over all Kittim and over all the land of Italy. Janus Saturnus reigned for fifty-five years. He died and was buried in the city of Genova.[24]

When Janus Saturnus died, Picus Faunus[25] reigned after him for fifty years, and he too built a very huge palace in the plain of Canpania. When Picus Faunus

---

21. Here Zepho replaces Heracles, who killed the cattle thief Cacus near Rome (*Aeneid* 8.185–275), as already noted by Gagnier in his Latin translation (Oxford, 1706), 4; and by Breithaupt in his 1710 Hebrew edition, 13n25. [Cf. J. P. Small, *Cacus and Marsyas in Etrusco-Roman Legend* (Princeton, NJ, 1982). SB].

22. This description of Cacus is a medieval expansion of Virgil's *semihomo* (*Aeneid* 8.194). Cf. Roman sacrifice of a he-goat to Janus.

23. The monster was called Janus and therefore its destroyer, Zepho, absorbed the name. Cf. Talmudic story in *y. Avodah Zarah* 1. The author has merged the holiday of Hercules with the holiday of Janus (Janus is called *geminus* = twin in Latin) on January the first. See note 21.

24. Medieval Latin legend that Janus founded Janua.

25. Picus and Faunus were two kings. The dates for the Roman kings follow Jerome, *Chronicle* (2005), 100. [Available at https://tertullian.org/fathers/jerome_chronicle_03_part2 .htm. SB]

died, Latinus[26] reigned after him; he clarified the Latin language and its letters. He too built a palace for himself. He made many ships and went to war against Asdrubel (Hasdrubal), son of Agneas, whom Yaniah bore to him.[27] He wished to take his daughter to wife by force just as Agneas had done to the Kittimites when he took Yaniah from them in war. Now Aspeciosa,[28] Asdrubal's daughter, was very beautiful. Her contemporaries embroidered her figure on their clothing because of her great beauty. A great war occurred between Asdrubal, king of Carthage, and Latinus, king of Kittim. Latinus captured their aqueduct that Agneas had brought them when he took Yaniah to Carthage.

Yaniah had taken sick, and her illness was hard on Agneas and his magnates. Agneas said to his wise men: "How shall I heal Yaniah's sickness?" His sages replied: "The air of our land is not like the air of the land of Kittim, nor is our water like their water. The queen became ill because of the change in air and water, for in her land she only drank water brought from *forma(e)*,[29] which her ancestors brought on aqueducts." So Agneas commanded that they bring *forma(e)* water from Kittim in a vessel, and they tested that water with all the waters of Africa. They found the water of Gukar[30] to be similar compared to them. Agneas commanded his magnates to collect hewers of stone by the thousands and myriads, and they cut stone without measure for building. The builders were very numerous and constructed a very huge aqueduct[31] from the spring of water unto Carthage, and these waters suited Yaniah for her needs: to drink, to bake, to do laundry, to wash, and to rinse every seed she ate. They also brought soil from Kittim in many ships along with stones and bricks. And with these they built palaces for her. All this they did from their great love for her. They used her magic to foretell the future and acquired blessing through her, and she became

---

26. Faunus's son identified above as Uẓi.

27. Johannes Codagnellus (thirteenth century) relates that Dido, wife of Aeneas, bore him two sons, Muyminus and Adriabal. The first name is Arabic and reflects Ishmaelite conquest of Africa; the second recalls Hasdrubal.

28. Apparently Yosippon's Latin MS had *speciosa* = beautiful, and the author understood the second word as the name of the daughter. J. Wellhausen, *Der arabische Josippus* (Berlin, 1897) [henceforth Wellhausen] identifies her as Sophoniba, daughter of Hasdrubal, son of Gisagon. [See Livy 30.12.11, 15.4, for the two Numidian kings who loved her.] Hence we cannot accept Wellhausen's correction of the name, but it is possible that this story echoes this woman.

29. In fifth-century Sidonius, *Ep.* 1.5.9, *formae* refers to the water pipes in the aqueducts.

30. Zucchara (modern Ein Gukr). The Arabic translation, other editions of *Yosippon*, and the commentary to *Chronicles* attributed to Rashi (at 1 Chron 11:17) misunderstood the phrase "waters of Gukr," and so the aqueduct stretched from Rome to Carthage.

31. 132 kilometers.

a goddess for them. When Latinus fought with Asdrubal and destroyed part of the aqueduct,[32] the Vandals were filled with zeal and spilled out their souls unto death; Asdrubal was killed in that battle. Then Latinus took Aspeciosa his [Asdrubal's] daughter to be wife and brought her to Kittim. Latinus ruled mightily, and the years of his reign were forty-five.

When Latinus died, Aeneas[33] ruled after him for three years. When Aeneas died, Ascanius (Ascianus)[34] ruled after him thirty-eight years, and he too built a large palace.[35] When Ascanius died, Silvius ruled after him twenty-nine years and built a large palace. When Silvius died, Latinus[36] ruled after him for fifty years. He fought with Alemania and Burgonia, sons of Elisha, and placed them under corvée. When he returned, he built himself a temple, Luẓiferi, which is Nogah (= Venus), the morning star, and he closed the temple of Saturnus, i.e., Shabbtai, and he brought its priests in fire upon the altar of Luẓiferi. When Latinus died, Aeneas Troianus[37] ruled after him thirty-six years. He too built a palace for his dwelling. When Aeneas Troianus died, Alba ruled after him thirty-nine years. When Alba died, Aviẓius (Aegyptus Silvius) ruled after him for twenty-four years and built a palace. When Aviẓius died, Capys ruled after him for twenty-eight years and built a palace. When Capys died, Carpento ruled after him for thirteen years and built a palace. When Carpento died, Tiberinus (Tiberius) ruled after him for eight years. When Tiberius died, Agrippa ruled after him for forty years and built a palace. When Agrippa died, Remulus ruled after him for nineteen years and built palaces. When Remulus died, Aventinus ruled after him for thirty-seven years. He fought against the sons of Riphat, who live on the river Lira (Loire), and against the sons of Turnus,[38] who live in Turonia on the river Lire. These too had fled from Agneas king of Africa[39] and built Turnus and Anbaza,[40] Aventinus subdued them and built a large palace

---

32. In 533 during Belisarius's reconquest, Gelimer, the last Vandal king, damaged the aqueduct (Procopius, *Vand.*, 2.1.2); Belisarius took him into captivity.

33. Above *Agneas*. King list is based on Jerome, *Chronicle* (2005), 100.

34. "Ascanius" in our published text. Flusser avers, however, that all MSS contain "Ascianus" and suggests this was in the author's Latin MS.

35. The author uses *heikhal* for both palace and temple.

36. Latinus Silvius follows Aeneas Silvius in Jerome's *Chronicle*, where he says he found the order reversed in one of his sources.

37. I.e., Aeneas of Troy; Yosippon follows his unknown source.

38. See H. Gross, *Gallia Judaica* (Paris, 1897), 216–18, for Tours.

39. Both the *Historia Brittonum* and *Yosippon*, using a similar source, relate that Brutus, Aeneas's grandson founded Tours (in some MSS Turnis or Turnus, as in *Yosippon*). Later he came to Britania, subsequently named after him.

40. Anbaza-Ambasia-Amboise; cf. Gross, *Gallia Judaica*, 62.

for his dwelling. When Aventinus died, Procas ruled after him for twenty-three years. When Procas died, Amulius ruled after him for forty-three years.

When Amulius died, Romulus ruled after him for thirty-eight years. In his days David smote Aram and Edom. Hadarezer and his sons fled and came to the land of Kittim. He gave them a site on the seashore and a place on the mountain. They built there a city and called her name Zorrento (Sorrento) after Zor,[41] from the clan of Hadarezer, who fled David. They also built for themselves the city of Ancient Albano[42] and dwelt there until this day. But a spring of oil welled up within the city Zorrento, and for many years the city sank and was covered by the sea; it is now between Napoli and New Zorrento. Nevertheless, this spring did not cease, for until now oil bubbles and floats atop the seawater, and the inhabitants of Napoli still collect it. Romulus had a great fear of David and built a wall around all the buildings of the kings who reigned before him. He placed all the temples and hills around [the city] within the wall, the circumference of which was forty-five miles, and he named the city Roma after his name, Romulus. They lived in great fear all the days of David. [Romulus] magnified the name of the Kittimites, who are called Romani from the name of the city unto this day. He built a giant temple to Jovis (Jupiter), which is the star Zedek (= Jupiter), making the fifth day a festival for Jovis, and he closed the temple of Luziferi. Romulus waged many wars, and there was a treaty between him and David.

When Romulus died, Ponpilius (Numa Pompilius) ruled after him for forty-one years.[43] When Numa Pompilius died, Tulius Ostilius (Tullius Hostilius) ruled after him for thirty-two years. When Tullius Hostilius died, Acus (Ancus) Marzius ruled after him for twenty-two years. When Ancus Marzius died, Tarquinius Priscus ruled after him for thirty-seven years. When Tarquinius Priscus died, Servius ruled after him for thirty-four years. When Servius died, Tarquinius ruled after him for thirty-five years. This Tarquinius[44] lusted after one of the women of Roma, but she was married so he took her by force. The woman was distressed and thrust a knife into her abdomen and died. Her brothers and her husband rose up and hid in ambush in the temple of Jovis. When Tarquinius came to worship in the temple of Jovis, the woman's brothers and her husband fell upon him suddenly with drawn swords and killed him. On that day, the Romans swore an oath that no king would rule over them in Roma. They chose

41. Latin of 2 Samuel and Chronicles have Sor (= Tyre) as Syrus (corrected to Zor by Yosippon), which may explain Surrentum's legendary foundation.
42. Perhaps a reference to older Albano.
43. List based on Jerome.
44. His son Sextus Tarquinius lusted (*armore ardens*) after Lucretia, according to Livy 1.58.1–5.

from the elders of Roma an Elder and with him 320 counselors, appointing them to govern and direct their realm.[45] The Elder governed with his 320 counselors, and they conquered the entire west.

After 205 years, great and terrible wars broke out between Babylon and Roma on land and sea because they aided Yavan (Greece)[46] in her war when they rebelled against Babylon at that time. They diverted the Tiber and paved the bed of the river from gate to gate, from its entrance into the city of Roma until the exit gate and from the exit gate unto the sea, a distance of eighteen miles; all of this was paved with copper. And from the gate of Roma that exits to the sea unto the gate through which the water enters is six miles, for three parts of the city are across the river and the fourth part on this side of it, and the river runs in the middle of the city. The inhabitants of Roma paved the bed of the river, and no boats or ships went to the king of Babylon, for they feared and trembled when they heard that Nebuchadnezzar had captured Jerusalem. They sent him a gift through their emissaries, and he made a treaty after the war. So, the war quieted until the rule of Darius, [when] they were again aroused to go to war.

---

45. Cf. 1 Macc 8, 15–16. Author apparently understood the word *senatus* (council of elders) as *senex* (old man) and translated it as *yashish* (cf. *sheikh*) [henceforth rendered Elder]. Author repeats 1 Macc's erroneous number 320 whenever he references Rome's senate. [Cf. Abraham's 318 men (Gen 14:14). SB].

46. Yavan is biblical for Ionia.

3. CONQUEST OF BABYLON

When God remembered all that He had spoken unto his servants, the prophets Isaiah and Jeremiah, regarding the future of Babylon, He stirred up against her two kings of great and noble nations, Darius, king of Madai (Media), and Cyrus (Coresh), king of Paras (Persia); and Cyrus became Darius's son-in-law by taking his daughter as his wife.[1] The two joined forces and, betraying the king of the Kasdim (Chaldeans), rebelled against King Belshazzar,[2] and a great war ensued. At the beginning of the war, the Chaldeans prevailed; but they had more dead than the Medes and Persians. These two kings reinforced their position and [refilled] their ranks and again challenged [the Chaldeans] to another great and mighty war; many died on both sides, and souls were spilled without number. The Chaldeans fled; Cyrus and Darius pursued them and smote them and crushed them unto a place one day's march from Babylon, and there Cyrus and Darius encamped with all their forces.

When King Belshazzar saw this, he sent forth the entire army of men of war and their thousand chiefs and with them a large and very great and mighty band of savage retainers [*paritzim*] from the palace of the king of Babylon. They went out from Babylon toward dusk and walked all night. By the morning watch, they began to smite in the camp of Cyrus and Darius; and the

---

1. Darius the Mede (Dan 11:1) was the son of Ahasverus (Dan 9:1). To correct somehow this unhistorical view of the Book of Daniel, the author makes the two contemporaries (cf. *AJ* 10.232, 248, and notes *ad locum* in the Loeb edition). *Yosippon* is an authoritative source for later biblical commentators. Cyrus and Darius were indeed related, as Josephus reported (*AJ* 10.248). Dan 6:1 ["Darius was sixty-three years old when he received the kingdom"] led the author to assume he was Cyrus's father-in-law.
2. The common medieval view of the four kingdoms held the Medes and Persians to be servants of Babylonia.

army became frightened. The Mede force fled. But Cyrus stood with his forces against the Chaldeans and fought with them, keeping them from pursuing the Medes. When night came, the fighting ceased, though the Medes and Persians continued to suffer many dead, for the officers of Belshazzar had defeated them.

These officers came to King Belshazzar in triumph, and he gave them a banquet and offered them many gifts of silver and gold. King Belshazzar was quite pleased with his thousand chiefs and sat with them to eat and drink, and they continued to sit all that day and all night. Now Belshazzar drank too much. When he was drunk, he commanded to bring forth all the golden vessels that were in the Temple of our God in Jerusalem. These were all the holy utensils that the Chaldean king Nebuchadnezzar took away with those whom he exiled from Jerusalem to Babylon. The king profaned the holy vessels and drank wine in them, he and his thousand chiefs, his consorts, and his concubines. Our God saw and was angry and became jealous for His vessels, and He sent the scribe from His throne to write a harsh epistle to the king informing him of the decree that the Lord our God had decreed against him, his life, and his kingdom. The writer came and wrote on the wall in vermilion by the king's candelabrum. These were the words that he wrote: CALCULATED, WEIGHED, AND DIVIDED, but the letters were in the holy script and the epistle in Aramaic language. The king saw the fingers writing, but the rest of the body [*golem*] he saw not, for the fingers were beautiful and terrible. Thereupon the king became very scared and frightened; all his limbs trembled, and his heart and all his bones rattled.

Daniel was brought before the king. He read him the letter and interpreted the words for him, saying to the king: "You acted very foolishly when you profaned the vessels of our God's house. Therefore, our God was jealous for His vessels and His temple and sent His messenger to write these words for you. These are the words that are in the letter: HISHEV SHAKAL VE-HIPHRISH, and this is their interpretation. HISHEV: our Lord counted the number of His enemy's days and curtailed them. SHAKAL: He weighed His enemy on the scales, and he was found wanting. VE-HIPHRISH: our Lord took away the kingdom from His enemy and gave it to Darius and Cyrus, who are warring with you, so that they share the kingdom between them."

When the king's officers heard this interpretation from Daniel, a man greatly beloved, a servant of God, the men became greatly afraid, and they rose and went each one to his home. The king remained alone with his eunuchs and household. He was agitated and frightened; sleep overcame him, but slumber haunted him; he slept like one of the dead in his nightmarish fright.

In the king's palace was a eunuch, the doorkeeper, one of the oldest servants of Nebuchadnezzar, honored and exalted. He thought to himself: "Is this not Daniel who interpreted to Nebuchadnezzar his dreams and was correct in all his words and none of his words failed? Now behold he has spoken against my lord King Belshazzar. I will cut off his head and with it appease Cyrus and Darius, kings of Media and Persia." That night, while King Belshazzar lay on his bed, the eunuch arose and smote the king, killing him, and he cut off his head and, carrying the head, fled to the camp of Cyrus and Darius, kings of Media and Persia; and giving them Belshazzar's head, he told them all that King Belshazzar did to the vessels of the House of God when he profaned them with wine at the banquet: how God sent his messenger, who wrote the letter, and Daniel, the greatly beloved, interpreted the letter, and how he chastised Belshazzar for the things that he did in daring to profane all the vessels of the House of God; therefore, God became angry and brought upon him the evil that your eyes see this day.

When Cyrus and Darius heard these words that the eunuch spoke, they bowed and prostrated themselves to God, Lord of the Heavens. King Cyrus said: "Blessed be God, Lord of these vessels and Lord of the temple that was in Jerusalem and in Judah, who exacted vengeance on the man who profaned his vessels, for since I heard[3] that He is Lord of all the earth and Lord of all the creatures and creator of all the world, so now I know [Ex 18:11] that God is greater than all the gods and in His hand is the dominion to remove kings and to raise up kings." King Cyrus vowed to build the temple of our Lord that is in Jerusalem and to send the exile from Babylon to Jerusalem and to restore all the vessels to the temple in Jerusalem.

After these events, Cyrus and Darius arose and went with a very great army and destroyed the land of the Chaldeans. They besieged Babylon and fought against her; they captured her and smote her with the sword: men and women, infants and babes, all the same; her young men they slew, and her virgins they trod under the hooves of horses; and all her princes and elders they strangled with ropes. All her pregnant ones [cp. 2 Kings 15:16] they split open, and all her nurslings they shattered with stones [cf. Ps 137:9]. So, our God had vengeance

---

3. The text from here until the beginning of chapter 7 has been collated from 3 different MSS. Other MSS tell another story about Darius's and Cyrus's siege of Babylonia for sixteen months, the death of Darius, enthronement of Cyrus over Madai and Paras, conquest of Babylonia, Cyrus's vow to rebuild the temple (this story was in Rashi's copy of *Yosippon apud* Dan 6:29, and possibly in the copy of Rabbenu Gershom). Hence, the longer story translated here was in the original *Yosippon* before the MSS were adulterated.

on Babylon and the Chaldeans for the spilled blood of His servants and revenged His people and His Temple and His city.

The two kings divided the whole kingdom of the Chaldeans. Darius took Babylon and its surrounding villages and the king's palace. He sat upon the throne of King Belshazzar and ruled in Babylon. King Cyrus took the entire kingdom of Chaldea outside of Babylon. At this juncture, the kingdom of Chaldea came to an end, and the kingdom of Media and Persia arose.

4. DANIEL IN THE LION'S DEN

Darius the Mede received the kingdom of the Chaldeans in his old age and reigned in Babylon [Dan 6:1].[1] And it came to pass when Darius was sitting on his throne, he sent for Daniel to be brought before him.[2] They placed a chair for Daniel, and he sat before Darius. The king said to him: "Are you Daniel?" He replied: "I am." He [the king] said to him: "Give me advice, and I will follow it, for the spirit of the Lord of the Heavens is in you. Pray, do not withhold your advice from me, for I have grown old and my strength has left me. For the ways of youth exhaust me, and wars have always weakened me, for I have begun my dotage and can no longer bear the burden of judging among men [Deut 1:2], whether to condone or condemn, for the matter is too heavy for me [Ex 18:18]." Daniel answered King Darius, saying: "Let the king charge three officials, men of strength and men of truth [cf. Ex 18:19] to bear the heavy burden of the people and judge between a man and his neighbor to ease from you [Ex 18:16 and 22] the weight of the people's burden and let the king rest in his house. Any important matter that is too difficult for them,[3] let them approach the king and he will judge; so, let the king and his throne be relieved and not be wearied further with the people's burden." The king did so and charged two army officers over the people; Daniel he appointed over the two to judge the people, and the king was at peace in his palace.

---

1. From here to the end of chapter 6 is lacking in some MSS (e.g., MS Jerusalem 8°41280, published by Flusser in 1979). [Cf. *Sefer ha-zikhronot hu divre ha-yamim le-yerahmi'el* (*The Book of Memory That Is the Chronicles of Jerahme'el*), ed. Eli Yassif (Tel Aviv, 2001), 254–57, which parallels the shortening of the feast story above. SB]

2. Expansion of Dan 6:2 based on Jethro's advice to Moses in Ex 18:14–27 and Deut 1:12–18.

3. Combines Ex 18:22 and Deut 1:17.

Darius sent a letter unto every land of his realm, saying: "The Lord of the Heavens[4] gave into my hand all the kingdoms of the earth, and the burden of bearing them weighs heavily upon me, for my spirit has reached old age. Therefore, I have taken counsel from Daniel, who has advised me with true counsel, so I hearkened to his advice and rest and relax in my house, and the bearing of the burden has eased. So now render honor to the God of Daniel and believe in him and seek him always and approach him, for he is great over all the gods. And let all the men in my kingdom know that I did this according to the counsel of Daniel. I have appointed two army chiefs over every land of my realm; unto them all the people will take heed in judgment to lighten the burden of the people from me.[5] I have appointed Daniel over these two officers to obey him in all that he will order them in judging the people and would not contradict his words and do all that he will command them. I have made him my deputy, and the two army chiefs I have placed under his command. He that disobeys the king's law shall not live." All the people gave heed to the king's command and to what would lighten his burden, and the king found peace in his palace. Daniel was second to the king; he was the one who went out and went in before the king. And the chiefs and the rulers and the nobles and the governors of state honored Daniel, for the spirit of his God was in him.

The two army chiefs, along with the other chiefs, the deputies, the rulers, and the magnates of the kingdom became jealous of Daniel. They all convened to slander Daniel by finding some libel to cause him to stumble before the king and the chiefs. They all agreed to inscribe a law and to make a covenant, saying "that every man whether great or small, chief or governor or commander of soldiers who will petition any god to ask or request or beseech anything from this day unto thirty days hence save for the king himself, will be food for the lions: neither will he be pardoned by the king, nor may he be ransomed by any amount, however high, to uphold an inscribed law." During all this, Daniel knew nothing of their plot, for they had furtively plotted against him, saying: "If we do not entrap him in the law of his God, we will not be able to trip him up." But they did not understand that just as Daniel was faithful to his God, so his God was faithful to him.

The men wrote these words that they had agreed on in a document, and each one signed it with his hand and sealed it with his seal in order to enforce the law of the document. The chiefs came to the king with the document in their hand. The king reached out and took it and read it in all innocence and did not

---

4. Cf. Ezra 1:2 and 2 Chron 36:23.
5. Also clumsy in Hebrew text.

pay attention to their deceitful plot against Daniel. And he authorized the law of the document with all that was written in it. And the king signed and gave it to the royal scribes to keep until it was needed.

After some days, the men prowled,[6] spying around Daniel's home to learn what he was doing so that they could find a pretext to slander Daniel as they had conspired. While they were walking to and fro near Daniel's house, they found a young girl playing by Daniel's doorway and asked her: "Where is Daniel, and what is he doing?" She replied: "There he is on the upper story of his house praying by the window that faces the House of God that is in Jerusalem and giving glory and praise to his God." The men took courage and went up to him to the upper story. There they found him kneeling, his palms extended toward heaven, for three times a day Daniel used to pray and give thanks to his God: for he who prays, speaks with God, and reads the Torah, God speaks with him. This is what Daniel did, and this was his custom daily. And so, when the men came to Daniel's house and he was praying, he was not afraid of them, nor did his heart fear the sound of their noise until he finished his prayer. Then they all fell upon him and seized him and brought him to the king.

When the king saw Daniel seized by the chiefs, he was anxious and greatly amazed, and he realized that on account of him they had established the law. The king said to the chiefs: "What have you done to Daniel? What is between you and him?" The men answered the king, saying: "Did we not write and sign before you, according to the law of the Medes and Persians that cannot be changed or broken, that everyone who bows down to any god during this entire month, save for the king himself, would be food for the lions? Behold, Daniel was found inside his house praying to his God against the king's commandment, and the laws of the Medes and Persians are not to be disobeyed. Now do not insult us by breaking our law. Give him to us that we may throw him into the lions' den, lest there be another affront against the laws of the Medes and Persians." The king answered the chiefs, saying: "You have conspired against Daniel. You must not provoke him. Leave him alone, for he is a Jew and his God is awesome and terrible and mighty, and he will demolish and destroy you!" But the chiefs held on to Daniel to destroy him and drop him into the lions' den. The king stirred to help him, to save him, but no one would help the king rescue Daniel, for all hastened to bring about his downfall to destroy him. But the king refused to listen to them, and the chiefs quarreled with the king over Daniel until sunrise.

When they saw that the king was with him, they all said to the king: "Let the king know and see, if he is not surrendered into our hands, we shall know that

---

6. Cf. Dan 6:12. This delightful episode is the invention of Yosippon.

you too violated the laws of the Medes and Persians." The king realized that they had plotted against him because of Daniel, so he gave up and surrendered him to them. The king said to them: "Tell me, if his God should save him from the jaws of the lions, where would you hide your shame and ignominy? You yourselves would substitute for him as food for the lions." They all answered the king thus: "So be it!" The king argued with his chiefs until daybreak. And the king said to Daniel: "Behold, these lords have conspired to cast you into the lions' den, and the Lord God of Heaven who has given unto you his spirit of holiness, he will stop their mouths from harming you. I am innocent before your God, for I sought to save you, but I could not."

They dragged Daniel and threw him into the den. Enclosed within the den were ten lions: their customary prey each day was ten sheep and ten human corpses, but they [the chiefs] had kept them without prey and fed them nothing so that they would hasten to devour Daniel. But when Daniel descended into the den of the lions, they greeted him with friendliness and licked him and wagged their tails and rejoiced to greet him[7] like dogs behave that rejoice at their master when he returns from the field. The chiefs rolled a huge stone to shut the den, and the king sealed the opening of the den with his ring and the rings of the chiefs, and each went to his house. Daniel continually praised the name of his God in a voice of thankful joy all the night unto the morning while the lions crouched around him and listened to the sound of his singing. But the king went to his house mournful and bitter; he ate no bread nor drank water or wine. Musical instruments were not played before him, as was the custom. He did not undress, for he mourned Daniel exceedingly. Sleep escaped him, for he was saddened because of the chiefs' plot against Daniel. In his anguish, the king said, as he tossed from side to side [in his bed]: "O let it be morning that I may see what has befallen Daniel."

It was on that day when Daniel was put down into the lions' den that Habakkuk, the prophet in the land of Judah, was coming from his harvesting toward evening, and he gave a feast [cf. 2 Kings 6:23] for his harvesters and was carrying their meal in his hand in order to serve them. Behold, his God spoke to him, saying: "Go and bring this meal to Daniel my servant in the land of the Chaldeans in the lions' den wherein he was lowered." And he said: "Alas, my Lord, who will bring me there at this time, for the route is too far for me?" Behold, an angel of God bore him by a lock of his head,[8] the meal in his hand, and he [the angel]

---

7. Prudentius (ca. fourth to fifth century) cites Hippolytus (ca. 202–4 CE) = Cathemerinon 4.46–51. Hippolytus may have been used by Yosippon's source.

8. Language of Ezek 8:3 and Vulgate to Dan 14:32 *capillo capitis*.

placed him inside the den by Daniel, and he ate and drank with Daniel. The angel took him out and brought him back to the place from which he [the angel] had carried him, even before the harvesters had finished eating. And Daniel continued to praise and exalt his God, for he was certain of His salvation. For he who prays to his God, speaks with his God, and reads the Law, his God speaks with him—and Daniel did not despair of his mercies.

Meanwhile, morning broke, and the king arose and hurried to the den. There the king heard the song of Daniel and the sweetness of his praise. The king could not speak with him, for his voice was broken by crying. The king got hold of himself and called: "Daniel! Daniel! Has God spared you from the lions' jaws and you were not devoured?" And Daniel answered: "Indeed God has spared me from the lions' jaws, for he muzzled their mouths, and they greeted me happily as if they were men of my household, for thus commanded my God in whom I trust; and a meal too was brought to me by Habakkuk in the spirit of my God. My lord the king, I did not sin against you, and no offense against you can be found in me; you will find neither treachery nor crime in me."

The king sent for the chiefs, Daniel's accusers; and they all came to the king, and he was standing by the den. He said: "Examine and observe the seal of your rings upon the den and say if it has been broken." They examined it and said: "It is as we have left it." The king commanded, and they rolled the stone from atop the den and hastened to raise Daniel out of the den, whole and unharmed, without injury. All the men were astonished at the wonders of the God of Daniel. They said: "The God of Daniel is the greatest of all gods." The king called his servants; they seized the chiefs who accused Daniel, along with their wives and sons, and cast them down into the lions' den. And even before they reached the bottom of the den, the lions rushed toward them [cf. 2 Sam 1:23], for they had not eaten since the day before, and they swallowed them; they gnawed and pulverized their bones. The lions roared at them in the den, and the sound of their roaring was heard from afar, and all the people trembled from their sound and said: "The lions have escaped the den." Then the king returned to his house, he and Daniel.

God added honor, greatness, grace, and merit to Daniel in the eyes of the king. The king ordered to be proclaimed throughout his entire kingdom:[9] "There is among all the gods no god like the God of Daniel, terrible in wonders and marvels. Who among you, of the people of his inheritance, may his God be with him and let him go up and rebuild the great House of God which is in Judah. I will give from my treasures gold and silver for all repair work until it is finished."

---

9. Language of Ezra 1:1 to supplement Dan 6:26–28.

He sent letters by mounted emissaries unto every city throughout his entire realm to let the Jews go and rebuild the House of God that is in Jerusalem. This was in the first year of the reign of Cyrus over the kingdom of the Chaldeans.

The king sent letters to all chiefs of the regions across the river and to the governors to be ready to join together to assist the Jews and supply all their needs in building materials: trees, stones, tailors, oil, wine, and every building need until they have completed the construction; also [he ordered that they be provided with] bulls and sheep for their sacrifices and that no man hinder them in all their work. And the Jews, every worthy man, rose to go to the House of God, about forty thousand. Among them, at their head was Ezra the Scribe and Eliaqim the priest and Yeshua and Mordecai and the rest of the family leaders of Judah and Benjamin. They proceeded unto the crossing of the river [Trans-Euphrates], and they came to Jerusalem and began to lay the foundation for the House of God.

When they [were] busy laying the foundations, evil men, enemies of Judah from the other nations, arose: Sanballat the Horonite, Tobiah the Ammonite, and Geshem the Arabian. They wrote an accusation against the Jews, servants of the Lord of Heaven, and sent a letter to the kings of Media and Persia, saying: "Let it be known to you that if the city of Jerusalem be built, it will be a snare for you and a great offense and a source of conspiracy against you, for from the earliest days the Jews inhabited the city, strong and hard men, harmful to kings and rulers throughout the land. For this Nebuchadnezzar besieged them and exiled them to Babylon. Then the kings were at peace and quiet, each in his place. Therefore, we have come to inform you about all these our beliefs, for we have eaten bread from the table of the king, and heaven forbid that we witness the downfall of the kingdom." When the letter reached the king, the work ceased until the second year of King Darius.[10]

------

10. Ezra 4:24. The author identifies him with Darius I (not Ezra's Darius II) to relate the rebuilding of the temple and the local opposition to Daniel for added dramatic effect.

5. DANIEL, BEL, AND THE DRAGON

While Darius was sitting on the throne of his kingdom, he sent for Daniel, servant of God, to see his wisdom and to know his advice. They brought him before the king, and he examined him, tested him, and he knew twice as much as he had heard about him. He rejoiced in him and loved him and appointed him his counselor just as he had been to Darius previously.

One day Darius celebrated the holiday of Bel, god of Babylon. The king prepared the offering to sacrifice to Bel, god of Babylon. This was the customary offering: one bull and ten male rams and one hundred doves and seventy round loaves of bread of [the king's] table and ten pitchers of wine from his table. This was his daily ration.

When the day came, they arrayed the table before Bel, and the king said to Daniel: "I wish you believed in the splendor of Bel, our great god, who will eat the array of this table." Daniel answered the king: "Let not the king's heart be deceived by Bel, and let it not mislead you, for he is vanity, and there is no spirit in him, for he is the work of a craftsman, so how can he eat and how can he drink? Only his priests eat the array of his table; also, they eat his offering and his burnt offering. Now, if you listen to my advice and hand over his priests to me, I will expose their fraudulence by which they deceive you and your people to bow down to vanity and nothingness." And the king said: "All right, let it be according to thy word [cf. Gen 30:34]."

Daniel ordered that the entrances to Bel and his temple and its gates be blocked and its gates be shut, except for the gate through which the king and Daniel came. Then Daniel said: "Bring me the ash!" They brought it, and he spread the ash on the floor of the temple. But the priests did not know what Daniel had advised to do. When they finished doing this, the king left with Daniel by the gate through which they had entered with their servants. Closing the gate, the king sealed it with his ring and with Daniel's ring. They went to king's palace and spent the night there.

In the morning, the king sent for Daniel to see and know what Bel did. They went to the temple gate and found the seals that they had sealed. The king said to Daniel: "Is there any damage to the seals?" He replied: "No." He ordered to remove them, and opening the gate, they saw the table. And lo, everything that they had arrayed upon it had been eaten, from bread unto meat, and the wine had been drunk. When the king saw, he fell to the ground before Bel and said: "Bel, great is your name in the world. Who is like unto you in majesty among the gods of the nations?" And Daniel answered him, saying: "Let not the king speak thus, for Bel is mud and clay and copper; and he neither ate nor drank. Just look at the ash that we spread on the floor and around the altar and the table; see these footprints: whose are these if not the eaters at Bel's table?" The king looked and, behold, footsteps of men and women and youth and children.

The king sent for and seized the seventy priests who served Bel. The king swore unto them: "If you do not tell me the truth, you shall die!" They showed him the hidden entrances through which they came to Bel in the night and ate the array of his table. The king understood their cunning; he ordered that the temple of Bel be razed to the ground.

Also, in those days the Chaldeans had as a god a great dragon that lived in a cave. They used to prepare an offering for him, which they brought at night, to be thrown to the dragon. When the dragon smelled the odor of the fat and the sacrifice, it rejoiced to come out for the offering and opened its mouth, as was its custom. They threw it into its mouth, and the dragon swallowed it, whereupon it swelled up and turned to reenter the cave. The chiefs said to the king: "Could Daniel mock even this god, which is a living god, as he did to Bel and his priests, and stop his service? Why does he not challenge this god? For if he challenges him, Bel and his temple shall be avenged."

The king said to Daniel: "Listen, Daniel, and take heed, and I will speak to you! Will you use your wisdom against the dragon, the great and powerful god, to destroy him as you did to Bel, who was lifeless? He is a living god, strong and powerful. Who will face him to do him harm?"[1] Daniel answered the king, saying: "Let not the king be deceived by him also, for he is an animal and may be subdued by the hand of man, for there is not in him the Spirit of God.[2] Now, if you will permit me, my lord the king, this dragon too I will smite and kill it without sword or staff or weapon, for it is a reptile that swarms upon the earth. And God enjoined the fear of man upon every animal, swarming and moving

---

1. Breithaupt adds the names of Daniel's three friends Ḥananyah, Mishael, and Azariah (45). [SB]

2. God is found in only two versions of our MSS and not in Jerahme'el. The phrase reverses Gen 41:38 and is an allusion to Bel being lifeless, lit. "in him there is no spirit."

creature, for he made man in God's image so that all shall fear him. And now, if it pleases you, give me leave to smite him and destroy him like one of the idols I had destroyed. Only do not let your chiefs harm me." The king said to him: "Go, do what you can." The chiefs were quite pleased at the king's command to Daniel to confront the dragon, for they said: "Now Daniel will be destroyed for he cannot stand before the dragon."

Daniel left the king and made for himself iron instruments like combs of flax and fixed them back-to-back so that their spikes were to the outside, honed and sharp all around. Then he wound around them all kinds of covering, fat and grease, all manner of fatty materials, and he also put a layer of sulfur and burned it until the spikes of the iron and the teeth disappeared and appeared as the offering [the dragon was used to]. Daniel threw it into the dragon's mouth. In its desire, the dragon hastened to swallow it, accepting it. When it entered its mouth and reached its belly, the fat and the grease melted from the iron spikes, and the sharp pronged points pierced the dragon's intestines. The dragon was weakened, its strength failed, and it died on the morrow.

Three days later, the Chaldeans and Babylonians came to seek the dragon for the regular offering, but he was not there. Only a stench rose from the cave. They broke into the cave, and behold, their god was dead, bloated, and stinking. The men were saddened; they were very angry with Daniel and said: "What has Daniel the Jew done to our two gods, destroying Bel and smiting the dragon? Now, if the king will hand him over to us, he shall be killed, and, if not, let it be known to the king that he shall not live." When the king heard that the masses conspired against him, he slew by sword their leaders and their chiefs, along with those who rose against Daniel.

6. THE STORY OF ZERUBAVEL

Daniel was quite old in years.[1] He came and bowed to the king; and he said to him: "Pray, my lord king, behold I have grown old, and I no longer have strength to handle affairs of the kingdom. Your people's rascals have humbled me in their hatred, for they lowered me into the lions' den twice, but my God, in whom I trust, saved me. They sought to take my life and kill me in their zealousness for their idols, but my God saved me from their wickedness along with three friends whom they brought to the furnace to be burned; and during all this the hand of our God was mighty to help us. Now, my lord king, I beseech you, permit me to go to my home to rest and to serve the God of my ancestors, for I have grown old and no longer have strength to govern."

The king replied to Daniel, saying: "And who would grant you this thing, to let you go, for you are a man of God, Lord of the Heavens, and how should my kingdom be governed when you have left me? Indeed, I know that you have aged and no longer have the strength to handle affairs according to the manner of chiefs, chiefs of the kingdom. However, if you give me another man like yourself, of your own people, knowledgeable and wise, full of the Spirit of God like you, who would be with me in your stead, as was your custom, then I will send you in peace to rest and relax in your house, though my soul knows that there is no one of your worth among all your people."

Daniel left the king at sunset and prayed to the God of Heavens to induce the king to allow him to go and serve his God. He slept that night, and rising early in the morning, he went to the community of the exiles ['adat hagolah], where he found Zerubavel, son of Shealtiel, son of Yekhoniah, king of Judah. Daniel raised him out of the [community of the] exile and, holding him by the hand, led him

____

1. Daniel's selection of Zerubavel is not in any known source and provides a good transition between the gesta Daniel and the gesta Zerubavel based on Latin 3 Ezra, chaps. 3–4.

to the king and presented him [Zerubavel] before him [the king].[2] Then Daniel said: "Here is a man worthy to be my replacement: he will be unto you just as I was. He is of the children of Judah, from the nobility, of royal seed, one of the sons of Shealtiel, son of Yekhoniah, king of Judah. He is a man of valor, full of wisdom and knowledge; in him is the Spirit of God [Gen 41:38], as much as in me; he is not inferior to me and will not be lacking; he will be as faithful an advisor to you as I; and you will permit me to retire in my place." The king believed all that Daniel related to him and sent him away. Daniel bowed before the king, and the king embraced Daniel and kissed him; then he commanded and gave him a present befitting the king; he gave him leave, and he left. So it happened that Zerubavel became the king's replacement for Daniel. Daniel distributed all that the king had given him among the poor men of the exile, and he went to his place, to Shushan, the capital, in the realm of Elam; there he worshiped God unto the day of his death amid his brethren, the community of the exiles there.

Zerubavel was a man of valor, successful, understanding, and wise, full of the spirit of wisdom, for Daniel had laid his hands upon him. He found grace in the eyes of the king, who loved him as much as he loved Daniel; he [the king] appointed him as leader [*nagid*] over all the chiefs and head over the two military chiefs who guarded the king.

One day when all the chiefs gathered to present themselves before the king according to their custom, the king said to them: "Have you ever seen a man like this Zerubavel, a man wise and prudent in the spirit of Daniel?" They replied and said: "The king's word is true!" In the afternoon, when the king would lie down after his meal, he lay down on his bed and slept. The two chiefs who guarded the king stationed themselves to watch according to their custom, and Zerubavel was with them as their head. They stood around the king until the time of his wakening, and the king was heavy in his sleep, for he was drunk with wine. The three lads were exhausted from standing guard, and one said to his companion: "Come let us tell riddles, words of wisdom, one by one according to his cunning, and let us write our riddles upon a scroll and place the scroll under the head of the king until he awakes, and he will see the scroll and will understand the meaning of its contents. And let the one whose words are deemed wiser than his two companions and his riddle more obscure than the riddles of his colleagues, let him be deputy to the king as he sits upon both his throne and chariot, and going out and coming before the king according to the high rank of deputy. Let all the utensils of his table be utensils of gold, and let a bridle of gold be put upon the cheeks of his horse, and also let the crown of deputy be put upon his head,

---

2. Cf. Lev 10:15; Num 5:25, 8:11, etc.

and let him take the gifts of a deputy from the king; let the king grant any of his requests, and he will be the friend of the king." All of them said: "Let it be so!" Then they made a covenant according to the law of the Medes and Persians that could not be dissolved. They brought a scribal inkstand and a scroll and cast lots among the three; and the lot fell to one, and he wrote upon the scroll:[3] "There is nothing so strong in the land as a king." The second wrote: "There is nothing as strong in the land as wine." The third, who was Zerubavel, wrote: "There is nothing as strong in the land as a woman."[4]

When they had finished writing their riddles, they placed the scroll under the king's headrest. Now, the king was awake, but his eyes were closed, and he was listening to the whisper of their words. When they put the scroll under the pillows of the king's headrest, the king rose as if from the end of his sleep and passed his two hands over his eyes and searched [beneath] his headrest.

He found the scroll of the book that the three lads had written and opened it and read it and closed it until all the chiefs and governors and nobles and lords of the state arrived. He called these three lads and said to them: "Let each one approach me with his cipher and make heard the interpretation of the words of his riddle. The one I deem most clever of you three, I will fulfill for him all that is written in the scroll, and honor him and raise him." The first one approached, read his writing and said: "Let the king and his chiefs listen to my words that I shall speak: There is nothing so strong in the land as a king." The second drew near and said: "There is nothing so strong in the land as wine." And the third, who was Zerubavel, said: "There is nothing so strong in the land as a woman." The king and his chiefs answered: "We have heard the words of your riddles; now offer your interpretations and we shall listen."

The first answered and said: "I pray thee, my lord the king, and I pray you, mighty chiefs. Do you not know the power of the king and the strength of his government, over the land and the sea and the islands and over all the nations and tongues, to put to death and to let live? If he commands his men to send out an army, they all go out [to battle] and would not turn back but advance toward death. And if he commands them to overthrow cities, they overthrow; [if he commands them] to level mountains, they level; and if [he commands them] to destroy walls, they destroy. And if they plow and plant and harvest the produce of the land, they offer up the choice part to the king before they eat from the

---

3. 3 Ezra 3:10–12. The author's clever inversion of the first two from his source, which moves from wine to king to woman and Truth, brings a new twist to the story.

4. Zerubavel's addition of Truth was a surprise since each was to speak on only one subject. The author's shortening of 3 Ezra 3:12 adds a dramatic element later and thus shows his literary skill.

produce, for they fear the king and all tremble in awe of him, for he is lord and hero over all, and no one disobeys his word and command. Therefore, believe my words, for there is nothing as strong in the land as a king." All those standing were amazed at these words.

The second answered and said: "I pray thee, my lord the king, and I pray you, wise men, although you all know of the power of the king and the power of his might in subduing and ruling in the land, and his terror and fear is upon all men, as you have heard with your ears. Yet, wine is stronger even than the king, for while the king is truly mighty, when he drinks, the wine rules over him and turns his heart to other things: to shout with joy and to sing and to dance and even to become a fool, for his heart was turned by wine to reject those who are close to him and to befriend those who are far, to put to death those who are loved and to honor strangers, even showing favor neither to father nor mother nor brother of his own flesh. Do you not know that the strength of wine is such that, if a man who has never studied a book drinks it, he will compose songs, while a man who is deaf will call out, and a secret that is kept will be revealed, and a hidden deed will be brought out into the open? Wine gladdens sad men and mourners and those whose spirit is disheartened and dying men; if they drink it, they will become happy and joyful. Worried men will sing, and those held in chains before execution will laugh if they drink wine. A drunk will brandish a sword at his companion, and he will challenge the shameless. Yet, when the wine has left them, they will forget all they did and no longer understand or remember, for the wine has left them, and they shall say: 'We did nothing.' And who will not believe that wine is not stronger than the king when it rules him, for the man's legs will be unable to walk, and his eyes will see what is not right, and his mouth will utter unlearned talk. You should know that wine is stronger than the king when it does thus." And the men who heard were very amazed.

Then the king called to Zerubavel, who was third, and said:[5] "Tell me now your riddle's interpretation [*pesher*] as your companions told me theirs." And he answered: "I will." Then he said: "Listen and take heed to my words, O king, and also you chiefs and nobles and governors and all the assembled people. Indeed, the king is stronger and greater than everything, and wine weakens the king when it rules over him and he is in its grasp. Nor can one deny either the strength of the king or the strength of the wine; yet, the woman is stronger than wine and the king and all the plants of the vineyards from which comes the wine. And why would not woman be stronger than the king, for she bore the king and nursed him and held him secure in her bosom and raised him and fed

---

5. The author parallels medieval interest in woman's omnipotence.

him and dressed him and washed his feces from him, and she chastened him, and she rules over him as a mother the son she bore, and her fear is upon him, and he fears her scolding voice, for at times she strikes him, and other times she rebukes him. And if she takes a stick to him, he runs from her outside because he is afraid of her. Until the lad grows to be a young man, he will not forget her awe, and he will not fail to honor her; and he will respect her at all times as a son respects his parent. Afterward, if he lifts up his eyes and sees a woman of beautiful appearance, he will lust after her beauty to make love to her, for his soul has cleaved unto her; he has set his heart upon her, and his love would not change for any price; and he would leave even his mother, who taught him, and his father, who sired him, and betray them for the love of a woman's beauty and her shape. Many men have committed folly for a woman's love and have been made fools and driven out of their minds for her sake, for they were fooled by her. Many were killed on her account and died and went down to hell proudly; many wise men were entrapped in her web and sages ensnared in her net. She will arouse a sword of enmity between brothers, lovers she will separate, and a man will betray his brother [because of her]. Do you not know and understand that if a woman of beautiful form passes before a man carrying a precious vessel, his eyes would peer upon her—at the beauty of her shape—because his heart turns after her? If she but utters a word, he will drop everything in his hand and, with mouth agape, would look upon her, for she caused his heart to be attracted to her. Who will not believe me about this and aver the truth of woman's strength? Tell me, for whom do you labor and for whom do you tire and for whom do you plunder and amass great wealth? Is it not for women that they may buy all kinds of precious articles, gold and silver and precious jewels and all kinds of expensive vessels, brocades of gold and myrrh and aloes and all kinds of spices and appealing incense? Will you not prepare all these for a woman? And if a man should break the law and go to a place of ambush in deserts or mountains or woods or on the seas and fight and murder and plunder and rob and pillage and kidnap and spill blood for profit, to whom will he bring the loot? Would he not bring it to a woman? Have I not seen the king sitting on his throne with the crown of his majesty upon his head and Apomenia, daughter of Absius the Makedonian,[6] his concubine, sitting opposite him, and she put out her hand and took the king's crown from his head and put it on her own head, and the king laughed with her. And when she got angry, the king hastened to soothe her so that her anger subsided. Who will not believe my words that

---

6. The Latin of 3 Ezra 4:29 has "Apemen filiam Bezacis mirifici," perhaps an indication that his Bible was garbled.

the woman is stronger than all for she enfeebled the strength of Samson and made David transgress and led Solomon astray and tempted him. Many has she entrapped, and numberless are killed by her; and her casualties are many. And even this you should know and learn, if one man governs the entire land whose inhabitants cannot be numbered, and all of them fear and tremble from him for he governs all of them, and over every woman is given a lord and king to rule over her and he lusts after her, but he cannot control and rule her. Even Adam, father of all those who inhabit the earth, his wife caused him to transgress the commandment of the Lord his God. She delivered him unto death with all his descendants after him; and also, in Noah's days, the heavenly angels acted foolishly and took wives for themselves. And who will not believe this when from the beginning of the world unto its end this fact has not failed to be, and [he will know] that I speak the truth. And now I will tell the king and all those listening that the king that rules the land is vanity, and the wine that governs the king is vanity, and vanity is the woman and her evil that rules over all three. The Truth rules everything in heaven and on earth, even in the seas and in the depths only the Truth has power against God and man. For in Truth's abode Falsehood cannot abide because heaven and earth were founded on the Truth and the Lord our God is Truth forever and ever."[7] And all the assembled people responded to the king and said: "Truth."

The king said to Zerubavel: "Come, approach me!" He approached the king, and the king, extending his hand, drew him near and, embracing him, kissed him before all the assembled people. And he said: "Blessed is the God of Zerubavel who put into him the spirit of Truth, for He is the God of Truth and He established His throne upon Truth, for there is nothing like unto His Truth and all else is vanity." And all the chiefs and officers and nobles and all the people exclaimed: "Indeed the Truth is greater than everything; and nothing in the world can stand against it, for it rules heaven and earth and everything is founded upon it; and true is the God of Zerubavel who put into his mouth the spirit of Truth, to praise and extol the Truth before God and man."

The king commanded to fulfill the law of honor that was written on the scroll, and all of it was fulfilled for Zerubavel, for he found more grace in the eyes of the king and the chiefs than his two companions. The king said to Zerubavel: "Ask whatever your soul desires of anything written in the scroll, and I will give it to you, even unto half the kingdom I will grant you." Zerubavel answered the king: "Pray let my lord the king remember the vow that you and King Cyrus swore to the Lord of Heaven to build His house and to return the vessels of His temple

---

7. 3 Ezra 4:38. Language from Ps 117:2 and Jer 10:10.

to their place and to allow the exile of the people of the Lord of Heaven to serve in His temple, which is named for Him, that they might pray to the great God, Lord of Heaven, on behalf of the king and his realm, for one may not delay the vow sworn to the Lord of Heaven."

The king commanded his scribes to hasten to write all that Zerubavel requested from the king to rebuild the ruins of Jerusalem. Also, King Darius sent to Cyrus, king of Persia, that he should join with him in fulfilling their vow to reestablish the House of God that is in Jerusalem. Cyrus sent forth a proclamation throughout his kingdom, saying: "Whosoever there is among you of all the people of the Lord of Heaven who has it in his heart to go up, to found and build—let him go up, and I will give from my treasures the cost of all the work until they have completed the building." The king's scribes wrote the word of King Darius, king of Media, and Cyrus, king of Persia, to the chiefs and governors who rule the regions across the river, the Edomites, the Tyrians and Sidonians and Samaritans and to Asaph, guardian of the forest [*pardes*] of Lebanon: "Let it be known to you that the Lord of Heaven stirred up our heart to send forth the exile of His people, whom Nebuchadnezzar, king of Babylon, exiled, and to return the vessels of the great and holy house that is named for the Lord of Heaven and to build His Temple and to raise up His altar and to offer up to Him daily sacrifices and to build the Sanctuary of the Holy of Holies and to establish the palace in good order and to rebuild the breach of Jerusalem's walls. Now, when this letter reaches you, make haste to lend your hands to assist them to fulfill all their needs of silver, gold and copper, trees and stones, builders, and tree cutters until they finish construction and to supply for the repair work everything that they ask from you, even wheat and barley and oil and wine for every need toward the work of repair and also for repairs of the altar to give young bullocks and rams, he-goats and sheep, pigeons and doves, fine wheat, oil and salt, and every maintenance for the altar and the work until it is finished." The two kings ordered the Edomites to lend a hand in the work of the House of God, because they had assisted the Chaldeans in destroying it, and to supply an annual tax of five talents of gold[8] to support the repair of the house until it and the holy city be completely rebuilt; and [they commanded] the Tyrians, Sidonians, Edomites, and the servants of the king in Lebanon who were under the command of Asaph, protector of the [royal] forest, to cut trees from the Lebanon and channel water from Lebanon to the sea of Jaffa, to complete the work of the House of God and let no man disturb them until they have completed all

---

8. Kaufman MS has fifty, as does *AJ* 11.61, while 3 Ezra 4:51 has twenty. The author adds the word "gold."

the work. The scribes wrote all these words just as the two kings commanded, and they fixed their seals and gave the letters to Zerubavel, son of Shealtiel, and to Nehemiah, son of Hakhaliah.

At that time, Darius, king of Media, fell ill, and the time of his death drew nigh; he sent for Cyrus, king of Persia, his son-in-law,[9] husband of his daughter, and he came to him, and Darius crowned him as his successor. Thus, Media and Persia became one kingdom. Darius the Mede was gathered unto his people, and Cyrus, king of Persia, succeeded him over the kingdom of Media and Persia. The lords of Media and Persia enthroned Cyrus, son-in-law of Darius, over the kingdom of the Medes and Persians. From that day hence, the kingdom of the Medes and Persians was united as one kingdom. And Cyrus sat upon the throne of the king of Babylon and of the Chaldeans.

---

9. Here the text continues from the two MSS (Urbino and G5 of the Geniza); and cf. MS Jerusalem 8°41280.

7. THE SACRED FIRE

In the first year of the reign of Cyrus, king of Persia,[1] God our Lord stirred up his spirit, and the king remembered his vow that he had sworn to send the exile and the sacred vessels from Babylon to Jerusalem. All the elders of the exile were called before Cyrus the king, who said to them: "Who among you of all the people of the Lord of the Heavens will be stirred to go up to Jerusalem, to the site of the footstool of the great and mighty God, to rebuild his house and his temple destroyed by Nebuchadnezzar, who did more evil than all the kings who were before him; let him go up and build, and may his God be with him when he is thus stirred. I, Cyrus, servant of the living God through whose command I was enthroned, will give of my wealth and of my treasures for all repair of the House of the great God by whose command I rule over the kingdoms of the Medes and Persians and who helped me destroy the kingdom of the Chaldeans."

Thereupon all the elders of the exile, including Ezra the scribe and Nehemiah, son of Hakhaliah, and Mordecai and Yeshua and the remaining heads of the exile, went up and came to Jerusalem and built the Temple of God according to the measure that the king had given them. They built the altar in proper form and arranged logs on the altar and placed [sacrificial] meat upon the logs, but they did not find the sacred fire.[2] Ezra the scribe and Nehemiah and Mordecai and Yeshua and all the heads of the exile prayed before God and said: "Master of all the worlds, You put into the heart of the king of Persia to render honor to Your city and rebuild Your Temple and send forth Your poor servants and priests to sacrifice and to offer up burnt offerings as

---

1. Cf. Ezra 1:1–5. Flusser defends his choice for the original *Yosippon* based on the three proclamations. See chaps. 4 and 6. [SB]
2. Cf. Latin translation of 2 Macc 1:19–2:7.

did our pious ancestors before You. Behold, we, Your servants, have come to this place and have prepared Your altar according to its measure, and we have slaughtered a sacrifice and have arranged logs upon the altar, and sacred meat we have given according to custom, but we do not have authority to sacrifice before You a strange fire, for the sacred fire is not among us, because Jeremiah, Your servant, and the chiefs of Your priests who went into exile in the days of Nebuchadnezzar hid it. Now, what shall we do, Lord of the Heavens? Give us advice and assistance, for the authority is in Your hands to aid and strengthen Your servants."

Now, while they were praying like this, it happened that there was an old man, one of the priests, and he remembered the place where Jeremiah had hidden the sacred fire. That old man went outside the camp, and all the old men ran after him; and behold, under the section of the wall was a cistern[3] with a great stone over it, and it was plastered over with whitewash. They broke the plaster and rolled the stone from atop the cistern and found at the bottom of the cistern water oily and thick and dense as honey. They returned and told Ezra. Ezra came to the cistern and said to the priests: "Go down and bring the water in your hands, but let not a stranger[4] touch it, only for priests of the seed of Aaron the priest, for that is the sacred fire." So the priests descended and brought the water with their own hands; and they went to the temple and poured the water upon the altar over the sacrifice and logs. Now, when they had done this, suddenly a most terrible fire burst out and kindled the flame; and the fire consumed and increased and was greatly strengthened so that the priests fled[5] from the house unable to withstand the fire. The fire increased and devoured the offering and the logs and encircled the whole house, purifying the vessels and the Temple. The fire in the house subsided, remaining only on the altar, where it belonged. From that day on, they put logs on it, and the fire continued until the second exile.

The Ark of the Covenant was not there, for Jeremiah the prophet had taken it with all the curtains that Moses, God's servant, had made in the desert and bore them to Mount Nebo and found there a cave and placed them inside it. The priests of that time pursued Jeremiah to recognize the place. When Jeremiah looked back and saw the priests, he was angry and swore an oath: "The place will not be known until I and God's servant Elijah come. Then we

---

3. 2 Macc 1:19. The author adds new data on the place and its form.

4. Author's literary expansion plays on "strange fire" above.

5. Variation on 2 Macc 1:22 and 1:31–32, exaggerated according to taste of the author's environment. Cf. 2 Chron 7:1ff.

shall return the Ark to its place in the Holy of Holies under the wings of the cherubim."

From that day hence, our ancestors offered up their sacrifices and their burnt offerings and their whole offerings and their daily offerings regularly. And the kings of Persia assisted them with gold and silver, wheat, oil and wine, and bulls and rams annually, for the kings of Persia loved the Temple of our God and His Sanctuary.

8. DEATH OF CYRUS

King Cyrus (Coresh) reigned over all the kingdoms of the earth, and our God strengthened his right hand, conquering nations before him, opening for him iron gates and breaking copper doors, giving him buried treasures just as He said through His servant Isaiah the prophet [cf. Isa 45:1–4]: "For the sake of Jacob, His servant, and Israel, whom He has chosen." Cyrus fought in the East and captured all the passes to Hodu (India) and in the south throughout the land of Kush (Ethiopia) and all the nations who live at the southernmost regions and in the west as far as Sepharad (Spain) and in the north all the land of Makedon and all the land of Caphtor (Cappadocia) and all the land of Alan and Elasar (Pontus) and the mountains of ALEPH,[1] which is the mountain of the bull [Mount Taurus], as far as the mountains of snow, which cannot be crossed. The rest of his deeds are written in the books of the kings of the Medes and Persians and in the book of Joseph the priest, who is Joseph ben Gurion,[2] who was exiled from Jerusalem in the days of Vespasian and Titus, his son, and in the book of the kings of the Romans.

Cyrus fought again with the king of the Scythians.[3] He went to Scythia, for they had rebelled against him.[4] The Scythians went toward him, and they fought

---

1. Ps 50:10 has *Eleph* (= thousand) where, according to the midrashim, *Behemoth* lives; *Chronicles of Jerahmeel* (trans. Gaster), LXXVIII(I), 234 has correct reading *Aleph* (= bull) as in Mount Taurus, whose Latin the author renders literally *har ha-shor*. Gen. Apoc. has *tor tora*.

2. One Genizah fragment has Josephus here. Yosippon, following Hegesippus's confusion, was also unclear whether Joseph ben Gurion was the original author or just one of the sources that were used. For full discussion of both possibilities found in various MSS and printed editions, cf. Flusser, *Josippon*, 2.74–79; and the introductory essays to this volume. Joseph ben Gurion and Joseph ben Mattathias were two separate Jewish generals in the war.

3. Hebrew *Sitim* (with ש—*sin*) from Italian pronunciation of *sc.*; already in Wellhausen, 48.

4. This section is based ultimately on Orosius, *Historiarum contra paganos libri VII*, 2.7, 1–6.

a great battle; the Scythians were routed and turned their backs to flee, but their king fell in that battle and Cyrus slew all the warriors of his camp. He pursued the survivors and came unto the citadel cities of Tamira, the queen, and her son. Cyrus saw that the Scythians had entered their cities: no one exited or entered, so Cyrus acted cunningly: he rose and, abandoning his camp, fled. The Scythians exited their cities with their king's son to pursue Cyrus. When Cyrus realized that the Scythians went out into the plain, the king wheeled about and, falling upon the Scythians, smote three hundred of them;[5] the king's son, Tamira's son, also fell among them. While the Scythians retreated to the mountains with Tamira, Cyrus captured their citadel cities and ruined them; he appointed commissioners in the provinces that he captured; then he set about to leave the land.

When the queen saw that her son was dead, the woman grieved exceedingly; hardening and setting her soul to die, she went and set an ambush and captured the mountain passes of the Scythians. It so happened that Cyrus, leaving the land of the Scythians confidently, paid no heed to an ambush; all his army crossed, and but only a handful remained with him; he passed the night there between two mountains and lay in that place. During that night, the woman suddenly fell upon Cyrus's camp and smote the camp of Cyrus, killing[6] two hundred thousand Persian warriors along with their king, Cyrus, in the battle. The woman was very cruel: she came upon the corpse of Cyrus like a wild beast, a bereaved she-bear whose cubs were killed. She cut off his head and put it in a goatskin that she filled with blood of the slain and said: "Drink and be sated, King Cyrus. Drink your fill of the blood you loved; for thirty years you have spilled blood without measure." King Cyrus found the end of his life fighting in the Scythian steppe, and this is no surprise,[7] for Saul, God's anointed, found the end of his life in war, and Yoashyahu (Josaiah), God's friend, ended his days in war as well.

King Cyrus was gathered to his people, and Cambysa (Cambyses), his son, reigned after him. He waged war against the kingdom of the Scythians and captured all the land of the Scythians; he killed Tamira, the queen, by sword, and all her descendants he eradicated and extirpated from the land. He ruled mightily over the Medes and Persians, and, capturing Damascus, he killed her chiefs by sword, for they had rebelled against him. Next, he went against Armenia and

---

5. Some MSS have three hundred thousand. Orosius has the queen send one third of her army to pursue Cyrus.

6. Hebrew *hiẕia* (spread out) translates Latin *sternere*.

7. Cyrus too is an anointed king (messiah) in Isa (45:1).

fought against them and subjected them under his rule, taking their sons from them as hostages. He fought against Egypt and captured it, subjecting the land, and he reigned mightily; fear of him was widespread throughout his kingdom. Our fathers served King Cyrus and all the kings of Persia who succeeded him in "sweet service," for they [kings of Persia] did not harm them nor oppress them; rather, they assisted them with silver and gold, with wheat, barley, and wine, rams and he-goats, given annually, for the kings of Persia loved the Sanctuary of our God that is in Jerusalem.

9. GESTA MORDECAI AND ESTHER

Only in the days of Ahasuerus was the memory of Judah nearly lost from the entire realm of Persia through the hatred of one Amalekite named Haman, who stole the heart of King Ahasuerus. Ahasuerus gave Haman license to act as he wished throughout the kingdom, even to wipe out the memory of Judah from the entire Persian realm, because Mordecai, a Jew of the nobles of Benjamin, did not rise before him. These [nobles] were the patricians, Benjaminite heroes, who accompanied their king, Saul, on the field of Amalek and delivered Amalek a mighty and powerful blow all the way from Havilah unto Shur,[1] a land of many days' journey. They slew more than five hundred thousand dead of the Amalekite people, all destroyed in King Saul's war against the Amalekite people; verily he slaughtered souls throughout the land of Amalek: men, women, and children, more than a hundred myriads in all. This is why this man, Haman, preserved a hatred against the Jews and especially against the tribe of Benjamin.

In those days, while Mordecai was sitting within the king's gate, he heard two of the king's eunuchs, gatekeepers, whispering as they plotted against the king, to kill him in bed and cut off his head and to bring King Ahasuerus's head to the king of Makedon,[2] for the nation of Makedon was stirred up against the kingdom of Persia. These are the names of the eunuchs: Bigthan and Teresh. When Mordecai told Esther and she told the king, the king ordered to record in the book of the chronicles of the kings of Persia Mordecai's faithfulness and the extent of his service that he had rendered to the king. After the eunuchs were beaten and hung on a tree, Haman became exceedingly angry that his aides

---

1. 1 Sam 15:7. Cf. Ginzberg, *Legends* 6.233–34, 462–64. I did not find a source for this datum.
2. Perhaps the author's assumption is based on the apocryphal additions to Esther, which he knew in Latin (16.10–14): "Haman the Makedonian sought to kill Mordecai and Esther and all their people in order to hand over the rule of Persia to the Makedonians."

were killed; so Haman sought to extirpate all the seed of Judah from under the heavens.

Mordecai understood Haman's intent, and he recalled the dream that he foresaw in the second year of King Ahasuerus's reign. He saw in the dream a loud and noisome din and a sound of thunder and the noise of terror throughout the entire land and fear and trembling among all its inhabitants. Two great dragons were calling each other to war, and all the nations of the earth ran to their sound. And behold, between them was a little people, and all those nations rose against this little nation to wipe out its memory from off the earth. That day was a day of darkness and gloom for the entire world; the little people was greatly anguished, and it cried out unto God. The dragons fought against each other with savage cruelty, and none could intervene or separate them. Mordecai saw a tiny spring of water passing between the two dragons, separating them from each other and from the fighting in which they were engaged. The spring grew and grew, and it became a gushing stream, like the great sea's stream that floods the entire land; he saw the sun shining upon the land, and there was light throughout the world; and that little people was exalted while the haughty were brought low, and peace and truth were established throughout the world.

From that day hence, Mordecai kept secret the dream that he saw [cf. Gen 37:11]. But when Haman oppressed him, Mordecai said to Queen Esther, his cousin: "Behold the dream that I told to you in your youth has arrived. Arise now and ask for mercy from the Lord of mercy, go to Ahasuerus and present your beauty before him, and stand up for your people and your family."

Mordecai the Jew prayed and said: "Let it be well known to the throne of Your glory, Lord of the entire universe, that it was not because my heart is haughty or my eyes proud that I did not bow down to this Amalekite, Haman, rather due to my fear of You that I challenged him by not bowing down to him, for I feared You, Lord of the Universe, and I could not give the honor due You to flesh and blood, and I did not want to bow down to anyone but You. For who am I that I should not bow down to Haman? For the salvation of Israel, I would have licked the shoe on his foot and the dust he treads. And now our God, save us from his hand, let him fall into the pit that he dug and be entrapped in the snare that he laid for the feet of Your pious, and let all know that You did not forget the vow that You swore to our fathers. For You did not send us into exile because of weakness, because You could not deliver us, but rather because of our sins we were sold and for our transgressions we were exiled, for we sinned against You. And now our God, powerful to deliver, deliver us from his hand, for we are greatly oppressed, and our eyes are upon You; to You we will flee to shield us and to stand in battle to fight for us against those who rise against us, and pray remember that we are Your inheritance, for ever since You divided the inheritance [Deut 32:8] to the nations and separated the sons of man, we became Your lot, for the lot that You have cast fell upon us and we became Your chosen. And now our God, why should our enemies say that they have no God, and they should open their mouths to swallow Your portion and praise their idols and vanities. Please, our God, deliver us and let them be ashamed of their idols and vanities; let them cover their mouth when they see Your salvation, God, and have mercy upon Your people and upon Your portion; do not close the mouths of those who praise You and who profess the unity of Your Name[3] evening and morning forever. Turn our mourning into gladness and joy; let us live and give praise for the good deliverance that You deliver us." And all the people of Israel cried out together to God on account of the oppression and trouble that Haman, son of Hamdatha the Amalekite, tormented them.

Esther, the queen, fled to God for she feared the coming evil. She removed her royal clothing and the ornaments of her splendor; she donned sackcloth and disheveled the hairs of her head, covering them with ashes and dust, and she tormented herself with fasting; she fell upon her face and prayed and said: "Lord God of Israel, who has reigned since the beginning of time and is the creator and maker of the world and ruler over it, help Your servant who is alone, who has none to help her except You. Alone have I lived here, and alone am I in the king's house, without father or mother. As a poor orphan seeks charity from house to house, so I have sought Your mercy from window to window in the house of King Ahasuerus from the day I was taken here unto this very day. Now, Lord, here is my soul, take it if it pleases You, and if you do not wish to take it, save Your flock from these lions [*Meg* 15b, cf. Ps 22:22] that have risen against them. For my father taught me and told me how You took our fathers from Egypt and killed all the firstborn of Egypt. You have led Your people away from them with a mighty hand; with outstretched arm you brought them across the sea as a horse in the wilderness [Isa 63:13]. You gave them bread from heaven and water from the flint rock, and meat to satiety You gave them. You smote great and noble kings before them, and how You bequeathed them Your good land. When our fathers sinned against Your great Name, You gave them into captivity, and behold, we are in exile unto this day. My father also told me how You spoke through Your servant Moses: [Lev 26:44] 'Yet for all that when they are in the land of their enemies [I will not cast them away]' etc. And now it is not only do they make us work hard, but they also say that it was not You who delivered us into their hands but thank their idols, and unto them they bow down, saying:

---

3. Language of the prayer book (the *kedushah* from the *musaf* service).

'You have delivered the Jews into our hands.' Therefore I, your servant, have abhorred them and detested them with a great hate. Just as a man loathes the menstrual rag, so I loathe my regal clothes and the royal crown upon my head, and I have not known joy from the day they brought me here except in you. Now my Lord, Father of orphans, support this orphan who trusts in You and give me mercy [when I come] before this man Ahasuerus, for I fear him as a kid fears a lion; humble him along with all his advisers and let him be meek and submissive before me through the charm and beauty that You give me, my God; put it in his heart to hate our enemies and love Your servants, for the heart of kings is in Your hand [Prov 21:1]. Lord, mighty and terrible and sublime, deliver us from the terror that I fear and that frightens me; let me come to him in Your name and leave him safely."

On the third day, Esther donned the clothes of her beauty and the ornaments of her splendor, and she took with her two of her servants. She placed her right hand upon one servant for support, as was the royal custom, and the other servant walked behind her mistress and supported her ornaments, lest the gold and the variety of precious jewels she wore touch the ground. She put on a joyful visage to cover the anxiety in her soul. She entered the inner court before the king and stood opposite him. The king was sitting upon his throne in royal garb, a gold vest shining bright upon him, with glittering emerald and turquoise and all the jewels of his splendor upon his garb. He raised his eyes and beheld Esther standing opposite him, and his anger burned against her that she had breached his law for coming before him without summons. When Esther raised her eyes, she saw the king's face, his eyes ablaze with the flame of the anger that filled his heart. The woman recognized the king's anger and his wrath; she was frightened, and her spirit grew faint, and she rested her head upon the servant who supported her right arm.

Our God saw this and took pity on the anguish of His people, and His soul was filled with compassion for the suffering of Israel and on the plight of the orphan girl who trusted in Him. He gave her grace in the king's eyes and added beauty to her beauty and magnificence to her fairness. The king rose with great haste from his throne and ran to Esther, embraced her, and kissed her and supported her with his arm. He said to her: "What is this fear of yours, Queen Esther, for this law of ours does not apply to you as queen, my companion, my wife." He took the gold scepter and placed it in her hand and said to her: "Why would you not speak to me?" And Esther said: "I beheld you, my lord, and my soul was frightened before your glory and before the grandeur of your splendor." As she spoke, she put her head once again upon the servant, for her soul was exhausted from the fast and her distress. The king was quite alarmed, and he wept before his wife, and all the servants of the king beseeched the queen, when they beheld the sorrow of their lord, to speak unto the king to gladden his spirit.

After these events, God worked great deliverance through the hands of Esther, the queen, and Mordecai the Benjaminite: they hanged Haman and his ten sons on a tree and slew by sword all those who sought evil against Israel. Mordecai was exalted from that day hence in the house of King Ahasuerus; and our fathers served in peace and quiet all the kings of Persia until Darius the second was king.

10. ALEXANDER IN JERUSALEM

During his [Darius's] reign, he waged war against the nation of Makedon and smote them in a major defeat and subdued the nation of Makedon with rigor[1] until Alexandros (Alexander), son of Philip, was made king: he exalted the name of the nation of Makedon, conquering all the lands of the East until the end of the earth. When the nation of Makedon was stirred up against the kingdom of Persia, Alexander went forth from Makedonia with a strong army and met Darius in battle and smote all of the nations who had a treaty with Darius; he conquered the land of Egypt and the land of Aram, advanced along the seacoast and conquered Acco (Acre), Ashkelon, and Gaza; then he decided to go up to Jerusalem to conquer it, for it had a treaty with Darius. He advanced with his army from Gaza until he came to an encampment[2] and camped there with his entire army.

That night, while he [Alexander] was lying in bed inside the tent, he raised his eyes and saw a man standing before him dressed in linen, his sword unsheathed in his hand—the sword's appearance was like lightning that flashes on a rainy day—and he raised his sword over the head of the king. The king was very frightened and said: "Why should my lord smite his servant?" The man said: "Because God sent me to conquer great kings and many peoples for you: I am the one who goes before you[3] to assist you. But know that you shall surely die because you dared to go up to Jerusalem to do harm to God's priests and

---

1. The author assumed that Ahasuerus made war on Makedon. Language of Lev 25:46. The Greek Romance of Alexander has the Makedonians pay tax to Darius. See A. Ausfeld, *Der griechische Alexanderroman* (Leipzig, 1907), 42–43. Yosippon follows *AJ* 11.317ff, for Alexander's tale.

2. Language of Ex 4:24 recalls the story of Moses in the inn. *AJ* 11.334, cites the dream in Dion, *Makedonia*.

3. So Isa 45:1 on Cyrus. Cf. *AJ* 11.334.

His people." The king said: "Pray, please forgive the sin of your servant [cf. Gen 50:17], my lord. If it displeases you, I will return [Num 22:34]." Then the man said to him: "Fear not, I will show favor to you! Continue your way to Jerusalem, and when you arrive before the gate of Jerusalem and you see a man dressed in linen like me, and the man has my form and likeness, hasten to fall upon your face and prostrate yourself before the man. Everything he says unto you, do it and do not disobey his command, for on the day that you disobey him, you shall surely die." The king rose and continued his way to Jerusalem.

When the priest heard[4] that King Alexander was approaching Jerusalem in anger, the priest was very afraid, along with all the people of Jerusalem; they cried out unto God and decreed a fast. After the fast, the Jews went out to greet him, to beseech him not to smite the city. The priest went out from the gate, he and all the people and all the priests, and the high priest stood before them dressed in linen. When King Alexander saw the priest, he hastened to get off his chariot and fell upon his face and prostrated himself before the priest and begged his peace. Now the kings, servants of Alexander, were angry and said to him: "Why do you bow down to a man who has no power for war?" And the king said to his servants, the kings: "Because the likeness and form of the man who walks before me,[5] subduing all the nations to me, are like those of this man to whom I have bowed down."

Following this, the priest and King Alexander came to the Temple of our God; the priest showed him the Sanctuary and the House of God, its court-yard, its archives,[6] its halls, and the place of the Holy of Holies,[7] the place of the slaughtering, and the place of the sacrifice. The king said: "Blessed be the God of this House, for since I have learned that He is the Lord of all and His rule is over everything and the life of every living thing is in His hand to put to death or to make live: happy are you His servants who serve him in this place. Now I will make a memorial for myself here and give craftsmen much gold to build my image and place it between the Holy of Holies and the House and may my statue

---

4. Several MSS designate him as Ḥoniah, while Josephus calls him Jaddus; b *Yoma* 69 and *Megillat Ta'anit* identify him with Simon the Righteous (or historically Simon the Sadducee). [The sages shortened the *vav* to a *yod* to make him one of theirs "righteous," צדיק ← צדוק. SB] Further on, however, the author follows Josephus naming him Yado (= Jaddus).

5. Yosippon's words are closer to b *Yoma* 69 and *Megillat Ta'anit* than to *AJ* 11.333–35.

6. Or treasury, 1 Chron 28:11.

7. Cf. *AJ* 11.336, for original, which the author expanded. For version in *Megillat Ta'anit*, cf. *Hebrew Union College Annual*, vols. 8–9 (1931–32), 330. The correspondence seems to be coincidental.

[*golem*][8] be a remembrance in the House of this great God." The priest said to the king: "The gold that your lips offered, give it to sustain the priests of God and the poor of His people who come to worship Him in this House. I will make for you a better memorial than you spoke: all the children born to priests in this year throughout the land of Judah and throughout the territory of Jerusalem will be called by your name, 'Alexander.' That will be a remembrance for you when they come to perform their service in this House, for we do not accept in this house any statue or picture." The king heeded his words and gave much gold to the House of God, and unto the priest he gave great presents.

The king asked the priest to inquire of God on his behalf whether he should go to war against Darius or cease [from war]. The priest said to him: "Go, for surely he has been given into your hand." He brought before him the Book of Daniel and showed him the writing within it concerning the ram that butts against every wind and concerning the he-goat that ran to the ram and trampled it to the ground. He said: "You are the he-goat, and Darius is the ram; you will trample him and take his kingdom from his hand." The priest thus strengthened him to go against Darius. Alexander wrote letters according to the vision that he saw and what the priest said to him, and he sent them to Makedonia and to Rome.[9]

Alexander left Jerusalem to go to war against Darius, and he passed by the Ammonites. Sanballat the Horonite went out to greet him and prostrated himself before the king; he [Sanballat] received him in his house and made a banquet for him and all his chiefs and gave him much silver and gold. Then he [Sanballat] asked his permission to build a sanctuary on Mount Gerizim for Menasseh the priest, his son-in-law who had married the daughter of Sanballat—he was the brother of Iddo, the high priest in Jerusalem—for Menasseh was unwilling to banish his wife from his house, as had his brothers, who banished their foreign wives. Thereupon the community of Hasidim[10] removed him from serving as priest in Jerusalem; so he went with his wife to Sanballat, his father-in-law,

---

8. "It" is feminine, translating *statuta* with the meaning of "form."

9. Rudolf von Ems (thirteenth century), *Alexander*, ed. V. Junk (Leipzig, 1928–29), 9861–84, has a slightly different version of the priest's offer, that the Levites would perpetually name one of their sons after the king, while the priest offered that all the priests would so name their son. Rudolf had a different version of the story. In any case, the mention of Rome suggests strongly that the tale refers to the attempt of Gaius to have his statue set up in Jerusalem, as opposed to Alexander, who accepted the priest's offer, in contrast to the Roman custom to so honor their leader.

10. *AJ* 11.306, has the "elders of Jerusalem." Thus, Yosippon places the *ʿadat Ḥasidim* of the Hasmonean period (chap. 16) already in the period of Alexander and also identifies the Hasidim with the Essenes.

and lived with him. For this reason, Sanballat asked the king to build a sanctuary on Mount Gerizim so that his son-in-law might be priest there. Whereupon the king said to him: "Build the sanctuary that you requested, only beware lest it become a snare for the priest who is in Jerusalem." Then the king went on his way to wage war on Darius, and Sanballat built the sanctuary on Mount Gerizim. He said to Menasseh, his son-in-law: "Here is a temple for you as it is written in your[11] Torah: 'And you shall give the blessing on Mount Gerizim' [Deut 11:29]." So Menasseh, brother of Iddo, became priest on Mount Gerizim. This sanctuary became a stumbling block and an obstacle, a snare, and a trap for the Sanctuary of God in Jerusalem and for its priests, for many of the evil men [*paritzim*] of our people went to Mount Gerizim annually to celebrate their festival according to their tithes and contributions and sacrifices and abandoned the Temple of God in Jerusalem. So, this sanctuary became exceedingly wealthy for many years, until the reign of Horkanus, son of Shimon the Hasmonean, who destroyed this temple and returned the entire rite to the Sanctuary of our God in Jerusalem. This was the Hyrcanus who circumcised Edom and brought them into the covenant and shackled them in the chains of circumcision.[12]

Meanwhile, Alexander[13] had gone to war against Darius, and Darius went out to confront him with a strong army. A great battle broke out between Persia and Makedon, and the entire army of Persia with Darius, their king, fell in one day, and Alexander captured the kingdom of the Medes and Persians. Wherever he turned, he acted harshly:[14] he conquered all the East and opened all the mysteries of India and came unto the Mountains of Darkness and went unto the end of the entire earth and ruled over the whole East unto the Pillars of Eracleos (Hercules)[15] and unto the Sea of Asphalt (Bitumen),[16] ruling over all the

---

11. I.e., "Yours" as a Jerusalem priest and not mine, I being a "foreigner" according to your Torah.

12. A favored phrase that seems to be the author's original reading of Ps 149:8. [My thanks to Steven Ballaban for the reference. The sentence is not in the Hominer edition: Ḥayyim Hominer, *Josiphon of Joseph Ben Gorion ha-Cohen*, 4th ed. (Jerusalem, 1978), 33. SB].

13. At this point, the Kaufman MS and other versions of *Yosippon* begin the Alexander Romance (see appendix), which is found independently in MS Parma 1087.

14. Language of 1 Sam 14:47. From here to "all the end of the earth" is dependent on Agrippa's speech in chap. 60, thus indicating that the author did not compose his book seriatim.

15. Greek genitive form (Ἡρακλέους) of Heracles (= Gibraltar), showing that the author's Latin source was based on a Greek original. Similar passages in *Excerpta Barbari* [*Chronica minora*], ed. C. Frick (Lipsiae, 1903), 270—a translation from the Greek to Latin in the Merovingian period—and *Historia Alexandri Magni*, ed. W. Kroll (Berlin, 1926), 3.27.2, 3.33.3. Who is guilty for placing Gibraltar in the east?

16. The Mare Asphalticum (Dead Sea) is an error instead of Mare Atlanticum, which must have been the original description of Alexander's western border.

nations just as a shepherd rules over his flock. He was in the East, and knowing the day of his death, he divided the entire earth among four leaders [Dan 7:6] of his tribe:[17] these are the Troiani (Trojans),[18] four shoots of Yavan (Greece);[19] he made them sovereigns throughout his realm, and they became four kings. These were the four heads of a leopard [Dan 7:6] that devoured the people of Judah. Were it not for the mercy of our God who stood in the breach and stirred up his priests, then the memory of Judah would have been lost from upon the earth. Alexander divided the land among them, and he enclosed all the northern tribes with iron bolts and a very strong construction[20] from sea to sea so that they could not get out and cause destruction in the lands of his realm. Alexander died in the East, and these four leaders ruled the whole world.

---

17. Cf. Hippolytos, commentary to Dan 4:3.

18. This word is found only in three MSS (New York, Rothschild, and Jerusalem) and deleted from others as not understood by copyists. For Troiani (Trojans), see chap. 13; and Chronicle of Frediger [Trojans = Makedonians = Phrygians = Franks]. Yosippon relies here on sound medieval scholarship for their being descendants of Trojans.

19. Perhaps the author read "quattuor propagines Graecorum" in his Latin source (now lost). *Propagines,* meaning "descendants," appears in the Latin translation of Gen 40:10 and 12 and Joel 1:7, where the Hebrew has "serigim." Perhaps the author recalled the Hebrew when he found the term *propagines* in his source. See chap. 37n on the influence of Latin translation on the Hebrew of *Yosippon.*

20. Chap. 88 uses the same terminology for the Alans (based on *DEH* 5.50).

II. GESTA HELIODORUS
(ELIODORUS)

In those days, Seleucus[1] ruled over the nation of Makedon; he was a merciful man[2] who governed peacefully over the people of Judah, and the land was quiet [cf. Judg 3:11] all his days. Yerushalem (Jerusalem) was quiet and deep in peace; all her pious sons, the Hasidim, served God and obeyed His laws and commandments at the behest of Onias, the high priest, who guided them in every matter and in every custom. There lived then a scoundrel from among outlaws [*pritsai ameinu*] of our people named Shimon of the tribe of Benjamin. Shimon went to Aram, to Apollonius, who had been appointed over all Aram, and said to him: "I have come to you to tell you about the wealth of the Temple in Jerusalem, in the treasury of the house that is in it, for there is no end to the quantity of gold and precious stones that is in Jerusalem's treasury; and it is fitting that all this should be in the treasury of Seleucus." When Apollonius heard this, he went to Makedonia[3] and told the king all that Shimon had said to him and tempted the king to take the gold of the Temple of God. King Seleucus sent Eliodorus (Heliodorus), his army chief, to Jerusalem with a strong army and ordered him to take the gold of which he had been told.

Heliodorus made the journey, and when he arrived in Jerusalem with all his officers and troops, Onias the priest said to him: "Why does my lord come to his servants?" Heliodorus answered, saying: "On account of your wealth, the

---

1. Yosippon apparently identifies Seleucus I (one of the four heads) with Seleucus IV. [This chapter follows basically 2 Macc 3 with considerable dramatic expansion. It begins with the story of Heliodorus, as does the Coptic Arabic text (via the Latin version) in Henry Cotton's *The Five Books of the Maccabees in English* (Oxford, 1832), 278. SB]

2. *Ish raḥamim* translates Latin *pius* for different rulers (see chap. 28).

3. The author substitutes Makedonia for the Seleucid kingdom and its capital in Damascus.

gold and precious stones that are in the treasury of your Temple, as the king was told." The priest answered, saying: "There is no gold in the treasury save for the gold that King Seleucus and other kings gave to the treasury of our God for the relief of orphans and widows, in return for which we pray to our God for the well-being of the king and his sons." Heliodorus did not listen to the priest and set guards around the Temple until the following day.

The city was in tumult, and there was much wailing and an exceedingly bitter outcry; the priests called out to God, and the elders and their wives and the chiefs and their wives threw themselves in the dust and afflicted themselves with fasting and withheld bread from the children, even milk from the nurslings.[4] They cried out to God to protect His treasury and the pledge deposited in His House. Even the virgins, who live secluded within their father's houses, stretched out their hands heavenward toward the window of their houses and cried out unto God. And what shall we say about Onias the priest? He tormented his soul, he cried and mourned, he removed the clothes of his splendor and donned sackcloth and ashes. Everyone cried and wept for him; for the man was distressed, and the look on his face betrayed the anxiety within his heart.[5]

On the following day, Heliodorus came with all his troops and, marching into the Temple of our God, entered the Sanctuary.[6] God caused him and the men accompanying him to hear a sound of thunder and noise, a powerful roar, a fearsome sound that splits mountains and shatters rocks. All Heliodorus's troops ran out and hid wherever they could, and he remained alone. He lifted his eyes and saw a terrifying man dressed in golden clothes, shining with precious stones and girt with weapons made of gold, and riding a great horse leaping and prancing into the Sanctuary. He [the horseman] ran to Heliodorus, and the horse kicked him with its hoof. It knocked him down and stood over him. He commanded two young men dressed in linen, whips in their hands, to lash Heliodorus violently. These two lads stood over Heliodorus, one on each side, and lashed him mercilessly with whips. The man was struck dumb and hovered between life and death. The young priests entered and bore him on their shoulders out of the Sanctuary and handed him over to his troops; they led him to his tent, where he fell upon the bed and lay dumb, not opening his mouth either to speak or to drink.

---

4. Not in source. See *Yosippon*'s influence on the Jewish chronicles of the Crusades: *Sepher Gezeroth Ashkenaz u-Ẓarfat*, ed. A. M. Haberman (Jerusalem, 1945–46), 47. See also Pseudo-Philo's *Biblical Antiquities* 30.4, ed. G. Kisch (Notre Dame, IN, 1949), 199.

5. 2 Macc 3:16. The author uses the language of Isa 3:9; cf. b. *Yebamot* 120a.

6. Heb. *va-yavo el ha-kodesh*, which should correspond to the *adyton* (Greek for innermost sanctuary restricted to the highest priesthood), Latin *adytum*. [SB]

The elders of Makedonia went to Onias the priest. They wept and pleaded with him and said: "Please, my lord, pray for your servant Heliodorus and for all of us, your servants who came with him, that we shall live and not die; for we know that there is no god save your God, for all the gods of the nations are vanity and emptiness, but your God is the one who made the world, and the soul of every living creature is in His hand." The priest prayed to God and offered holocausts and sacrifices; and the two young men, the ones who had beaten him in the Sanctuary, appeared again before him [Heliodorus] and said to him: "Rise and go to Onias the priest and prostrate yourself at his feet, for it was on his account that God was merciful to you." Heliodorus rose and went to the priest and, prostrating himself before him, blessed God and the priest and gave gold and silver to the treasury of the House of God. He quickly fled, going to Makedonia to King Seleucus. The king said to him: "What happened to you in Jerusalem?" To which Heliodorus replied: "Do you have any enemies who seek your life? Send them to Jerusalem and let them enter the Temple, and there they shall die, for a great and terrible God reigns in that place, and He destroys all the enemies of Jerusalem and Judah." He told the king all that he had seen, so Seleucus would no longer send anyone else to Jerusalem to do her harm, and he sent an annual gift to Jerusalem all the days of his life. The kings of the world loved to send gifts and to honor the Sanctuary that is in Jerusalem.

12. TRANSLATION OF
THE SEPTUAGINT

Ptolemy the Makedonian, who was made king over the kingdom of Egypt,[1] was a wise and prudent man who loved reading books. He commanded two of his chiefs to collect many books. These are the names of the chiefs: Aristeas and Andreas. They collected the books of Media and Persia and books in all the languages. The king said to them: "How many books do you have?" They said to him: "995."[2] Ptolemy laughed and said: "Come, let us add another five and make it a thousand!"[3] Aristeas and Andreas said to him: "Please, my Lord, we have labored in vain on these books because there is nothing of value in them.[4] If it please the king, let him write to Jerusalem to the [high] priest, and let him

---

1. The author identifies Ptolemy I, whom the author recognizes as one of the heads appointed by Alexander (chap. 10, end, and chap. 11, note 1; cf. *AJ* 12.2) with Ptolemy II; the story follows *AJ* 12. For a thirteenth-century genizah version, see Dan Greenberger, Steven Bowman, and Naḥum Ilan, "From the Quill of Ḥananel ben Shmuel," *Ginze Kedem* 13 (2017): 9–23 (Hebrew section). [Biblical Talmi (Josh 15:14) rather than later Hebrew Aptolomeos. SB]

2. In *AJ* 12.13, Demetrios of Phaleron responds to Ptolemy that he had already collected two hundred thousand and that soon the number would reach five hundred thousand. Yosippon's Latin source has twenty thousand and fifty thousand. The author reduced the figures even further based on the size of his contemporary libraries. [See now D. Wasserstein, *The Legend of the Septuagint* (Cambridge, UK, 2006) and following note. SB]

3. The additional five is based on the Jewish legends that indicate only the Septuagint translation of the Torah. [However, the author may well be playing here on the verse at 1 Kings 5:12 (4:32 in English version), where Solomon's songs number 1,005. SB] Later in the story, the author will aver that all twenty-four books of the Bible were translated, which allows him the opportunity here for the king's sarcasm.

4. Cf. *AJ* 12.14, where Demetrius calls the king's attention to the Jewish books. The following is the author's opinion. His *ta'alah* is more common as the rabbinic *to'eleth*.

send you some of the sages in Jerusalem who know the Greek language, and they will translate their Torah for you, for it is holy writ, while all the writings and books that we have written are worthless."[5]

The king sent letters and an offering to the officiating priest and inquired about this matter. The priest sent seventy priests with Elazar at their head[6] (this was the Elazar who was tested in the days of Antiochus and killed for the Lord his God).[7] When Elazar came with seventy priestly translators to Egypt, Ptolemy gave them seventy houses and separated them from each other,[8] assigning to each a skilled scribe. The priests translated all of the Torah, and the rest of the scriptures, twenty-four books in all, which the seventy elders rendered from the holy tongue to the Greek language.[9] Elazar brought their work to the king, who read each man's translation, and behold, all the translators understood and explained the text in exactly the same way.

The king was very happy[10] and, bringing forth much silver and gold, gave it to Elazar and the seventy sages and sent them to Jerusalem. On that day, he also set at liberty 150,000 Judaeans and gave to each one 150 gold drachmas. The king sent an offering to the house of our God, a pure gold table, its weight one thousand talents, on which was engraved the land of Egypt and the River Shihor-Ye'or (Nile), which is in Egypt,[11] and how it flows and waters the whole of Egypt.[12] Into the table, he set every kind of precious stone:[13] no table like this was seen in the entire world. King Ptolemy sent it as an offering to the great and terrible God, Lord of the world.

------

5. The author uses the root *PRSh*.

6. *AJ* 12.56, notes that not all were priests. Elazar was not the high priest at the time.

7. On Elazar the martyr, cf. chap. 14. For the phrase designating the martyr "he was tested (and found complete)," see chaps. 24 and 35.

8. The author follows the (oral or written?) Talmudic story here from b. *Meg.* 9b, rather than *AJ* 12.103–4, which has all of them in one house.

9. The author uses the same root *PRSh*, which here is better rendered as "interpreted." His source has the seventy translate only the five books of the Torah.

10. Having finished with the Talmudic story, the author returns to *AJ* 12.110.

11. The author's Latin translation had the Meander River, based on that translator's (*AJ* 12.71) misunderstanding of "to meander"; the author restored the Nile on the basis of the biblical reference to the Nile as Shihor (Josh 13:3). Hence the duplication "Shihor-Ye'or."

12. Einhard, in *Vita Caroli Magni* (Florence, 2014), chap. 33, writes that Charlemagne had three such tables.

13. The author's language is influenced by 1 Kings 6:21 (*zahav sagur*) as well as the Latin *includere* (to close = *lisgor*); Latin *AJ* 12.66, details inset stones (*clusi*).

13. THE DECREES OF ANTIOCHUS

After many years, Antiochus[1] reigned over the nation of Makedon, and Ptolemy, king of Egypt, was gathered to his people, and another Ptolemy ruled after him. Antiochus, king of Makedon, waged war on him [Ptolemy II], defeated him, and killed him. He conquered all of Egypt and ruled over the entire land.

In those days, great and terrible wars began to beset the people of Judah, for once King Antiochus had defeated Egypt, he became very haughty and ordered every people throughout his realm to worship an image [cf. Dan 3:5], that is, a graven image of King Antiochus.[2] All the gentiles consented and worshiped it. Then the outlaws of our people came, Menelaus and Simon and Alcimus[3] and the other wicked men among our people, and they stirred up Antiochus to do evil unto Israel.

A vision appeared to the people of Jerusalem, and for forty days, they saw between earth and sky the image of fiery horses and their riders bearing in their hands weapons of war made of gold, fighting against each other for forty days. The wicked of our people came to King Antiochus and said to him: "Behold, a miracle has appeared in Jerusalem. They say that Antiochus the king is dead, and they rejoice at the downfall of our lord." The king became very angry and came unexpectedly to Jerusalem and put her to the sword, killing many in the city of Jerusalem and exiling a great multitude, scattering its entire community of Hasidim. The Hasidim fled to the forest and ate grass like beasts, hiding like animals in the forest. For it was not enough for King Antiochus that he killed

---

1. Cf. *AJ* 12.234. Antiochus IV Epiphanes (175–64); Ptolemy V Epiphanes (204–181); Ptolemy VI Philometer (181–45).

2. Not in primary sources, but cf. Jerome on Dan 11:33 (*PL* 25, col. 569), following perhaps 1 Macc 1:54.

3. Menelaus is Simon's brother (2 Macc 4:23); Alcimus is later. [See B. E. Scolnik, *Alcimus, Enemy of the Maccabees* (Lanham, MD, 2006). SB]

and exiled; when he left the land of Judah, he left behind commissioners to oppress the people of Judah, and he left Philip from the refugees of Phrygia (who are the Trojans from whom the Romans are descended,[4] and Philip was of that generation). The king left him to oppress the people of Israel, and he commanded him, saying: "Whosoever consents to worship the image of the idol that I set up and eats pork, let him live! All who refuse, kill without mercy, and prevent this people from keeping their Sabbaths and from circumcising their sons!" The king went on his way to Makedonia, and Philip, who was a powerful man, advanced throughout the land of Judah and did as the king commanded: he kept the Torah and all service of our God from the people of Judah and let live all the evildoers and outlaws of our people, and he killed many of the community of Hasidim.

In those days were found two women who circumcised their boys: the women were hung by their breasts;[5] they and their sons were dropped from atop a tower, where they [fem.] splattered and died.

---

4. 2 Macc 5:22 has *Philippum genere Phrygem*, which the author identified with Troiani. See chap. 10.

5. Cf. 2 Macc 6:10 and 1 Macc 1:64. The author adjusted his sources to the cruelties of his own age. Cf. also A. Wertheimer, *Battei Midrashot* (Jerusalem, 1950), 1.281; and A. Jellinek, *Beit HaMidrash*, 2nd ed. (Jerusalem, 1938), 1.148, where women suffer such punishments in Gehenna.

14. DEATH OF ELAZAR

Elazar, chief of the priests,[1] was seized; he was the Elazar about whom we wrote that he went to Egypt in the days of Ptolemy. They brought Elazar before Philip, and Philip said to him: "Elazar, O wise and understanding man, please do not transgress the commandment of the king: eat from the meat of his sacrifice." He replied: "Woe unto me if I reject the commandment of my God in order to fulfill the commandment of the king." Philip summoned him privately and said to him: "You know that I have loved you for a long time, so now I take pity upon your soul and your old age. Please, take some of the meat of your sacrifices from which you eat and eat it before the people, and they will say that you have eaten from the meat of the king's sacrifices, and you shall live and not die."

When Elazar heard this, he showed everyone the value of his greatness and the holiness of his glory, and he said to Philip: "Today I am ninety years old, and at my age it is not fitting to worship my God in deceit, nor may I deceive men. If the young men say that Elazar at ninety years rejected the law of his God, then they too will disobey it and be lost. Now, heaven forbid that I should disgrace my holiness and sully the purity of my old age or weaken these youths who are with me and enfeeble them so that they say that Elazar at ninety sinned against the rule of his God and chose to be a slave to the vanities of gentiles, so let us do the same. For though I might escape this day from your hand, how could I be saved from the hand of my God, from whom neither the living nor the dead may escape, for he has the power to kill the living and quicken the dead? I shall die bravely and leave behind courage for my people, and my young men, when they see this humble death, they will consent to do likewise and will die for the honor of their Torah as I so humbly died."

---

1. 2 Macc 6:18 has "one of the chief scribes."

When Philip heard these words, he turned completely cruel, commanding his men to torture and beat the old man and to profane the pious Ḥasid. As they beat him mercilessly, with all manner of blows, he groaned and said: "O Lord my God, who has brought me to this old age, You know that I could have saved myself from this humble death, but I did not so desire for I love it. And now, the violent blows are too hard for me, and I have not the strength to endure; but because of my fear of You, they are trifling in my eyes and are as nothing, and I suffer them with courage." And with these words he ended his days and returned his soul,[2] bequeathing courage to his people and strength to his young men.

---

2. There is no hint of *kiddush hashem* (martyrdom) in this phrase. See S. Lieberman, "Roman Legal Institutions in Early Rabbinics and in the Acta Martyrum," *Jewish Quarterly Review* 35 (1944): 49–52; Zunz, *Literaturgeschichte der synagogalen Poesie* (Berlin, 1865), 641–42. [See also S. Shepkaru, "From After Death to Afterlife: Martyrdom and Its Recompense," *Association for Jewish Studies Review* 24 (1999): 2–3. SB]. Compare the dignity of Elazar to that of Calasiris *pace* Moses Hadas's analysis in his translation of Heliodorus's *Ethiopica* (Ann Arbor, MI, 1957), ix. The phrase appears throughout *Yosippon* (chap. 15, end) in various contexts and means "to die." [On the phrase *shilem naphsho*, see S. Shepkaru, *Jewish Martyrs in the Pagan and Christian Worlds* (Cambridge, UK, 2006), chap. 4, note 86, which suggests a possible cultic allusion to *shlamim* sacrifice. Chap. 18, however, clearly supports Flusser's argument to the contrary. SB] *Yosippon* usually glosses *leshalem*, "to pay," for *lehashlim*, "to complete."

15. DEATH OF THE MOTHER AND HER SEVEN SONS

Seven brothers and their mother were seized[1] and sent to the king, for the king had not yet gotten far from Jerusalem; and for the sake of the abominable, stinking, and putrid flesh of swine, they were cruelly torn to pieces, their flesh flayed by a bull [whip].[2]

When the first was brought before the king, he said to the king: "Why do you keep on talking and trying to teach us? We have already learned from our forefathers. Behold, we have prepared ourselves to die for God and for His Torah." The king became furious and commanded to bring a copper pan, and they put it on the fire. He commanded to cut out his tongue and cut off his hands and feet and scalp and put them into the pan, which was on the fire, before his brothers' eyes; and the remainder of the body they threw into a big copper cauldron, which was over coals. As he [the first son] was about to die, the king ordered to cool the cinder beneath the cauldron,[3] lest he die too quickly, in order to frighten his brothers and mother. Now, these were encouraging one another, and each strengthened the other when they saw that their brother died for God and His Torah; and they said to each other: "This is what Moses, God's

1. 2 Macc 7:1. The mother is unnamed here. Christian traditions in *Les livres des Maccabées*, ed. F. M. Abel (Paris, 1949), 381–82. Rabbinic tradition calls her Miriam bat Tanḥum (or Menaḥem) or Ḥannah. The earliest version of *Yosippon* [version C] to call her Ḥannah was extant in 1160–61, as does the Vatican 408 MS of version B. [See now Sela, *Arabic Josippon*, 141–44. SB] See 1 Sam 2:5 for Ḥannah, which may be source for this midrash on the martyrdom of the woman and her seven sons; see also *Pesikta Rabbati* on Miriam bat Tanḥum and Samuel's mother, Ḥannah.

2. In the Latin text before the author, *taureis*, "by whips made of bull's hide."

3. Text (2 Macc 7:5) has *iussit ignem admoveri*, which the author understood as *le-hasir ha'esh mi-tahat ha-sir*, i.e., reading *amoveri* for *admoveri*.

servant, said in his song: 'He will have compassion for His servants' [cf. Deut 32:36 in Latin]. God will regret[4] all the evil that he intended to do to His people, and he will have pity on them." Thus died the first [son].

They brought the second [son] and said to him: "Take heed and obey the king's commandment! Why should you die in dire agony like your brother?" He [the second son] replied: "Hasten the sword and quicken the fire. Do not do less to me than you did to my brother, for I do not fall short of my brother in piety and fear of God." The king ordered them to sever all his limbs and put him into the pan that was on the fire. He said to the king: "Hear me, you who are so cruel to God's creatures, did you give us the souls that you are now taking [from us]? Can you bind them in your clothing? Behold, they are going [back] to God, who gave them, and into the light that is with God, and we shall live long lives without termination or end,[5] when He raises the dead of his people and the slain amongst his servants." Thus died the second.

The third was brought forth. He looked at the king, extended his right hand toward him, and said: "Why do you try to frighten us, O foe and enemy? All this has come upon us from heaven, but we will take it upon ourselves with love. You are contemptible in our eyes, and all your torments are as nothing to us, for it is from heaven that we hope for honor and grace, and he will reward us for our labors." The king and all his chiefs were astonished at the nobility of the lad's spirit. Thus died the third.

Then the fourth was brought, and he said to the king: "Why should I waste words with you, O wicked man? We shall die for God, and he will bring us back to life, yet for you there will never be resurrection or life." Thus died the fourth.

The fifth was brought, and he said: "Do not say in your heart that God has abandoned us, for out of his love for us He has brought us to this honor. Whereas you, who insult and profane, God has aroused you to do to us all that you do, because he hates you; for he will yet wreak great vengeance upon you and your seed, and his anger will burn against you and your entire household." The fifth died.

The sixth was brought before the king, and he said: "We know our faults, for we have sinned against God, and now, we who have given our souls unto death as an atonement for our people, behold we shall die; but you who have dared to do such things to the servants of our God and to wage war against God, he will wage war against you and uproot you from the land." Thus died the sixth.

---

4. 2 Macc 7:6. Note pun on verb *hitnaḥem* and its alliteration with the closely related verb *yeraḥem*.

5. *Sof veketz*, which glosses as "in life" (fem.) for *vita*.

There remained yet the seventh and he a young lad. The saintly mother[6] who saw her seven sons killed in one day, her heart feared not, nor was her spirit shaken. She stood bravely over the corpses of her slain sons, and lifting up her voice, she cried out, saying: "My sons, O my sons. I know not how you were formed in my belly; I gave you neither spirit nor soul, nor did I bring you forth from my belly or rear and raise you. Your sacrificed[7] flesh that you received from God, and all your bones he formed; he wove the sinews and covered them with flesh and made hair grow and breathed the spirit of life into your noses. All this you have given up for his sake, and he shall give it back to you and renew your bodies[8] and reward you for your labors. Blessed are you for all this, my sons."

The king was very ashamed that the woman had bested him, and the king said: "Bring forth the seventh one: being a boy, we might be able to tempt him with words to do our will, lest the woman boast and say: 'I have defeated King Antiochus by encouraging my sons to die for our God.'" He commanded them to bring forth the seventh, the boy, and the king implored him, vowing to make him rich with silver and gold, with flocks and many slaves, and to make him his deputy [*amicus*] and give him authority throughout his kingdom, but the boy spurned the words of the king.

The king summoned the boy's mother and said to her: "Good woman, take pity on this boy and have mercy upon the fruit of your womb; tempt him to do my will, and he will be left for you." The woman answered: "Give him to me, and I will tempt him with my words." He gave him to his mother, who led him aside somewhat, kissed him, and mocked the king's indignity and his shame. She said to her son: "My son, forget that I carried you in my belly for nine months and nursed you for three years, and after I nursed you, I have fed you bread to this day and taught you the fear of God. So now, my son, observe the heavens and look upon the land and the sea and the water and the fire, for by the word of God they were made, and man who is flesh and blood is as nothing compared

---

6. 2 Macc 7:20. The Hebrew *kedoshah* is usually translated as "saintly"; however, the Latin root carries a suggestion of martyrdom that is not necessarily evident in the text. The author elsewhere uses the root *KDSh* to render the Latin *pius*.

7. 2 Macc 7:23. "Flesh" in feminine from Latin *caro* or Italian *la carne*. The following passage derives from Ezek 37:10 and 8; cf. also *Megillat Aḥimaaz*, ed. B. Klar, 2nd ed. (Jerusalem, 1974), 94; cf. Shabbetai Donnolo, *Sefer Hakhmoni*, ed. D. Castelli (Firenze, 1880), 12 (dated 946). Yosippon inverts the order and makes "flesh" precede "bones"; "flesh" (*basar*) has the meaning of "body."

8. Contemporary medieval Italian Hebrew used *golem* as a synonym for "body" (see chap. 2). The author uses *gviah* for body, more commonly "corpse."

to Him.[9] Fear not, my son, this cruel man; die for God and follow your brothers. Would that you could now see your brothers' place and the grandeur of their glory before God. Go, my son, and join your brothers, and you will share their glorious destiny, and I will come there with you and rejoice with you as if on your wedding day,[10] and I will be with you in your righteous destiny."

While she was still speaking, the boy answered, saying: "Why delay me and keep me from following my saintly brothers?[11] I do not obey the king because our God's Torah, which he gave in the hands of his servant Moses to the people of Israel, whom you have cursed and blasphemed, you cruel enemy of God. Woe unto you, enemy, woe unto you! Where will you go, and where will you flee? Where will you run, and where will you hide from the hand of our God, you wicked foe and enemy? For He shall resurrect and glorify and exalt us above every nation, but you who have conspired to do this thing, to raise a hand against his servants, better for you if you had not been born, nor come forth from the filth of the stupid woman who bore this fool Antiochus who brought such evil upon himself, for you have done us only good. And if we suffer a little and bear these troubles in this world, behold, we are going to eternal life and everlasting light in which there is no darkness and to a life in which there is no death. But you, execrable to all mankind and abominable to our God, when our God wreaks vengeance upon you, you will die an unnatural death amid great afflictions and descend to the depth of Sheol into the darkness of hell, where there is no life and no light but darkness and the shadow of death, and there is no rest there or relief, only torment and oppression, fire and brimstone; this will be your portion from God and your fate from our Lord, O wicked and blood-stained man. And our God will have mercy upon His people. Until now He has shown His anger, but from now on He will no longer be angry at His people, for He regrets all that He has done to us before, for [though] He has acted in truth and righteousness and we have acted wickedly, He will once again have mercy on us and will raise us to eternal life."

---

9. 2 Macc's polemic against *creatio ex nihilo* is lost in the author's translation.

10. The author adjusts his source (2 Macc 7:29) to the theme of martyrdom as marriage, e.g., Binding of Isaac. For later midrashim, see Sh. Spiegel, "Meaggadoth ha'aqedah," in *Alexander Marx Jubilee Volume* (New York, 1950), 632–36 (Hebrew section). [In light of this later emphasis on comparing sacrifice and martyrdom to marriage, the sacrifice of Jephtah's daughter in Judg 11, which is based on the binding of Isaac, takes on a new dimension. See now Y. Feldman, *Glory and Agony* (Stanford, CA, 2010), index, s.v. "Female Sacrifice." SB]

11. The Hebrew is *kedoshim*, which is translated as "saintly" in the text when designating the mother. Flusser does not deal with this sobriquet (nor in the author's Maccabees, although the cult of the Maccabee saints, in Antioch, was widespread in Byzantium). [SB]

King Antiochus was furious that [the boy] did not obey him and so added tortures more cruel than those that he had inflicted upon his brothers. The seventh died as well. Then their saintly mother[12] stood over their corpses and raised her palms to heaven and said: "O my sublime God, Lord of the world, let me, your maidservant, come with my sons to the place that you have prepared for them." And as she was saying this, she returned her soul,[13] her spirit left her body, and she fell upon the corpses of her sons and went with them.

12. 2 Macc 7:41 does not describe her death, so the author could only embellish the contrasting peacefulness of her demise. [For the phrase "their saintly mother" (*imam hakedoshah*), which Flusser surprisingly does not discuss, see Shepkaru, *Jewish Martyrs*, chap. 4, note 89. SB]
13. For this phrase, see chap. 14. Here it means "to die" and has no hint of martyrdom (see chap. 18, where it is used for Antiochus IV).

16. THE TIMES OF MATTATHIAS (MATITYAHU BEN YOḤANAN) THE PRIEST

The king went on his way to Makedonia and commanded Philip and his officers, whom he left in the land of Judah, and said to them: "Obliterate all memory of the name Judah from the land and kill everyone who calls himself a Jew; but everyone who sees fit to be of our people and calls himself a Greek, let him live!"[1] Philip and the chiefs who were with him did as ordered; he wiped out all those whom he found observing the Torah. Only those who fled with Mattathias ben Yoḥanan to Mount Modiin[2] were spared, for Mattathias would not suffer the disgrace caused by the uncircumcised; he was zealous for his God and wept, saying: "Woe is me, my mother, that you bore me to see destruction of my people!"[3] He sent forth Yehudah (Judah), his son, to exclaim secretly throughout the cities of Judah, saying: "Whoever among you [Ex 32:26] is with me and whoever is for the Lord, my God, to me!" There gathered unto

---

1. The pressure to convert, not in the sources, is identified with national assimilation since Antiochus IV. Yosippon was aware of the Makedonian persecutions of Jews in southern Italy under Basil I, which also aimed at forced baptism. [See R. Bonfil, *History and Folklore in a Medieval Jewish Chronicle: The Family Chronicle of Ahima'az ben Paltiel* (Leiden, 2009), 77–80, 260–70. SB]

2. *Har Hamoda'it* is the same in Talmud (M. Jastrow, *A Dictionary of the Targumim, the Talmud Babli, and Yerushalmi, and the Midrashic Literature* [New York, 1886], 159, s.v.); but the near contemporary Hebrew translation of 1 Macc has *be-har ha-moda'i* (cf. *Kobetz 'al Yad* 7 [1896–97]: 7), of which the author may have been aware.

3. Yosippon conflated two verses, Jer 15:10 and Lam 3:48, to create this moving plaint; see note 5 below: Flusser identifies only the first part from Jer and references 1 Macc 2:7 without mention of the second part from Lam. [SB]

him the powerful community of the Hasidim,[4] to whom Mattathias said: "Why should we continue to waste words! There is nothing left now but prayer and war. Be strong and let us be strengthened. Let us die in battle and not die as sheep led to slaughter."[5] All were strengthened by Mattathias's words and said to one another: "To your tents, O Judah.[6] Rule now your land! Enough of you, King Antiochus! Your sword is sharp, O people of Judah; beware, O nation of Makedon!" And from that day forward, the yoke of the nation of Makedon was removed from the people of Judah.[7]

When Philip and the king's chiefs heard of these things, they went against them [the Yehudim] with a great force.[8] On their way, they found about one thousand Yehudim, men, women, and children, all of them in one cave observing the Sabbath. They came to the entrance of the cave and said to them [the Yehudim]: "Come out and profane the Sabbath and obey the king's command, and you shall live and not die." But they said: "We shall neither go out nor profane the Sabbath! Today let heaven and earth bear witness on our behalf that we shall die in our innocence." Philip commanded to bring fire and place it at the entrance of the cave; they put logs on it, and the cave filled with smoke; and they [the Yehudim] all died in the smoke.

The king's officers went to Mattathias on Mount Modiin and found him girded with weapons, he and his sons and brothers and only a few of the community of Hasidim with him, for they had gone to bring their wives and children to Mount Modiin.[9] The king's chiefs approached Mattathias with words of peace and said: "O Mattathias, a man honored among your people, obey the command

---

4. 1 Macc 2:42: *synagoga Assidaeorum* translated as *'adat ha-ḥasidim*, rather than *kehal Ḥasidim* as in Ps 149:1. See chap. 10. Matityahu's words are the author's own.

5. Yosippon's own conflation of Ps 44:23 and Isa 53:7. This verbatim clarion call was evoked directly or indirectly by Abba Kovner in Vilna during the Holocaust. See Y. Feldman and S. Bowman, "Let Us Not Die as Sheep Led to the Slaughter," *Haaretz, Literary Supplement*, December 7, 2007, 4 [Hebrew and English versions]. See note 3 above. [SB]

6. Cf. 1 Kings 12:16 and 2 Chron 10:16.

7. The national liberation is advanced to the inception of the revolt. 1 Macc 13:41, however, dates it to Shimon's leadership.

8. The author adjusts the order of his sources in 1 Macc 2:29–38 and 2 Macc 6:11. The figure one thousand is from 1 Macc 2:38, and the cave reference is from 2 Macc 6:11. [The story of the one thousand rebels is discussed by Shepkaru with relevant literature in "From After Death to Afterlife," 5–6. SB]

9. Evidence of the author's historical sense. Having anticipated the revolt to the events at Modiin, he resolved the difficulty he caused by splitting Matityahu's forces, himself armed at the sacrifice of the pig and his supporters escorting the women and children out of danger.

of the king, and you shall live and not die." But Mattathias replied proudly and said: "I will fulfill the commandment of my King—now you fulfill the commandment of your king that he commanded you!" The king's officers became scared and fell silent and did not say a word, for they wondered how they could seize Mattathias and kill him as they had killed the rest of the Hasidim. One of the Yehudim who was with the king's chiefs, one of the bandits and wicked ones, replied: "I am amazed at the officers of the king and his army. How long will you be silent and not fulfill the king's command? Let us have vengeance upon Mattathias, who has dared not to obey the king's command." As he said this, he unsheathed his sword and cut off the head of the pig, took it in his hand, and went to the altar they [the traitorous priests who supported the usurpers (supporters of Antiochus) in Jerusalem] had built to sacrifice to the vanities of King Antiochus. He placed the head of the pig upon it and burned incense to the images of the king.

When Mattathias saw this, he became very angry, and his furor burned within him: he unsheathed his sword and leapt onto the Judaean offering the sacrifice and struck him on the neck with his sword. His [the Judaean's] head flew aloft and fell before the king's chief, who had drawn near to speak with Mattathias, and his body fell upon the altar, by which he had been standing. Mattathias killed him, and the king's chief he cut down with his sword and put to flight the remainder of the chiefs and slew[10] many of their crowd. Then he sounded the ram's horn to give the signal for battle. He was the first to raise his hand against the kingdom of Makedon, and he was the one who commanded us to fight on the Sabbath, and he is the one who will be our intercessor in this matter. It is written in the book of Joseph ben Gurion haCohen. Mattathias went forth with his sons and brothers and with them the great congregation of the Hasidim; they pursued the sinners, beat them, and crushed them until not even a remnant was left of them in the land of Judah; and they circumcised the boys; so God achieved a great salvation through his [Matthathias's] hand.

As the day of Mattathias's death drew nigh, he summoned his five sons and encouraged them, saying: "My sons, I know that henceforth great wars will oppress the land of Judah because the Lord God aroused me to do battle for our people. Now, my sons, be zealous for your God, for His temple, and for His people; make war and do not fear death, for, if you should die in your war, you will be received among your fathers and share with them their reward, for all our ancestors who were zealous for God received from him honor and grace.

---

10. *Silah* in Lam 1:15 (as in Latin translation and Septuagint) as synonym for "kill."

Did not Pinḥas, our father,[11] receive the covenant of salt [Num 18:19] because of this? And the remainder of our fathers who were zealous for God received their reward from Him." He summoned Shimon, his son, and said to him: "I am aware of the wisdom that God has placed within your heart. Do not withhold your counsel from this people; be like a father to your brothers, and they will heed your[12] every counsel and every word, for our God has given you courage and counsel." And Mattathias spoke on: "Summon Judah, my son, to me!" They called him, and he came and stood before his father. He said to him: "My son Judah, you are called Maccabee because of your bravery;[13] I know my son; I know that you are indeed a man of war and God has given you strength and bravery and a heart like that of a lion that flees before nothing. Now, my son, honor [Prov 3:9] the Lord for the wealth that He has given you; fight His battles and make war without sloth. Laze not to go unto every corner of your land, into the east and west and north and south, to take the land from the hand of the uncircumcised; be for this people 'general of the army' [*sar ẓava*] and 'anointed for war [*meshuaḥ milḥamah*].'" Bringing forth a flask of oil, he [Mattathias] poured it over his [Judah's] head,[14] anointing him for war. All the people shouted for joy and sounded the ram's horn, saying: "Long live the messiah!" And having completed commanding his sons, he [Mattathias] died and was gathered to his people.

---

11. 1 Macc 2:54. The author skips directly to emphasize Pinḥas, the ancestor of the Hasmoneans and the "first" Zealot (*kanai*).

12. 1 Macc 2:65: *ipsum audite.* The author caught well the pun on Simon's name, and perhaps this reading should reflect this even more, as in the New York MS: *ve-elekha shim'on,* as opposed to *ve-elekha yishme'un.*

13. Source has *Iudas Machabaeus fortis viribus.* מכביי (MKhBYY) was standardized in tenth-century Hebrew (*Yosippon* and 1 Macc), but the Yemenite MSS of *Megillat Antiochus* have מקבי (MaQBAY so vocalized); cf. Wertheimer, *Battei Midrashot,* 1:313, 323. Menaḥem Zvi Kadari, "The Aramaic Megillat Antiochus (I)," *Bar Ilan Annual,* vol. 11 (Jerusalem, 1963), 93; also *The Jewish Encyclopedia* (New York, 1905), s.v. "Maccabees"; and R. Marcus, "The Name *Makkabaios*," in *The Joshua Starr Memorial Volume* (New York, 1953), 59–65, which is one of the last essays to appear before Flusser's seminal Hebrew article "The Author of *Sepher Yosippon,*" *Zion* 18 (1953): 109–26 (in Hebrew), where he suggests a provenance from the Hebrew מקוה. [SB]

14. For title *meshuaḥ milḥamah,* see m. *Sotah,* chap. 8. Yosippon's assumption is dependent, according to Flusser, on the ninth-tenth-century Hebrew Maccabees, which reads, "Yehudah Makhabyy rose after him and his brothers helped him and anointed him with joy in place of his father to be *meshuaḥ milḥamah.*" The Latin of 1 Macc 3:1 reads, "se conjunxerant," which the Hebrew translator read as *unxerant* and translated "he anointed him." See A. Neubauer, *Mediaeval Jewish Chronicles* (Oxford, 1895), 1.166, 168.

17. EARLY DAYS OF YEHUDAH (JUDAH) THE MACCABEE

Judah, his son, called Maccabee, succeeded him. His brothers and his father's entire household supported him, and the whole community of the Hasidim was with him. Judah rejoiced in fighting the battles of Israel: he donned a breastplate[1] like a hero and girded himself with his weapons, and in his strength he appeared like a giant.[2] He shielded the camp of Israel with his sword and pursued its enemies, trampling their lives into the ground [Ps 7:6] and singeing the sinners with the flames of his mouth. The wicked were stunned from fear of him, and all the evildoers were frightened of him, like cattle dread the roar of a lion on the day when he roars to devour his prey. Jacob was glad about his deeds, and Israel rejoiced with his actions, and great kings were afraid. Yehudah's name spread throughout the world, and his wars were recounted unto the ends of the earth. Blessed be his memory among the people of Israel. May there be peace upon the birthplace of his righteousness [Isa 15:2] and blessing upon the bed of his holiness, for he did not spare his soul from death for the sake of Israel, the people of God. And he went from city to city and killed all the wicked people of Judah who terrorized the people of Israel.

Apollonius, chief of the army of Makedon, heard these things and said: "Who is this who has dared to rebel against our lord the king?" He assembled a great and mighty army of Makedonian warriors and came to fight against Israel. Yehudah went out to meet him, and a great battle ensued between the nation of Makedon and the congregation of the Hasidim. During the battle, Yehudah saw

---

1. The author mimics the poetic style of 1 Macc 3:3.

2. *Ke-yelid 'anak* renders *sicut gigas* and hence "giant" seems to be the correct translation. [The Byzantine Meyuḥas ben Eliahu, in his commentary on Genesis, identifies the "*anakim* as 'Greeks,'" no doubt based on the name of one as Talmai, which is also Yosippon's preferred spelling for Ptolemy. SB]

Apollonius standing within the ranks of the Makedonians, and in the force of his rage, he raced toward him in the thick of the battle, hacking to his right and left and before him. He felled the warriors of Greece just as the harvester fells his sheaves and the bundles of his harvest, and reaching Apollonius, he struck him with his sword and laid him out on the ground. The Greeks and the warriors of Makedon turned their backs and fled, and Yehudah pursued them with the congregation of the Hasidim, smiting them a mighty blow and taking their booty. Yehudah took the sword of Apollonius and fought with it all the days of his life.

When Seron, chief of the army of Aram, heard of this, he said: "I shall make a name for myself and go fight against Yehudah!" He gathered all his army and came to Beth Horon. When Yehudah was told, he said: "We must not delay; let us go against them even though our brothers the congregation of the Hasidim have left us. If we wait for them to return, then our enemies will say that we are afraid of them." Yehudah advanced against them [the Makedonians] all night, and at daybreak they saw an immense force, and they said unto Yehudah: "How can we fight against this multitude when we are so few?" Whereupon Yehudah said: "Call upon heaven, and you shall be saved for the battle is God's!" Yehudah came from the flank of the [enemy] camp, leapt upon them suddenly, and engaged them in battle. Seron and his army panicked and fled; Yehudah pursued after him and caught up with him and smote him, and he slew on that day many of Aram; and fear of Yehudah fell upon all the nations. When King Antiochus heard of these events, he was enraged and mustered his people and all the nations under his sovereignty—an immense multitude. He divided his force and taking half of it went to the land of Persia, for at that time the Persian nation had rebelled against Makedon, seeing that the people of Judah had rebelled. The king gave half of his force to Lysias, an important member of his family of Makedonian royal descent, and said to him: "You are aware of all that Yehudah, son of Mattathias, did to two chiefs I had and to their entire army. Now go and smite all the inhabitants of the land of Judah! Behold, I am sending Eupator, my son, with you, while I will go to the land of Persia and uproot the Persian nation, for they have rebelled against me!"

King Antiochus went to Persia and left Lysias as tutor to his son to fight in the land of Judah. Lysias chose Ptolemy and Nicanor and Gorgias, valiant men, and he sent with them forty thousand warriors and seven thousand cavalry; the entire forces of Aram and Philistia joined them as well, and they invaded the land of Judah to destroy her.[3]

---

3. 1 Macc 3:38–39 and 41. The Latin of 1 Macc 3:41 has *terra alienigenarus*, reflecting Septuagint *allophyloi* to render Philistines, as did the Hebrew translation of Maccabees, and

When Yehudah and all the elders of Israel heard of this, they declared a fast, donning sackcloth and putting dust on their heads, and called out to God. After the fast, Yehudah mustered his army and placed over them captains of thousands, captains of hundreds, captains of fifties, and captains of tens, and he took the field to confront all the invading armies. A call passed through the camp: "Whoever has planted a vineyard or has built a house or who has betrothed a woman or is fearful and soft-hearted, let him go and return [Deut 20:5–8]." So the people returned, and there remained with Yehudah seven thousand young men, and of the brave men of Israel, all brave in battle, only one out of every hundred, men who would not avert their face nor flee from anything.

Yehudah went out to confront Nicanor, who brought with him a multitude of merchants, for he thought to sell them the Judaean boys and girls from the captives whom he planned on taking from the land of Judah, and he came haughtily toward Yehudah. Yehudah went out from the 'adat Ḥasidim with him and called out to God, saying: "My most high God, You [who] have ruled from the beginning of time and rule even now, who puts an end to wars and in whose hand is power and might to elevate and to bring low, subdue and humiliate this people before the humble of your people, for You it is who subdues peoples beneath us [Ps 47:4] and nations under our feet." Then, after the prayer, the priests [Num 10:8–10] sounded the holy trumpets, and the entire army cheered, and Yehudah leapt hurriedly into battle and dealt a mighty blow on Nicanor's camp. They fled before him, and Yehudah pursued after them, smiting all the way, and they dispatched nine thousand souls in that battle. They returned and took their spoil; they took the gold that the merchants brought to purchase the youth of Israel and divided it among the poor. And they rested there in that spot, for this battle took place on the sixth day.

Yehudah left that place and went to Bacchides and to Timotheus and waged a great war with them; twenty thousand warriors of Makedon he laid out[4] in that battle. Bacchides and Timotheus fled; Yehudah pursued after them, but he did not catch up with them, for they came to Astoroth Karnaim [Gen 14:5]. But Yehudah did catch up with Philip, that Philip who did the evil in the land

---

Yosippon guessed correctly here, even though Flusser denies that he read that Hebrew version of Maccabees (which seems to contradict his position in chap. 16, note 13). The Vulgate's Psalms always translates Philistines as *alienigenae*. See further chap. 19.

4. Yosippon uses the verb *hitsi'a*, which is a rare usage here, and no alternate readings are listed by the editor. The Hominer edition does not have this sentence (see Hominer, *Josiphon*, 84, second paragraph). Our translation follows 2 Macc 8:30 (8:37 in the Hebrew translation of I. Frankel [Berlin, 1922–23]). See now D. R. Schwartz's annotated translation *The Second Book of Maccabees* (Jerusalem, 2004), 189. [SB].

of Yehudah.[5] As Yehudah drew near, Philip turned from the road and entered a nearby house. Yehudah commanded them [his men] to knock the house down upon him and burn him there with fire. Thus, he avenged Elazar and the blood of the Hasidim that Philip had spilled. They returned to strip the corpses and sent the booty to Jerusalem. Nicanor had fled from there and escaped, for he had shed the purple garment that he wore and donned the rags of poverty, wherefore he was not recognized; he went to Makedon and related to Lysias everything that had happened to him.[6]

---

5. 2 Macc 8:32 has Philarches, whom the author identifies with Philip. [See chap. 13. The difficulty whether it is a name or title is discussed by Schwartz, in *Second Book of Maccabees,* 190, who translates *philarches* literally as *rosh hashevet,* i.e., a title. SB]

6. 2 Macc 8:36. The author assumes that he reported to Lysias, whom Antiochus delegated while in Persia.

18. DEATH OF ANTIOCHUS THE WICKED AND THE DEDICATION OF THE HOUSE OF GOD

At that time, King Antiochus returned from Persia in disgrace, for the Persians had forced him to flee. When he reached Ecbatana, he was told all that Yehudah had done to his chiefs when he smote them. Antiochus was filled with wrath, and he became exceedingly angry, and he raged and cursed, saying: "I will come to Jerusalem; I will make it a graveyard; I will fill it with the corpses of the slain." He gathered his entire army—chariot corps and cavalry and an immense horde.

God was jealous for His people and His city and His Sanctuary. Remembering all the evil that Antiochus had done to His people, He demanded the blood [price] for the Hasidim from Antiochus himself. So God struck him with boils and with a sickness of the intestines, but he was not subdued by the sickness and said: "Hurry the chariots; hasten the cavalry; quicken the foot soldiers; and I shall go to Jerusalem, for I will do my will as I have spoken, and who can resist me? Are not the sea and the land mine, to change their nature as I please, to make the sea land and the land sea?" When he had finished speaking, he rode upon his chariot and went with all his army, a very great army, and with him were many elephants and a very great force. On the road, when his chariot was passing by an elephant, the elephant trumpeted, and the horses bolted. They slipped the traces and overturned the chariot; Antiochus fell from the chariot and broke all his bones, for he was a heavy and fat man. God added woe to his sorrow and made all his flesh stink. The flesh of Antiochus gave off an odor like the smell of a corpse's flesh left upon the field during summer. His servants carried him on their shoulders for a short while, then threw him to the ground and fled from him, for they could neither approach him nor bear the foul stench that exuded from the flesh of that blasphemer and curser and enemy of God.

When all the force and he [Antiochus] himself could no longer stand the foul stench that exuded from his flesh, he knew that the hand of God afflicted him. Humiliated and subdued, he said: "Righteous is God who humbles the mighty and who has humiliated and subdued a wicked one like me this day because I did all the evil that I did unto His people and His Hasidim. Therefore, all these evils have afflicted me." He swore an oath, saying: "If God will heal me from this disease, I shall come to Jerusalem and fill her with silver and gold and spread purple clothes throughout her streets; and I shall give all my treasures to the temple of the great God; I shall circumcise the flesh of my foreskin and go throughout the land calling out loud: 'There is none like the Lord God of Israel in all the world.'" But God did not listen to his prayer nor hearken to him, for throughout the journey of the cruel Antiochus, his disease remained, his flesh tore from his bones, and finally his intestines fell out upon the ground; and he paid with his life,[1] dying in shame and disgrace in a foreign land; and Eupator, his son, reigned in his stead.

Yehudah, son of Mattathias, and the congregation of the Hasidim came to Jerusalem and destroyed the altars that the uncircumcised had built, and they purified the House of the gentiles' idols. They built a new altar, gave meat for the sacrifice, and arranged wood, but they did not find the holy fire. They called unto God, and fire came forth from the stone upon the altar,[2] and they put wood upon it. This fire lasted until the third exile.[3] They dedicated the altar on the twenty-fifth of Kislev and set forth the Shew-Bread and lit the candles and praised God by reading the Hallel [prayer of thanksgiving] for eight days.

---

1. *Shilem naphsho* means "to die" and has no special use as martyrdom (see chap. 14).
2. The author expands on 2 Macc 10:2 from the story of the sacred fire in chap. 7 with no reference to the Talmudic story in b. *Šabb.* 21b.
3. The author's addition. According to chap. 7, this should have been the "second exile." The midrash *'eser galuyot* lists the Roman exile as the ninth.

19. YEHUDAH'S WARS

After the dedication, Yehudah went to the land of Edom, and Gorgias confronted him with a very strong army. Yehudah attacked Gorgias's camp, and they fled before him; Yehudah pursued them with his young men, and they slew on that day twenty thousand men of Edom.

Gorgias fled and went to Timotheus in Arav,[1] for the king had appointed him over all Arabia. Timotheus went forth with 120,000 of the forces of Makedon and Arabia and invaded the land of Gad and Gil'ad [cf. Josh 13:25], killing many of the people of Judah. They [the people of Judah] sent a letter to Yehudah, saying: "Come up and save us for the sword of Timotheus is annihilating us." Yet another letter came from the Galilee, saying: "Come up and save us for the sword of Tyre and Sidon, and the Makedonians who live there, is annihilating us."

When Yehudah heard these words, he called unto God with fasting and prayer,[2] and choosing some warriors from among the Hasidim, he hastily crossed the Jordan. Shimon also took three thousand Judaean warriors and raced to the Galilee and fought a major battle. He struck down eight thousand and saved his brethren in the Galilee; he took the spoils of the eight thousand that he had killed and returned to Jerusalem. Yehudah, the anointed warlord [*meshuah milhamah*], crossed the Jordan and came to Gil'ad to face Timotheus; he found him fighting against the city on Mount Gil'ad[3] and challenged him to battle. A great battle ensued, and they confronted each other, for the army of Timotheus was great and

---

1. Arav refers throughout the text to the Nabataean areas of Transjordan and not to the Arabian Peninsula.

2. Not in source. Version C has instead, "Shimon said to his brothers, 'You go to Gilgal and I'll go to Gil'ad,'" which is similar—a coincidence?—to 1 Macc 5:17.

3. Dathema in 1 Macc 5:9, which perhaps the author forgot or ignored when he reached 5:29.

numerous[4] and the people of Yehudah were few in number. Now Yehudah called to God from the heat of battle; he lifted up his eyes, and, behold, there were five young men mounted on horses all dressed in gold, and two of them were standing in front of Yehudah, one on each side, protecting him with their shields, and three were fighting against the camp of Timotheus. When Yehudah saw them, he realized they were sent from heaven to aid the Hasidim, and he encouraged his young men and pressed the army of Timotheus and drove into Sheol 20,500 of his army. Timotheus fled from there along the Jordan, with Yehudah after him, attacking all the while. From there he [Timotheus] fled along the seashore and came to Gaza. Timotheus took up a strong position in that place and prepared for battle, for all the force of Philistia had gathered unto him. Yehudah drew near that place and pounced upon him [Timotheus] as a lion pounces upon a flock of sheep. Timotheus turned tail to flee, and all his armies scattered, and the Hasmonean army pursued them, smiting and crushing them completely.

Timotheus entered Gaza and closed the city all around and fought from atop the wall. Yehudah with all the Hasmonean youth approached the city to fight, and they fought against it for five days. On the fifth day, Timotheus's men climbed up the great tower and cursed and insulted the anointed warlord, uttering abominations that we cannot relate. Twenty of the Hasmonean youth became zealous due to the insults of their abusers; they took their shields with their left hand and their swords with their right and ran toward the wall. They leaned the ladder on the wall and went up one after another, and, leaping into the city over the wall, they struck the men upon the wall, clearing a space for their comrades, and all went up. These twenty came into the city and descended to the street, and, raising a cry, they killed many, leaving their corpses on the ground. They came to the gate and fought at the gate from within and from without, and the entire Hasmonean army approached the gate. They lit a fire, the gate collapsed, and Gaza was captured. They captured alive those who had cursed the anointed warlord and burned them. They smote Gaza with the sword and killed all her males, slaughter without cease for two days; Timotheus fled and hid in one of the wells and was not found. But they found his brothers Chaereon[5] and Apollophanes and brought them to Yehudah. He ordered that their heads be cut off. They took the spoils of the city and came to Jerusalem singing, praising, and giving thanks, praising God through David, king of Israel: "Give thanks unto the Lord for He is good, for His mercy is forever [Ps 106:1]."

---

4. 2 Macc 12:20 has 120,000 infantry and 2,500 cavalry but only 6,000 soldiers with Judah. The author conflates Timotheus's wars.

5. Vocalized in the Jerusalem MS as כריאן.

20. THE WAR WITH LYSIAS

When Antiochus heard of this (this is Antiochus Eupator, son of Antiochus, called Epiphanes, who did evil against Jerusalem, who killed the Hasidim, and who died of the great afflictions, as we wrote above), he sent Lysias, his cousin, with a force of eighty thousand cavalry, eighty elephants, and an immense army; they invaded Judah and Jerusalem and fought against Beitar[1] and, building a siege wall around her, began to batter the city with an iron ram and with catapulted rocks. Yehudah and the entire Hasmonean army were living in the forests and mountains due to the Greek force. Yehudah said to his young men: "Let us welcome our God with fasting and entreaties, and let us go against the Greek army fighting at Beitar." After the fast, he sounded the ram's horn and, giving the war signal, went with all his young men to the aid of their brethren who were in Beitar.

When they came to Jerusalem and arrived at the Temple, they offered up burnt offerings and sacrificed peace offerings and called upon God. They went out from Jerusalem to go to Beitar, to the Makedonian camp. Yehudah said to his lads: "Be strong, and we shall be strengthened for the sake of the people of God and for our brethren; we shall die together bravely and not see the evil that shall befall our people." When he had spoken such words, he lifted his eyes and beheld between heaven and earth a man dressed in gold, riding a horse; the appearance of the horse was like a flame, and in the hand of the man was a spear. His back was toward the Hasmonean army, and his front faced the Greek camp; his hand outstretched to smite the Greek camp. Yehudah said: "Blessed is God who sent His angel to save His people and smite the enemy camp." They hastened from there, and, arriving at Beitar, they charged into the midst of the Makedonian camp, terrorizing it. They killed eleven thousand foot soldiers and

---

1. Bethsura in Latin is Beth Tsur not Beitar.

sixteen hundred cavalry of the Makedonians there. Lysias fled with all his army in shame and disgrace. Now Lysias knew that the Lord was fighting against the enemies of Israel, so he made a treaty with Yehudah. These are the words of the letter that Lysias sent to the army of Judah: "Lysias, Commander of the army and Viceroy to King Antiochus to the Anointed Warlord Yehudah and all his army, greetings. Let it be known to you that I have received your letters from Yoḥanan and Absolom, the messengers whom you sent, and all that they said to me I have done. I read the letter in friendship, and I have fulfilled all that was written in it, and I have passed on to the king on your behalf all the messages you have sent me; I have made a reply to Yoḥanan and Absolom, and also I have instructed the messengers that I have sent to you to speak to you words of peace."

These were the words of the letter that the king sent to Lysias, his cousin: "King Antiochus to Lysias, my brother, greetings. Let it be known to you that I have received and read in friendship the letter that you sent to me regarding the Judaeans. My father died and is no longer among men but was taken to be with the angels. I seek the well-being of my entire kingdom, making an end to wars and establishing peace. I have heard that the Jews did not wish to obey my father and abandon their Law; therefore, they prevailed with the sword and killed my father's choicest[2] and his dignitaries. So now extend to them your right hand and seal a pact with them, and they will know that, out of my wisdom and the goodness of my heart, I will let them live and preserve their Law according to their wishes."

These were the words of the letter that the king sent to Yehudah: "King Antiochus Eupator to Yehudah Anointed Warlord and to the rest of the people, greetings. Let it be known to you that I have enacted a decree in every city and among every people of my realm with regard to the Jews, not to oppress them but to allow them to preserve the rites of your Law; and for everything my father did originally in error, forgive us. And if we have erred, behold, we have sent to you Menelaus to speak words of peace."

---

2. "Abandon their law" is the author's note re: accepting the Greek rite. [*Meshamnei avi*, literally "my father's fatcats," with pun intended by the author. SB]

21. THE JUDAEAN-ROMAN COVENANT

In those days,[1] God began to magnify the fourth kingdom over the third kingdom, that is, the kingdom of the Romans, who were aroused against the kingdom of Greece, and he magnified the name of the Romans among all the kingdoms. This is the fourth beast that Daniel, the "man greatly beloved" [Dan 7:7], foresaw that devoured, crushed, and trampled the rest underfoot. This nation of Romans devoured and crushed all the kingdoms.

They [the Romans] fought King Antiochus of Greece,[2] who had 120 elephants, an immense army, and numerous horses and chariots. The Romans broke him in battle, subdued him, and made him pay tribute to them.

These are the ones who broke the pride of Anibal (Hannibal),[3] king of Africa, who ruled in the city named Carthage, for Hannibal had come with a very large army, as many as the sand on the seashore, and with him a whole Berber force[4] and all the armies of Kush, Put, Lub (Libya), and many [other] nations. He crossed the sea strait between Africa and Spain, invaded Spain, and broke the pride of the nation of [Visi]Goths. He traveled from there throughout the whole land of Germania, which is the land of the West,[5] and broke the

---

1. See letters in 2 Macc 12:31 and 1 Macc 8. Already identified by ancient Jewish sages as the Roman Empire.

2. 1 Macc 6–7. Yavan refers to Antiochus's entire realm, including Makedonia.

3. The author begins excursus on Hannibal (Anibal, in the author's Italian dialect) from an unknown medieval source probably derived from Livy; cf. *AJ* 12.414.

4. North African Berbers and Arabs attacked southern Italy during the author's time. See chap. 46.

5. Hannibal was never in Germany; however, the author (or his source) may have referred to the lands of the Germanic peoples, i.e., the West, as Germania.

pride of the Franks and Saxons and all the inhabitants of Germania, and he subdued the Bretons, who live by the ocean [*yam Okianus*]. He traveled from there, invaded Italy, and fought the Romans. The Romans advanced against him, and a major battle was fought, and an immeasurable number of Romans fell there on that day. The Romans fought another eighteen battles with Hannibal over ten years, but they could not stop Hannibal.[6] Finally they mustered a whole army of warriors led by two dictators [i.e., consuls], one named Aemilius and the second Varos (Varro), who went to fight Hannibal. They found him making war against the city of Canusium, a large city, and they fought by the River Aufidus.[7] An immense battle ensued there; and on that day, ninety thousand of the most valiant Romans fell dead. Aemilius, a valiant Roman, ended his days in that battle; but Varro fled and took refuge, entering Benusia (Venusium), the city that sits between the mountains and the plain.[8] Also in that battle, forty thousand corpses of Hannibal's troops were spread out [in the field]. Hannibal pursued the Roman force unto the gate of Roma; he besieged the city for eight years, building houses before the gate, and fought for the city.[9]

The counselors of the city said to one other: "Let us open the gate and cross over to Hannibal and make a covenant with him; so we shall live and not die." This they intended to do.

There rose up from the city a youth named Sipio (Scipio),[10] and he said to the 320 city counselors: "Heaven forbid that we should do this and cross over to Hannibal." They said to him: "So what can we do? We have not been able to stand our ground against Hannibal for the past eighteen years." Whereupon Scipio said: "Let us take counsel: give me about five valiant legions, and I will

---

6. Cannae in 216 BCE. Hannibal's invasion 218–213.

7. In August 216, the consuls C. Aemilius Paullus and L. Terentius Varro (the author corrects to Varus) with eighty-six thousand men found Hannibal in Cannae, which the author identified with nearby Canusium (the author's Greek *Kanosi*, modern Canosa), both cities on the River Aufidus, in the province of Bari. Despite Muslim destructive raids in the ninth century, the author still knew Kanosi as "a large city."

8. Cf. Livy 22.49.12 and 14. The author knew the city of Venusium (Byzantine *Benusia*, modern Venosa), still a Jewish metropolis in the tenth century with extensive catacombs (Hebrew epitaphs published by D. M. Cassutto, "Venossa (H)," *Qedem* 2 [1945]: 99–120). [See now D. Noy, *Jewish Inscriptions of Western Europe*, vol. 1, *Italy (Excluding the City of Rome), Spain and Gaul* (Cambridge, UK, 1993); and C. Colafemina, "Hebrew Inscriptions of the Early Medieval Period in Southern Italy," in *The Jews of Italy. Memory and Identity*, ed. B. D. Cooperman and B. Garvin (Bethesda, MD, 2000), 65–81. SB]

9. Note the proverb *Hannibal ante portas* (from 211 siege).

10. L. Cornelius Scipio (the author's Italian *Sipio*) was a hero at nineteen after Cannae and thirty-one as consul in 205, successfully arguing for invasion of North Africa. On the number 320, see chap. 2, end.

go to his land of Africa and fight against it and destroy it; perhaps he will then leave you and come to me to save his land from my hand; then there will be relief for you."

And they did so. He [Scipio] took thirty thousand valiant Romans and marched to Hannibal's land, which is Africa, and fought, killing Asdrubal (Hasdrubal), his [Hannibal's] brother; he cut off his head and brought it to Roma.[11] He mounted the wall and said to Hannibal: "Why have you coveted our land and did not come to save from my hand your own, which I have ruined? Behold, here is your brother's head!" And he threw his brother's head at him. Hannibal recognized his brother's head, and, hardening his spirit and strengthening his heart, he fortified the position and swore: "I will not desist from besieging the city until I have captured it!" He continued to besiege it for many days more.

Scipio continued to advance in Africa, destroying the whole country. He came to Carthage and laid siege to it. The Carthaginians sent a letter to Hannibal in Roma, saying: "Why do you covet a foreign land while your land is being taken from you? If you do not come quickly and save us from the hand of Scipio, we shall open the gate at once and surrender the city of Carthage and your entire household to him."

Hannibal, upon reading this letter, wept and lifted the siege on the city. He went to Aufidus, where his boats were waiting, and killed there innumerable Romans—men, women, and children—from the captives he had with him. Boarding a ship, he sailed to Africa with all his army. Scipio came to confront Hannibal, and a great battle broke out, and Scipio defeated him in that battle. Up to fifty thousand men were killed in that battle, and he beat him three times in that battle. Hannibal fled from Scipio to Egypt,[12] and Scipio pursued him to Egypt; Ptolemy handed him over to Scipio, and Scipio brought him with great honor to Africa. When Hannibal arrived in Africa, he drank deadly poison and died and was buried there. Scipio conquered all the land of Africa and every source of silver and gold there,[13] and the nation of the Romans was made greater than all the nations of the earth.

---

11. The consuls M. Livius Salinator and C. Claudius Nero killed Hasdrubel in battle in 207 near Metaurus (Umbria). Livy (27.51.11) reports Hannibal in Apulia when Claudius Nero ordered the head thrown into his camp.

12. Hannibal fled Carthage (Romans demanded his surrender) in 195 to Antiochus III, king of Syria (defeated by Romans in 190), thence to Crete, and finally to Prusius, king of Bithynia, in Asia Minor, where he poisoned himself when Romans demanded his surrender (ca. 183 or 182). Cf. Jerome, *Chronicle*, 219.

13. Cf. 1 Macc 8:3. Mines in Roman Spain.

These are the words of the letter[14] that the Romans sent to Yehudah, son of Mattathias: "Quintius Memmius Titus Scipius Manilius,[15] commanders of Roma, to Yehudah Anointed War Leader [*meshuaḥ milḥamah*] and to all the elders of Yehudah (Judaea): Greetings. Let it be known to you that we have heard of your valor and your battles, and we have rejoiced. All that Antiochus and Lysias gave to you[16] and all that they have written unto the Jews we shall write thus throughout our land. It suits you to be known as our friends and renowned and not [friends] to the Greeks, who persecuted you. Since we shall go against Antioch in war, hasten to send us a letter [saying] who are your enemies and who are your friends."

These, then, are the words of the treaty that the nation of Romans swore with the people of Yehudah: "Let each one love and unite and aid his comrade, the nation of Romans and the people of Judaea on land and sea forever. If war be waged against the nation of Romans, let the Judaeans assist them according to their strength and not give unto the enemies of the Romans either weapons or wheat or any sustenance, just as the Elder and the 320 counselors decreed.[17] And if war breaks out against the nation of Judaea, let the Romans assist them according to their strength and not give to the enemies of the Judaeans any weapons, neither wheat nor any sustenance. And neither shall they take from the Judaeans any sustenance but rather come to their aid in any crisis that they have, and neither add to these words nor subtract just as the Elder and his 320 counselors decreed."

---

14. The author returns to 2 Macc; letter in 2 Macc 11:34.

15. Quintus Memmius and Titus Manilius; the author adds Scipius, based on his Hannibal excursus.

16. 2 Macc 11:35. Source recalls only Lysias's letter to the Jews (2 Macc 11:16–21; see chap. 22); author adds Antiochus here to hint at the two letters of Antiochus Eupator in 2 Macc 11.22–26 and 27–33; see chap. 20.

17. The author's misconception based on 1 Macc 8.15–16.

22. YEHUDAH'S WARS

After this, the land was quiet for eight months. In those days, Yehudah began to judge his people and put away the wicked from among his people. At that time, in all the coastal cities from Gaza to Acco, Judaeans lived among the gentiles of Makedon. The inhabitants of Jaffa and Yavneh perpetrated a great wickedness, deceiving the Judaeans who dwelt in their midst to board their ships with their wives and sons to go play together at sea; they trusted them and went. But when they had reached a deep place, they drowned some two hundred souls.

When it was told to Yehudah, he wept and proclaimed a fast and, racing to Jaffa, besieged it, and the Lord gave it into his hand. He separated the Judaeans from it, then he smote the city with the sword—male, female, infant, and babe—and he burned the city. Thus, he did with Yavneh, and he burned all the ships of Jaffa and Yavneh; the fire could be seen all the way to Jerusalem and the flames for 240 stadia. Thus, he exacted vengeance for the blood of the children and the women who drowned in the sea.

He departed from there and went to the desert of Arav[1] and smote the people of Arav, trampling many people of Arav in battle, and he set tribute on them. Then he went, returning to the land of Yehudah, passing to a city of Caspin, a city greatly fortified, settled by a diversity of gentiles. They trusted in their fortification and, cursing Yehudah, uttered words against the army of Yehudah that we cannot relate. Yehudah said: "O Lord Shaddai, who gave Jericho into the hand of Joshua His servant by the trumpeting sound of your people, give into our hand this day this city that I may exact vengeance upon them for the curses that they swore against our people, O Lord." He took his shield in his left hand and, drawing his sword, leaped against the city gate. All the Hasmonean youth raced after him, and they smeared the gate with pitch, heaped brush upon the

---

1. *Midbar Arav*: Edomite territory in southern Jordan.

pitch and thorns of the desert, and ignited the gate; and it burned and fell to the ground. The Lord gave the city into his hand, and he caused a slaughter in it that has not been done since ancient times; a pool of blood two stadia in length by two stadia in width flowed out from the city like a lake of water.

He departed from there and went 750 stadia; Timotheus went out to confront him with 120,000 infantry and one thousand horse. Yehudah prayed to God and went against Timotheus with ten thousand Judaean young men.[2] A huge battle ensued, and Yehudah killed thirty thousand of Timotheus's men. Timotheus turned tail to flee, and Dositheus, commander of the army, pursued him with Sosipater of the young men of Israel. They captured Timotheus alive and brought him to Yehudah. Yehudah commanded [them] to cut off his head from him. Now Timotheus wailed greatly and entreated him, saying: "My lord Yehudah, don't kill me, for many Judaeans live in my land, and I swear unto you that I will do good unto them all the days of my life."[3] He swore an oath to him [Yehudah], so Yehudah had mercy on him and did not kill him, permitting him to go his way; and Timotheus, keeping his sworn oath, did not harm the Judaeans for the rest of his days.

Yehudah departed from there, going toward the desert, and attacked the king's force that entered Arav; he smote them, causing them to flee, and killed twenty-five thousand of them. He departed from there and went to Ephron, which was a large city, and besieged it; God gave it into his hand, and he killed in it twenty thousand. He departed and went six hundred stadia [ris] to a city named Sitopolis (Scythopolis, i.e., Beit Shean). Now the Scythopolitans were greatly afraid, and they went out to greet him, entreating him with tears, and said to him: "Our master, Anointed Warlord, ask the Judaeans who dwell among us how we have behaved well toward them. Even in the days of Antiochus the cruel, many Judaeans took refuge among us, and we preserved their life." The Judaeans dwelling among them also bore witness to this; Yehudah blessed them and left them. Yehudah returned to Jerusalem three days [cf. Exodus 19:11] before the holiday of Shavuoth [Pentecost].

After the holiday, he went out against Gorgias, the Edomite general, leaving with three thousand infantry and four hundred horse. A battle ensued, and some of the Hasmonean warriors fell there on that day. Dositheus, commander of the army, was injured, struck on his shoulder, and the Hasmonean young men were nearly pushed back. When Yehudah saw the collapse of his young

---

2. In 2 Macc 12:19, Yehudah's officers killed this many.

3. Timotheus actually refers to hostages related to Yehudah's soldiers. The Latin was unclear to the author.

men, he prayed to God and encouraged his young men. He sprang ahead of his men, smiting the army of Gorgias, killing many. He called and said: "[I am coming] to you, Gorgias!" and leaped upon him, stretching forth his hand to smite him. Gorgias turned around to flee from Yehudah. He threw away his weapons and ran away. Nobody encountered him after that, nor was he seen again, alive, or dead. Some say he was wounded in battle, fled to Marisa in the desert of Edom, and died. Yehudah returned and smote all of Edom, destroying all their cities and subjugating them.

Images of the gentiles' idols were found under the clothes of the youth of Israel who were slain in battle, and they brought them to Yehudah. Yehudah knew that this was the sin for which they fell in battle, and he said: "Blessed is the God, the Revealer of the secret, who made manifest these hidden things." The army was encouraged to serve God in holiness and purity, and he returned to Jerusalem.

23. ANTIOCHUS EUPATOR'S WAR

When Antiochus Eupator heard of all the battles that Yehudah had waged and the cities that he had captured, he broke the treaty that he had with Yehudah and came with an army as numerous as the sand of the seashore, and with him chariots and cavalry and twenty-two elephants;[1] Lysias, his cousin, was with him with a huge army; he invaded the land of Judaea and besieged Beitar.[2] Yehudah and all the elders of Israel called unto God with fasting, weeping, and entreaties, offering up burnt offerings and sacrificing whole offerings.

That night Yehudah took with him all the Hasmonean youth and infiltrated the king's camp at night.[3] He destroyed four thousand of the king's warriors and killed the largest of the elephants. At dawn, the king advanced in battle to confront Yehudah, and the fighting was very intense. Yehudah saw one of the elephants with gold armor larger than all the other elephants—he thought that the king was sitting upon it, and he called, saying: "Who among you, my lads? Who among you [will come to me]?" Then Elazar,[4] one of the Hasmonean youth, sprang forward and ran toward the elephant, killing all who came against him from among the king's warriors, and he smote right and left, the dead falling all about him. He dove into the depth of the fighting, and reaching between the elephant's legs, he stabbed its navel with his sword, and the elephant plummeted upon him. He died for the Lord and for his people. He left a glorious act to those hearing about him and mourning to his people. Eight hundred of

---

1. According to 2 Macc 13:2; 1 Macc 6:30 has thirty-two elephants. The last phrase is not in MS Jerusalem.
2. 2 Macc 13:15 and 1 Macc 6:31 have Bethsura, which is Beth Ẓor. See chap. 20, beginning.
3. Cf. Gen 14:15. The author puns on the first phrase of sentence.
4. Macc 6:45. Only later versions (B and C) of *Yosippon* add "his brother." The author did not know that Elazar was one of Yehudah's brothers.

the king's nobles fell in that war, apart from a great multitude of the men of the army, killed in battle.

The king ceased from battle and went to his tent.[5] He was told thus: "Behold, Philip has revolted in your land, and also Demetrius, son of King Seleucus, is coming from the city of Roma with a huge army, to take the kingdom from your hand." The king feared greatly and made peace; he made a covenant with Yehudah and embraced him and kissed him and swore, he and Lysias, his cousin, saying: "We shall not go up against Jerusalem any more in war for the rest of our lives." The king brought forth gold aplenty and gave an offering to the House of the Lord in Jerusalem, and he seized Menelaus the wicked, the Judaean who had brought his father, Antiochus, to Jerusalem to do all the evil that he did there. [It was this Menelaus who brought King Eupator to Judaea.] Now the king was furious against him and said: "Seize him!" There was a tower in that place[6] fifty cubits high and below it ash and cinder without measure. The king commanded, and they raised Menelaus upon the tower and binding him hand and foot, threw him down, drowning him in the depth of the ash. He sank into the depths of the ash, dying for his cruelties and his sins, for he had done many abominations before the altar of God, whose cinder and ash were holy; therefore, the wicked one was punished by dying of suffocation in the ash. Righteous is the Lord, who renders unto man according to his ways and according to the fruit of his deeds!

The king went his way to Makedonia. And Yehudah began to judge his people and do righteousness and justice.

---

5. The author misunderstood the Latin of 2 Macc 13:18: and understood *tentabat* from *tenta* = *tenda* = tent in Italian.

6. Yosippon posits that Menelaus was killed in Judaea. The Latin has only *in eodem loco*. The Greek of 2 Macc 13:4 and *AJ* 12.385, identify Beroea in Syria.

24. NICANOR'S WAR

At that time, Demetrius, son of Seleucus, came with an army of Romans and fought against Antiochus Eupator; he killed Antiochus and Lysias and ruled in Antioch, which belonged to Makedon. Alcimus the priest, a wicked man who ate the flesh of pork in the days of Antiochus, went to him [Demetrius], and Alcimus said to Demetrius: "May the king live forever! How long will you fail to do justice unto your servants who are in the land of Judaea? For Yehudah, son of Mattathias, has prevailed upon us by his sword and with him his army of Judaeans called Hasidim;[1] and he has killed us because we rebelled against their Law, while we have accepted your Law."

Alcimus said many things, infuriating Demetrius, and Demetrius sent Nicanor, commander of his army, with a strong force and with him chariots, cavalry, elephants, and infantry without number. He came to Jerusalem and sent to Yehudah words of peace, saying: "Let us greet each other in friendship and speak together words of peace to each other." Yehudah was not alarmed by his words and went to Nicanor. Nicanor went out to greet him; he embraced him and greeted him. Chairs were brought and placed for the two of them, and they sat and spoke words of peace. Then Yehudah commanded his young men, the Hasmoneans, to approach with their arms, for he said [in his heart]: "Lest the enemy leap upon me suddenly," and the young men stood about him as Yehudah had commanded. They stood up from the chairs and went to their tents. Nicanor and Yehudah returned to Jerusalem, and a battle did not take place. Nicanor was fond of Yehudah and said to him: "It is fitting for a man like you to take a wife and beget sons." So Yehudah took a wife and begot a son.

Alcimus beheld their friendship and returned to the king, telling him what happened. The king wrote to Nicanor, saying: "If you do not send me Yehudah,

---

1. *Assidaei Judaeorum*. [See J. Kampen, *The Hasideans and the Origin of Pharasaism* (Atlanta, GA, 1989). SB]

son of Mattathias, bound in chains, know that you shall surely die!" Yehudah learned of this and, leaving the city at night, blew the ram's horn, giving the signal to war; all the Hasidim warriors and the Hasmonean army gathered about him; and he went to Shomron (Samaria) and stayed there.

Nicanor came to the Temple of God and said to the priests: "Bring forth the man who fled from me, and I will send him to the king bound in chains." The priests swore, saying: "He has not come here, nor have we seen his face recently." Whereupon Nicanor cursed the Temple of God, also he spit at the Sanctuary, and extending his right hand, baring his forearm toward the Temple, he said: "I shall destroy this Sanctuary, leaving not one stone upon another, for I shall dig up and overturn all its foundations." Then he left in great anger. The priests wept between the porch and the altar,[2] saying: "O Lord, who has dwelt in this House since ancient times, You are still indwelling, for here is Your throne and here the footstool for Your feet and all Your worship. Nicanor has dared to curse Your House and Your dwelling place, Your strength and the Temple of Your glory [Ps 52.1]. Take vengeance upon him and let all know that he spoke villainy; therefore, let him die like a villain."

Nicanor was searching every house in Jerusalem for Yehudah and sent five hundred troops to the house of Raxias (Rasius)[3], the Elder of the Hasidim, who was tested in the days of Antiochus the cruel and was proved perfect,[4] for he bore willingly blows and many torments and was called "father to the Jews" and "judge in Jerusalem." When Nicanor sought to manifest the enmity that he had in his heart for the Jews, he sent forth to bring him [Raxias] to him; they surrounded the house to capture him, and the old man hastened and, taking the sword, stuck it into his belly, ran to the wall, and threw himself down into the midst of Nicanor's troops. The troops moved back to make space for him, and falling to the ground, he was broken. But he got up and, passing the troops, stood on a large rock, and from the excess of blood that flowed out from him, he went out of his mind; he grabbed his intestines with both hands and threw them on the troops and, calling unto God, died and was gathered to his people.

When Yehudah heard these things, his anger burned within him, and he sent unto Nicanor, saying: "Why do you tarry? Get out to the field [of battle], and I will show you the man whom you seek within the city; behold, here he is for you in the valley, on the plain." Nicanor assembled all his army and went to confront

---

2. The author uses Joel 2:17 to translate 1 Macc 7:36.

3. Also, variant RAXIAS.

4. *Buḥan . . . venimẓah shalem* (see 2 Macc 14:38), the author's flowery phrase (from *Avoth de Rabbi Natan*) for one who dies for *Kiddush hashem*. See chap. 12 (Elazar) and chap. 35 (Honi). The pun was intended by the author. [SB]

Yehudah on the Sabbath. The Judaeans who came with Nicanor spoke to him, saying: "Our lord, do not act maliciously! Respect the Giver of the Sabbath!" Nicanor said: "So who is it who gave the Sabbath?" And they said: "God, whose dwelling is in heaven, and His government is over the whole world." Nicanor cursed and spoke with such malice that it is not proper to write.

Yehudah heard and said to his young men: "How long will we tarry to go to war to wreak vengeance on this cursing and blaspheming man, for who is this dead and castoff dog who has desecrated the strength of the glory of Israel? [cf. Ps 52:1]." Yehudah marched off to Nicanor in anger and great zeal, and Nicanor went out to confront him with a strong force and a mighty hand. Yehudah called out unto God and said: "O Lord my God, You sent an angel into the camp of Sennaharib, whose servants[5] stood without the city and vilified you, and You smote 185,000 of his men: the dead we counted, but the killer we saw not; all the more [you should punish] this man who stood in Your house and vilified Your power and Your glory!"

A great battle was waged on that day. During the battle, Yehudah saw Nicanor, his sword drawn in his hand, and Yehudah called out, saying: "[I am coming] to you, Nicanor!" He ran at him in the fury of his anger. Nicanor turned tail to flee from Yehudah. But Yehudah overtook him and smote him with his sword, hacking him in two,[6] hurling him to the ground. There fell on that day in battle thirty thousand of the Makedonian army, and the rest fled. Yehudah pursued them with his young men blowing the ram's horn, and they went out from all the cities of Judaea to confront them; they smote them and crushed them, and not even one of them was saved. They returned to strip the fallen, and they found gold, precious stones, and much purple. They cut off Nicanor's head and his arm that he had stretched out against the Sanctuary of the Lord, and they hung them before the gate; for this reason, its name is called the Gate of Nicanor unto this day.[7] The people rejoiced greatly, praising God in the words of David, king of Israel: "For [the Lord] is good and His grace is forever." From that day hence, they made that day a holiday, a festival, and a day of wine drinking on the thirteenth day of the month Adar, one day before Purim. Yehudah judged[8] all his people, enacting justice and righteousness in the land.

---

5. 1 Macc 7:41; Isa 37:6; 2 Kings 15:6.
6. The Greek version has Nicanor's head and arm cut off only after the battle (see below); Yosippon's translation is based on an unclear Latin version.
7. The author erroneously connects the Greek officer with the famous gate of the philanthropist.
8. Cf. 1 Macc 7:50. The style is similar to chap. 23; compare also the first lines of chap. 22.

25. YEHUDAH'S DEATH

A year past, and Yehudah's time to die drew near; God commanded that Yehudah end his days and be gathered to his people, the Hasidim. Bacchides came against him with thirty thousand Makedonian warriors and suddenly attacked Yehudah; he was at Lisah (Laisa) with some three thousand men. And all who were with him fled, but Yehudah remained with his brothers and eight hundred young men from the youth of Israel who did not turn tail or retreat;[1] these were Yehudah's comrades, tested in every battle that Yehudah had fought with the gentiles.

Bacchides came with fifteen thousand and arrayed for battle to Yehudah's right, and he arrayed on his left the remaining fifteen thousand of the army; they raised a great cry against Yehudah from his right and his left. Yehudah saw that the battle was dire, and he recognized that Bacchides stood on his right, for all of Bacchides's heroes were there, and the right wing was with him; so Yehudah raised a cry and sprang into battle, his brothers joining him along with the remaining Hasmonean heroes, and he ran toward Bacchides. A great battle ensued, and at the beginning of the battle, thousands of Makedonian casualties fell as corpses to the ground. During the battle, Yehudah saw Bacchides standing in the midst of the army, and he ran to him in the fury of his anger, smiting his warriors, knocking many dead to the ground, killing all those who stood in his way: from the right and the left, corpses fell without number. Now the men that Yehudah killed on that day were many, until there was no room except in that spot, so that Yehudah stomped upon the dead, trampling over them as he advanced against Bacchides with his sword drawn, dripping blood. Bacchides

---

1. 1 Macc 9:5. [The author's style deliberately negates 2 Chron 29:6; cf. S. Bowman, "*Sepher Yosippon*: History and Midrash," in *The Midrashic Imagination*, ed. M. Fishbane (Albany, NY, 1993), 280–94. SB].

beheld the face of Yehudah and, behold, his face like a lion standing over his kill striking fear and trembling, and Bacchides turned his back to flee, heading toward Ashdod.[2] Yehudah pursued him, beating him and all who were with him, killing fifteen thousand men in the battle. Bacchides fled and took refuge in Ashdod. Now the [Makedonian] force that was to the rear of Yehudah found him tired and exhausted, and they fell upon him; Bacchides too went out from the city and surrounded him on every side, and many more fell dead. Yehudah too fell on that day upon his many victims that he slew, and Shimon and Yonathan, his brothers, took him and buried him on Mount Modiin, and all Israel mourned him for many days.

---

2. Called Mount Azotus in 1 Macc 9:15, which the author simplifies with the 'road (*derech*) to Ashdod'.

26. THE DAYS OF YONATHAN AND SHIMON

After the death of Yehudah, the enemies of God's people increased all around, and Yonathan girded the authority of his brother. The other deeds of Yehudah, his bravery and his wars, are written in the book of Joseph ben Gurion, the book of the Hasmoneans,[1] and the book of the kings of Romi.

When Yonathan received the authority, he went with a few men to the Jordan. Bacchides pursued Yonathan with a large army and, coming upon him on the Sabbath, pressed him against the waters of the Jordan. When he saw that Bacchides was pressing him against the water, he went into the water with his men. Bacchides crossed after him with all his force and caught up with him, attacking him from all sides. Yonathan stretched forth his right to strike Bacchides, forcing him back and making him retreat. So Yonathan split the army of Bacchides, and he fled to Beer Sheva,[2] which is in the desert, and rebuilt the ruins of the city. Bacchides came against him with force and besieged the city for some days, and they were greatly distressed. Shimon said to his brother Yonathan: "How long will we choose this wretched life? Let us choose death and go out against our enemies." Yonathan came out of the city that night and smote Phaseron,[3] who accompanied Bacchides, in his tent, and he smote Odaren and his brothers, who had come with Bacchides. Then Shimon opened the gate and, with a strong force of Judaean young men with him, went out and smote the camp of Bacchides, casting to the ground many dead; they burned the rams, the catapults, and all the equipment that they had brought to destroy

---

1. Joseph ben Gurion is Josephus: Hasmoneans via the Latin Vulgate of Maccabees.
2. The author could not identify Bethbessan in the source.
3. Both Phaseron and Odaren are tribal names reduced here to personal names.

the city. Bacchides fled, escaping toward the desert; Yonathan pursued him, and they caught up with him. Bacchides entreated them, promising to release the prisoners, and swore an oath to them. So they let him go, and, releasing all the prisoners, he did not venture to invade again the land of Judaea.

At that time, Yonathan's authority was strengthened; he judged his people and reigned secure. After Yonathan's death, Shimon seized the authority of his brother Yonathan and fought from every side to confront Antiochus's force, and the latter, with the rest of the army, went in another direction, so he [Shimon] turned against their rear. Two of Antiochus's officers came between Shimon and his young men, one on one side and the other on the other, and Shimon smote Antiochus's force that came against him; not one escaped from him. Israel dwelt in peace all the days of Shimon, everyone under his vine and fig tree.

Ptolemy, Shimon's son-in-law, killed Shimon at a drinking party and, seizing his wife and two sons, put them in chains. The days that Shimon governed God's people were eight years, and he died and was gathered unto his people. The rest of his deeds and bravery and his wars we have not written here; behold, they are written in the book of Joseph ben Gurion haCohen, in the book of the Hasmoneans, in the book of the kings of Roma, and in the letters that the Roman nation, the Persian nation, and the kings of Makedon [i.e., Spartans] sent him.

27. ORKANUS (HYRCANUS) AND TALMI (PTOLEMY)

After Ptolemy killed Shimon, he sent forth to kill Yoḥanan, Shimon's son; he was the Yoḥanan called Hyrcanus, for when Yoḥanan had killed Orkanus (Hyrcanus), a great king at the time of his father, Shimon called his son Yoḥanan "Hyrcanus," after the name of the king he had killed, for his strength and bravery.[1]

When Hyrcanus heard that his father was killed, he fled to Gaza.[2] Ptolemy pursued him and came before the city gate of Gaza, and the inhabitants of Gaza closed the gate and did not let Ptolemy enter the city to do harm to Hyrcanus. So Ptolemy turned and came to Dagon and stayed there.

After this, Hyrcanus received the authority of his father and, offering up burnt offerings and sacrifices, brought out an army against Ptolemy, his sister's husband, and was victorious in battle. Ptolemy closed the gate of the city called Dagona, and the youth approached and besieged the city with all kinds of weaponry: with an iron battering ram, with rampart, and with weapons of destruction; so the city came under siege. Now Ptolemy, being besieged, brought Hyrcanus's mother and his brother up into the tower and beat them and tortured them before his eyes, with whips and all manner of punishment and torture. When the young Hyrcanus[3] saw the beating of his mother and his brother, he took pity and wept and cried, and he withdrew his multitude; the sounds of war were silenced, the flame of battle subsided, and he withdrew from

---

1. That a man is named for his actions is based on Jerome's *Chronicle* (*Eusebius Werke*, vol. 7, *Die Chronik des Hieronymis. Griechischen Christlichen Schriftsteller* 47 [Berlin, 1956], ed. R. Helm, 146). [The biblical mentality sees meaning in every name; or as one could put it, the Hebrew *šem* underlies the Greek *semeion*. SB]. Cf. chaps. 16 and 37.
2. 1 Macc 16:19 and 21 have Gazara. The author shifts here to Josephus.
3. *BJ* 1.58; *DEH* 1.1.17, in the author's idiosyncratic reading.

the city. The mother was stretching out her hands and imploring her son, not for pity nor for mercy but rather to [re]ignite the flame of battle, to sound trumpet calls, to bring back the battering ram, to raise up the rampart, to multiply rocks and encourage slingers, to draw bows and shoot arrows, to kill people, to mine the wall and overthrow the city and capture his enemy to exact revenge upon him, for his mother said: "If with my death I would exact vengeance upon the enemy, I would not consider this death like any other death. Be strong, my son, be strong, son of my womb and son of my vows [Prov 31:2], and let your battle be strong against this city and destroy it. Then we shall have vengeance for [the death of] your father from his son-in-law, an adversary and an enemy; for pity of your mother, do not forget the murder of your holy father;[4] do not pity your mother by forgetting your father and sinning against your God."

When Hyrcanus heard the words his mother cried out [to him], the lad's rage was ignited, and he ordered [his men] to raise a shout, sound the trumpets, and raise the tumult; the multitude rose to draw bows and shoot arrows and multiple stones and build a siege wall and raise up a rampart and place ladders; and he brought the ram and smote the tower, and the wall was about to fall. The people cried out from the city, and their cry rose up. Now Ptolemy was very pressed, and in his desperation, he brought up once again Hyrcanus's mother and his brother upon the tower against which he [Hyrcanus] used the battering ram; he tortured them severely and whipped them cruelly and threatened to drop them if Hyrcanus did not withdraw from the city.[5] The youth saw his mother beaten and tortured, and he wept and took pity. Then his mother again said to him: "Weep not, my son! Weep not! Fight your war; let your heart not soften! And if you feel compassion for your mother, why does your heart not move remembering your father and [your] revenge for him? Avenge yourself upon his enemy and his vengeance!" The lad Hyrcanus, remembering his father, was filled with rage and zeal, and he pressed the city with a mighty hand. But when he saw his mother suffering, he stayed his hand from destroying and slaughtering in his compassion for his mother. The lad did not know what he should do, for when he remembered his father, he was angry—but when he

---

4. *DEH* 1.1.7. *Avikha hakadosh* surely is not a martyr in the religious sense. See chap. 15 on the application of this term to Maccabees. *Kadosh* not in Hegesippus. Further on, he calls the father "pious" (*heḥasid*) and his mother "saintly" (*hakedoshah*). It is difficult under these rhetorical examples to extrapolate this usage in terms of martyrdom. While the author could be drawing on some contemporary usage of *sanctus*, it may refer to his priestly origin, which the author designates as *kedoshei adonai* (chap. 5) [SB].

5. *BJ* 1.57; *AJ* 13.231; *DEH* 1.17. The author transferred Ptolemy's speech from the beginning of story to heighten the dramatic tension.

saw his mother, he felt pity. He grew furious when he remembered the pious one [*heḥasid*], and he had compassion when he saw his saintly mother [*imi hakedoshah*]. The war within the lad's heart was greater than the war that he fought against the city. For he said in his heart: "They will count against me all this evil the enemy does to my mother."

In those days, the seventh year arrived, that is, the sacred year that the Jews celebrate,[6] as they celebrate the seventh day; therefore, Hyrcanus ceased from the war and returned to Jerusalem. Ptolemy's cruelties increased greatly against those very ones whom he had used to save his life, and he gave the command to kill Hyrcanus's mother and his brother. Then Ptolemy fled and took refuge in Philadelphia.

---

6. Josephus's explanation of *shnat shmittah* for the non-Jewish reader; cf. *BJ* 1.60; and *AJ* 13.234.

28. HYRCANUS AND ANTIOCHUS PIUS

Antiochus bore a grudge against Shimon for killing his chiefs, and, mustering an army numerous as the sand of the sea, he invaded Judaea with a mighty hand in the fourth year of his reign, which was the first year of Hyrcanus, king of Judaea. Hyrcanus closed up the city, and he laid siege to Jerusalem for many days, but he could not prevail against her due to the height of the walls, the fortification of the towers, and the strength of the youths who inhabited the city. Antiochus built 130 towers to the north of the city,[1] each with turrets, and he put warriors from his troops on their turrets, and, mining the wall of Jerusalem, he collapsed it.[2] The Jews charged quickly toward the fallen wall and smote all the Makedonian warriors who dared to invade the city. They left through the breach in the wall and fought with Antiochus's force; they chased him from the camp and overturned the towers that Antiochus had made. Antiochus retreated twenty stadia from the city and made his camp there.

The holiday of Sukkoth arrived,[3] in which it is the law for the people of God to offer up burnt offerings, to sacrifice *qorbanoth* and thanksgiving offerings [*zevaḥim*], and to praise the name of God with four kinds of trees. Hyrcanus sent messengers to Antiochus, saying: "Give us a truce for eight days,[4] and let us celebrate the festival of the Lord our God." He replied and said:

---

1. The location is only in the Greek version. B. Niese in his edition of Josephus argues that the towers had to be in Yosippon's Latin MSS.
2. The author loosely reads *AJ* 13.239.
3. For this explanation (not in chap. 27), cp. chap. 31. *DEH* 1.5 mentions the *qorban Sukkot*.
4. The author adds the extra rabbinical day of *ḥag ha-aẓereth*.

"Celebrate your festival, but let me have a portion in it with you." Antiochus sent an offering to God: one bull, its horns adorned with pure gold, and he sent gold and silver, vessels full of spices, all this an offering to the Temple of the great God.

The gatekeepers took this offering and brought it to the priests, and the priests hoisted it in the temple. This Antiochus acted better than Antiochus Epiphanes, for Epiphanes set his heart against Jerusalem; and when he had taken Jerusalem, he entered the Temple of God, but he did not act well, for he slaughtered the pig in the Temple and fouled the altar and threw the pig's flesh in every corner of the Temple. For this, God struck him with a sickness, and he died of his evil diseases, as we wrote above, while this Antiochus, called Pius, acted righteously and honored the Temple of God. Hence, the Jews rebelled against Epiphanes and did not serve him further, but this one was called Pius for he was a merciful man.[5]

Hyrcanus saw that he [Pius] had set his heart to worship God, so he sent envoys to him to make a treaty with him, and he made a treaty with him. He received him in Jerusalem, making a great feast for him and all his servants; he gave him three hundred talents of gold, and he left to go to his land. King Hyrcanus claimed the hidden gold in Jerusalem; he opened one of the graves of David, king of Israel, and took from there three thousand talents of pure gold, but he left there much gold.

King Antiochus departed from Jerusalem and went to fight with King Arsak (Arsaces) of Persia, and King Hyrcanus was with him. Joseph ben Gurion said in his book: "On this matter I found as witnesses other writers who wrote books; I found written thus in the book of Nicolaus of Damascus: 'Now King Antiochus went out against Arsaces, Hyrcanus accompanying him, and they came to the Lyko (Lycus) River and fought against Indat (Indates), general of the army of Arsaces, king of Persia, forcing him to flee, and he smote the Persian force, and many died. Antiochus built there a great construction as a trophy for this exploit.'"

They traveled from there to go to Arsaces, but Hyrcanus stayed on the road for two days because of the Sabbath and the holy day of Shavuoth that followed upon the Sabbath; for this reason, Hyrcanus stayed on the road for two days.[6] Antiochus went by himself with his camp and did not wait

---

5. *AJ* 13.243–44. *Ish raḥamim*, literally "a merciful man," which the author uses for royal figures, designated Pius in sources, e.g., Seleucus, Pompey, Augustus, and Vespasian. See chap. 11 (beginning) and chap. 78.

6. *AJ* 13.251, amended by the author for explanation; *AJ* 13.252 for Shavuot is *quinquagesima festivitas* (Pentecost).

for Hyrcanus, so that Hyrcanus would not gain honor for warring against the Persian king.[7] Antiochus attacked Arsaces, king of Persia, and fought with him, and many Greeks fell in that battle, and King Antiochus ended his days in that battle.

---

7. The author's erroneous assumption. [For a historical discussion of an interpolation into *Yosippon*, see M. Pucci, "On the Tendentiousness of Josephus' Historical Writing," in *Josephus Flavius: Historian of Eretz-Israel in the Hellenistic-Roman Period*, ed. U. Rappaport (Jerusalem, 1982), 117–29 (Hebrew), xi–xii (English summary), esp. 124; and M. Pucci, "An Unknown Source on a Possible Treaty between Hyrcanus I and the Parthians" (in Hebrew), *Zion* 46 (1981): 331–38. SB]

29. HYRCANUS'S WARS

When Hyrcanus saw that Antiochus had died, he ceased from his campaign against Arsaces; changing direction at Aram Tsuvah, he came to Midbata and besieged it for six months; the Lord gave it into his hand, and he placed it under tribute. He turned from there to Samogan (Samoga) and captured it and all her environs. He returned and came to Sh'khem (Sychima) and smote it, for it did not open its gates before him. He smote Mount Gerizim and destroyed the temple that Samballat had built for Manasseh, his son-in-law, brother of Iddo, chief of the priests; Hyrcanus destroyed it two hundred years after its construction, overturned its foundations, and smote the Kutim (Samaritans) of Mount Samaria.

He marched to the land of Edom, where he smote Ḥaverah (Abora) and Mareshah of Edom and humbled the pride of Edom, placing them under his yoke until the exile, for the king captured them and chained them in the bonds of circumcision,[1] circumcising the flesh of their foreskins. From that day hence, they were circumcised and preserved the observance of the Torah of God until the exile. The king did so unto all the gentiles whom he conquered.

After God had made his path successful, he sent envoys to Roma to renew the treaty with the Roman leaders. These are the words of the treaty that the Roman leaders renewed with Hyrcanus, king of Judaea: "Fannius, son of Marcus, and Lucius and Mallius,[2] sons of Mentius, Gaius Sempronius, son of Falernus, and the rest of the Roman leaders and the Elder who is with us to Hyrcanus, king of Judaea: peace. Let it be known to you that we have received your letters, which we have read with affection, and we inquired about your well-being from your envoys Dositheus and Apollonius and Todoros [Diodoros], good

---

1. Phrase from *AJ* 13.319, also used chap. 10 (see note there) and chap. 49.
2. The author often splits one name into two men.

and wise men, and we have honored them; they sat with us in front of the Elder, and everything that they requested of the Elder he gave them, and we [were of one mind] with him. All of the territory that Antiochus took by force from your land will be yours, and everything that Antiochus did and everything that he commanded will be annulled. The cities of his land that you captured in war will be yours. We have written letters unto every nation to receive with respect the envoys that you have sent to us, and we have dispatched with them our legate named Fannius,[3] to whom we gave a letter; further, we spoke to him our words dictating words of peace for you, as the Elder decreed and his 320 advisers decreed."

In those days, the kings of Makedon were fighting among themselves; King Hyrcanus traveled with his entire army. They encamped before Samaria and besieged it, building a siege wall against it. A great famine occurred in Samaria until the Samaritans and the Kutim [were reduced to eating] the corpses [and] carcasses lying on the road.[4]

King Hyrcanus left and went to Jerusalem due to the Fast of Kippur to atone for the people of God, for he was both king and priest, and he left his two sons, Antigonus and Aristobulus, in charge of the army in Samaria, against whom Antiochus, king of Makedon, invaded, for he had come to the aid of the Kutim to save Samaria from Hyrcanus's sons, and he fought against them. A great battle ensued with King Antiochus, and King Antiochus fled from the young men, the sons of Hyrcanus, taking refuge in a city called Sitopoli (Scythopolis = Beth Shan).

On that very day, Hyrcanus was in the House of the Holy of Holies[5] praying on behalf of the people of Israel, and afterward he mentioned his sons, for he worried lest they had died by Antiochus's sword. He heard a heavenly voice [*bat kol*][6] speak out in the Holy of Holies: "Do not be saddened and do not worry for your sons, Priest Hyrcanus, for this day your sons have done battle with Antiochus, and they have defeated him, putting him to flight and dealing a decisive blow to his army. Now you, Hyrcanus, fear not, finish your worship in peace, for you have come in peace, and you shall go in peace." Hyrcanus left the

---

3. *DEH* 1.1.9.

4. The author loosely reads *AJ* 13.266.

5. The author assumes that it was Yom Kippur.

6. [*Bat kol*, the still small voice that represented divine communication, a substitute for prophecy. Cf. *Encyclopedia Judaica* (Jerusalem, 1972), s.v. SB]. b. *Sotah* 33b does not place him inside the Sanctuary, whereas the Tosephta assumes that he was engaged in the Yom Kippur service. Perhaps the author's assumption is based on *AJ* 13.282, which has him alone in the Sanctuary.

sanctuary and related all these words to the attending people, but the people did not believe, so they sent horsemen to the camp in Samaria and found that everything said by Hyrcanus was true.

The Kutim sent [messengers] again and brought Latiro (Lathyrus), son of Cleopatra, queen of Egypt, and with him Gallimander[7] and Epicrates, Makedonian officers, and they came to the aid of the Kutim to rescue Samaria from Hyrcanus's sons. King Hyrcanus left Jerusalem to confront the army of Egypt and dealt them a very great blow, killing many, and he smote Gallimander too, who died there. The survivors turned and fled for their lives; and the kings of Makedon and Egypt ceased from helping Samaria and the Kutim any further. The king returned [from these battles] and came to Samaria and besieged it for one year. The Lord gave it into his hand, and he killed all of its males with the sword and leveled its walls to their foundations.

At that time, God magnified the name of Judaea throughout the inhabited world. Cleopatra, queen of Egypt, also dismissed the Egyptians from her armies and appointed Ḥilkiah and Ḥananiah as generals over all the army of Egypt, for her son Lathyrus had rebelled against her, and the Egyptians abandoned her and joined Lathyrus. Ḥilkiah and Ḥananiah the Jews, Cleopatra's generals, went forth against them,[8] fought with them, and subdued them to the queen's rule. Lathyrus fled before his mother and went to Cyprus, one of the islands in the Mediterranean, and dwelt there. Hyrcanus fought against all his surrounding enemies and subdued them; thus, Israel dwelt in peace in the days of Hyrcanus, every man under his vine and under his fig tree, and they multiplied and increased in number and became very strong.

---

7. *AJ* 13.279, has Callimander.

8. Based on *AJ* 13.328, which has Lathyrus ruling over Cyprus after his exile from Egypt; the author assumes that his flight came after his defeat by Ḥilkiah and Ḥananiah.

30. HYRCANUS AND THE PHARISEES (PERUSHIM)

In those days,[1] when King Hyrcanus was sitting on the throne of his kingdom in Jerusalem, the holy city, the king made a great feast for all his chiefs and servants and the warriors of the army of Judah and Benjamin. The king was sitting at the table with the sages of Israel—the Pharisees who explained the Torah—for Hyrcanus was one of their disciples. When Hyrcanus's heart was gladdened with wine, he said to the sages, that is, to the Pharisees: "You know that I am your disciple, and if you should see me turn from the path, reprove me and return me to the correct path, for it is befitting that you do so." The Pharisees answered, saying: "Woe unto us that we see such a thing, for we are this day witnesses that you are a righteous man, and you walk along the straight path, for you are king and priest."[2]

Hyrcanus was pleased with their words.

Sitting there was one of the Pharisees named Elazar, a contentious man and an evildoer, and he called out, saying: "Let King Hyrcanus live forever! If you really wanted to be righteous as you have said, renounce the priesthood and let the crown suffice you." Hyrcanus replied, saying: "Why should I renounce the priesthood?" Elazar answered: "Because your mother was taken captive in the days of Antiochus Epiphanes and thus became defiled. Therefore, it is not befitting for you to enter the Holy of Holies." The king became furious; joy turned into strife and their mutual affection into hatred.

---

1. *AJ* 13.289; and *Kiddushin* 66a. Flusser continually cites Talmudic parallels, but it is uncertain whether Yosippon knew the text from either oral or written sources. The sentence is nicely styled on Esth 1:2–3. [SB]

2. Hyrcanus was not king; cf. *AJ* 13.288. See chap. 29.

A rich and great man of the Ẓedokim (Sadducees), by the name of Yehonatan, was sitting there, and he said to the king: "Did I not tell you, 'Do not rely on them, for lies are in their mouths,' and now they have commanded Elazar to curse you." The king said to the Pharisees: "You judge this matter wherein Elazar has cursed me." The Pharisees answered and said: "Whipping and beating him should suffice, for the Pharisees cannot issue a death sentence." Yehonatan replied, saying: "Did I not tell you that this curse was made with their knowledge and will?" From this day hence, Hyrcanus rebelled against their teachings, for Yehonatan convinced him to be a Sadducee.

The king gave the command, and they proclaimed throughout the land of Israel: "Every teacher who teaches the code of the Pharisees shall surely die." Hyrcanus killed [many] of the people at that time; whereupon the people's hatred rose against him and his sons in those days.

Joseph ben Gurion said: "Now let me explain what caused the quarrel and controversy that befell the people of God. For the Pharisees used to say: 'Let us preserve the Torah, which our forefathers, the sages who explained the Torah, transmitted to our hands.' Those who taught in those days constituted two groups: the Sadducees, who did not believe in any tradition and interpretation but in the Torah of Moses alone; and the Hasidim[3] were the other group in those days. For these controversies, there was much fighting and much blood shed among the people of Israel, for the poor [*dalath ha-'am*][4] supported the Pharisees, save for the rich and its warriors[5], for they were collaborating with the king and the Sadducees."

Joseph ben Gurion said: "In those days, King Hyrcanus asked, inquiring[6] of God about his sons—which of them would be king and sit on his throne after him. He had three sons: Aristobulus and Antigonus, two who were loved by their father, and a third, Alexander, hated and detested by his father, who had banished him to the Galilee, and he could not see his father's face. When Hyrcanus put his question to the Lord, the Lord spoke to him in a dream during the

---

3. That is, the Essenes. *AJ* 13.298, mentions Essenes. *Yosippon* is the first source to derive the name Essenes from the word *Hasidim*. He earlier identified them as the Hasidim in the Hasmonean revolt and who existed already in the days of Alexander the Great (see chaps. 10 and 16 and chap. 24, note 1). The Hebrew is rather clumsy here.

4. *Populares* in the Latin of *AJ* 13.298. *Populares* also designates the opposite of *patricii*; see the following note.

5. *Copiosi vel divites*; the author adds "nobles" based on his conclusion that the Ẓedokim provided the army leaders (cf. chap. 34). In the *Festschrift to Gedalyah Alon* (Tel Aviv, 1970), 144, I suggest that his contemporary society also influenced him.

6. *Vayidrosh mipi adonai. DRSh* is the biblical verbal root for direct approach to God by priest, king, and prophet. [SB]

night, saying to him: 'Raise your eyes and look upon your son who will succeed you and sit upon your throne.' He lifted his eyes and looked, and, behold, his son Alexander was standing by him. So Hyrcanus woke up and wept and asked again of the Lord, but He did not answer him further [cf. 1 Sam 28:6]."

King Hyrcanus was gathered unto his people, and the days that he ruled were thirty-one years. The rest of his words and mighty deeds and wars that he fought, the cities that he captured from Aram, the mighty deeds that he did against Makedon, subduing Edom and circumcising the Edomites, they are written in the book of Joseph ben Gurion and in the book of the kings of Romi (Roma).

31. THE DAYS OF ARISTOBULUS THE FIRST

Succeeding him [Hyrcanus] was his son Aristobulus, the one called Great King,[1] for he greatly expanded the border of Israel. He fought against Tyre and Sidon,[2] killing men without number; he circumcised the flesh of their foreskins and subdued them under the rule of Judaea until the arrival of the Roman general Pompey. This was Aristobulus who defiled the priesthood and downgraded it by placing the great crown of kingship on his head.

While sitting on the throne of his kingdom, he was incited to cruelty; he bound his mother and brother in chains, for he was jealous of his mother and his brother regarding the kingship. He loved his younger brother Antigonus and clothed him in purple and bestowed many royal honors on him; he sent him to war with his entire army of warriors to fight against any nation that rebelled against King Aristobulus. Antigonus went and fought the king's wars wherever his brother, the king, sent him. Antigonus defeated all the rebels who had raised their hand against the king, killing many men and slaying great multitudes; then he returned and entered Jerusalem in triumph.

King Aristobulus fell ill with a sickness, and his illness was very severe. Antigonus heard on the way that his brother, the king, was sick; so when the lad arrived in the city, he did not go to the palace but went to the Temple to pray for the deliverance of his brother, for he could no longer stand his brother's suffering.

---

1. *BJ* 1.70, and *AJ* 13.301, identify Aristobulus as the first Hasmonean king. The author adds "great" since he had already designated Yoḥanan Hyrcanus as king. See below for elaboration.

2. *Ẓor* is Hebrew for Tyre. The author's unknown source is inaccurate.

That day happened to be the festival of Sukkoth, in which it is a law unto the Jews to receive in honor and to praise God with four kinds of trees. A great crowd of men of Israel was there, and Antigonus passed through with his troops into the Temple court in the midst of the crowd; he was girt with battle gear and dressed in silver armor embroidered with gold;[3] the lad was very handsome in appearance and good looking, and all the people were amazed at his beauty and looks.

A man named Yehudah was there, one of the most important Hasidim.[4] He raised his eyes and saw that Antigonus was passing in the court of the Temple. Yehudah said to his disciples:[5] "I would rather die today than see the death of this lad Antigonus; would that I shall die and not witness his death, for I foresee that Antigonus will die this day in a place called Straton's Tower." His disciples said to him: "Rabbenu, you have spoken falsehood, for the Straton's Tower you mention is some six hundred stadia [ris] distant from Jerusalem, and it is midday already. How could what you said come to be?" He replied, saying to them: "My sons, I wish I were wrong about this matter!" With this statement, he fell to the ground and was silent and, behold, slept like a man exhausted and wearied from the great anxiety that was in his heart.

After this, wicked men went and told the king as follows: "Behold, Antigonus, your brother is coming to kill you; he is standing in the Temple court in battle gear, dressed for war, arrayed with his troops to attack you suddenly and seize you and all your entire household." The king became very alarmed and set guards at the gates and in the streets and at all the pathways to the king's house. He ordered the guards, saying: "Anyone who dares come to me girt with weapons of war, neither ask him nor answer him but draw your swords and kill him instantly. As for the rest of the people who do not have weapons, do not kill them, only prevent them from coming to me, for I am sick, excepting only Antigonus, my brother: he alone may come to me, and I shall question him and examine him concerning the rumor that I heard, whether it be true or false." Thus, the king commanded the guards at that time. All the guards were warriors well trained in war. Following this, the king sent greetings to his brother Antigonus, saying: "Throw off your breastplate and take off the weapons of war from your loins; hasten to me and don't tarry!" But the queen, Aristobulus's

---

3. So contemporary Byzantine battle dress. Yosippon regularly uses feminine from his Italian, here "armor" from *la corazza*.

4. See chap. 30, notes.

5. *BJ* 1.79; *AJ* 13.312. *DEH* 1.7 has Yehudah request death for his earlier erroneous prophecy. Yosippon brings the prophecy forward to Yehudah's encounter with Antigonus in Jerusalem, dramatically altering the intent to pity for the lad's imminent death.

wife, and her counselors of wickedness changed the king's message to cruelty; she called the king's emissary and said to him: "When you go to Antigonus, speak thus to him—'Your brother heard that you have donned the trappings of war and girded weapons of battle, and the king is eager to see the trappings of war that are upon you, and he has commanded that you come to him girt with weapons of battle and dressed in the trappings of war." The emissary went and told Antigonus all that the queen, Aristobulus's wife, had commanded him. The lad believed [him] and went confidently, for he trusted the love of his brother, the king. As he was going through the pathways to the palace, hurrying to his brother, the king, dressed in the trappings of war and girded with the weapons of battle, behold, along the path was a tower called Straton after the name of the city six hundred stadia distant from Jerusalem; this tower in Jerusalem was also called Straton's Tower, and it is adjacent to the king's palace. Antigonus passed this place confidently when the king's guards leaped upon him with their drawn swords and struck him, spilling the innocent blood of the lad who had neither sinned nor rebelled. They killed the innocent and righteous one on that spot just as the sage Yehudah, one of the most important Hasidim, had said.

Later on, when Aristobulus was told that his brother was killed, his compassion for his brother was stirred, and he wept and cried in an exceedingly great and bitter outpouring. He beat his breast with both his fists and, flinging himself to the ground, ruptured a lung in his bosom;[6] the streams of blood [Lev 12:7] in his chest opened, and the king began to vomit blood from his mouth. Vomiting blood day after day into a gold basin, he gave the basin to a boy, who was to carry it to the king's physicians.[7] The boy carried the vessel, and, passing the spot where Antigonus, the king's brother, was killed, behold, the dead man's spilled blood still stained the marble pavement; all the stones of the floor were colored with the blood of Antigonus. The boy's feet slipped, and he slid, overturning the basin and spilling the king's blood over the blood of his murdered brother; and the blood of the king mixed with the blood of Antigonus, his brother. The king's troops shouted and scolded the boy, saying: "Wicked one, what have you done, spilling the king's blood over the blood of his slain brother?" The boy answered, saying: "I did not do this intentionally, for I slipped on the marble; that is why the basin in my hand overturned and the blood was spilled, as you see."

------

6. The author changed his sources to describe a medical condition that he understood, perhaps indicating that the author was a physician.
7. For a fragment on diagnosing from vomited blood, see S. Müntner, *Rabbi Shabbetai Donnolo* (Jerusalem, 1949), 144.

When Aristobulus heard the sound of the crowd's shouting, he asked:[8] "What is this noise these troops make, and what is the sound of this rebuking and quarrelling that I hear?" But his troops and the eunuchs serving him were silent and did not answer him at all. Because they were silent, the king became more distressed[9] over the matter. The king asked again more persistently, as kings do: "Tell me what the crowd is shouting about, and if you do not tell, you shall surely die!" They answered and told the king what had happened, namely, that the blood was spilled over the blood of his brother.

The king sighed and cried out, saying: "Blessed be the righteous judge, the true judge, and blessed be the Avenger of innocent blood in that the blood of the wicked was spilled over the blood of the righteous who was killed." The king said to his body: "How long, wicked body, will you imprison the soul and not let it take leave to join the souls of my people? Rather, you cast my blood and spilled it out, sacrificing it,[10] giving it to lap up to the devils who are with Satan, for they have incited and driven me in this affair to do such things and to kill my brother." As he was speaking these words, he ended his life, died, and was gathered to his people. The days that he reigned were one full year. All Judah wept for him exceedingly, for the Jews loved him because he was beneficent and victorious, for he vanquished a great nation called the Ituraei and circumcised the flesh of their foreskin, subduing them under the yoke of Judah. The Greeks called him Aristobulus Philelleni, that is, beloved[11] of Greeks. And the rest of his words and mighty deeds are written in the book of Joseph ben Gurion and in the book of the kings of Roma and in the book of Strabon of Caphtor and in the book of Timagenes the Jerusalemite.[12]

---

8. *BJ* 1.83; *AJ* 13.315–16, with the author's dramatic emphasis.

9. The author misunderstood the Latin expression.

10. I.e., for the souls of the mother and the brother whom Aristobulus killed.

11. The author prefers the form *ahuv* (= beloved), instead of the literal "friend" (*ohev*). See chap. 47. [SB]

12. In different biblical translations, Cappadocia is identified as Caphtor. In *AJ* 13.319, Strabo cites Timagenes (actually he was from Alexandria in Egypt). It is not clear where the author derived his Jerusalem origin.

32. ALEXANDER YANNAI'S WARS

Alexander, his brother, succeeded him. He was the Alexander whom his father, Hyrcanus, hated, and Alexander ruled just as the Lord had spoken to Hyrcanus in the night dream. After being freed from the bonds in which his brother had imprisoned him, he sat upon the throne of his kingdom and led an army against Talmaida (Ptolemais), for the people of Ptolemais (Acre) had rebelled in those days.

Gaza revolted at that time, and King Alexander went against Ptolemais and besieged it, and the city came under siege. The inhabitants of Ptolemais sent [a message] to Lathyrus, Cleopatra's son, who was living in Cyprus from fear of his mother, Cleopatra, saying: "Come and save us from Alexander, king of Judaea, who is fighting against us, and we shall be your servants." But Lathyrus refused to come to their aid, for he feared to fight with the Jews, since he remembered the defeat that Hyrcanus, king of Judaea, had inflicted upon him in battle when he went to the aid of the Kutim in Samaria. For this reason, he was afraid to come. The envoys of Ptolemais said to him: "Do not be afraid to come to save your servants, for if you cross over [the sea] and go with us, other kings will join to aid us; Zoilus, king of Sidon,[1] and other kings will come to our aid." With these words, they convinced Lathyrus; coming by ship, he went with them, and all his force was about thirty thousand men. Alexander broke off and left Ptolemais before Lathyrus.

Lathyrus and all his army came to Ptolemais, but its people did not receive him, for a wise man named Demaeretus[2] came and spoke to the elders of Ptolemais, saying: "Would it not be better for you to suffer the yoke of Alexander, who is a Jew, than to let Lathyrus, a foreigner, rule over you?" As a result of

---

1. Zoilus was not king of Sidon.
2. Latin MSS have both Demaeretus and Demaenetus.

hearing his words, they changed their minds and did not accept Lathyrus, and Lathyrus feared greatly. Zoilus, king of Sidon, sent him messengers: "Come, let us join forces and go to war against Alexander, king of Judaea!"

Alexander also sent messengers to Lathyrus, saying: "Let there be a covenant between me and you, and do not lend a hand to aid Zoilus, king of Sidon, my enemy; let there be peace between me and you!" He [Alexander] sent him [Lathyrus] a gift of four thousand talents of silver, and Lathyrus accepted Alexander's friendship. Then Alexander went to war[3] against Zoilus, fought with him, killing many, and Zoilus fled from him. Alexander took all his land from him and returned, arriving in Jerusalem in glory and victory.[4]

After these events, Alexander sent a secret message to Cleopatra, Lathyrus's mother, saying: "Behold, your son Lathyrus rebelled against you, and he is camped opposite me. If it pleases you, hurry and come with your army, and I will go out with all my force, and we shall capture him according to your heart's desire." Lathyrus heard of this and became exceedingly furious and enraged; he invaded the Galilee on the Sabbath and captured Sochton,[5] a city in the Galilee. Those whom he killed in it and those whom he led into captivity were about ten thousand souls. From there, he went to Sipporin, and many of Lathyrus's men were slain in that place. He departed from there and went to make war on Alexander.

When Alexander heard of these things, he gathered fifty thousand Judaean warriors and chose from them six thousand heroes with copper shields who were called *ecatonta machos*, one against a hundred. King Alexander went out on that day from Jerusalem with pride and might, and he encountered Lathyrus on the rivers of the Jordan. Alexander said to his warriors:[6] "Let us fall upon him suddenly, for the river is behind him, and if they flee from us, behold, the river will block their way, and having no refuge, they will all die to the man." Alexander trusted in his valor rather than trusting in God, Lord of his fathers.

Lathyrus and his men were most frightened of Alexander and his warriors. There was in Lathyrus's army a man named Philostephanus, and he divided the troops, for Philostephanus was a wise man skilled in war and trained in fighting. When Alexander and his army attacked Lathyrus's army, the battle broke out, and many were slain from Lathyrus's camp. They fought from morning until noon: the Jews were victorious, and a great number of Makedonians were

---

3. The author misunderstood *AJ* 13.335, which has Lathyrus defeat Zoilus.

4. In *AJ* 13.335, Alexander asked Lathyrus for Zoilus's land, which led the author to understand that Lathyrus gave it following Zoilus's death.

5. Asochiton, and in some MSS, Asochron.

6. *AJ* 13.340, which the author changes to Alexander's speech to his soldiers.

slain. He [Alexander] smote half of Lathyrus's army facing them, but there still remained Philostephanus with half the army that he had divided, and they did not approach the fighting until afternoon. In the afternoon, Philostephanus advanced with half the army to fight against the Jews and Alexander. He found them tired and weary; so he dealt them a great blow, and thirty thousand of the Jews, all of them warriors, fell on that day. The survivors fled to the mountain [cf. Gen 14:10], and Alexander fled from the battle to Jerusalem. The defeat of the Jews at that time came about because they trusted in their own valor rather than in God, Lord of their fathers.

It was evening when Lathyrus entered one of the villages of the Jews and found women and children. He commanded to slay some women and children and ordered to cook their flesh in a cauldron in order to terrify the people of Judaea so that they would say of them that they ate human flesh.

At that time, Queen Cleopatra went forth to do battle with her son Lathyrus, and Alexander went out to greet her and ask her for peace; he gave her gold and silver and told her all the evil that Lathyrus had done in his land; and Alexander joined with Cleopatra to fight against Lathyrus. When Lathyrus heard, he fled before them; he boarded a ship and fled to Cyprus. He abandoned his army on the seashore, where Ḥilkiah and Ḥananiah, Cleopatra's Jewish generals, killed them, and the queen returned to Egypt.

King Alexander went with his entire army; he invaded the plain of Aram[7] and fought against Gadira (Gadara); he besieged it for ten months and captured Gadara and its surrounding villages. He marched from there to Ḥamat (Amathus) and encamped there. It happened on that night that Theodorus with his warriors came out of Ḥamat and, falling upon the Jews' camp, cast ten thousand Jews dead to the ground. When the Jews arose at dawn,[8] they fought against Theodorus and put him to flight, dealing his army a great blow, and he fled from before them; and then the king captured Ḥamat and its surrounding villages. He marched on and encamped against Raphis (Raphia) and captured it and its surrounding villages. From there, he marched and encamped against Anthedona, besieged it, and captured it and its villages, and then returned to Jerusalem.

A year later, he led an army against Gaza, encamped before the city and besieged her, for the king remembered the evil of the people of Gaza, that the Gazans were allied with Lathyrus in fighting against the Jews. Apolodotus, Gaza's general, rose with twelve thousand warriors and, making a night attack

---

7. *Humilis Syria* (low, shallow) for *Coele Syria* (hollow of Syria).

8. *AJ* 13.357; *BJ* 1.87; and *DEH* 1.9.2 only relate that notwithstanding, Alexander continued his march.

on the camp of the Jews, dealt them a great blow. But the Jews maintained their position until morning light. When morning came, the Jews raised a great cry and pressed the Gazans, smiting them and pushing them unto the gate of Gaza; and the whole road was littered with Gazan corpses; the king built a dike against Gaza, and the city came under siege.

The Gazans sent [a message] to Hartas (Aretas), king of Arav, saying: "Come up and save us from Alexander and the Jews who are fighting against us, and we shall be your servants." Aretas, king of Arav, came with his army to the aid of Gaza. When Alexander heard that Aretas was coming to war against him, he left a commander [*nagid*][9] to guard Gaza, and he [Alexander], with the rest of the army and all his warriors, went out to confront Aretas, king of Arav. A battle broke out, and Alexander was victorious. Aretas fled from him and went to his land to Desert Rock [Petra], and many of his men were killed at that time. The king returned to Gaza and besieged her for one year.

At that time, Pysimachus (Lysimachus) rose up and killed Apolodotus, his brother, commander of Gaza. The Gazans rose up to kill Pysimachus, but Pysimachus hurried to the gate and, opening the gate of Gaza, called in Alexander and the Jews. The Jews rose up and, raising a cry, passed through the gate and captured the city. Alexander entered the city and commanded his warriors to kill all the inhabitants of the city without mercy, and he smote all her males with the sword; only Pysimachus and all his household did he let live.

Five hundred leaders of the city fled to the temple of Apollinus (Apollo). When Alexander was told, he brought them out of the temple and commanded that they be killed in the midst of the city. He burned the temple of Apollinus, and all its priests he burned with fire inside the temple.[10] The gold statue of Apollinus[11] was thrown into the fire at the king's command; after some days, they [Alexander's warriors] collected the gold from the fire. The king returned to Jerusalem and sat upon his throne and reigned in peace.

---

9. *Nagid* in Hebrew, a well-represented term in tenth- to eleventh-century sources, e.g., Saadia Gaon, commentary to Dan 9:27.

10. The author assumed that Alexander would destroy any pagan place. Cf. *Royal Frankish Annals*, s.a. 772, for Charlemagne's destruction of the Saxon idol at Irminsul, of which the author may have been aware. *Templum Apollinis* is similar to that in the *chansons de geste*. Perhaps the author made up his own version of the name.

11. Mediaeval Christians accused Muslims of worshipping gold statues of Muhammed and Apollin. He may have heard the name from Christian slanders against Muslim raiders in the author's homeland, southern Italy.

33. ALEXANDER AND THE PHARISEES

During the festival of Sukkoth, the king went to the altar according to the custom of priests, whereupon the Pharisees—the sages—began to play with *ethrogim*[1] and with palm branches and to hit each other with *ethrogim* and palm branches in joy and glad-heartedness, for it was a law of the Jews to sport with citrus fruits and dates. One of the Pharisees dared to throw an *ethrog* and strike the king. The king's troops got angry and said to the Pharisees: "Why do you disgrace the king by throwing *ethrogim* and palm branches at him?" They said: "This is no disgrace, for it is a law unto us to do so." The exchange led to curses, and they reproached the king, saying: "Son of the defiled woman, the priesthood does not befit you, for your mother was defiled." The king got very angry,[2] and his ire blazed within him, and he put forth his hand over the altar and said: "Sword!" The king's troops drew their swords and killed six thousand Pharisees dead in the courtyard of the Temple. The king commanded, and they built the wall of acacia wood[3] between the altar and the rest of the Temple. From that day hence, the people were prevented from coming to the Temple, so the people

---

1. Josephus relates that the people rebelled against Alexander and pelted him with *ethrogim* and even bad-mouthed him, saying that he was the son of a polluted woman since she had been a captive. The author's interpretation derives from *DEH* 9.2, which expands on *BJ* 1.88, and led the author to connect that to *AJ* 13.372. The question remains whence he derived the law that allowed the Perushim to hit each other with citrons and palm branches. Was this a local custom in the author's time?
2. *AJ* 13.373, with dramatic effect of the author, who creates the verbal exchange. [The command "sword" is in the singular in Hebrew. The corresponding verbal root is intransitive in Hebrew. The image recalls Ex 14:21. SB]
3. The author adds "acacia" from the biblical desert worship tradition. [This wall developed theological symbolism as the iconostasis in Christianity. SB]

stood in the courtyard of the Temple, and only the priests entered the Temple, as the law commands.[4]

After these events, Alexander gathered all his army and marched against Desert Rock; he smote the Arab people and captured the fortified cities of Arav. From there, he marched against Madaba and captured it and smote Moab and subjugated it to his rule. Then Ḥamat rebelled at that time, and the king went against Ḥamat, destroying it, and he also killed Theodorus, who was in Ḥamat. Then he returned to Jerusalem.

War broke out between Alexander and the Pharisees, and the fighting dragged on for six years. In those years, Alexander killed fifty thousand Jews who supported the Pharisees. Alexander summoned all the people and said to them:[5] "Purify your hearts and cast the hatred from your midst and do not hate me, and I will do justice just as you tell me." The Jews called out to the king: "If you would die, perhaps [then] we would cleanse our hearts, for you are a man of death and a sentence of death is upon you."

They rebelled against King Alexander and went to King Demetrius of Makedon, called Eucaerus,[6] and brought him to battle against Alexander; Demetrius came and encamped at Shekhem. Now Demetrius had a force of forty thousand Makedonian warriors and three thousand cavalry.

When Alexander saw that the Jews rebelled against him, he hired six thousand troops of Makedonian warriors, and taking twenty thousand Jewish warriors, who were with him, went to confront Demetrius, while from every Jewish force they gathered to aid Demetrius. Demetrius sent [men] to persuade the troops that were with Alexander to return to him, but he failed; Alexander in turn sent [men] to entice the Jews who were with Demetrius to return, but he [too] failed.

Fighting broke out and Alexander's troops fell in the battle, and Alexander remained alone, for all his troops fell on that day. But they killed many of Demetrius's troops, for they fought to the death and did not retreat, and so all died. Then Alexander, alone and deserted, took flight to the mountains. About six thousand valiant warriors of Israel rallied to him, while many Jews who had been with Demetrius's army fell in with him to help him, but Alexander feared to fight further with Demetrius. Demetrius, however, fled from Alexander, for he saw that a great horde of Jews fell in with him to aid him.

---

4. *BJ* 1.90; *AJ* 13.375; *DEH* 1.9.4. The sources relate his return to Jerusalem after the Arabs defeated him.

5. *BJ* 1.92; *AJ* 13.376, with dramatic embellishment.

6. The Greek text and some Latin MSS preserve the derogatory name Acaerus (the tardy one), but the Latin translation of *AJ* has the more complimentary Eucaerus found in author's MS of *BJ*.

There was another battle between Alexander and the Jews who supported the Pharisees, and he slew many of them in the fighting. The survivors fled to Beth Shemesh;[7] he captured the city and, seizing eight hundred leading Pharisees, took them to Jerusalem. While sitting at a drinking feast in a lofty place with his wives and concubines, he commanded that they crucify eight hundred Pharisees; for this reason, the Jews called Alexander Thrakidas.[8] And Alexander ruled mightily over the Jews.

After this, he gathered his army, marched, and encamped against Dim (Dion) and captured it. From there, he departed to Ḥasmon (Essemon) and captured it with a mighty hand. He marched from there and besieged Gaulana (Gaulam) and Seleucia (Seleucus) and captured them, and he captured also Gamla and the hill [lit. valley] of Antiochia, the great city, where he killed Demetrius. He returned and entered Jerusalem three full years after he left for war; the Jews received him with honor and paid him great respect, praising him for his valor after the manner of the Greeks.

At that time, the Jews invaded the land of Aram and ruled over it and all the territory of Edom and all of Moab and Amon and all the land of Paleshet (Philistia) and all of Arav (Arabia) unto Desert Rock. Now these are the names of the cities that King Alexander did not destroy after he captured them; those of the seacoast were Straton's Tower, Apollonia, Ashdod, ʿAza [Gaza], Antidones, Raphis (Raphia), Rhinocora, and Hebron,[9] Marasha (Marisa), Sitopoli (Scythopolis) of Aram, Gadera, Gaulan, Seleucia, Gabala of Moab, Ḥeshbon, Madaba, Baḥoron,[10] Megan, Onzora (Ein Zora), Cilicus, Aulon,[11] and Pellan. These are the cities that he did not destroy, for they entered a covenant with him, circumcising the flesh of their foreskins, and dwelt in their cities, but the king destroyed the rest of Aram's cities.

At that time, King Alexander became sick, and his sickness was "fourth fever" [*quartanus typus*]; and even though the fever dragged on for three years, he did not desist from war. He led an army against Rigba (Ragaba) of Gerisin (Gerasa)[12] and besieged it for many days, for the king's wife and his concubines had joined the army.

---

7. *BJ* 1.96–97: Bemeselis; *AJ* 13.380: Bethomis; *DEH* 1.10.3: Bemeselel.

8. *AJ* 13.383. Thracians were considered savage and bloodthirsty from Thucydides (e.g., Mycalessos) to Tacitus.

9. *AJ* 13.396. For the following list, see A. Shalit, "Alexander Yannai's Conquests in Moav," *Eretz Yisrael* 1 (1951): 1–19; and Marcus, "Name *Makkabaios*," 65. Hebron = Abora.

10. Lembaoronem, a Latin corruption of Lemba, Oronaim. The author's MS probably had Baoronem, which he read as the accusative of Baoron.

11. Cilicum Aulon, which the author read as two names.

12. *In monte Gerasenorum* (in the mountains of the people of Gerasa).

When the day of his death arrived, Queen Alexandra, King Alexander's wife, approached him and said: "You know the hatred between you and the Pharisees; your sons are small, and I am a woman. Who will come to my assistance?" Alexandra wept before the king, and the king said to her: "Come and I will give you an advice; follow it, and all will be well for you and your sons after me. When I die, hide my body from all the army until you have captured this city, and when you shall have captured this city, anoint my body with spices, lest the corpse putrefy, and carry me to Jerusalem as if [I were] a sick man; do not reveal the secret save to the eunuchs loyal to you. Now, when you have arrived in Jerusalem, summon the Pharisees, my enemies, and reveal the secret to them, hand over my corpse into their hands, and say unto them: 'Behold, your enemy Alexander is dead, and here is his body. Do unto it what you deem fit; if you prefer to cast it to the dogs, then cast it; do unto it whatever you deem proper.' If you speak thus to them, they will honor me greatly and will bury me with respect, for I know their nature: they will not bear a grudge of hatred against me, since they are merciful;[13] they will help you to rule the kingdom, for the people listen to them, since they have power over the people who do their will. Do everything they command you to do and follow their advice; turn neither to the right nor to the left, and you shall rule until the boys grow up."

The queen did so and, capturing the city, went to Jerusalem and summoned the Pharisees, saying to them all that Alexander, her husband, had commanded. The Pharisees summoned the people, and they buried the king with honor; they spoke to the people, and they crowned Alexandra, Alexander's wife, as queen over all Judah. The days that King Alexander ruled over all Yehudah were twenty-seven years, and he died and was gathered to his people. The rest of his words and his mighty deeds are written in the book of Joseph ben Gurion and in the book of the kings of Roma. And the king lay with his ancestors, and his wife Alexandra succeeded him.

---

13. The author's addition.

34. QUEEN ALEXANDRA'S DAYS

While sitting on the throne, she [Alexandra] called the masters of the Pharisees and gave them authority over all the people. She sent for and brought the masters of the Pharisees from every place whither they had fled in the days of her father-in-law, Hyrcanus, and in the days of her husband, Alexander; she released all the prisoners from prison; and she obeyed the Torah [teaching] of the masters of the Pharisees, which her father-in-law Hyrcanus and her husband Alexander had disobeyed.

When the queen saw that her two sons were beginning to mature, she gave the priesthood to Hyrcanus, for Hyrcanus was meek and humble, and she made Aristobulus, her younger son, general of the army, for he was a handsome lad, strong in hand and light of foot; she appointed him as head of the Sadducees to be general of the army. The queen sent to all the kings whom her father-in-law, Hyrcanus, and her husband, Alexander, had conquered, and she took their sons as hostage. The queen ruled in peace and quiet, and there was neither adversity nor trouble in her days; and all the kings surrounding her sent offerings of gold and silver annually to the queen, all her days.

There was peace and truth in the days of Alexandra; only the masters of the Pharisees inspired controversies and strife with the Sadducee chiefs. The Pharisee masters came with her son Hyrcanus and spoke to the queen: "Long live the queen. Be strong and mighty forever! Give into our hands Alexander's Sadducee counselors who advised him to crucify the eight hundred Pharisee masters whom your husband, Alexander, crucified." She said to them: "Do unto them as you see fit!" The Pharisee masters went and killed Diogenes, the Sadducee chief, and, along with him, they killed many others.

The Sadducee chiefs came with Aristobulus, her younger son, and spoke to her: "Sacred Queen,[1] forget not all the trouble that our leaders suffered in the days of your husband, Alexander, and all the trouble that we suffered with him and the great and terrible battles that we fought serving with him, how we put our lives on the line for his sake, how we had no concern for ourselves for the sake of his life, and how we fought his wars to save him from those who sought his life. Now why should we die like sheep led to slaughter, having committed no sin or iniquity, while you elevate the enemies of your husband, Alexander, and humiliate those who loved him? When you humiliate us, your enemies, and Aretas, king of Arabia, [those] who were afraid of our valor and our wars will rejoice. For if someone had brought up our names before Aretas and before your enemies, they would have shaken in fear and trembling throughout their settlements, even from sight of our faces. Heaven forbid that we should rebel against you or raise a hand against your commands, for you are queen and mistress. But you should know that we shall not bear the yoke of our enemies the Pharisee masters, and we shall not die like sheep led to slaughter at their hand. If it pleases you, we shall leave Jerusalem for the other cities of Judah and live in humility, and we shall no longer see the evil befalling our people." They gave their voice to weeping, and the queen, too, wept before them.

Aristobulus opened his mouth and spoke to his mother, uttering curses and maledictions, speaking all his mind to her. The queen, like a woman, did not know what to do, so she said to them: "Leave Jerusalem, choose for yourselves cities from among the cities of Judah, and dwell in them: do not live in Jerusalem with Pharisee masters, for they are your enemies." And they did so. The Sadducee chiefs left Jerusalem along with veteran warriors and took cities for themselves, dwelling in them for fear of the Pharisee masters.

In those days, Damascus rebelled, for Ptolemy, called Minaeus, rebelled there by not paying the tax to the queen as he was supposed to. The queen sent her son Aristobulus with an army of the people[2] who supported the Pharisee masters, for the army of the Sadducees and the Hasidim was not with them; they went forth from Jerusalem and went to Damascus, returning in utter disgrace.

At that time, Tigran (Tigranes), king of Armenia, went forth with three hundred thousand dressed in armor and an immense horde, to invade the land of Yehudah. The queen and the people were exceedingly afraid of Tigranes; she

---

1. *Malkah kedoshah*. Not in the author's source. Contemporary Christian rulers—Saxon emperors, Merovingian and Frankish kings, and Byzantine emperors—were called "august Caesars."

2. I.e., a mass levy of undisciplined Perushim supporters (chap. 30) who were easily defeated, and not the veteran troops of the Zedokim or the consecrated veterans of the Ḥasidim.

sent messengers to greet him and a gift, and they found him fighting at Acco, that is, Ptolemais. Tigranes was pleased by the messengers and the gift and asked for the peace of the queen; he praised her and blessed her and made a pact with the queen's messengers.

At that time, it was reported to Tigranes that Lucullus, general of the Romans, pursued Mithridat (Mithridates) but failed to catch him, for he took refuge in the mountains of Persia, so Lucullus returned and invaded Armenia. When Tigranes heard this, he hurried and went to Armenia to deliver his land and save her from Lucullus. Tigranes said: "It is better for us to protect our land than to covet a foreign land."

In those days, Queen Alexandra fell ill with the sickness from which she would die. Aristobulus saw that his mother's death was drawing nigh. He left his wife and sons in Jerusalem, along with [his wife's] family, to be of assistance to him in the city, and taking one servant with him, he left Jerusalem at night and went to the cities of Yehudah where the Sadducees, his father's allies, lived. At the beginning of his flight, he came to Giv'ah (Gabatha), a place where his friend Galestes, a valiant Sadducee, dwelt, and he [Yehudah] accompanied him [Galestes] from Giv'ah to muster the Sadducee army.

The queen was told that her son Aristobulus had fled and that he was going to muster an army. Again, they [the Pharisees] came and told her: "Aristobulus has captured twenty-two cities in fifteen days." Then the queen and the entire nation of Yehudah were struck by fear and terror, for all the rest of the inhabitants of the cities fell in with him [Aristobulus] to help him. The queen ordered to seize Aristobulus's wife and his sons and all his wife's family, placing them under the guard of the watches [of Levites] of the Temple,[3] lest they attempt to flee.

After this, the mighty and strong arm of the warriors of the Sadducees and Hasidim, veterans of the army of Yehudah, increased exceedingly,[4] and, joining Aristobulus, they assembled on the field, blowing the ram's horn and giving a signal to war, for a great multitude from Mount Lebanon and from the Galilee[5] and from all the land under the rule of Israel were gathered to him. Hyrcanus and the Pharisee elders trembled. And the queen, too, was greatly afraid of her son Aristobulus; she was struck by worry and then became ill with the sickness of which she died.

---

3. *BJ* 1.118: Baris, later called the Antonina Fortress.

4. The author's two opposing ideologies were each supported by a military force: the Ẓadokim and the Hasidim against the Perushim never existed during the Second Commonwealth. The author clearly sympathizes with the Hasidim.

5. Trachonitis in original.

The Pharisee elders came before the queen and with them her elder son, Hyrcanus, and they said to her: "It would be a great sin for us to do anything without your advice as long as you are still alive, sacred queen [*malkah kedoshah*], for your son Aristobulus has frightened us greatly, because he comes against us mightily to wipe out our name and kill his elder brother. So now, sacred queen, give your counsel and your aid." The queen answered and said:[6] "Away with you, leave me alone, for my soul is sore weary, for I am on the threshold of eternal life and about to return my soul unto the King who gave it. And you, do what you wish. Here is gold and silver for you and many treasures; here is an army of warriors in my palace. Do as you will, for I cannot advise you in this matter as I am going the way of all flesh." As she uttered some such words, she ended her life, and she died and was gathered to her people.

The days that she ruled were nine years, and all her days were seventy-three years. She was a woman who weakened her nature,[7] and she neither sinned nor rebelled against her God, for wisdom and understanding and cleverness were in her. Out of her great wisdom, she, from time to time, knew the future,[8] but she was not wise in elevating her husband's enemies and humiliating his friends and allies. Therefore, after her death, there arose in her house tribulations and sorrows, and wars burst. But in her days, the land was quiet, for she did not covet another land. She just preserved well the lands of the nations that her husband, Alexander, and her father-in-law, Hyrcanus, had conquered, restoring them to Israel; those did not escape her grasp until the day of her death. Here ends the record of Queen Alexandra.

---

6. *AJ* 13.429. The author has modeled the material. Note further that *leshalem nafshi*, "unto the King who gave it," meaning "to return my soul" here, cannot refer to martyrdom.

7. The author understood *succubuit* as "to be tripped up in sin" and so inverts the source's praise as "a woman who never failed due to the weakness of her sex." The Hebrew is clumsy.

8. The author misunderstood *AJ* 13.431, which says that she calculated the present more than the future.

35. CIVIL WAR BETWEEN HYRCANUS AND ARISTOBULUS

Now it seems right to me[1] to relate the deeds that happened after her, for it is proper that every writer who writes books and relates ancient matters write in good order, lest the deeds that occurred be forgotten. Moreover, it is proper for the man who produces books to write words of truth, for thus commanded Joseph ben Gurion, the priest who is chief of the authors of all the books that were written, except for the twenty-four sacred books and the books of wisdom that Solomon, king of Israel, and the sages of Israel made. I collated words from the book of Joseph ben Gurion and from the books of other authors who wrote the story of our forefathers, and I collected[2] them in one scroll.

Joseph ben Gurion wrote thus in his book: In the 173rd year of the Olympiadas,[3] in the days of Quintus and Hortensius and Metellus,[4] generals of Roma—when they renewed the covenant that their fathers, officials of Roma, had with the nation of Yehudah, as it is written on a copper tablet in Jerusalem and in Roma—in the days of those chiefs, a great war broke out between the brothers Hyrcanus and Aristobulus, Alexander's sons. This war was waged by the Jordan near Jericho; men without number were killed, and many of the

---

1. In *AJ* 14.1–3, Josephus elaborates on his method as a responsible historian, which Yosippon summarizes before adding his own methodology.
2. Common phrase (from *'gr*) among the author's Italian and Byzantine contemporaries, viz., Donnolo, *Sefer Hakhmoni*, 5; *Megillat Aḥimaaẓ* (ed. Klar), 51; and Ioannes Skylitzes, *Georgius Cedrenus*, vol. 1 (Bonn, 1838), introduction.
3. *AJ* 14.4. Josephus has "in the third year of the 177th Olympiad." The author did not understand dating by Greek Olympiads or by Roman Consuls.
4. *AJ* 14.4. These were two men: Quintus Hortensius and Quintus Metellus Creticus, whose names signified the year (69 BCE), which dating system the author did not understand, so he calls them "generals," which they also were, instead of more accurately "consuls."

people of Israel were slain. Aristobulus and his warriors pressed Hyrcanus's army, and they could not withstand the pressure of Aristobulus and his warriors, nor could they bear the heat of fighting, so they turned their back and fled toward Jerusalem. Aristobulus was victorious in the battle, pursuing them with his warriors, smiting all the way to the gate of Jerusalem; and the survivors of Hyrcanus's army joined with Aristobulus.

Aristobulus and his warriors and the entire army of Yehudah were fighting against Jerusalem to tumble its walls to capture Hyrcanus, who had taken refuge within it; they encircled the city with a mighty hand and girded her with men like a girdle about the waist. Hyrcanus, in his anguish, the war weighing heavily upon him, brought forth Aristobulus's wife and sons from the prison where Queen Alexandra had imprisoned them. Hyrcanus seized the woman and her sons as hostages to save his life from his brother's sword for the sake of his wife and sons.

The elders of Israel and the elders of the priests left and went to Aristobulus's camp, and they wept and pleaded with him not to devastate the city but to make a covenant with his brother so that Aristobulus would be king over all the people of Yehudah and Hyrcanus, his brother, would be priest in the Temple of God and subject to the house of Aristobulus as his deputy. Aristobulus agreed, and so it was done. Aristobulus entered the city and received the kingship; he made a treaty with Hyrcanus, and they entered the Temple of God and swore an oath to each other. All the people saw this, and each man went to his city and to his land, and the war ended.

Meanwhile, Hyrcanus had an ally named Antipater, a wealthy man great with gold and silver, with much property and many servants.[5] This man was also a valiant warrior, wise and clever in all fraud and deceit, a schemer. This Antipater was commander over the entire nation of Edom,[6] for when Hyrcanus had gone to the land of Edom and subjugated it, as we have written above, King Alexander appointed this Antipater over them, though still a youth.[7] Antipater had married a woman of royal Edomite seed, and she bore him four sons. These are their names: the first Phaselo (Phaselus), the second Erodes (Herod)—he was the Herod who ruled—the third Pherora, and the fourth Joseph; and the name of his daughter was Shlomit (Salome), and his wife was

---

5. *AJ* 14.8. See description of Abraham (Gen 26:14) variously translated as "a large household," better as "many slaves" (New English Bible), but it also recalls Joshua 22:8—such wealth from war booty.

6. *AJ* 14.10. Actually it was his father, but the Latin text is unclear.

7. *AJ* 14.11: *iunior Antipater*. Having absorbed the father into the son, the author translated this phrase literally.

Cypris the Edomite. For this reason, writers say that this man was an Edomite, but Nicholaus [of Damascus] the author said that this Antipater was of the Judaean nobility, of those who came from Babylonia to Jerusalem in the days of Nehemiah and Ezra the scribe.

Since the man had become Hyrcanus's close ally, Aristobulus sought to kill Antipater. When Antipater heard of this, he was very afraid of Aristobulus. He spoke to the heart of the warriors of Yehudah and seduced them with words, saying: "I have a word to you, saints of God,[8] for I have seen violence and oppression among the holy nation, much sin, great transgression, and the essence of evil; truth is absent, and there is no righteousness. How is it that the younger rules the elder in that Aristobulus rules today and seized the kingdom, neither through God's will nor through the will of his people's elders but rather through the sword and weapons of war and through spilling the blood of God's people. So now, Israel, heed my words and love righteousness and truth!"

As he continued to speak, he stole the minds of elders of Israel. And Hyrcanus, too, he incited in private: "Choose flight and flee, for your brother Aristobulus is plotting against you to kill you, for his advisers have counseled him thus: 'As long as your brother Hyrcanus lives, your kingdom will not be stable, for he is your elder brother; only when you shall have killed him will your kingdom be stable.' They advised [him] to kill you." Hyrcanus listened to these words but did not believe, for he was blameless and upright and very meek.

When Antipater saw that Hyrcanus did not heed his words, he would not cease to utter such words to him day and night; also, he spent gold and silver and hired friends to speak to him according to Antipater's words. And finally, he had seduced him with his cleverness and encouraged him to flee, saying to him: "Be silent until I go and secure a place for you wherein you shall find refuge." Antipater left Jerusalem and went to Desert Rock to the palace of Aretas, king of Arav, who was pleased to greet him, for he was his ally from long ago. And he made a pact with him and took an oath from him that he would not hand over Hyrcanus to those who sought his life. Antipater returned to Jerusalem and told Hyrcanus everything that he did. He left Jerusalem with him at night and traveled for many days unto Desert Rock, to the palace of Aretas, king of Arav, who went out to greet Hyrcanus with chariot and cavalry; he received him with great honor, and he stayed in his palace for many days.

---

8. *Kedoshei adonai*, which may be a sobriquet for warriors who became *eo ipso* potential martyrs; here the Latin *sancti* may be an influence, but Yosippon uses the term for the Sadducees and Hasmoneans who were of the priestly class, and so a literal reference seems obvious here.

After this, Antipater began to incite the king of Arav to come with Hyrcanus to Jerusalem to fight against Aristobulus in order to restore the kingship to Hyrcanus. But Aretas refused to fight against the Jews, for Alexander had defeated him three times in battle and had taken from him all the fortified cities of Arav. Antipater said to him: "Don't be afraid to go up with us, for we have with us the mighty hand of Israelite warriors to fight against Aristobulus." Aretas answered and said: "If you return to me all the land and the ten fortified cities that King Alexander took away from me, then I will join you to fight against your enemies." So Hyrcanus swore an oath to return to him all the land and these ten cities. Aretas agreed and mustered an army of his warriors and marched with them to do battle against Jerusalem with a force of fifty thousand cavalry and an immense army. He marched from Desert Rock and invaded the land of Yehudah. Aristobulus went forth to confront him, and a mighty battle broke out on that day.

On the day of the battle, a great horde of Judaean forces joined Hyrcanus and Antipater to help them. Aristobulus, seeing that a great multitude of the Judaean army fell in with Hyrcanus, left the army and returned to Jerusalem alone and desolate, for all his force had joined with Hyrcanus and Antipater.

Aretas, king of Arav, marched and camped against Jerusalem accompanied by the mighty and very strong army of Yehudah and Arabia, and he encamped to the north of the city. And they fought against Jerusalem, the entire army of Yehudah and the entire army of Arav; only the people of Jerusalem and the priests were with Aristobulus. From day to day, the battle waxed and increased, and the noise of battle grew until the fifteenth day of the first month [i.e., Passover], when many Hasidim and Sadducees left the land of Yehudah and went to live in Egypt to celebrate Passover because of the wars in the land of Yehudah.

At that time, the army of Yehudah and the army of Arav surrounded Jerusalem from every side. And a man was hiding himself in the midst of the army of Yehudah, and his name was Ḥoni, a righteous man and beloved of his God who was tested and found whole; he used to come to his people's aid and pray on behalf of the people of God. When there was no rain from heaven, this man Ḥoni used to pray and request rain from God, and God would consent [to] him and not ignore his request. Ḥoni did [this] so many times when there was drought in the land of Israel.

On the day of the battle, they [the army of Yehudah] found Ḥoni hidden in the Judaean camp; they led him before the leaders of the Jews, and he stood amid the people. The leaders and the people said to him: "Pray against the evil done unto us; perhaps God will heed your request as he responded to your request for rain and will deliver Aristobulus into our hand and the priests that are with him." Ḥoni answered, saying: "You are the people of God, and they are

His priests. I will pray for you, but also for his priests I will pray. For I will neither curse nor revile the priests of God." They pressed him and said: "Pray as we
demand, and if not, know that you shall surely die!" In his anguish, he raised his
eyes to heaven and spread out his palms and prayed: "God, Lord of the Heavens,
King of all the world, all life is in Your hands and the intent of the thoughts in
the heart of man; straighten the thoughts of Your people and Your priests, and
direct their hearts toward You, and do not do the will of one against the other
to do harm but only good, for this is Your people and these are Your priests." As
he prayed with these words, the wicked of Judaea fell upon him and killed him.
God did not delay His vengeance and afflicted the Judaean camp with a plague,
and a great number died for Ḥoni's [spilled] blood.

After this, the priests on the wall spoke to the people, saying: "O Israel,
people of God, lend your hand to the Lord of your fathers and to his Temple;
give us sheep and rams and he-goats, and let us sacrifice a peace offering [*zevaḥ*]
according to the law, for today is Ḥag Hamaẓoth [Passover], and let not the
burnt offerings and peace offerings cease from the altar of God lest there be sin
upon you." The army called out and said: "Give us gold, for each and every ram
one thousand gold drachmas and the same for every sheep and he-goat, and we
shall fulfill your request!" Aristobulus and the priests gave the gold willingly.
They lowered the gold from the wall and gave it to the army, who took the gold
but did not give the sacrifice; rather, the wicked ones and the sinners against
God stole the sacrifice. The priests prayed over the fact that the army stole God's
sacrifice, and God did not delay the vengeance and smote the army with a great
famine. The famine increased greatly until an ephah of wheat [*modius tritici*]
sold for eleven gold drachmas.

36. ROMAN INTERVENTION AND POMPEY'S SIEGE OF JERUSALEM

In those days, Pompey the Great, Commander of the Army of Roma, advanced with a great army against Tigran (Tigranes), king of Armenia. He sent Scaurus, one of his servants, commanding him to take control over Aram. Scaurus went to Damesek (Damascus), where Aristobulus sent him envoys asking for his assistance. Hyrcanus too sent him messengers asking for his assistance. But Scaurus was unwilling to assist Hyrcanus; rather, he wanted Aristobulus's friendship, since he [Aristobulus] had given him four hundred talents of gold. Scaurus took the gold and sent a letter to Aretas, king of Arav, at Jerusalem, saying: "Leave Jerusalem, and if you do not, know that the Romans will come against you!" When Aretas read this letter, he left Jerusalem and went his way, accompanied by Hyrcanus and Antipater, for "the helper will stumble and he who is helped will be ashamed" [cf. Isa 31:3].

Aristobulus came out of Jerusalem with a small force and pursued Aretas, Hyrcanus, and Antipater and caught up with them in the Valley of Capiron, where he fought and defeated them in battle, killing six thousand warriors of the army of Arav and also many of the Judaean army of Hyrcanus; and in that battle, he also killed Cephalon, Antipater's brother. Aristobulus then returned to Jerusalem and ruled over all Yehudah.

After these events, Pompey the Great also came to Damascus, and all the nations sent him envoys. Aristobulus, too, sent him as a gift a vine of gold weighing five hundred gold talents and also a garden of gold, called Terpon[1] by Joseph ben Gurion. And Joseph ben Gurion says: "I saw with my own eyes this vine and

___

1. τερπόλη, a delight. R. Marcus (in Josephus, *AJ* 14.35, Loeb Classical Library [Cambridge, MA, 1966]), suggests that its Hebrew name was *eden* = delight.

this garden as a statue in the Temple of Iovis[2] in Roma; there was an inscription upon the vine as follows: 'This is the vine that Aristobulus king of Judaea sent as a gift to Roma.'"

After these events, envoys came to Pompey from Hyrcanus and from Aristobulus; Hyrcanus sent Antipater, and Aristobulus sent Nicomedes. Nicomedes pleaded with him [Pompey] to lend his hand to Aristobulus, for he had given him four hundred gold talents. Antipater too, when he saw that Nicomedes persuaded him [Pompey] to aid Aristobulus, spoke to him privately, saying: "Why do you come to the aid of Aristobulus and accept a bribe from him? Is it not better for you to rule over such a populous people as this nation of Judaea? You will gain a reputation and might, and you will have done a great deed such as your fathers did not accomplish. If you will help Hyrcanus obtain the kingdom, he will be your servant, and all the people of Yehudah will be your servants." When Pompey heard these words, he rejoiced exceedingly and told Antipater, saying: "If such is your desire, be silent until I tempt him with words; perhaps Aristobulus will come to me, for I fear to challenge him in battle lest he wage war in the mountain passes to prevent us from [invading] his land. Rather, wait until he comes to me, and I will deceive him and go with him to Jerusalem; then I will give the kingdom to Hyrcanus, but only if you give me an annual tax."

Whereupon Pompey called Nicomedes and deceived him, saying: "Tell Aristobulus, your lord: 'Thus spake Pompey, Commander of the Army of Roma: Hasten to me and do not tarry. I am here in Damascus. I will await you until you come to me, and I will secure the kingdom of Judaea in your hand, for thus decreed the Elder and his 320 counselors.'"

Now these are the words of the letter that Pompey sent to Aristobulus: "Pompey, Commander of the Army of Roma, to Aristobulus, king of the royal seed of the priests of God: Peace. Let it be known to you that I have received the vine and the garden that you sent to me, and I sent them to Roma. The Elder and his 320 counselors were pleased, and they gave your offering to the Temple of Iovis. They praise you there and pray for you in that place. The Elder has written to me to strengthen the kingdom in your hand. Now if it pleases you, hasten to me in Damascus, and I will fulfill your wishes as seems proper and fitting to you." This letter is written in the book of the kings of Roma.[3]

Aristobulus went to Damascus unto Pompey the Great, hero of Roma, along with Hyrcanus, Antipater, and the Judaean elders who supported Hyrcanus and Antipater. They said to Pompey: "Judge thou, O great general and man of

____

2. Josephus copies Strabon, who reports this.

3. The letter and the whole story are the author's addition.

mercy, for Aristobulus has oppressed his elder and has usurped the kingdom with sword and javelin and by war, nor did that suffice him, for he ruled by force over the people of Judaea and has smitten all the nations, our neighbors, friends of ours from yore, treading upon them as if in a wine press and spilling much blood in their land, and he is cruel to his people and to foreigners." Antipater brought forth one thousand elder witnesses, and they testified to [the truth] of these things.

Aristobulus responded and said: "Indeed, I know that he is my elder brother, but he is lazy and weak, and it is not fitting that he rule. I did not covet the kingdom, nor do I love to rule, but I saw the people of Judaea in its need at the death of our mother, the queen. All the servants of Judaea, conquered by our forefathers, rebelled and disobeyed, and naught was left but ruin. When I saw this, I accepted the kingdom and fought with them, bringing them under the yoke of Judaea. And further, my father commanded before his death that I should be king after my mother, for he saw the laziness of Hyrcanus and his lack of sense." Aristobulus brought forth witnesses who testified to these things. The witnesses whom Aristobulus brought were young men, all of them dressed in royal blue and purple and all of them adorned with gold and precious stones.

Pompey was amazed[4] at the magnificence of the youths and at the splendor of their beauty, and he said to his elders: "The men of this people are all kings! Blessed be the king who will rule over this people, and blessed would we be if able to govern this people! Our name shall be known in all lands, and fear and awe for us will fall upon all the nations when we shall have subdued this powerful people."

Pompey marched from Damascus to Jerusalem accompanied by Aristobulus and Hyrcanus. During the march, while the camp rested, Hyrcanus quarreled with his brother Aristobulus over the kingdom, and the inhabitants of the cities that Aristobulus had captured also came and cried out to Pompey how Aristobulus conquered them and subdued them. Pompey summoned Aristobulus and ordered him to return the cities to their owners and to give his signed statement to their residents that he would not invade them again. Aristobulus obeyed and, returning the cities, signed his text [cf. Isa 14:5] and did all that Pompey had commanded him.

Hyrcanus continued to quarrel with Aristobulus over the kingdom, whereupon Pompey said to them: "Be silent until I come unto your cities, then I will know what I will do for you!" Aristobulus despised Pompey and left without

---

4. In *AJ* 14.45, Pompey condemned Aristobulus, but the author misunderstood *stupere* here and expanded his rhetoric accordingly.

asking his permission; he came to Delon, from there[5] to Pilam (Pella) and Sitopoli (Scythopolis), and from there he traveled to Alexandrona (Alexandrium), where he remained. Pompey was enraged and diverted against him [Aristobulus] all the forces that he had planned to send against Persia. Pompey pursued him, catching up with him at Alexandrium, and besieged the city. Aristobulus's sages said to him: "Why are you rebelling against the Romans, who rule over nearly all the world, when you see that we have no support from our people, who have joined with them?" Aristobulus heeded them and, going out to Pompey, asked him for peace. He quarreled again with his brother over the kingdom, and again he left and entered Alexandrium against Pompey's order.

On the following day, Aristobulus came out of the city and, sounding the ram's horn, rebelled [against Pompey] and went to Jerusalem, with Pompey in pursuit with all the forces of the Roman army and all their might. They marched until they came to Jericho, city of fragrance,[6] and encamped there, for in that place grew *balsamo*, an excellent unguent[7] that is [called] *panag*.[8] As Joseph ben Gurion haCohen says: "This tree is not seen anywhere else in the world save in Jericho, and many kings, even the kings of Egypt, took cuttings from that tree wishing to [grow it] in their own land. But the tree did not take [root] and desiccated; and this tree remained in Jericho until the destruction of the Temple; when the Temple was destroyed, then this tree was transferred from Jericho to Egypt and other places."

After this, Pompey rose early and left Jericho for Jerusalem. When Pompey beheld the height of the city's walls and the loftiness of her towers, how her stones shone and the glitter of her lattices, the magnificence of her beauty and the luster of her splendor, Pompey went mad viewing the grandeur of the city and said: "Who will sling a rock and who will shoot an arrow against this holy city? Blessed be the king who shall rule over this city!"

After this, Aristobulus went out to him [Pompey] and asked him for peace, for he repented that he had rebelled; Pompey received him and made peace with him. Aristobulus said to him: "All that you command me, I will do; and all that you assess me, I will give; only aid me in the matter of the kingship and do not humiliate me before my enemies!" Pompey said to him: "Bring me the vessels of gold of your temple and the precious stones; I will send them to Kittim, to Roma, to the Temple of Iovis, then I will fulfill all your wishes!" Aristobulus

---

5. *AJ* 14.48, has Pompey traveling; the author is in error.

6. Pun on *raiyah* (fragrance) and *yeriho* and the fragrance of balsam.

7. *AJ* 14.54. See 2 Kings 20:13 (cf. Rashi *ad locum*).

8. In Jerome's Vulgate, *balsamum* translates *panag* in Ezek 27:17. Yosippon's usage influenced later Hebrew commentators and linguists.

consented to do so, and Pompey sent Gabinius, a valiant and mighty warrior, [one] of the heroes of Roma, to take the vessels and the precious stones from the Temple of Jerusalem. But the people refused to give what Pompey asked and chased Gabinius from the city, and many Roman warriors died in the fighting within the city.

Pompey was furious and put Aristobulus under guard and bound him with chains; then he approached the city to fight against her with a mighty hand. He saw that the city was well fortified from every corner, for it was situated on a very high mountain save for the broad approach at its north; Pompey arrayed all his battle weapons there; and his whole force was with him, a mighty and very strong force, for the entire army of Roma that had been sent to Persia and Media was assembled at Jerusalem. The Jerusalemites sallied suddenly to attack Pompey, and raising a great cry, they rushed to his camp, killing many. The valor of the men and the swiftness of the youth so dismayed Pompey that he considered withdrawing from the city.

Fighting broke out within the city of Jerusalem between the supporters of Hyrcanus and those of Aristobulus. Hyrcanus's men ordered the gate opened to receive Pompey into the city, while Aristobulus's men prevented him from entering. The fighting inside was stronger than the fighting outside, and many of Yehudah died in that fighting. When Pompey heard this, he approached the gate, and the Jews themselves opened the gate and received Pompey with all his force within the city.

Pompey captured Jerusalem and the king's palace; only the Temple of God he did not capture, for the priests had closed the gates of God's Temple: they seized the approaches to the Temple and fought mightily. Now that month was the fourth month,[9] and the priests fought until the seventeenth day of it. On the day of the fast, while the priests were offering up the meal offering [cf. 1 Kings 18:36] and sacrificing the peace offerings and the burnt offerings before God's altar, Pompey too offered up the ram to batter the tower of the Temple, and, crushing the tower, it [the ram] knocked it to the ground. Thus, they opened the inner recesses of the Temple; the first to ascend were Cornelius and Faustus, sons of Sylla,[10] and they entered the Temple when the priests were sacrificing the peace offering and the burnt offerings before God. Following Cornelius was Furius and his men, and behind Furius came Fabius with a strong force

---

9. *AJ* 14.66, has Jerusalem taken in the third month of the siege on a fast day; the author assumed that this was the seventeenth of Tammuz and corrected accordingly.

10. *BJ* 1.149 and 1.154, has Cornelius Faustus, the son of Scylla. Faustus Cornelius Sulla, the only surviving son of Sulla the dictator, was Pompey's son-in-law.

of Pompey's warriors, their swords unsheathed in hand. They marched into the Temple, smiting about the priests of God. But the priests did not fear, nor did they dread the drawn swords, nor were they agitated by the flashing spears, nor were they agitated by the shining spears, nor did they tremble at the corpses falling dead within the Temple, for the priests walked over the corpses to celebrate God's service: to offer His peace offerings, to hallow His holocausts, and to offer His *qorbanot* [sacrifices]. The priests said to one another: "Strengthen yourselves and be strong, O priests of God, and let us be killed before His altar, for it is fitting that we die in our watch and not leave the Service of God nor cast His work away!" God's priests continued without fear or dread in the eye of the battle's storm just as a man might walk in the midst of peace. When a priest of those sacrificing the peace offering fell, his colleague would come and take the *qorban* from his hand and offer it up; and when they [the warriors] had slain him as well, his companion would come and replace him as he had done for his colleague until all God's service was completed by the priests on the day of the fast. Thus, they [the warriors] slaughtered the priests, all of them wearing the ephod garment and dressed in holy vestments, and the corpses of the priests fell upon the carcasses of their peace offerings, and their blood intermingled with the blood of the peace offerings, and they died in holiness before the altar of God.

Joseph ben Gurion in his book spoke about the affair of the priests, saying: "I spoke no lie in anything that I have said about the priests of God, and anyone who reads my book and does not believe my words, let him go and read other authors' books, for many authors bear witness to this. Behold, it is written in the book of Nicholaus of Damascus and in the book of Strabo of Caphtor and in the book of Titus (Livy), the author who wrote Pompey's deeds, and in the books of many others." Joseph ben Gurion added still more things that we have not written here. Now when the last of the priests [was] dead in the Temple, Pompey's generals entered the Sanctuary and remained there. These are their names: Gaius and Antonius and Marcus Tullius Cicero,[11] who was an author and wrote in his book everything he saw about God's priests and his Sanctuary.

After this, Pompey, accompanied by many others, entered the Temple; he saw the Holy of Holies and took pity, touching nothing in the Sanctuary, for they found a great many golden vessels and two thousand talents of gold drachmas. Pompey wished to touch nothing that he found in the Temple; he ordered the

---

11. *AJ* 14.66, dates the events by the incumbent consuls, Gaius Antonius and Marcus Tullius Cicero (63 BCE). The author, not understanding this dating system, made three generals out of the two consuls: Gaius and Antonius. The author assumed Cicero was an eyewitness and wrote his observations.

rest of the priests to purify the Temple and to offer the sacrifice, to sacrifice burnt offerings, and so they did.

He gave the kingdom to Hyrcanus and killed the supporters of Aristobulus; he took Aristobulus and bound him in chains to lead him to Roma. All the cities of Aram that the Judaeans took in battle he returned them to the Aramaeans; and all the territory that the Hasmonean kings had conquered Pompey returned to its inhabitants; and all the nations that were subdued to Jerusalem for ages he freed them from being servants of Jerusalem. Jerusalem, mistress over all the cities, became subject to Roma, and, too, the nation of Yehudah, a kingdom of priests, was subjugated.

Thus spake Joseph ben Gurion, saying: "All this came upon us from the brothers Hyrcanus and Aristobulus, for they initiated this evil in Jerusalem, and we became slaves to Roma. Henceforth we sank from greatness and became subdued."

37. ROMAN CIVIL WARS

Pompey[1] returned to his land, to Roma, bringing with him Aristobulus with his two daughters and two sons, for the third [son], Alexander, had fled and taken refuge. Pompey left as governor[s] in the land of Israel Hyrcanus and Antipater, and he left with them Scaurus, to whom he gave the whole of Egypt. Pompey went [on] his way to Roma, and Scaurus marched to Desert Rock to the Arab nation, accompanied by Hyrcanus, Antipater, and all the army of Judaea. With their advance, they subdued the Arab nation under Roma, for Antipater had persuaded them, since he had been for some time a close friend of the Arav king.

While Hyrcanus and Antipater were at Desert Rock with Scaurus, commander of Pompey's army, to fight against Arav, Aristobulus's son Alexander escaped from Pompey, entered Jerusalem, and rebuilt the walls of the city that Pompey had destroyed and, gathering a strong force of Jews, fought against Hyrcanus and Antipater and routed them; nor could Scaurus stand against him.

Gabinius came from the city of Roma to the land of Aram; and when he heard all that Aristobulus's son Alexander had done—that he fought against Scaurus and killed many Romans and routed Hyrcanus and Antipater and rebuilt the walls of Jerusalem that Pompey the Great had destroyed—Gabinius came against him with a heavy force of Romans and Aramaeans and, in addition, Hyrcanus's and Antipater's large and strong Judaean army. Antonius, who is Marcus—(for two names are a sign of valor, and he was a hero and an experienced warrior)—joined with them also, and all these generals came to do battle against Aristobulus's son Alexander in Jerusalem.

Alexander came out to confront them accompanied by a small force of some ten thousand infantry and fifteen hundred cavalry and fought a battle with these

---

1. This chapter follows mainly *AJ* 14, with additions from *DEH* 1.19; cf. *BJ* 1.

generals; six thousand of his warriors died in the fighting, and he fled with the rest of his men and entered Alexandrium. Gabinius came to the city and fought against it. But he [Alexander] made yet another sortie from the city and, making a surprise attack on Gabinius's camp, killed many of them. Marcus Antonius joined the battle, forcing Alexander back and chasing him into the city and losing many of his men in the fighting. Gabinius besieged the city and fought against it. Alexander's mother came to him (she was the wife of Aristobulus) and pleaded with him in tears to make peace between Gabinius and Alexander; and he agreed, so Alexander went out and made peace with him.

Gabinius divided the kingdom of Judaea into five units, with Hyrcanus as ruler in Jerusalem: he placed in Gadara a governor for the second unit; in Ḥamath (Amathus) a governor for the third unit; in Jericho a governor for the fourth unit; and in Sipporin (Sepphoris) in the Galil a governor for the fifth unit. All this Gabinius did in order to douse zeal in the kingdom and put an end to wars in the land of Judaea, but he did not succeed.

At that time, Aristobulus and his son Antigonus escaped from the city of Roma to the land of Judaea and arrived at the border of the land of Judaea, where a great crowd of Judaeans fell in with him; Pitholaus, commander [*nagid*] of Jerusalem,[2] joined him with one thousand warriors, for he remembered his former glory. When Aristobulus saw the great multitude with him, he separated out the poorer mass, choosing eight thousand valiant warriors who would not turn their backs nor retreat for any reason. He went forth to confront Gabinius in battle; Gabinius came with a very strong force of Romans and Judaeans to battle against Aristobulus. He [Aristobulus] fought against him [Gabinius] with his eight thousand veterans [*giborov*] and dealt the Roman horde a very great blow, killing many of the Roman force. Also seven thousand of Aristobulus's veterans died in that battle, and Aristobulus remained with his one thousand veterans. [With them] he burst through the Roman force, smiting as he advanced, until he took refuge atop the mountain. The Roman force pursued him and overtook him, so Aristobulus turned around and fought against them for two days.

On the third day, his one thousand veterans fell, after having killed many more of the Roman army. Aristobulus remained alone, fighting, and killing many. They wounded his head with a great many wounds, for the bronze helmet on his head was split open, and he fell to the ground. They captured him alive and bore him to Gabinius, who healed him from the blows and, binding him

---

2. The author reintroduces biblical title *nagid* for *Dux Hierosolymorum* = ὑποστράτηγος ἐν Ἱεροσολόμοις; see chap. 39, note 3.

again with chains, led him to Roma to the Elder and his 320 counselors.[3] The days that Aristobulus ruled were three years and six months, a precious man, a hero, generous, handsome, and good looking.

Afterward, the Elder sent Aristobulus's sons from Roma to Jerusalem, for he took pity on Aristobulus's wife, their mother, Gabinius having written to him of the woman's wisdom; for this reason, the Elder in Roma took pity on her and sent her sons and daughters to her.

Gabinius crossed the Euphrates River and fought against Persia and Media [Parthia] and subdued them, for Pompey the Great had conquered them, but when Pompey left, they rebelled. Gabinius went and subdued them, subjecting them [to Roman rule].

At that time, the Egyptian people rebelled and deposed Ptolemy as king of Egypt, for the Egyptian people said: "We shall no longer pay tax to Roma."[4] Ptolemy sent for Gabinius to help him. The latter came with all his army to help Ptolemy, king of Egypt; and Gabinius sent for Hyrcanus and Antipater to aid him. Antipater went forth from Jerusalem with a very heavy army, the army of Judaea and Benjamin, and went to aid Gabinius, whom they found in Damascus on his return from Persia. Now Gabinius ordered him to precede him to Egypt to open the road for him; Antipater led the way and fought the Egyptian guard, smiting them a very great blow, and opened the road. Then Gabinius came to Egypt and restored Ptolemy to his kingdom.

At that time, when Antipater was with Gabinius in Egypt, Aristobulus's son Alexander continued to rebel. He gathered a large force of Judaean young men and invaded Mount Gerizim and smote the Roman guard that Gabinius had left there; he extirpated also all the Romans from the land of Judaea. When Gabinius heard this, he sent Antipater to speak words of peace unto the ears of the people who rebelled. Antipater went and convinced the people, restoring them to Gabinius, but Alexander paid no heed to him and, taking with him thirty thousand Judaean young men, went to Mount Tabor and arrayed for battle against Gabinius; ten thousand of his [Alexander's] lads fell, and he fled with twenty thousand. Gabinius marched back to Jerusalem and returned the kingdom to Hyrcanus; he also made Alexander governor over all the people of Judaea. He left there and returned to Roma.

A year past, and the Elder and his 320 counselors heard that Persia and Media had rebelled, so they sent there Grassus (Crassus) with a very heavily armed force. Crassus came to Jerusalem and entered God's Temple, where he

---

3. See chap. 2, end.
4. The author uses both Roma and Romi.

stretched forth his hand to take the gold that was in God's Temple, two thousand talents of gold drachmas. In those days, the high priest[5] was Elazar, a righteous and devout man, and he said to Crassus: "Why do you stretch forth your hand to despoil God's Temple, to take the gold that Pompey did not touch nor other generals? Swear to me that you will not take the gold, and I, for my part, will give you one beam of gold whose weight is three hundred gold minas." On that beam were hung all the clothes of blue and purple that covered the gate of the Holy of Holies. This is why the beam was hidden from everyone's eyes and was not seen. Crassus swore to him [Elazar] that he would neither touch nor take any of the gold in the Temple, save for the beam alone, so Elazar the priest gave him the beam, made by a master craftsman, its weight three hundred minas of gold. The weight, according to the words of Joseph ben Gurion, was two and one-half pounds, which is thirty ounces, and one ounce is sixty measures, according to Joseph ben Gurion. But when Crassus had taken the beam, he broke his word, returned, and took all the gold in the House of God, two thousand talents' worth of gold drachmas and all the golden utensils, more than two thousand talents of pure gold.

Joseph ben Gurion said: "Many enemies and haters who despised the nation of Judaea will not believe my words regarding the wealth of our God's Sanctuary, but my words are true; there is no lie in them. Many great kings had sent to the Temple of God from year to year an offering of silver and gold vessels, and in those days, there were a great many very wealthy Jews. Many authors have borne witness just like me, including Nicholaus of Damascus,[6] and also Strabo of Caphtor spoke about the wealth of the Jews, saying: 'Mithridates, king of Armenia, attacked the city called Coö (Cos), on the frontier of the land of Asia and took the gold that Cleopatra Queen of Egypt had deposited there.' He also took the gold that the Jews had dedicated to send to the Temple of our Lord, and the weight of the gold that only the Jews living in the land of Asia dedicated [to the Temple] was eight hundred talents. For there was no gold from the land of Judaea there nor from the land of Alexandria, just the gold from the land of Asia."

After Crassus took the gold that was in God's Temple, he went to battle against Persia and Media and fell with all his army in one day. The Persians were victorious and, invading Aram, took it from Roma, until Cassius, the Roman general, a valiant man, came and invaded Aram and redeemed it from Persian

---

5. Hyrcanus was High Priest.

6. Not here in source but mentioned with Strabo (Caphtor = Cappadox: Cappadosia in chap. 31) in *AJ* 14.104.

oppression, returning it to the rule of Roma and chasing the Persian army out of Aram. Cassius returned and, entering the land of Judaea, found the people of Judaea fighting against Hyrcanus and Antipater: he assisted the two, and the kingdom was pacified under Hyrcanus. Cassius left there and, crossing the Euphrates, wielded his sword against Persia and Media, waging great battles against Persia and Media until he restored them to Roman rule, just as Pompey the Great had subdued them before, for Pompey had subdued twenty-two kings when he was in the East.

38. THE STORY OF JULIUS CAESAR

In those days,[1] a pregnant woman died in the city of Roma, the wife of one of the 320 counselors in Roma. Upon her death, the child wiggled in her womb and struggled, so they took a sword and cut the woman's stomach open and took the child out from her womb. The child lived and grew, and they called his name Julius, for he came from his mother's bowels in the month of Ab [roughly the month of July]. They also called his name Caesar, for his mother was cut;[2] and "cut" in the holy tongue is "caesar" in Latin.

That boy was valiant in war, and when the Elder sent Pompey to the East, he had sent this Julius Caesar to the West to subdue the kings of the West. Caesar fought in the West to subdue the Frankos (Franks) and the Brikatos (Britons), and all the pride of the West to the Ocean; then he returned to Roma, a hero in triumph. His heart filled with pride, and he said: "I will become king over all Roma!" But the Elder and his 320 counselors said: "We shall not accept a king over us, for a king has not reigned over Roma since the days of King Tarquinius, who raped a man's wife, and the woman became quite vexed and stabbed her belly, committing suicide. Since then, our fathers have sworn an oath never to place a king over them, and henceforth until now, no king has ruled over us these many years. And you, why should you disobey our ancestors' commandment? Your comrade Pompey was also a triumphant hero in the East, where he conquered twenty-two kings and also subdued the nation of Judaea, a great and

---

1. This chapter continues to follow *AJ* 14, with occasional additions from *DEH* 1.22.25 and 2.25. The well-known unhistorical legend that Julius Caesar was a caesarean birth has a nice pun on *caesare* (to cut) or *caedere*.

2. Yosippon's Latin source goes back to the sixth-century Byzantine Greek chronicle of Malalas. Caesar derives from his *gens* name, while his mother, Aurelia, was still active into his late thirties.

noble nation, but he did not seek kingship. So, now, know that we will not accept you, nor will you rule over us."

Caesar said in his pride: "Nevertheless I shall rule over you; you will be my servants and I your king!" He challenged Roma in war, and men without number were killed; he ruled mightily and placed a royal crown upon his head; and being called Julius Caesar, he ruled as "Caesar." That is why all the kings who ruled after him were called by his name, "Caesar."

When Pompey, who was in Cappadocia, heard that Caesar ruled in Roma and had exiled the Elder and his 320 counselors, he assembled all the kingdoms of the land under his control to come fight against Caesar. When Caesar heard this, he brought forth Aristobulus from prison and gave him an army of two legions, twelve thousand men, commanding him to march into Aram and to incite the people of Judaea to join them and pressure Pompey from the rear. When Pompey heard of this, he greatly feared Aristobulus, so he sent a letter, and the matter was known to his allies in Jerusalem. The Jerusalemites sent men to greet Aristobulus in Aram with words of peace; they ate with him and drank, and they gave him a deadly poison to drink and killed him there.

Pompey crossed over to Kittim[3] and fought with Caesar, and many fell dead. Pompey retreated from before Caesar, and Caesar pursued him, caught up with him, and killed him; now Caesar ruled over all the territory of Roma.

Caesar crossed into Aram[4] and sought to enter Egypt, but the Egyptians would not receive him, for Pompey's generals were still among them. Mithridates, king of Armenia, came to help Caesar, and he encamped in Ashkelon, for the people of Pilosio (Pelusium), a great city on the frontier of Egypt, did not receive him.

When Hyrcanus heard that Caesar invaded Aram, he feared greatly, for he had been a loyal supporter of Pompey for a long time. So Hyrcanus said to Antipater: "Come let us send warriors to aid Mithridates, who is located in Ashkelon; perhaps we shall find favor in the eyes of Caesar." Antipater took a strong force of Judaean warriors and went to help Mithridates, who was pleased to greet him; the two joined forces and went into Egypt and, encamping at Pelusium, fought against it. Mithridates attacked the city walls, while Antipater attacked the gate; Antipater captured the gate and, entering the city with his Judaean warriors, smote the city with the sword and plundered it.

They marched on until they came to a city called the city of Oni (Ḥonia); there they found Egyptian Jews who had settled in Egypt, a very strong force

---

3. *AJ* 14.127. Caesar did not kill Pompey.
4. *AJ* 14.137, has Caesar in Syria.

that would not let Mithridates and Antipater pass into Egypt. Antipater showed them the letter in which Hyrcanus had written words of brotherhood and peace, that they should support Caesar and accept Mithridates; the Egyptian Jews did so and received Mithridates. Mithridates and Antipater marched from there, arriving at a place called Delta; here the whole army of Egypt, a great and mighty force, confronted them, and a massive battle ensued. Mithridates panicked, turned about, and fled, and his right wing surrendered.

When Antipater saw the flight of Mithridates and the defeat of his generals, Antipater raced with three thousand Judaean youths and rescued Mithridates from death; he turned back the entire Egyptian force, and they retreated before him. He pursued them and inflicted a huge defeat on them, pressing them as far as the banks of the Yeor (Nile). Egyptians fell by the sword on the banks of the Nile, and whoever survived Antipater's sword died in the Nile. Antipater captured the whole kingdom of Egypt, and Mithridates was with him.

Mithridates informed Caesar of Antipater's valor and victory in Egypt: that he had humbled the pride of Egypt and returned them under Caesar's rule; that he had fought and was beaten in battle; that he had been severely wounded and then healed. When Caesar heard about it, he loved greatly Antipater, praised him, and sent envoys to bring Antipater to him in honor. Mithridates and Antipater went to Caesar in Damascus.

When Antipater came before Caesar, Caesar said to him: "I have heard of all the hardship that has befallen you and the glory and victory that you accomplished in Egypt for our sake and how you restored Egypt to our rule; now it is our pleasure to honor you for your strength and bravery." Then Antigonus, son of Aristobulus the young, came and wept before Caesar and told him all about his father, Aristobulus: how Pompey's allies in Jerusalem, on the advice of Hyrcanus and Antipater, gave him deadly poison to drink. Aristobulus's son Antigonus added, saying to Caesar: "You know that my uncle Hyrcanus and Antipater were Pompey's loyal companions and his counselors, and they are your enemies."

Antipater answered Caesar and said: "I have indeed been Pompey's loyal companion, for he rendered good to me, and he had the authority of Roma at that time, and I fought his battles, but this war, which I have fought now and in which I placed my life on the line and [in which] I restored all the pride of Egypt to Caesar's authority, I did not fight in Pompey's name, for I knew that Pompey was dead; rather, I fought in Caesar's name and was severely wounded, as you can see with your own eyes today." Whereupon Antipater proceeded to strip off his clothes and show his flesh and head wounds. He continued: "Let my wounds answer for me as trustworthy witnesses and let my blows respond for me that in Caesar's name I fought this battle, and I did it all after Pompey's death."

Caesar answered Antipater and said: "Peace upon you, hero of Judaea and peace upon all who seek your health and well-being, for your wounds bear witness to your glory and your blows have testified to your strength! Now I appoint you over all my warriors until I fight against the nations across the Euphrates and have subdued them; then you shall return to your land and to your city." Caesar set Antipater over the army of Roma on that day and hence until he subdued all the pride of the East and all the land of Hind (India); then Antipater returned to his land and his city, Jerusalem, the holy city, and Caesar went his way to the city of Roma. Thus Joseph ben Gurion: "Now even many writers bore witness, like me, to Antipater's glory at that time: so too spoke Nicholaus of Damascus, and so too spoke Strabo of Caphtor, and many other writers bore witness."

39. ERODES (HEROD) BEFORE THE SANHEDRIN

At that time, Antipater returned to Jerusalem to Hyrcanus, king of Judaea,[1] who had sent him. Hyrcanus had rebuilt the walls of Jerusalem that Pompey had destroyed, and he ruled securely. But Hyrcanus was blameless and upright and very lazy in all practical matters, and Antipater was alarmed at Hyrcanus's sloth, so he placed his sons over all Judaea at Hyrcanus's command. He took his eldest son, Phasael (Phaselus),[2] and placed him as *nagid*[3] over Jerusalem, and he took his second son, called Herod, and placed him as *nagid* in the Galilee, and he was still a youth of fifteen years.

At the same time, a bandit left Jerusalem, a youth called Hezekiah, chief of the robbers.[4] This man was a robber [*paritz*] and a bandit who, in his sweep [Jer 22:17], despoiled all Aram, regularly killing their youth by sword, destroying all their fortified cities, and desolating all their land without mercy. In every place where there were Aramaeans (Syrians), Hezekiah plundered them, accompanied by many young robbers; all the Aramaeans were terrified of his oppression, and they could neither withstand nor survive against him.

---

1. Hyrcanus was officially High Priest and Ethnarch; the Jews called him king.
2. Compare early Carolingians: Charles Martel (recalls Maccabee/Hammer) and Pipin as *major domus.*
3. *Nagid*: see chaps 32 and 37 (here translating *dux*). The title *nagid* was resurrected as a political term in the eleventh century. [Neither M. Cohen, *Jewish Self-Government in Medieval Egypt* (Princeton, NJ, 1980), 5ff and 12ff, nor Flusser, *Josippon, ad locum*, discusses Yosippon's early usage. SB]
4. *AJ* 14.159; *DEH* 1.26.1; *princeps latronum* (*lystis* in Josephus) rendered as *sar ha-priẓim*, all negative usage.

While Antipater's son Herod was commander and ruler of the Galilee, Sextus, Caesar's cousin whom Caesar had placed in command of all the land of Aram, sent him a letter saying: "Sextus, Caesar's nephew, to Herod, Antipater's son: Peace. Let it be known to you that we have heard that you were appointed commander in the Galilee, and we are pleased. Recall now Caesar's love for your father and his respect for him, and fight Caesar's war; for Hezekiah, chief of the robbers from your land, has despoiled all the territory of Aram over which I am commander, and the Arameans cannot withstand him. Go now, fight him, kill him, and you will receive a huge gift from Caesar and from me." Herod obeyed Sextus; he marched forth and encountered Hezekiah while he was coming confidently after he had smitten Aram: he [Herod] smote him [Hezekiah] and killed him and all his lads, the robbers. When Sextus heard of this affair, he sent a gift of silver and gold to Herod, and all the Arameans too sent him gifts of silver, gold, and precious stones, because he had fought against Hezekiah and killed him. For this reason, they honored him, and the lad became very wealthy with silver and gold, for the Arameans had enriched him because he saved Aram from Hezekiah's oppression and had killed him.

The leaders of Judaea heard all that Herod had done to Hezekiah, and the men were greatly saddened and said to Hyrcanus: "How long will you suffer the burden of Antipater and his sons, for the entire kingdom is in their hand, and they do everything that they wish, for Antipater is ingratiating himself with the kings of Roma[5] with your wealth and treasures; his son Phasael is *nagid* of Jerusalem, and everything that he seeks to do in Jerusalem he does, and you have no part in the rule of Judaea save for the name because the whole kingdom is in their hand? Furthermore, his son Herod[6] killed Hezekiah, a valiant and ruthless man, whose terror was upon all the nations, and all our neighbors trembled from fear of him; he was beloved of his people and a terror for all the nations. Now bring Antipater's son Herod to trial before the sacred Sanhedrin[7] in Jerusalem, before the seventy sages in Jerusalem, and let them render a sentence of death, for he is deserving of death." After repeating these things to him daily with the mothers of Hezekiah's lads whom Herod had killed, who cried unto Hyrcanus whenever he came to God's Temple, [reminding him] that Herod had killed their sons, Hyrcanus consented and sent for Herod to come stand trial before the seventy sages who constituted the sacred Sanhedrin in those days.

----

5. *Romanis principibus*. The author understood *princeps* as ruler or governor rather than Rome's generals.

6. *AJ* 14.167; the author's nationalist encomium of Ḥizkiyahu.

7. Perhaps reflects a Christian *sancta synodus*.

When Antipater heard this, he sent to his son Herod, saying: "Whereas Hyrcanus, king of Judaea, has called you to come unto him, hurry and do not tarry, but take care lest you come unarmed and alone; rather, [come] with troops. Yet when you come to the city, do not come with a large army lest Hyrcanus say that you have come against him to do battle. Come with a few men, [but] all of them veterans [*gibborim*]." Herod did as his father commanded him; he came with a small number of men, but all of them veterans; and he stood before the judges and before the Sanhedrin. Standing before them, dressed in purple, his head coifed,[8] surrounded by troops and girt with sword, all the judges and the men of the Sanhedrin were frightened; they were silent and said nothing, and everyone who spoke against him before he came were silent and did not say a thing.

Then spoke Shamai (Sameus), a disciple of Hillel the elder, and said to the Sanhedrin (according to the report of Joseph ben Gurion),[9] "I have something to say before you, God's holy ones, for this day I have seen a new thing among you. Every sinner who stands before you has to stand dressed in black, his hair full of dust, begging you for mercy for his sins; but this lad,[10] Herod, stands before you dressed in purple, his hair coifed, surrounded by troops, and girt with sword; and if he is condemned in trial, he will return and kill us. Nor am I surprised at Herod, for he did all this only to save himself from death; it is you who have sinned, for you pardoned his transgression. Because you allowed him to act this way [see Ex 23:5], the day will come when this Herod, whom you showed favor at trial, will soon rule over you and will kill you in return for your showing him favor at trial. Moreover, he will have no mercy for Hyrcanus, who took pity on him, for he will kill him and receive his kingdom."

When Shamai had spoken these words, Hyrcanus said to the men of the Sanhedrin: "Let us go home, for the day has passed, and on the morrow, we shall return to the place of judgment to investigate and know the verdict of this trial." Hyrcanus spoke this thing only to save Herod from the trial, for he saw that the college of judges was of one mind, to pronounce a sentence of death against Herod. Hyrcanus rose up and went to his home, and all the judges went each to his home. That night Herod left Jerusalem with his troops and fled to Damascus in Aram to Sextus, whom Gabinius had appointed over Aram, and told him all that had happened to him in Jerusalem; and Sextus appointed him *nagid* over Aram.

---

8. Eloquent rendering of clumsy Latin.

9. Sameus in *AJ* 14.172, is not Shamai, Hillel's opposition.

10. *AJ* 14.173; *optimus iuvenis* continues Josephus's irony.

At the new year, Herod gathered all the army of Aram and came against Hyrcanus in battle. His father, Antipater, with Phasael, his brother, went out to greet him, and they said to him: "You are not repaying Hyrcanus in the same coin as he paid you, for he saved you from death, and the only reason he brought you to trial was through the counsel of evil advisers, for he loves you like his own son. Now leave him alone lest you be guilty before God, and, if you do not desist, do not say in your heart that you fought against Hyrcanus and won, for all wars are from God: He gives valor to whom He desires." When Herod heard this, he returned to Aram, having shown his valor.

40. THE ROMAN LEADERS' AFFECTION FOR THE PEOPLE OF JUDAEA

After these events,[1] Hyrcanus sent messengers to Roma to renew the covenant with Julius Caesar.

Now it seems proper for us to relate the love the Roman leaders showed to our fathers because of their strength and valor and their faithfulness, for our fathers were valiant and faithful. For this reason, all the kings of the earth loved to make a treaty with them because of their strength and valor. Also, the kings of Persia and Media sent them offerings and many letters to Jerusalem. Joseph ben Gurion wrote down only a few of their letters, because he did not want to write too many of the letters of the gentiles that were sent to Jerusalem; only the letters of Roma did Joseph ben Gurion write word for word, and I was too lazy[2] to copy all of them, so I wrote only a few of their letters as I found them written in the book of Joseph ben Gurion.[3]

Now these are the words of the letter that Julius Caesar sent to the Roman generals in Tyre and Sidon to protect the land: "Julius Caesar, king of kings, to the generals of the Romans in Tyre and Sidon: Peace. Let it be known to you that I have received the letters of Hyrcanus, son of Alexander, king of Judaea; I have been pleased by his letters and his loyalty, and I send you copies of all the words that were written in Hyrcanus's letters. I send them to you so that you write them in Latin or Greek on copper tablets and put them in the

---

1. Text continues to follow *AJ* 14.
2. The author skips *AJ* 14.211–64. The phraseology is an ancient and medieval literary affectation (cf. *AJ* 4.266).
3. Cf. Flusser's introduction in *Josippon*, 2.3–6.

Temple of Iovis in Sidon in a prominent place. Let them be read frequently, lest the words in the letters be forgotten, to inform everyone of the friendship of the nation of Romans and the nation of Judaea. For Hyrcanus, king of Judaea, and his people, the nation of Judaea, were a strength to the nation of Romans: when I fought in Egypt, he sent Antipater, the hero of Judaea, who saved Mithridates from death, smiting the pride of Egypt and opening for us all the entire land of Egypt; the Jews helped us in all our battles as far as the land of India. For this reason, I, Julius Caesar, have commanded all the inhabitants of the seashore from Gaza to Sidon to pay an annual tax for the Temple of the great divinity that is in Jerusalem, except for Sidon; for the Sidonians, according to their custom, give to the Temple of the great divinity in Jerusalem 20,575 measures of wheat every year. All the land of Lydia,[4] which the Roman generals and Pompey the Great gave to the kings of Aram, I have commanded to be taken from the kings of Aram and restored to Hyrcanus, son of Alexander, king of Judaea. And all the land up to the Euphrates and across the Euphrates that the Hasmoneans had taken in war and that Pompey had returned to their owners I, Julius Caesar, have commanded to restore to Hyrcanus, who is in Jerusalem. Their forefathers had taken it by the sword; therefore, let all that they took in war be theirs. Now every king and officer who shall overturn my covenant and who shall maliciously disobey my commands, that king or officer shall die by the sword, and his land shall be made waste, with neither man nor beast living in it."

The envoys whom Hyrcanus sent to Roma sat with Julius Caesar before all the envoys of the nations who came to Julius in those days. All the envoys of nations spoke to him standing;[5] only Hyrcanus's envoys sat with him as equals [cf. Gen 2:18] to watch the horse and chariot races[6] and the wild animal fights that were performed before Julius and the *nudi* [gladiatorial] fighters,[7] and everything else that was performed before him to gladden his spirit. These are the names of Hyrcanus's envoys: Lysimachus, son of Pausanius; Alexander, son of Todros (Theodorus); Patroclus, son of Chiriah (Chaereas); and Yonathan, son of Oniyah [Onias].

We did not copy here many similar letters that we found in the book of Joseph ben Gurion, for his book of the year 508[8] after the destruction

---

4. Latin Lydia, but Josephus (*AJ* 14.208–9) intends Lod.

5. Cf. contemporary Byzantine imperial diplomacy.

6. Chariot races were the most popular sport in Byzantium.

7. Paired gladiatorial contests called *monomachi*.

8. The medieval date for destruction of the Temple was 68 CE: the author's Latin Josephus source was dated 576 CE.

of the Temple is full of such letters. Now we have written and translated[9] from the book of Joseph ben Gurion haCohen in the year 885 of the Destruction Era.[10]

---

9. I.e., translated. This MS, called Hegesippus, contained *AJ* 1–16 only of Josephus' 20 books.

10. This dates, according to Flusser, the original of this MS of *Sefer Yosippon* to 953 CE. My thanks to Benzion Wacholder for pointing out that placing Destruction Era dates inside a text is an important rabbinic injunction; cf. *Seder Olam*, in Neubauer, *Mediaeval Jewish Chronicles*, 2.66, chap. 30, middle. The phrase צֵא וחשב ‎ (= "go and calculate" to the destruction of the Temple) is the mnemonic prescription for scribes from early Talmudic times to the fifteenth century; [cf. *Tractate Avodah Zarah* (MS J.T.S.), ed. Sh. Abramson (New York, 1957), fol. 9a; also *Yalkut Shimoni* on Dan 8.]. This scribal tradition suggests two alternatives: either 953 is the year of authorship, as Flusser has argued, or the scribe added it from the MS he copied. MS Rothschild, where it appears, is dated post 1470. If the latter case, the authorship of *Yosippon* or at least this Italian version should be antedated to between 576 and 953, although chap. 1 is clearly from the beginning of the tenth century and DE dates appear on epitaphs in the ninth century. See Reuben Bonfil's incisive review of Flusser's work in the Israeli Hebrew daily *Davar*, "Sepher Yosippon: Historia ke-Sifruth," September 28, 1981, 13–14; and Bowman, "Dates in *Sefer Yosippon*." [SB]

41. DEATHS OF JULIUS CAESAR AND ANTIPATER

At that time,[1] when Julius Caesar was praying in peace and security in the Temple of Iovis in Roma, ambushers from Pompey's remaining supporters rose up against him, and together they stabbed thirty spears in his trunk and side, killing him inside the temple. These are the names of the men who killed him: Cassius and Brutus.

Then Cassius left Roma and, crossing the sea with a very strong army, invaded Asia and despoiled her; he left and marched into the land of Judaea and extorted[2] from the land seventy talents of gold. When Antipater saw that Julius Caesar was dead, he sought to avenge him and fight against Cassius, but he was not able since Cassius had with him an immense and powerful army consisting of many nations. So Antipater divided the whole land of Judaea between his two sons to collect the tax and pay Cassius. Herod brought the tax, which his father had given him, and gave it to Cassius to avert him from the land of Judaea; thus, he found favor in his eyes and he loved him like himself. Cassius took the gold from the land of Judaea and went to Makedonia,[3] since he was afraid to return to Roma, having killed Julius Caesar.

Then the leaders of Judaea plotted to murder Antipater, and Malkiah (Malachus) arose and sought to kill Antipater. When the matter became known to Antipater, he mustered his troops and warriors to fight against Malachus. Malachus was greatly afraid of Antipater and swore allegiance to him, and Antipater

---

1. The author uses a different source for Caesar's murder than *AJ* 14.270.
2. Literally fined or punished.
3. *AJ* 14.277, has Cassius go to Syria. He later died in the land of Makedonia (so the author called the Seleucid realm) in the Vale of Philippi (see chap. 42).

believed his word and became his friend. Then the two met at a feast before Hyrcanus, and Malachus bribed Hyrcanus's chief cupbearer with much gold; he [the cupbearer] gave deadly poison to Antipater and killed him. Antipater died, a great and valiant man; this is where he ended his days and reached the [final] frontier to his life. Thus received his fate a man who defended the people of Judaea and the holy city with his sword.

When Herod heard all that Malachus had done to his father, he [Herod] came against him [Malachus] with a strong force to exact vengeance for him [Antipater]. But his brother Phasael prevented him, saying: "Lest there be massive fighting and much blood be shed within Jerusalem," and he advised him to kill Malachus through a ruse. Herod sent to Cassio [Cassius] and informed him of everything that Malachus had done to his [Herod's] father. Cassius answered Herod, saying: "Avenge your father against Malachus. When I shall have come to Tyre, and Hyrcanus and Malachus have come to me, come with your brother to me there and avenge yourself on Malachus!"

When Cassius arrived at Tyre, Hyrcanus came to him with all the leaders of Judaea and Malachus, Phasael, and Herod, for Malachus had sworn an oath to them, saying: "I am innocent of your father's blood, for I was not in the plot for his death." The boys pretended to believe him, but secretly they plotted to kill him, for they knew that Malachus swore falsely, for he had killed their father. Accompanying Hyrcanus to Tyre, they came to Cassius, who made a feast for them, and they sat with him. Now Cassius had ordered his troops, saying: "Everything that Herod commands you, obey; do not ignore him lest you die!" After they had eaten,[4] they lay down for an afternoon rest, and later that day toward sunset, Cassius went down to the city gate; they made room for him, and he sat before the gate. He [Cassius] called Hyrcanus and Malachus, and they sat before him; and he also summoned the brothers Phasael and Herod, and they sat before him. Herod made a sign to the Roman troops, and they leaped upon them [the four men] with drawn swords, raising the swords over the four of them, but they killed only Malachus; they did not touch Hyrcanus and his officers.

Hyrcanus was petrified and lost his mind from fear. After a while, as soon as his mind returned to him, he asked Herod, "Why was Malachus killed?" Herod said: "I don't know, but Cassius ordered to kill him." Hyrcanus answered and said: "Surely this Malachus was a wicked and evil man." Hyrcanus said these words only out of fear.

---

4. The author's picaresque description explains why Malachus (Malichus in *AJ* 14.292) was killed outside the city.

42. ANTHONY'S DAYS

After these events occurred, Cassius went to Macedon[1] to confront Octavianus, Julius Caesar's nephew, and the noble Antonius, who came from the city of Roma to fight against Cassius to exact vengeance for Julius Caesar from Cassius, who had killed him.

At that time, great fighting broke out in the land of Judaea, for Filis (Felix) came from Damascus accompanied by a heavy Roman army to rule over the land of Judaea. Phasael, Antipater's son, said[2] to Felix the Roman: "Go back to Damascus, over which Cassius appointed you, since you have no portion in the land of Judaea!" But Felix did not listen, so [Phasael] killed many from his force, and Felix himself nearly fell in battle, but he fled and took refuge in a small town. Phasael captured the town and also seized Felix, but he did not wish to kill him, so he released him, and he left.

Cassius was fighting against the youth Octavianus and against the veteran Antonius; an immense battle occurred there [Philippi], and on that day, more than one hundred thousand corpses died in battle. Cassius fled, and Octavianus and Antonius pursued him and smote him and killed him. Octavianus succeeded his uncle Julius Caesar as ruler; this was the Octavianus called Augustus because he extended [Roman] dominion beyond everything that preceded him, for Augustus in Latin translates in the holy tongue as "he added." For this reason, all the kings of Roma who ruled after him were called Augustus, and also they were called Caesar after his uncle Julius Caesar.

When Octavianus Augustus and Antonius had defeated Cassius and Brutus in the land of Makedonia in the valley of Philippi, they entered the territory of Ephesus. Hyrcanus sent envoys to them and with them an offering of a royal

---

1. *DEH* 1.28.6 has Makedonian War.
2. The author's addition with an ironic inversion of Gen 12:1f.

crown and precious jewels. They gave it to Augustus and to Antonius, his comrade, and renewed the treaty that had been between Hyrcanus and Julius Caesar. They asked Augustus to return the captives exiled by Cassius from the land of Judaea and permit the Jews who were sold in the days of Cassius to be set free and [permit] all the remaining Jews living in the land of Greece (Yavan) and all the land of Asia to live in peace and security. Augustus and Antonius granted all that Hyrcanus requested.

These are the words of the letter that Augustus and Antonius sent to Hyrcanus, king of Judaea, saying: "Octavianus Augustus, king of kings, and Marcus Antonius, his colleague, to Hyrcanus, king of Judaea: Peace. Let it be known to you that we have received your letter from the hands of Lysimachus, son of Pausanius; Joseph, son of Minaeus; and Alexandrus, son of Todoros, envoys whom you sent to us in Ephesus to sign a treaty with us; we made a treaty with them as you desired, and we are pleased at your health and deliverance. Until now, we have fought with Cassius, who acted wickedly in plotting to kill Caesar, and we have punished him for the evil of stretching out his hand against Caesar, as a man who has stretched his hand against the sun[3] to bring it down to earth. For this reason, we fought with him great and mighty wars and defeated his wickedness in the valley of Philippi; and we killed him and Brutus, his colleague. Thus, Asia was rescued from their hand just as a woman is freed from her birth pangs[4] on the day she gives birth and just as one who is sick is preserved from the burden of his sickness. For they trod down the whole of Asia like mud of the streets in their wicked oppression; and they did not have compassion on the innocent nor on the shrines or the cities, nor did they keep the oath they swore; and they ruled in the land of Makedon. Cursed be the land of Makedon, which received them and which hid their evil between her thighs just as a prostitute hides the man who whores with her under her skirts; so the land of Makedon hid the wickedness of Cassius and Brutus that they did against the Judaeans and all our peoples. Let it be known to you that the wicked and the despoilers who destroyed the whole land were killed. Now let King Hyrcanus rejoice and all the people of Judaea with him, and let Jerusalem, the holy city, be gladdened, let the priests of God, the great and noble divinity, in the sanctuary of Jerusalem, be glad, and let them take the offering that we sent; let them pray for the life of Augustus, king of Roma, and Antonius, his colleague, for I, Augustus, have extended my rule throughout the land from the sea beyond India unto the western sea that is beyond the land of Britonia (Bretagne) that is

____

3. I.e., Julius Caesar; emperors were likened to the sun.
4. The analogy is better in Hebrew than in Latin.

the Ocean. And in every place where there may be found slave or maidservant of the seed of the Judaeans, let them be set free without ransom, but rather by the command of Augustus and Antonius, his colleague. And now live [long] and prosper, you and all men of our *pax* [*romana*]."[5]

After this, Augustus returned to the city of Roma and sat upon his throne. But Antonius was still in Ephesus, and he sent a letter unto the officers of Roma stationed in Tyre: "Why do you not restore the land that you took from Judaea in the days of that wicked Cassius? Know now that the sword will be upon you swiftly if you do not restore the land to our allies the Judaeans. And if you do not hasten to make peace with them, woe unto your land, and I, Marcus Antonius, make this oath to you, which I will not recant!"

After this, Antonius marched into Aram, and Cleopatra, queen of Egypt, went to him, and Antonius lay with her and fell in love with her. Cleopatra diverted Antonius with her sorcery, and Antonius did all that the queen requested from that day hence, for she deceived him with her sorcery.

Then a hundred nobles of Judaea came to Antonius and slandered[6] Herod and his brother Phasael, saying: "These sons of Antipater took the kingdom from Hyrcanus and left him naught but the name [of king]." Antonius asked Hyrcanus if that were the truth. Hyrcanus answered: "Heaven forbid! Phasael and Herod are my servants; they are most faithful to me." Antonius was pleased at Hyrcanus's words, for he loved the lads for their father's sake, since Antonius had been boon companion to Antipater, their father.

With the arrival of Antonius at the fortified city of Tyre by the sea, many of the nobility of Judaea continued to come to him to slander the youths. Antonius grew angry with them and put fifteen of them into prison. He grew angry against those shouters who cried out to him against Herod and his brother Phasael and killed many of them, for he was partial to Phasael and Herod; he elevated them and honored them and sent them to Jerusalem in honor. Antonius returned to Roma after he had conquered all the kingdom of Persia.[7]

---

5. [The author's addition. The first part of the phrase is still in use in some Hebrew circles. The second part *anshei shlomeinu* has a different emphasis in religious circles: "our brethren." Leonard Nimoy introduced the first part in the popular *Star Trek* series, his source is unknown. SB]
6. Indicates the author's diaspora background; see chap. 50, note 11.
7. Unhistorical but anticipates the following story about the Persian king.

43. THE WAR WITH ANTIGONUS

After these events, Aristobulus's son Antigonus went forth from Jerusalem and rebelled against his uncle Hyrcanus; he went to Persia accompanied by a large force of Judaean nobles; and he went to Pagorus (Pacorus), king of Persia (i.e., Parthia). Antigonus promised him one thousand talents of gold and eight hundred women, the most precious in Judaea, in return for helping him take the kingdom from Hyrcanus and kill Herod and his brother Phasael. Pacorus heeded the words of Antigonus, Aristobulus's son, and mustered a great army, the army of Persia and Media. They invaded Aram and captured it and smote all the Romans they found there, the men of Antonius, general of Roma. Pacorus, king of Persia, sent his cupbearer with a heavy force to Jerusalem, accompanied by Antigonus, Aristobulus's son. The king of Persia commanded them, saying: "Thus you shall do when you to Jerusalem: call out peace for the city and peace for the people until you have entered the city, but when you have entered the city, begin fighting, smite Hyrcanus and Herod and his brother Phasael, and give the kingdom to Antigonus." The chief cupbearer of the Persian king and Antigonus, Aristobulus's son, marched to Jerusalem; they called out peace for the city and peace for the people, then they entered the city and began fighting with Hyrcanus within the city.

Herod and his brother Phasael divided the positions between them: Herod received the king's palace to protect it, while his brother Phasael mounted the wall to defend the parapet; meanwhile the Persians and Antigonus's followers began smiting among the people and looting the city. Herod descended from the king's palace along with his lads; he began fighting in the city streets with the men of Persia and with Antigonus's men; and he dealt them a very great blow, forcing them to flee. Phasael also descended from the wall and smote all those standing opposite him; they fought with strength and defeated the Persians and Antigonus's men. After seven days, the chief cupbearer summoned Herod and Phasael and said to them: "How long will this fighting continue in the holy city? Desist from this battle and go call on Pacorus, my lord; join with him and let his hand be with you, for it is better for him if you were his allies, for you are valiant, than for Antigonus to be his ally, whose valor does not equal yours." Herod did not believe his words, while Hyrcanus and Phasael did believe his words. They did just as the chief cupbearer had spoken to them and went out to meet Pacorus, whom they found in Damascus of Aram. He received them publicly with honor, but in secret he planned to seize them, so he put guards over them at night to imprison them in chains. Hyrcanus and Phasael arose at night, and, behold, ambushers surrounded the house with their weapons, but they did not know that they were there because of them.

Then Ofellius and Saramalla, rich men of Aram, came to Phasael and related to him all the deception of Pacorus, king of Persia: how Antigonus had bribed him with one thousand talents that he promised to give him and eight hundred women from the nobility of Judaea. The rich men of Aram said to Phasael: "Here is a ship all ready for you to set sail. Get going and save yourself," for Pacorus was located on the seashore at that time. Phasael refused to flee and leave Hyrcanus, so he approached Pacorus, king of Persia, and said to him: "You broke your pact! Now we know[1] that there is no faith among the Persian people, as we have heard with our ears and seen with our eyes concerning the plot that you prepared against us. If you are a man in need and have no gold with you, behold, here is Hyrcanus, who can give you double anything that Antigonus promised; just do not act against men with whom you sealed a pact."

When Pacorus, king of Persia, heard this, he swore an oath, denying [the allegations] and promising them with words, saying: "False rumors and lies you have heard about me, for I did not think this, nor did it cross my mind to do such things!" They [Hyrcanus and Phasael] returned and rested safely, and while they were lying down there, Persian troops fell upon them, captured them, and imprisoned them in chains. When Phasael awoke, his hands were bound with iron. Phasael jumped about and leaped and sought to draw his sword but could not, for his hands were bound. And he looked and, behold, a large stone, so he ran to the stone and, leaping high above the ground, smashed his head on the stone in the frenzy of his anger and died. Just before he died, a woman told him that his brother Herod escaped, and Phasael rejoiced, saying: "God, You have made me happy in my death, for I know that I have an avenger of my blood, who will take revenge." And with these words, he died and was gathered to his people.

---

1. The infidelity of Parthians was proverbial: "there is no loyalty among the People of Paras (= Parthians)," from an unknown source. Cf. *DEH* 1.29.4. [SB]

When Herod heard all that Pacorus, king of Persia, had done to Hyrcanus, king of Judaea, and to Phasael, his brother, while he was in Jerusalem, he took his mother and his mother-in-law and his betrothed Miriam, the daughter of Alexander, Aristobulus's son, and her mother, Alexandra, Hyrcanus's daughter, whom we have mentioned above, and the girl was exceedingly beautiful in appearance and lovely to look at. Herod mounted the women on horses and mules and left Jerusalem at night for the land of Edom, accompanied by ten thousand warriors of Judaea.

While they were on the way, the women and children cried; his [Herod's] mother turned around and stopped the cart[2] in which she was riding, for the women said: "Let us die in Jerusalem, the holy city, and not distance ourselves from her." Herod unsheathed his sword and sought to kill himself, for he feared lest the enemy come and take the women. His lads ran and took hold of his hands, saying to him: "It is a disgrace for a man like you to kill himself without honor; let the women pass before us, and we shall stand here until the arrival of the Persian army that left Jerusalem to pursue after us, then they'll know whom they're chasing." When they finished speaking, the women passed by, and Herod stood together with all his men of war, about ten thousand men.

Before long, the chief cupbearer of the Persian king appeared, accompanied by a large and strong force of Persian troops, and Herod fought with them, he and his men, smiting them, spreading them over the ground, and making the chief cupbearer flee to Jerusalem before Herod. Also, many Judaeans of Antigonus's pursued him and caught up with him and fought with him, but they were defeated by him, and he dealt them a very great blow. At that place where Herod smote the Judaeans, he made a city and built a great palace[3] in the first year of his rule, and he named the city Herodion, which is sixty ris distant from Jerusalem.

Herod continued on his way to the land of Edom, and his brother Joseph went forth to greet him and take counsel with him; they brought the women into the fortress [*mezudah* = *Masada*] of Edom and placed wheat and water and wood in the city and [to] Joseph, his brother, and the men of war. He commanded the rest of the army to disperse throughout the land of Edom to find sustenance for themselves, giving them gold drachmas for their needs, and he, with but a few, continued his way to Desert Rock to Maluk (Malachus),[4] king of

---

2. The author dramatically reverses the story in *AJ* 14.356. Her refusal to flee replaces Josephus, where it is an accident.

3. *Aula oportuna*; the author usually renders palace by *heykhal*.

4. Malachus was in Petra, the author's *sela midbar* (Isa 16:1). The author usually drops the Greek ending in foreign names, e.g., Malachus to Malkiah in chap. 41 and Malok below.

Arav, for Malok was a longtime ally of Hyrcanus and Herod. But Malok did not remember the boon that Hyrcanus had rendered him, and he prevented Herod from entering the land.

Herod set his mind to go to the land of Egypt, so he advanced in that direction; Malok regretted what he had done to Herod, that he had rendered him evil for good. He [Malok] sent envoys after him [Herod] to bring him back and honor him, but they did not catch up with him, for he had come into Egypt unto Cleopatra, queen of Egypt. The queen received him with great honor and sought to make him general of her army. But Herod refused, for he was in a hurry to go to Roma, so the queen gave him a large sum of wealth and ships to bear him to Kittim, which is Italia.

Herod boarded a ship, but twice he had to return to Egypt, because it was winter and the [contrary] winds were too strong. But on the third attempt, the wind corrected, and he crossed the sea. The ships arrived at the great harbor[5] of Brudision (Brundisium), a city on the tip of Italia, and the official[6] of Augustus, king of Roma, was there; he [the official] received him [Herod] with honor and gave him horses and men who escorted him to Roma.

He [Herod] went and stayed at the home of Antonius, Marcus Antonius, his ally, and he told Antonius all that had happened to him: how Antigonus rebelled against Hyrcanus and bound him in chains and clipped his ear to disqualify him from being priest; how he killed his brother Phasael, joined with Pacorus, king of Persia, disgraced the kingdom of Roma, and relied on the kingdom of Persia. When Antonius, Augustus, and the Elder in Roma heard that Pacorus had disgraced the kingdom of Roma, they took counsel together and did not delay the matter; they summoned Herod and placed a royal crown on his head and commanded the people to sound the trumpet. They sounded the ram's horn and raised a cry and shouted, saying: "Herod reigns in Judaea and in Jerusalem, the holy city!"

Augustus and Antonius went out, with Herod between them, and entered Antonius's house. Antonius prepared a great feast and called Augustus and the Elder and all the Roman senators [*ziknei Roma*, lit. elders]; they ate and drank and rejoiced greatly over Herod being crowned king. They registered that day as the beginning of Herod's reign, signing a pact with him and inscribing the treaty on a bronze tablet, which they placed in the royal temple in Roma so that the covenant could be read for all time.

---

5. Tenth-century Brundisium (the author's Greek *Brudision*) was the major port for Byzantine southern Italy. *N* is swallowed in the local dialect.

6. Perhaps contemporary Byzantine official policy.

After these events, Antonius and Herod took ship to come and fight against Pacorus, king of Persia, and against Antigonus, king of Judaea, and with them were many ships and boats and a strong, mighty, and well-armed force. Antonius disembarked at Antiochia and crossed to fight against Pacorus. Herod went to Talmaida, that is, Acco, and with him was a very strong and large contingent of the Roman army, and accompanying him were Ventidius, Machaeras, and Silon, Roman warriors whom Antonius sent with him.

At that time, Antigonus and all his force were encamped at *meẕudah* (Masada) of Edom, in which were all the household of Herod: his mother, his mother-in-law, his betrothed, and his brother Joseph. The people of the city were thirsty for water, for Antigonus had destroyed the aqueduct to the city, so the people considered opening the gate. Joseph, Herod's brother, considered fleeing to Malok, king of Arav, for he heard that Malachus regretted refusing to receive Herod when he fled from Antigonus. But God prevented him from fleeing when He made it rain on that night, filling all the cisterns with water, so he [Joseph] refrained from flight.

Then Herod left Acco, that is, Talmaida, with the officers of Roma whom Antonius had sent with him, and he came to Masada against the camp of Antigonus. His brother Joseph went out from the city and joined with him; they fought against Antigonus and defeated his army; and Antigonus retreated to Jerusalem. Herod brought his whole household from Meẕudah, and when his army of many Judaeans, a very large contingent, joined him, they came to Jerusalem and laid siege to it, accompanied by the Roman generals whom Antonius sent to assist him. But the Roman generals were unwilling to fight against Antigonus, and they disobeyed Antonius's order, for Antigonus had given them a bribe. But Herod did not miss their aid, for there was with him a great host from all of Judaea, and all the men of Galilee joined with him to assist him. Herod laid siege to Jerusalem and fought against Antigonus. He gave the order to his army to encircle the city; they surrounded the city, he and the Roman generals Ventidius, Silon, and Perdelius,[7] but they had secretly taken a bribe from Antigonus and did not want to expose the matter.

Herod approached the wall and, calling out in a loud voice, said: "Listen and give ear to my voice, dwellers of Jerusalem, the holy city, and the Hasidim who are in it and all the people great and small! Far be it from me that I fight against the Lord our God, against His Temple and His city, and against you the people of God, but only against Antigonus, who acted maliciously and wickedly

---

7. The author's misreading of *per Delium* (through Delius) as a name in the accusative and so his Perdelius.

in handing over his uncle Hyrcanus to the Persian king, clipping his ear, maiming him, and desecrating the anointed of the Lord and sending him into exile. He had taken no pity on the old nor on his father's brother; also he killed my brother Phasael and sought to give all the beautiful and precious women of our people to the king of Persia; he has done great evil and sinned against God. Now hand him over, him alone, and let him die according to law, and I will desist from [fighting] you and make peace with you, and we will be one people."

Antigonus, calling out from the wall, said: "Give ear and listen, you generals of Roma who came to help the wicked. If I and my father's house have sinned, the rest of the priests did not sin; nor is it fitting to make the priests lose their honor and the kingdom that their fathers took in battle, when they took their lives in their hand and saved the people of God from Antiochus and from all their enemies around; and they delivered their soul to death, dying for the sake of God and His people. It is proper for their seed to rule; it is not proper that Herod rule, a slave of our house,[8] who is not completely of the seed of Judaea, for his mother, Kiprin the Edomite, bore him to Antipater, general of the army of Judaea. When Hyrcanus sent him to collect the tax from the land of Edom, at that time, he took her as his wife and begot through her this wicked one. And now, if it is not proper for me to rule, choose [a king] from the priests, and let him rule according to the law." Herod answered harshly to Antigonus, and they came to curses and reproaches. Antigonus ordered his troops to shoot arrows at him [Herod] from the wall. They chased him away, and he stood opposite.

Herod saw that winter was nigh and the camp could not encamp against Jerusalem due to the winter and the snow, so he marched to Shomron with all his camp, including the Roman generals. Then he made a great celebration for his marriage, for he had taken as his betrothed Mariamme[9] of the Hasmonean line. After the marriage, he collected much wheat, [with] which he supplied the Roman generals and troops all their needs for the winter season.

After this, Antigonus sent his army of bandits from Jerusalem, and they went to the Galilee, where the bandits of Galilee joined them; they stayed, looting and killing many of the people of the Galilee, because they [people of Galilee] had made peace with Herod. When Herod heard, he marched against them [Antigonus and the bandits] suddenly and caught them in Sipporin in the Galilee,

8. Renders *privatus*; b. *Baba Batra* 3b denotes Herod a slave of the Hasmoneans, but R. Bonfil asks, Did Yosippon know the Talmud? (private communication); *eved* can also mean "servant" in Hebrew, while *privatus* is generally a nonofficial or private person in medieval Latin.

9. MaRYaMI is a Hebrew rendering of *DEH*'s Mariamme. Peter Morvyn's English version of *Yosippon* (1558) calls her MaRIMI. [SB]

and a large battle ensued, many falling on both sides. Herod's right wing collapsed, and they turned their backs to flee. When Herod saw that the battle was difficult—he was fighting on the left wing—he hurried and regrouped to confront the bandits and made them turn around and flee from him. Herod pursued them and smote them with the sword, [making] a very great tumult, and there remained of the bandits only those of the Galilee, who fled to the caves and hid there. There was no room for Herod to attack them, for the caves were midway up a very high mountain, and the only way up was a narrow path, for there was a very deep valley below the hill;[10] and from above, the top of the mountain stood over the caves like a very steep tower. When Herod saw that he could not approach them, he turned and climbed to the top of that mountain with all his army and encamped there. He commanded the smiths to make iron chains; he also had large wooden baskets made and had them bound with iron chains; he filled the baskets with regular armed troops; bread and food too he had placed in the baskets; and he gave them long scythes to pull the bandits out from the caves. He had the baskets lowered from the top of the hill and had them set against the entrance of the caves, and the bandits were afraid to exit from the caves.

Then one of the lads, girt with sword, grabbed the iron chain from which hung the basket with both his hands, and hanging on the chain, he jumped into the cave and killed many of the bandits; he grabbed their corpses with the scythe and hurled them into the valley. And all the lads did likewise, killing the bandits in all the caves, but their wives and children lived. The king captured the caves; only one cave remained because they [the troops] did not lower a basket to its opening.

Inside was an old man[11] with his wife and seven sons, and the old man stood at the entrance of the cave and said to his sons: "Come out!" and one went forth, and the old man drew his sword and killed him, and also the second and the third until the last of them. Even though Herod the king took pity and cried out and pleaded with the old man that he should not kill his sons, the old man did not listen to the king; rather he vilified and cursed the king. After this, he killed his wife and cast her into the valley after her sons, then he killed himself and fell into the valley on the corpses of his sons, and so he died.

After these events, when Herod was told that Antonius had fought against Pacorus, king of Persia, and, having killed him, was now situated on the Euphrates,

---

10. Accurate description of the Cliffs of Arbel. [SB]
11. *AJ* 14.429. This is an interesting parallel to the woman and her seven sons, but here military martyrdom or honor suicide supersedes religious martyrdom. [SB]

Herod went to greet him. He [Herod] found a great crowd that wanted to go to Antonius, but they could not because there were Arabs (Araviyim)[12] on the road killing everyone whom they found going to assist Antonius. When Herod heard this, he went with his lads and found them [the Arabs], fought them, and smote them with the sword, and he opened the road; and all those who wished to go to Antonius went to him, and the king took all their booty and went. Then Antonius sent a chariot force and cavalry and a crown of gold as a gift to King Herod for his help by killing the Arabs and opening the road. The king went to him, and Antonius went out to greet him and embraced him, kissing him and rejoicing with him greatly.

After Marcus Antonius smote Pacorus, king of Persia, he set out for Egypt. He gave Sosio (Sosius), general of his army, and a very heavy force of mighty and very strong Roman warriors to King Herod. He sent a letter throughout Aram, saying: "Marcus Antonius, king of kings,[13] to all the leaders of Aram: Let it be known to you that Herod, Antipater's son, was made king over Judaea at the command of Octavianus Augustus, king of kings, and myself, Marcus Antonius, as the Elder advised. Now beware lest you abstain from sending your men of war to his assistance when he comes to fight against Antigonus, for if you do not hurry to go to his aid, a sword against you and a great plague, for I, Marcus, swear on my sword, and I will not revoke my word!"

After this, Herod and Sosius went to war against Antigonus, and with them were a Roman force and all the army of Aram. On the way, Herod was told that his brother Joseph had died in battle, for Pappus, a hero of Jerusalem, killed him when the king of Jerusalem had sent him [Pappus]. Pappus smote the whole Roman army that had come earlier with Herod and made their officers flee. But Joseph, Herod's brother, stood fast because he did not wish to flee, and, fighting against Pappus, he fell and died in the battle; and there fell on that day thirty-six thousand[14] of the army of Roma whom Pappus killed. He cut off the head of Herod's brother Joseph and sent it to Jerusalem to Antigonus; Herod's brother Pherora bought it with fifty talents of gold and buried it in the tomb of his fathers.

These things were told to the king, but he already knew of the matter because he had seen everything that happened to his brother in a dream. The king grieved

---

12. Renders *barbari*, the author's Berbers of North Africa, who participated in raids on southern Italy; see chap. 21 and chap. 46.

13. The author thought that Rome had two kings at that time. Compare corulers in Byzantium and the Carolingian Empire.

14. *AJ* 14.449, has six cohorts (Latin *sex turmae*; *turma* was a smaller division of cavalry). The author calculated on the basis of the six-thousand-man legion.

a little but did not delay his vengeance. He left Sosius with the whole army and took twelve thousand Romans and twenty thousand Jews and entered Lebanon and crossed the Galilee; he turned from there and went to fight against the army that Pappus had sent to confront him. He found them in the far reaches of the Galilee and dealt them a very great blow from midday unto the evening, a very great blow.

In the evening, when the king ordered his lads to eat and drink, he with his household came to a large[15] house. When the king was eating, the house fell suddenly upon him and his household, but the king was not killed nor even wounded—neither he nor anyone of his household. For this reason, all the people believed that he was God's beloved,[16] as Joseph ben Gurion related.

On the morrow, he went out to fight against Antigonus and Pappus, who opposed him with a very numerous camp, and a battle ensued. Antigonus fled to Jerusalem, but Pappus stood and fought against Herod; and many were killed that day; Pappus too, hero of Jerusalem, was dealt a blow and was wounded in that fighting. Pherora cut off his head and bore it before his brother King Herod; the king commanded that they bury it. As for the lads who fled from the battle and hid in the local houses, the king commanded that they [his men] destroy the houses over them [the warriors who had fled], so the king exacted vengeance for his brother. In the evening, the king commanded his troops to eat and drink, and he with two servants went to a bath that was in that place, and some of Pappus's warriors who had fled from the battle were hiding there. As the king approached the bath and was naked, one of them came out before him with his sword drawn in his hand; he went out and fled, and the second man also went out, and the third, and they did not harm the king, for they all ran away. And even more the people believed that he ruled through God.

From there, he marched on to Jerusalem with all his camp, and an additional thirty thousand Judaean nobles joined him. Sosius, whom Antonius had sent to assist Herod, came again with a very large army and a strong force and with him a Roman force and two kings of Aram; they encamped against Jerusalem in the third year of Herod's rule after he was made king in Roma. They fought again against Jerusalem at the beginning of the fourth year of his rule. They fought many battles, for many times Antigonus and his army came out against them in battle and smote them a very great blow, but they [Antigonus's army] were not

15. The author misunderstood *ad superiorem domum* (upper story).

16. Such miracles contributed to Herod's popular mystique at the beginning of his reign and probably gave support to the Herodians who accepted him as a messianic figure. [See Epiphanius's *Panarion* 1.20, trans. Frank Williams, vol. 1 (Leiden, 1987), 48–49; and *Royal Frankish Annals*, s.a. 817. SB]

able to make them [Herod's army] withdraw from Jerusalem, even though many times they burned the dikes with fire and won valiant victories outside the wall.

Herod's army overcame Antigonus's army and chased its men into the city, within the walls. For Antigonus had very few men with him, as many had fallen in battle.

Twenty[17] Judaeans from Herod's lads rose up at night; they placed ladders on the wall and climbed atop the wall, and Sosius's warriors climbed up after them, for the sentries on the wall were lying exhausted. Having climbed the wall, they slew the sentries and ran to the gate. The men that were with Herod and Sosius raised a cry and broke the gate, and the people of the city were terrified, and Jerusalem, the holy city, was captured.

Herod and Sosius and all the army entered the city and dealt the inhabitants a great and mighty blow and had no pity on either young man or virgin nor old man and woman. Herod became angry at Sosius's officers and said to Sosius: "If all the people will be killed by the sword, whom will I rule?" When Sosius heard this, he sent a messenger throughout the camp, saying: "Whoever kills one more soul in Jerusalem shall die!" Sosius's officers ran to the Temple and sought to open the Temple and see the Holy of Holies, but they could not, for King Herod drew his sword and, standing before the Temple gate along with his lads, chased the Romans away from looking at the Holy of Holies. The king said: "We had better die than let gentiles see the secrets of God that are in the Holy of Holies." Then the king gave to Sosius and his officers from his property silver and gold as payment for their aid that they rendered him, and the remainder of the booty in the city he rescued. At that time, Sosius gave to God's Temple a large gold crown, for he feared lest God punish him for fighting in God's city. All this came upon Jerusalem, the holy city, in the days of the Roman officers Marcus Agrippa and Canidio Gallus (Canidius and Gallus)[18] in the year 185 of the Olympiada in the fourth month on the day of the Fast.[19]

After this occurred, Sosius went to Antonius with Antigonus in chains. Herod sent silver and gold aplenty to Antonius to kill Antigonus because Herod feared lest the kingdom be restored to him [Antigonus]. It happened that when Antigonus was killed, Herod was then secure over all Judaea.

---

17. Expansion of *AJ* 14.476; similar to Gaza in chap. 19.

18. The text splits one name, Canidius Gallus, into two men, a common error of the author.

19. *AJ* 14.487, has in the third month of the 185th Olympiad. The author's correction is to the fast day of 17 Tammuz.

44. HYRCANUS'S DEATH

Finally, when he [Herod] ruled as his heart desired, he honored all the Jews who had given him a hand and had assisted him. He highly honored Hillel the Elder, chief of the Pharisees, and his disciple Shamai,[1] for they had from the beginning stirred up the people to enthrone Herod, saying: "He is from God because of the people's sin, better that he be king before he sheds blood aplenty within Jerusalem." Therefore, Herod honored the Pharisees and all his supporters, but for his enemies, he had no compassion and killed them with the sword, and he took their gold and silver and put it into his house; and he amassed gold and silver aplenty. Moreover, he fought against all the surrounding hostile nations, defeated them, took their gold and silver, and put it into his house.

He set sentries at the gates to search all who left Jerusalem: and whoever had any gold, the sentries took it; and the sentries even searched the dead as well, lest they hide the gold in their caskets when they bore them to the graves. Thus, Herod waxed richer than all the kings who preceded him during the period of the Second Temple.

In those days, Alexander's son Hyrcanus, who had ruled in Judaea, was in exile in the land of Persia: he was the Hyrcanus who was exiled from Jerusalem when Antigonus, his brother Aristobulus's son, banished him to his friend Pacorus, king of Persia: they marched him to Babylonia into the multitude of Jews who lived there, and he dwelt among them. The Jews who lived in

---

1. *Pollio Pharisaeus*, whom the author identifies with Hillel the Elder; usually identified, however, with Abtalyon, *av beth din* (president of the court) and teacher of Hillel the Elder. *Samaeus discipulus eius* was already identified with Shamai (Hillel's opponent; chap. 39) rather than as Hillel's disciple. Shemaiah was Abtalyon's colleague and *nasi* (minority leader), the fourth pair (*zugoth*) of Pharisaic leaders; Hillel and Shamai were the succeeding fifth pair.

Trans-Euphrates accepted him as king, honoring him as God's anointed; nor did Hyrcanus lack anything of the royalty that he had in Jerusalem, save for the Temple of God. When Hyrcanus heard that Herod, son of Antipater, his boon companion whom he had magnified and had loved as his son, was made king, he, Hyrcanus, craved to come to Jerusalem, for a longing for the Temple of God seized him.

Herod heard that Hyrcanus was in very great honor in Babylonia, and he feared lest schemes arise and the kingdom be restored to him. So he sent envoys to the Persian king, saying: "Hyrcanus, who is with you in your land, he it was who raised me, and he is as important in my eyes as my father, and he is pious; yet today he is in the exile to which Antigonus, his brother's son, banished him to Pacorus, who ruled Persia before you. Now that I have been made king in Judaea, I remember his mercy and beneficence that he rendered unto me. Behold, I send you a present of gold and silver; please do not prevent him from coming to me; and I will honor him, repaying and redeeming unto him the boons that he rendered unto my father and me. And if you do not send him, know that great battles will come to you via the Romans and Judaeans."

When the king of Persia heard this, he sent to Hyrcanus in Babylonia, saying: "If you desire to go to Jerusalem, I will not prevent it, but I advise you, watch out for Herod, for he is a bloodthirsty man, lest he ruin your old age!" Also, the Jews who lived in Babylonia spoke to Hyrcanus with these words: "Don't think in your heart that Herod sent to bring you to him out of love; rather, it was from jealousy over the kingdom. For never have kings ever rewarded anyone who had rendered them good when they were in disgrace, since honor changes them and majesty turns their heart. Surely you know that you cannot officiate as priest in Jerusalem because of the blemish that Antigonus, your brother's son, inflicted on you when he clipped your ear. Stay with us, for you lack nothing with us; here, in our eyes, you are like a king; stay in your place and do not meddle anymore in the wars of Jerusalem!" But Hyrcanus did not wish to listen to them. So Hyrcanus went to Jerusalem. Herod with full entourage went out to greet him, embracing him and kissing him, and brought him to his house; he honored him greatly in public and continuously fêted him, publicly calling him "my father"—but in secret, he schemed to take his life.

When Alexandra, Hyrcanus's daughter and mother of Herod's wife Mariamme, whom she bore to Alexandrus, son of Hyrcanus's brother Aristobulus, heard, she, Alexandra, said to her father, Hyrcanus: "My father, guard yourself against Herod, for he does all this unto you only to kill you. Heed my words: flee to Malok, king of Arav, lest this bloodthirsty man ruin your old age with a sword!" But Hyrcanus was not willing to listen to her. Nonetheless, she urged him greatly [cf. Gen 19:3] and badgered him. They summoned Dositheus, one of the Judaean nobles whom they trusted, and revealed to him the secret, for Dositheus was Herod's enemy because he had killed his brother; for this reason, they revealed the secret to him and gave him a bribe. Hyrcanus sent a letter with him to Malok, king of Arav, at Desert Rock, that Malachus secretly send him men and horses to stand by the Asphalt Lake[2] as escort for Hyrcanus, in flight from Herod, to Malok, king of Arav.

When Dositheus received the letter, he found an excuse to become a favorite of the king; he gave Herod the letter sealed with Hyrcanus's signet and revealed the whole secret that Hyrcanus and his daughter Alexandra had told him. When the king received the letter from Dositheus, he praised him and blessed him, giving him a great gift of gold and silver, and he said to him: "Go on your way to the place where Hyrcanus sent you, and take with you the letter, sealed with Hyrcanus's signet, that he gave you. When you get the letter from Malok, king of Arav, bring it to me; then show me the men and horses that he sends for Hyrcanus, and I will capture them."

Dositheus did all that the king said to him: he went to Malok, king of Arav, then he returned to King Herod and gave him the invitation that Malok sent to Hyrcanus. When the king [Herod] received this letter, he sent troops to the Asphalt Lake and captured the escort that the king of Arav sent for Hyrcanus.

The king called the seventy elders, and he questioned Hyrcanus whether there was a pact between him and Malok, king of Arav. Hyrcanus said: "There is no pact between myself and him!" Then he said: "What envoy did you send, and what letter did Malok send to you?"

He replied: "No letter came to me, and I did not send an envoy!" The king produced Dositheus and the letter and Malok's men whom he had captured and the horses, and he exhibited them before the seventy elders. Then he commanded one of his troops to cut off Hyrcanus's head,[3] and the trooper smote him, cutting off his head. Hyrcanus died, a righteous and good man and old who, when he was reigning, did no evil to anyone but who experienced many troubles from his youth. For, when his mother died, and Hyrcanus, having received the kingship, had ruled three months, his brother Aristobulus fought against him and took the kingship from him; and after three years, he was restored to his kingship and ruled for forty years. Antigonus, son of his brother Aristobulus,

____

2. *palus bituminis*: the Dead Sea in Vulgate to Gen 14:10.

3. The author's source only has him kill the man.

fought against him and, capturing him, clipped his ear[4] to bar him from being priest and exiled him to Chaldea. After three[5] years, Herod, whom he had raised on delicacies, ruled; he [Hyrancus] hastened to come to him, and coming, he died as we wrote above. He was eighty years old when he was gathered to his people.

---

4. The source has that he only blemished the ear.
5. "Three" is lacking in two MSS as well *AJ*.

45. ARISTOBULUS'S DEATH

After these events,[1] Mariamme and Alexandra became greatly saddened, and they hated Herod exceedingly because he had killed the old man. King Herod gave the priesthood to Ḥananel, one of the ignoble priests, for he was not of the Hasmonean seed. Alexandra sent to her friend Cleopatra, queen of Egypt, wife of Antonius, hero of Roma, that she speak to Antonius to send envoys to Herod to command him to take the priesthood from Ḥananel and give it to Aristobulus—a youth of fifteen years, handsome and of good appearance and unmatched in beauty and form among his contemporaries—he was brother to Mariamme, Herod's wife, and Alexandra's son whom she bore to Alexandrus, son of Aristobulus. Queen Cleopatra acceded to her friend Alexandra's request and pleaded with her husband, Antonius, to send envoys to Herod to take the priesthood from Ḥananel and give the priestly authority to the youth Aristobulus.

Antonius sent Gellius, one of his officers, to Jerusalem to Herod to fulfill the wish of Cleopatra, his wife, and Alexandra, her friend, and Gellius came to Jerusalem and spoke to Herod in such vein. But Herod refused to give the priesthood to Aristobulus, saying: "There is no precedent to depose a living priest from his honor and to install another in his place."

When Gellius was in Jerusalem, he saw the youth Aristobulus in his form and beauty, and he also saw Mariamme, Aristobulus's sister, a beautiful woman of exceedingly lovely appearance, and he was taken aback at their beauty, for he had not seen their equal among the nations, and Gellius said to Alexandra: "From whom did you bear these? It was not a man who had union with you but rather an angel of the gods; only thus could you have born such children. Now

---

1. The author returns to the point in chap. 42 where he skipped forward, adding this sentence for transition.

heed my words and engrave their figure and embroider their image[2] and send it with me to Antonius; when he sees the image of the youths, he will fulfill your desire." Alexandra followed Gellius's advice and sent the image of the youths to Antonius, the hero of Roma, who was sojourning in Egypt.

When Antonius beheld the images of the youths, his lustful vices burned; and he sent a letter to Herod, saying: "Marcus Antonius, hero of Roma, to Herod, king of Judaea: Peace. Remember the boon that I rendered you when I assisted you to be enthroned over all Judaea. Now do not delay to send me the youth Aristobulus, and if you do not send him quickly, know that the Romans will make war against you!"

When Herod saw this letter, he knew it was because of the licentious vice of Antonius's lust for the youth, so Herod hurried to bestow the priesthood upon the youth. He wrote to Antonius: "The youth cannot leave the city for he is high priest in place of Ḥananel. Verily, if the youth should leave the city, the Jews will be stirred to major riot and much blood will be spilled, for they would prefer to die rather than give over the youth." When Antonius heard this, he ceased to demand the youth.

King Herod removed Ḥananel from the priesthood and gave it to Aristobulus, his wife's brother, and he but a youth of sixteen years. Formerly, high priests had served until their death, but Antiochus, the one called Epiphanus, was the first to profane the priesthood by removing the high priest and installing Onia (Onias) in his place; the second was Aristobulus, who removed his brother Hyrcanus; and the third time was when Herod cast Ḥananel out of the priesthood and gave it to his wife's brother in order to quiet the quarrels and strife among his household. Herod did this, but it brought no rest in his house, for his mother-in-law and his wife hated him because he had killed the aged Hyrcanus.

Herod secretly commanded to guard his mother-in-law, Alexandra, for he feared she might stir up the people against him. Alexandra sent to Cleopatra, her friend, for aid, and Cleopatra invited her to flee from Herod and come to Egypt. Alexandra made two coffin-like boxes to leave Jerusalem among the coffins of the dead that left Jerusalem for burial in Hebron or in other places. Alexandra lay in one box and her son in the other box in transit from Jerusalem to go to the port of Yafo (Joppa), where Cleopatra had sent ships to bring her and her son to Egypt.

One of Alexandra's advisers, called Sabion, told the king, and the king commanded Sabion, saying: "Carry the boxes that contain Alexandra and her son

---

2. See chap. 2. Embroidered portraiture was an important Byzantine art form. The Hebrew root *RKM* is the source for the Italian *ricamo*, as in *ricama a mano*. [SB]

just as Alexandra told you, but as you bear them covered as they are, bring the boxes before me, and I will seize them inside the boxes." Sabion did so accordingly and bore the boxes before the king. The king opened the boxes, and behold, Alexandra and her son were within them. The king reproved Alexandra and said to her: "Are you not ashamed to try such tricks?" The king reproved her with many words, yet the king forbore even this offense.

Next year, during the festival of Sukkoth, the high priest Aristobulus, dressed in high priestly garb, mounted the altar to perform the sacred service of the high priest. When the people beheld the youth in his garments of office, in his appearance and beauty, his image likened to an angel of God, the people rejoiced greatly and wept out of great happiness, blessing God and the priest. King Herod was very worried and said to himself: "If I do not remove this lad quickly, the kingdom will be restored to him, for the heart of all people is to enthrone him."

After the holiday, the king left Jerusalem with his entire household and went to Jericho, a great city, site of the excellent perfume balsamon,[3] for which fragrance the city of Jericho was named, according to Joseph ben Gurion. When the king went to Jericho, he made a large feast for all his nobles and servants, while Mariamme, the queen, also made a feast for all the noble women who came with her. The king returned to the feast and spoke with Aristobulus, the high priest, who was sitting next to the king—all his nobles and servants were sitting according to their rank—and the king rejoiced and all his servants exceedingly.

After the feast, during the afternoon, the king with the youth Aristobulus and the king's officers went out to the gardens, to the springs to watch the king's servants swim, for broad and very deep pools of water filled by springs were there. The king stood over one pool and watched his servants swimming in the water and playing. The lads began to dunk one another, and the lads called to the youth Aristobulus—the king's plot—and they said to him: "Pray, come on down to play with us in the water!" The youth Aristobulus said to the king: "Let me go down and swim in the water with the boys." And the king said: "Why should you go down?" He [Aristobulus] begged him [Herod], and the king said: "As you wish." The lad went in and swam in the water with the jesting lads, and the king went home. The king's servants played with Aristobulus in the water until dusk, and they dunked him in the water until they drowned him by this ruse of King Herod.

When the people heard that Aristobulus had died, they raised their voice and wept, and along with them wept all the king's officers and servants. Alexandra

---

3. *Balsamon* is Greek form; chap. 36 has the Italian form *balsamo*. See there for the author's pun.

and Mariamme, the queen, wailed, and Mariamme said to the king in public: "How solitary[4] I remain of all my family since you took me with your sword, and you pitied neither my sire's hoary head[5] nor my brother's youth; desolate am I of all my family." She wailed exceedingly before the public, and King Herod also wept, for his compassion was stirred by the beauty of the youth, and he made a great show over his burial, rendering him great honor in his death. Alexandra, the youth's mother, sought to kill herself, but she chose life in order to find some scheme to exact vengeance against Herod. From that day hence, Mariamme uttered not a word to Kiprin, the king's mother, nor to his sister Shlomith due to her hatred for them; she cursed them continuously and insulted them for the shame of their family, saying that they were mixed breeds, since Kiprin was an Edomite, from Judaea's servants. Kiprin, the king's mother, and his sister Shlomith as well despised her. Shlomith constantly libeled her to the king, but the king did not listen to her words, nor did he reprove his wife Mariamme because of his love for her, for the king loved her beyond any other love. Since Mariamme was confident in his love for her, she cursed and insulted the king's family.

---

4. Same style re: Esther (chap. 9); cf. Lam 1:1.
5. Cf. *DEH* 1.37.2 and also 1.36.2.

46. WAR WITH THE ARAVIM (ARABS)

At that time,[1] wars broke out in Aram, Armenia, and Persia. They had rebelled against the kingdom of Roma, for Marcus Antonius, hero of Roma, now situated in Egypt, had oppressed them by giving them as a gift to his wife Cleopatra, since Antonius fulfilled her every wish and command like a slave. She seduced him to take away the lands of kings and give them to her, to take their silver and gold and give them to her, and so Antonius did; he killed great and noble kings and gave [all] to her. Furthermore, she incited him to kill the king of Judah and the king of Arav and give their land and booty to her. This time, however, Antonius thought it over, and a little of his sense returned to him, just as the madman's sense returns to him when he is cured of his illness. Antonius said: "It is not good to kill great kings, for we cannot kill them without the ruin of Romans and bloodshed; Herod, king of Judah, is our friend and our ally who was enthroned at the counsel of Augustus, who is in Roma, and the Elder and his 320 counselors; it would not be a proper thing to do." But on the king of Aram, Antonius took no pity and gave her his land and its spoil; and he set out again and killed many.

He marched out to fight against Persia, and Cleopatra went with him, accompanying him as far as the Euphrates. There the queen turned back to Egypt and entered the land of Judah, where King Herod received her in Jericho, city of fragrance, site of excellent perfume, and made a great feast for her and her servants. The queen tempted him to lie with her, but King Herod refused and took counsel with his advisers whether he should bring her to one of his royal rooms to kill her in order to save many from her wickedness. But his advisers prevented him, saying: "Heaven forbid such deeds, for if you kill her, great battles would break out between you and Antonius." When the king heard, he refrained

---

1. This chapter follows *AJ* 15; and *DEH* 1.32ff.

from such actions and, giving her silver, gold, and precious stones befitting a ruler, accompanied her to Egypt, and the king returned to Jerusalem.

Antonius fought in Armenia and captured it; from there, he marched against Persia and captured it. Antonius brought Artabazes, king of Armenia, and Arsaces, king of Persia,[2] bound in chains with all their precious jewelry and gave them to Cleopatra as maidservants. For this reason, all the nations hated Antonius, for God gave into his hand great and noble kings, but he disgraced them and gave them into the hand of his wife.

After these events, Cleopatra incited Antonius to fight against Octavianus, called Augustus, who ruled in Roma and governed from beyond Hodu to Briktania (Britania),[3] even unto the ocean in the West. Antonius arrayed an immensely powerful force to fight against him in the year 187 of the Olympiada,[4] for he heeded his wife Cleopatra. King Herod gathered a massive and strong force of Judaeans and all the nations that he had conquered and in addition a great many ships and marched to Egypt to aid Antonius, to go with him to Kitimah (Italy) to fight against Octavianus Augustus.

When Herod came to Egypt, Antonius said to him: "Don't come with me lest these kingdoms rebel against me when I go to Kitimah to fight against Octavianus, but it is good that you be our defense over here; go and conquer the land of Arav, for its king has rebelled." When Herod heard these words, he mustered much cavalry and infantry, invaded Arav, and devastated the land of Arav with fire and sword.

Cleopatra sent Athenion, general of her army, to assist Herod, saying to him in secret: "Be of one counsel with the king of Arav and, when you approach to battle and the fighting begins, stand behind the Judaean camp and smite their camp from the rear. The Judaeans will be in the middle, and they will fall with Herod, their king; thus, I will take the land of Judah and rule over it." Herod marched to the land of Arav with Athenion, and Athenion sent these words secretly to the king of Arav; the king of Arav went out to confront him with a great and numerous army. King Herod stood in camp and sent the army of Judaea out against the king of Arav, and a major battle broke out. The Judaeans were winning at the beginning of the fighting and dealt a great blow against Arav. As the Arabians fled from them, Athenion smote the Judaean camp [*kiti*] from the rear, just as the queen had commanded. The Judaeans turned, and behold, there was fighting from the rear; the Judaeans turned around to fight

---

2. The author thought that Hegesippus meant two different kings.

3. Some MSS have "Briktania" for "Britania"; see chap. 68.

4. The author did not understand Josephus's Olympiads; 187th Olympiad, *AJ* 15.109.

against Athenion and the Egyptians. They were caught between the Aravians and the Egyptians: on the one side the former, and on the other the latter, and Judaeans in the middle; the Judaeans suffered a great defeat, many falling in the fighting. King Herod hastened[5] to leave his army with his horses and cavalry; he smote Athenion and routed him, and also he smote mightily among the Aravian force, killing many, pursuing them unto their fortified cities; then he returned to Jerusalem.

Meanwhile, a great and powerful earthquake, the like of which had not occurred since the days of Uzziah, king of Judah,[6] shook the whole land of Judaea in those days. Many died throughout the land, and many cattle as well died in the earthquake; ten thousand men, women, and children also died in the environs of Jerusalem, in addition to those who died in the cities of Judaea. King Herod panicked, as did the whole nation of Judah: the king's heart felt faint, and the heart of the people felt exceedingly faint, so they sent messengers to every surrounding nation and made peace all around. Herod sent messengers to make peace with the king of Arav. But the king of Arav seized Herod's envoys and slaughtered them before the city called Desert Rock, his kingdom's capital. He mustered all his force, the army of Arav and a Berber force,[7] an army as numerous as the sand on the seashore, to invade the land of Judaea to destroy her, for he heard that all the pride of Judaea had died in the earthquake.

When the king heard that the king of Arav had slaughtered his messengers, he wept, and his heart was greatly saddened. Summoning all his officers and warriors and the whole army, he spoke to them thus: "Saintly ones of God, holy nation, my brothers, my friends, listen to what I say unto you this day! I know that a great sorrow has come upon us this year; therefore, I feared to speak directly to you, lest my words cause you suffering and lest they be a burden unto you, for you are in embittered spirit, but listen and attend my words! Like the sons of Hasidim,[8] we have fought until now to show our strength and valor to take booty and spoil: sometimes we were victorious, sometimes we were defeated, as is the way of the world, but we defeated all our neighbors, and we took their land and property. But now we shall go out to battle not for property or for booty but for vengeance, because innocent blood was shed; they killed our envoys that we sent to make peace with them. Now I would be amazed if

---

5. *AJ* 15.120; *DEH* 1.32.5; the author exaggerates Herod's successes.

6. The author's addition; cf. Amos 1:1 and Zechk 14:5.

7. The author's addition. See chaps. 21 and 43.

8. The author dramatically combined *DEH* and *AJ*; cf. *DEH* 1.32.6.

you fear their numbers; you know we have defeated them in every battle. If you say that your heart has softened because of the earthquake, on this point you are intimidated for naught—it did not disadvantage us but rather benefited us since it brought Aravians forth to battle. For if this earthquake had not occurred, they would not have come to fight us, but they heard that we perished in the earthquake, and they come confidently. And a further sign for you that this war is the will of God: consider the dead who perished in the earthquake; no warriors died, not even one, rather old men, women, and children. They took courage from our trouble, but they were confident in vain.

"Woe unto the haughty man who trusts not in his own strength but in his enemy's ruin! For in a flash, man's lot is changed; from distress man goes to security and from defeat to strength and from security to distress and from valor to defeat, for man's fate is subject to change: power is not eternal nor defeat perpetual. Therefore, it is not proper for a man to be confident on a good day nor fearful when he has a bad day. We learn this from what has happened to us: we have defeated the Aravians in the first battle, nor did they withstand us in the last, for they fled; next Athenion smote us from the rear and were defeated, while they who fled came back against us and turned around to fight us. So now the anxiety that you feel is not fear, for valor shall determine the outcome. If you fear from the houses that fell in the earthquake and killed souls, [know that] if God sought to afflict us further, surely He would be able, for who could withstand Him, but it was His to afflict us and purify us of our transgressions. We have been cleansed of sin and offense, for the earthquake has purified us, and God will not afflict us further, for after wrath comes mercy.

"Now be strong and strengthen your hearts, O holy nation, as did your ancestors! And if our flocks have died, our enemies' counsel and faith have died, for they raised their hand against our envoys. They transgressed and rebelled not only against our Torah but against all the laws of every people, Roman law, Greek law, and even against their own [Berber] law have they transgressed and rebelled. They raised their hand against sacred men, for envoys are sanctified; Greeks call envoys angels [*aggeloi*], and we too call them *mal'akhim*, that is, God's envoys who make peace between nations to prevent bloodshed.

"Now be strong and bold to exact their vengeance as God commanded us, for their blood calls out to God. Let us hasten to war with God's will, before God takes revenge in another way. Let us hasten while yet their blood helps us, for God's angels are with us and will fight with us over the spilled blood, and they will help us against the enemy."

When the Judaeans heard these words, they were stirred up to battle. King Herod saw that the people's heart was united to fight against Arav, and he offered up burnt sacrifices and peace offerings [*shlamim*] to God, Lord of Israel. He crossed the Jordan with an immense force of many chariots and cavalry from the army of Judah and Benjamin, all of them warriors who would not turn their backs; and he went to the land of Arav. The king of Arav went forth to confront him and with him an army as numerous as sand upon the seashore; they arrayed for battle, and five thousand of Arav fell in the first battle. They stood fast, but another four thousand fell.[9] The Judaeans pursued the Aravivans unto the camp; the Aravians closed ranks, and the Judaeans could not break their ranks, for the Aravian camp was closed all around, and the Aravians fought within their camp.

King Herod set the Judaean camp in front of the Aravian camp, blocking them from leaving camp to draw water for five days. The Aravians thirsted for water exceedingly and sent messengers to King Herod with an offering in hand to plead with him to cease the fighting and allow them to exit the camp to draw water. But Herod did not accept their gift, nor did they see the face of the king, for the king had hardened his spirit to exact vengeance against them. The Aravians said to one another: "Let's go out and fight, for it is better for us to die in battle than to die of thirst!" They went forth and arrayed for a major battle. The Judaeans went forth to confront the Aravians, and the battle flared; the Judaeans killed seven thousand Aravian dead in the initial fighting. The Aravians turned their backs and fled unto their fortified cities with Herod and his army in pursuit; he dealt them an immense blow, and many Aravians were slain on that day on the way to their fortress cities, a great defeat that cannot be described. King Herod captured Desert Rock and all their fortress cities; and the Aravians became Herod's slaves all of his days. The king returned to Jerusalem in peace with the entire Judaean army, for not one of them was missing; they gave thanks and praise to God, their Lord, making an offering in the Temple of God, for they brought much booty with them, very great wealth that they took from Arav and from the Berbers.

---

9. *AJ* 15.156, has forty thousand Arabs captured.

47. HEROD AFTER THE DOWNFALL OF ANTONIUS

In those days, Antonius fought against Octavianus Augustus, and Augustus had the upper hand and defeated Antonius. Thus, all dominion fell into the hands of Augustus, and he came by ship to Rhodes to invade Egypt.

When Herod was told that Antonius had perished, he was greatly saddened and, taking his life in his hand, went to Augustus in Rhodos, a Greek city, to greet him with an offering. He put all his household in order: he gave his mother, Kiprin, and his sister Shlomith to Pherora, his brother, commanding him to bear them to Masada of Edom; Mariamme, his wife, and Alexandra, her mother, he gave to Joseph, his sister Shlomith's husband, and to Somi (Somoemus) of Tyre,[1] commanding them to take the women to the city called Alexandrium; he commanded them, making them swear an oath, that if they should hear of any calamity from him, to kill Mariamme, his wife, and her mother, Alexandra. He boarded a ship and went to Augustus, king of Roma, for Augustus considered killing Herod because of his loyal friendship with Antonius.

When he came to Augustus, he did not remove any of his royal insignia, save for the diadem alone, and said to Augustus: "If because my friendship with Antonius you are wroth with me, I do not hide it from you but rather admit it before you. It is true that I was loyal to Antonius, and were he still alive, I would still be his friend, for he helped me and made me king. And everything that my mouth says about my love for Antonius, I would have shown my hand in battle had I crossed with him to Kitimah. But I did not cross, nor was I in the battle, for I could not due to the war with the Arabians and due to the bad advice that his wife Cleopatra gave him—not to take me along with him. For this reason, I

---

1. *Ituraeus*: the author restores from *Ẓor* (= Tyre).

did not raise my sword against you, nor did I fight against you, not from fear of war nor from cowardice, nor did I abandon him as one who abandons a friend in his hour of need; rather, it is my shame that I was not with him. Moreover, even though I was not beside him, I did send with him an army of troops and ships bearing weapons with much grain and food. Had I been with him at the field of battle in the vale of Akẓio (Actium) in the land of Kittim (Roman Epirus), you would have seen with your eyes all the love I had for him. But I was not there.

"Behold I hide nothing from you, lest I appear as one who would abandon his friend in his time of need, for your judgment is heavier upon me than your fighting; I fear your judgment, but I do not fear your fighting. For in judgment a man's strength will not help him; rather, he will be trapped in his sin; for this reason, I want to show you my love for your enemy. See now that even though you have overcome Antonius, and he is defeated and flees, were I to find him, I would not abandon him but rather help him. For he was defeated through his lack of sense, and you won with your force and were victorious with the help of Roman warriors, but even more you won and were victorious through your counsel. He was vanquished with the weapons of war, but even more was he vanquished by his lack of judgment: his Egyptian wife, Cleopatra, vanquished him; love for the Egyptian vanquished him, the bed of illicit lust vanquished him, and his wife controlled him with her magic charms. He did not listen to my advice to kill her, for she was his enemy who incited him to fight against you. Had he listened to me and killed her, then it would have been better for him; then I would have come with him to fight against you. And had he fallen, I would have raised him up, and had he fled, I would have made him stand, and I would have shielded him. But in all this he would not listen to me; he abandoned me; I did not abandon him, for it was he who put the crown of kingship upon my head. I have come to you, and I have removed it from my head; but my judgment and my strength I have not removed. And even as I stand in your judgment, as long as I am still alive, I am an enemy to all my enemies and faithful[2] to all my friends, for we have many friends; therefore, my friends trust and rely on me in time of trouble."

When he had spoken these words, Augustus answered, saying to Herod, king of Judaea: "It is fitting that you continue to rule over what you now rule, for you are faithful to your friends and you maintain your loyalty and you are not ashamed to reveal your love for Antonius, our enemy. But from now on, be our friend, and we will give you a reward[3] for your loyalty, twice as much as

---

2. The author regularly prefers *ahuv* for *ohev*, e.g., chap. 31, end.

3. Biblical *shohad* used as gift, as in chap. 44.

Antonius gave to you. For I, who defeated him in battle, will now defeat him with my generosity and give you all that you ask of me. For Antonius did not pay you according to your worth, for he listened to his wife and did not heed your advice, since he preferred her magic charms and did not trust you; his lack of judgment made him our enemy. Now do not be surprised for what he did to you, so he did also to me. Because of his wife, he abandoned me and became my enemy. So now it is fitting for a man like you to take many presents by reason of your power, for you have fought our enemies, a powerful people, and you have conquered the Arabian nation. Now all our enemies are your enemies and all our allies your allies."

Then Augustus took the diadem of kingship and put it on Herod's head and doubled the size of the kingdom over which he ruled. Herod accompanied him as far as Egypt, and Augustus gave him all the kingdoms that Antonius had given to his wife. Augustus crowned Herod king there. Augustus gave him moreover four hundred troops, warriors of the people called Galli (Gauls),[4] and he honored him greatly.

---

4. *AJ* 15.217; Cleopatra's former bodyguard.

48. MARIAMME'S DEMISE

Herod returned safely to Jerusalem but found his household in alarm,[1] for Joseph and Somi of Tyre, whom the king had appointed to guard his wife Mariamme, had revealed the king's secret plans in which he had ordered to kill his wife Mariamme when he went to Augustus were any calamity to befall him, lest another man possess her after his death. When the woman heard this, she was very vexed, and when he told her all the honor and majesty that befell him, the woman did not rejoice, nor was her face glad, nor did she listen to his words; rather, she cursed his family. When Herod saw the hatred that she had for him, he was very unhappy, for the king loved her very much.

The day came when Mariamme, the queen, had a quarrel with the king's sister Shlomith, Joseph's wife, and the queen vilified her and her family. Shlomith denounced her [Mariamme] to the king, saying: "When you were with Augustus, my husband, Joseph, lay with Mariamme, the queen." But the king did not believe her, for he knew his wife to be a virtuous woman of long standing. But because of the hatred that she had for him, the king took these words a little to heart, and, summoning his wife, he asked her: "Tell me please what is this hatred that you feel toward me without cause, for you do not love me as before, while I love you above all women; I swear to you that, from the day I knew you, I have felt no lust for another woman but you." Mariamme said: "If you have loved me as you say, who has heard the like of someone who loves yet kills; if love, why kill? Why did you command Joseph to kill me on the day you went to Augustus?"

When the king heard this, he was greatly shaken; he stopped hugging her and shouted: "Surely the word I have heard is true! Here is the sign that Joseph

---

1. This chapter conflates *AJ* 15; and *DEH* 1.37 (based on *BJ* 1).

did not reveal my secret unless he had lain with her!" The king left the palace and slept in another house.

When Shlomith, the king's sister, saw that the king believed what he heard about his wife, she called one of the king's eunuchs, of the cupbearers, and gave him a bribe of silver and gold. Putting words in his mouth, she said to him: "Take this deadly poison and go to the king and whisper in his ear these exact words: 'Mariamme, your wife, summoned me and gave me silver and gold, and also she gave me this drink, which I have in my hand, and she said to me: "Go and serve this drink to the king, for it is a love potion to restore the king's affection to me so that the king shall love me."' And when you utter these words, if the king is shaken and says to you: 'Where is the drink?' you say to him: 'Here it is in my hand; for this reason, I am telling the king and brought the drink in my hand—let the king examine it whether it is good or bad and lest it harm the king.'" The eunuch went to the king and spoke all that Shlomith had commanded him. The king was anxious and said: "Where is the drink?" And the eunuch said: "Here it is in my hand." Then he handed the vessel that contained the poison to the king, and it was tested before the king. A man condemned to death was brought before him; he drank from the contents in the vessel and died at once.

The king ordered to seize his wife Mariamme and his sister's husband Joseph and Somi the Tyrian; he seized also one of Mariamme's eunuchs, ordering that he be severely tortured in order to confess. The eunuch did not confess about the matter of the drink, but he did confess the hatred that his wife felt toward him by reason of what Joseph and Somi told her revealing the king's secret. The king commanded to kill Joseph and Somi, and they were killed. As for Mariamme, the king commanded that she be kept in custody until he would send for and assemble the seventy elders[2] to bring her to trial to condemn her to death.

Shlomith and her counselors hastened to the king and said: "Let it be known to you, O king, if Mariamme would live for one more day, the people will rise against you, for the queen's servants will gather from all places, and they would not allow her to be killed without tumult and fighting." The king said: "Do as you please!" So they dragged her to be killed outside the city.

Alexandra, her mother, came out and called out: "Come out, rebellious woman who rebelled against your husband!" She reviled and cursed her, crying and wailing—but Alexandra spoke thus only in deceit, to live a bit after her, so that she might exact vengeance for her [Mariamme] and devise a plot to

---

2. The author's mistaken reference to Sanhedrin; his source has *iudicium colligens familiarum* (a court of his household).

kill Herod. Other women too reviled and disgraced her [Mariamme], for they thought her guilty.[3] And Mariamme answered not a word but remained silent and walked proudly to her death without fear or dread, like a woman going to a house of mirth; her face changed not, nor did she adjust the pace of her gait.

Thus, the queen spurned death like her family, the Hasmoneans, and she showed everyone the dignity of her family and the greatness of her ancestors. She bared her neck for the sword and was killed and was gathered unto her people, the woman who surpassed all woman in beauty and appearance, and in fear of the Lord, she superseded all the women in her times. Only humility was lacking in her, for she constantly cursed the king when she saw that he had sinned; but as far as beauty is concerned, no man could relate the greatness of her beauty, as described in the book of Joseph ben Gurion.

Nor did God tarry to avenge Mariamme, for He smote the king's household with a plague, and many of the king's servants and many of his officers and chiefs also died; all the cities of Judaea suffered the plague in those days. The people prayed [cf. Num 16:22] and said: "Lord of the universe, You should not kill many from amongst Your people [as punishment for the sins] of one!" And God healed the people, and the plague abated.

Herod regretted killing his wife; the king's anger changed to passion, and the king, yearning exceedingly for his wife Mariamme, recalled her name constantly as if she were still alive. He commanded her servants to make her a perpetual feast and to arrange a chair for her at the king's side, as when she lived. The king fell seriously ill because of his love for Mariamme and because of his longing for her; he could not suffer the longing and nearly died from longing. When Alexandra saw that the king was ill, she plotted to kill him. The king heard and commanded to kill her at once.

Herod's sons Alexander and Aristobulus, whom his wife Mariamme had born him, were in Roma in those days to learn Roman letters.[4] When the boys heard, they were greatly saddened and very angry that their mother was killed, but we shall relate their deeds later.

---

3. The author misunderstood *AJ* 15.234.

4. The first stage of acculturation here; *litteratus* (intellectual) occasionally meant "one who knows reading and writing (Latin)."

49. KING HEROD'S GREATNESS

When the king recovered from his illness, he gave his sister Shlomith as wife to Costobarus, an Edomite. He made him *nagid*[1] over Edom, for all the Edomites were circumcised since the days of Shimon's son Hyrcanus, who had circumcised them and imprisoned them in the chains of circumcision.[2] Costobarus, ruling now in Edom, sought to free Edom from the Judaeans, so he refashioned Edom's ancient idol[3] and sent [messengers] to Egypt to ask for chariots and cavalry to rebel against Herod. When Herod was told of this, he sought to kill him, but his mother and his sister begged him for mercy, so the king had compassion on Costobarus on this occasion.

Afterward, Costobarus and his wife Shlomith had a quarrel; she slandered him to the king and begged the king to tell Costobarus to write her a bill of divorce. The king ordered her husband to write her a bill of divorce in obedience to the command of the king but not according to the Torah of Moses, for a man could leave his wife only if he hated her [cf. Deut 24:3], but a woman could not leave her husband, as Joseph ben Gurion related in his book.[4]

Shlomith spoke to the king about the men[5] whom Costobarus hid in a village that belonged to him: they were of the Hasmonean seed, of royal descent, and they were hidden for twelve years since the day Herod took Jerusalem. Shlomith

---

1. *Nagid* for Latin *iudex* here, elsewhere for *dux*; cf. chap. 39.
2. See chap. 29.
3. Costobarus (in *AJ* 15.253) was scion of the priests of Keze (Qozah, a divine archer, later syncretized with Apollo; cf. Marcus *ad locum*); the author assumes his reconversion perhaps based on his familiarity with contemporary tribes that adopted Christianity and reverted to their pagan beliefs when they rebelled.
4. *AJ* 15.259 has her send him a *get*, which seemed unlikely to the author, so he changed his source accordingly. Her slandering him in *AJ* 15.260 took place after the divorce.
5. Sons of Baba or Sabba(s). Herod wiped out all the family of Hyrcanus, his potential rivals.

told the king, and he commanded that they kill Costobarus and the men whom he hid; he also killed Lysimachus and Dositheus of the Judaean nobility; he did not leave anyone who could resist his sins: thus, he profaned the Torah.

He built in Jerusalem theaters[6] of marble and white stone and engraved upon them the image[7] of the nations he had conquered; he built a hippodrome in the large valley with chariots for the horses; he built a cage for wild animals and put into the cage lions, bears, leopards, wolves, and wild boars; he cast sheep and cattle to stir up fighting between them and also men to fight with the wild animals: sometimes the wild beast overcame the man, and sometimes the man overcame the wild beast, and the king gave great wealth to the winners. This was joy to the gentiles, but to the Jews, sorrow.

Ten men, a blind man and his comrades, became zealous, and they leaped at the king with drawn swords. But the king already knew of the matter since he was told one day before the event. They were not able to kill him because, when they ran toward him, the king's troops surrounded them and killed them. The informer, however, sinned against the king three days later, so the king commanded to cut up his flesh and cast it to the dogs.

Herod did many things and built many cities: he rebuilt Shomron in length and breadth according to its original plan and called it Sebastia; and he built within it a temple [dedicated] to Augustus, king of Roma. He built Caesarea of marble and beautified the city exceedingly. He built a port for it and a haven for incoming ships, and he built a great city and many cities that cannot be numbered [Gen. 16:10].

In the thirteenth year of his rule, there was great famine in the land of Judaea and among the nations that Herod had conquered and subjected to his rule. But there was great surfeit [*Sanhedrin* 97a] in the land of Egypt. The king brought forth all his treasury of silver, gold, and precious stones to help the people, for the people were impoverished exceedingly due to the famine, and the king did not spare any of his ornaments of royalty. He sent to Egypt and collected wheat as numerous as the sand of the sea, distributing it on the shores of Yafo and Caesarea, and he made it cheap and plentiful in his land. Augustus, king of Roma, sent a letter to Petronius in Egypt to send a fleet of large vessels and ships bearing wheat to sell in the land of Judah, in addition to the ships [with wheat] that he sent as a gift to Herod, king of Judaea. Petronius sailed with many ships, and

---

6. Cf. *AJ* 15.268; *biraniyoth* (pl.), lit. "palaces"; cf. *b. Pesah* 118b. The author's source recommends seeing the theater and amphitheater. [The author perhaps knew Capua's amphitheater. SB]

7. Lit. "a picture"; *AJ* 15.272 (276) speaks of *trophaea Gentium*.

he found [the market] cheap in the land of Judaea; and they sold it cheaply, as Augustus commanded,[8] and so Herod fed all the land of Judaea.

The king ordered the bakers to give bread to the aged and the sick, and to the remainder of the people, the youth, he gave wheat. Thus, the king did all the days of the famine. The king fed the people all the days of the famine and also fifty thousand foreigners who came to him because of the famine, and the king fed eighty thousand *homers* (and a *homer* was ten *ephahs*)[9] to other strangers from his own wealth.[10]

The people of Judah loved him from that day hence, and all the nations surrounding him and those afar loved him, and his name went forth throughout the lands; he shielded his people like a wall, saving them from famine. The people forgot all the evil that he did before and praised him as they saw him in a time of trouble and did not speak evil of him but only good. His enemies too spoke no evil of him out of fear and terror, for he frequently changed his royal clothing and went among the people in poor clothes so he would not be recognized. He spoke with the people and examined them, and when he found one who loved him, he honored and enriched him, but when he found one who was his enemy, he killed him with harsh torments.

He made the people swear and bound them in oath, but many did not wish to take the oath; but they could not escape him until he made them swear allegiance to him. At that time, he crushed those people who did not take the oath. Only the Pharisee masters, Hillel and Shamai and their colleagues, he did not force to swear since they were loyal to the king. For on the day that Herod and Antonius besieged Jerusalem, these Pharisees persuaded the people to let Herod into the city and to enthrone him, saying: "For the sins of the nation he will surely rule!" [cf. Job 34:30]. This is why he did not bring them under oath. Also, the teachers of the Hasidim he did not bring under oath for the sake of Menaḥem, the teacher of the Hasidim, for Menaḥem was a wise and righteous man in those days, and there were many like him among God's people in those days.

Josephus ben Gurion relates in his book: "I have many things to write of the wisdom of God's people, for they were wise: nowhere in the world were there

---

8. The Hebrew is creative: the verb *hudal* is passive, made from the adjective *dal*, for poor; the word *zol* implies the ships' merchants found the markets cheap. Cf. *AJ* 15.299ff.

9. *Corus autem habet modia Attica decem* (*homer* = *cores* = ten Attic *modia*); cf. Marcus *ad locum*.

10. *AJ* 15.314, has Herod give to foreigners over ten thousand *cori* and throughout the kingdom eighty thousand *cori*.

wise men as in God's people, and wisdom only reigned among God's people.[11] Through this Menahem, all the nations would recognize and know how wise were the other colleagues of Menahem," as written in the book of Joseph's wisdom, for Joseph ben Gurion wrote books of wisdom, books in which he did not write about wars but only about wisdom.

When Herod was a lad going to the sages to learn, Menahem was sitting in the assembly of the elders, the sages, and in the college of righteousness.[12] Menahem saw the lad passing, and he rose and prostrated himself on the ground before the lad and said: "Long live the king!" But the lad thought that he was laughing at him and cursed the sage. The sage grabbed him and slapped his buttocks just as they slap lads and said to him: "You shall surely rule, and great wealth will increase in your kingdom. When you sit upon the throne of your kingdom, remember the slap I gave you, for it is a sign to you of the transgressions that you will sin in the future and do great evils—but you will also do good things; so listen to my advice: seize the good and leave off the bad! But I chastise you for naught with much talk; I foresee the future that you will not leave off wickedness!" Then Menahem wept and wailed and, seizing him again, slapped him on the buttocks, and he went his way.

When Herod ruled just as the sage had spoken, he remembered all these things and, summoning Menahem, said to him: "What you said has come true, so I know that God's wisdom is in you. Speak now and inform me of the years I will reign: how many will I live, and how many I will rule!" But the sage was silent and did not answer. When the king saw that he did not answer at all, he was much alarmed and said to himself: "Verily this sage knows that my days draw nigh; that is why he is silent." Then the king asked him again: "Tell me, please, will I rule ten years?!" Menahem answered and said: "Ten and also twenty and even thirty and more." And the king said: "How many more?" But the sage was silent and did not answer him further about these matters. The king rejoiced over Menahem's words and believed him, honoring him and giving him great wealth. Such is the wisdom that existed among God's people in those days.

---

11. Based on Latin Eccl 24:1–16 (cf. Hebrew original: *Sefer Ben Sira Ha-Shalem*, ed. M. Segal [Jerusalem, 1958], 1–18).

12. *Ḥavuroth ha-ẓedek*: title known from tenth-century academy in Jerusalem; academies in Italy called *ḥavurah*. *Megillat Aḥimaaẓ* (ed. Klar), 36, 44, 80, 89, 44; Bonfil, *History and Folklore*, 308–9 and note. Title may also derive from the then recently (ca. 800) discovered Dead Sea Scrolls. Flusser's introduction to *Josippon*, 2.108ff. [SB]

50. HEROD'S CONSTRUCTION

In the eighteenth year[1] of King Herod, after having smitten all the kings around him, after having built all the great cities and the fortresses, and Lord, God of Israel, having relieved His people from all its enemies around, King Herod gathered all his chiefs and warriors and the rest of the people and spoke to them these words: "Give ear and listen [Deut 31:30], people whom God has chosen to be a nation precious to Him among all nations for the love of your ancestors and for the oath sworn to them and the covenant He sealed with them. For these He has rescued us in many wars, and He has conquered for us many nations and mighty kings, except for the kings of the Romans, who are our friends and comrades and lords over all the kingdoms.

"And now my brothers and friends, God has given us peace all around and has granted us relief, as you see with your own eyes today. Why should we not repay Him according to His deeds and His good acts which He has rendered unto us and done for us; why should we be lazy and not rebuild His Temple and His House like the First Temple? For our ancestors who returned from the exile built it narrow and not according to the measure of the first [Temple]. But it is not proper to denounce our ancestors in this matter,[2] for they were slaves to the kings of Persia and they built according to the measurements that the Persian kings allowed them. Afterward they were slaves to the kings of Greece until the Hasmoneans arose and were liberated and seized the kingdom, but they could not build the Temple because of the wars that occupied them. Now there is no foe [*satan*] or obstacle [*pegʻa rʻa*], and I have built great cities to magnify your name: I did not build them in my name, for I am one man while you are a great and mighty people.

---

1. *AJ* 15.380; cf. Rashi to b. *Baba Batra* 3b.
2. The author's opinion expressed by Hebrew for "derogate" or "slander," translating Latin *accusare* (*AJ* 15.386), as in chap. 42.

"Be strong and of good courage, my brothers and friends, and let us build the House of God just like the First Temple according to its length and breadth and height; let us act and be successful!"

The people were silent and said nothing, for they feared lest the Temple be torn down and the building delayed. When the king saw that the people feared lest the Temple be torn down and the construction delayed, the king said: "We will not tear down the Temple before we arrange all the materials for the reconstruction of the Temple."

And so the king did, arranging all the material to rebuild the Temple from his wealth and from his treasures: wood, stones, carts to carry the stones, gold, silver, and precious jewels, ten thousand skilled artisans and one thousand priests to enter the sanctuary, the place where no foreigner could approach. He arranged everything and presented it to the people. When the people saw that the king had arranged everything, they rejoiced and said to the king: "Let us act and succeed!"

When the king saw that the heart of the people was united to build God's Temple, he razed its foundations and set [new] foundations of huge stones and built the Temple upon them.

The Temple that King Herod built was 100 cubits long, 100 cubits wide, and 120 cubits high; only he increased the building's height by a further 20 cubits[3] of the Temple's roof: and the foundations stood upon 20 cubits below [ground level].[4] The stones of which the king built the Temple were white as snow. The length of one stone was 25 cubits, 12 cubits wide, and 8 cubits high: the same measure for all the stones from the Temple's foundation unto its tip; the Temple rose loftily and could be seen from afar.

He had the Temple decorated completely: its doorposts and its thresholds, and he made the locks of silver. He made curtains for the doors: he made a curtain for each door according to the measure of the door; thus he did for every door, and the curtain was gold weave, blue and purple and crimson, precious stones and gold speckles; and he set on the curtain a wreath of flowers made of gold. He made the Holy of Holies[5] its length and width as it was before and set it along the width of the Temple as the law orders.

The king made columns of silver; their pedestals of silver and their hooks he made of gold. He made a vine[6] of pure gold and set it on the tops of the columns,

---

3. The author adjusted the roof assuming that the building was a cube.
4. In the source, twenty cubits sank after the foundations dried.
5. Cf. 2 Chron 3:8; 1 Kings 6:3; Ezek 41:4.
6. *AJ* 15.395; cf. m. *Middot* 3:8. The Hebrew is a model of style.

one thousand talents of pure gold its weight.[7] The vine was a work of art: its twigs,[8] its leaves and its flowers of shining gold, and its clusters were of greenish gold, and its grapes and grape-pips and grape-skins [cf. Num 6:4] were made of precious stones and all of it [intricate] lacework. The vine amazed the eye of all who beheld it and brought joy to the heart of anyone who saw it; and many of the Roman authors testify that they saw it at the destruction of the Temple, as Joseph ben Gurion related.

He made the inner hall and set it along the width of the Temple;[9] he built in front of it two walls[10] and bound [its stones] with iron from outside, and no one else knows the skill for this work anymore. And the king made a level place around the Temple and filled every hollow and so made the whole place level.

He surrounded the Temple with four halls.[11] He made the East Hall and set it along the east side of the Temple, its back facing the east and its front facing the Temple, its length 250 cubits,[12] its width 100 cubits according to the measure of the Temple, and its height 120 cubits. He made the courtyard in front of the East Hall and made it all covered with tiles.

He made 160 columns in four rows, 40 columns to the row, and the length of each column 50 cubits,[13] its thickness one-third of a cubit [*ulna*], the same measurement for 160 columns; and between each column 15 cubits; and the length of the courtyard 720 cubits, for he extended the construction toward the Kidron Valley.[14] He made vaults over the valley and built bridges and pavements above the vaults; building the construction over them, he raised the building considerably above the valley to the front of the Temple and made it with three roofs.[15]

Joseph ben Gurion related: "All those who stood in those days on the third roof and looked into the valley's depth could not see the vale's bottom because

---

7. Doubles Aristobulus's gift to Pompey (chap. 36).

8. See D. T. Rice, *Byzantine Art* (New York, 1968), 462–64.

9. Language of 1 Kings 6:3; 2 Chron 3:4, 8.

10. *AJ* 15.396 has the walls of the Temple's inner portico.

11. The author's influential misunderstanding of *quadriporticus* (= square hall) as "four halls" (e.g., Rashi, b. *Yoma* 23a). The author's Temple was a huge building, surrounded by four buildings forming a cross around it. His Temple then resembled a Byzantine cruciform church. [See the Church of the Apostles in Constantinople built in 536–546 (Procopius, *Buildings* 1.4.9–13), the model for Venice's San Marco, built in 1063–1095 (Rice, *Byzantine Art*, 99). SB]. See Flusser, *Josippon, ad locum*.

12. Based on Latin of *AJ* 15.400.

13. *AJ* 15.415 has 50 feet.

14. The mention in *AJ* 15.412 of a very deep valley to the east is the author's Kidron Valley. It is unclear whether the author assumed similar rows of columns in the other courtyards.

15. Vaults and roofs added to support the hall over the valley.

of the great height of the construction, for it was dark underneath and so the bottom could not be seen."

The king built a wall of silver between the hall and the Temple; he made a gold door in it, hanging over the door a sword, its weight one talent of pure gold; and he wrote upon the sword: "The foreigner who draws near shall die."[16]

He made the South Hall and set it along the southern side of the Temple, its back to the south and its front facing the Temple, its length 250 cubits, 100 in width according to the measurement of the Temple, 120 cubits high; and he set the courtyard before it. He made the hall high above the courtyard, and he enclosed the courtyard[17] and joined it to the eastern courtyard and made the gates as he made the eastern courtyard.[18] He made the hall in the west, where the sun sets, with its back facing the west and its front facing the Temple, its length 250 cubits and 100 cubits in width according to the measure of the Temple. He made the courtyard of the west and set it facing the hall toward the setting sun and made four gates in it: one gate looked out upon the palace of King Herod with the valley between [the Temple and the palace] in which there were three roads: two roads went outside the city, and one went down by terraces to the valley and then turned and climbed up to the city, for the city above the Temple appeared like a theater surrounded by a great valley from its entire southern side. He made the hall of the north and set it along the north side of the Temple, its back facing the north and its front facing the Temple, in length 250 cubits, 100 cubits in width according to the measurements of the Temple, and 120 cubits in height. He made the courtyard and set it along the North Hall, its length about 720 cubits and its width according to the measure of the hall and the Temple, its length and breadth according to the length and breadth of the eastern and southern courtyards. The halls and the courtyards were of one size, all three of them. Only the fourth courtyard alone was not of the same size, for the place was rocky; therefore, the king did not lengthen it [to the length of the other three].

The king set in [the fourth courtyard] four gates to the west, and four gates he set in the southern courtyard to the south and four gates in the northern courtyard. He set twelve gates for the three courtyards. But in the eastern courtyard the king set one great gate through which we entered with our wives and children. We entered it in those days only in holiness and in ritual purity, entering and walking upon the pavement of the courtyard before the hall facing the

---

16. Josephus's observation; see Num 1:51, 3:10 and 38, 18:7.
17. The author's intent is unclear, but apparently the entire courtyard was so enclosed. The South Hall parallels the East Hall above and the West Hall and the North Hall below.
18. Similar to the error below, where the North Hall is also 720 cubits.

Temple. Only we men entered the hall, for the women did not enter it, and into the House we did not come, for it was the place of the priests, and they, the priests did not come in the Holy of Holies save for the high priest once a year. But we saw everything that was in the Temple while we were standing within the hall[19] in those days: all the gold work in the Temple while the gate of the Temple was open as far as the courtyard. The gold vine and all its work, all the golden works that were in the House, all the trophies that the king had inserted into the wall of the Temple, the booty of the nations that God gave into his hand, these too we saw and rejoiced, just as Joseph ben Gurion describes.

All the work was finished at the end of eight years,[20] for in those eight years God did not let it rain on Jerusalem during the day, only at night, lest the construction of the Temple be hindered, according to the words of Joseph ben Gurion. King Herod offered up to God three hundred bullocks as burnt offerings; in addition, he donated sacrifices of burnt offerings and peace offerings in abundance,[21] for on the day of the king's annual feast—the anniversary of his receiving the kingdom—on that day, all the work for the House of God was completed. The king made a festival for the House of God for one full year, a feast[22] throughout that year in all the cities of Judaea. The people rejoiced exceedingly and praised God with joy and praise and with musical instruments: harps and lyres, ram's horns and bugles, and trumpet blasts over the construction of the House of God [cf. Ps 149], may it be rebuilt swiftly in our days, amen amen.

We have written only a little of the construction of the House because it was a prodigious enterprise. Therefore, we did not write of the half or even a third of it, for Joseph ben Gurion did not write in just one book about the construction of the House; he wrote in the *Book of the Wars*[23] and in his *Book of Wisdom*.[24] He wrote many books: books of wisdom and books of polemics and apologetics[25] in which he reproached gentile writers who slandered Israel. He refuted their words, overcoming them and vanquishing them and speaking well about his people and his family.

____

19. Josephus, not the author, speaks here as an eyewitness to the Temple. [See Judah ibn Mosqoni in Bowman, *Jews of Byzantium*, 136. SB]

20. *AJ* 15.421, has one and a half years; the complex was completed just prior to the Roman war.

21. The author erred: "others gave according to their capability."

22. Sloppy combination of several sections for this observation.

23. The author relied on *AJ*, despite *DEH*'s description of the Temple.

24. The author thought Josephus did write that book based on *AJ* 3.14.

25. I.e., *Against Apion*, but the author may not have actually read it.

51. HEROD'S SONS

After these events, Alexander and Aristobulus, Herod's sons whom his wife Mariamme bore him, came from the city of Roma. The lads came full of furor and ire over their mother's killing. They had support and power from their wives' families—for Alexander had married Glafyra, daughter of Archelaus, king of Cappadocia, and Aristobulus had married [Beronici], the daughter of Shlomith, Herod's sister. But they did not honor the king, their father, due to the hatred that they harbored against him for their mother's sake.

Herod recognized in their faces the evil of their heart, and also many gossipers warned the king to beware of his sons, saying that they would ever seek to avenge their mother. The king was shaken, so he brought to his house his son Antipater, whom Dositis [*filius Dosidis*] had born him; she was his first wife, whom he married before he reigned, and she was from a young family [*mispaḥah ẓe'irah*]. Herod had cast out her and her son long before because of his love for Mariamme, his wife, but now when he saw that Mariamme's sons hated him, he restored Dosis and her son Antipater to the palace. He set Antipater over his entire house and designated him as his successor. Antipater had continuously beseeched the king, saying: "I am from a young family since my mother is from a poor family, whereas my brothers are from a noble family, and they seek to kill you and me as well." Now Antipater was rather clever in doing evil and for plotting ill.

The king was quite angered, and he went to Roma, taking with him his son Alexander, and brought him to be judged and punished by Augustus. Alexander chose his words wisely before Augustus and his father; both were sitting together. He said: "Indeed I am greatly grieved for the death of my innocent mother, for it is not man alone[1] that feels grief and anxiety for his parents' ruin;

---

1. Cf. Latin of *AJ* 16.110.

even animals and cattle, too, pity their flesh and blood and their relatives—and how should I not feel compassion and anxiety when I remember the womb that I came from? But heaven forbid that I desecrate my father's [honor], for a mother's honor is like unto a father's honor, and as desecrating the mother would bring death to the son, so too would desecrating the father bring death to the son. But Antipater, my brother, he it was who inflamed my father's anger against us to kill us just as our mother was killed." He spoke many such words weeping and crying, and Augustus, king of Roma, and all his officers wept over Alexander's words.

Augustus begged Herod to have mercy on his sons, to have compassion for them and not be cruel to them. He seized Alexander and cast him at his father's feet, beseeching Herod to embrace his son and kiss him. Herod was reconciled to his son Alexander, embracing him and kissing him, as Augustus bade him. Augustus gave Herod a great gift of gold and silver, and the king returned to Jerusalem.

The king summoned the army and said to them: "Listen, my friends, I went to Roma to Augustus to join him in a trial to judge with him, for I did not want to judge alone which of my sons would succeed me. Both he and I decided that my three sons would be colleagues in the kingdom and all three would be enthroned after me, for Antipater is firstborn but his mother was not of a noble family, while the mother of Alexander and Aristobulus came from a noble family. Therefore, they will not rule over one another; rather, the three of them will be colleagues. You are witnesses this day with the Lord that I have given the kingdom to my three sons, for the Lord has given me an immense and extended realm. Honor my sons as is proper, not more than is proper while I still live, but be loyal to my sons, and I will reward each and every one of you according to his deed. Beware[2] of speaking evil and of evil councils, and don't speak excessively with my sons, for always much talk and feasting brings man to evil counsel, and words engender anger in the heart, and from anger man comes to evil thoughts. Just as the wind stirs up a calm sea and makes it storm, so evil words enrage hearts of men. You, my officers and warriors, advise my sons well and say good things to them, lest they rebel against their father and sin against God. And you, my sons, respect your father that your days may be long, and let each love his brother!" He kissed the three of them again in front of the army, bound them in one love; then he left the army, and each one went his way.

But the jealousy within Herod's house did not abate, for Mariamme's sons said: "It is not proper for Antipater to be our colleague, since his mother was

____

2. The author adds the speech; note contemporary Constantinopolitan politics.

from a low-class family." Antipater also was clever in doing evil. He flattered his brothers to their face by speaking peace to them, while he set men in hiding to report his brothers' words to his father. The spies reported what the youths said and did not say, for Antipater paid the spies.

Antipater's entire actions were to join company with wicked and evil counselors, sitting with evil men and treading the path of sinners. He would sit to eat and drink with them, and he bribed them to bear false witness against his brothers, saying that they wished to kill their father, the king; they came and told the king just as Antipater said. Antipater retorted deceitfully to his father: "Let the king not believe these words, for there is no evil in my brothers' hearts!" Thus, he deceived the king, who believed him, and through his cunning, he captured the king in his snare.

He bribed the king's brother Pherora as well and his sister Shlomith, to slander his brothers, for the king heeded their advice exceedingly and did nothing without their counsel, for Pherora, the king's brother, annually gave the king one hundred talents of gold from a Trans-Euphrates province.[3] The king loved him very much, and he gave him in marriage his wife's sister, and after her death, he gave him his daughter as wife. But Pherora tormented her through an affair with his concubine, so the king became angry with his brother, even more so because Herod was told by slanderers that he sought to give the king poison to drink. They also slandered Shlomith, saying that she sent a letter to Silio (Sylaeus), the king's enemy, to whore with her. But Pherora and Shlomith were quickly reconciled to the king, and all the king's anger poured out on Alexander's head, for Antipater hired wicked ones who said to the king: "We saw Alexander standing with his sword unsheathed in his hand to kill Antipater."[4]

Antipater called to the king and said: "My father, you know that until now I have stood by my brothers and spoke well of them in your presence—but now, behold, my brother Alexander has risen against me to kill me!"

Three of the king's eunuchs, one the king's cupbearer, one who brings dishes before the king at mealtime, and one who guards the king's bed came and said to the king: "Alexander came and gave us a bribe of much gold and further offered to lie with us as a woman. When we refused to heed him, he said to us: 'How long will you rely on this old man Herod, my father, the hair of whose head has already fallen out from old age? Trust in me and do my will, and I will give you great wealth on the day I reign as king, for soon I shall kill my father and rule, for I have a strong and mighty force of Judaean warriors who will help me kill him.'

---

3. The source excludes income from the Trans-Euphrates province.
4. The source has *pater* = father; the author's MS probably had Antipater.

When Herod heard, his anger burned within him and, seizing many of his servants, killed many of them. He also seized Alexander and imprisoned him in chains and iron bands and put him under guard. He seized also many of his servants, supporters of Alexander, and commanded to beat them and torture them cruelly so that they should tell the truth and reveal the secret of the plot that they had made with Alexander. Many of them who did not confess died in agony and harsh torments. But one of them, who could not suffer the blows, confessed and said: "It is true that Alexander and Aristobulus devised a plan to kill the king during mealtime when the king was busy eating and sits secure. Alexander and Aristobulus would leap upon him with unsheathed swords to kill the king and flee to Roma to take refuge until they would find favor in Augustus's eyes and request from him a force to come fight against Antipater, the king's son." When the king heard, he believed and seized Aristobulus, putting him in chains along with his brother Alexander.

When Alexander saw that he had become hateful to his father, he wrote four letters. He wrote libels in them slandering his brother Antipater's advisers and the king's brother Pherora and the king's sister Shlomith, saying: "It is true that I have sinned, but Pherora and Shlomith are the ones who incited me in these matters. Pherora has been the king's enemy since the day he had a quarrel with his wife, the king's daughter, on account of his concubine whom the king turned out of his house; from that day hence, he was the king's enemy." He wrote many more things about him [Pherora]; he also slandered Shlomith over the adultery that she committed with a certain young man;[5] he wrote many such things against the king's officers and counselors; and he sent these to the king.

At that time, Archelaus, king of Caphtor, father of Glafyra, Alexander's wife, came to the assistance of his son-in-law Alexander to save him from his father's hand by wisdom and cunning, for he knew that he could not save him either by fighting or begging. When he arrived at Herod's palace and faced him, he shouted in anger, saying: "Does my son-in-law Alexander, the murderer, still live? Where is he? I shall remove his head from upon him with my own hand, for as he is his father's enemy, so too is he my enemy, for he had no compassion on his father—so how could he have compassion on me?! Show him to me! I will take his bowels in my hand, and I will give my daughter to another man if she has not sinned. But if she has sinned, she too will die with him, for I did not give her to be an accomplice to the murderer. I am surprised at you, O king, if Alexander still lives, for it is not proper to delay vengeance on him from day to day. It was God who brought me to you to join with you in this revenge; on the day you

---

5. *DEH* 1.40.9 unclear; Josephus clearly indicates Alexander.

kill your son, I shall also kill my daughter. I gave her into your hand to be like a daughter to you, but she loved the wicked one and sinned against you. Therefore, there is a death sentence upon her since she did not tell you of the wicked one's plots. Let us hasten and kill the two of them, for it is not fitting to have mercy upon them. And if you have mercy upon your son, come, let us change places and roles: you kill my daughter, and I will kill your son, the murderer."

When the king heard the speech of Archelaus, he believed him, and his anger against his sons abated somewhat; he accepted Archelaus's loyalty and agreed to eat and drink with him in friendship. Thus, Archelaus deceived the mind of the king, who trusted him like a brother. When Archelaus, king of Caphtor, saw that he found favor in the king's eyes, he spoke to him, saying: "Pay attention to my words, King Herod. For what reason did your sons seek to raise their hand against you, and what did they lack with you? They lacked neither gold nor silver, nor did they lack kingship, for kingship too you gave them. They did not think evil against you except the counsel of wicked men and with the counsel of Pherora, your brother. For just as they incited you against the boys, so too they incited the boys against you and stole their mind, and they also stole your mind because you are old and wish to live in peace. They stirred up strife in your house between you and your sons and did not let you live in quiet and tranquility; they are the counselors of evil, sowers of strife, who deceived your old age and destroyed your sons."

The king listened to Archelaus's words, and his anger against Alexander and Aristobulus abated, but his anger flamed exceedingly against Pherora. When Pherora saw that the king's anger burned against him, and when he realized that the king listened to Archelaus, Pherora went to Archelaus, begging him to speak with his brother, the king, to forgive his sin. Archelaus said: "I will speak about you to the king, but when you come before the king, do not hide your sins; confess all that you have done and the strife that you incited between the king and his sons." Pherora came before the king and, falling to the floor at his feet, confessed to all that he had done, saying: "For the sake of the concubine whom the king separated from me, I became angry, and I did all this." Archelaus said to the king: "Bear the sin of your brother, for you two came forth from the same womb. I too have a brother who rebelled against me, but I forgave him. For what should a man do to his own flesh? If his hand hurt a man or his leg or if one of his bones hurt him, it would be fitting for him to take medicine to strengthen his limbs, since it is not good to cut off his own flesh." The king listened to Archelaus and, forgiving his brother, was reconciled to him. The king said: "You have come to us just as a doctor comes to the sick and heals him of his illness, so you have healed, and you have abated the anger in my heart against my sons. I beg you to forgive Alexander, my son, and do not take from him your daughter Glafyra, for I have loved her as my daughter. My son Alexander is a wicked man, but your daughter is a wise woman, and she will chastise him with words until he listens to her and no longer sins."

Archelaus said to Herod: "Let me to take her away from him and give her to one of your servants, but not to Alexander, for I hate him exceedingly." The king said to Archelaus: "Bear his sin on this day and forgive him!" Archelaus said: "I shall do according to the word of the king."

After this, Alexander and Aristobulus came before the king, and the king embraced them and kissed them; Archelaus too embraced Alexander and kissed him, and the sadness changed to joy and to feasting. By this deception, Archelaus saved Alexander from his father.

The king made a great feast and gave to Archelaus seventy talents of gold and a gold bed with precious jewels, handsome eunuchs, and a concubine beautiful and lovely to behold; her name was Pannychis. He commanded all his officers to give him a present, and they gave him great wealth. He went his way, the king accompanying him as far as Antiochia, whereupon the king returned to his home.

52. DEATH OF HEROD'S SONS

A man of Laconian seed named Euryclaus (Eurycles)[1] came to Jerusalem, a greedy man who loved gold; he brought the king an offering, and the king gave him double his offering. This was not enough for him, so he stood before the king and served him; he found favor in his [the king's] eyes, and the king received him among his advisers.

Euryclaus saw the hatred between Herod's firstborn, Antipater, and Mariamme's sons, Alexander and Aristobulus, and Antipater hired Euryclaus to slander his brothers. Euryclaus tempted Alexander with words and said to him:[2] "It is proper for you to reign alone over all Judaea, for you are a young warrior, a hero, and of a noble family. It is not fitting that Antipater be your partner in rule, for his mother was from a low-class family." Thus, he tempted the lad, and the boy told him all his thoughts and the cunning of Archelaus that saved him from his father, and Alexander uttered words against his father to Euryclaus and vented his spirit as boys would do.

Euryclaus went and told the king, saying: "It is not proper for me to hide all the wickedness that I see in your house. Your sons plot evil against you, as your son Alexander told me: 'How long will God not exact vengeance against my father, who killed my mother and her whole family and destroyed the whole kingdom!'" And the advice that Archelaus's father-in-law told him was to kill his father, for he was the blood avenger of his mother and his grandfather,[3] whom

---

1. Eurycles of Sparta; cf. *AJ* 16.301; *DEH* 1.41.2 has *Lacon genus* (from *BJ* 1.513); Pausanius (2.3.5, Loeb edition *ad locum*) praises him as "the builder of the finest baths in Corinth"; cf. St. Caratzes, *Les Tzacones* (Berlin, 1976), 75n22. [SB]

2. Author collapsed Eurycles's deceptive arguments to Alexander: Antipater had the right to rule from father and Alexander from mother.

3. *DEH* 1.41.3 errs *pace BJ* 1.525; Alexander's mother, Mariamme, was Hyrcanus's granddaughter.

Herod killed. Euryclaus related things that Alexander had not spoken and said: "Let it be known to you, O king—that your sons plotted with your officers to kill you while you were sitting peacefully."

The king investigated the matter and found nothing. But he did find a letter, written in the name of Alexander and Aristobulus, sent to one officer in one of the walled cities, saying: "When we have killed our father, we shall flee to you, and you receive us in your walled city until we have gathered our supporters." The king seized the officer and tortured him cruelly to make him confess, but the officer did not confess, and nothing was discovered. The king, in his great anger and ire, ordered his sons Alexander and Aristobulus to be bound in chains; he gave Euryclaus fifty talents of gold, and he [Euryclaus] went his way.

In those days, Herod went to Tyre by the sea; from there he came unto Caesarea, and to every place that he went, he dragged his sons with him bound in chains. All his force and his army had mercy and felt compassion for the boys—but their father had no pity. Within the camp was a valiant warrior who, from his youth, was skilled in war and grew old in active service; he had a son who was a supporter of the king's son Alexander and was his friend. Because of his son's love, the man took pity on the king's son Alexander when he saw him being dragged in iron chains; he cried out and said in a loud voice: "Mercy is lost, pity has gone, and truth is wanting!" He said to the king: "Woe unto the father like you, who has no pity for the sons of his loins. You believe your evil counselors. For they are your enemies who seek to remove your sons from you and leave you alone and deserted without sons, and then they will rise up against you and kill you. Where is your wisdom, Herod, and where is your heart that you do not understand how your evil counselors enticed you, arousing you to shed your sons' blood?" So Tiro finished speaking to the king in this way.

The king's advisers said to the king:[4] "Let it be known to the king that by speaking these words Tiro has only shown the hatred his heart feels toward you. This Tiro plotted with the man whose task is to shave your beard, saying to him: 'As you are shaving the king's beard with a sharp razor, when you pass the razor over the king's hairs under his beard, slice his throat and kill him, and Alexander, the king's son, will give you great wealth as a reward for your action.'"

The king ordered to seize Tiro and his son and Tryfon, whose task was to shave the king's beard; the king commanded that Tiro and Tryfon be beaten cruelly and harshly. When Tiro's young son saw his father's beating and harsh torments, his compassion for his father was aroused, and he said to the king:

---

4. *DEH* 1.41.11 has Tiro and his comrades seized and among them Tryphon, the king's barber, who slandered himself with the author's statements of the king's advisers.

"If you take pity on my father and do not torture him further and forgive him, I will tell you everything and reveal all the secrets." The king said: "Behold, I have forgiven your father and will not do him any harm; just tell me the truth." The boy answered: "It is true that your son Alexander incited my father to kill you, but my father did not wish to raise a hand against you;[5] he asked Tryfon to do the things that you have heard." The boy said these things to save his father, but it did not help him.

The king summoned all his officers and servants and spoke unto their ears about Tiro and Tryfon and stirred them up against them; on that day, the army killed Tiro and his son with staffs before the king. As for Alexander and Aristobulus, his sons, whom his wife Mariamme bore him, he commanded that they be taken to Shomron, which was renamed Sebastia, and, at their father's command, the two of them be hanged on a tree,[6] and they died.

---

5. The author's correct appreciation of the psychological situation.
6. Renders *strangulantur*.

53. THE WICKED ANTIPATER

Herod's son Antipater, whom Dosis, his wife, had born him, rejoiced. He rejoiced over his brothers' downfall, and for this reason, the hatred of the whole people was aroused against him. Nor did Antipater cease from deceptions and plots when he saw the children of the murdered Alexander and Aristobulus begin to grow up. Alexander's sons were Tigranes and Alexander, named after his father, whom Glafyra, Archelaus's daughter, bore him; and Aristobulus's sons were Herod, Agrippas, and Aristobulus, after his father, whom Beronici, daughter of Shlomith, the king's sister, bore him; and two daughters, called Erodiades (Herodias) and Mariamme. Antipater saw that the king changed his attitude toward his slain sons' children to take pity on them.

The day came, and the king gathered his officers and warriors and said to them: "I know that I have reached old age and my days are drawing nigh, and I continuously see before me the children of my slain sons, and I cannot look upon them save with tears and weeping for I am the one who brought upon myself this weeping; by my own hand, I removed them from before me in my anger. Now I have mercy upon their children because they are little and because they are orphans; therefore, I have commanded that they be given helpers who will be like fathers to them." The king spoke to his brother Pherora: "You, Pherora, betroth your daughter to the first born of Alexander, and you be unto him as a father." He said to his son Antipater: "Betroth Aristobulus's daughter to your eldest son. Also, my young son Herod will betroth the other daughter of Aristobulus." The king grabbed their right hands and, putting one hand into the hand of the other, arranged the marriages. All those standing before the king rejoiced, except for Antipater, who was very angry, as his face showed, over the fact that Alexander's son took Pherora's daughter, for Pherora was the king's brother and wielded great authority, and also Archelaus, king of Caphtor, was the grandfather of Alexander's boy; Antipater feared lest they might help Alexander's boy.

Antipater wept before his father and said to him: "What did I gain by your giving me the kingdom while you gave the power to Alexander's boy by giving him your brother Pherora's daughter, and he is the son of the daughter of Archelaus, king of Caphtor? How can I survive before these two powerful men?" But his father said to him: "I have ordered that you reign after me; so why fear, when the entire kingdom is in your hand?"

Antipater was afraid of all the king's sons, for the king had nine wives who bore sons and daughters; only two were barren and did not bear children, but the others bore sons and daughters. Dosis, his wife, bore him Antipater; Mariamme, his wife also, bore him Herod the Younger; his wife Malthacis bore him Antipas and Archelaus and a daughter, Olympiades (Olympias); his wife Cleopatra, the Jerusalemite, also bore him Herod and Philip; also Herodipallas[1] was his wife, and she bore him Phasael. Moreover, the king had daughters, one named Roxane and the other Shlomith; and their mothers, the king's wives, were Phaedra and Elpis. Antipater feared all the families of the king; so he allied with the king's brother Pherora and gave him a gift of gold and precious jewels. These two wicked men, counselors of evil, joined together and entreated the king and, stealing his mind, canceled the marriages that the king had made for the children of the slain. Antipater and Pherora were accustomed to feast daily, and the two plotted together often.

One day the king got angry with Pherora and said to him: "Get to your house. You may not see my face again!" So Pherora, the king's brother, went and sat in his house and did not see the face of the king. The king sent his son Antipater to Roma to Augustus, king of Roma, to request his peace.

In those days, Pherora, the king's brother, fell ill with a sickness of which he died, and he sent to the king, entreating him to come to him to grant amnesty to his family and his sons. The king had compassion for his brother and went to him and wept over him. When he died, he made him a state funeral and brought him to Jerusalem and buried him in the grave of his fathers with great honor. But the king did not forget the rumor[2] that his brother plotted to poison him, a rumor he had heard while Pherora was still alive. Wishing to discover the matter, he seized his brother's eunuchs and his maidservants and ordered them to be tormented cruelly with all kinds of beating and harsh torments.

One of the maid servants, who was in agony, cried out and said: "O Lord of the universe [*Deus omnipotens*] in whose hand is every living thing, you have the power and might to save us from these cruelties for we are dying without guilt

---

1. The author's MS apparently ran the two names together.
2. Actually, the rumor was that Herod had poisoned Pherora.

and without sin. O Lord of the universe, turn this sin upon the head of Dositis, Antipater's mother, who did all these wicked things by regularly feasting the king's brother Pherora and the king's son Antipater in her house; when they had left the king's feast, they would come to the house of Dosis, Antipater's mother, and sit drinking every night plotting against the king. [They planned that] Antipater will go to Roma and Pherora will stand by the king[3] [and] serve him a deadly drink to kill him. Antipater will come from Roma to reign, for he said: 'If we do not kill him, we shall not escape his hand, just as his sons whom he killed were not saved from his hand. And upon whom will he take pity, who had no compassion for his wife whom he loved and her sons? We have no choice save to distance ourselves from him and to run away from this evil beast, for he made me king in deceit. But when shall I rule? He still looks like a lad, while I have already aged and white hairs have begun to sprout on my head; and who will know who will die first, I or he? And further, the children of my murdered brothers have begun to grow up, just as when you cut off the serpent's head and his head lives and bites. His young son Herod, whom Mariamme bore him, is loved by his father. I know that he will not give me the kingdom; he just deceives me and seeks not good for me but rather ill, for he is an enemy to all his sons, his wives, his brothers, and his entire family. Behold, his brother Pherora, who from his youth served him, is his enemy, and he said to me in secret as follows: "Don't be friendly with your uncle and don't speak with him; I will give you one hundred talents of gold for he is an enemy to all men." Pherora said: "Who can bear his wickedness? Perhaps if we turned into animals and beasts that live in the forest and in the field, we could be saved from his hand: for a man who does not have compassion for his sons, how can he have compassion for his brother? There is no relief or deliverance other than our right hands and our swords. Be strong and let us strengthen ourselves to kill him before he kills us!"'"

The maid servant spoke all these words to the king and saved her life and the lives of her friends from the cruel beatings, for the king believed her words concerning the matter of the one hundred gold talents that was said to have given to Antipater, for no one had heard of this matter except for Antipater. For this reason, the king believed Pherora's maidservant.

The king ordered Antipater's secretary, a loyal servant, be seized and cruelly beaten. When he could no longer bear it, he confessed and said: "It is true that Theudion, friend of Antipater, the king's son, sent from Egypt a small vessel, full of deadly poison for the king to drink. Antipater took the vessel and gave it to Pherora and said to him: 'When I go to Roma, give this to my father lest they say that I killed him.' Pherora took the vessel and gave it to his wife for keeping."

---

3. The source has Pherora go to Perea.

The king sent for Pherora's wife, saying: "Take in hand the vessel that contains the deadly poison that my brother gave you to keep and hasten to bring it to me!" When the wife heard, she said to the men whom the king sent to her: "Wait until I bring it, and I will go with you to the king!" The woman went to the roof of her house to fetch the vessel, but fearing to go to the king, she threw herself from the top of the roof to the ground; but she fell not on her head but on her side and did not die. This was from God's doing in order to repay Antipater in kind for what he had done to his brothers.

They brought the woman before the king on her bed, and the king said to her: "Pray tell me please the truth lest I cut your flesh and cast it to the dogs. If you reveal the secret and speak the truth, I will pardon you and all your household."

The woman answered and said: "Hear, O king, whom God has chosen; He is witness that I shall not hide anything from you now, for why should I conceal from you now, and for whom would I preserve the trust? For I did not reveal my husband Pherora's secret while yet he lived, not even were my neck to the sword, but he escaped from your hand and went to the place where the servant has refuge from his master, so why should I hide anything from you? Or [should I hide it] from love of Antipater, your wicked son who has brought me to this ruin?"

She said: "Remember, O king, the day that you came to your brother, on the day he was ill from his fatal illness, and you wept upon his face with tears as brothers are wont to do, and when you stopped in the evening and went to your majesty's bed to lie until morning, that very night your brother called me and said: 'My wife!' I said: 'Here I am, your maidservant, my lord!' He said: 'Did you see the tears that my brother wept over me?' I said: 'I saw, my lord!' He said: 'I was trapped in that wicked Antipater's snare, for he waylaid me and trapped me with his wiles just as a man stalks the bird, for I considered killing my brother, the king, who raised me and treated me well, thus repaying wickedness for good. Now go and bring me the vessel with the deadly poison that the wicked Antipater gave me and pour it out upon the ground before my eyes so that Antipater may not find it to kill my brother, the king.' I brought the vessel and spilled out the poison in it on the ground before him, but I left a little in it and saved it in the same vessel in order to show you, for I feared this day that has come upon me now." The woman raised her hand and held out the vessel to the king; the king took the vessel from the woman's hand into his hand and pardoned the woman; then he commanded the physician to treat her and sent her home. At that time,[4] the king sent a letter to Roma to Antipater, saying: "Come and don't tarry, for I cannot rule the kingdom without your being here!"

---

4. King summons Philip and Archilaus in *DEH* 1.44.7.

54. DOWNFALL OF THE WICKED ANTIPATER

In those days,[1] the king's sons Archelaus and Philippus were in Roma along with Antipater, who, being jealous of them, sent a letter to the king saying: "These sons of yours are also your enemies, for they spoke evil against you before Augustus and his officers." The king wrote back to him: "Truly I know that they are my enemies, but hasten to me and do not tarry, bring your brothers with you, and I will exact vengeance against them; I will make you king before I die."

A full seven months after the king sent the letter, Antipater came from Roma and, arriving at a city called Torinti (Tarentum), heard that Pherora, his uncle, had died. He wept and mourned deeply—sobbing not out of love for Pherora but because he was left alone with no one to help him kill his father. From there, the ship sailed, arriving at the port of Caesarea, and, hearing that the king had demoted his mother from the status of queen mother, Antipater was seized by great panic.

When Antipater realized that his entire secret was revealed, he considered fleeing by ship. But every one of the eunuchs[2] with him craved to go home, saying to him: "If you flee, your enemies will slander you in every way before the king; it is not good that you give such opportunity to your enemies. Rather, when you go to the king, all your enemies will fall, and those who slandered you will fall into the pit that they dug. When the king sees you, he will raise you high and magnify you as in days gone by, and he will bring low your detractors." He believed their counsel and, disembarking ashore from the ship, began to wade on foot toward the land—but no one went out to greet him. Some feared lest

---

1. The author loosely follows *DEH* 1.44.1 through 1.45.
2. Renders *amici* (friends) and also reflects the author's contemporary world.

they be punished by the king, while others [stayed away] because of the hatred that they had for him; therefore no one went forth to greet him, and he saw that he was trapped like the fish caught in a net.

From there, he traveled to Jerusalem and found no one along the way who would speak with him, and also, the king's guards accompanied him lest he flee. He entered the city and went not to his house but up to the king's house; he arrived suddenly and fell at the king's feet; but the king hid his face lest he see him. Antipater rose and sought to embrace his father, but the king repelled his son's embrace and said: "Murderer! You are not ashamed to embrace the one whom you sought to kill, and you approach me with blood-stained hands! First, wash your hands clean if you can and cast off the rumor that I have heard about you! Tomorrow you will come before me along with Varo (Varus), the envoy whom Augustus sent, and speak your piece; even though you are a murderer, still I have given you a chance to speak on the morrow, and I will calmly listen to your words." Antipater left the king in fear and trembling and went home; not knowing heads or tails about the matter, he was totally shaken up.

His mother came to him with his wife, and both explained the matter to Antipater. When Antipater heard, he began to pull himself together, [planning] how could he save himself with words from the accusation with which he was charged.

On the morrow, the king sent for and assembled his officers and friends and also gathered all the detractors who spoke against Antipater; he sent for and summoned Varus, the Roman whom Augustus had sent to seek King Herod's peace. As Varus sat before the king, the king said: "Have you heard, Varus, how my son Antipater rose against me and sought to kill me?" And Varus said: "Let the king judge with mercy!"

The letter that Dosis, Antipater's mother, sent to her son was read out before the king: "Your father has heard all about your plot to kill him. Be on guard lest you come here without strength and force! Request a force for yourself from Augustus, for here there is neither relief nor deliverance save with a mighty hand and fighting."

The king sent for Antipater and brought him [Antipater] before him [Herod]. When he [Antipater] came, he fell heavily at his father's feet just as a man drops from a sword blow. The king commanded those who were standing before him: "Be silent!" And all the people hushed.

The king began to speak: "No righteous man in the land would suffer this wickedness or one forbearing to endure Antipater's treachery. I know, Varus, that you despise me because I sired such sons and killed two of them, but those two sons, as I understand, died innocent; they did not sin against me;

rather, I killed them through this one's slander. Nor did they sin against this one, so he hated them for no reason; he incited me against them in his jealousy and envy that their mother was from an important family and the kingdom was rightly theirs. But I acted like an ignoramus and made this dunce king—while he turned enemy to his brothers and stole their senses to provoke them against me; they turned against me because of this Antipater's words. And I too, through this Antipater's tongue, turned enemy to my sons. It is true that I killed them, and they died, to their father's grief and to their brother Antipater's joy; and I weep over my sons [cf. 2 Sam 19:1] while he rejoices over his brothers. How could I not weep, O Varus, when I constantly behold in my house my sons' widowed wives? I killed my sons because they rose against me over the kingdom that I gave to this one, and now I see their orphaned sons all the time and their widowed wives. But nothing can be done, for I extirpated all from the inner circle of my house and made room for this wicked one. Nor was it enough for him that he killed his brothers through his wicked counsel and deceit: he sought to kill me. I brought all this upon myself because I raised him up over all my sons and made him king to succeed me. Nor did he wait until the day of my death from God's hand but was lustful and hastened to rule by spilling his father's blood and so repay me evil for good, he whom I loved, this hateful and abominable one, to whom I gave sovereignty while yet I lived. I also gave him 350 talents of gold and sent him to Roma to be befriended by Augustus, king of Roma. God forbid you should say that his brothers, whom I killed, had risen against me as this one has; rather, this one has done all the evil, this bloodthirsty deceiver.

"Guard yourself, Varus, protect yourself lest you heed the sound of his pleadings and lest you have pity because of his tears. For this one is skilled in deceiving and stealing the senses, as he stole my senses and stirred me up against his brothers in his continued slanderous mutterings against them. He guarded me in deception and brought me to bed, watching all around over me to appear like a protective wall in everyone's eyes—but in secret, he was like an ambusher and an enemy. I trusted him; I put my soul and my bones in his hand! How did I escape from his hand? It seems to me that I am alive, but I am not alive because I am dead; only in a dream am I alive. Who will believe that I escaped the hand of one whom I put in power over me, and who would believe that this one, whom I loved and made precious and great above all my sons, would rise up against me? For this reason, I weep, O Varus, that I remain alone, and I cry out, for I have beheld great sorrows that the sons of my loins rose against me. But I shall not pardon the multitude of sins and the plentiful spilling of blood, nor shall I have mercy for anyone who would thirst to drink my blood; and even were I to find this sin among all my sons, I would not pardon nor have mercy!" The king spoke this in furor and anger, choking his voice in his ire, and was silent.

Antipater raised his head a little from off the ground just as a man hit by a sword would raise his head. Opening his mouth, he said: "My father, your very contentious and accusatory words will help me and stand by me as an advocate, and just as you sought to do me wrong, you have justified me with your words. Verily, as you said, I was your protector—how could I murder when I was on guard? How could I keep watch to harm you when I watched over you lest your enemies hurt you either openly or in secret? And who does not know that God will exact vengeance upon a man who seeks evil against his father?! Even if I were the most ignorant of creatures, even I knew this. And if I did not fear God, I could learn from what happened to my brothers, lest what happened to them could happen to me. According to your words, they sought to kill you because of their jealousy and envy for me, namely, that you made me king over them, and they were from an esteemed family. They were afraid because you made me king; therefore, they stood against you to do you harm, and they died for their sin. As for me, it is not proper that I rule, for I know of sovereignty only from your hand, so why would I have plotted to kill you? To receive kingship? But you already made me king. Because of hatred? But you already love me. Because of my dishonor? But you already honored me. These, my brothers, were angry because you made me king, and if you had given them sovereignty, they would not have risen against you. Out of fear, they sought to raise their hand against you, for they saw how you had made me king. But I, just as your voice testifies in my behalf, did not fear, for I was crowned king and sat in confidence, and I was not afraid, save from you alone.

"What would have incited me to kill you? If poverty—for poverty tempts a man to kill a person to take wealth—but you already gave me great wealth, and you sent me to Roma, where I saw kings who came there to seek the peace of Augustus, who is Caesar; kings like me they were, but they were not rich like me. Moreover, that Augustus who is Caesar, I reconciled him with you and made him your friend so that he did not support Sylion (Sylleus), who was fighting against you, even though Sylleus gave him gold aplenty to supply him with a force to fight against you. But the king did not wish to listen to him when I went there, for he favored me, and Caesar became your friend and turned into an enemy of Sylleus. And who revealed the secret of others who plotted to kill you? Only I revealed their secret. How could I, who seized Corintho (Corinthus), who ambushed you, be a murderer? Did I not seize him? Did I not torment him with harsh blows and sound thrashing to confess? And he did confess and spoke the truth, and I exacted vengeance against him. Had I been silent and quiet, I could have killed you with my silence—but I saved you from his hand, just as you know. Even if brutality lives within me or the snake's fury, I would have to don humility from your benefices and your mercy that you rendered me, from your plentiful goodness that you removed my brothers as kings before me and that you crowned me, though it were not fitting for me to rule. Not only did you crown me your successor, but I ruled alongside you and took a portion of your kingdom.

"Woe unto me, how ruined, who, because of the multitude of your munificence and the beneficences that you have rendered unto me! For this reason, jealousy has been stirred up against me! Woe unto me, a simpleton, that I left you and went, giving opportunity to those who were envious of me and dominion to those who lay in wait to ambush me! For when I went for the sake of your life, I put my life in danger [see Judg 9:17]. But I did not go to satisfy my craving, nor was it for me to consider the way [cf. Prov 15:9]; it is yours to calculate the path, so you sent me. For you I have lived, my father, not for myself, lest Sylleus disgrace your old age and take the kingdom from you while you yet lived and lest Caesar be alienated from your friendship. Behold, Caesar, who sits in Roma and rules throughout the land, will testify in my behalf; even though he is not here, he knows my wants and my words that I have spoken about my father."

Antipater called out and said: "Caesar, Caesar, even though you are not here, answer me and give testimony in my behalf before my father as to what I spoke in your ears about my father and what you, O Caesar, said about the murderers who stood before you in judgment! Did you not exact vengeance upon them? Did you not hate the murderers? And how did I speak before you, to murder my father? Speak and testify, O Caesar, all that you have heard. Though you be in Roma and I in Jerusalem, I am being punished before my father without you, and you are not here. But you are here, for your letters are here and your letters are in my hand, which every murderer shall fear and every hater of murderers will choose. Accept, O my father, the letter of Caesar, your friend, and it will teach you how I helped you before him! Accept the letter of Caesar that calls for your peace, written with the right hand of Caesar, a right hand that has done no evil to you, that put the royal crown upon your head! Who would hate me more than Caesar if he found such a sin in me? But heaven forbid it! It was because of Sylleus that I left, lest he do harm to you, for you sent me. Remember, father, that I did not want to go; I saw already those who were jealous of me digging a pit at my feet. But I did accept the hardship of going for the sake of your salvation, and I loved rather than hated the hardship for your sake. But I am distressed by the hardship here before you, whereas I was not distressed by my hardship on the road [Exod 18:8]. I call out to

Caesar, not that he should hear my words but that his letters should acquit me from this charge. Here I am, my father, I traveled, going from Caesar's presence and coming before you; I hurried to come before you. Perhaps I should not have left you then, but you sent me, and I went.

"Here I am, my father, and here are my witnesses. Don't say that I have brought you human witnesses, for some men fear to testify to the truth, while others take a bribe, but my witnesses, who will testify for me and bear evidence on my behalf, do not fear you nor hide the truth. They will not take a bribe to bear false witness and deceit like men, for all men are deceitful [Ps 116:11]. Behold, now I call three witnesses before you, and these three will testify in my behalf: neither heaven nor earth nor the sea will have mercy [cf. Isa 9:18] on a man who rises up against his father's blood. I came traveling under the heavens, so why did the sky not harm me and strike me with lightning and kill me? Also, I crossed the sea traveling in the midst of currents of water, so why did it not drown me? I went forth on the land, back and forth upon the earth, so why did it not open its mouth and swallow me as it did Dathan and Abiram,[3] who rebelled against Moses, who did not sire them? And Absolom when he was fleeing from the battle to save his life, the land did not permit him to flee and commanded one of her trees; it seized him by the hairs of his head, hanging him until his murderer came and killed him. Thus, he was not allowed to flee to his father, for, had he come unto his father, he would have been saved. Behold, here I am, I have come before you, so why should I die?

"David exacted revenge for the killing of his son and commanded that the murderer be killed, but I shall not wait for vengeance upon my enemies. But in one thing, suffer my face and heed my voice: do not give me over to others to exact vengeance against me; before your own eyes exact vengeance against me without mercy. Do not search my face anymore but bring forth my intestines and ask them. Bring forth my guts and ask them if they plotted evil against you. Take out my heart from my bosom and cut it with a sword, chop it into pieces, and seek all the secrets that are in my heart. Spill out my blood and, as it oozes, ask it to speak the truth to you. And further, let all my flesh and bones be examined with fire to find the truth and seek and examine, investigate, and ask well of all my members if it is true that I thought to do you harm or not. Now, what are you waiting for, father? If you have pity on your son, cleanse me of the accusation—and if you do not have mercy, hasten to exact vengeance against me! If you say in your heart: 'I will not raise my hand against my son because

---

3. Also from *DEH*; but see the Jewish oath from Byzantium cited by J. Starr, *Jews in the Byzantine Empire, 641–1204* (Athens, 1939), doc. 109, 163f. [SB]

he is my flesh and my bone,' it was not your bone and your flesh that sought to raise his hand cruelly against you."

When he had finished speaking, all those who were standing before the king lifted their voices and wept. Only the king did not weep. Then Nicolaus, the author,[4] loyal friend to the slain youths, Herod's sons, this Nicolaus, the author, responded at the king's command. He spoke to those who were weeping from Antipater's words, revealing his cunning before them as follows: "For what are you crying, and for whom do you have pity? If you have compassion and pity, pity the youths, precious sons who died for nothing, whom this one killed through slander and wicked cunning! For if this one should be spared, the king's whole house will fall into ruin, should this one who killed his brothers and also had no compassion on his father be spared." Nicolaus then sweetly raised his voice like those who keen over the dead. He called to the slain and said: "Awake, Alexander, get up, Aristobulus, and behold your enemy, who seeks to escape with words. He killed you, innocent ones, by bringing false witnesses to testify against you when he wrote letters full of lies to punish you by slandering you to your father; and his father did not think he could lie against his brothers. Now let him surely die who killed his brothers, he who advised his father to distance them from him lest he see their death, so he killed them from afar. If this one should be spared, all the king's sons will die. For this one is skilled in mixing deadly poisonous drinks and in stealing people's sense to deceive men; Pherora, the king's brother, was faithful to the king and very loyal, but this cruel one stole his sense and converted him to the king's enemy."

Nicolaus spoke many more words to unfold his wickedness upon him and to bring forth all the evils that he committed upon him; then Nicolaus finished speaking and was silent.

The king said to Varus: "Ask him if he has anything to say!" But Antipater did not respond further, save that he said: "God will be a witness that I am innocent of all this." The king said: "Bring the vessel that contains the deadly poison!" They brought the vessel that Antipater gave to Pherora. The king said: "Bring before me a man under sentence of death!" He [the condemned man] was brought before the king, and he [the king] commanded them to force him [the man] to drink, and they did so; the man drank and died at once. The king took from the potion and gave some of it to Varus to bring it before Caesar, so that Caesar might see the wickedness of Antipater.

---

4. *DEH* 1.45.1 has speech of Nicolaus of Damascus; the author's source already has "the writer."

The king commanded to bind Antipater in chains and put him in jail. Yet, even though he was in prison, he did not cease from deceit and slander. He wrote a letter in the name of Acme, maidservant to Caesar's wife Julius,[5] a letter full of curses and insults against the king, as if Shlomith, the king's sister, sent it to her friend Acme, as if Shlomith had cursed and insulted the king. When this letter was found, the king nearly killed his sister Shlomith, but another letter was found that Acme had sent to Antipater as follows: "Just as you instructed me, so I wrote a letter full of insults and curses to your father about Shlomith, his sister, knowing well that the king would kill her. Now you, send me the gold that you vowed to me if I brought such evidence to the king that he kills his sister." The king found this letter and saw that it was the cunning of Antipater to kill Shlomith just as he had killed Alexander and Aristobulus with his crafty letter.

---

5. Caesar's wife was Livia; Julia was his daughter. My thanks to the editor for the correction; the author in any case writes, "Julius, wife of Caesar." J. Gagnier, in his edition of a Latin *Josippon* (Oxford, 1706), 265, has in the margin, "sed Iosephus dicit eam fuisti in servitio Julia Caesaris conjugis." Not Hegesippus (1.45.3) or Yosippon or Gagnier or Flusser or this translator caught the anomaly of Josephus (cf. *AJ* 17.141), which is quite detailed and identifies Acme as a Jew, although Flusser does correct the name Julius to Julia, the wife of Augustus. [SB]

55. HEROD'S DEATH

In those days, King Herod fell ill, and his sickness lay heavy upon him; he wrote in a covenant[1] that his son Antipas be enthroned after him. He summoned Shlomith, his sister, and, giving her silver and gold aplenty, commanded her to execute his intent against the leaders of the people and their sons whom he had enclosed in the hippodrome [*ippodromio*],[2] to kill them so that many people would weep at the king's death.

The king was seventy years old when he fell ill, and his sickness worsened daily. He sought to exact vengeance against Antipater before his death, but he waited for the envoys that he sent to Augustus to tell him about Acme, handmaid to Augustus's wife Julius,[3] for Acme did it at Antipater's behest. Therefore, the king sent [a message] to inform Augustus to exact vengeance against Acme and afterward against Antipater.

There came the day when the sickness weighed heavily upon him, and he was greatly saddened, hating his life and craving death, so he said to his servants: "Bring me a sweet apple and put it in my hand!" And his servants did so. The king said: "Give me a *ma'akhelet*,[4] and I will pare it[5] with my hand, for this is how I enjoy eating it!" They put the *ma'akhelet* in his hand, and he rose a little, steadied himself by leaning on his left hand, and, raising his right hand with the

---

1. Latin *testamentum* means "will" here. The author, however, recognized the New Testament from Jeremiah's *brit ḥadashah*. See chap. 56.
2. Ablative case for *hippodromus*; *podromia* in chap. 49.
3. Julia. See chap. 54, note 5.
4. Jerome's Vulgate renders the author's *ma'akhelet* (a sacrificial knife in Gen 22 and Judg 19) *gladium*, and one might argue that the author merely restored the original Hebrew.
5. *Letaher* = lit. "purify." The allusion suggests that Yosippon adds a hint of human sacrifice to Herod's intended suicide. See S. Bowman, "*Aqedah* and *Mashiah* in *Sepher Yosippon*," *EJJS* 2 (2008): 21–43. [SB]

sword with which he pared the apple, sought to thrust it into his belly. Achiabus ran and grabbed his right hand and took away the *ma'akhelet* and saved him. Then all those who were standing before the king lifted their voice and wept, and also all the king's servants and his entire household cried out, weeping with a great cry; the sound was heard from afar, and the rumor went forth stating that the king was dead.

Antipater rejoiced at the sound of the people's cry, and he said to the official in charge of the prison: "Free me, and I'll go!" Not only did the official not free him, but he also went before the king and told him Antipater's words.

The king cried out in his anger and said: "Does the murderer yet rejoice and exult at my downfall and death?" He commanded executioners, and they killed him at the king's command. So Antipater died and was buried in the city named Ircaniah (Hyrcania), as the king commanded; he erased from the rescript of the covenant the name of Antipater,[6] whom he had made king with him; he enthroned Archelaus and inscribed him in the rescript of the covenant to be king after him.

After he killed Antipater, the king lived for five days; then he died and was gathered to his people. The days that Herod ruled over all Judah were thirty-seven years; Herod died a successful man: would that he was considerate toward his household as much as he succeeded, with God's help, outside it! Unfortunately, among his family, he was a man of strife [Jer 15:10]. He was successful from his youth, though royalty was not properly his by virtue of his ancestors. Nor was it enough that he ruled for many years, but he even gave the kingdom that he had not taken from his father to his son.[7]

He died and left his household weeping and wailing because he had killed his sons. But the edict that he decreed upon Shlomith and her husband, Alexander,[8] making them swear to kill the leaders of the people and their sons so that the masses would weep at his death, Shlomith did not do this. Shlomith spoke to the troops, saying: "The king commanded to open the hippodrome and set free the leaders of the people and their sons, for the king regretted the wickedness that he said to execute them"; so they [the troops] set them [the leaders] free, and they went to their homes.

After this, the whole army was gathered, and Talmi, a faithful servant of Herod, went forth and spoke unto the army fine and honest words; he showed

---

6. One MS of *DEH* has Antipater instead of Antipas, and so probably did the author's MS.

7. The source has "sons," but the author's MS identified only Archelaus as his heir. See previous note.

8. *DEH* 1.45.10 has Alexas, but some MSS have Alexander.

them the king's ring and said to the troops: "The king commanded to give the ring to Archelaus and crown him his successor." He opened the rescript of the covenant and read aloud to them how he commanded to enthrone Archelaus; and all the troops applauded, saying: "Long live King Archelaus!"

Archelaus went with all the people unto the city called Irodion (Herodion), which was two hundred ris from that place where he died. They bore the king's bier, upon which the king lay dead, and the bier was of pure gold, bedecked with precious jewels: the covering of the bier was of shining gold and purple woven with gold; the king's shroud was clasped in front at the shoulder, with a gold fibula bedecked with precious jewels, a diadem of gold upon his head and upon it a crown of the kingdom, and his scepter in his right hand. He was sitting upon the bier as if alive, and a contingent of troops before him, warriors of Judah,[9] and behind his troops, a guard of Germania—and Gauls are Franks[10]—all of them girt with sword and dressed in armor as on the day of battle. Those who were weeping and mourning were walking opposite, wailing as they went; and the remainder of the people following behind. The officers walked surrounding his bier, each with his jewels upon him, gold and precious stones, and girded with weapons; fifty of his servants dispersed myrrh and muscus[11] and all the fragrance of Arav along the entire way; and the king's sons led the bier. He was buried in the city of Herodion, as he had commanded; the road was two hundred ris distant; and they rendered him honor the whole way—but not all of them from love of him but rather from fear, for many of the people had hatred in their heart toward Herod and his sons. Even if a man fears to speak with his mouth, yet, in his heart, he is [free] to think about his government whether good or evil.

When Herod was buried, the people spewed forth their innermost thoughts and the hatred that they long had for him. They spoke against him openly, saying: "A burdensome and wicked man he was, whose trouble and yoke weighed heavily in the harsh decrees that he enacted against his people. Insolent and cruel, he did not rule but killed his nobility, stripping his people bare, not leaving a man any wealth through the tax that he extorted from us; he enriched foreigners and impoverished the Jews and brought troubles upon the Temple and sullied the Sanctuary. Happy are those who died early before they suffered Herod's cruelty, for during Herod's reign, trouble increased in Judah in fewer years since we returned from exile than the sorrow that we witnessed during

---

9. Renders *agmen Thracium*, which is faulty in several MSS; several MSS read Judah, and so the author's "warriors of Judah."

10. The author designates Gaul as Germania, as in chap. 21.

11. Musk, the prized perfume in vernacular *muscu*; cf. *Megillat Aḥimaaẓ* (ed. Klar), 40 [and Bonfil, *History and Folklore*, 318. SB]

the exile in the land of our enemies, the kings of Babylonia who ruled over us. This Herod troubled us in our land more than the hardships we saw in the exile of our enemies' land, the kings of Babylonia, for the kings of Babylonia sent us from exile to our land, but this Herod forced many out from our land into exile. Herod was crueler than Darius, more wicked than Artahshasta (Artaxerxes), and greedier than Media. Hence, we waited for the day of his death to gain freedom, but we were forced into slavery, since he made Archelaus king in his place; Archelaus committed all the evil that his father had done and added new ones. If Archelaus should rule, woe upon the king and upon those over whom he will rule, for we have a king whom we did not choose. Rather, it were better for us to be without a king than that Archelaus rule over us, for Archelaus is indeed like Herod; however, he ceased from ruling, and this one received the kingdom."

56. DAYS OF ARCHELAUS

Not only in Judah did Jews say such things, but also in Roma they slandered him [Archelaus] before Caesar and before the Elder in the temple of Apollinus (Apollo) that Caesar had built. Then Antipater, son of Herod's sister Shlomith, began to speak: "I am surprised at you, O Caesar, that you accepted Archelaus's words when he said to you: 'Help us and I will reign in Judah,' since he already made himself king and had not asked your permission, for he sat on the royal throne in Judah without your judgment. What right has he to ride on a chariot all of gold, if not because he made himself king? Why did he put a royal crown on his head, if not because he made himself king? And why did he dare to sit on the throne on high, and from atop the throne to bless the people, and surround himself with troops, as is customary to kings? Was it not because he made himself king on his own and did not wait for your judgment? Did not his father, Herod, reign according to the judgment of Caesar and the Elder as it was written upon the tablets of the covenant between you and us? Whereas before his illness befell him, while he still had his wits about him, he made his son Antipa(s) king, then, when his illness bore him down and his senses departed from him, he made Archelaus king, a madman who on the day he ruled acted as is customary to madmen: he entered the Temple of God on Passover and came with his troops and oppressed the people. When the people complained,[1] he gave the order to his troops, and each unsheathed his sword; they laid out nine thousand corpses of the people of God in the Temple on Passover. This is the sacrifice of peace offering that Archelaus made at the beginning of his reign.

"Have mercy on us, O Caesar and O Elder, and remove from us this cruel king. For it is not proper that one rule in Judah save he be from the seed of Judah

---

1. *DEH* 2.1.2 has them ask for a remission of the tax burden. Josephus (*AJ* 17.218) records three thousand Jews massacred.

from the nobility of royal descent—but this Archelaus, Herod's son whose mother was an Idumean,[2] why should he rule? Antipater the Great, Herod's father, who fought the battles of the first Caesar and was respected in Caesar's eyes and in the eyes of all the Romans, never asked for the kingdom, for he knew that it was not proper for him: but his son Herod ruled on account of the people's sins. Nor did it suffice him that he ruled, but he who had not received the kingdom from his father gave it to his son."

Shlomith's son added many more words to slander Archelaus: "Now, O Caesar and O Elder, give us leaders from your land as you gave in Aram, and we shall obey them and not rebel."

Nicolaus, King Herod's secretary,[3] answered, saying to Shlomith's son: "O most restless family![4] This one [Antipater] speaks foolishly and not ethically. Not by these words will you rouse envy against Archelaus, for this is your wont to destroy peace and stir up wars. If it is your intent to instigate wars and raise a hand against the kingdom of the Romans, why do you slander Archelaus? And why are you amazed if it is written in the tablets 'the last who ruled before the first'?[5] Since the sovereignty is Caesar's, this was done many times if he seeks to enthrone the last over the first; it is proper that Caesar enthrone whom he chooses and not whom you choose. You will accept whomever Caesar chooses! Herod, his father, also chose Archelaus. When did Herod do better, on the day when he angered Caesar or on the day that he assuaged him? For on the day that he crowned Antipa(s), Caesar was angry; but on the day that he crowned Archelaus, Caesar was agreeable: for everything that is judicious will be sustained. Consider well, O Caesar, do you believe your father's words who made you king, or do you not believe him who commanded that you be ruler and king after him? For your father knew the future, and thus you will know the future. Dominion is in your hand to enthrone as you see fit."

Caesar listened to their words and took council with the Elder, then he gave the authority to Archelaus—but he did not give him the kingdom. He said he would give him the kingdom only if he would be loyal, since by then Caesar had been told that the Judaeans were already stirred up to rebel.

---

2. The source has only *Idumaeus genus*; the author follows Nicolaus of Damascus rather than Josephus and assumes that only Archelaus's mother was from Edom. See chap. 35.

3. In chap. 54, Nicolaus is identified as the author; here the reference may or may not refer to him as Herod's secretary. The author uses the same word *sopher* in both places.

4. *Inquietissima natio* refers to the people of Israel.

5. The author misunderstood the source's reference to the precedence of later wills (*testamentum*) over earlier wills.

Archelaus entered Judah and committed many outrages and ruled for nine years. When he heard of the death of Yovav (Iuba), king of Luv (Libya), who had married Glafyra, wife of the slain Alexander, Herod's son and Archelaus's brother, Archelaus sent for Glafyra, who already had sons from his brother Alexander, and took her to wife after Iuba's death. When Archelaus took Glafyra, his widowed sister-in-law,[6] and brought her to his house in Jerusalem, the woman had a dream; behold, her first husband, Alexander, was standing before her. Glafyra passionately desired to embrace him, but Alexander pushed her away and said: "Leave me alone and do not touch me! Are not you ashamed to embrace me, for after me you bedded with Iuba, king of Libya; nor was this sufficient for you, but you bedded my brother Archelaus and came into my house to my shame to bed him in front of me." And he swore an oath, saying, "I shall not bear this shame until I shall exact vengeance upon you and my brother Archelaus, who committed this disgrace with you!" The woman awoke and told the dream to her servants. Glafyra lived for two days after her dream: then she died and was gathered unto her people, two days after seeing the dream.

Archelaus too saw in a dream: behold, nine ears of corn, full and good, standing on one stalk,[7] and he raised his eyes and looked, and behold: one large bull was standing opposite the ears of corn; the bull[8] put out his tongue and licked off the ears and swallowed them. He awoke from his dream and related the dream to one of the sages. The sage said to him: "Nine years of corn are the nine years that you ruled, and the bull that you saw lick off and swallow the ears of corn is Caesar, king of Roma, who will take your kingdom in this year." After five days, Caesar's force[9] came up against him, bound him in chains, and led him to Roma, where he died. Antipas, his brother, ruled after him and changed his name to Herod.

---

6. The author uses *yevamato*, which is a violation of Leviticus law. However, as the author carefully notes, she had borne Alexander sons, and therefore she was not subject to the levirate law. Hence, the author's usage here should be considered a slanderous charge, if not a reflection of his social reality; already condemned in the DSS 4QMMT.

7. The author's addition based on Gen 41:5 and 22.

8. Idiom from Num 22:4: to lick clean, i.e., devastate.

9. The author's source has a legate arrest Archelaus for trial in Rome and exile to Vienna in France (*DEH* 2.2.3), where he died.

57. PAULINA'S AFFAIR

In those days, Caesar died,[1] and after him ruled Tiberius Caesar, a wicked man who sent Pilatus, an officer of his army, to Jerusalem with the image of Tiberius in his hand. When Pilatus sought to bring the image into the city, the people stopped him, saying, "No image of a man shall enter into the holy city." Pilatus, the army's general, became angry and killed many of the people by sword, but also many of his troops were cast as corpses to the ground. In fact, in the days of Tiberius Caesar, not only in Judah were outrages committed, but also in Roma, the city of his reign, were many obscenities committed.[2]

Now I will relate one of the obscenities committed in Roma in the days of Tiberius Caesar. In his days, there was a woman in Roma beautiful in appearance and very lovely to look at. This woman was full of grace and beauty above all women, for everyone who saw her left off his work to look at her; many lusted to lie with her, but they could not, for she was chaste and faithful to her husband. Her name was Paulina, and the woman was regularly in her house of prayer. A youth named Mundus, Tiberius Caesar's chief charioteer, saw her, and his love burned within him like fire over the woman's beauty. He propositioned her to lie with him for the price of twenty thousand gold drachmas, but the woman refused to heed him and revealed his secret, telling it to her husband.

When Mundus saw that Paulina did not listen to him, he went to the priest of the temple that was in Roma in those days. In that temple, there were two images

---

1. *DEH* 2.3.2 (from *AJ* 18.66–80) with several adjustments including the removal of Mundus's servant Ida, who engineered the seduction, and further allusions to the Virgin Birth. Caesar (Augustus) died in 14 CE.

2. *DEH* 2.3.4 = *AJ* 18.65–80. The author uses this story of Paulina as a mask for the story of Mary and her Virgin Birth. Jesus was born in Augustus's time and died under Tiberius, as the author learned from *DEH* 2.5.2, where it follows the Paulina episode, and is clearly hinted at by the author when he cites Luke 1:28 below.

of gods, one named Isidis (Isis) and the second Anubis (Anub), and Anubis was more important than Isis in the people's eyes in their superstition.[3] The youth went to the priest and gave him one thousand gold drachmas[4] to deceive the woman to bring her to the temple at night in order to fulfill his lust with her.

The priest went and spoke to the woman as follows: "Thus spake Anubis, the great god: 'Come to my temple, and lie down in the presence of mine altar, and I will rise in the night and speak to you secretly, for I have loved you that you shall be my prophetess.'" The woman rejoiced greatly and told her husband, and her husband said to her: "Who can deny what divinity requests?"

The woman went to the temple, and her maidens prepared her in the presence of the altar, and the woman lay down, and her servants left the temple, for thus the priest had commanded. And it came to pass while she was lying down that the youth rose from the rear of the altar in the image of Anubis and entered beneath her clothing and fell [upon her] kissing without surfeit. The woman awoke and asked of him, saying: "Who are you?" He said: "I am Anubis; I have come for the sake of your love." Then the woman said: "If you are a divinity, why do you lust for the woman? Can a god meld with the woman?" Whereupon the lad said: "He can, for Akimena (Alcmena), a beautiful woman like you, indeed received a god upon her and bore him Iovis,[5] a god like me; also Leda, another woman, did likewise, and many other women too who bore many gods." The woman believed and said: "Blessed am I among maidens if my god will love me!"[6] For that reason the woman did not deny what the youth requested, and he lay with her unto morning; he left her in the morning,[7] and she went to her house quite happy.

She related to her husband all that had happened to her in the temple, and the man rejoiced exceedingly, saying: "Blessed are we for god has visited us!"[8] Also all the women blessed her and said: "Blessed art thou, Paulina, for you have conjoined with divinity!"

Somewhat later after this, Mundus went and spoke to Paulina, saying: "Blessed art thou, Paulina, for you have conjoined with Anubis, the great

---

3. Actually, the opposite was the case.

4. The author's assumption; *DEH* has him say that it cost Mundus nothing; in *AJ* 18.74, Mundus promised the priest fifty thousand drachmas.

5. Jupiter sired Herakles through her.

6. The author understood *DEH*'s clear hint to Luke's Gospel (1:28 in Latin version and 1:42) linking the story of Mary to that of Paulina and emphasizes it several more times (see above). Cf. *AJ* 18.74; and Song of Songs (Canticles), chap. 6.

7. Only in *AJ* 18.74; Yosippon had only *AJ* 1–16.

8. The author's addition (cf. Luke 1:28) follows the Latin *visitare* rendered by the Hebrew *liphkod*.

god! Learn from now that just as you did not refuse the God his request,[9] so too you should not deny a man's petition [cf. Isa 54:2]! Just as you did not hide your secret parts from god, so henceforth hide them not also from man. For Anubis is a great god who gave me what you denied me, and that which you refused me he gave me, for he gave me his appearance and his name, and also he brought you into the temple and gave you to me to fulfill my lust with you. What have you profited that you did not do my will in my desire for you and did not take twenty thousand gold drachmas that I had brought you? Behold, god gave me free without money what I asked of him. And I in my own name, Mundus, could not accomplish my desire—yet when I changed my name to Anubis, I accomplished my desire. Learn, Paulina, from now to fulfill my desire henceforth!"

When the woman heard, she saddened exceedingly for she was done wrong; she went and told her husband, but he had no response to castigate his wife, for he had commanded her to go to the temple. When the king heard, he killed the priests and also destroyed the temple and drowned the idols in the river Tibiris (Tiber).

But he did not kill the youth, saying: "His love burned him and his lust overcame him"; rather, he exiled him to a distance.[10] Therefore, we have written this disgrace that was done in the days of Tiberius Caesar to inform, for in every land of his rule in his days, outrages such as these were committed.

---

9. In the source, Mundus says this disparagingly. Hebrew style from Jer 49:10; same language in chap. 78.

10. Cf. Roman punishment of *relegatio* banishment.

58. DECREES OF GAIUS

In those days, Herod's son Archelaus died,[1] and Antipas, his brother, ruled after him, changing his name to Herod. He too acted wickedly in outdoing his predecessors; there was no shameful vice that he did not do, and he ruled for twelve years.[2] He took his brother Philip's wife while the latter still lived and while she already had sons from his brother, yet he took her for a wife. He killed many sages of Israel, including Yoḥanan, because he [Yoḥanan] had said to him [Antipas]: "It is forbidden to you to take your brother's wife!" So he [Antipas] killed him [Yoḥanan]; he was the Yoḥanan who performed baptism before anyone. The king of Roma exiled Herod to Spain (Sepharad),[3] and he died there. Agripas, son of Aristobulus, the slain son of Herod the Great, succeeded him, and he reigned twenty-three years.[4]

In his days, Tiberius Caesar died, and succeeding him was Gaius, who acted wickedly and outdid all who preceded him. This was the Gaius who called himself divine, commanding that altars be built for him throughout the land, recalling his name as god, and everyone swearing an oath in his name just as in the name of the gods. All the nations were willing, so they built altars to him, swore oaths in his name, and recalled his name as god. Only the Jews were not willing to obey him and were stirred up to war, saying: "Let us die together and not obey him!"

In those days, the people of Egypt sent an envoy to Gaius named Apion, and likewise the Jews sent Philo as their envoy, a wise man who composed many books. Apion argued before Gaius, saying: "All the nations recall your name as

---

1. The author's assumption. Archelaus was exiled to govern in Roman Provence; Antipas governed only in the Galilee.

2. There is no source for this figure. See chap. 64. The style is unusual for *Yosippon*.

3. *DEH* 2.5.4; *AJ* 18.252—actually to Lugdunum in Gaul.

4. The source for this incorrect figure is unknown.

god, building altars in your name and swearing oaths in your name as if it were the name of god. Just these [Jews] alone do not build altars to you and do not mention your name as god and do not swear oaths in your name."

Philo began to speak:[5] "Truly we do not build an altar except to God our Lord, and we do not recall the name of other gods, save for the Name of God. Nor do we swear an oath to any other name save in His Name, and we do not sacrifice to other gods except to God alone; ere [this], we would offer up our lives to death, for we are not willing nor will we obey your words!" Gaius became furious with Philo and cast him out from his presence in disgrace.

He said to the Jews who were outside waiting in Gaius's courtyard as follows: "Your hearts will not gladden this day, for it is a sorrowful time,[6] since Gaius is very angry, but there is a cure and aid for the affair. Come, let us return to the ancestral aid, the first, to our forefathers' help,[7] to the Lord our God; let us proclaim a fast and call a solemn assembly [cf. Joel 2:15] in the land of our enemies!" The Jews proclaimed a fast in the territory of Roma and called a solemn assembly for three days [Esth 4:16], and they cried out unto God, Lord of their fathers; and God answered their fast and prayer.

On the third day,[8] God stirred up the spirit of his troops against Gaius, and they leaped upon him with drawn swords, cutting him and chopping him into so many pieces until there was nothing to be buried,[9] and the dogs ate his flesh because he was not buried. Thus, God avenged Himself against Gaius.

Gaius Caesar died, and Claudius Caesar succeeded him. Claudius dismissed Philo and the Jews with great honor, and they went to Jerusalem and destroyed all the altars that had been built to Gaius throughout the land of Israel. Agripas, king of Judah, was highly honored in the eyes of Claudius. Agripas died, and his son Agripas succeeded him and ruled for twenty years;[10] Claudius Caesar also died, and Nerus (Nero) Caesar succeeded him.

---

5. There is no source for Philo's response.

6. Cf. contemporary Jewish attitude toward such decrees.

7. Cf. Morning Service in the Hebrew prayer book, the reading of the *Shema*; *Mekhilta*, ed. Ish Shalom (New York, 1949), 28; *Mekhilta*, ed. Horowitz (Frankfurt, 1949), 92; *Sepher Gezeroth Ashkenaz u-Zarfat* (ed. Haberman), 26, 72f.

8. The author's dramatic linking of murder to fast.

9. Cf. Suetonius, *Caligula*; and cf. the fate of Jezebel.

10. I did not find this length of Agripas's reign in the sources. It is correct, however, if we calculate his reign from 50 CE until the destruction of the Temple.

59. BEGINNING OF THE REBELLION AGAINST THE ROMANS

In the days of Agripas, son of Agripas, fighting broke out throughout the land of Judah and Aram,[1] for Elazar, chief of the bandits, oppressed the entire land of Aram and destroyed her. For twenty years, he did not cease from despoiling, exacting booty, and killing people, and he spread out throughout all Aram a dense layer of dead corpses. In Judah too, he killed many until Felix, general of the Roman army, came against him with a heavy force and smote his bandits and, capturing him, bound him in chains and marched him to Roma. But even though Felix sent the bandit Elazar to Roma, he did not cleanse the land from blood, for hatred increased among the people, loathing and killing each against his brother.

A great evil sprang up within Jerusalem in her streets and markets and in the Temple of God. Anyone who hated his neighbor[2] would hire against him an assassin from the bandits and in his hand a short sharp sword, double bladed, called a *sica*.[3] The bandit would hide the knife under his clothes and enter within a crowd in the market or in the Temple and, finding the man whom he sought to kill, approach him in the crowd and, drawing alongside him, stab him with the knife, killing him, and no one would know who stabbed him. This is what the *sica*-bearers [i.e., *sicarii*] did daily among the people. The people, who saw death continually before their eyes but not the killer, sighed at the groaning of the mortally wounded; hence, they called this death "blind death" that has no

---

1. The author's addition, with no source for the assumption.
2. Only found in Greek *AJ* 20.165; it seems to me probably the author's assumption.
3. The author's addition. Hebrew *sakin* (a knife); the author assumed that these were the *sicarii* (from *sica*, which has a similar sound).

eyes. Now the people were greatly afraid of the bandits, the *sicarii*, for the *sicarii* were swift and quick in their work and deft in killing a person slyly. They would interact and be friendly with a man for a day or two until he trusted him so far as to walk with him in the crowd, then he would stab him with a knife and kill him; then he would lament for him before the crowd, and it was not known who had killed him. Many died through this simple method and this sly wickedness.

Thus was killed by a *sica* the righteous and pious Yonathan the priest; he fell and died in a crowd of people in the Temple court, but it was not known who stabbed him; many like him from among the Hasidim were killed in those days. Fear of the *sicarii* exceeded the fear of war, and the people went about within Jerusalem armed with weapons and wearing armor because of the *sicarii*, but many of the poor had no armor and feared the party of *sicarii*; so they left Jerusalem with their wives and children and walked hither and yon because of the murderers. The bandits said to Felix the Roman: "Behold, these men left Jerusalem to rebel against the kingdom of the Romans"; he sent a force after them and smote them with the sword, and not one of them survived.

At that time, the Jews and Romans were stirred up to war, for the Jews rebelled against the Romans because of Florus, general of the Roman army, who tightened his yoke over the Jews. Florus did not omit any wickedness in his actions in Jerusalem: spilling of blood, adultery, violating virgins, disgracing women, usury, robbery, and cruelty.

At that time, Beronike, King Agripas's sister, came into the Temple to worship God; she looked, and behold, Florus was pressuring the people because of the tax, killing many of them in the Temple court. The lady, sister of Agripas, the king, went out because her compassion was stirred over her people, and she wept, pleading with Florus to have mercy on the people, but Florus had no pity. Rather, he laughed, making fun of the king's sister standing barefoot in the Temple, and she was an object of derision in Florus's eyes.

Elazar ben Anani, high priest,[4] was there, and so it happened when Anani was high priest that Elazar, his son, being a youth and very stout of heart, saw the evil that Florus did among the people. He sounded the shofar, and a band of youths and bandits, men of war, gathered around him, and he instigated battle, challenging Florus and the Roman troops; Elazar overcame Florus and killed all his troops.

Florus fled from Jerusalem and went, alone and abandoned, to King Agripas in Egypt, for King Agripas had just come from Roma, and he was in Egypt on his

---

4. The name should be Elazar ben Ḥananiah; apparently the story is the author's: *BJ* 2.332, has Florus leave Jerusalem for Caesarea.

way to Judah. When Agripas was coming from Egypt, his sister Beronike went forth and told the people to go out and greet the king, and she sent a missive to her brother, the king, that the king should be of assistance to his people. The people too went forth sixty ris from Jerusalem to greet him, and they bowed down to King Agripas, and he in turn greeted the people; he entered Jerusalem accompanied by two Roman officers with a huge force.

When King Agripas entered Jerusalem, all the people cried out to the king and said: "Save us, O king, and let your hand be with us to help us, for we will not serve the Romans any longer!"

60. AGRIPAS'S SPEECH

When the king heard, he pitied the people and had compassion for them, but it appeared wicked in his eyes that they spoke of rebellion against Roman sovereignty. He assembled the people in the enclosure of the Temple courtyard and spoke in their ears in the following words: "Listen and give heed, my brethren![1] I know of the great pain and sadness in your hearts, and I too am grieved and worry with you because we are too weak to fight against the Romans. But if you heed my advice, then it will go well for you, for deliverance will succeed the advice. Bear a bit longer the yoke of the Roman officers until I send a letter of greetings to Nero Caesar, and he will remove these officers from over you; do not hasten to sally into freedom, for many in their search for freedom will fall in hard labor. Many of our people who are wicked and worthless seek to cause a war; they rejoice in fighting, for this is their forte, and the good ones who seek peace will fall because of their wickedness. Therefore, heed my words: whoever is wise, let him understand for himself; and whoever is a simpleton, let him learn from my words! Therefore, let there be quiet among you while I speak, for if you are silent and keep quiet, then it will be good for me and for you, for I shall speak my words gently and you shall listen and understand. But if you are not silent and raise your voice to quarrel and heckle, you will realize two evils: you will cut off the speech from my mouth, and also you will cut off listening from your ears, and you will not hear my words. But be patient until I send a letter to Caesar, and he will remove from you these policemen and send moderate [*modesto*] policemen; for if they are moderate policemen, consider this as freedom and not slavery, but if he is a malicious policeman and harsh, this is slavery. So be patient and do not embarrass them. Even if they are wicked, it will be their disgrace to act wickedly in public if you do not embarrass them; but in secret, they do evil;

---

1. Loose paraphrase of *DEH* 2.9.1; style from Deuteronomy.

but if you embarrass them, they will become impertinent and do evil in public. Whereas they used to be judges and policemen, they will change to oppressors and enemies, for a bad policeman is preferable to a righteous enemy, the former devouring men in secret but the latter destroying men in public: so don't provoke them!

"Know and understand about wild animals under the control of men in iron cages: lions and bears and leopards, if you don't touch them or incite them, they will rest and neither harm nor destroy. But if you enter their territory and provoke them, pulling their ears, making them angry, won't they cause harm, destroying and killing people? Know and understand from disease: if at the onset of high fever you take medication, you will irritate it more, but if you leave it alone for a while, it will subside by itself; then you can take medication and make it go away.

"So now be patient lest you arouse against you Caesar and the whole kingdom of the Romans. Caesar seeks not your harm, nor did he send these policemen to harm you, but his eyes cannot see from west to east, and his hand cannot reach from Roma to here, for he is flesh and blood. But if you wait for me while I send envoys to Caesar, I shall take away from you these policemen peacefully, without war or bloodshed.

"If you dare to fight against the kingdom of the Romans, you will not prevail, because God has raised them over the whole earth; from one end to the other they rule, and all the nations shall serve them until their end comes too. All the nations are considered the servants of the Romans, and they fight against you as their auxiliaries.

"Give ear and listen, and I will recall for you the names of the nations whom the Romans conquered; nor are they ashamed to serve them. A nation called Athenae who live in the land of Yavan, a people strong and noble, burned their houses and their cities lest Sersen (Xerxes), king of Persia, descend upon them, for Xerxes invaded them with a gigantic force, mighty and very heavy and innumerable. The territory of Asia could not bear the mass of his force; the sea seemed too small to him to contain the horde of his ships and the land too narrow to bear the multitude of his force. For Xerxes said: 'I will tread with the mass of my force in the midst of the sea and make it dry land, and also I will go with the multitude of my ships into the midst of the lands and make it a sea,' for his heart was arrogant due to the multitude of his force. The Athenae went forth to confront him, and they fought him, and many corpses died from the multitude of his force; Xerxes, he too fled from before them and entered a small boat and escaped. Now these Athenae who overcame Xerxes and conquered many nations are slaves to the Romans.

"As for the nation of Lakedaemon, which performed many heroic deeds, one of the Roman officers, named Agisilah,[2] subdued that nation, and they enjoy serving the Romans, their master.

"The nation of Makedon and the nation of Afriki (Africa), ruled by two noble kings who had conquered all the peoples of the lands and subdued them, now they have no shame to be slaves to the Romans. Previously they sought to subdue the nation of Romans, and now the latter are their masters: now these two nations—Makedon and Africa—are slaves to the Romans. Philip's wealth did not help him, nor Alexander the Great's bravery. For Philip stayed in the land of Makedon, subdued by the Romans, and he served them; and Alexander the Great did not want to serve the Romans; knowing that he could not fight against them, he went forth from the land of Makedon, fleeing from the Romans and distancing himself from them, albeit he conquered in every place that he went. Wherever he turned, he caused harm [cf. 1 Sam 14:47]: he conquered the whole East: all the land of Persia, all the kings of Media, all the kingdoms of Caspia, all the kingdoms of Hodu; he opened up all the mysteries of India and all the treasuries of gold, and he came unto land's end. All this he did to get far from the West, lest he serve the Romans; he escaped—for he was gathered to his eternal home. But the kings who ruled after him served the Romans, and all the booty that Alexander took from the East and all the wealth that he found, after his death, his heirs, who ruled after him, gave it to the Romans.

"It is no surprise that Alexander crossed into India and governed as far as the ocean. The Romans rule as far as the ocean, and from the nations who live among the waves of the ocean, they took booty as far as the land of Briktania (Britania). As for the power of the Roman [subjects] who dwell in the West among the Okianus waves, about whom the world knew nothing, yet the Romans found them and subdued them under their yoke. They had always lived alone hidden among the Okianus waves and never knew slavery, but now like all the nations, they serve the Romans. When the Romans first invaded them, they fought the very Okianus, for no ship went on the Okianus from days of yore, but the Romans taught it to carry ships like every sea, for the Romans came in ships upon the Okianus as far as Britania and placed her under corvée.

"What can be said of Anibal (Hannibal), king of Africa, how many nations he conquered, who opened the secret pathways of mountains, paved roads, and captured cities? On many occasions, he also overcame the Romans and defeated them, but the Romans held fast and fought him continuously until he abandoned his weapons and fled. Nor did he stand fast but escaped to the

---

2. King Agesileus of Sparta was not a Roman officer.

land of Prusion.[3] Whereas he was a victor at the beginning and a pursuer, he became a fugitive like a slave; nor did he escape from their hand, for they captured him.

"The nation called Gallos (Gauls), a nation mighty and strong of heart called Frankos (Franks), tall and handsome, thinking nothing of death facing them, these live within great walls, not walls of stone, nor of wood construction, but natural walls: to the east, high mountains that a man cannot cross, and to the west, the Okianus, and in the south, a great and deep valley, and over the valley, a mountain like a tall mast,[4] and in the north, a very great river named Rhinus encircles all the land of Germania wherein the Gauls live, through which no one passes with ships. But Romans circled round and went up the high mountains, a mountain upon which was the column of Ercules encircled by clouds, but the Romans crossed it and descended into the land of Germania; they fought with the Gauls, defeated them, and subdued them. Until the Romans came against them, they were haughty and said: 'Would that the river Rhinus were not before us, for the river stands before our power; if the river were not there, then we would have gone forth in our strength and conquered the whole world.' But now they rejoice over the river Rhinus and say, 'This river hides us from the Romans.' No longer could the Gauls get drunk [on imported wine brought] via little boats, [called] *gallie*.[5] Rather, Roman ships and a powerful Roman fleet ply [the river] and proceed as far as Bicornis Sea;[6] they humbled all the nations across that river, which had not known slavery, and taught them to serve.

"And the nation called Iliris (Illyrii), which has the source of gold in their land, what advantage did they have? Their gold did not suffice them to exit from slavery to freedom, for they serve the Romans. The Pannonius nation, of what advantage is their wealth since they give it as a tax to the Romans? Of what advantage that they boasted over the river Pactolus, that is the Danube,

---

3. See chap. 21, end; the author added a Greek suffix to Prusias (of Bythinia) to designate an eastern country.

4. Strange Hebrew translation for *praerupta Pyrenei*.

5. The author's anachronism for *caupuli Germanorum* as *gallie* (French) from *galea* (Italian). Greek *gálea* is dated to the reign of Leo VI by Zvi Ankori, *Karaites in Byzantium* (New York, 1959), 174n18. The French (*galie, gallie, galle, gallee, gualee, gualie, jalie, gellee*) first appears in the *Chanson de Roland* (ed. J. Bédier, 1922), v. 2625 and 2729, which makes *Yosippon* the first to cite this French term, *gall'e*, as wine carriers on the Rhine. Flusser suggests a contemporary pun: Why are these boats that bring wine to France called *gallie*? Because they bring wine to intoxicate the *Galli*. *Chronicle of Ahima'az* (ed. Bonfil), 279, line 13 and note, has *aliah* in local dialect.

6. *Bicornis amnis* means a wide river (poetic: "two horned").

which spews forth gold when it surges;[7] for this gold does not suffice for what they pay annually to the Romans.

"Let us speak of the East: of what help to the inhabitants of India are the precious stones in their land, for they [stones] are not for them [inhabitants]; rather, they give them to the Roman treasury. Similarly, of what help is it to the people who have fine wool in their land if they cannot sell it but rather have to give it to the Romans annually? And also, Persia and Media, of what use is their arrogance and pride? True, they subdued many nations, but now they are subjected to the Romans and give over their kings as hostages to the Romans; they too changed and are now ruled as slaves,[8] and they bring the Romans clothing, gold ornaments, and elephants as a tax like all the kings.

"What shall we say of Egypt, a great multitude and a rich country that is hotter than all the lands and does not worry about drought, for the Nile waters it, for she has a novel grace, a land fat and full: for four months, she feeds her lords, and for seven months, she nourishes her inhabitants? And what shall we say of the city of Alexandria, which a noble king built and called her after his name to bring trade and merchandise to enliven her inhabitants, and a river encircles her like a wall to assist her against the enemy? Who can rebel against the Romans like the Egyptians, all of whose rich who give tax to the Romans number ten times 50,700[9] excluding the people of Alexandria, and yet they do not seek to rebel, for they give tax lest the Romans carry them to a distant land?

"The nation called Lacedaemon who offered their lives to death,[10] dying for their land rather than serving the king of Carthage, but there remained of them Philaenis and his brothers;[11] they fought against the king of Carthage and did not serve him, but they do serve the Romans. What shall we say of the nation called Syrtes,[12] rumor of whom terrifies the earth,[13] who ruled a third of all the earth from the Atlantic Sea, from the Pillars of Hercules, as far as Yam Suf and from there as far as Kush their kingdom stretched, yet they too serve the Romans like all the nations?

---

7. Not knowing the river Pactolus, mentioned immediately after Pannonia (modern Hungary), the author assumed the Danube.

8. The source has princes and noble hostages to be Romanized.

9. The author multiplied his source's 50,700 by ten.

10. *DEH* 2.9.1 relates a confused version of the rivalry between Cyrenaica and Carthage (Sallust, *Jug.* 79).

11. See previous note. *Yosippon* mistakenly has them as Lacedaemonians (i.e., Spartans) from the unclear relation in *DEH*. They did die for their country.

12. Actually refers to two bays on the North African coast.

13. The author's source refers not to fear of a nation but to the sound of the waters in these bays.

"Who counted the great mass of nations living in Carthage of Africa who received the yoke from the right hand of Sipius (Scipio), hero of Roma. This very Carthage accepted upon herself to give tax to Roma twice a year because she did not rely on the mass of her inhabitants.

"Creta is the name of a state in the sea that contains one hundred cities, all fortified, a land good and fat around which the sea girdles like a wall. One of the Roman generals overcame her and conquered her, and many of her inhabitants fear the bundles of sticks—spears[14]—that are in the Romans' hand.

"Asia and Pontus too with the kingdoms of Bosphoron (Bosphorus) are subdued under Roman control, and while ships did not cross in that stream,[15] yet Romans subdued them with four mighty navies, placed them under corvée, and made a treaty with them.

"What shall we say of Armenia, which they protect not only their borders but also spy out the gates of every nation around her lest they frighten the peace and rebel against the Romans? All the nations serve them, and you by yourselves will rebel?

"Where are the mighty deeds of your battles and the valor of your troops; where is the victory of your ships that will race upon the sea to fight against the Romans, whom even the elements serve?

"How good it is to speak the truth: behold how all the earth unto its frontiers is the kingdom of the Romans. Their rule stretches beyond the ocean, and they found other land among the islands of the ocean, the land of Britania, who have no portion with mankind, but they taught them servitude, for the ocean gave them transit, and they crossed through it. What do you say about Euphrates, who has them on both sides, they are in the service of the Romans? Every corner of the East and every corner of the North and all the mass of nations who live in the North as far as the mountains of snow that do not permit passage to any man save the Romans; and every corner of Teiman unto the mountains of sand, they plant their land, and the Romans reap their harvest. All the land of the West as far as Gaditan (Cadiz), who received the Romans as new travelers [*novi hospites*], and in the place where no ship ever came, there their ships come and make commerce in order [for Cadiz] to give tax to the Romans. Parthus (Parthia) too, their partners by treaty, will not assist you, for Romans also tightened their yoke upon them.

"Don't say in your heart that the Romans are indeed like the Egypt and Arav, with whom you are accustomed to fight, for Roman weapons are different from

---

14. *Fasces,* which the author understood as "spears," not knowing why the inhabitants should fear these symbols of Roman power.

15. Latin *pelagus,* which the author translated to Hebrew *peleg.*

their weapons and their wealth greater than the wealth of all the nations, for they took the wealth of every nation. And do not trust the fortifications of the walls of Jerusalem, for the Romans shattered the ocean wall."

Agripas continued to speak many more words, which we have not written here. Agripas spoke further, saying: "It is good for you, my friends, it is good for you as long as a ship stands in the harbor to protect your lives from the storm, for when the ship enters the sea's current, one cannot be protected against the tempest from the sea's current nor the waves in the current, for there is no haven to rest except tempests and fear of death." And he said: "Set in your hearts lovers of your land and love of your sons and your wives; place in your heart love of your Sanctuary and love of your priests and have pity upon them lest you destroy everything through your action. Pay attention to my words, for I have spoken in your ears the salvation of your souls: I have told you the peace that I have chosen for myself with the Romans. If you heed and make peace, I am together with you, but if you choose war, you are by yourselves; if for peace, you and I are together, but if for war, without me."

61. THE BANDITS TAKE CONTROL OF JERUSALEM

Agripas raised his voice[1] and wept, the elders and the sages with him also wept, and Anani (Ananias) the priest wept too. Meanwhile, Elazar[2] ben Anani, accompanied by[3] a strong band of youths from the bandits,[4] suddenly leaped with drawn swords upon the Roman officers who were with King Agripas and killed the officers and their masses who were with Agripas in Jerusalem and Judah.

Th elders and sages separated and seized Mount Zion, for they did not want to be with the youths in one plan. Now the battle waxed between the bandits and the sages; the bandits seized the Temple of God, and their position became superior to that of the sages. When King Agripas—he was in camp outside the city—saw that the bandits were in charge, he sent his two officers, Darius and Philip, along with a force of three thousand cavalry to help the elders and the peace party fight against the bandit youths. The peace party trusted the king's forces coming to help them; they joined with them and fought for seven days and, overcoming the bandits,[5] routed them, pursuing them and smiting them as far as the Temple.

---

1. The author follows *DEH* 2.9.2–2.10.5 in this chapter.
2. *DEH* 2.9.3 relates that the governor forced Agripas from the city. Elazar is mentioned in *DEH* 2.10.1 as Elazar, son of the high priest, while in *BJ* 2.409, his father is named also.
3. Not in source. *DEH* 2.10.1 speaks only of the capture of Masada and massacre of the Romans there and that Elazar, son of the high priest, ceased the Temple offerings.
4. The author refers to the revolutionaries as bandits throughout the text. The Vulgate for Ezek 18:10 and Jer 7:11 has *latro*, which means "bandit."
5. Not in sources. The author wanted to clarify the situation, namely, that the revolutionaries controlled the Temple but the people in the Temple had not allowed the revolutionaries to enter it.

The king's officers entered the Temple along with the king's troops, smiting the bandits, but the bandit *sicarii* leaped upon them from the rear, infiltrating the king's force in the Temple. They stabbed with their knives here and there among the king's force, for the king's troops held spears and great swords according to the custom of war, whereas the *siccrii*, since *sicae* were small, came from below and stabbed beneath their [the king's force's] armor. Thus, many of the king's force who entered the Temple died. Since the bandits had the upper hand, the king's force left Jerusalem, and with them the king's officers, Darius and Philip; the sages and elders and all the peace party left with them and went to King Agripas.

Elazar ben Anani and the bandits came to rule over Jerusalem, and they wreaked havoc in Jerusalem. They burned the palace of King Agripas in Jerusalem, looting his treasuries and all his cherished artifacts. They burned too all the promissory notes and loan contracts that were in the king's palace, and they burned the palace of Beronici, the king's sister; so their rule strengthened in Jerusalem.

62. DEATH OF SHIMON OF SITOPOLI (SCYTHOPOLIS)

In those days,[1] Aramaeans and Jews lived together throughout the cities of Aram; and war broke out between Jews and Aramaeans in all the cities of Aram. The Caesareans brought a Roman force to the city and killed all the Jews whom they found there. The Damascenes too formed a plot to kill the Jews among them; they concealed their secret and did not utter their plan even to their wives, for many of them kept the Torah of the Jews. One night, the Aramaeans rose up and, seizing the roads and entrances to the city, killed ten thousand Jews, for each man of Aram had his weapon in hand, while the Jews lay naked in their beds, not knowing what they had plotted against them.

When the Jews who lived in the land of Judah heard everything that the Aramaeans did to the Jews in their land, every man of Judah girded his weapons and raced to Damascus like lions and bears, like a bereaved animal furious and enraged. They smote Damascus with the sword, male and female, from elder unto babe and child. Thus they did to numerous of the cities of Aram. They smote them with the sword and had no mercy upon elder and woman or pity upon the child. They killed all of them in cruel wrath, for their iniquity and sin aroused them to such cruelties that they killed Aramaeans within their cities, a great spread of naked and dead elders and murdered women, along with slain men, and babies and nurslings killed at their mothers' breast, for there was no one [left] to bury [them]. The land of Aram reeked from the stench of her slain, for the Jews destroyed the whole land of Aram. If not for Cestius, commander of the army of Rome, who saved Aram from the Jews, memory of Aram would thus have been lost from all of Aram Ẓovah.

---

1. The author follows *DEH* 2.11.1–2.17 in this chapter.

After this, the Judaean force was marching on its way from Aram to the land of Judah when they arrived in Sitopolis[2] of Aram to fight against her, for it remained the [only] Aramaean fortified city. In this city, Jews and Aramaeans lived together. The Judaean force came before the city and called to the Jews living within: "Peace." The Jews living in Scythopolis, however, did not respond to their brethren's "Peace" but rather with curses and swords, for they were united with the Romans and Aramaeans, and many were from the tribe of Levi.[3] The Judaean force said: "We come for your safety and to assist you to fight against the Romans." And they replied: "We do not accept your greetings and your aid." When the Judaean force beheld this, they marched on to Jerusalem accompanied by great booty, countless gold, and silver that they brought from Aram.

The Aramaeans who lived in Scythopolis said to each other: "Behold, the Jews will return to fight against us, and perhaps these Jews who live among us will assist them and hand over the city to them, so doing unto us what they did to the rest of the cities of Aram." They said to the Jews who were living in their midst: "We have heard that the Judaean force will return to fight against us; now you leave the city with your women and children and stay in the forest, which is close by the city, until the invading Judaean force leaves us." The Jews did so; they left the city and sat in the forest.

There was a lad named Shimon, a roughneck [*paritz*],[4] tough and ruthless, tall and broad-chested,[5] strong of arm, powerful and brave, who destroyed many of the people of Judah, killing many of God's people in order to find favor in the eyes of the non-Jews. He sold many of God's people to foreigners, for when the Judaean forces came to destroy Scythopolis, Shimon constantly went out to confront them, killing many of them, turning them back; thus, Shimon prevented the Judaean force from doing any harm to Scythopolis.

As Shimon was sitting safely in the forest, and with him his father, Shaul, a noble man and elderly, and many elderly inhabitants of Scythopolis, Romans and Aramaeans assembled a numerous force and killed all the Jews found in Scythopolis. They came into the forest to kill Shimon, his father, and all his family, after they had slain thirteen thousand souls in the city.

---

2. *DEH* 2.17. Scythopolis is Beth She'an, which the author renders in Italian dialect with *sin*, translating the *sc* and the ending resembling Napoli. The author, as will be seen, places the city in Syria.

3. *DEH* has *tribule collegium*; apparently the author's MS had *tribu Levi*.

4. The author calls him *paritz*, his term meaning "bandit" (for "revolutionary"). Perhaps he read *praedo* (bandit) for *praeditus*.

5. Lit. "broad heart," generally an idiom for generosity that does not fit here.

Shimon looked and, behold, a horde of Romans and Aramaeans were coming against him, so he unsheathed his sword and ran against them, smiting them a great blow, forcing them to retreat. Yet another great horde massed against him. When Shimon saw the great horde coming against him, and he alone with unsheathed sword in hand, he called out, saying: "Hear ye, Romans and Aramaeans, inhabitants of Scythopolis, and I shall speak unto you. Surely you are fighting against me with right and justice, and you will have no pity on me who saved you from the Judaean force, which I did not allow to destroy your city and kill you, your wives, your sons, and your daughters by the sword as they did unto the rest of the cities of Aram; I fought your battles and killed many of my people and my family in order to find favor in your eyes; I gave you their blood as surety; I have kept a bond of friendship with foreigners but enmity for my people; I have killed many of my people, fathers and sons, for your sakes; and you in justice and righteousness reward me like this! Now I shall die, but in anger and great rage; and I will exact vengeance upon myself for having killed my comrades and my friends. I shall kill myself with my own hand to avenge my brothers' blood that I spilled and so show my strength and bravery lest you exalt yourselves over me in my downfall and say: 'We killed Shimon.' Now I will kill myself by my own hand like a murderer whom the Torah[6] puts to death."

And speaking so, his eyes filled with blood, his mouth foamed, and his rage burned in him, and he cast his mercy aside and scorned compassion. He took his father, brought him forth from the midst of the people, and slew him, and after him, he killed his mother, so that they would not plead for the children. Then his wife ran desiringly and willingly, baring her neck to the sword so that she would not see the death of her sons. Then the children ran and offered their neck to the sword lest they see the death of their mother. The cruel one hastened and smote, killing her and her sons with one blow rather than give them to enemies; so he killed his entire household. He gathered their corpses, mounting their corpses like a man victorious in battle who would not see any of his house fall into the hands of his enemies, for he had killed them all, and raising his right hand in the sight of all, he killed himself as well. Shimon did this to show his strength and bravery, because he had preserved friendship with foreigners and hatred for his people; therefore, he died such a strange death.

---

6. The author translates *sacrilegium* (sacrilege) as *sacer* (holy) *lex* (law) and thus derives "Torah" (sacred). Shimon killed himself as he deserved, as did Saul. Cf. *Leviticus Rabbah* 26:7 and *Genesis Rabbah* 65:27.

63. CESTIUS'S WAR

It happened after this[1] that Agripas went and told Nero Caesar, king of Rome, all these things, how the Jews rebelled and how they killed the Roman officers and all their force. Nero Caesar, called Augustus, sent to Cestius, commander of the army of Rome, stationed in Aram, who had a strong contingent of the Roman army, for he was fighting against the king of Persia; he smote him and restored the kingdom of Persia to Roman rule. Nero ordered him to go up to Judaea to offer the people peace and to appeal to them to restore the treaty.

When Agripas related these things directly to Cestius, Cestius rejoiced over these words of Agripas, since he found a pretext to exact vengeance upon the Jews for their having spilled considerable blood of the Roman force and of the inhabitants of Aram. Cestius mustered a force numerous as the sand of the seashore and invaded Judaea. At the beginning of his campaign, he smote a city named Zebulon, for her inhabitants were afraid, abandoning the city and fleeing to the mountains. When Cestius came to the city and saw the beauty of the edifice, he ordered to torch it and smote the people in it with the sword. Nor did this sate his soul, so he went to Yafo with a heavy force and, fighting against her by land and sea, captured her and killed eighty-four hundred men in her streets. From there, he marched to Caesarea and fired all the city's environs, killing all the people found outside the city. When the men of Sipporin went out to greet him with entreaties and declarations of peace, he had pity on them and did not fight against the city. He entered the city and did no harm to it, and the bandits in the city fled to the mountains.

When Cestius left Sipporin, the bandits made a surprise attack and killed two hundred warriors of his horde. Gallus[2] too, an officer in his army, was

____

1. The author adds these events in order to link the previous chapter to the war of Cestius.
2. Josephus identifies him as an officer named Caesennius Gallus.

wounded in that battle, but he fled and so did not die. Cestius turned about and fought with the bandits, and they fled from him; but Cestius pursued them with his horses and cavalry, engaging and killing many of them, and the rest fled to the mountains [Gen 14:10]. Gallus returned to Caesarea to be treated for the wounds that the Judaean bandits had inflicted upon him. Cestius with his whole force, numerous and mighty, marched from there to a city named Antipatridis (Antipatris) to fight against her, and there he found a Judaean camp that had gone out to confront him. When the Judaean camp saw the size of Cestius's camp, they declined battle and went to Gibeon,[3] which is fifty ris distant from Jerusalem. They arrived on Friday and spent the Sabbath there. Cestius pursued them with all his camp as far as Gibeon, encamped against Gibeon, and fought against her.

After the Sabbath, during the morning watch,[4] each man girded his weapons and went forth from the city and, raising a cry, arrayed for battle with Cestius's camp. They spread out 515 horses and their riders of Cestius's warriors dead upon the ground and a great many infantry, and twenty-two Jews fell in that battle as well. In that place was seen the strength of Monbaz (Monobazus), a Judaean youth, and Cenedaeus, who first smote the Roman camp.[5] Cestius and Agripas sent messengers to Jerusalem to Elazar ben Anani to make peace, but Elazar did not accept; in fact, he killed one of the envoys. Elazar mustered the priests and the army to go forth again to battle against Cestius.

---

3. *DEH* 2.14.5 has Gabao, which the author correctly identifies, although the following events are not as accurate.

4. The source has Jews fight the Romans because it was the Sabbath, but the author misunderstood the word *posthabita* as "afterward."

5. The author knew the form "Monbaz" from the Talmud [directly or indirectly? SB]

64. VESPASIAN IS SENT TO FIGHT AGAINST THE JEWS

These are the priests who ruled during the Second Temple:[1] Matityahu ben Yoḥanan,[2] having smote the Makedonians, officiated as high priest for one year and died. Yehudah, his son, called Maccabee, officiated after him for three years,[3] and he died in battle. Yehonatan, his brother, officiated after him for eighteen years, and he too died in battle. After him, Shimon, his brother, officiated for eight years, and Ptolemy, his father-in-law slew him [Shimon] at a drinking party. Yoḥanan, his son, officiated after him: he was called Hyrcanus, for when Yoḥanan smote a king named Hyrcanus,[4] his father nicknamed him Hyrcanus; and he ruled twenty-one years[5] and died. Aristobulus, his son, reigned after him for one year: he was called king because he began placing the crown of monarchy upon his head; and he altered the priesthood, profaning it to a monarchy 480 years and three months after Israel returned from Babylonia. Then he died, and Alexandrus, his brother, ruled after him for twenty-seven years; when he died, the Jews enthroned Alexandra, his wife, and she ruled for nine years and died. After her Aristobulus, her son, ruled for three years: in his days, Pompey, the Roman commander, invaded Jerusalem, captured him, bound him in chains, and brought him to Rome. Hyrcanus, his brother, ruled after him for forty years: in his days, Antigonus, his brother's son, rebelled and, with Persian

---

1. List is based partly on *DEH* 2.13 and partly on Jerome's *Chronicle* or perhaps one of its genealogies.
2. He was never high priest, but such an assertion can be found in rabbinic literature (cf. prayer *al ha-nisim*).
3. Cf. Jerome, 141; Judah was never high priest.
4. See chap. 27, beginning, derived perhaps from a variant MS.
5. Jerome has twenty-six years, while chap. 30 has thirty-one years.

aid, raised his hand against Hyrcanus, captured him, bound him in chains, brought him to Babylonia, and cut off his ear so that he could not be priest and king; and Antigonus ruled for three years. In his days, Herod fled from Jerusalem to Rome, mustered a force of Romans and came to Jerusalem. Antigonus died in the third year of his reign; Herod ruled after him for thirty-seven years and died. After him, Archelaus, his son, ruled for nine years, and the king of Rome bound him in chains. After him ruled Antipas; he changed his name to Herod and reigned for ten years.[6] The king of Rome exiled Antipas to the land of Spain[7] for taking his brother's wife while he yet lived, and he died there. After him, his son Agripas, son of Herod the Great, ruled for twenty-three years, and he died. Agripas, his son, ruled after him for twenty years, and throughout the days of his reign, the war between the Jews and the Romans did not quiet down until the exile of Judah to Rome: this is the exile of the Destruction of the Second Temple in the twentieth year of King Agripas in the fifth month, which is the month of Ab, on the ninth day of the month.

In the days of Agripas ben Agripas,[8] Nero Caesar ruled over Rome and sent a gift of offerings and sacrifices to the House of God to offer up in his name as had done the kings of Rome who ruled before him. But Elazar ben Anani the priest stood up and cast out Nero's gift from the House of God, saying: "We will not profane the Sanctuary of our Lord with the gifts of foreigners." He sounded the shofar and arrayed for war[9] against a Roman army force that was stationed on duty to watch over Jerusalem; one of their officers died, and many casualties fell there of the soldiers of Kittim. However, one officer was seized alive, for Elazar ben Anani had sworn not to kill him, but he violated his oath and killed him. After this, King Agripas fled to tell King Nero of the wickedness that was done in Jerusalem. Nero detailed Cestius with a heavy force to accompany him; they invaded the land of Judaea, seized a few forti-fied cities and Yafo, and destroyed them; then they and Agripas went up to Jerusalem. Elazar ben Anani the priest went out to confront them with the rest of the priests and most of the army. They met them between Jerusalem and Yafo and arrayed for battle against them, and many casualties fell there. The priests fled to Jerusalem; Cestius and Agripas pursued them with the rest of

---

6. In chap. 58, he reigned for twelve years, while Jerome (p. 171) has twenty-four years.

7. Actually, to Gaul; see *AJ* 18.252.

8. Free paraphrase of *DEH* 2.10.1, which does not speak of Nero's gift. Cf. Talmud, *b Gittin* 56a, which differs in the following from *DEH* (*pace BJ* 2.49) and Yosippon, who relies on him but only lists the refusal of the priests to accept a gentile offering.

9. The author's transition back to the outbreak of the war. He skips through his source, and this accounts for his inaccuracies.

the Roman army unto the gates of Jerusalem and encamped against Jerusalem for three days.

On the fourth day, the priests sallied forth suddenly from Jerusalem with the rest of the army and smote five thousand infantry and one thousand cavalry in the camp of the Romans; the Roman camp was terrified by the priests, who pursued them and overtook them on the slope. Now, the priests and the army stood there for four days and killed many of them. When Cestius and his army saw that they could not retreat from the Jews, they chose forty Roman lads and stationed them between their camp and the priests' camp. Cestius commanded them, saying: "Stand all night; sound the trumpets and burn the fire so that we can escape from them, and don't withdraw before morning." The Judaean camp saw the fire and, hearing the sound of the trumpets, thought that they were a Roman camp: when they rose early in the morning, behold, the Roman force had fled [about] a three-day march during the night. The priests pursued them along the Caesarea road and found all their weapons cast aside along the way where the Romans had thrown them to lighten themselves for flight. But the priests did not gather the castaway weapons; rather, the army pursued after them [Romans]; they caught up with them and smote them unto the gates of Caesarea. Both Cestius and Agripas took refuge in the port of Caesarea, whence both fled to Rome, came to King Nero, and told him all that had befallen them. While they were speaking with him about these matters, a messenger arrived from Persia and reported to Nero saying that the Persian king and his army and all his servants have rebelled, and no longer would they honor serving the Roman king. Nero became very frightened when he saw that all his subjects were rebelling against him from all sides.

At that time, Vespasian, commander of the force that Nero had sent to the West, arrived; he had subdued Ashkenaz,[10] Britannia, Saxonia, and Ascotia, to submit to the yoke and serve Nero, king of the Romans. When Vespasian arrived, King Nero told him all the evil that the priests in the land of Judaea had done unto the Roman force and that they had killed their people and their

---

10. The source has Gallia. The author is the earliest source to identify Germany as Ashkenaz. In Jerome's *Exordium* to his *Chronicle*, where he comments on the family of nations in Gen 10, the text identifies *Ascanaci gentes Goticae*. This is an interpolation by a later author (contemporary to the Goths) who added it between 381 and the beginning of the sixth century. Therefore, it appears that Ashkenaz already was applied to the Gothic tribes in their own time. L. Wallach, "*Zur Ethnologie* אשכנז—*Deutschland*," *Monatsschrift für Geschichte und Wissenschaft des Judentums* (1939): 303, suggests that this identification derives from the similarity of sound Ashkenaz Scanza (i.e., Scandinavia), which, according to Jordanes, was the home of the Goths. The name Ashkenaz does not appear in chap. 1 of *Yosippon*. See Flusser's introduction to *Josippon*, vol. 2, section 16.

troops in the land of Judaea just as Cestius and Agripas, king of Judaea, had related.

After these events, King Nero sent Vespasian, commander of the force, and Titus, his son, with him to invade the land of Judaea. He commanded them, saying: "Thus you shall do when you arrive in the land of Judaea: capture their fortified cities and destroy them, wiping out everything that you find, and do not restrain your hand from man, woman and child, elder and suckling, from annihilating them without mercy." Vespasian and his son Titus crossed the sea, and with them all the Roman force and their choicest warriors, arriving at the port [*maḥoz*] of Antochia.[11]

---

11. *DEH* 3.3.1 has Alexandrea, which the author corrects *pace DEH* 3.5.1 but misspells Antiochia as Antochia.

65. JOSEPHUS'S CAMPAIGNS IN GALILEE

When the Jews heard these things, they chose three experienced officers as commanders—Joseph ben Gurion;[1] Anani, the high priest; and Elazar, his son—appointing them over the land and dividing among them the land of Judah by lot and giving them fighting Jews for support.[2] The third of the land that fell by lot to Joseph ben Gurion, for he had been anointed as warlord [*meshuah milhamah*], included all the territory of Naphtali and Mount Galil and beyond. The second lot, Jerusalem and all her environs, went to Anani (Ananus), the high priest, [his task] to strengthen the walls and prepare for battle against Vespasian [cf. 1 Kings 9:26]. The third lot, all the territory of Edom from Elia unto Yam Suf,[3] went to Elazar ben Anani the priest and with him Yehoshua. The rest of the land from Jericho unto Gilad toward the Euphrates River and, across the Euphrates, all the land of Aram Naharaim went by lot to Menasseh. They set the rest of the nobles of Judah and the priests over the fortified cities from the boundaries of Jerusalem toward Egypt.

Vespasian, traveling with his whole army from Antochia, arrived and encamped in the land of Aram Ẓovah and, in counsel with his officers, decided:

---

1. This is not Josephus who is mentioned later (*DEH* 3.3.4) without designation of his father. Based on this, the author identified the historian Josephus with the Joseph ben Gurion mentioned here and throughout the text is consistent in this designation. The historian Josephus was the son of Matityahu, but the latter's name was not mentioned either in *DEH* or in *AJ*. While it is mentioned in *BJ* 1.2.568, there is no reason to assume that the author knew *BJ*, which was not available in Latin.

2. Hebrew is unclear.

3. The author adds the geographical gloss. Eilat was a port in the tenth century. Yam Suf is traditionally the Red Sea (lit. the Reed Sea). Cf. 1 Kings 9:26.

"Let us go first against Mount Galil!" When Joseph heard that Vespasian planned to ascend the Galil, he left Jerusalem, went up to the Galil, and rebuilt the destroyed cities, strengthening the walls, their gates and their bolts, and their palaces. He appointed army commanders at the head of the people, over thousands, over hundreds, over fifties, and over tens, and supplied the people with all manner of weapons. He taught the army trumpet signals and bugle calls: what sound to muster for battle, what sound to assemble, and what sound to disperse; all the trumpet calls of war he told them [Cf. Exod 18:21 and Lev 10:1–10]. He commanded the army, saying:[4] "Hear O Israel [Deut 20:3],[5] today you are about to join battle with your enemy. Let not your courage falter. Do not be in fear or in panic or in dread of them. Fear not death, but let your heart be strengthened and have courage to fight on behalf of your people and your land, lest you be exiled from her. Fight for the Sanctuary of God, lest it be desecrated with the defilement of gentiles, for death in battle is better than life in exile. And when you are arrayed in battle and you see a casualty fall from among your heroes, be zealous for God, saying: 'Let us choose death over life so that your war will succeed'; because by dying for God our Lord and for His covenant together, you shall proceed to the Great Light [Isa 9:1]."[6]

When he had done speaking these words to the army, he chose from Judah sixty thousand infantry and a few cavalry; of these, he selected six hundred special battle veterans, men of status, one per hundred and ten per thousand and one hundred per myriad who would neither turn tail nor fear the sound of battle. Then Joseph sounded the shofar and went to the cities of Agripas in Judah to capture them. He came and encamped against Tiriyah;[7] this was the city of Agripas, where he had his caches of silver and gold and weapons.

When Joseph arrived, he stood before the gate of the wall and offered peace to the ears of the people on the wall, saying: "Open the city and hand over to me all the treasures of Agripas and all his precious things and live, and you shall not die. Is it not better for you to be with the destiny of God's Sanctuary and its portion than to be of aid to Agripas, who has joined our enemies and strengthened their hand to fight against God's Sanctuary and the people of His legacy?" The people heeded Joseph and opened the city gate; he entered there, and they made peace with him, handing over to him all the treasures of

---

4. Speech is the author's creation. In the source, Josephus gives his troops practical advice.

5. Cf. m. *Sotah*, chap. 8.

6. On this phrase, cf. Baer, "Hebrew Sepher Yosifun," 192n19. The phrase is from Isa 9:1 and used in the Vision of Baruch (48.50) as well as the Slavic Enoch (65.10).

7. The author continually and mistakenly identifies Taricheae as Tiriyah, a city between Acco and Shefar-Am.

Agripas, for Joseph's words seemed good to them, and they too wanted to be included in his destiny.

At that time, Joseph was told that the Tiberians had rebelled; they separated out from the entire people the men of Jerusalem and threw off command of Joseph, becoming slaves to Vespasian, who appointed over them one of the officers of Kittim. When Joseph heard these things, he left his camp in Tiriyah; he took with him six hundred youths to go to Tiberia and came against them suddenly. Arriving at the seashore near Ginasar, he found there a great many boats prepared to assist the Romans and Vespasian, commander of Rome; Joseph commanded to smash them, scattering them hither and yon in the sea. When the Tiberians saw the boats scattered in the sea, they said that these too were Joseph's force; and all their troops fled to the city, closing the city gate behind them.[8]

Joseph approached near the wall below the city gate and called out to the ears of the people, saying: "What is this conspiracy that you hatched against me—that you void a covenant that we made to God, and you betray the vow that you swore by Israel's God that we fight together against our enemies?" The people answered Joseph from atop the wall as follows: "Please, sir, hear the words of your servants: Heaven forbid that we be of aid to the Romans; rather, we should be of assistance to God and His Sanctuary and the people of His destiny. But there are in our midst wicked men who made a treaty with the Romans, and they brought them to the city." The men opened the city gate, and Joseph, entering with his men, began to seize the wicked men there. He arrested about six hundred men and sent them to Tiriyah, the city that he had taken; and the remainder of the wicked ones who gathered against him he smote with the sword.

He also seized alive Vespasian's officer, the commander of the city too,[9] and bringing him outside the city, Joseph commanded one of his warriors to cut off his hands. The commander pleaded with Joseph, saying: "Cut off one hand please, but let the other one live." He became a laughingstock in the eyes of Joseph and his warriors. Joseph answered, saying to the warrior: "Give him your sword and let him cut off his hand: let him choose which will live and cut off the other." The commander took the sword from the warrior and, putting his left

---

8. The source has them open the gates and go out to Josephus. The author apparently misunderstood the phrase *portis reseratis*.

9. *DEH* 3.3.8; *BJ* 2.621–44 (= *Vita* 170–73) has this punishment imposed on Cleitus, the Israelite who led the revolt against Josephus in Tiberias. The author understood the word *princeps* in Hegesippus as "officer" rather than "ringleader" and so made him a Roman.

hand on the rock, smote his left hand with his right hand and cut it off. Joseph cast him toward Vespasian's camp to show his scorn for the Roman camp.

It happened after this that the men of Sipporin also rebelled and, plotting against Joseph, made a treaty with Vespasian and the Roman force. The matter became known to Joseph, and he went to war against them with all his camp. The city was stronger than he, and he could not prevail against her, for he had earlier raised her walls and strengthened her towers as well; so he encamped against the city and besieged her.

At that time, the inhabitants of Jerusalem heard that the men of Ashkelon had rebelled and offered to make a treaty with the Romans, so they sent against them Niger and Sila (Sylas) the Babylonian and Yehohanan, one of the warriors of Jerusalem,[10] with a multitude of the poor [*dalath haarez*],[11] and they came to Ashkelon and besieged her. Now there was within the city one of the Roman officers named Antonius, a strong man and a battle tested veteran. During the morning watch, before a man could recognize his comrade, Antonius sallied from the city to the Judaean camp and smote them a great blow; ten thousand Judaeans fell there.

But the remainder stood their watches until dawn, and these did not retreat from their places, saying: "Better for us to die fighting than to flee before our enemy," and they took courage in their position. When morning came, the Judaean survivors drew up for battle to confront Antonius; many of the Roman force died; and also among them fell Sila the Babylonian and Yehohanan the Jerusalemite. And their number was eight thousand men.

Niger alone escaped because he hid in a grave. The Roman warriors pursued Niger but did not find him, for he disappeared before their eyes, so they set fire in the forest around the grave in which he hid. The fire devoured the forest wood all around but did not touch the grave, and Niger survived there until he was safe from the Romans. The Jews sent another large army from Jerusalem to come to Ashkelon to bury the dead; these came to Ashkelon and buried the dead, and they searched for Niger's corpse, but it was not there. While they continued to search, Niger called out to them from the depths of the grave in which he was hidden, saying: "Here I am," and the army rejoiced in finding Niger. The Romans remained closed up in the city, for they were afraid of the multitude of Jews who came to bury their dead; and having buried their dead, the army raised Niger and brought him to Jerusalem.

____

10. The source has only Iohannes Essaeus, i.e., was an Essene.

11. *Dalath haarez* (lit. lowly peasants), a phrase used by the author for the Pharisaic mob that fought the Sadducees in the days of Alexander Yannai. [SB]

Joseph gathered his strength, determined to fight against the people of Sipporin; he smote all the army found outside of the city and torched all the hinterland villages and her environs. Thus he did to all the cities that made a treaty with the Romans: the people he smote with the sword, and their houses he set ablaze. Joseph spilled much blood in the Galil among all the people who made a treaty with Vespasian. He destroyed them without respite and set the cities aflame, and their remnant, their children, and their women he led into captivity to Jerusalem, and those Roman troops found there he smote with the sword.

66. BATTLE OF YODPHAT

When Vespasian and his son Titus heard about all the harm that Joseph inflicted upon them in smiting their troops in the Galil and in killing their allies, he [Vespasian] became very angry, his wrath burned in him, and he marched to Aptalmaiita,[1] which is Acco. King Agripas of Judah was there and with him forty thousand battle troops, and he joined Vespasian's army with all his force. Romans too without number and with them the rest of the gentiles and the multitude of the nations: Aram Ẓovah, Aram Naharaim, Shin'ar, Ashur, Paras, Kasdim, Arav, Makedon, all the Orientals, Miẓrayim too, Luv, Sva, Dedan [Gen 25:3; 1 Chron 1:32],[2] and all the states near and far, for all of them cast off the yoke of the Jews and rebelled against Jerusalem and her king; and they were one with the Romans and with Vespasian to help them and to fight together against Judah and the inhabitants of Jerusalem, except for Edom, for they were servants to the Jews. They did not come to the aid of the gentiles who fought against Jerusalem, for before this, Hyrcanus had circumcised them; therefore, they preserved[3] the covenant of our God and did not rebel against Judah. So there were within Jerusalem thirty thousand Edomite battle troops to defend the city walls, watches of Edomites who guarded the city in shifts assigned by lot.

After these events, Vespasian moved with all his camp and army from Acco, entered Galil, and encamped there. Joseph was told that the Roman camp was indeed camping on the ridge of Galil. When he heard that Vespasian

---

1. *DEH* 3.3.8.1–2; elsewhere the author writes Talmaida; Akko is added by author. [Ptolemy in biblical Hebrew is Talmi (cf. Judg 1:10). Here the author transliterates the initial P as APH, which is common in medieval and modern Hebrew. SB]

2. Biblical Sheba and Dedan. Cf. Gen 25:3; 1 Chron 1:32. The author evidently recalled how the Greek-speaking Jews of southern Italy pronounced them. Cf. Septuagint *ad locum*.

3. *Shamru mishmereth brith* is literally "preserved the duty of the covenant."

approached, he retreated from Zipporin and went to Tiberias. Vespasian sent a great army to pave the roads, level the ridges, straighten the winding pathways, and improve the trails in order to make a track for his army. This matter was told to Joseph, and he went forth[4] against them, smiting them and destroying them by sword.

When Vespasian heard all that Joseph had done to the Romans, he took his entire army to battle him in Tiberias.[5] When Joseph saw that Vespasian was coming with all his force to [do] battle, Joseph retreated and came to Yodphat (Jodaphat),[6] a city in the Galil, and shut up the city after him.

At that time, Vespasian sent envoys to Joseph, saying: "Thus spoke Vespasian, commander of the force of Rome, of what use is it that you shut yourself up inside the city walls? Come out to me and make peace with us, and we shall make a treaty with you: you will serve the king of Kittim, and you shall live and not die, both you and the people with you."

Joseph sent to him, saying: "Give us a few days grace, and I will speak to the ears of the people as you have spoken; perhaps they will listen to me." Vespasian left Joseph alone. Joseph sent messengers to the people in Jerusalem, to the priests, the nobles, and the rest of the army, saying: "Vespasian sent to me, saying, 'What use is it that you stiffen your necks against us, for all of you shall fall by the sword and the survivors exiled from your land to go into captivity, and your land will remain a wasteland without inhabitant? [cf. Jer 32:43]. Now listen to my voice and come to me, and make peace with us and live, and you will not die; rather, you will eat the good of your land, for living is better than death.'" The inhabitants of Jerusalem sent to Joseph, saying: "Do not dare to make peace with them; just be strong and brave to fight with them until you finish them off or until you die in battle, both you and the army with you, but don't you join with the gentiles!" When Joseph heard the words of the Jerusalemites that they sent to this effect via messengers, he went out to array for battle to confront Vespasian and the Roman camp.

Vespasian began to fight with the Jews by taking the city Gadarana (Gadara) in the Galil. He destroyed it, smiting with the sword until not even a remnant survived of the men, women, children, babes, and even nurslings, saying: "I will exact vengeance for Cestius and his army who fell in the land of Judah." He marched from there and came to Yodphat (Jodaphat), the city where Joseph

---

4. I.e., to Yodphat, but the source does not mention where.

5. The source has Yodapat or Yodpat.

6. Jotapata. The author knew the form Yodapat/Yodaphat, which is Talmudic. The style is quite biblical.

was; and it happened on the first day of his encamping against Yodphat that he gave all his army food and drink and girded them with weapons of war.

On the morrow, the Romans trumpeted the signal for battle and encircled the city. Whereupon Joseph came forward and blew the shofar for battle, and he with all the army of the Jews who were with him went out and fought against the camp of the Romans at the foot of the mountain from dawn to dusk.

When evening came, they ceased fighting; the Jews disengaged from the Roman camp and entered the city, while the Romans returned to their tents and to their camp. Now there fell on that day a huge force from both sides, for the Romans came in pride against the Jews, saying: "We shall subdue them like all the nations whom we have captured." But the Jews dared to oppose them, saying: "We shall die together in zeal for the Sanctuary of our God, and we shall be strengthened to fight for the sake of our people and our land." For this reason, a large number fell there on that day.

The fighting strengthened on the second day and the third and the fourth until on the fifth day it was as strong as on the first day; and all the gentiles who were in the area joined the Roman camp to assist them, but the Jews who survived within the city continually decreased until there remained only a few. Joseph's youths and warriors fell in battle, so Joseph closed the city gate to fight with them [Romans] from the wall.

Vespasian besieged the city for many days, diverting the aqueduct outside the city so that its inhabitants became very thirsty. When Joseph saw that there was no water in the city, he took clothes and dipped them in the water of the city pools, spreading them out over the rim of the wall to show the Roman camp that they indeed had water, lest the Romans boast and say that they had no water.

Vespasian commanded to build a dike against the wall, and he moved a ram up to it—this is the iron battering ram that destroys walls—and he began to butt the city wall with the ram. Now this is how the ram with which they knock down walls works: they bring a big thick beam and put on the end of the beam an iron helmet in the shape of a ram's head whose weight is half[7] that of the beam, and they hang the beam between two poles with ropes; the tops of the poles are tied together, while their bases are planted in the earth with the head of the ram against the rim of the wall in front, and at the beam's rear are iron rings fastened to it with ropes tied in them. Now when they sought to knock down a wall, they would pull the ropes of the beam and send it butting against the wall; the wall would quake and move and fall to the ground.

---

7. The source has "from the middle of the ram," by which the author understood the battering head to be half the beam's weight.

As they butted Yodphat's wall, Joseph saw the wall beginning to move, so he took sacks, filled them with straw, and hung them with ropes from the rim of the wall to intervene between the ram and the outer wall, lest it reach the stones of the wall, for the straw was soft; therefore, the wall was protected from the iron, for every soft thing opposes the hard. Vespasian commanded to send scythes and cut the ropes of the sacks, so that the straw fell on the ground; and again, they continued to butt the wall with the ram.

There was upon the wall a valiant warrior, a priest named Elazar. When he saw them begin to butt the wall with the ram, he lifted a huge rock from off the wall and, raising it high, dropped it on the tip of the ram, breaking it, and it fell to the ground. Then Elazar climbed down the wall and took the ram's head and threw it inside the wall. The wall there was low; therefore, Elazar could descend to take the ram's head. He smote the army that was with the ram, and the rest of the army fled from him. The archers shot arrows at Elazar, and five arrows transfixed him; and the men on the wall stretched out their hands and pulled, lifting Elazar to the wall. The men in the city raised a great shout that Elazar had succeeded in smiting the Roman camp and took the ram upon which they had relied. At that time, Elazar died in high praise for fighting on behalf of his people like a hero, and all the people mourned greatly over Elazar. They buried him in Yodphat, rendering him great honor in his death: for his teaching, for his bravery, and for his dying.

When the Judaean youths saw what Elazar had done and had died with renowned name, two of them became zealous, men of understanding, one named Netira and the second Philippus, and, opening the city gate, went out to fight; they smote and destroyed a great many among the Roman force, and they too died fighting.

When Joseph saw that the fighting had become very heavy, he sallied and smote the Roman camp a great blow, setting aflame the dikes and the iron rams with all the siege weapons. The fighting waxed fierce, and the Roman force began to flee, for they saw that the Judaeans were sacrificing their lives unto death: and the Roman force no longer could withstand them. Vespasian came forward and emboldened the heart of his army, strengthening them; and they stood in battle, fighting Joseph on that day until sunset.

The fighting became exceedingly fierce; Vespasian was shot in the right leg; and all the warriors of Kittim became terrified when they saw the blood flowing from Vespasian's leg. When Titus saw that his father was wounded, he ran in alarm to his father's aid, and his father said to him: "What is this that you are frightened? Take hold and exact vengeance for your father!" Titus and his father, Vespasianus, fought on that day a very forceful battle: there fell on that day many dead from the warriors of Kittim; a very great many of Joseph's men fell, and only a few remained with him as he went back into the city.

On the morrow, the Roman force arose and took their stand at the dike by the iron ram that Joseph had burned and arrayed for battle against the city. The city Yodphat [cf. Jer 50:9] grieved for her heroes, for they all fell in battle. There remained only Joseph and a few men with him, and they went up upon the wall, and the women too ascended upon the wall, for there were no more men left for fighting. Vespasian's men shot a huge rock in a catapult that impacted on the belly of a pregnant woman and carried the child out of her belly about half a ris. They loaded the catapult a second time, and the stone hit one of Joseph's warriors on his head, slicing off the man's head; and a wedge of his head went a distance of one ris with the stone.

At that time, one of the Kittim warriors came and stood under the rim of the wall opposite Joseph, for he thought to himself, "Perhaps I could shoot Joseph with my arrow." Joseph looked at him and shouted toward the warrior, saying: "Don't kill him!" Startled, the man turned around, and the Jews poured boiling oil from atop the wall upon him; his skin melted off his flesh, and he went skinned throughout the Roman camp.

Vespasian continued to fight against Yodphat for forty-eight full days, but the wall was mightier than they, and they could not capture it until the remainder of the survivors within became so exhausted that they could no longer persist and protect the whole city wall. Afterward, Titus and Sabinus came at night and climbed the wall, for the guards had ceased to watch any longer. After they had climbed the wall, a great many troops of Kittim mounted behind them. They broke the bolt of the gate, and the whole Roman force entered Yodphat, sounding a great war cry inside the city. When the Jews heard the sound of the shout, they woke up in fear and dismay, and each, seizing his sword in hand, went out into the city streets, and behold, a Roman force had entered the city. So they fought and died, fighting where they stood, saying to one another: "Let us die fighting and not be taken alive."

Joseph arose, and forty of his surviving warriors left the city with him and fled to the forest, where they found a cave that they entered, hiding themselves there within the cave. All the men of the city were consumed in the fighting, for they did not believe the covenant of the Kittim, because one Jew asked of a Roman: "Let me live." The latter swore to him, saying: "Thus will God do unto me and even increase if I kill you. Come out to me." The Jew called out, saying to the Roman: "Give me your right hand, and I will trust in you." And the Roman put forth his left hand, giving it to the Jew. But the Jew did not notice that it was his left hand because he was scared. So, when the Roman gave him his left hand, he grasped it, but the Roman held a javelin in his right hand and killed him. The Jew, however, had no javelin in his right hand, for he had cast his weapons away; therefore, he died. When the Jews saw that the Roman did not keep his pledge and was not faithful to his vow, and the Jew died, they said: "Let us die together for the blood of our brother and not have faith in the covenant of gentiles." So all died together, and with their death, they killed many of the Romans in that fighting, even more than they had killed previously, and the city was subsequently taken.

67. JOSEPH SAVES HIS LIFE

Joseph and forty men were hidden in a cave, so Vespasian sent Pavlinus [Gr for Paulinus] and Gallicanus to Joseph, saying: "Come out to me and live, and you shall not die."

When the men who were with Joseph saw that Joseph was inclined to go out to the Romans, they said to him: "We are surprised at you, for you were chosen from myriads of a priestly people and a holy kingdom and appointed as commander of the army at the head of your people, and your eyes have seen the disgrace of your people and the shame of your flock on this day, and you can live? How can you still desire living? Is not death preferable to life on such a day? Is it because of their mercy upon you that they do not kill you? Do they summon you to benefit you? Only in order to capture you alive so that they may boast, saying: 'Behold, we have captured alive your anointed warlord.' Then they will say: 'We have the upper hand.' Now, if you were not to die by their hand, they will have no victory, nor will they find anything to boast about, for they had neither captured you nor killed you. Is it not better for you to die by your sword than to die by their sword or to live and hear the shame of their abuse? Do not trust them, for they will not let you live out of goodness or mercy; rather, they will preserve you for shame, which is worse than death, so that they may boast over you in the disgrace of their abuses. And now have you set your heart to live after the loss of your people and your brethren, for what desire would you choose living?

"Where is the word of Moses that he spoke before God: 'If You destroy them [cf. Ex 32:32], blot me out from your book that You have written'? Where is Aaron, who stood between the dead and the living, standing firm like a hero before the angel, and he was handed over unto death for the sake of his people, lest they fall in the plague? Where are our kings Shaul and Yehonatan, his son, who fought on behalf of God's people and died for the sake of God and His people? Could not Shaul have lived and be saved? Yet he did not desire life but rather chose death over living when he saw that his army had been routed in battle; for this reason, he did not separate from his brethren, both he and his son Yehonatan, the beloved and sweet ones [2 Sam 1:23]. Pray, remember the righteousness of David, God's anointed [*messiah*], who said [2 Sam 24:17]: 'Let Your hand be against me and against my father's house, for I have sinned and acted perversely; but these sheep, what have they done?'

"Where is the holy Torah, which is hidden in your heart? Are you not priest and anointed who taught us the Torah? How can we love our God with all our heart and all our soul if we do not die for his covenant with his servants who are killed for His name? Have you not testified for us[1] many times saying that every man who would die in battle[2] for God and for His people and for His Torah, his destiny will be with God to go to the Great Light[3] without seeing the enveloping darkness? Are you not Joseph, who shouted in battle in the fighting at the Roman camp: 'I am Joseph, priest and anointed warlord, who has given my life to death in behalf of the people of God.' And now with your going out to them alive, what will you answer then? Will not shame [cf. Obad. 10] and disgrace cover you, since every word from your mouth is a lie? Did you not say to the people:[4] 'Fight until you die in battle, for if you die for the sake of God's sanctuary and for his Torah, your deaths will be an atonement for your souls, and you will go to the Great Light'? If what you said was truth, why do you save your soul from death, from following your people who have gone to the Great Light?

"But until this day you have been a hero in fighting over all the gentiles; indeed, when they hear tidings of you, they tremble and become sick from fear of you, and now you would give yourself to be captured by Romans like one of the wretched maidservants? Is it not your disgrace and shame and the shame of God's people that a general of the king, a priest and anointed one such as you,

---

1. The author's addition (cf. Talmud, *Berakhoth* 54a); cf. Baer, "Hebrew Sepher Yosifun," 193. Based on *DEH* 3.16, the author develops the idea that a man who dies in a holy war will be rewarded in the world-to-come. This idea is expressed by both Josephus and Hegesippus. One may however assume that the author learned this idea from his Christian neighbors who fought against Muslim invaders. See following note.

2. Similarly, Pope Leo IV (847–855) promised eternal reward to those who died fighting Arabs in southern Italy.

3. See chap. 65, among others, for this widespread phrase.

4. Not in the source, but these words do parallel the text above. The author adds another idea, that death in a holy war is atonement for the souls of those who fell fighting the Muslims in southern Italy, as on the flag of Pope John VIII (872–882); i.e., both Christian and Muslim warriors became martyrs.

should be bound in the chains of the gentiles? And further, all those who see you alive from this day and hence will say as follows: 'Is this not the man who surrendered his city, his warriors, and the troops of his host and the rest of his people to death and saved only his own life to live?'"

When they had finished speaking to him these words, each unsheathed his sword and approached him inside the cave, saying: "Look and listen, Joseph, if you consent to heed our voice, we shall kill you first as a lord and hero and general, but if you refuse to die with honor, know that we shall kill you like one of the enemy who comes against us."

Joseph began to speak to them: "Surely I know that you speak justly, and who would wish such a life? I wish God would summon my soul and take her unto Him, for He is the one that places my spirit within me. Who will release what he confines [cf. Job 12:14]? Is He not the one who confines and releases, for He is the Living God and breathes into our corpses life's breath; He makes us live that we may be alive before Him? He is the one who deposited the spirit of life within us, and He confines it. And now how could we release that which God confined? Do you not know that this soul is a deposit from God, and we are servants, and He has given it to us? If we should cast it away ere it is demanded, will He not be angry with us, and we would be cursed without finding rest with Abraham, our father?

"Did Abraham, our father, go to God without summons? Was he not first summoned and afterward departed, and similarly with all the righteous ones? Did not God first summon Moses, his chosen one, saying to him: 'Ascend Mount Abarim' [Deut 32:49], so he ascended, nor would he have gone up had he not been called? Thus, no one can complete his life if it is not demanded of him.[5]

"Now pray learn from Job, for when he says: 'Let the day be lost on which I was born,'[6] couldn't he be choked and die or harken to his wife's voice when she says to him: 'Curse God and die'?[7] Even he showed patience with the severe boils and the malignant leprosy [cf. Lev 13:51] that plagued him until his soul was required from him, and he returned it when summoned. Truly he sought a way to die, but from God's hand, not his own hand, for did he

------

5. The author's addition. On the phrase *lehashlim nafsho* (complete his life), see chaps. 14 and 18.

6. *DEH* too cites Job 3:3. In the following the author adapts Job's example in his own style.

7. The Hebrew of Job 2:9 reads literally, "Bless God and die." However, there is a long tradition, already in the Septuagint, to read the word "Bless" as a euphemism. The woman's words are not cited in the source. Here too the author uses his biblical knowledge to fill out the omissions in his source.

not say: 'They wait for death, but it comes not [Job 3:21],' and he did not die until his end came. Also, another pious one [i.e., David] said: 'Release my soul from prison' [Ps 142:8], for he knew that the soul is imprisoned, and who will release her save God who imprisoned her? He hath given it, and He will take it away.

"I know how goodly and pleasant is death at the end of one's task or in battle, for it is honorable and precious in God's judgment if we were to die at the appointed time by God's hand, or, if during fighting at our enemy's hand, we will be considered righteous. But if we take our own lives, who will speak for us, and who will justify us? Will not our righteousness and our hope be lost? And if you seek to die by a weapon, better for you to die by our enemy's weapon and not let our own hand kill one another.

"But I wish that we could die by our enemy's hand after they swore to us to let us live, thus betraying their oath and killing us; then all who hear of it will say: 'Was it not from fear of them that they killed them?' and we would have a good reputation. But even if we were righteous to subdue them in battle—for it was due to our sins that they subdued us—yet they swore to us to let us live and afterward they betrayed their oath and slew us, would not such a death be better for us than to die like villains?

"And now if we should kill one another, we would be labeled murderers, for we would have murdered each one his comrade. And if anyone of us were to kill himself, he would be considered a suicide just like King Shaul, whom you praised, since he was not enthroned over Israel save by their wish, as they said: 'Give us a king and let him rule over us.' For this reason, God turned away from him, for he did not fulfill God's request; for this reason, God anointed David over His people while Shaul was still alive; therefore, he [Shaul] chose death because he could not live. And so I imagine that from cowardice he did this, for he said: 'Lest these uncircumcised ones come and mistreat me' [1 Sam 31:4]. So now understand and know that since he did not take pity on his son, how could he have had mercy for his own life?

"Why did Aaron [Deut 17:13] stand between the dead and the living? Was it not to stay the plague that he stood before the angel to avert the pestilence from his people? But now I, though I am not Aaron, rather, merely one of his descendants, did not spare my soul from death for I knew that it was better for me to die at the hands of my enemies than to die by my own hand.

"And now even if my soul fears the piercing stabs of my enemies, you should know that I am faint of heart only out of my great wickedness; nevertheless, I would stand fast before them like a professional soldier who would not retreat before the weapons of death. And you too know this powerful people who subdued all the kingdoms of the world. Did I not muster for battle against them like a hero and even delivered them a major setback by my holding fast for forty-eight days in this tiny city Yodphat? Did I not say: 'Perhaps I could drive them away from Jerusalem lest they advance against her'?

"If you say: 'Let us choose death rather than be slaves to our oppressors,' I agree with you and will not separate my soul from dying with you. However, it is good to be free and live, for death is good in its own time, while living is good in its own time. Now behold, men call us to life. If at the moment of dying a man should flee from the battle, he would be considered a coward, and he would be disgraced; but if at the threshold of living, that man should go to die, he would be thought a fool. And if in a moment of fear a man should surrender his life to death, this is not might but rather fright. For thus foolish women would act in the moment of their terror when they knew that calamity would overtake them; they would die from timidity, or they would fall from atop the city's height to die, or they would strangle, or they would stab themselves and die immorally. Yet the valiant man who does not retreat before anything, he would not act thus, for how would his bravery be known if he did not stand before every evil that confronted him?

"Look upon the animals, the lions and all the forest beasts who fight unto their death. Is it not for the sake of saving themselves from death? Are not their weapons their teeth, their claws, and their fangs? Do they destroy or injure themselves? Only if something attacks them do they fight to their death or until they save themselves. We too seize our weapons when we fight against our enemies either to die or to live. So now how can we die each by the sword of his brother?

"Look at the shipmaster. Why should he suffer the storm and be alert through the night and keep watch day and night and battle against the waves if not to save his ship? If, out of recklessness, he would draw near the breakers and smash up on the rocks, what would they say of him? Would they not say about him: 'Behold, a wicked scoundrel who destroys his ship and loses his men'? And the king, were he to assign his precious vessels to his appointees, would they not preserve them until he recalled his vessels and demanded them from their charge, then they would return them to him? But if they abandon his vessels before he demanded them from their charge, would they not anger him, and he be furious with them? And if a man should come before the king before the end of his watch, would he [the king] not rebuke him [the man] and say to him: 'Why is it that you have come?'? Indeed, all souls belong to God. He has given them in His mercy, and He will take them at His will when they have fulfilled their end, then the soul will go to its rest. But if the soul should go before its time,[8] He would not accept it, nor would it find rest, and for all of its life it would wander and roam, since it was banished before its appointed time.

"Do you not know that if a man had a servant who was insolent, rebellious, mutinous, and stubborn, when bad times would come upon him and he sees that he is in dire straits, he would go and hang and be strangled and die or stab himself and die? Do you not know that this would be his judgment: to cut off his right hand that killed him and also to decree that he not be buried because he committed suicide?" Thus spake Joseph, spreading his palms upward: "And now El Shaddai, You are our father, You have fashioned us in Your faith, and You direct all of us through Your manifold mercy; all of us are the creation of Your hand, and You rule over all Your creation, for You have made everything, and You direct everything wherever You desire [cf. Prov 21:1]. Now if it is good in Your eyes to take the soul that You have given me, take it, for it is in Your hand; You have given it, and unto You it will return; take it according to Your will, for I will not cast it away, nor will I be considered before You as a suicide. In Your hand is every living thing and the breath of all mankind, for just as man cannot live without judgment [Job 12:10], so too he cannot die without judgment."

Although Joseph spoke at length, the men who were with him did not heed his speech, for they sought to die. When Joseph saw that he could not turn them around and that his words had no effect in their ears and that they did not listen to him, he spoke to them cunningly, saying: "If you seek to die by the sword, it is better that you die by lot. Pair up, if you will, and cast lots before me, and the one upon whom the lot falls shall die by the sword of his comrade. We shall do so until we are finished together, and we shall die and not live, nor will we see the disgrace of the Sanctuary of God and the exile of our people."

They did so, and the men obeyed him, and they stood in pairs and cast lots before him. When the lot fell upon one, his comrade stabbed him and he died; and another stood, and the lot fell upon his comrade, and he killed him. Thus, they all did until everyone had fallen by the sword and only Joseph and his comrade remained. And his comrade said to him: "Come let us cast our lots also that we may be gathered to our brothers." But Joseph answered his comrade and said: "Why should we cause harm to ourselves? If I kill you, I would be considered a murderer, and if you kill me, you too will be considered a murderer, and we shall have abandoned our hope with God, our Lord, for all these have died immorally." When the man heard Joseph's words, he ceased to speak of such

---

8. Cf. *DEH* 3.17, 217–18. The author understood his source to allude to a popular belief about the wandering souls of suicides. Cf. Macrobius, *Comm. in somnium Scipionis*, 1.13.9–10; and Baer, "Hebrew Sepher Yosifun," 197.

things, for he was in awe of him. This is how Joseph was saved from the sword of his comrade.

Just at that time, Nicanor the officer came and took Joseph and his comrade and led them to Vespasian. When the Roman camp saw Joseph, they shouted a very great cry: part of the army rejoiced that Joseph was captured, saying: "Hurrah! Hurrah!" and part of the army grieved in bitterness, saying: "Is this not the hero whose dread destroyed the whole Roman force and the tidings of his bravery went throughout the whole land? How could he be captured? And we, how can we win if such a one as this is captured in the bosom of his land? How can we be saved in a foreign land?" And Vespasian's son Titus began to whistle and shake his head and said: "Who knows, perhaps we too shall be captured just as this one was captured." Consequently, he took pity on him [Joseph] and spared him from dying by the sword.

68. BATTLES IN THE GALILEE

After this, Vespasian marched from there with all his camp and went to Acco, and from there he marched to Caesarea, the great city King Herod had built. When the Caesareans saw Joseph, they cried out to Vespasian, saying: "Kill him, for if he lives, he will provoke major battles on you." But Vespasian did not heed their call to kill him.

It was reported to Vespasian: "Behold, the men of Yafo were going in ships to the islands and to the lands of your dominion to plunder and rob, to kill and destroy your people." So, he lay in wait for them until they went, and afterward, he came to Yafo, encamped against her, and captured her, for there were no men of war there. When they came back from the islands, they found the Roman camp within the city. These sought to leave the sea for the dry land, and behold, a very great stormy wind broke all the boats, for there was no harbor and the boats butted against the rocks in the sea. Some of the army was lost, and the survivors, the Romans stabbed them even before they reached land, and they died. The number of the dead men who drowned in the sea were four thousand, excluding those who died in Yodphat, for there fell in Yodphat forty thousand Judaeans.

Vespasian sent his son Titus with Valerianus and Traianus. They went and encamped against the fortified cities that encircled the Galil and captured them. All who made peace with him lived, but those who were stubborn and fought with him died fighting in battle. And all the people who were in Agripas's portion, they returned them to him except for Tiriyah (Taricheae),[1] for they destroyed her inhabitants, took her booty, sold the women and children, and they captured all the cities of the Galil.

---

1. Taricheae from *DEH* 3.23.1; for the form, see chap. 65.

They [Romans] went from there to Gamla, the city at the head of the mountain, for which reason it was called Gamla (Camela);[2] it was the choice of the cities of Agripas,[3] and also the city Seleucia, a land of forests, streams of water, and all kinds of fruit-bearing trees.

Agripas said to Vespasian: "Please, let us not destroy this city, for I will go and speak in the ears of the people and call them to peace. Perhaps they will listen to my voice, and they will live and not die." So Agripas went to them and called them to peace, and they answered him, saying: "Pray approach a bit and speak with your servants." When he neared the wall and was speaking with them, they dropped a huge stone upon him, and the stone fell upon Agripas's shoulder, breaking his arm, and he fell to the ground; and his servants drew near and carried him off. When Vespasian saw that they had disgraced their king and raised their hand against him, then he encamped against the city and fought with her because the Jews had disgraced their king.

The Jews said to one another: "Be strong, and let us be strengthened in our battle, for we have no more hope of living after we have raised our hand against the king." They fought against the Roman camp; the Romans set up the iron ram against the city wall and butted it, and the wall fell to the ground. Vespasian entered the city and with him a numerous and great army; Vespasian commanded them, saying: "Thus you shall do: stand all the night around the wall as a watch until the morning, and when it is the morning, we shall capture her." But they did not heed their lord's command, for they entered within the city during the night. The Jews rose against them inside the city, closing around them the entrances of the city without retreat, and the Jews smote them there a very great blow such that nary any of those who entered the city with Vespasian survived. Only Vespasian was saved with ten men and an officer, Butsio.

When morning came, Vespasian fled from there, for his warriors had fallen, and the Jews pursued after him, killing Butsio, his officer, who was a hero in the Roman camp. Vespasian retreated from there into the mountains with the remainder of his camp and sent Titus, his son, to the land of Aram to bring back the Roman force that he had sent to invade Persia, and Titus brought them to the land of Judah.

After this, Vespasian and Agripas went to the city of Seleucia and smote her until there hardly remained a remnant to her. After he smote Seleucia, he came

---

2. *DEH* 4.1.1 has Camela, which the author understood as referring to a camel; the author missed this interpretation by perhaps misunderstanding his source's *a superioribus* as a high place.

3. According to *DEH* 4.1.2, Agripas besieged the city for seven months; the author did not read his source too carefully.

to Cischala[4]—it [alone] remained of all the fortified cities of the Galil—and he encamped against her, for a great number of bloodthirsty men and destroyers in the land was gathered there.

Now in that city, there was a man named Yoḥanan. He was enlightened in books,[5] also cunning of heart with a penchant toward evil, a man of [silken] tongue and counsel to evil thought to spill blood and to do every wickedness, to tempt and seduce many from the path, and to lead astray toward all that God hates, to anger us to take the booty of those seduced by him, lying in ambush, spilling blood, coveting every wealth. The man grew rich from the booty of the oppression,[6] and wicked men, murderers, robbers, and rebels like him gathered unto him; he filled their hands with riches, and they joined him, becoming like his brothers.

At that time, Titus came on a mission from his father, Vespasian, for he was sent to make peace with the city, summoning her to peace so that she make peace with him. Titus spoke peace unto the ears of the inhabitants of the city, and the city elders were willing to make peace. When Yoḥanan saw that the city elders wanted to make peace with Titus, he appointed his brethren who had joined with him to guard the walls to prevent the elders from speaking with the Romans. Then Yoḥanan replied to Titus, saying: "Tomorrow is a holy day of God for us. Leave us alone for two days,[7] and on the third day, we will render you our words." Titus acted accordingly; he left them alone for two days. On the third day, Yoḥanan rose up during the night, he and his men, and fled the city; and Titus did not know that Yoḥanan had fled.

Titus rose early on the morrow and spoke to the men of the city, saying: "What is your intent? Tell me." The men opened the gate of the city, and Titus entered, and they received him with joy. When he asked for Yoḥanan, he was told that he had fled during the night toward Jerusalem. So he sent pursuers after Yoḥanan, and they hastened in going, but they did not overtake him; they caught only a few of the people who had left to escape with him—men,

---

4. Gischala (Gush Ḥalav); one MS has Cischala, however, which the author used.

5. Based on the words *studia* and *doctus* applied to Yoḥanan in the source, which, however, are used in a different sense by *DEH*, who disparages Yoḥanan. *Yosippon's* words perhaps influenced the Crusade chronicles (cf. *Gezeroth Ashkenaz ve-Ẓarefat*, ed. Habermann, 12). The author's style is strictly biblical in his string of infinitives; see following note.

6. The phrase *hon ha-hamas* also appears in the 1 QS 10.19 (The Manual of Discipline), which has other stylistic parallels to this passage based on biblical influence.

7. The author's gloss is based on his misunderstanding of his source's *ebdomadis sacrae dies*, i.e., the Sabbath. Diaspora Jews celebrated holidays for an extra day since the date of the holiday was set in the land of Israel and the pace of communication allowed for doubt as to the actual date.

women, and children, the old and the weak. The pursuers killed all whom they caught and looted the booty that was with them. Thus, Titus captured all the cities of the Galil and appointed officers over them.

Vespasian removed from there to Mount Tabor. This is the Tabor whose height is thirty ris, and the mountaintop is a mesa extending twenty-three ris. Vespasian sent his officer Plagido (Placidus), who captured the mountain and the city atop it. Up to here is the chronicle of the battles that occurred in the Galil and the land of Israel. Many of the gigantic battles and awesome deeds that were done there we have not written, for they were many, but now we would relate the battles of Jerusalem and how it was besieged.

69. INTERNAL BATTLES WITHIN JERUSALEM

When Yoḥanan the Galilean fled to Jerusalem,[1] he found there countless wicked scoundrels, murderers, and reckless bloodthirsty men, for men of war had gravitated to Jerusalem from everywhere to assist God's temple; Anani the priest had received them and brought them into the city. They grouped around Yoḥanan the Galilean and joined with him, giving him their advice and support.

Yoḥanan plotted with these scoundrels to attack the wealthy people, to kill them and seize their wealth. It happened when they seized one after another of the city's notables, they would say to him: "Did you not send letters to the Roman camp to Vespasian to surrender the city to them?" And speaking such words in front of the people, they would bring scoundrels to bear false witness against him so that he would be sentenced to death. They did so to Antipas and to Libia (Levias), good and honest men of the city's notables, and took all the wealth of their household, their silver and gold and precious things, to be sustenance for the scoundrels.

They banished the high priests from their watches and ousted them from the crown of the holy [service]; and they cast a lot, saying: "Who will officiate as priest?"; they mocked the priesthood. The portion fell to one of the priests, named Pani ben Penuel,[2] a rustic tiller of the land who did not know the priestly way—for it was not proper for such a man to be priest. Yet they appointed him high priest, for they mocked and scorned the priesthood.

When the men of faith and truth in Jerusalem saw that the scoundrels had taken over, they assembled and volunteered to fight against them. The people

---

1. Chapter follows *DEH* 4.6.1 to 4.10 with author's additions.
2. Apparently the author's MS read "Phanuelis"; the source has "Phanis filius Samuelis."

were zealous for God and took a stand against the scoundrels and fought them. Now the fighting grew fierce between the people and the scoundrels, and the fighting became fiercer throughout the city streets, its markets, and within the Temple of God and the Temple court, until the city was filled with the dead and the stabbed, for there was no street or market or courtyard where there was no fighting. The people overcame the murderers and scoundrels; the people's zeal was great, and they began to overpower them. When they [scoundrels] saw that they could not hold out against the volunteers, they all ran into the Temple of God. They closed it behind them and remained within the Temple.

When Anani the high priest and the rest of the Hasidim and the people saw that the scoundrels retreated to the Temple to save themselves, they commanded the people, saying: "Leave them alone. Don't fight with them within the Temple, lest God's Temple be profaned with the blood of corpses!" and the people desisted. Anani the high priest counseled to set guards from the people's warriors at the gates surrounding the Temple to prevent them from leaving the Temple, and the number of guards that he set up against them were six thousand, bearing swords, carrying shield and lance, breastplate, and helmet.

Anani the high priest had such a thought: "Behold, these scoundrels are shut up in God's Temple. We cannot touch them within the holy Temple of God; moreover, it would be damaging for the people of God to kill each other." He sent envoys to Yoḥanan the Galilean, chief of the murderers, a scoundrel, to make peace.

But Yoḥanan and his band of scoundrels refused to make peace with Anani, for they had sent to Edom to come to Jerusalem to their aid—for the Edomites had always been strong and fierce, but they yielded to Judaean control ever since King Hyrcanus had crushed them, circumcising them and putting them under conscription as troops guarding the walls of Jerusalem, and the rest of them were subjected to the Jews. When Yoḥanan sent for an army of Edom, Edomite warriors came during the night—some twenty thousand men girt with fighting gear. When Anani and the people heard the sound of the Edomite camp during the night, he, Anani, mounted the wall and asked them as follows: "Who are you?" They answered him, saying: "We are of Edom. We came to seek God in His Temple and also to seek the peace of His people."

Anani answered them, saying: "You did not come to seek God; rather, you have come to assist Yoḥanan and the scoundrels. Would it not be better for you to come to the aid of God and His temple and His people than to help these murderers and sinners who spilled the blood of righteous ones and the Hasidim and the innocent in the city of God? Their wickedness in the city of God is worse than the wickedness of the Romans. [It has made us] say: 'Would that our death be at the hands of the Romans rather than at the hands of Judaeans like us!' And if you have come to help them, you have sinned against God for coming to assist them, for they trampled upon God's people like wine treaders [cf. Isa 63:2], and they have made God's Temple a house for murderers and the dwelling place of the wicked. Now, if you have come to seek God, why are you girt with your fighting gear? Not for your sake have we closed the city gates preventing you from entering the city; we have shut it only because of the weapons, for they are tools of destruction. Now if you desire to enter the city, strip off your weapons and come in peace."

The Edomites said to him: "We are amazed at the priests of God's Temple, the elders of His people and His officials. Are we considered as enemies that we are denied entry into the city? Do you not know that Vespasian approaches? For this reason, we have donned our fighting gear to come to aid God and protect the city, as we have always done."

As they were speaking further in this vein, behold, there appeared a very great cloud, powerful lightning, strong noises and immense thunders, darkness and obscurity, and the sound of thunder encompassing all, hail, and flaming fire. The people fled from atop the wall, for they could not hold on. Anani, however, said that these noises, the lightning, and the thunders were sent by God to fight in behalf of Jerusalem. Therefore, each man went to his home, and they did not know these noises were to the detriment of Jerusalem and the people.

When the scoundrels shut up in the Temple saw that the soldiers had fled from the gates they were guarding and also that the people atop the wall had fled each to his home, they rose up, opened the doors of the Temple, and went out from there; they went through [the city] to the gate of the wall and looked right and left, but there was no one; so they took in their hands large cleavers and hacked at the bar of the city gate until they broke the lock. Whenever the sound of the thunder intensified, they increased their efforts to break the lock of the gate and its bar. And when it ceased, they too stopped, until they opened the gate of Jerusalem.

The Edomite force entered the city and roamed throughout the city during the night and came unto the Temple. They brought forth the scoundrels who were left there and formed one army; and they killed on that night eighty-five hundred fighting men of God's people, in addition to a great many of the poor. When the morning came, they turned against the rich, to imprison them, and they summoned the judges of the people, seventy elders of the Sanhedrin. Yoḥanan the Galilean, the scoundrel, said to them: "Why do you not sentence these rich people to death, for they struck a pact with the Romans to surrender this city into their hands?"

At that time, they seized one of the important men of the city, named Zechariah, a wealthy and righteous God-fearing man. He [Yoḥanan] said to the elders: "Sentence this man to death, for he was in league with our enemies to hand over this city to them." When the priests and the elders heard the words of Yoḥanan and his men that they sought to kill Zechariah, they wept bitterly. When Yoḥanan and his men saw that the elders refused to kill Zechariah because he was righteous, they boldly took him from the midst of the elders, brought him up to the top of the tower on the wall that faces east, and threw him down from there. Zechariah fell from the wall to the depths of the Valley of Yehoshaphat and died. The elders feared Yoḥanan and were very terrified, for he said to them: "If you do not judge all whom we bring before you according to the sentence we desire, know that you too will die the same death as Zechariah."

They [scoundrels] seized a wealthy and righteous man beloved by all the inhabitants of Jerusalem, named Gorgon; this man was a valiant and experienced soldier, a volunteer in all the battles against the nations who fought against Jerusalem. When the gentile warriors drew near to fight against the Judaeans, Gorgon would go forth to confront them, killing them and putting them to flight. For this reason, all his body, his face, and his head were full of scars from the many battles that he fought for the House of God. But because he was unwilling to obey the voice of Yoḥanan and join his faction, he [Yoḥanan] seized him [Gorgon] and said: "You will surely die!" They brought him forth outside the city to kill him there. Gorgon begged them: "I beg you to do me the great mercy of burying my corpse." They answered him and said: "If you had been held your peace, we would have buried you, but since you have spoken, we will kill you, and you will not be buried, but rather we will throw your corpse in the field for the birds of the sky." As he was pleading with them, they struck him and he died, and, throwing his corpse in the field, they reentered the city.

70. VESPASIAN'S ENTHRONEMENT

Vespasian,[1] ruler of the Romans, came to Caesarea and camped there, for he said: "Let's not hurry to attack Jerusalem, until they have fought each other to the death within the city. Perhaps their might will be broken through fighting and famine." Vespasian was an expert in warfare, and he camped in Caesarea for many days.

The people in Jerusalem were fighting with Yoḥanan and the men who gathered unto him, until the people suffered casualties without number: some fell by the sword; others were stabbed with knives, for some of the murderers [i.e., *sicarii*] held their knives in hand, hiding it under their clothing. A murderer would approach a righteous man and, suddenly, without [the victim's] knowing, stab him, and he would fall and die, not knowing who smote him; more people died this way than in battle.

In those days, Yoḥanan sent a force of fighting men from Jerusalem. They went to the cities that had made peace with Vespasian. They destroyed and smote the city's inhabitants, every Judaean and Roman found there. And taking all the wealth of the cities, they went to Gadara across the Jordan and stayed there.

At that time, all the inhabitants of Jerusalem, the priests and the rest of the people, sent peace terms to Vespasian: "Give us your hand to help us, for the wickedness of Yoḥanan and the murderers with him is unbearable. They have destroyed countless in the city of God." The people of Gadara also sent to Vespasian similar words, saying: "Yoḥanan's men destroyed everything that they found, from man unto cattle, without leaving a remnant, [for] now he came against us to annihilate us." When Vespasian heard the message of the people of Gadara, he came to their aid and not to Jerusalem.

---

1. Chapter follows *DEH* 4.11–4.26. The author uses biblical *peḥah* (= pasha) and consistently writes "Vespasianus."

When Yoḥanan's men who were camping in Gadara were told that Vespasian was coming against them, they smote the chief of the city of Gadara, named Doliso (Dolesus), and left the city to flee toward the forest. Vespasian sent the officer Placidus after them; he caught up with them and smote many of them.

Placidus returned from there, and while on his way back to Gadara, he found on the banks of the Jordan a great mob of poor people [*dalath haarez*] who sought to go up to Jerusalem to find refuge there. He pressed them to the river and smote 13,000 of them. The rest of the crowd fell into the Jordan: 92,200 men, women, and children. And also sheep, cattle, camels, and donkeys without number died in the water, until the flow of the Jordan was stopped by the multitude of carcasses and the corpses of men and beasts. Then the waters of the Jordan widened and overflowed their banks to the fields and into the vales, for the cadavers stopped the Jordan from flowing. All these corpses were swept to the sea of Sodom, the sea of slime [*Asphaltius lacus*], and the bodies of the dead, corpses of man and beast, covered the surface of the sea.

Following this, Vespasian departed from there, marched to the land of Edom, and captured two fortified cities, one named Legaris and the second named Caphartor. He smote ten thousand men of these cities and took the rest of the people captive. He marched from there to Ḥamat Gader (Amathus), where there are hot springs. Then he turned toward Shomron and came unto Jericho and began to rebuild all the cities that he had captured, to reconstruct their walls, and to station within them fighting men and guards to assist him in the siege against Jerusalem.

He marched to Caesarea to gather his entire army and people to go against Jerusalem to besiege it, and lo, envoys came from the land of the Romans from the city of Roma and told him that Nero the king had died and Galba succeeded him; yet within six months, the Romans had struck him [Galba] down and enthroned in his place Vitellio, a drunkard.

When all the Roman officers with Vespasian heard this, they became angry and very enraged, saying: "Why was Vespasian not enthroned, a valiant hero who captured many nations, great peoples, mighty kings, and has grown old fighting? And now, although it is more fitting that Vespasian be king, they enthroned a drunken villain."

All the Roman officers with Vespasian rose and said to him: "Rule over us!" But Vespasian refused to heed their pleas that he rule over them, so they forced him to sit upon the throne of the kingdom and put a crown upon his head. When he put forth his hand to remove it, because he did not want to rule, they drew their swords and said: "Know that if you refuse to rule, you shall surely die!" Seeing that they did not desist from him and fearing lest they kill him, he ruled over them.

71. THE BEGINNING OF SHIMON'S DEEDS

Meanwhile, the fighting in Jerusalem increased,[1] and much blood of God's people was spilled within her by Yoḥanan the scoundrel and his bloody henchmen.

There arose in the midst of Jerusalem a bloody scoundrel named Shimon of Judah, and he began to imitate Yoḥanan's habits, spilling innocent blood and looting and robbing in Jerusalem. Anani had previously cast him from Jerusalem. Due to his great wickedness, Anani cast him out of the city, whereupon Shimon went and joined up with bandits. But Shimon thought to himself: "It is disgraceful for a man like me to be a thief and a bandit." So he went throughout all the cities of Judah, calling out in the streets of the cities: "Whoever among you is a slave seeking to be free, whoever is a murderer seeking to be saved, whoever is oppressed seeking liberty, whoever is stubborn and rebellious, let him come to me; let him throw off himself the yoke of law!" And some twenty thousand gathered unto him.

When the lords of Jerusalem and the priests heard how the wickedness of Shimon was great and that his power to do evil increased, they said to one another: "Let us send against him valiant men experienced in war to fall upon him suddenly. Perhaps they will be able to smite him or capture him before his wickedness increases and he be added to our enemies who fight against us and be another obstacle for us." They sent a great force against him. They advanced toward him suddenly, reaching his force at night, where they found him camped in planted fields destroying the crop of the land, and they began to smite Shimon's force. Shimon arose against them during the night and dealt them a very great

---

1. Chapter follows *DEH* 4.22.1 to 4.33 with author's additions.

blow. Whereupon the men turned to run away on the road to Jerusalem, and Shimon pursued them, smiting them all the way to the gates of Jerusalem, and a great many of them fell along the way.

Shimon went to the land of Edom to take it from the Jerusalemites, and he fought against Edom. They resisted him, and neither could overcome the other, so each returned to his camp. Shimon was very angry and said: "Better is my death than my life, for I could not capture Edom." He encamped on the border of Edom and sat there contemplating whether to renew the war against them.

While he was considering his intent, behold, Yaakov the Edomite came unto him, and he was a valiant man in Edom, a fighter, and a murderer. When he came to Shimon, he made a pact with him, saying to him: "I am handing over Edom to you. Now rise up early in the morning and wage war against them. When you see that I come toward you, point your spear to me, and I will turn toward my people in retreat. I will put terror in their hearts, and they will flee. You will pursue them and capture Edom." And so they did. When Edom saw that Yaakov fled from the battle, they all turned to flee from Shimon, and he pursued after them, smiting many. He captured Edom, and they became his servants.

Shimon marched from there and with him forty thousand Edomites and Judaeans. He came to Hebron and captured it and took all the wealth of the city. And taking all the warriors of Judaea with him, he marched from Hebron to the villages around Jerusalem, destroying their crops and their harvest, their standing grain, and their sheaves [Exod 22:5].

When Yoḥanan heard, he wanted to go out from Jerusalem to fight him [Shimon], but he was afraid of him and did not go out but ambushed him on the road. And lo, Shimon's wife left Jerusalem to go to him with her slaves and maidservants. Yoḥanan captured her and brought her to the city. Yoḥanan and his men grew arrogant for capturing Shimon's wife and said: "Now he will fall into our hands." When this was told to Shimon, he too captured many of Yoḥanan's men and cut off their hands, every right hand, and sent them to their master. Shimon sent to Yoḥanan as follows: "Let my wife go, for if you do not free her and I capture this city, I will cut off their hands and feet." The people were afraid of him and sent him his wife, so he refrained for some time from the evil he intended to do to the people of Jerusalem.

After these events, Vespasian was told that Galba, the king enthroned after Nero Caesar, was killed and that Vitellius ruled in his place. Vespasian remained quiet in Caesarea for some time.

Shimon turned toward Edom, taking along his wife. When he entered Edom, he began to loot their possessions, until they had nothing left, and he amassed great wealth. He left Edom and came to Jerusalem, and with him all the force of Edom and Judaea that rallied to him, and he encamped against the gate of Jerusalem.

Yoḥanan [and his men] were in the city. Their iniquity spread within the city, each killing his neighbor and committing adultery with his neighbor's wife; whoring spread within the city. Also, some of the army shaved their beard,[2] grew long the hair of their head, and dressed in women's clothes according to their custom, for the sake of adultery, and this iniquity became a scandal. No one went out or came in; for whoever went out died in the field by Shimon's sword, while in the city, he died by Yoḥanan's sword.

When the people saw how great Yoḥanan's evil was within the city, they assembled to do battle with him. They fought, and many of the people fell. And had not the Edomite force within the city come to aid the people, Yoḥanan would have killed all of them. The people took counsel to bring Shimon into the city to help them so they might overcome Yoḥanan. They sent Amitai the priest to Shimon, to bring him into the city. But Shimon rejected their deceit, saying: "I do not desire to come into the city because you hate me" [cf. Judg 11:7]. They pleaded with him, so he came with all his force to Jerusalem. But Shimon broke the pact he had made with the city people to assist them. And there was fighting between Shimon and Yoḥanan every day.

When Vespasian heard that Vitellio had died in the city of Roma, he divided his army; he took half the army to go with him to fight in Roma, and half the army he left with Titus, his son, to besiege Jerusalem.

At that time, Vespasian ordered to take the chains from Joseph, saying: "I remove the chains and iron fetters from you, and you will be an adviser to my son Titus, for he had compassion on you and would not kill you." Joseph answered: "It is a disgrace for me and all my people to remove the iron fetters from our prisoners with a key; rather, we break and smash the iron fetters from our captives. If you smash them and break them off me, I will be a faithful adviser to him all the time." He took him with him to Alexandria[3] and broke off the chains and iron fetters from him.

In those days, Vespasian sent for Antonius and Mucianus to come to Roma. They fought with Vitellio for many days and [finally] killed him: eighty thousand Romans fell in Roma in that fighting. When Vespasian heard that Vitellio was defeated and his officers whom he had sent there controlled [the city], he

---

2. Not in the source and forbidden to Jews. Actually, Hegesippus says the opposite.

3. *DEH* 4.25 has Josephus freed in Berytus.

hastened to go to Roma to renew his kingship.[4] When Vespasian went to the land of Romania,[5] he left Titus, his son, in Alexandria, and with him half the Roman army, commanding him to go to Jerusalem to lay siege to her.

Titus marched from Alexandria and encamped at Nicopolis. From there he proceeded by ship and went to Tanis. From there he traveled to Eraclea and, marching from Eraclea, came to Pelusion (Pelusium). He marched from there through the desert and came to Baal Iovis,[6] which is in the desert. From there he marched to Rinocori (Rhinocorura). From Rinocori he proceeded to 'Aza (Gaza). From there he went to Ashqelon and came to Yavneh. He marched from Yavneh and encamped at Yafo. Marching from Yafo, he encamped at Caesarea and stayed there until he gathered all his army of Romans and the rest of the gentiles who came to help him fight against Jerusalem, and he sat in Caesarea until the end of the winter.

---

4. *DEH* 4.33.2; Latin Ben Sira (Eccl 46:16). Cf. 1 Sam 11:14, which influenced the medieval concept of *renovatio imperii*.

5. *DEH* 4.33.2. Romania is the contemporary name for Byzantium since the sixth century; the Ottonians referred thus to Italy.

6. *Casi Jovis Templum*; temple of Baal Zaphon, as author correctly glossed.

72. FIGHTING BETWEEN THE BANDITS

In the first year of Vespasian,[1] who was made king of the Romans' realm, fighting increased among the inhabitants of Jerusalem, intensive internal fighting; fierce in its cruelty was the ceaseless strife. Nor did the fighting diminish during the days of the winter, as was customary, for summer and winter the battles of Shimon and Yoḥanan continued, and there was a third, Elazar. Now, some of the noble and valiant youth who were in Jerusalem—Yehudah, Ḥeẓron,[2] Shimon, and Ḥizkiyahu—joined up with Elazar. They seized the Temple and all its surroundings including the adjacent courtyards and set some of their troops in ambush as guardians over the Temple boundary. Yoḥanan gathered to him a very large mob, for he was determined to hold his position with all his troops. His position was in the depths of the lower part of the city. Therefore, they were hit by arrows and rocks projected from the heights of the city to destroy Yoḥanan's men. Shimon too seized a position for himself in the high part of the city, and all his force was below the high part that he seized for himself. Thus, there was a three-way battle within the city, with no peace or quiet or rest all over the city. Fighting continued day and night, man against his brother. Numberless were those who fell in the fighting, and no one could count the mass of slain. The blood flowed in the streets and flooded in the Temple like the wash of rain until it covered the threshold of the Temple gateway. The corpses of the slain fell one upon the other, for Yoḥanan was in the middle and Shimon at the very height of the city, and Shimon pressured Yoḥanan through Elazar, for Yoḥanan was in the middle between Shimon and Elazar.

---

1. *DEH* 5.1.1 to 1.5.
2. The author misread his source's *Ezeronis Simon*, Shimon, son of Ḥeẓron.

Now, the three-way battle continued to wreak havoc exceedingly, for the forces in the city's height hurled rocks upon the army in the lower part of the city. Those in the lower part of the city, when they too cast rocks at the army in the city's height, their rocks came back at them and added to their casualties. A great and numerous crowd of priests and volunteer Judaeans assembled at the Temple to prevent fighting in the Temple. And the fighting men[3] smote many of them, so that while the priests were offering up the sacrifices, they were being killed upon their offerings. The corpses of the priests fell upon the carcasses of the beasts that they were sacrificing. And many of the rest of the people, who had assembled in the Temple, also fell by the sword. Innumerable human corpses within the Temple of God were cast off to be trodden under foot, for the corpse of the priest fell upon his offering, his hand holding onto his sacrifice, and the corpse of the stranger fell upon the priest's corpse, the unclean corpse upon the corpse of the pure, the corpse of the wicked upon the corpse of the righteous, and the murderer's corpse upon the corpse of the pious. Their blood mixed together inside the Temple of God until the blood flooded throughout the Temple: and the blood of the ignoble mixed with the blood of the noble, the blood of the adulterer with the blood of saints. And the blood of good and evil, of pure and impure, intermixed so that there was a lake of blood in the Temple of God. Not only blood [was there] but also the fat of human corpse and intestines and bowels of the stabbed who fell in the Temple of God.

When the fighting men challenged one another to do battle, saying: "Come over, let us fight," one could not cross over to the other because of the great number of corpses, and blood, and the fat melting over the stones of the Temple pavement—for the Temple floor was not like the surface of the earth where blood when spilled is absorbed by the dust; not so was the Temple floor, which was paved with marble: therefore, the blood stayed upon the Temple floor, and also the human fat was melting over the marble. When a warrior went toward his opponent to fight, his foot would slip in the fat of the corpses and the blood of the cadavers in the Temple, and he would fall, and his opponent would come and stab him, then he too would fall. The one who feared fighting would come to a bad end until they fell by the sword, while the one determined to harden his heart would hold on. There was no pity over the faint of heart. And so the fighting was exceedingly heavy. When the fighting men got tired and sought to rest, there was no respite and no quiet. Elazar and Shimon were able to rest, but Yoḥanan could not rest, for Elazar was on one side of Yoḥanan and Shimon on the other. For this reason, Yoḥanan had no rest, for he was in the middle.

---

3. Free paraphrase of *DEH* 5.1.3; the author's Hebrew was insufficient.

When Shimon and his men would cease from fighting Yoḥanan, Elazar and his men would attack him; so Yoḥanan did not have one day's rest. Day and night they fought against Yoḥanan, for when Elazar's men had arrows, they would shoot them at Yoḥanan, and when the arrows were finished, they would rush upon them with swords with no quarter. Thus, the slain were ever increasing, and when they tired of attacking with swords, they would hurl fire at each other, and those burned [to death] in the houses were without number. The sound of war filled the city; the houses collapsing from the fire were full of grain, corn, pure oil, and all kinds of victuals. Four plagues[4] contended with each other throughout the city of Jerusalem: blood and fire, devastation, and famine. There was no rest or flight and no relief. Everywhere there was wailing and lamenting, crying, and weeping, keening of women, moaning of the stabbed, the groaning of the elderly, crying of boys and babes. Life was so hard that all said: "Blessed are all who have died before, and woe unto those who live on a day such as this and see this evil."

---

4. *DEH* 5.1.5; cf. John 6:1–8 or Ezek 14:21 for possible influence.

73. JOSEPH'S LAMENTATION OVER JERUSALEM

Joseph lamented this lamentation[1] and said: "How has this city of your people, blessed above all cities, been destroyed? How have your hands fought to destroy your own people and yourself, you who formerly used to vanquish your enemies without weapons of war? Rather, the hosts of angels [*angeli*] fought your battles for you. The waves of the sea too fought against your pursuers, and also the land swallowed your enemies and destroyed those who rose against you. The thunders of the heavens would also destroy your foes, and the stars of the heavens [cf. Judg 5:20] from their courses fought against your enemies.

"Awake, O Moses, and behold your people and the flock that God gave you, to lead in the righteousness of your faith. Awake and behold how they have turned their hand to destroy their [own] soul. Look upon the people of God for whom you raised your staff and split the sea; its waters became dry land before them, and they passed through upon dry land, the people for whom you pleaded to feed them bread from the heavens in their hunger, and at the time of their thirst [cf. Lam 2:19], when they were faint unto death, you brought forth water for them from the flint rock. Awake now, Aaron, O holy one of God. You who stood like a hero before this people and met the destroying [plague] not letting it approach the living; it returned unto its slain and drew not near to the living among your people. Awake, O Joshua, who stunned the very heights of Jericho's walls with the sound of your trumpeting and the sound of the ram's horns of God's priests. Behold the people for whom you have conquered—many nations and mighty kings, and now they are destroying one another. And you, David, why do you sleep? Wake up and arise with all your harps and lyres to sing

---

1. Hegesippus (*DEH* 5.2) keens over Jerusalem; the author's style from Lamentations.

the holy canticles, demand the words of your canticles that have ceased from the mouth of this people in their wickedness. Behold their chiefs who have changed themselves into destroyers unlike you, David, who offered your life for their lives [cf. 2 Sam 24:17], saying: "Pray let your hand be against me and my father's house and do not destroy among this people." Awake now, Elisha, who drew through your prayers an army of Aram and brought it to a fortified city, and you ruled over it without sword or fighting, smiting with blindness, darkening the light of their eyes, and you changed their hatred to love. You fought with your prayer, causing the camp of Aram to hear the sound of horses and chariots and riders [2 Kings 7:6], and Aram and their troops retreated due to the prayer that you poured out on behalf of your people. And now, shepherds of Israel, where are your prayers and your supplications that you poured out on behalf of this people to avert from it wrath and fury.

"How you have changed, Abode of the Holy and Sanctuary of the Holy of Holies; you have become as a platform for the dead. Your dead have fallen within you. And you, Jerusalem, city of God, you have changed into a stranger, like a city wherein neither God nor was His holy Temple within it, for the holy Temple has become a den of murderers and a refuge for bandits. And all who flee to it are killed within it—Anani and Yehoshua, chiefs of the priests, were killed within it: they who were holy chiefs of the honored in the people of God, who were entreated by nations, now their corpses fell within the Temple and without burial, they became food for birds of the sky and for dogs.[2] They fell, not through the wickedness of their deeds; only because they reproached your sons did they fall within you. And your own hands brought upon you this calamity wherein priests of God and His prophets were killed within you: Zechariah was slaughtered in front of your Temple and lay without grave,[3] and the earth covered not his blood nor the blood of Anani and Yehoshua until much blood was spilled to avenge them, a flood of the blood of your youths and valiant men.

"How has their understanding been reversed and flows backward[4] and become like images of idols that do not see or hear or understand? For all living things and creatures on Earth fight those who fight them in order to be saved from their enemy's sword, but your sons have reversed [this], each man falling by the sword of his brother.

---

2. Cf. 1 Kings 14:11, 16:4, 21:24 but in an opposite context.

3. Apparently Hegesippus knew the legends on the blood of Zachariah (in addition to Matt 23:35 and Luke 11:51), whereas the author did not.

4. *DEH* 5.2.1. *Yosippon* balances this colloquialism with paraphrases of Ps 114:5 and Ps 115 (and prophetic parallels).

"Where is the pride of your might, Jerusalem, who has not bowed your shoulder under gentile yoke and broke the yokes of Egypt and Midian and Philistines (Palestini) and Aram and Ashur (Assyria) and Kasdim (Babylonii) and Persia and Media? Where is the heroism of the Mekavvim,[5] sons of Hasmonaeans, who with few men succeeded in destroying the valiant men of Babylonia and the army of Persia? They killed Demetrius and Antiochus, filling the land with corpses of the slain, for they chose death over life rather than heed the call of sinners, and they offered their lives unto death, not for their sons and daughters nor for their precious possessions but for the Temple of God, lest it be defiled with their abominations. Where is the staff of God, the holy staff that flowered on the day of your joy, but now the flowers of the staff have dried, for faith is dried and Torah is abolished.[6] And where is the compassion of the holy people and their mercy for their brethren? How did they become so cruel? Where is their great mercy that made them bury their dead with honor? And now behold their slain and dead cover the surface of the land, and there is no one who buries, for there is no peace for the buriers because others would come and kill them, and they die without a grave. For this reason, father does not bury his son and son does not bury his father and brother does not bury his brother, for they set watches over the dead lest they be buried. And when one goes to bury, he falls and dies in the field, and there is no one to bury him.

"And you, Sanctuary of God's Temple, your fragrances used to drip from above, and the scent of your incenses wafted afar, and the odor of your mixed unguents spread throughout the land. How have they all changed [their hearts] to fill you with human corpses? You reek from the blood of the slain. Your streets are filled with the stabbed and those who died from hunger. Your paths are filled with dead. The living who are left in the city are as good as dead, for their soul is disgusted by the smell of human corpses. Many will die, and many will sicken and will not cure.

"David said [Ps 79:1]: 'God, gentiles have come into Your portion and have defiled Your holy Temple.' Would that this were done by gentiles and not by Your sons [fighting] against each other, whose hands filled the Temple of God with the defilement of corpses of the slain, ever growing with no one to bury, for they were prevented from burying; and when one wished to bury the dead, a

---

5. *Macchabaeorum fides*, but in one MS *Macchaveorum*, which the author transliterates as "Mekavvim" ("to hope" for the Salvation of Israel). See chap. 16n13.

6. A metathesis of this verb, אפסה, gives the word for gathered or collected, אספה, in some MSS.

bandit would come and smite him, and he would die so that both of them would remain upon the surface of the land.

"And they continued to commit new evil: when a man would wish to take vengeance on his neighbor [Lev 19:18] and would find him dead, he would cut up his corpse in order to exact the vengeance of his hatred. Then the evil of the stench of the dead man's corpse would overcome the living and [strike him with] an incurable sickness. All this has come upon them,[7] because they have abandoned God's law, because they have broken the covenant that He sealed with their fathers, because of the treachery that they committed against the God of their fathers by spilling innccent and righteous blood in God's temple. Therefore, our groans have multiplied, and the sound of our cries has magnified, bringing with it endless mourning, for there is no end to our wickedness that we have done, and the Lord our God has been long suffering while we have continued to act faithlessly: therefore, He has poured out His wrath upon us."

---

7. The author removed *DEH*'s Christianized polemic.

74. BEGINNING OF TITUS'S WAR AGAINST JERUSALEM

After these events,[1] Titus returned to Jerusalem after his father had gone to Roma. Titus hastened to fight against Jerusalem so that he could return to aid his father; he came with a heavy force to Shomron, and the men of Gofna received him. Then he marched from there and came to Elon (Aulona), thirty ris from Jerusalem. He left his camp there and, taking with him six hundred cavalry, came to Jerusalem to reconnoiter the place and learn the height of the wall, to understand the power of the people and their strength, to investigate the power of the bandits who glorified in fighting, and to offer peace to all who would make peace with him.

As he came and approached the wall, he saw that no one came in or out through the gate, for the bandits lay in wait outside the city on the road of Titus' approach. And when Titus had passed with all the army behind him—he had advanced with but a few—the bandits rose from their ambush at Helena's tomb, and they charged and smote in the midst of Titus's army. They separated Titus from his warriors, surrounding him, and two of his warriors fell there. And [the bandits] sought to capture Titus alive. When Titus saw that the bandits had surrounded him and that he had no way to rescue himself, he realized that he could not open a path except with the steel in his hand, that is, his sword, for his warriors had left him, so he cut through the knot of bandits and escaped, for they sought to take him alive, and he would smite anyone who drew near to capture him.

Upon Titus escaping from the bandits, they regretted [their plan] and said: "What have we done not killing him?" Then they threw [lances and javelins] at

____

1. Chapter follows *DEH* 5.3 *et seq.*

him, but they did not reach him, for God protected him to give Jerusalem into his hand, and he returned to his camp, for the heart of kings is in God's hand.

During the morning watch, [Titus] approached the city with all his army and said to his officers and warriors: "Embolden your hearts and be strong, for you have come to fight against a strong and mighty nation, unlike other nations whom we have fought against in the past, for I have investigated, and I know the extent of their might and their cunning in war." Then he arrayed his army and ordered them to close-knit formation, one unit hard by the other so that the units could not be separated or unsheathe their swords, for their battle line was ordered straight across. He commanded those in front to beware lest they stumble into one of the holes or pits or one of the bushes on the way, for it was dark. He came unto Har Hazeitim [Mount Olivet] and camped there opposite Jerusalem above the brook Kidron, for the brook was between the city and the mountain, and his camp was six ris away from the city.

When morning came, the people looked and, behold, a Roman camp atop Har Hazeitim. The bandit chiefs made peace with each other in order to direct their wickedness against the Romans. They swore an oath to each other and opened the gate; the bandit chiefs went out of the city with all the fighting men and, raising a war cry, attacked the Roman camp. They brought great confusion into the army, and it retreated before them, for they had sallied rather suddenly against them. But Titus cried out to his army, and the Romans took heart, making a stand opposite the Judaeans to do battle; and many fell on both sides, but the Romans could not hold their position before the Judaeans. Titus and his warriors who were with him, however, encouraged their men to stand against the Judaeans, so the Judaeans stopped pursuing the army of Kittim, and the Judaeans, with all the fighting men, returned to the vicinity of the wall. Titus was furious at his army and waxed angry at his warriors for panicking before the Judaeans. Titus fortified them, saying, "Behold, the brook Kidron separates us from the troops of Jerusalem." So they set their faces toward the wall, trusting in the brook. Then the bandit chiefs divided the fighting men, and they sent forth an army of warriors, commanding them to outflank the Roman army and come upon it suddenly; so they [bandits] outflanked them [Romans] and, coming from their rear, attacked them, forcing them to retreat from their position.

Titus turned around at the sound of the trumpet blast of the Judaeans attack.

The battle was taking place at the flank of his army on the other side of Har Hazeitim. He was alarmed by the sound of the fighting. Just then the bandit chiefs opened the gates of Jerusalem and went forth with all the fighting men from the city attacking Titus and his army, smiting them a very great blow, nor did they turn their backs to withdraw, for they persisted to smite them until they put the Roman camp to flight to the top of Har Hazeitim; also many of Titus's warriors and his officers fled and did not stand against them, save for Titus alone.

His warriors pleaded with him, saying: "Pray take refuge with us on the mountain lest you fall by the sword of the Judaeans and all of us would be destroyed, for you are our master and the gods have made you our leader throughout the land; and now, should you fall alone, would we all not die? Of what value would your blood be if you should die like one of us?" But Titus did not listen to them and held his position and did not turn his back to retreat, saying: "I would rather choose death with honor rather than life with shame." Then he turned toward the Jews coming against him and drove them away from him by fighting and also chased away those who attacked his flank.

When the Judaean fighting men saw that the Roman camp stood fast in battle against them, they turned from against the Romans and with all their strength risked their lives in an attempt to kill Titus; and the fighting there was great and exceedingly intense, and a great many fell on both sides. On that day, Titus's warriors fell, and Titus too nearly fell in this battle; and had not the remainder of his warriors come back to him and saved him, he would have died on that day. The Judaeans returned to their position by the wall across the brook of Kidron, and the Kittim on that day fled three times before the Judaeans.

75. FIGHTING WITHIN AND WITHOUT

At that time,[1] the external fighting quieted while the internal fighting flared up within the city, man against man. On the first day of Passover, Yoḥanan, the chief of bandits, came into the Temple of God with all his warriors. The priests and the people received him in honor. When he had come into the Temple, he and his men stripped off their cloaks, and behold, they were wearing breastplate under their cloaks, their swords upon their hips; they attacked the priests and the people in the Temple; they seized the doors of the Temple and began to kill, turning their hearts to cruelty, not respecting the aged or listening to the plea of those who entreated them or having compassion for babes and sucklings or upon women and children, for Yoḥanan was angry with Shimon and also Elazar ben Anani and with the chiefs of the bandits, saying: "Let no one be considered as chief in this city save me!" When Shimon and Elazar heard what Yoḥanan had done, these too rose up and smote many of Yoḥanan's men.

When Titus was told that the Judaeans conspired among themselves and were fighting within the city, he drew near to the city with all his army and found some of the Jews standing outside the city, and they said: "Approach and enter the city because we cannot live with these bandits: save us please from their hand, and we will be your servants."[2] But Titus did not believe their words, for previously he had seem them fighting against him with one heart, hastening to rescue each other in the fighting, so he did not believe their saying to him: "Come and save us, and we will be your servants." While he was still speaking with them, behold, a sound of tumult within the city and the outcry of fighting

---

1. Chapter follows *DEH* 5.5.1 to 5.8 with the author's additions.
2. Pun on Passover *haggadah*, where Israelites pray thus to God.

men, some of whom said: "Open the gate and let Titus enter and capture the city," while others shouted: "Close the gates lest the Romans enter." And when the Romans heard the voice of those telling them from atop the wall: "Hurry and save us from the hand of these bandits so that we do not die," many of the Roman camp ran to the gate of the city, and as they approached the wall, they [Judaeans] dropped stones upon them from atop the wall and shot them with arrows.

The Judaeans and the people who were entreating Titus outside the city to save them from the bandits turned to fight with Titus's men who came to the wall and smote them; the Romans retreated, and the Judaeans pursued after them unto the tomb of (H)Elena. Now the Judaeans began to mock the Romans whom they pursued and to deride them like fools, for laughter is not proper in battle, and they began to beat upon their shields in front of the Romans to scoff at them. This angered Titus's warriors, and they wanted to return and attack them, but Titus prevented them, not letting them [warriors] go at them.

Titus assembled all his officers, servants, and advisers and spoke to their ears, saying: "I know your bravery, for you are greater than all the nations, not only in bravery, for with wisdom and understanding and counsel, you rule over peoples. I am not surprised at the Judaeans who say one thing and do the opposite, who swear an oath and break it. I am surprised only at you that they can fool you with their bravery and their cunning, for this you were routed two and three times since you harkened not to my commands, and you rebelled against my orders. For while it is unfitting to violate the king's command and disobey his words, you have disobeyed my orders and you have violated my orders. Do you not know[3] how one of our people rose and slew his son because he went to war without his father's permission? And you have disobeyed my words; therefore, you deserve a death sentence!" Titus spoke other words of reproach to his army that we have not written. All of his officers and warriors bowed to him, [asking him] to pardon the sin of disobeying his commands. And so he did and forgave them, reproaching them, saying: "You will no longer disobey," and they said: "No!"

After these events, when Titus saw how the heart of the Jerusalemites turned against each other and each attacked his neighbor, Titus approached to do battle at the walls of Jerusalem. He commanded that they [his men] block all the wells and ditches and burrows that were about the wall, and they filled them with dirt to straighten the way for the fighting men.

---

3. The author recalled Manlius Torquatus and mistakenly understood a reference to the father who executed his son for disobeying his order by attacking the enemy.

While Titus was doing that, the Judaeans did not come out to drive him away from the wall as before, for Shimon took for himself ten thousand valiant Jewish bandits and five thousand Edomites with Yaakov, the Edomite leader [*nagid*] of Edom, and Shimon the younger, the Edomite leader. Shimon assembled all these and went against Yohanan, chasing him toward the courtyard of the temple. Yohanan stood at the entrance gate to the Temple and with him eighty-four hundred warriors, bearing swords and wearing armor. Shimon and Elazar joined forces to besiege Yohanan, neglecting to fight the Romans for the deliverance of the city and fighting each other instead. Meanwhile, the Romans were establishing a position for their army around the wall, while the rest of the people who were [caught] between these three chiefs were like lost sheep, for the chiefs terrorized them. This one took for himself men from this lot and that one from that lot. They divided the people like sheep; when the Roman attacks became heavy upon them, they all joined the fighting, but when they had driven off the Romans, they returned to fighting against each other.

76. JOSEPH'S WORDS ON JERUSALEM

Joseph called out and said:[1] "Jerusalem, O Jerusalem, a Canaanite king founded you, a mighty king called Malki Ẓedek (Melchizedek), for he was a righteous [ẓadik] king, and you were added the name[2] Jerusalem because of the Temple of God that was built in your midst. Canaanites lived within you formerly until King David came and drove out the Canaanites and settled Hebrews in their place, and also he built within you the palace of his residence. Moreover, he set his heart upon building within you the Temple of God, but God prevented him via His messenger the prophet, and he left to Solomon, his son, all that he had prepared. Solomon reigned in his father's place and completed building God's Temple, and he placed in it gold and silver and precious stones in great quantity. For this reason, kings and princes of the Earth envied him, for the construction of your Temple overshadowed everything, and his renown exceeded everyone. The floor of your Temple was of marble, shining like glass. And its servant [priest] was dressed in four colors: crimson thread in the image of the heavens that are above this sky, for it is of fire; light blue and byssus for the earth, for they grew from it; and purple from the sea, for it was collected from the sea. When the priest came to the service dressed in these four colors, he would say before the Lord of Everything: 'Behold, I have come before You in four images of Your world, and let it be considered as if I were bringing before You the entire world.' Moreover, his attire was adorned with refined gold and precious stones according to the image of the tribes of Jacob, whose name was called Israel, and his loins were girt with linen pants to cover his nakedness, for

---

1. Chapter continues to follow *DEH* 5.9 *seq.*
2. The author misunderstood pun on Hierosolyma: "holy" or "temple."

it was proper that the priest be the most modest of men when he stood to serve in the two sanctuaries, the outer sanctuary and the inner sanctuary that is the Holy of Holies; for in the outer sanctuary, the priests and Levites convened to serve, but no one came into the Holy of Holies save the high priest once a year, for there was the ark of the covenant of God, which contained the two stone tablets while the First Temple still stood. There was the staff of Aaron, which brought forth blossom and planted a shoot [Num 17:23], and opposite the sanctuary were fourteen steps, from which the sign was shown to Ḥizkiyahu (Hezekiah) [cf. 2 Kings 20:9; Isa 38:7]. Jerusalem was better fortified than any city, mistress over all states, for mighty kings have founded it and many rulers built it. Herod increased its loftiness and its excellence and built for it yet another wall, calling it Antonia after Antonius the Roman. How you are laid low[3] and many nations overpower you, laying siege on you."

---

3. The author adds the ending and changes his source's third person to second person to make the story into a lament.

77. THE WAR ON THE WALL

After this,[1] Titus passed opposite the wall to decide where he could break through it into the city, and he saw a level site opposite the tomb of Yoḥanan, the high priest. Titus took up position at this spot, he and Nikanor (Nicanor), his army chief; he sent Nicanor to speak words of peace to the people upon the wall. When he had finished offering the people peace as his master had commanded him, one of the Judaeans stationed on the wall shot him with an arrow and killed him. It angered Titus very much that the Judaeans shot the officer he had sent to speak peace to them, so he prepared for battle against the city with all the weapons of war and destruction, and they dragged the iron ram to butt the wall, for it destroys walls.

When the Judaeans saw that the ram was dragged to butt the wall, the men were shaken and terrified, and the three bandit chiefs, Shimon, Yoḥanan, and Elazar the priest, and the rest of the bandit chiefs made peace. They opened the gate of the city and went out to the field of Yoḥanan's tomb and chased away the Roman camp from the weapons of destruction that they had prepared to destroy the wall. They set fire to all these wooden weapons and burned them; also, they burned the battering ram and some of the batteries, for Titus and his warriors saved a few of the batteries, but the rest they set ablaze.

On that day, the Alexandrians in Titus's camp fought to save the batteries from the Judaeans; but the Judaeans overcame the Alexandrians. Titus hastened, racing with the choice of his warriors, drove away the Judaeans, and killed twelve of them.

At that time, Yoḥanan fell, one of the Edomite chiefs, for the Kittim tricked him into talking with them, and an Arab shot him in the back and killed him. The Edomite troops mourned for him exceedingly. That night they rose up,

---

1. Chapter follows *DEH* 5.10, 1 to 5.14.

with some of the bandits from Shimon's and Yoḥanan's warriors, and went to the three wooden towers that Titus had raised against the wall. They slew the Roman detachments there, and the rest fled. Then they chopped the legs of the towers, which fell to the ground, and many of the Roman camp died there. Titus heard the sound of the tumult from the falling of the towers; he was greatly alarmed, and all his army as well; they fled because of the sound of the falling since they did not identify the noise.

When morning came, Titus assembled his entire army and approached the city wall while the Judaeans were still fighting within the city. Titus brought up the destroying ram and battered the wall, breaching it and demolishing it, and the wall fell to the ground—this was the outer wall. And the army within that wall withdrew behind the second wall.

At that time, Titus commanded to demolish the whole wall, which they had toppled, and to remove the stones far away, lest they be an obstacle to his camp. The leaders of the Judaeans saw that Titus had captured the outer wall and that there remained [only] two walls, for there were three walls to the city. So they made peace with each other and divided their fighting assignments: the watch of Yoḥanan, the bandit chief, was from the corner of Antonia to the north of the Temple. The section of Shimon was from the corner of the field of the tomb of Yoḥanan, the high priest. And these stood with all their valiant warriors against the Romans.

Now the fighting grew heavier at that time, as the Roman army was fighting more fiercely to glorify their name, while the Judaeans fought more fiercely, because they saw that their end drew nigh. Titus stood before his warriors to encourage them, saying unto them: "Do your utmost this day, and I will give unto each man who fights on this very day silver and gold and honor."

One of his warriors, named Longino, came within the contingent of Judaeans standing outside the gate and smote the man positioned against him upon the mouth, and he died. He continued to smite another, stabbing him in the side, and he died. Then Longino ran back to the Roman camp. The Judaeans were not pleased with this event. Their anger blazed in their hearts. Shimon stood before his warriors and spoke to them, declaring: "Whoever flees from battle shall die and his household be destroyed!" Titus told his men to fight, lest any fall. Then he left the scene of the fighting opposite Shimon and went to the corner of Yoḥanan's position, for they had raised the battering ram there, since the site there was level.

Titus commanded to batter the second wall, but a Judaean from among the bandit warriors, named Castor, a man of war, took up position atop the wall, and shooting arrows, he smote many from the Roman camp and made many flee. Now this man Castor was with nine warriors, his comrades. When Titus positioned the battering ram against the wall, Castor called from atop the wall, saying to Titus: "Pray, my lord, have mercy upon this breached city."[2]

When Titus heard Castor's shout, he commanded his warriors to cease fighting. Then he called to Castor and said: "Come out to me and live." Castor answered Titus, saying: "Behold, I will convince my nine comrades, and we shall come out together." But he was deceptively misleading Titus.

He [Castor] was saying to his nine comrades before the eyes of the Romans as follows: "Come on, let's go and take refuge in Titus's camp." His comrades knew, however, that he was deceiving the Romans and drew their swords and smote him upon his armor. As he fell before the eyes of the Kittim—and they did not know that they had done this deceptively in order to prevent the battering ram from drawing near the wall—someone from the Roman camp shot an arrow and struck Castor in his nose, the arrow passing through his nose. Castor cried out, speaking unto Titus: "Is this my reward for seeking to run to you, and I am shot with an arrow? Now, my lord, send me one of your officers, and I will come down to him: I will accept your word from him, and I will come unto you."

Titus said to Joseph: "Go and seal a pact upon our word with him; bring this man to me, and he will live." Joseph replied to Titus: "Why do you send me unto him? How have I, who served you wholeheartedly, sinned against you?" for Joseph understood Castor's guile.

Titus sent for Aeneas, one of his veteran officers, and said to him: "Go to Castor and give him our word[3] so that he will come down to me." Aeneas went to Castor and said to him: "Come on down to me, and I give you my word: we will go to the king's son." Castor answered him, saying: "Prepare your lap so I can throw down to you this gold I have, and then I will come down, lest the men of the city know [of it] and take it." Aeneas spread his cape to receive the gold that Castor had mentioned. Castor lifted a huge stone with both his hands and dropped it on Aeneas. But Aeneas saw it, dodged it, and so escaped, but the stone fell on his companion, and he died.

Titus was very angry over this: he brought the ram near to the wall and butted it, and the second wall fell.

When Castor saw that the wall had fallen, he looked and saw a house on fire; he dropped into the burning house and died, for he chose death over life. Now the Romans advanced within the second wall, and the bandits went out against

---

2. *Prutsah* is an interesting pun on *peritsim*. [SB]

3. Rare use of *he'emin* as causative: "to make someone believe." [SB]

them with the rest of the warriors and engaged in close combat. The Jews got the upper hand, smiting very many in the Roman camp, and the survivors of Titus's army fled to the first wall, which they had previously destroyed.

At that time, Titus seized his bow and shot arrows against the Judaeans, and not one of his arrows hit the ground, for all of them hit people. Despite this, the Romans were driven away outside the city, for the Judaeans had the upper hand until the fourth day, and on the fourth day, a great force of all the gentiles assembled around Titus to assist the Romans. The Judaeans sallied to confront them outside the city, but the gentiles got the upper hand against them, and they retreated; they pursued them unto the inner wall and closed them in.

78. JOSEPH'S SPEECH TO THE PEOPLE OF JERUSALEM

On that day, Titus commanded his army to retreat from the wall to the outskirts of the city and to let the fighting abate for a few days in order to call the Judaeans to peace, saying: "Perhaps they will bear the yoke of the Romans and live—and not die," for he had compassion upon the city and upon God's Temple, not wishing to destroy it. He desisted from fighting for five days; and on the fifth day,[1] he came against the city gate.

At the time of his advance, behold, Shimon and Yoḥanan prepared flaming pots to burn the destructive weapons that the Romans had made. And they all agreed to fight heroically with one heart. When Titus saw that the Judaeans were determined to take a stand and strengthened themselves to die fighting, he began to speak peace to them and to plead with them, saying: "Behold, I have taken two walls of the city, and there remains one wall. What is the point of your stubborn resistance? For I shall capture the third wall as well, and I shall ruin this city; you shall be destroyed with it, and I shall demolish the Temple of God, your Lord."

He sent unto them Joseph the priest to speak in their ears words of peace in Hebrew so that they would believe and trust. Joseph went and stood before the gate of the wall, for he feared to draw near the wall, since he knew that he was abhorrent in the eyes of the people because he submitted to Titus and lived. Joseph called out in a loud voice and said: "Hearken unto me, all Hebrews, and I shall speak into your ears what is good for you." Joseph began to speak to the people, saying: "It was proper at the outset for you to fight as you are fighting now, before this calamity came upon you, while your cities were standing and

____

1. *DEH* 5.14.4 to 5.17 with the author's additions.

your territory full of people, before you lost your warriors in battle, waging war upon a mighty and powerful nation that governs over all peoples and has subdued throughout the world; and they rule over the nations that once ruled over you, and the latter have become their slaves. Now you fight with them foolishly and not wisely, for you have set your hearts to defy them, and you do not know that you are extending the calamity upon yourselves until the holy Temple will be destroyed. Take pity and have compassion upon the altars, lest they be pulled down, and upon the sanctuary, lest it be destroyed, and upon the Temple, lest it be rooted out, and upon the peace offerings and the daily offerings, lest they cease, and upon the perpetual flame, lest it be put out, for we have sinned against God, the Lord of this sanctuary, and have rebelled against Him.

"For this, He has turned away from us, for fighting within His sanctuary, killing His priests and His holy ones, and we have spilled much innocent blood within His house. Behold now, the destroying weapons are readied to knock down the Temple, and the fire is prepared to burn the Temple. Behold, the gentiles, your enemies, are taking pity upon the Temple of God and upon His Sanctuary, not wishing to destroy it; you too have compassion, so that the destroying weapons be removed from you.

"And now what are you relying on? Have they not demolished two walls, only one remaining? And if you should say: 'We rely upon our God,' He is not with us, for He has turned away [from us] to assist our enemies; for they have honored His great Name, and they fear him, while we have rebelled against Him. By this you shall know that the Lord is with them, that they rule over all nations except for places enclosed by snow or heat where there is no road to transverse. Now what do you hope for: Has not the Lord given every people and kingdom into their hand? Is it not their time to rule until the end of their destiny? Has He not given dominion unto them, and He assists them, and He is with them to assist them all the days of their destiny? Do you not know that at the beginning it was the people of Egypt, and He gave them dominion over all the nations? Afterward He turned away from the people of Egypt and He was with you, giving you dominion over many nations, for He was with you and with your kings. After this, He turned away from you and gave dominion to the Kasdim and Ashur (Assyrii) and Persia and was their support, for they are all His handiwork. Now He has abandoned them, and His support is with the Romans; He is with them to support them for many years; and He has given them dominion over nations that ruled over them previously.

"Now why do you fight against the rulers over nations who have opened the secret of the passes to Hodu and to all the islands of the Great Ocean, which is beyond Hodu? They rule over the reaches of east and west, from the ends of

Britania unto the sea of Oceanus, and also set the *limes* of their authority unto the islands of Ascotsia, which is in the sea of Oceanus, and over all the territory of Saxonia, which is enclosed in lakes.[2] Saxonia's inhabitants are a great people, tall like giants of great height, fighting men and valiant in all ways—who were wont to say: 'We would rather all die than serve foreign kings.' Yet the Romans came and subdued them, and they became their slaves. And now with your saying: 'Let us die and not suffer the yoke of gentiles upon us,' why don't you ask about the times of your earliest ancestors who preceded us, whether they were free without lords or whether the yoke were removed from them? Did not Jacob, our father, bend his shoulder to live in Egypt in a strange land, serving them lest he die of hunger, he and his household and twelve sons from whose loins we have sprung? Was not Yehudah there, the noblest of Yeshurun's sons, after whose name we are called Yehudim? For who could subdue him, so noble and great, yet even he bent his shoulder and served Egypt, lest he die of hunger. And Joseph was there, the worthiest of men, who suffered to serve at the house of Pharaoh to sustain his father's household. Had Joseph truly wanted to return to the land of Canaan, who could have stopped him? Benjamin was there, who was restored to the house of Joseph by cruel deceit, for he forced him to serve. Despite all this, he did not sin; rather, he bent his shoulder to serve, for it is no disgrace for a man to serve one greater than he. Your ancestors were slaves until Moses came and freed them with God's word. You served Egypt twice. And you served the kings of Ashur for many years, and also the kings of Persia you served a very sweet slavery. And after them, you served the kings of Makedon, a harsh and violent slavery, until there arose a family of noble Hasmoneans, and God saved you through them from the hand of Makedon.

"And now, what shame would it be for you were you to bend your neck to serve the Kittim? Did they not subjugate those who had subdued you and were your lords, overpowering them and becoming your friends? Rather than loving the Italians as you should have, you have become their enemies. Did you not know that the Kittim governed Ashur, which used to rule over the whole world, and they also govern Egypt, to whom you used to be slaves? And now if the Egyptians plow the fields of their land, would not the Romans reap their harvest? Consider the kings of Makedon, who knew no masters and who also ruled the entire land of Hodu; now, behold, they are slaves to the Romans. Once Pyro ben Achille (Pyrrhus, son of Achilles), a hero of Makedonia, became haughty and fought against the Romans; they subdued the pride of his arrogance, and

---

2. The Saxon historian Widukind (ca. 925–973) repeated this description from Hegesippus, whom he thought was Josephus.

he submitted his shoulder to their yoke. And about the Philistines, what shall I say to you? Does not the youngest of the Roman generals govern over all of Philistia? And now is it not an honor for you to serve alongside the Persians who are your fellows after they were your lords?

"Tell me, pray, when were your ancestors free? Was it not from the day they left Egypt until the reign of Saul ben Kish that you were free, because the Lord was your King? Yet you rejected God your King from being your king, for you chose for yourselves a man as king like all the nations [cf. 1 Sam 8:5]. And from then until this day, you have been slaves, for you served Saul and the rest of the kings. And after the death of Saul, you served David, the great king, who governed over every nation bordering upon you. And after his death, you served Solomon, his son, and, after the death of Solomon, the kingdom was split for many years until the kings of Kasdim came and exiled you from your land. And how good was Coresh (Cyrus), king of Persia, who restored your captives to your land? Nor did he restore you alone, but also all the vessels of the Sanctuary service he restored with you, and it was deemed to his merit. After his death, the kings of Makedon rose against you and oppressed you harshly. Then God aroused His priests, the sons of Hasmonai, to deliver you from their hand, and He magnified your name, and you became comrades and confederates of the Romans, and friendship grew in your hearts for many years. After this, you rebelled against the priests of God, the sons of Hasmonai, and you chose for yourselves a man from among you; his name was Herod, who tightened his yoke upon you; then Herod died, and Archelaus ruled over you, and he hardened his yoke over you. Then you rebelled against him and said that we will not serve kings of Judah any longer; rather, we shall serve Roman kings. Of your own will, you bent your shoulder before Caesar Augustus, because he was a man of compassion and mercy—for which reason his name was called Augustus, for he augmented compassion to his people and was not cruel. You served him just like all [other] peoples, without shame, and you became renowned, for you served a good king.

"Now look at all the creatures of the Earth: at man, at beast, at animals, at birds and swarming things, and at fish of the sea, for the greater rules over the smaller [Gen 25:23]. There is no shame to any smaller [being] to fear its superior: for the bull fears the lion, and the ram fears the bear, and the goat fears the leopard [cf. Isa 11:6], while the hawk fears the eagle, and the dove fears the hawk. Consider [even] the lowliness of beasts: how the bull exalts himself over the cows and bulls smaller than it, and the ram over sheep and the billy goat over herds of goats. And if you acquiesce in subservience to the Romans, what would you have to lose, since they do not lord over you as the gentiles who had lorded over you previously? And the beasts and fowl about whom I told a little, they rule each other, and the greater cannot rule over the lesser unless the smaller in his meekness bends his shoulder, [allowing] the greater to rule over it. So now cover yourselves with meekness and become like all the creatures."

While Joseph was speaking to the people upon the wall of Jerusalem, they raised their voice, vilifying him and cursing him from atop the wall, and they shot many arrows at him to kill him.

When Joseph saw that they did not perceive his words and counsel, he began to give them proofs from Scripture. Joseph called out and said to them: "O rebellious ones, what good is your support of this Temple in which you have spilled much innocent blood and have profaned it with your swords? Pray tell, rebels, when did you conquer with sword or spear?

"Remember your father who sired you, Abraham, with what did he vanquish Pharaoh and subdue him when he took his wife, with sword or with prayer? Was it not with his prayer to God that he vanquished Pharaoh and not with fighting? For he dared to call God and cry to him, and He returned to him his wife pure and untainted? For Abraham would rest in peace, whereas Pharaoh was tormented by pains and great afflictions. Sarah too, Abraham's wife, whom Pharaoh coveted, whom he took in order to commit an outrage, to uncover her secret parts, but could not prevail, for God did not permit him to accomplish any of this as he desired. Instead of uncovering her flesh, he covered her completely in luxurious [ornaments]—silver and gold and precious stones. Thus, while Abraham was still sitting in his house relying upon God, behold, Sarah entered dressed in gold and silver, covered in all sorts of precious things and also in the virtue of her modesty, pure and unsullied.

"And what shall we say of Isaac, his son, when the Philistine king chased him away? He had with him his father's 318 trainees who had smote five kings, and many of them were his household servants. And he had courage to fight the Philistines, but he did not want to do battle, trusting instead in the spirit of humility. Now, the Philistines who had chased him away came and were gracious toward him when they saw that the hand of the Lord was with him, for who can relate the favors of God and the wondrous deeds that He performed for our fathers?

"Jacob, our father, when he fled from his brother Esau, carried nothing with him save his staff and supplies for the road and also his weapons, and through his prayer, God assisted him in his going and in his returning, for he wrestled with the angel and prevailed.

"And what shall we say to you about Moses, our shepherd, a man of God? How did he vanquish Pharaoh and all his army? Was it not with prayer and the staff of God in his hand that he broke the pride of Pharaoh and his sorcerers, and with it did he not smite Egypt with ten plagues, and with it did he not rent the sea along twelve pathways? Then, when Pharaoh drew near with all the army of Egypt, Moses did not fight him with weapons, but rather through his prayer did Pharaoh and his army sink into the great bottom of the sea. Moses sang a song of thanks while the warriors of Egypt perished in anger and rage because they sought to fight against Moses and Israel with weapons of war, with horses and chariot, but Moses fought them with his prayer. Therefore, they were overthrown in the sea [Ex 14:26] while Israel celebrated in song and praise.

"And who does not know that prayer is better than weapons of war, for prayer accelerates God's assistance, whereas weapons of war [rely on] human bravery. Do you not know that when Joshua, Moses's servant, crossed the Jordan, he was a warrior? [And yet] how did he overwhelm the walls of Jericho? Was it not through his prayer and God's priests, who blew the ram's horns? And also, when he demolished the city, not leaving a soul, save Rechab, the good harlot [*bona meretrix*], and all who fled to her house? Did you not know that Gideon's prayer assisted him in smiting the multitude of Midian, Amalek, and the people of the east [Bnei Kedem] with three hundred men? Without his prayer and supplication, which he poured out before God, what could three hundred men be considered against Midian and Amalek, a powerful people as numerous as the sand of the sea?

"Consider God's ark, which the Philistines took: Could our fathers recover it with sword or fighting? Was it not by prayer and supplication that the ark was restored to its place?

"And in the days of Ḥizkiyahu, king of Judah, when Sanherib, king of Ashur, came and deprecated God's sanctuary, and his heart's malice and arrogance soared high, how was he brought low? Not by fighting but by prayer, for Ḥizkiyahu arose and adorned himself with the ornaments of prayer, for under the shield he donned sackcloth, and under the helmet ash, and instead of arrows prayers, and his prayer soared where no dart would rise. In the one prayer, which Ḥizkiyahu poured forth, 185,000 men fell. The dead we counted, but the slayer we saw not.

"When the king of Judah, the king of Israel, and the king of Edom [cf. 2 Kings 3:9] allied together and went to war on Moab, their spirit wearied in the desert out of thirst. Of what use were their weapons of war or their courage? Was it not through Elisha's prayer that water sprang for them in the desert, a river in the wasteland? Also, through Elisha's prayer during Aram's attack upon Shomron, did not God sound in the ears of Aram the tumult of horses and riders [cf. 2 Kings 7:6], and the whole army of Aram retreated, for the sound of a driven leaf chased them [Lev 26:37]. His prayer too turned the famine in Shomron to plenty, until thirty ephahs of fine flour was sold for one piece of silver [cf. 2 Kings 7:16]; thus, through prayer our ancestors always overcame.

"Did Israel not prevail against the horde of Amalek when Moses spread his palms heavenward; and Joshua's prayer caused the sun to stand still at Giv'on [Gibeon] until evening changed into noon and the army of Israel prevailed against their enemy? Had it not been for his prayer that halted the sun, night would have intervened between Israel and their enemy.

"Samson too, before he sinned, it was his prayer that was his power, and when he sinned, he fell like any man. So too Saul, God's chosen, when his ways were pure, his prayer was his strength and valor, yet when he sinned, God turned away from him.

"And David did not lose his power from childhood to the end of his days, for he would rely on prayer; he did not wish to fight against his brothers or his own people. Thus, he gained strength over his enemies, for in his refusal to raise a hand against his brothers, every nation feared him.

"Asa (Asaph), king of Judah, with a small army set out to confront the Kushites [cf. 2 Chron 14:8ff], and he prayed to God, entreating Him as follows: 'We know not what we are to do; our eyes are upon You.'[3] God harkened unto his prayer and smote a million Kushites [2 Chron 14:8].

"Deborah too with her prayer brought deliverance to Israel, and many women stood in prayer, and they lived to [see] deliverance.

"Don't you know [cf. 2 Chron 25:11–15] what Amatsyahu, king of Judah, did when he fought with Edom? He smote them with the sword and brought ten thousand of them into captivity with their gods? He entered Jerusalem and erected the gods that he took from Edom, sacrificing and offering libation to them, saying: 'For you have delivered me, and because of you, I captured Edom.' Therefore, he was caught [cf. 2 Chron 25:23] like a fox when he went to battle with Yoash, king of Israel.

"Every calamity that ever came upon us was our own fault, for the Lord our God is righteous in all and His judgment is upright, for enemies did not harm us as much as we harmed our own selves. The gentiles who took all our precious things and the vessels of our Temple kept them in a state of purity until the time that they restored them, while we desecrated them by our treacheries and by the innocent blood that we spilled out in the Sanctuary of the Lord our God. Moreover, in our exile to the lands of the gentiles, we sought God and learned the laws of the Torah and taught the gentiles to obey them.

---

3. The author brings the prayer of Yehoshephat (2 Chron 20:12) instead of the similar prayer of Asaph (2 Chron 14:10).

"But now we sit in our own land, yet our heart is divided, and our wickedness is turned against each other; we have forgotten the words of the Torah and its laws; for exile increased our fear of God and His Torah, while controversy has removed the Torah from our midst and hardened our hearts from fearing of God.

"Who has caused us this entire calamity? Did not our own hands do this to us, because our heart was divided, and our inner strife immediately brought blame upon us? Who first brought Romans against Jerusalem? Was it not Hyrcanus and Aristobulus who were divided, and each betrayed his brother? These brought the Romans against Jerusalem. And who brought the Roman generals Antonius and Sossius against Jerusalem? Was it not Herod in his fighting with the Hasmoneans? Who summoned Caesar to rule over you? Was it not you and no one else?

"And now why have you rebelled? Sure, Florus, the Roman general, oppressed you; it would have been more fitting to bring him to trial before Caesar and not rebel and make war. You rebelled against Nero Caesar because he acted wickedly toward you; so now, why do you rebel against Vespasian, who is a merciful man[4] and has so far done nothing bad to you? It would be proper to make peace with him and to bear his yoke, for you know his might and his compassion. Whom would it have been proper for him to harm if not me for all the trouble that I made for him? For who emptied his sword and spear more than me, since I engaged in battle with them at the beginning, and I destroyed many of them, but I did not do all this from my own heart's desire. I knew too that it was not proper for me to fight him, yet when I saw that all of you had taken counsel to fight against them and you sent me to battle, I fought with all my heart. You know how I fought on behalf of the city of Yodphat! Was it not with all my might that I braced myself to persevere in war on behalf of my people and on behalf of the city until the catapulted stones and arrows covered me and the fire enveloped me—yet I continued to strive? But now, here I am in their hands, and they have not repaid me in kind for the evil that I did unto them but rather rewarded me. Many times I sought to escape to you before the Romans captured me, but I could not. Now, I thank God that He did not lead me to be with you in the wickedness that you are doing on this day in killing righteous ones and spilling the blood of innocent, poor, and pious men within the Sanctuary of God. For if I were with you, or were my fate with your evil, or were I to die by your sword, then would my mother's heart be stirred in lamentation and grieving, and also I would have lost my hope.

---

4. Here *ish raḥamim* renders *benignus*; in chap. 28 *pius*.

"And now what are you hoping for? For the signs and wonders that were done in the days of our fathers? They are not [to be expected], for our wickedness has increased, and there is no righteousness. By this you shall know that God is not among us, for before these battles, the waters of Shiloah [Siloam] were nearly dried up. But now with your doing battle and all the nations assembled against us, behold, the waters of Shiloah are flooding like a stream to sustain and aid our besiegers. So now do not wonder at my saying to you that God is not among us. Pray ask, behold, and know which man who daily sees in his house controversy, contention, jealousy, strife, and anger and does not flee nor retreat from his house to find rest. And now God our Lord was in our midst when we preserved His Torah and His commandments, but when we abandoned His Torah and contaminated His Sanctuary, spilling the blood of righteous ones in His House, making his Sanctuary a place to spread corpses, continuing to commit every abomination, He has turned away from us. For His glorious Name will not dwell in a place of pollution and impurity, only in a holy place. And we have profaned His Temple and desecrated His Sanctuary, so how could His glory dwell among us? Did He not command us in the desert with respect to Korah, Dathan, and Abiram: 'Separate yourselves from among this congregation!' [Num 16:21] for He did not want good to mingle with evil, nor righteous with wicked among men. This God is Truth, so how could His glorious Name dwell in the midst of a congregation of sinners and murderers?

"So now why should I mince words, for I see that the day of our calamity is approaching, the downfall of the city wall and the burning of the Sanctuary? But you harden your hearts like iron when you see the ruin of our people and the destruction of the city of our joy, and there is no hope. Yet you revolt more and more [Isa 1:5] since you have no mercy. It will be considered as if you destroyed the Sanctuary by your own hands, for all this calamity is your own doing. You brought the fire upon the edifice of God's Sanctuary, which noble kings and saintly prophets built for God, and you have destroyed it by your own hands.

"Would that your heart were of stone, for stones are hewn by water and rocks of the catapults are consumed by much blood,[5] but your heart would neither yield nor soften to the fear of God. But if you continue to do evil, and if you have no compassion upon God's Sanctuary, have mercy upon your sons and daughters and upon your wives and children, lest they go into captivity.

"Even though I am here within the Roman camp, am I not still in your midst and with you, for my precious wife, who is from an esteemed and well-born

---

5. The author's source alludes to signs foretelling evil, viz. "dripping drops of blood." His "stones hewn by water" reflects contemporary Latin literature.

family, is with you, and also my saintly mother [*imi hakedoshah*] is among you? So now if you do not find my words trustworthy, for you think that I say these words to deceive you, [do this]: if you hear me and my words turn out to be false, kill my saintly mother, and my beloved wife, my soul's delight, put to death, nor spare my own life, and let their blood be as surety to you."

When the people heard Joseph's words, some of them were moved, and they wept before Joseph, for their heart inclined to his speech, and Joseph too uttered his speech to the people weeping and lamenting, with many tears and in a bitter voice.

79. TALE OF THE MAKEDONIAN LAD

Titus[1] gave the command, and they [the Romans] set free at that time all the Jewish prisoners in his camp; also, they sent forth all the slaves whom the Romans bought from among the captives, for Titus's compassion was stirred upon hearing Joseph's words. Some of the prisoners that Titus released entered the city, nor did he prevent them.

The majority of the people desired to go out to Titus to make peace, until the bandit chiefs, Shimon and Yoḥanan, arose and appointed men over the gates and commanded them, saying: "Every man who sets his face to leave the gate to go to Titus, kill him." Thus, the bandits' guard strengthened over the people, preventing them from going forth to the Romans, and every man that they captured leaving the city to go to the Romans, they smote him with the sword and looted his house. Jerusalem was shut off completely, with no one exiting or entering.

The famine was severe in Jerusalem, and the bandits searched houses and chambers to find food for their sustenance. Whenever someone prevented them, he was struck and killed. The food was consumed from the city, for the bandits finished the people's food until they had to collect dung from the garbage to eat, and in their seeking here and there, they fell and died from hunger. Whoever found grass or herbs or greenery or a rat or a snake or anything, they would eat it to sustain their life, for the famine was intense against them. Whoever had wheat, he feared to grind or bake, lest it become known to the bandits and they take it; so they would eat the wheat in secret. And in the houses wherein there was food, the men of the household would snatch the food

---

1. Chapter follows *DEH* 5.17–20.1 with the author's additions.

by force from each other: the father seizing the food from the son and the son from the father, and the mother from the hand of her son and the son from the mouth of the mother. Whoever left the city to collect weeds to sustain himself, the Kittim would find him, and he would die, until the people ate every crawling thing of the earth, from rat unto lizard and snake, mole and tortoise, cat, and dog. Disease increased among the people, and they died without burial. And if they found the carcass of a horse or any cattle within the city, many would scrap over it until numerous corpses fell fighting over it.

It would happen when men left the city with their children and their wives to find weeds to sustain themselves that the Romans found them and slaughtered the children, saying: "These children, after a time, will grow, and they too will bear arms and fight against us just like their fathers." Hence they slaughtered them, and the Romans prevented the mass of poor from leaving the city. When they wearied and no longer could keep [the people] back, many did leave on account of the famine; and the Romans began to smite among them and hang them on crosses opposite the gate. The Romans did this every day, and the number of those hanged daily on crosses was five hundred souls. Shimon and Yoḥanan also did likewise to any whom they found among their troops or among the nobles who sought to go out to the Roman camp. They also seized him, smote him, and hanged him on the cross over the wall opposite the Roman camp until even the Romans took pity upon the people. Titus commanded not to hang one more Jew upon a cross, for his compassion was stirred.

Yet, despite all this, Titus ceased not to entreat them, saying: "Listen to me, please, and live; have pity upon your people. Why should you destroy them through hunger and thirst through siege and stress?" When they heard Titus's words, they were emboldened to do evil, to strengthen their heart to be cruel toward the people. They insulted Titus to make him angry, lest he continue to speak in such manner to the people anymore, saying: "It is better for us to die by sword, by hunger, by fire as free men for God's Sanctuary and for his Temple and not to bear the yoke of the Romans. For what advantage would it be for us to live a few days longer and see the destruction of God's Temple? Would it not be better for us to die in this misfortune and go forth to the Great Light, to the repose of Gan Eden?"

When Titus beheld this, he commanded to bring forth the ram to the wall to butt it and demolish it, to save those who were trapped under the control of Shimon and Yoḥanan and to kill the latter.

It happened that when they drew the ram near to the wall, a hero was there with Titus, a good lad, by the name of Comagino, son of Antiochus the

Makedonian,[2] who had come to aid the Romans. He was swift of foot and a seasoned warrior but lacking common sense. He called out, saying to Titus: "I am amazed at the horde of your camp that were mighty [enough] to conquer every land and every nation. Why do they tarry and hesitate to smite the Judaeans who are standing outside the wall?" Titus chuckled and said to him: "Just as these words come from your heart, why do you tarry? Go; unsheathe your sword against them!"

Now the lad was incited and, summoning all his Makedonians, engaged in battle with the Jews with arrow and lance. But the Judaeans were stronger than the Makedonians, and they smote among them, both those Judaeans outside the wall and those stationed atop the wall, and they continued to smite the Makedonians until there fell many corpses. But the lad escaped, for he was swift of foot, so he returned and came to Titus. This lad was of the seed of Alexander the Great.

Whereupon Joseph said[3] that whoever would desire to be like Alexander, it is fitting that he be a hero like him, then he will fight against a strong people. For Alexander fought against one city: he came alone at night, leaned a ladder on the wall of the city, descended into the midst of the city, and smote its inhabitants all night long by himself. When morning came, his camp heard, and they said: "What is the noise?" When told that the king was inside the city, they ran and hacked the city's latches and saved their king. But David, our king, performed even greater valor and bravery, for Alexander fought within the city, while David fought within the camp of giants [Rephaim] [cf. 2 Sam 21:15–17]. When Abishai (Abessa) heard that David was fighting against the giants [Nephilim], he hastened to run to David's aid and found him fighting by himself, smiting in the camp of the giants. One of the giants came and encircled David to smite him from behind. When he [giant] raised his hand to smite him [David] with the sword, Abishai ran and blocked his blow with his shield. David turned about and smote the giant [Naphil], and he died [cf. 2 Sam 21.17]. Hence, we know that the iniquities of the city saved Alexander so that the city would be given over into his hand, while the Holy Spirit saved David. The Makedonian's son understood that it was not from lack of power that the Romans ceased to fight against the Jews at that time but rather from prudence.

---

2. His military unit was called "Makedonians." He was not descended from Alexander (below).

3. I.e., in his book, *DEH* 5.19.

80. SIEGE OF JERUSALEM

After these episodes,[1] Titus divided his force into four camps: these he stationed around the wall and set up four rams to butt the wall all around. They set up one ram opposite Antonia, and the ram's length was thirty cubits.[2]

On that night, Yoḥanan, chief of the bandits, sallied with his troops and excavated the soil under the wheels of the ram's cart; they placed slabs under the wheels, plastered pitch, oil, and sulfur, and set it afire. But the ram's guards did not know, for they were asleep; the fire ignited the ram's legs, and it fell upon those who were stationed there, and they died. The Kittim camp took fright and said, "We can no longer fight against this city for they have burned all the weapons of destruction," and the bandit chiefs mocked them over these words. Now Titus was angered exceedingly and commanded [his troops] to maneuver the three remaining rams to there and set them against the outer wall.

As they did this, four Judaean youth became zealous, filled with fanaticism for God's Temple, and each said to his comrade: "Come, let us volunteer for the Name of God our Lord, and we shall make a name for ourselves on this day." These are their names: Teptius the Galilean and Megassarus and Yuvamnus and Iras.[3] They girded on their battle gear and went forth against the Roman camp standing [guard] over the three destroying iron rams. The heart of the four lads filled with zeal and anger, fury, and rage, and they went against the Roman camp without fear or dread, just as a man would come among his maidservants without trepidation; they smote those surrounding the rams and routed

---

1. Chapter follows *DEH* 5.20.1–24 with the author's additions.

2. Actually, the ramp's height was thirty cubits, not its length.

3. *Adiabenus et Agiras* means a man of Adiabene known as Hagira (in Aramaic; *BJ* 5.274, has Ceagiras). The Latin is unclear. One MS has *ac habens* for Adiabenus; Agiras is variously spelled.

the remaining army. They plastered the legs of the rams with inflammable plastering and set fire to the rams, emboldened to make a strong stand until the rams were burned and fell to the earth. The Romans shot a heavy volley of arrows and destructive missiles like rain aplenty at them from afar, for they were afraid to draw near to them; they did not move or retreat from the site of their stand until the rams finished burning. Titus ran with all his camp to save the rams from the fire, but they could not, for Shimon and Yoḥanan and the rest of the warriors sallied against them. They shouted to confront them and routed them from approaching the rams; and the four lads did not die. But there fell there a great many of Titus's warriors.

The Roman camp assembled, for the Judaeans were invading their camp and forcing them away from the city. The valor of the Judaeans became known exceedingly on that day, for the Romans could no longer maintain their position against the Judaeans with the sword, so they shot arrows at them from a distance.

When Titus saw that all his camp had fled, he shouted out, saying to his army: "Shame on you, Romans, a disgrace on such a day to retreat before the Judaeans, whose land we have captured and whose walls we have breached. They have nothing more than battle weapons and but a few, while we are many and accompanied by many nations. So now if they volunteer to die for their land and for the Sanctuary of their God, why don't you too volunteer to make a reputation for valor for yourselves?"

It was on that day that the Judaeans returned to the city, while a huge horde from all the gentiles assembled to aid the Romans. Titus took counsel with his army and all the gentiles who joined them, saying: "Come, let's besiege the city without fighting, for their food is all gone; perhaps the famine will finish them." So he closed the exits of the city, for he feared lest they sally against them suddenly, and they lay siege to the city, closing the surrounding roads and setting guards about day and night.

The famine increased in force among the inhabitants of Jerusalem and the fighting men. But for the famine, the city would not have been captured, for many would go to bury the dead, and the living would fall upon the dead and die, and there was no one to bury, for there was place neither for buriers nor for buried. There were many who threw the dead into pits, and they too fell among them and died. Many, while they were yet alive, went and made graves for themselves, lay down in them for a day or two, and died there, for there was no one to bury or anyone to weep, for weeping had ceased and tears had finished and voices had silenced before the intensity of the famine. All the streets of the city became filled with dead, both within a house and without, and there was no one to collect, no one to bury, no one to weep, no one to raise alarm. And the tales of famine increased until it is wearisome to recount.

When Titus saw the corpses of the dead who had died from the famine cast away uncounted like dung into the Kidron Valley, he was terribly dismayed. He spread his palms heavenward and called out, saying: "Gods of the heavens, cleanse me please from this guilt, for I did not desire to cause it; I beseeched peace, but the bandit chiefs refused, and they brought all this calamity upon the people."

81. DEATH OF AMITAI

At that time,[1] the scoundrels went and told Shimon, saying, "Behold, Amitai (Matthias), the high priest, who brought you to this city, seeks to leave for the Roman camp." Shimon sent and seized Amitai and his four sons, but one of his sons fled; so he caught Amitai with his three sons.

Amitai begged Shimon not to let him live but to hasten to kill him before he sees the death of his sons. But Shimon hardened his heart and did not heed his plea. Thus, Amitai fell by the hand of Shimon, he who had brought him to Jerusalem, and it was not proper for Shimon to reward him such evil for good.

Shimon commanded [his troops], and they stood Amitai on the wall opposite the Romans, and he said to him: "Why don't the Romans save you from my hand since you sought to take refuge with them?"

Amitai begged him to let him kiss his sons before he died, but Shimon did not permit him to kiss them. Then Amitai raised his voice and said to his sons: "My sons, I brought this murderer to this city; therefore, I too am considered a murderer like him, for I brought this upon myself and upon you. From that day, a death sentence was upon me because I brought a bandit into the city of God. I said perhaps he would be an asset to this city, but he turned into a stumbling block for us and a snare for everyone in this city. Nor was one murderer in our midst enough for us, but another murderer was brought in to destroy and consume us. Nor did I bring him to this city out of friendship for him; rather, all the priests and the people sent me to bring him here. Now all the people who used to be free are crushed as slaves to him who lords over them as he wishes, both he and Yoḥanan, his accomplice. Therefore, we brought them to us to subdue the criminal bandits in the city, yet behold, they continued to commit crime after crime and evil after evil."

---

1. Chapter follows *DEH* 5.21–22 with the author's additions.

So Amitai continued and said: "Why do I persist still speaking like a man who has acted justly? For I have sinned against God and His people and the holy city in that I brought you to this city. I should have been sentenced to death by stoning because I brought you to lord over God's people. And it would be proper for me to be rescued from their hand because I caused them evil while unto you I brought good. Had I contemplated fleeing to the camp of the Romans, I could have escaped, for I did not stumble within the city. For before we brought you to the city, Yoḥanan was a stumbling block to this city, and therefore we said: 'Behold, Shimon will be of assistance to us and also to chase away our oppressors'—but behold, you have turned into an oppressor. We said: 'Perhaps he will finish off the murderers'—and lo, you have become yet another murderer; or to subdue the bandits—and lo, you have become a bandit; or to rescue innocents—and lo, you have spilled innocent blood; or to retire weapons of war—and lo, you have increased warring within the city. Before you came here, the bandits in the city used to kill a man secretly, for they were afraid of the people, and now behold, you have killed the valiant of the people in public with a haughty hand.

"Who strengthened himself to the advantage of our Roman oppressors? Was it not you who destroyed the valiant of the city? Whereas Kittim smote but a few outside the city,[2] you killed many inside the city. Whereas Titus sought to make peace with us, for he had compassion upon us, you refused to make peace, and you instigated fighting against us. Whereas Titus commanded his army and warned them lest they set fire to God's Temple, you with your own hand set a fire in God's Temple. On the day that you fought with Yoḥanan—that day was God's holy day, on which one did not fight—he [Titus] turned away from us, saying: 'Go celebrate your holy day.' But you profaned God's holy day with your fighting in the Temple, you spilled the blood of God's priests, and you extinguished the perpetual flame with their blood. Everything seemed to me as if I had done it because I brought you to this city. Behold, now God's vengeance will fall upon me in my old age since by your hand I will go down in grief to hell. For every calamity perpetrated within this city was committed by the two of us: by me, for in my excessive foolishness I gathered you into this city, and by you, because you continue to spill innocent blood.

"And now, Shimon, I thank you that you will kill me ere my eyes behold the burning of God's Temple, but I condemn you for killing my sons before my eyes. Would that, just as I shall not see the burning of God's Temple, so I would not

---

2. The author's MS apparently had *paucos* (few) instead of *pacem* (peace); *DEH* is more positive toward the Romans.

see the blood of my sons spilling upon the earth before my eyes. For this reason, we abhorred Yoḥanan because he destroyed old men and did not respect old age, and now behold, you kill old men and destroy young ones. Yoḥanan, while killing the elders of the city, used to play his music with lyre and harp, and you, while murdering old men with young and fathers with sons, trumpet the loud blast of the shofar."[3]

After this, Amitai spoke to Shimon's servant, who was holding him [Amitai], the killing axe in his hand, and said to him: "Be quick, fulfill Shimon's order, and smite the sons with the axe before the father's eyes so that I may hear the sound of your brutal blows smiting sons before their father's eyes. Yet I will bear what I see, though unwillingly, because you are the smiter; even against your will, you smite. Would that Shimon the killer allow me to kiss my sons and embrace them while I still live. So now pray, let your mercy be magnified; if you should kill me after my sons, don't separate my corpse from their corpses, so that my corpse may cover their corpses and I spare them from the birds in the sky. Perhaps they will eat my corpse alone and not eat my sons' corpses. Let my mouth and tongue fall upon my sons' blows, and I will hug them violently, lest this cruel one separate me from them. And even if he would separate our carcasses, he could not separate our souls.

"And now we have wept enough; of what use is weeping. Go now, precede me, my sons, and I will come after you according to the strength of my old age, and I know that you have the strength of youths. Wait up a bit for me and let me reach you. Go please and find a resting place for us for the rest of time, for with all my strength, I desired to precede you to prepare this resting place, but I was not permitted. So now if you yourselves go along this path and find a resting place, the locals will give you fine hospitality, for they will see that you are innocent. Were I to go before you to the resting place, they would not have given me fine hospitality, for they would loathe me according to the wickedness of my deeds, that I brought Shimon to God's city. So now, my sons, go please; do not linger, for this is not something new; rather, it was done like this earlier in the days of the Hasmoneans. The woman who sent her seven sons before her; they went and prepared a resting place for themselves and their mother, for in front of her, each would embrace his brother and then die for God and His covenant. Their mother watched and rejoiced opposite them, and afterward she followed

---

3. The author misread *senectus* and assumed the following from his source: *Iohannis nos cera terruit, Simonis latrocina delectaverunt* (Yoḥanan's beeswax terrified us, whereas Shimon's injustices comforted us). The word *cera* (wax) was unclear and occasionally corrected to *cithara* (a stringed instrument); attested in two MSS of Hegesippus. The author therefore has Yoḥanan fiddling and Shimon trumpeting.

her sons with great happiness. They were killed by the cruelties of Antiochus, and we, by Shimon's cruelties. If only we too could be in one resting place with them! And if we cannot enter their resting place, then let us be their neighbors, for they died in their righteousness, and we shall die in our innocence.

"Comfort ye, comfort ye [cf. Isa 40:1], my sons, and hurry please, and we shall get out of this swarm of murdering bandits! And should Jonathan, who was killed before his father, happen to meet you while you are on your journey and should Saul also meet me and ask me about God's people, you will say to Jonathan and I will recount to Saul that this people that you have known, before whom the waters of the sea split, the sun stopped on their behalf, and the Jordan flowed backward for their sake, the people who trod through the depths of the sea, and clouds dropped their food from above, the wilderness gave them its waters, and they were covered with heaven's clouds, in place of their trustworthy shepherds, a swarm of bandits and murdering chiefs has lorded over them, Shimon, the bandit chief, and with him troops of Edom, our slaves. Thus, you shall say to the righteous ones who preceded you, choosing death with God's people rather than living in shame in gentile uncleanness. Also, in such words we shall relate to those righteous ones who died in the days of Matityahu, the high priest, rather than fight on the Sabbath. For Shimon not only gave battle on the Sabbath, but on the Sabbath, he killed God's priests within the Temple on the altar of His sanctity. And were Yeḥoniahu (Jehoniah) to hear these things, he would cry out greatly that Shimon is ruling over God's people, and on his behalf, Jerusalem was destroyed, and for him, the Temple was burned. Yeḥoniahu surrendered himself and his household into exile without handing over God's Sanctuary to be destroyed. Did not Yeḥoniahu act better than Ẕidkiyahu (Zedekiah), who, for the sake of God's Temple and the holy city, accepted captivity and exile lest the Kasdim raise a hand against Jerusalem? But Ẕidkiyahu persisted in his foolishness and, betraying his oath, strengthened his heart against God's wrath, nor was he subdued until God's Temple was destroyed, God's people went into captivity, his sons slaughtered before his eyes [cf. 2 Kings 25:7], and the Kasdim blinded his sight; then he too went into exile. The sorrow of Ẕidkiyahu was greater than the sorrow of Yeḥoniahu and my own sorrow, for Ẕidkiyahu lived for a long time after his sons, while I go together with my sons; for this, my heart is comforted. And the king of Kasdim, who took pity on Ẕidkiyahu,[4] giving him provisions and honor after he had slaughtered his sons and blinded his eyes, would it not have been better for him to die, together with his sons, and

---

4. The author misread his source, which refers to Yeḥoniahu.

not to live after them? But to his bad luck, he had compassion upon him and did not kill him. So the compassion of the king of Kasdim harmed him more than his cruelties, in that he let him live after his sons: therefore, the king of Kasdim let him live so that the warmth of his heart that warmed up over his sons would die down. There is no remedy for this pain save death; then the soul will rest from grief's sorrow."

Amitai called out and said to the slayer: "Hurry up, smite me while my sons are still moving their hands and feet before they die; perhaps we may die together. For it is better for us to die than to see God's city like a grave and her crowd slaughtered in her midst."

Amitai cried out to God and said: "I beseech thee, O Lord, who is incomprehensible and awesome, don't kill Shimon amid the flock of Your people. Rather, kill him alone and separated, captured by these who seek his life, he and his sons together. Let his fate not be with Your portion [people], nor let his destiny be with the Temple of Your Sanctuary. Let him see his sons in their captors' hand, and afterward let him behold their death, then let him too die for the wickedness of his deeds and let his eyes look upon the exile and the captivity and let him pay with his life.[5]

"Let Shimon know that my fate was better than his fate, for I was gathered with my sons, and my eyes did not behold exile, nor did my sons go into captivity, nor did I see the burning of God's Temple. Yet he will see all this with his eyes, and his soul will die languishing [cf. Deut 28:65]."

Amitai said to the slayer: "Hurry up, smite me while the blood of my sons is still damp upon the steel, before it dries, and let my blood mingle with my sons' blood; let it soothe me as medicine and as salve. Also smite me facing the Romans, for they will exact vengeance for me and be witnesses for me on such a day, for I was their enemy and not their ally. Would that I were Shimon's enemy at the beginning just as I was the Romans'! And would that I had fought against Shimon just as I fought against the Romans and had stopped Shimon's wickedness over God's people! Now, O Lord, inscrutable God who dwells on high, judge and reprove! [cf. Prov 3:11–12]."

When he had finished speaking, Shimon gave the command [to his troops], and they struck the three sons of Amitai facing their father, and they died. After this, Amitai was struck, and he died with his sons.

Even while the carcasses of Amitai and his sons were being thrown from atop the wall, Shimon commanded, and they killed Ḥananiah, the high priest from a clan of honored priests, and his carcass was thrown down upon Amitai's carcass.

---

5. *Yeshalem et naphsho*, i.e., die; see chaps. 14 and 18.

At that time, Aristeus the scribe, of noble stock, was also killed in the place where Amitai had stood, along with fifteen righteous and innocent men who died by Shimon's violence.

It happened while Shimon was smiting these righteous ones that eleven nobles of Jerusalem, well born, passed by and saw how these righteous ones were being killed, and they said to one another: "How long will God look upon the wickedness of Shimon that he is doing in this place and remain silent and not seek the blood of the righteous and the pious from his hand?" This conversation was heard and related to Shimon; he killed them too on that day.

82. THE BATTLES OF JERUSALEM CONTINUE

When Elazer ben Anani the priest[1] saw that Shimon's wickedness had increased within the city, and he had annihilated the righteous and the pious from the city and there was no more hope, he dispatched [a force] and seized the wall of Masada; then he went and sat there to guard it. When Yehudah, captain of the thousand, guardian of the tower, saw what Shimon had done, he cried to the Romans to come to him; perhaps they would save these men. But the Romans did not believe him, as they said: "They are mocking us as they did previously," but he was shouting at them in good faith; still they did not come.

At that time, Shimon gave the command and killed Yehudah and his men, and he cast their corpses outside the walls opposite the Romans alongside the corpses of their brothers. Shimon said to the Roman officers: "Here are the men who sought to go out to you; pray take them and let them be with you!" And Gurion, Joseph's father, was imprisoned in Shimon's house, bound in chains and iron fetters, and no one could come into contact with him.

It so happened at that time that Joseph came up opposite the wall facing the tower wherein was his father; and Joseph passed by, his eyes scanning the tower, when a small rock came at him from atop the wall, hitting him on his head, and he fell to the ground. The bandits rushed to go out to capture him; the Romans saw that Joseph had fallen, and Titus hastened and ordered to save him before the bandits reached him. They did so, covering him with their shields from above and around against the slings and arrows; thus they saved him, and

---

1. Chapter follows *DEH* 5.22–27 with the author's additions. The author's mistaken assumption that Elazar ben Yair was Elazar ben Anani is from *DEH* 2.10.1. See chap. 89 (beginning).

he did not die. And the bandits in their rush to capture Joseph sounded a great trumpeting.

Joseph's mother heard the sound of their trumpeting, and she was told that they were shouting for joy over her son Joseph because they had gone out to capture him. She ran and mounted the wall and raised her voice in weeping and lament and in bitter voice, saying: "To this has my anticipation come, and so my expectation that I hoped to live after my son Joseph! But I did not succeed in burying him, yet I myself expected that he would bury me, but now it is beyond my capacity to bury him. O would that I could die, for I did not desire life after my son's death. Now would that my death be with him, and let me cover him with my garment that is upon my flesh so that one garment will cover two dead." She mounted the tower and, spreading her palms heavenward, cried out in a loud voice; her cry increased, and her soul embittered exceedingly. The bandits were laughing at the sound of her cry while the whole Roman camp wept over her, sobbing. And she said to the bandits: "Why don't you kill me too, for I gave birth to Joseph, whom you killed. Did I not nurse him from my two breasts, and I raised him? So now why do you let me live?" She continued to weep until the whole Roman camp opposite her wept, and many of the Jews who were in the city wept at her voice.

When Joseph heard the voice of his mother from atop the wall, he drew closer to the wall, valiant Romans with him covering him, their shields over him to protect him. Then Joseph called out and said to his mother: "Don't be afraid, my mother, for I have escaped. However, I wish I had died today before beholding the burning of God's Temple and the destruction of His people. For the souls in the bodies are like prisoners under siege, and when the soul leaves the body, it goes free, for as long as it [the body] is still alive it is entrapped."

On that day, a great many men with their wives, their sons, and their daughters left the city, for they had overcome the bandits' guards; and they went out to the Roman camp. Titus commanded, and they gave them sustenance, food and drink, but many of them could not open their mouths for food, as their jaws had hardened from the long days of famine, so that when the bread reached their innards, they died. And the children, seeing the bread, would fall upon it and bite the bread with their teeth, and they expired and died. When Titus saw that the people were dying when they ate the bread, not having eaten bread for some time, he said to Joseph: "What shall I do for your people who are dying when they eat the bread?" Joseph answered him, saying: "This I have seen that when a man fasts for three or four days and there comes time for him to eat, they give him first milk or fine meal; perhaps that will strengthen the intestines and they gain control; then he can eat the bread." Titus ordered, and they

[Romans] did so, and many of the people lived, but many died from [excessive] bowel movement.[2]

When these Judaeans went out from Jerusalem, some of them had swallowed gold and fine jewels to hide from the bandits. It happened when they left for the Roman camp that when one of them went off to his needs by himself, he would search his excrement in order to find the gold and whatever else he had swallowed. While they were doing this, some of the Aramaeans [Syrians] and some of the Arav men saw them and said to one another that they should ambush them, seize them secretly, split open their guts, and they would find within their intestines gold and precious stones. The Aramaean men and Arav men began to do this evil against the Judaeans, and those who were so split numbered two thousand souls.

When Titus heard of this wicked thing that Syrians and Araviim were doing, he fumed and became very furious and summoned all the officers of his camp; they assembled to him, and he looked, and behold, their weapons were covered with gold. He said to them: "Remove this gold from your weapons, for this gold has instigated the Syrians and Araviim to do this abhorrent thing, this scandalous wickedness," and they did so and removed it. At that time, Titus commanded, and they chased the Syrians and Araviim from the camp, preventing them from perpetrating this wickedness again. But if they were to find a Judaean outside the camp at a distance and the Judaean alone, no one seeing him, then they would kill him and split him open.

In those days, Menaḥem [Manneus], one of the guardians of Jerusalem's gates, counted, tallying the number of dead that were taken for burial just from that gate, excepting those cast out in the city streets or in the cisterns or in the Kidron Valley and excluding those who fell by the sword whom they brought out from the rest of the gates. Just from the gate of Menaḥem alone, their number was 115,880, all of these nobles who were buried, the remainder of the people being cast out upon the earth. The Jewish leaders who left to Titus related the number of dead that were taken for burial from every Jerusalem gate during the period of the famine and in battle as 600,000, excluding those who died in the houses and remained there for there was no one to bury them, and excluding those who died in the streets, for there was no one to collect them, and excluding those who died in the Temple and in the courtyards of Jerusalem without number.

In those days, the famine worsened within the city, and hunger began even among the bandit chiefs, until they were eating their horses' dung and all the

---

2. The author's medical addition. [Such too was the tragic fate of many of the survivors of World War II concentration camps. SB]

leather gear of their chariots and weapons. The bandit chiefs sought to find a fresh tree branch or vegetable or grass to eat, but there was none, for Romans had cut down every tree surrounding Jerusalem for thirteen miles, and there remained not a tree uncut in any garden or any place, for surrounding Jerusalem, there had been gardens and orchards without number and also every fruit-bearing tree of every variety of fruit trees. All of them were cut down, so that the entire surrounding land was like wilderness and wasteland. And it happened that everyone who came from afar of those who had seen previously the forests of Jerusalem and the gardens and orchards would look to the right and there was no tree and turn to the left and there was none, and he was horrified and wept with bitterness and lamentation.

The Romans again approached the wall to fight, and the bandit chiefs sallied against them, and these were hungry and grunting; a great many of them and also of the Roman horde fell there. No longer now were the bandits able to burn the ram as previously, for they could not summon strength to withstand the hunger; but if they were to burn the ram time and again, the Romans would have marched away from Jerusalem, and then the bandits would have said that the Roman horde lost heart besieging Jerusalem. This is why the Romans strengthened their heart not to retreat from the bandits and fortified guard posts and sentries, saying to each other: "Be strong and let us be strengthened in battle, for it would be a shame and a disgrace for us to retreat before these starving ones, since they are dying." The bandits returned to the city, and the Roman troops came and butted the wall with the iron ram, and the inner wall fell to the ground; the Roman horde broke out in a long fanfare saying: "We have captured the city."

The Judaeans too raised a cry within the city, for they had built another new wall in place of the wall that the Romans demolished, and they built it in the area of Yoḥanan's watch opposite the breached wall.

When the Romans heard the Judaeans' shouting, they looked, and behold, another new wall with the bandits and the Judaeans standing upon it; they were quite dismayed; their joy changed to anger, and the Romans were disheartened to fight again, for they despaired of capturing the city. Titus said to them: "Behold, their wall that they have built is not a dry wall, for they built it quickly. Now, while the clay is still damp, bring the ram to it and butt it so that this one too will fall, and we shall capture the city and depart."

The Roman horde went up on the wall that they had breached and stood atop it. The Judaeans and the bandits were standing on the new wall facing them, and they were close by each other, so they fought there between the two walls, and the Judaeans gained the upper hand, chasing the Romans from the breached wall.

When Titus saw how badly it was going for the Roman horde, he called to his officers and said to them: "Don't you know that all labor and all fighting and all else, its ending is more difficult than its beginning? If at the finish of the labor your hands slacken, behold, you have labored in vain [cf. Isa 49:4, 65:23]. Look upon the ship that plies the sea, crossing every lane until it enters the harbor, and entering the harbor, the sailors' hands weaken and let it slacken. Will it not be battered against one of the rocks or cliffs and be broken up and everything on her be lost? What would be the advantage then to those sailors of slackening their hands?

"But if they strengthen their hands to the work, they will enter the harbor and dock in the place of their choice at rest and repose. And likewise, all the builders, if they do not fulfill their work or complete it for the slackening of their hands and leave it insufficient, will they not lose their pay and their labor be in vain? Further, I shall speak to you about farmers: if they plow their land, plant it, watch over the seed of the field until the ears of corn are ripe, and harvest time arrives, if their hands slacken and they do not reap, will they not lose their hard labor and their sustenance? And you who have fought against this city for a long time, and many of your officers and warriors have fallen, and your hands have been strengthened until this day; now behold, the walls are breached and thrown down to the ground, the people destroyed by fighting, plague and famine, and there remains this new wall. What would be the value of all that you have done previously if you seek to abandon the battle? It would have been better for you to have left it at the beginning before your numbers diminished, before your heroes died, before your troops fell. But now that all this has been done, if you were to leave the battle, what further desire would you have for living? Would it not be better for you to die? Did you not come to this city in the days of Nero Caesar to fight in his name, lest you bring shame upon him? Now that Vespasian, my father, who is more valiant than Nero, rules, will you let your hands slacken? Is this not a shame and a scandal for you today?

"Why do you not learn bravery from these Jews, whom the sword, the famine, and the plague have destroyed, and they die without hope, yet still they fight like animals? Do you not see that every day one or two of them come and spill out their lives against our camp and kill many in the camp, and afterward they too die? And they do this only to make a reputation for bravery for themselves." And he spoke to them further in such vein.

83. THE BATTLE IN THE AZARAH

While he was still speaking with them,[1] behold, one of his warriors, named Sabino, a fighting man since his youth and bold of heart, said: "Who among you will volunteer with me against this people and fulfill the command of the king's son?" He raised his shield in his left hand and his unsheathed sword in his right; and eleven of his warriors went with him, all of them proven fighters. Titus was amazed at Sabino's courage that he dared to act thus.

The Judaeans stood over the breach in the wall, the place from which the Romans were chased away, and when the Judaeans saw Sabino and his comrades coming against them, they began shooting arrows at them and casting stones. Despite this, Sabino did not retreat from before them, nor did his heart soften. Sabino came and clove unto the Jews where the wall was breached. As he drew near, one of the Judaeans smote him with his sword, and he fell upon his face; and the sound of his falling was heard. He recovered and got to his knees while the Judaeans went toward him. Sabino, still fighting, was struck, and he died, for fighting was more precious in his eyes than life. And three of his warriors died there, while eight of them fell alive though dying, and the Romans raced to them and rescued them; but on the morrow, they too died.

The Roman warriors grew angry and envied what Sabino did; during that night, twenty of Titus's warriors made plans to make a reputation for valor for themselves, saying: "Come, let's go from the corner of the city breach." They told it to Titus's standard-bearer, and he too came with them, and they mounted the city breach during the night. The Jews did not know, for they were lying exhausted and enfeebled from the hunger. And so it happened that when the Romans called out, the Judaeans were alarmed, for they came upon them suddenly.

____

1. Chapter follows *DEH* 5.28–31 with the author's additions.

When Titus heard the sound of the shouting, he too took some of his lads and went to the wall. The Judaeans woke up early, and behold, Titus was on the wall. Then the Romans mustered against them, and some of them mounted the wall, while others stood at the breach; and others came through the cavern that opened into the city, for this was the underground way by which to enter or exit the city.

The Judaeans drew up for battle with the Romans inside the Azarah, which is the courtyard of the Temple, and all of Titus's warriors and Roman lads descended there with unsheathed swords against the Judaeans, for they bore no weapon other than swords. The Judaeans too did likewise and willingly battled with sword; and they approached each other with sword.

Then major fighting, the like of which was never within Jerusalem, happened there, each cleaving to his enemy, and all were afoot, swords smiting one another with no retreat or turning, for each man was fused with his foe. Such a falling of corpses, stabbers upon stabbed, and the sound of tumult was heard from afar. The strikers shouted, the struck groaned, the sound of swords clanging as sword clashed against sword, the sound too of human bone struck by the sword, and the sound spread afar. The Romans took courage, saying: "Behold, this is the day we have hoped for." But the Judaeans held fast, saying: "There is no retreat outside, so we shall die for our God, for His Temple, for His Sanctuary: on this day, we shall be considered as a burnt offering." The courtyard of the Azarah filled with the blood of Romans and Judaeans from the morning unto the fourth part of the day, the blood spreading over the face of the courtyard like a pond of water. Corpses were cast down without number, and most of the corpses were from the Roman horde.

One of Titus's warriors, named Gulianus [Iulianus], one of the most valiant of the Kittim, looked up, and seeing the Judaeans were getting the upper hand over the Romans, he fumed and filled with rage and fury as he beheld Romans retreating from the Azarah away from the Jews, for they remained but a few. Gulianus ran to confront mighty Jews pursuing Romans to the edge of the Azarah. He raced toward them unto the corner of Antonia and stood before the Judaeans, preventing them from passing after Romans. The Judaeans returned to the Azarah, and Gulianus too followed them inside the Azarah. Then one of the Judaeans smote with his sword upon Gulianus's shield, which was on his arm; and seeing that the Judaean had smote him, he gathered his strength to leap from the ground according to military tactic, but his foot slipped on the stones of the floor of the Azarah, and he fell to the ground, for his feet were shod; hence he fell. Now this is not the rule of bravery, for if a warrior seeks to kill his enemy, it is proper for him to beware of his enemy and be watchful for the blow, to be protected lest he be struck, and to the slayer, to be on guard lest he be killed and not say in his heart: "My bravery will perform wonders, and I will be mighty and not fall"; for Gulianus did not go like a man advancing against a warrior like himself, but in his arrogance, he went like a man going to the playing field. And so, at the moment when Gulianus fell, he got to his knees and fought a little; and they smote him and he died. Titus longed for Gulianus to come back in glory, but he did not, for he fell and died.

When Titus heard that Gulianus fell and died, he too sought to enter the Azarah to fight, but his warriors did not let him, for they feared lest he too fall. So the hand of the Judaeans was strengthened on that day over the horde of Romans who had entered the Azarah, and the corpses of Romans multiplied there without number. The Judaeans stripped Gulianus along with the Roman corpses, and they took their weapons from them. These are the names of the valiant soldiers of the Judaeans who performed this heroism on that day: from Yoḥanan's portion, Elasah[2] and Yiphtaḥ;[3] from Shimon's portion, Milkiah[4] and Ya'akov *nagid* of Edom;[5] and from the third portion, Arisimon[6] and Yehudah with the rest of their brethren. They were those who continued to smite among the Roman army on that day within the Azarah, routing them and closing them up within Antonia, standing over the gate of Antonia, preventing them from exiting and from entering. Now Titus knew that Antonia was a snare for the Romans and gave the command, and they destroyed it.

---

2. Alexa; the author recalled the biblical Elasah (Jer 29:3).

3. Gyptheus; the author decoded the biblical Yiphtaḥ (Jephthah).

4. Melchius, and in one MS Melchia.

5. *Iacobus Idumaeorum dux.*

6. *BJ* 6.92, has Ari Simon, i.e., Simon, son of Ari. Several MSS, as common in *Yosippon*'s sources, run the names together as one.

84. THE BATTLE WITHIN THE CITY

On the morrow,[1] the Jews celebrated their holiday of Shavu'oth;[2] Titus approached the Temple, and Joseph was with him. Titus called out to Yoḥanan and to the bandit chiefs in a loud voice, Joseph interpreting Titus's words for them. Titus called out and said to Yoḥanan: "How has this Temple sinned against you that this calamity will afflict it, destroying it? If you laud strength and valor, come forth with your warriors to the field and let us fight there. Now, is this day not the day of your celebration? Why do you fight in the site of the sacrifice and the offering and profane your God's Sanctuary? We do not fight against the Temple, for it is the House of God; rather, our fight is with you and not with the Temple. Now, if you say that we can no longer fight, subdue your neck to us and bear our yoke. But if you say: 'Come, let us fight,' let us go and enter the field and there engage in battle: Why should you cause the sacrifice of your God's service to cease?"

When Joseph had translated Titus's words to the Jews, all the people were silent; they did not answer, for Yoḥanan's and the bandit chiefs' order to them was not to answer them a word. Then Yoḥanan called out and said to him: "No sacrifice offered up in this Temple can be better than our flesh and blood, for we are fighting for our God; we shall be considered before Him as a daily offering acceptable before God; we shall die free men within the holy city."[3]

Titus answered Yoḥanan and said: "This city is a holy city and the Temple is a holy Temple, but you—sullied and sinners—you have defiled the Temple of your God, and His Sanctuary, and His city in which you have spilled

---

1. Chapter follows *DEH* 5.31–36 with the author's additions.
2. The author interpreted Hegesippus to mean Pentacost, while Josephus (*BJ* 6.94) indicates 17 Tammuz.
3. *venehshav lifanov ke-olath tamid leratzon venamutu ḥofshim bitokh ʿir hakodesh*; *DEH* has *civitas dei*.

innocent blood. You have killed His priests within the Temple, so how would you be innocent enough to be considered as offerings and sacrifices? Now, you have become abominable in His eyes, for every sacrifice with blemish is unacceptable before Him, whereas you are filled with every blemish and sin and guilt, so how could you be acceptable as a sacrifice before Him, saying: 'We are pure'? Would it be all right in your eyes if someone were to come and snatch your table from in front of you? Wouldn't that be wicked in your eyes? Yet you, why did you prohibit the sacrifice of the men of your God from the Temple and fill His house with corpses to be trampled upon? Who would see and not weep over the mass of your corpses that died because of you and your crony Shimon, for they have increased beyond number, yet still you say: 'God is with us!'

"It is proper for valiant men to fight on behalf of their people and their city and their land—and I did not come to destroy your country or to ravage your land or to wipe out your cities or to annihilate you; I came only to summon you to peace and to have mercy upon you if you were to obey us and turn your shoulder to our yoke as you were before.

"For who among all the nations can be as compassionate as we to do good, to enact *ḥesed* [mercy]? Did not Hannibal, king of Kartagina (Carthage), go with all his force, invade, and trample our land, destroying our fortifications and annihilating the mass of our troops by sword, he and his army? He besieged us for many days, as we have done unto you; and after all this, we captured him, and we had mercy upon him and did well by him. Likewise, we did unto Antiochus the Makedonian and the rest of the nations whom we captured.

"Don't you yourselves preserve the memory of Yekhonyah [Iechonias], your king, because he took pity upon the holy Temple and the Sanctuary of your God without making it a wasteland? He had compassion upon you, lest you go into captivity or die by the sword; and he surrendered himself and his house to the king of Kasdim in order to spare you from the hand of the gentiles, but you had no compassion. Now, I strike this covenant with you before the God of this house, and let it be a witness between me and you that I will give you Joseph and a few of my honored officers. Let them be as a security in your hands, and you will make peace with us; you will bend your shoulder and subdue your neck to serve us like all the nations; you shall live and not die; and the service of your God's Sanctuary will not cease." Whereupon Joseph wept a great lament before the eyes of the bandit chiefs over the words of Titus because he had compassion for them.

When Joseph saw that he could not turn the bandit chiefs to peace, he called out and said to them: "I am not surprised at this city, which is going to be a wasteland, for I know that her end is coming. Yet I am surprised at you, for you have read and you understand the book *Vision of Daniel*,[4] for behold, all of his words came true. Has not the *tamid* stopped and the anointed priest[5] been cut off and all the words of Daniel been fulfilled?[6] While your eyes see, your heart does not believe."

When Joseph finished speaking, the bandits had hardened their heart and paid no heed to his words, yet many priests and nobles left that day and went to the Roman camp and stayed there. Titus sent them to Gofna (Gosna), which he gave to them as a haven, and he commanded to feed them there and watch over them, lest the Roman troops do them harm. Now many sought to leave Jerusalem, but the bandits prevented their leaving: perhaps their sin was to be expiated by dying along with the city alongside the rest of their brethren. The bandits closed up the exits of the Temple and the city, lest anyone go out to the Roman camp.

When it became known to Titus that many of the Jews sought to leave and take refuge with him but the bandits prevented them, Titus approached the breach in the wall accompanied by Joseph. When the people saw Joseph, they cried out a huge lament and said: "We know our sins, which we have transgressed, and the compassion the king's son has for us. We wish to leave and take refuge with him, but we are not able, for the bandits prevent us." When the bandits heard their words honoring Titus, they raced at them with swords to kill them, while the Romans ran to save them.

Fighting broke out again within the Temple between Romans and Judaeans, and the Romans were pressed toward the building of the Holy of Holies to take refuge there; the Judaeans pursued after them and killed them there within the holy place. From outside the Temple, Titus called out to Yoḥanan in a loud voice, for Yoḥanan was within the Temple. Titus said to him: "Is it not written in the Torah of your God: and the stranger who draws near, let him be killed for the sake of this Sanctuary, for none other may draw near to there than the

---

4. Note the Byzantine Hebrew apocalypse *Ḥazon Daniel* that dates from the second decade of the tenth century, according to R. Bonfil, and deals with the Byzantine reconquest of southern Italy. Bonfil, "La visione ebraica di Daniele nel contesto bizantino del secolo X," *Rivista di Studi Bizantini e Neoellenici*, n.s. 40 (2003): 25–65. Josephus and Hegesippus, of course, refer to the biblical Dan. The *tamid* is the daily offering from above. [SB]

5. Cf. Dan 9:26; the author's emphasis distinguishes from *DEH*'s Christian interpretation of this verse as referring to Jesus. Compare Saadia Gaon, *Book of Beliefs and Opinions* 8.8 (trans. Rosenblatt, New Haven, CT, 1948), 321, sharing perhaps a similar source to *Yosippon*.

6. Hegesippus recalls the "abomination of desolation" (Dan 9:27, 11:31, 12:11), while the author alludes to the cessation of the *tamid* (Dan 9:26–27, 12:11); tradition applies these verses to the destruction of the Temple (cf. b. *Ta'anit* 4.6).

high priest alone once a year, for it is the Holy of Holies, and the one who takes refuge in it do ye not let live? Even so, you are spilling there blood of the uncircumcised, who are abhorrent to you, and also blood of Jews your brethren. And God your Lord will be a witness for me that I was unwilling and had no heart to demolish this house; rather, your wicked deeds will demolish it. Would that you agree to make peace with us, we would honor this Temple, and we would leave you alone; alas, your heart has strengthened like iron, to your detriment."

When Titus saw that no one paid attention to his words, he went and chose from among his warriors thirty thousand battle-tested veterans[7] and commanded them to go to the Azarah, courtyard of the Temple. He sought to go down with them, but his officers prevented him, saying: "Take your stand in an elevated place, and when the warriors shall see you, then they will strengthen their heart and fight. Don't go to the Azarah, lest you die with the others, and then all of us will be lost." Titus appointed Kirialis (Cerealis) over the thirty thousand warriors whom he sent to enter the Azarah against the Jews at night to smite them while they were still lying and exhausted. But the Judaeans set watches and knew that the Romans were coming against them, so they rose and took up positions all night to confront the Romans, but they did not fight, for who fights in the predawn when a man cannot distinguish his comrade?

When it was morning and the Judaeans were sharing the watches over the gates of the Azarah, they fought a fierce battle over the gates, and the fighting lasted for seven days. When the Romans got the upper hand, they pressed the Judaeans into the Azarah, pursuing after them; and when the Judaeans took strength and gained the upper hand, they chased the Romans from within the Azarah, pursuing them as far as Antonia. They continued to do so for the seven days of fighting. After this, Titus commanded, and the Romans ceased fighting, withdrawing from the Judaeans, for Titus commanded to demolish the wall of Antonia in order to widen a place for all the forces of his camp; and they did so.

---

7. *DEH* 5.35.1 reads *triginta electis uiris singula deputat bellatorum milia.*

85. BATTLE OF THE FORTRESS

The famine[1] was very severe in Jerusalem, and there was no sustenance, so the Judaeans began to go out, everyone who dared go at night to steal horses and donkeys or any edible beast from the Roman camp, to be food for them. Finally, the Romans set watches around their camp against the Judaean raiders who acted thus daily. The Judaeans saw that they set watches, and no one could steal anymore.

At that time, some of the Judaean youth went out, girt with their weapons of war. They came to the East Gate and demolished the wall that Titus had built, for Titus had built a wall in the orchard garden[2] opposite the East Gate, lest the Judaeans sally suddenly and smite his camp, as they used to do regularly.

Then these youths sallied from the place that they had destroyed and ascended from there to Har Hazeitim [Mons Oliveti], where they found considerable cattle, horses, mules, and donkeys; they smote the guards with sword and drove off everything they could. Then they raised a great cry, and the Roman camp saw that the Judaeans were driving off their cattle, so they rose up and ran after them to fight. So those youths split into two groups—one drove the cattle, and the other stood upon the roadway opposing the Romans—and a major battle erupted. The Judaeans were fighting for their lives against famine to rescue some food for themselves, while the Romans were fighting for the shame done to them, and many casualties fell there. Then the whole gentile horde that was in the Roman camp rose up to attack these youths, who, when they saw such a numerous army against them, fled toward the city. The Roman troops pursued after them but did not capture them; only one of the lads was captured alive,

---

1. Chapter follows *DEH* 5.36–39 with the author's addition.
2. Based on variants in the author's MS: two MSS have *pomarium* (orchard; cf. Vulgate, Eccl 2:3) for *DEH*'s *pomerium* (wall).

and they brought him to Titus. Now the name of the man who captured the lad was Pedanius, and the Roman warriors boasted and lauded Pedanius so that he became great in Titus's eyes.

It so happened that among these youths was a contemptible man, short of stature, by the name of Yonatan. He turned his face and looked back and saw that, lo, Pedanius had captured the lad, and he filled with rage. Now he was standing next to the grave of Yoḥanan the priest outside the city facing the Roman camp. He called out to Titus and to all his camp and said: "Who among you brave fighting men will come to me? For my hands will fulfill my words, and it will be known whose is the valor on this day, whether to the Romans whether to the Jews." Yet, while he was abhorrent in the eyes of the Romans and they held him in contempt, nonetheless they feared to go out against him, saying: "If we kill him, it will not be counted as glory to us, for he is contemptible, but if he should kill us, then it would be a disgrace to us."

Yonatan called out and said to them: "How will Roman valor be considered among us on every battle front? Have you not been routed before us, and we smacked you like our maids so that you fled from us? And now how would you be deemed if not for the gentiles who join you daily and assist you? For already you should have been fodder to us except that our own swords have devoured us, each killing his comrade and everyone his brother to our detriment; therefore, we remain few in number. Now who among all your heroes will dare to come against me, who am despised of all Jews, so that you may know that we are the mightiest and bravest?"

One of Titus's warriors, named Pudens, volunteered to go out against him—and so it seems that he was Pedanius who had captured the lad alive and brought him to Titus. And it happened when Pudens went out to Yonatan that Yonatan wounded him and killed him. Therefore, Pudens bequeathed glory to Yonatan, and to the Romans, he bequeathed shame and disgrace.

Moreover, Yonatan did not give glory to God in his smiting of Pudens, for he became arrogant and began to dance about and jeer at the Romans, saying: "Come, send out another to me, and I will kill him." And he danced about, insulting the Romans, and behold, Purion[3] the Roman shot him with an arrow and killed him. It is fitting for a man killing his enemy [to do so] without rejoicing or boasting but rather to give glory and praise to God, who saved him from his enemy's hand, for who knows what will be at the end?

---

3. *DEH*'s *centurionem Priscum* appears in several MSS as *prius eum* or *priuscum*. Not recognizing a name, the author made one up from *centurionem* or perhaps from a garbled MS *purionem*.

After this, the Judaeans saw that the wall of the Temple was also breached, the last of the city's three walls; now they knew there was no hope, so they counseled together what to do.

There was at the side of the Temple a very large fortress,[4] one of those that King Solomon had built and to which the Second Temple kings had added cedar logs to heighten its walls, covering it with cedar, so that the fortress was quite enlarged. The Judaeans went and coated the cedar logs of the fortress with an inflammable plastering of pitch, sulfur, and naphtha, and they continued coating them. Then they went and incited the Romans to enter the Temple to do battle, retreating before the Romans toward the corner of the fortress. The Romans pursued, following them into the fortress; however, they exited from another place; and also more of the Romans who pursued them brought ladders, leaned them against the wall of the fortress, and mounted the roof, until they said: "We have captured the fortress."

When the fortress was filled with Romans both within and upon the building, one of the Judaeans volunteered—he had been hidden within the fortress—and set fire to the cedar logs that the Judaeans had plastered, and all of them ignited. The fire burned the entire Roman army within the fortress, while the Judaean escaped. The fire spread throughout and unto the heavens, and there was no escape for the Romans, for the huge flame encompassed them.

The Judaeans stood outside around the fortress with all their weapons so that not one of them [Romans] could escape; all the Romans who came there burned to a crisp, and those who were incinerated constituted a very large force.

When Titus heard the screams of those who were burning, he and his warriors ran, but they could not save them, for the fire had grown very large. And Titus began to weep, crying greatly, both he and his men. Those who were above on the roof of the fortress, seeing their lord, Titus, opposite them weeping and the fire separating the fortress from Titus, said: "Let us die before Titus." They fell off the roof in front of Titus, and they too died, for the roof was very high, and there was no way to descend, and the fire consumed the logs. The Judaeans stood opposite the gates of the fortress, and when they saw someone escape from the fire and try to flee the flame by the gate, the Judaeans met him with sword and smote him and he died. They did to all the survivors, until the last.

One of the Roman nobility, of patrician family, by the name of Longus, was there inside the fire; and the Judaeans called him, saying: "Pray, escape to us so you may live and not die." Though he sought to leave, yet he feared, for they

----

4. *DEH* 5.38.2 has *porticus* for the author's *birana* (cf. 2 Chron 17:12, 27:4), a walled fortress; cf. chaps. 49 and 50, for *theatrum*.

did not let any survivor live, so he unsheathed his sword and thrust it into his abdomen, and he died.

Also, one of the Roman nobility named Artorius, was there inside the fire. He looked, and behold, his friend stood at a distance opposite him outside the fortress, and his name was Lucius. Artorius called to him from within the fire: "My brother, my friend, run and save me!" And Lucius called back to Artorius: "How can I save you from inside this huge fire?" Artorius called out, saying to Lucius: "My brother, stand please, and I will fall upon you, and you will catch me, and if it should happen in my falling upon you that I should die, you will inherit my patrimony, and if I live and you shall die, your sons will inherit my patrimony." So Lucius ran and stood under the wall of the fortress, and Artorius fell upon him from the top of the roof, and in his falling upon him, both died. Titus commanded that they write their oath and their covenant, which they had vowed before their deaths, and they wrote it in blood upon the sword, to be an elegy for them. And great vengeance was exacted there against the Roman warriors.

The fire spread and burned the entire fortress unto the site of the palace of Ḥizkiyahu (Ezechias rex), king of Judah, which was near the Temple. So the Romans retreated from the Temple and from the city and went to their camp, their horde diminished in number, for Jerusalem had destroyed them.

Many more gentiles gathered to Titus to assist the Romans; and they encamped around Jerusalem, saying: "We shall not be able to capture Jerusalem by sword but, rather, by famine." So they laid siege to her all about, and there was no food within Jerusalem.

86. A MOTHER'S CRUEL ACT

There was a woman in Jerusalem,[1] one of the daughters of the gentry; her name was Miriam [Maria], and she was from across the Jordan. With the intensification of the war in the days of Vespasian, she went up to Jerusalem with the pilgrims, taking her menservants, her maidservants, and much treasure.

During the famine in Jerusalem, the bandits searched the houses to find sustenance and, entering this woman's house, took everything that she had, from food unto fodder. And when hunger weighed heavy upon her, she desired to die, but her end came not, and the woman began to collect everything she could find to eat from the earth, from chaff unto straw, but there was none.

She had a son; and it came to pass that when the hunger was intense upon her, descending into the very marrow of her bones, all her compassion changed to cruelty. When the woman heard the sound of the boy crying for bread and there was none, she said: "What shall I do for you, my son? For all about is wrath and in every corner famine; outside the sword wreaks havoc, and in the chambers fear [Deut 32:25]. The bandits get the upper hand; our enemies too increase in force: here fire, here collapse, here famine, here plague, and I am powerless to feed you, my son. And if I die, to whom will I leave you, and you so tiny? I used to look forward to your growing up and taking care of me in my old age and at my death burying me, or if you die before I die, I would bury you with honor like a mother the son of her belly. Now, my son, what shall I do for you, since there is no grave to bury you, and you live as if you were dead? Let me choose for you a grave within my belly lest the dogs eat you. And I will be a grave for you, and you will be sustenance for me, in place of the respect that you have to

---

1. *DEH* 5.40.1 expands *BJ* 6.201–13, which the author follows from *DEH* 5.42. This story is probably a midrash developed by Josephus based on Deut 28:57 and elaborated by Hegesippus and Yosippon. [SB]

honor me; feed me please your flesh and provision my old age before the famine devours you; repay your mother what she gave you, for from her intestines you went forth, and there you will enter, and I will bring you to the innermost part where the breath of life was blown into your nose; and that which left my intestines from below I shall return from above. O my most precious, whom I love with all of my heart, make my soul live and become food for your mother and thereby disgrace the bandits who took away our sustenance. And now, my son, heed your mother's voice, refresh my soul, have compassion upon me, and let your portion be in Gan Eden; become for me a sate and a shame, so it will be said that his mother killed him and ate him."

When she had spoken to her son some such words, she seized the child in her hand and faced the other way, and she cut him with the sword and killed him, and her face was averted and her eyes saw naught, and she took the child's corpse and dismembered it, and she roasted it and cooked it, and she ate and preserved the remainder.

The odor of the child's flesh wafted through the street, and the people smelled it, saying: "What is this smell of roasting flesh?" The scent went to the bandit chiefs, and they came to the woman's house in anger, saying to her: "Why do you eat, and we die from famine?" And the woman called out and said to them: "Don't be angry at your servant! Behold, I have saved your share. Sit please, and I will set the table before you, and you will eat your share that I have reserved for you."

She set the table before them and said: "Eat your meal, and here is your share that I saved for you: here is the child's hand and here his leg and here his cut-up pieces before you. And do not say that he is the child of another woman, for he is my son, and I gave birth to him, and I ate him, and also I saved your share."

The woman raised her voice[2] in bitter lamenting and wept over her son, saying: "My Son, my son, how sweet you were to me while you lived. With your death, you have sweetened me, for you have provisioned me against the famine, and you have resuscitated my life. You have provided prey for my old age, and also you have saved me from the wrath of the murderers who came against me in anger, and now these are my friends, for they sit at my table." The woman said to them: "Eat please. Why do you detest my food? Eat and replete, for my son has sated me; taste please, and see how sweet my son is. Don't let your compassion be stirred more than mine. Don't let your heart soften more than mine, for it is a disgrace to fighting men to let their heart be softer than a woman's heart. If you refuse to eat of my sacrifice, I will eat it and be a shame upon you on such

---

2. The author's addition. Hebrew recalls 2 Sam 19:1 and Gen 7:33f.

a day that my heart has overcome your hearts, for such a table as this is fitting to set before valiant men such as you. I arranged this meal, and for your sake it was prepared, for you caused me to set such a table as this, since it would have been proper for me to take pity upon my son more than you. And because you plundered my house, I was forced to host this fête."

This affair was heard throughout the whole city, and the Jews grieved exceedingly, and also the bandit chiefs were humbled by this matter, for this thing was shocking in their eyes, and all of the people sought to die because they were dismayed over this malevolence. And many of the people left Jerusalem with all they had to the Roman camp.

When Titus heard of this matter, he was much awed, and he stood up, spreading his palms to the heavens, and said: "Lord of the Heavens, the hidden things are revealed to you. You know my heart's secrets: I did not come to this city to fight but to summon her to peace. How many times have I requested peace, but they did not agree, and I continued to beseech them, but they did not turn their ear, and I sought to take pity on them so they might live. When each fought against his brother, I called out to save them; we came and found wild animals cruel to their brethren. And above all the evil that they did, this evil has been greater, for the woman ate her son. I too have heard[3] of this people's valor and Your love for them and that Your Name dwells in their midst, and You have chosen from them pious ones and have brought them to You in heaven, and You split the sea for them and the waters of Yam Suf were split before them, and the waters of the Jordan flowed backward for their sake, and the sun stood still for them when they fought against their enemies until You delivered them, and upon chariots of fire You brought their prophets up to heaven, and You smote the horde of Ashur while they reclined upon their couches. All this I know, O Lord God: and now this people against whom I fight, I thought that they had trusted You, but they do not trust You. Now behold, You see that they do not trust in Your deliverance, but they rely on their sword and their fighting; they take pride in themselves over your signs and wonders that You performed for their good ancestors, but these become boastful and say: 'No ruler can subdue us, for the sea was split for us and the bitter waters sweetened for us, and our bread descended from the heavens, and our water rose from the ground, and the Jordan flowed backward before us, and the heavens stood still for our sake, and they and their host fought to assist us.' These things You did for their ancestors in their righteousness, while

---

3. The author praises the Jews in a reversal of his source. The author may have misunderstood Titus's *ferocitas* (savagery) as bravery; however, it may have been a deliberate misreading, since Josephus was translating.

to these in their wickedness You smote in our battles in order to permit their territory to become wasteland and their cities a ruin. So now let us hasten to depart from the midst of their territory, lest we be destroyed in their malevolence, for our eyes behold Sodom, which is within their border, overturned and their waters become bitter with harsh blows. They have hardened their heart like iron, saying: 'Let us be cruel of heart like our ancestors,' for Abraham, their father, had but one son, and he had no pity upon him; rather, he went to slaughter him. But I do not condemn him; rather, I am amazed how he could not take pity upon his son. And one of your kings did slaughter his only daughter."[4] And he uttered many such taunts and blasphemies.[5]

When he finished speaking, they brought the ram to the wall. At that time, many of the bandit leaders went out to him to make peace.

---

4. The author's source too speaks of Bat Yiphtaḥ, summarized in several MSS; cf. Flusser, *Josippon*, 2.351, *ad locum*.

5. See the excellent study by Carson Bay, "The 'Maria Story' in Greek, Latin, and Hebrew: The *Teknophagia* Episode (*BJ* 6.201–13) in Josephus, Latin Josephus, Rufinus, Pseudo-Hegesippus, and *Sefer Yosippon* with Introduction, Texts, Translations, Notes, & Commentary," *Judaica* 3 (2022): 1–105.

87. BURNING OF THE TEMPLE

One of the Temple gates[1] was closed, and its door was covered with silver; the Romans set fire to the gate, and the timbers of the door burned, and the silver fell to the ground. When they opened the gate, behold, they saw a way leading to the Holy of Holies. Titus gave the order prohibiting his army from the Holy of Holies, commanding his men:[2] "Leave this house alone until we take council." Then the Roman officers said to Titus: "If this house will not be burned, we shall not be able to conquer this people, since they will die for its sake." Meanwhile, some of their warriors stood there to guard the Holy of Holies until they had taken counsel.

When the Judaeans saw that they [Romans] had retired from there but left guards, they ran against them with sword and smote them. When Titus heard all that the Judaeans had done, he led all his warriors and went against them and smote many of them; the survivors ran to Mount Zion.

On the morrow, the Romans gathered and set fire to the Holy of Holies from outside; they took beams and stood them against the golden gates of the Holy of Holies and set them ablaze. The gold heated, and the door timbers burned and fell to the ground. The Holy of Holies opened in the fifth month on the tenth of the month; this was the day on which it was opened in the days of the Kasdim (Babylonii). When they opened the gate, the Romans trumpeted a loud blast,

---

1. Chapter follows to *DEH* 5.45 with the author's additions.

2. *BJ* 6.236–43, relates the council over the fate of the Temple and Titus's argument not to destroy it. Some scholars doubt Josephus's apology for Titus. *DEH* 5.42.2–4 adjusts the story to concern for the spread of the flames beyond the Temple. Yosippon, misreading his unclear source, set the council for the next day. Thus, the author has Titus protect the Temple only because the decision was postponed. Modern scholars disagree about the council. See further discussion in Flusser, *Josippon*, 1.410–11n [and Martin Goodman, *Rome and Jerusalem* (London, 2007), 440–44. SB]

and Titus ran with all his might in order to put out the fire in the Holy of Holies, but he could not, for the army was too numerous; he shouted out to them, but they gave no heed, for they came en masse like a torrent of water, and the smoke thickened and spread.

When Titus saw that he could not clear away the army, he unsheathed his sword and began cursing his army officers and smiting the foreigners with the sword so that they disperse from there, but he could not. Many of the other gentiles who came to their aid died there, for Titus smote them, but the people ever increased. Titus shouted at them until his throat was parched and he could no longer shout. And the priests fought until they could no longer raise their arms. When the priests saw that there was no salvation, they threw themselves into the fire within the Holy of Holies, and many of the Judaean warriors accompanied them, and they burned, saying: "There is no life after the burning of God's Holy House." And Titus smote to prevent it, but none listened to him, for there were many gentiles, and he became weary and exhausted and dropped to the ground with no strength left. When he saw that he could not save [it], he rose and entered within the holy place to behold the beauty of the Holy of Holies, and gazing upon the glory [*kavod*] of the Temple and its grandeur, he believed that it was the House of God. Then he said: "Now I know that this is the House of the God of Heaven and the dwelling place of His Glory, and not for naught did the Judaeans battle over it unto its destruction.

"Also the gentiles coming from the ends of the Earth with silver and gold and every precious vessel to worship the God of this house, do not come for naught, for the glory of this house is greater than the temple of Romans and all the gentile temples that I have seen."

Meanwhile, the fire intensified to ignite the Holy of Holies. When the bandit chiefs saw the Holy of Holies afire, they too went and burned all the remaining houses in the city, which were full of every precious wealth. They destroyed the rest of the Temple building, saying: "After the Holy of Holies is burned, what desire is there in living or leaving house or building?"

At that time, one of the Judaeans stood and prophesied falsely, saying to the bandits: "Take strength and stand at arms, for now the House will be rebuilt by itself and not by the hand of man.[3] Pray take heart and fight, for on this day, the

---

3. *DEH* has the *pseudopropheta*'s prophesy God's continued dwelling in the Temple, whence he will banish the enemy and the fire. Flusser suggests that author's statement is perhaps from *Seder Olam Rabba* (ed. Ish Shalom), 150. D. Flusser, "Two Notes on the Midrash on 2 Sam. VII," *IEJ* 9 (1959): 99–104.

House will be rebuilt." When the bandits heard this, they engaged the Romans, who smote them, and the bandits fell. And many of the poor [*dalath ha-'am*] upon whom they [Romans] had taken pity at the beginning, they killed them like sheep to the slaughter, because they heeded the words of the false prophet and paid no attention to the signs that were performed in Jerusalem.

For a year before Vespasian came, a single great star shining like unsheathed swords was seen over the Temple. In those days, when the sign was seen, it was the holiday of Passover [Pascha], and during that entire night, the Temple was lit up, illuminated like the light of day, and thus it was all seven days of the Passover. All the sages of Jerusalem knew that it was a malevolent sign, but the rest of the ignorant people said that it was a benevolent sign.

At that time, they [Judaeans] brought a female calf for a burnt offering, and it happened when they dropped her to the ground to slaughter her, behold, she gave birth to a sheep. Moreover, a sign was seen in the East Gate, for the East Gate was large and very heavy; it did not open until twenty men came in the morning and opened it and twenty men in the evening closed it, and the sound of the gate's hinge was heard from afar. And it happened in those days that they [Judaeans] found the gate completely open by itself without the hand of man, nor could they close it until there gathered a huge number of people, and they closed it. And also, regarding this sign, the sages of Israel and the priests said that it was bad sign, while the rest of the people said that it was a good sign. It happened after this that there was seen over the Holy of Holies from above for the entire night the outline of a man's face, the like of whose beauty had never been seen in all the land, and his appearance was very awesome.

Moreover, in those days were seen chariots of fire and horsemen, a great force flying across the sky low to the ground coming against Jerusalem and all the land of Judah, all of them horses of fire and riders of fire. When the holiday of Shavu'oth came in those days, during the night the priests heard within the Temple something like the sound of men walking, the sound of many men's marching feet walking within the Temple, and a terrible and mighty voice was heard speaking: "Let's go and leave this House."[4]

Four years before the war, there was in Jerusalem a man from the rabble[5] named Yehoshua ben Ḥananyah [Iesus Ananiae filius], and he began to call out in a loud voice beginning on the holiday of Sukkoth, saying: "A call from the East and a call from the West and a call from the four winds, a call against

---

4. *DEH*, 393, has *transimus hinc*. The author's Hebrew is a reversal of Isa 2:2 on the "end of days."

5. Hebrew pun on *ruricula vir*.

Jerusalem and a call against the Temple, a call against the groom and bride and a call against all the people," until all the inhabitants of the city hated him and cursed him and beat him, but he did not cease to call out with such a voice. The head of the city seized him and said to him: "Why do you shout so and call out in such a way?" And he commanded to beat him, yet he continued to call out in this manner. So he left him alone, for he considered him as a madman. He went forth, calling out: "Woe unto Jerusalem, alas upon Jerusalem," until the day of the war. And when the war happened, he began to call out: "Woe unto me, woe upon me." And he did not cease to call out such a word until a small stone[6] came at him, striking him on the head, and he died.

In those days, a missive written upon a flint from ancient days was found, and they [Judaeans] read it, and behold, on it was written as follows: "At the time when the building of the Temple is finished and it will be square [*tetragonum*], then it will be destroyed." When Antonia was captured and the Roman force destroyed it, they [Romans] breached the corner of the Temple, and the Judaeans hastened to rebuild the Temple's breach; when they [Judaeans] had finished the building, behold, the Temple was square. But they did not remember the words of the missive upon the stone; for this reason, the words of that missive were found to be true. Also, there was found written on the wall of the Holy of Holies as follows: "When the building of the Temple shall be square, then a king will rule over Israel,[7] a king who will rule and govern throughout the land." For this reason, some of the people said that he will be Israel's king, but the sages of Jerusalem and the priests said that he will be the Romans' king.

When the Roman force entered the Temple and the Judaeans retreated to Mount Zion, the Romans carried their idols [*signa*] and stood them in the Temple and sacrificed to their lord, Titus; they offered libations to him, lauding him with great noise, insulting and blaspheming exceedingly.

---

6. *Fundibalus* probably came from a sling; the author's *even yad.*
7. "Square" reference added by the author from a mistaken assumption. The source has "a king from the land of Israel will receive rule over the world."

88. END OF THE BATTLE OF JERUSALEM

At that time, a small boy[1] descended from the priests to them [Romans] and called out to the Roman commander over the Temple, saying: "Give me water so I may drink." The commander took pity on the boy, for he found favor in his eyes; he commanded, and they gave him water and he drank; the remainder he snatched and ran away and, going up to the priests, gave them to drink. The commander chased after the boy before the eyes of his army, but he did not really want to capture him since he pitied him, for the commander appreciated what the boy had done. He said: "How well done was this boy's theft, and how I do love it." The whole Roman force was amazed at what the boy had done and that he had escaped.

While the Romans were pouring libations before Titus, behold, some of the priests who were captured at the Temple were beseeching Titus lest he kill them. He said to them: "Why do you choose life rather than die with your brethren who died for the sake of the God of this house when they burned in its fire?" He commanded, they struck them, and they died.

Both Yoḥanan and Shimon sent peace offerings to Titus and a plea requesting that they be allowed to live. Titus responded and said to them: "You tarried to ask this thing, and now you request to live? Why should you survive from the entire horde of your people, after you finished off your people and destroyed this city through your manifold wickedness, and too the Holy of Holies was burned? After all this you seek peace? Did I not seek this thing from you on many occasions, but you did not agree? Time and again I called you to peace, for my soul pitied the poor of the city who were enveloped in hunger, the dead thrown outside the city without burial, yet you stiffened your neck until all the

---

1. Chapter follows *DEH* 5.45–51 with the author's additions.

people was destroyed. Now, what is the benefit of my letting you live?" And he scorned and ridiculed more than we have written.

He said to them: "While you are still girt with weapons of war and with spear in hand, you beseech me? Cast away your weapons of war and then entreat. Did we not capture the city, the Temple as well, and even burned the Holy of Holies? Now what do you hope for? Have you any resistance left? Throw away your weapons of war, and you shall live!" Whereupon the bandits called out to Titus, saying: "We have sworn by our God that we shall not bear your yoke; now if you deign to release us, we shall leave the city and go to the desert."

Titus waxed furious and said: "Is your heart still full of pride? You are captured in our hands, and still you say: 'We have sworn not to bear your yoke'? Have you not sworn that you will die? Why do you go back upon your oath? Keep fast in your death watch, for you reject life! [cf. Deut 30:19]." At that time, Titus commanded, and they went against them with swords; and they strengthened their heart and engaged in battle.

At that time, Zerah[2] descended and with him the king's sons and his brothers, and many of the nobles and leaders of Jerusalem bowed down to Titus, and he received them.

When Shimon and Yoḥanan saw that Zerah had gone with the king's sons and his brothers to Titus, they went to the king's palace and destroyed it, setting it on fire along with everything that was there. They set ablaze all his treasures so that the Romans would not take them. From there, they descended to the Temple[3] and found there two officers; these were the commanders whom Titus had appointed over the Temple, one infantry commander and one over the chariots; they smote the infantry commander but captured his comrade alive. And he beseeched them, saying: "Lead me to Shimon," and they did. When they had led the commander to Shimon, he ordered to kill him, but the executioner delayed, and the commander leaped, falling down the incline of the mountain, and so escaped to Titus. But Titus banished him from his presence because he had not fought to the death and had not been taken alive. Now Titus was angry over what they had done and commanded to kill all the surviving Judaeans; the Romans began and, raising their hands against the people, filled the houses and streets with corpses.

When Shimon's Edomite warriors saw this, they sent to Titus to request their lives and to escape to him. When Shimon was told, he ran against them

---

2. *DEH* 5.46.2 has Iaza, a diminutive of Izates, king of Adiabene (35–60 CE), who revolted from Rome and converted to Judaism along with his mother, Helena (cf. *AJ* 20.17–96); both fought in the revolt and finally surrendered to the Romans. Two MSS of Hegesippus have Zara, translated here as the biblical Hebrew Zerah.

3. *DEH* 5.47.1 has *in aulam*, i.e., only one incident, not two.

and smote their chiefs and leading men, but the rest of the Edomites escaped to Titus, who treated them well. Titus commanded to stop those who were smiting the people, and they ceased.

At that time, Shimon and Yoḥanan retreated and hid in one of the hiding places; when the Judaeans saw that Shimon and Yoḥanan ran away and hid themselves, then all their leaders and the heads of the people descended and took refuge with Titus. Titus commanded to let them live and to have mercy on the survivors except for the bandits, for the bandits fought to the finish in battle.

At that time, the priest Yehoshua ben Shabbtai came to Titus with two gold candelabra and gold tables and golden vessels, the goblets, the spoons, the shovels, and the libation bowls along with priestly clothes, ritual garments adorned with precious stones and many fine jewels, and he gave all this to Titus. Pinḥas, guardian of the chambers, also was captured, and he revealed to them the treasuries of the purple, the vestments of the holy priests, all the beds of spices with all the gold vessels of the House of God, and he gave all these to Titus. Nor was it proper for him to have acted thus but rather to die with the rest of his brethren, the priests who died for God and were burned up in the firing of His Sanctuary. At that time, Jerusalem was captured with all its precious things, and they demolished the wall of Mount Zion.

At the end of three days, Yoḥanan's soul was exhausted from hunger, and he arose and went from his hiding place to Titus; Titus commanded, and they marched him throughout the camp in shame and contempt, cursing him while he was bound in chains. At the end of seven days, he died through strangulation[4] and pain.

After this, Shimon also came forth from his hiding place, for the hunger was fierce upon him; he rose and, donning royal clothing and purple, appeared in the midst of the Roman force. When they saw him, they feared to approach him. He said to them: "Go, summon the commander in charge for me." They went and called Rufo, who was from the city of Taranto.[5] When the officer came to Shimon and said to him: "Who are you?" he answered: "I am Shimon. Bring me now to your lord, Titus," and they brought him. When Titus saw Shimon, he commanded to march him throughout his camp, cursing him while he was in shackles; and after this, he commanded, and they killed him.[6]

---

4. Rare forms *tashnuk* and *denak*. See Flusser, *Josippon, ad locum,* for references.

5. Terentius is his family name. Similar error in Macrobius, *Satur.* 3.18.3 (ed J. Willis, 1970), 1.212.

6. *DEH* has Yoḥanan and Shimon kept for the triumph in Rome.

The number of people who fell by sword at the hands of the Romans and by the bandits' hands, all the Jewish people both near and far who came to celebrate God's holy day in Jerusalem and fell by the sword, numbered one million one hundred thousand; and those who went into captivity with Titus were ninety-seven thousand. The bandits died in battle, and their remnant was captured alive. And it came about that when Titus marched from Jerusalem, he took with him a captive people that he had captured. In every city in which he made camp, he cast some of these bandits to lions and wild beasts to eat until all the bandits were finished.

It happened in those days that there was a people from beyond the land of Ararat, and the name of the nation was Alan. They were totally enclosed since Alexander the Great had closed them up, for surrounding their land were mountains and cliffs; therefore, he locked them up with bars of iron and a strong construction, and they were shut up inside their territory until the day that Jerusalem was captured. In that year, there was famine in their territory, the land of Alan, and they sent to their neighbors, the nation called Yrkanos [Hyrcani], who opened the end of their enclosing gates, and they went out to plunder and loot. They set out toward the land of Media and took horses with them, and they rode, pulling more horses to the rear, and they entered the land of Media. When Pacarus, king of Media, heard that the Alanos were invading his land, he retreated before them and fled to the mountains, abandoning his property, his sons, his wife, and his concubines. The Alanos came and seized them; and Pacarus, king of Media, sent to them one hundred talents of gold to ransom his wife and sons, and they did so. They left his land and turned to go, returning to their land. But Mithridates, king of Ararat, went forth[7] to confront them, he and all his army, for he said: "Perhaps I may be able to drive them away from my border before they destroy my territory." When they came, Mithridates, king of Ararat, fought with them, but they threw a strangling rope at him,[8] and the rope fell over his neck, and it caught, and he was captured. As they ran, so he ran after them with the rope, lest he be choked; unsheathing his sword, he cut the rope from his neck and escaped. When Titus heard of this event, he sought to go against them [Alanos], but he could not, for his warriors were devastated in Jerusalem and he feared to go against them, so he set out for Romania and went to Antochia (Antiocheia).

---

7. *DEH* 5.50 has Armenia; Vulgate to Gen 8:4 and 2 Kings 19:37.

8. The author's paraphrase. Latin has *laqueolo* (= lasso).

89. BATTLE OF MASADA

He heard[1] that a large army of Judaeans had assembled at Masada [*meẓudah*],[2] and with them Elazar ben Anani,[3] who had been in Jerusalem—he had escaped from Jerusalem during the fighting and had gone to Masada; therefore, many of the Jews gathered around him. When Titus heard that the Judaeans had rallied to Elazar ben Anani, he sent there the Roman commander Silva with a strong and heavy force from the Roman horde. Silva went to Masada and besieged her, butting the wall with an iron ram and breaching it, and he captured the city. When the Judaeans saw that their wall was breached, they constructed a wooden wall inside the [breached] wall, but the Romans set fire to it and burned it. In the evening, the fighting men disengaged, and the Romans retreated from the Judaeans, for the night was dark.

Elazar summoned the Jewish leaders who were with him, and he spoke unto their ears, saying: "Draw near to me please.[4] Behold, O seed of Abraham and kingdom of priests, who have overcome their oppressors in the past, now what can be done about this situation, against the numerous horde attacking us and not suddenly, as our eyes behold? Therefore, it is fitting for us to relate the strength of our ancestors and their valor, which was before from days of yore. Pray understand and be enlightened that unto everything there is an end, a fate, a time for all fighting: sometimes to pursue and sometimes to retreat, sometimes to be strong and sometimes to submit, and there is no shame in submission, for there is a time for everything. Alas, everyone who has courage, who strengthens his heart without allowing fear in his heart, this one is considered a hero. And

---

1. Chapter follows *DEH* 5.52–53 with the author's additions.
2. The word *meẓudah* in Hebrew (*Miẓadah*, *Masada* in Greek) literally means fortress or acropolis.
3. Confusion of Elazar ben Anani and Elazar ben Yair; see chap. 82.
4. *DEH*'s style from 1 Pet 2:9; the author's from Ex 19:6.

now, if you strengthen without fear of death, this day you will be considered heroes and men of valor, for you will be blessed throughout the land.

"Pray understand what Abraham, your father, did who took his son, his only one, to offer him to God and did not think in his heart that he would kill him but rather only thought and knew that He would let him live.[5] Pray remember what Yoshiyahu (Iosiam), the righteous king, did when he refused to live in this vain world. He chose to live an eternal life in the world of righteousness because he did not desire to live in this world. He craved only to go to the Great Light, for he looked at the multitude of our sins until he could no longer endure; therefore, despising such life, he engaged in foreign wars. Did not Pharaoh Nekho (Nechao) say to him: 'I did not come to fight against you and your people but rather against the king of Kasdim.' But Yoshiyahu did not listen to him and did not turn to retreat; rather, he set his face to go to the Great Light. So, when he took up a position against Pharaoh's force, he was wounded and died, but he had no fear of death. How,[6] then, could we fear death or spare our flesh from any blow? Yoshiyahu was a righteous man, and he fell in battle; and Pharaoh was a wicked man, but he succeeded in killing Yoshiyahu; this world was the destiny of Pharaoh, but the Great Light that is in Gan Eden was the destiny of Yoshiyahu. Therefore, we know that Yoshiyahu, who fell in this world, was a hero who went to the light of Gan Eden, and Pharaoh fell, for his lot fell to the dark places of Abadon.

"We know that a man is not paid the wages for his righteous labor while he is still alive in this world; rather, only after he fulfills the days of this world will he be paid the reward for his righteousness. In this world, we toil and become exhausted, but when we go there, we take the wages of our labor, for here is weariness and no rest, but there is rest and relaxation. There a man will reap the produce of his righteousness and consume it at leisure,[7] nor throughout the length of days in this world will mankind find grace.

"Understand further from Hevel (Abel), who was killed by Kayin (Cain), that Hevel did not live out his days in this world, for Kayin killed him, and when Kayin had killed him, he was gathered to eternal rest and endless everlasting peace. And Kayin, who lived out his days after Hevel, was a wanderer and went at

---

5. See my comments on *midrash aggadat bereshit* in Bowman, "Jewish Responses to Byzantine Polemics 9th–11th Centuries," *Shofar* 28, no. 3 (2010): 103–15. [SB]

6. The author substitutes this question for *DEH*'s biblical parallel. *Niba'et* is a rare future use of this niphal conjugation. Jerusalem MS has *liphhod* for Flusser's *liphhot*, perhaps a *lapsus calami*. [SB]

7. The author's words based perhaps on contemporary Christian sermons: *fructus iustitiae* [James 3:18; Phil 1:11] or *fruges iustitiae* [2 Cor 9:10]. The Latin is ultimately from Amos (6:12) *pri tsedakah* (fruit of righteousness), Greek καρπὸς δικαιοσύνης.

his end to the dark places of Abadon and to eternal burning.[8] So now, if we should live, our lives would be bad lives, for all our days are vanity and toil. And the soul [*nephesh*], while yet in our bosom, is considered like a prisoner in jail, for while it is still in the flesh, it remains tormented, but when it leaves, it rejoices and worries not. As long as it is within the flesh, it does not lack weeping and lamenting, grief, and torment, worry and toil, and vanity, for it is the spirit of life locked up in the flesh. It is bound in sinews and bones as if in chains and fetters; it is this spirit that sustains the flesh, which itself is from the dust of the earth; the dust does not sustain the spirit; rather, the spirit watches over the flesh and examines its deeds. As long as it is in the flesh, the flesh does not behold the spirit, nor does the spirit behold the flesh, for the spirit is hidden from the flesh of the body. Even if all-seeing eyes were made for the entire flesh, it would not behold the spirit or know when the spirit entered the flesh or when the spirit left the flesh. For the soul's spirit is from heaven, and all flesh is from the earth, for every soul lives bodiless, but the body cannot live spiritless. If the spirit should enter the flesh to visit us just as a man visits a friend, we live, and when the spirit leaves, the flesh dies. And the soul, if it were willing to obey the flesh in its craving, this would be the death of the soul; but if it were not willing to obey the flesh to sin, the soul would go on to live and the flesh would die. Therefore, the soul rejoices when it leaves the flesh, just as a prisoner who leaves prison and as a slave who flees his master. For as long as the soul is in the flesh, it is considered as a slave bound to harsh masters, and work burdens him, but when it goes forth, it rejoices, for it returns to Gan Eden [Paradisus]. For the soul resembles a servant in service to a great king, and the king sends him to serve a stranger, one of his men, and he [king] gave him [servant] to serve him [stranger] for a number of days. Whereupon the servant went and served the man as his lord had commanded him, and at the completion of a number of days, the servant returns to his master happy and rejoicing, for he is returning to his place and to his rest. He knows that the stranger will no longer govern over him, for he is the king's servant, and the stranger cannot rule over him with rigor. And so our souls are with us for the days we live, and after this, they go and return to their rest, to the place of the Great Light [*caelestis gratia*]."[9] And he continued to speak to them with such words that we have not written.

He spoke further to them about the sages of Hodu, that if one of them should die, they are prevented from weeping and keening over him, for they say: "Has not the soul gone to the place that gives life, that is, the place of eternal life?" "And other

---

8. Cf. Targum to Isa 33:14; *Seder Eliahu Rabbah* (ed. Ish-Shalom), 108; *Targum Yonatan* to Gen 27:33.

9. *Caelestis gratia* (heavenly grace) becomes the author's Great Light. See chap. 65.

peoples listened to them and believed that there is hope beyond—and we who have known the mercy of God our Lord, is it not proper for us to believe that there is hope beyond our end? Now, if your souls so love living in this world of vanity that you seek to surrender to the Romans, you should have surrendered to Titus, who is king, as did the remnant of your brethren, and not to Silva who is a servant.

"And now, why do you crave this life where you see your elders being dragged by their beard and hoary hair and your sons and your daughters crying out to you—and there is none to save them—and your daughters in the hands of the sullied uncircumcised—and there is no help—and your wives laid before your eyes while you are bound in fetters, and your eyes too behold this thing?

"What is the worth of living in such life? If you had craved life, you should have listened to King Agripas when he said that we cannot rebel against the Roman king or raise a hand—but you did not heed. Now that you raised your hand and killed Florus and rebelled, all this great calamity has come upon you. They have destroyed all our wealth, Jerusalem is captured, the Temple destroyed, all of our territory has become desolation and a hissing, and everyone who passes by shall be astonished and shall hiss [cf. 1 Kings 9:8] over this calamity that has befallen us. Now we remain alone like a beacon atop a mountain and an ensign on the hill [Isa 30:17]. Why then choose living?" And he continued to speak at length to them in such words, and all the people wept facing him in bitter and great lament.

When he finished speaking, Elazar keened this dirge, saying: "Where is the great city, capital of the people, Jerusalem? Where is the beauty of Zion, the holy city? Where is the honored and awesome Sanctuary? Where is the holy Temple that sanctifies the refuge? Where is the Holy of Holies, the holy place where no foot of man may tread save for the anointed high priest but once a year? And now, O Jerusalem, who used to be full of people, besplendored by all the kings and beloved of God, and in you was established the royal throne; your marketplaces and your streets were paved with marble, your walls flashed with marble too, and all your courts were built with marble as well; all your gates were covered with gold and silver; your shrines were founded for glory and for grandeur; and your priests within you like the ministering angels atoned for your people with acceptable offerings—and now you are filled with corpses slain by the sword. Your sons who dwell within you and those who come to you from afar from the ends of the Earth celebrating your holy days, they too fall within you. How you have fallen from the summit of your height, and how you have been burned and demolished unto your foundations, and you remain devastated sitting alone. How callous the eye that can look upon you, and the heart that beholds you is stronger than iron, seeing how you have become a grave for corpses; all your streets and courtyards are devoid of living, for the bodies of corpses fill them up rather than the living. And the fire's ash covered the sun's eye within you blotting the sun. Your elders sit opposite their sons' corpses to keep the birds of the skies away from them, and their hoary hair is filled with ashes instead of honor. While from the women there remained few of your daughters, shut up within your thresholds, not that they may live but that they may be profaned and sullied in your midst. Who would see all of these things and choose life? Would that [cf. Jer 9:1] our death be early rather than we see this shame, or would that I had no eyes rather than see these evils! Behold, we are alive on such a day, and our sons and daughters yet live with us; and behold, our adversaries have cast lots for them to divide them as slaves and maidservants.

"Now, why do we not remove this plunder from the hand of our besiegers, lest they succeed in doing anything like this; this day will be considered as our glory, for we have been born to die, and our end is death. Is it not better for us to die in honor and leave as free men without seeing this abomination on such a day? Now offer yourselves willingly; please, take pity on your wives and children, your elders, your sons, and your daughters—not pity that they go into captivity and groan in the hand of their captors and there is no deliverer, for you have lost their portion of life, but have pity on them that you kill them with your hands, and they will be considered[10] as a burnt offering [*qorban olah*] acceptable to God, and the offering of the holy [*terumat hakodesh*] not be profaned by gentile menstruation. And after we had done this deed, let us go forth against our adversaries and fight and die in our valor[11] and not be taken in chains like slaves in the hands of these uncircumcised; we shall no more look upon our elders dragged by their beard, our wives and children profaned before our eyes, our sons crying out, and it is not in our power to deliver [them] [cf. Prov 3:27]."

The men rose and collected their wives and their sons and their daughters: and they kissed them and embraced them and said to them: "Is it better in your eyes to die upon your land rather than go into captivity in the land of your enemies and die there before the idols of the Romans?" And the people moaned through that night, crying and mourning and lamenting and keening, crying with great weeping, the men and the women and the children.[12]

---

10. The author's addition, *nehshavim leqorban olah lerazon*. So Yohanan in chap. 88. Cited similarly in the twelfth-century Hebrew Crusader chronicles.

11. The author is unique in having them die fighting at Masada, which is more praiseworthy than officers' suicide in Yodphat cave and Josephus's surrender (chap. 66). [Thus, the history of *Yosippon* ends in a blaze of glory amid the rage of tragedy. SB]

12. The shorter of the two endings apparently is the original; the longer ending is in rhymed prose. *DEH* MSS also have different sentences at the end. The prayer "Let it be thy will" at the end may be a later addition. The shorter version has a longer prayer in rhymed prose with citations from Ezek 25:14, Isa 66:13, Isa 11:12, Deut 30:4 and Zeph 3:20.

When the morning came, they took their wives and their sons and their daughters

and slaughtered them on the ground and put them in the cisterns and threw dust upon them. After that, the men went forth from the city and engaged in fighting with the Roman camp, and they [Judaeans] killed many of them [Romans] without number. The Jews fought until all of them were finished in the battle, and they died for God and his Sanctuary.

Up to this point, the wars of the Second Temple. Woe unto us that the city of our joy has been destroyed, the house of our desires ruined, our Temple burned, and we have been exiled from the portion of our ancestors, and we could do nothing. May it be the will of God our Lord that He remember the oath of our ancestors. May he rebuild our city, and may he renew our Temple. May he gather our dispersed and collect our banished and return our captives. May he hasten our messiah and hurry our redemption. May he cause our enemies to fall and humble those who hate us. May he exact our vengeance and fulfill for us the verse as it is written: "I will wreak my vengeance upon Edom through my people Israel," etc., and as the verse: "As a mother comforts her son, so I shall comfort you, and in Jerusalem you shall be comforted." And may he fulfill for us the verse as it is written: "He will hold up a signal to the gentiles and assemble the exiled of Israel and gather the dispersed of Judah from the four corners of the Earth"; and as it is written: "Even if your exile be in the farthest heaven, from there the Lord your God will gather you; from there He will take you"; and as it is written: "At that time, I will bring you, at the time I will gather you; for I will give you renown and praise among all the peoples on Earth when I return your captives before their [Heb: your] eyes, says God."

to slaughter them on the ground that they be considered as burnt offerings acceptable before God, because for his Name, they went, lest they be killed before the Roman idols.

They did just as Elazar ben Anani the priest had told them: each man belted on his fighting weapons, and each man gathered his wife and children to the square of Masada, and each kissed the members of his household and embraced them, and they wept upon each other in great lamenting. Then the priests and the elders called out and said to the women and children as follows: "It is good for you to weep and die here rather than die amid the idols of the Romans." Then the men drew their weapons and slew their wives and their sons and their daughters, and they cast them into the cisterns in Miẓuda, and they closed them up and filled them with soil. And the army moaned throughout that night in weeping and lamenting and great grieving and with much mourning.

They rose early in the morning, and all of them went out together as one man from the city in savage fury and fought against the Roman horde, and they killed many of them without number, until all of them were finished in the fighting.

Up to here, the end of Jerusalem, the holy city, and the people of God and his portion. May it be the will of the God of heaven that He may have compassion upon us and upon His people and upon His city and upon His house and upon His Temple and upon His Sanctuary and upon His portion, swiftly in our days. Amen.

APPENDIX: TITUS

I. Titus set officers over the survivors and took some 90,000 with him into exile.[1] The number of those who fell in Jerusalem was 1,108,000, those whom he settled in Romi subject to his father were 1,500, and those whom he settled

---

1. The two passages on Philo and Josephus are taken from the manuscript of Yeraḥme'el. The passage on Philo is found in the body of the text of *Sefer Yosippon* as an addition to chap. 58; the passage on Josephus is found in the same manuscript following the appendix on the exile of the Jews by Titus that appears at the end of *Yosippon*. In the introduction to our book [vol. 2], we showed that the *Sefer Yosippon* in the manuscript of Yeraḥme'el is Yeraḥme'els own copy, and he lived in twelfth-century Italy. Since the passage on Philo appears in the body of *Sefer Yosippon*, it is certain that it is the creation of Yeraḥme'el himself; the second passage, found as noted at the end of *Sefer Yosippon*, correctly identifies the Yosef ben Gurion the priest with Yosef ben Matia, that is, Josephus. Based on these factors, it can be concluded that it too is the creation of the same author who copied *Sefer Yosippon* prior to this passage; in other words, the passage on Josephus was also composed by Yeraḥme'el himself. The assumption that the two passages were composed by Yeraḥme'el is certain since both have the same character: both are Hebrew versions of a Christian source, based on Hieronymus's [i.e., Jerome's] *De viris illustribus*, which is essentially an encyclopedia of individuals important for the understanding of Christian literature. We may assume that the two passages were composed on the basis of a Latin source by Yeraḥme'el himself, but one may not exclude the possibility that Yeraḥme'el found these passages already in Hebrew garb and just copied them into his book. A. Neubauer previously published the two passages: that on Philo in his description of the Yeraḥme'el manuscript in his Bodleian Catalogue (p. 11) and that on Josephus in his *Mediaeval Jewish Chronicles*, 1.190–91; and from the latter, S. Krauss, *Das Leben Jesu* (Berlin, 1902), 1239, took the section on the beginnings of Christianity. Several MSS of *Yosippon* contain appendices that connect the history of the Jews in several lands with the destruction of Jerusalem by Titus. This appendix is preserved in two forms: (1) in the MS of Jerahmeel [ed. Eli Yassif, *The Book of Memory That Is the Chronicles of Jerahme'el* (Tel Aviv, 2001)], and (2) in the Mantua edition and two MSS. It appears that appendix 1 is the result of an abridgement, and appendix 2 contains perhaps particulars from the "exile" in Spain.

in Taranto and Odranto and other cities in Puglia about 5,000. Vespasian gave his son Titus the land of Africa, and he settled in Karthago 30,000 Jews alone, in addition to those he put in other places. He settled Joseph the priest in Romi with his family and gave him houses and a place for prayer.

II. Titus appointed administrators over the cities that made peace with him and left them in the land of Judah. Now the number of the captives that he took with him was 90,000.[2] The number of those of Jerusalem who fell by sword and famine—those who came from near and far[3] to Jerusalem and their dependents—totaled 1,108,000.[4] Those he settled in Roma and gave to his father [were] 1,500, and where he landed by sea[5] he left 5,000 in Taranto and Odranto[6] and other cities in Puglia.[7] Vespasian gave to his son Titus the land of Africa[8] and all of the land of Spain,[9] and he put in Kartina[10] 30,000 Jews, and in Ispalia,[11] his capital on the River Biti,[12] the rest of the captives, save for those in other places. And Titus ordered to warn them [i.e., the locals] lest they harm

2. Appendix 1 has "about 90,000"; and *Yosippon*, chap. 78, has 97,000.

3. See *Yosippon*, chap. 78, whence the author takes the phrase.

4. *Yosippon*, chap. 78, has 1,100,000. Evidently the author of the appendix thought 8,000 died of famine.

5. Here the author introduces the origins of the southern Italian communities. He understood Titus to have disembarked and left there five thousand Jews. *Megillat Ahimaaz* (ed. Klar), 12, relates that his ancestors were brought by ship to the River Po among Titus's captives.

6. See *Yosippon*, chap 78, for Taranto. Hebrew texts regularly record Odranto, which is an earlier stage of the shift from Hadrumentum to Otranto. B. Klar includes [*Megillat Ahimaaz*, 61] the famous praise of Odranto that paraphrases Isaiah: "For the Torah shall go forth from Bari and the Word of the Lord from Odranto."

7. Pulia is the Hebrew rendition of Puglia, the ancient Roman Apulia.

8. This is a fable that Vespasian gave to Titus Provincia Africa (modern Tunis); in Arabic Ifriqiyya.

9. Spain seems to be a late addition to appendix 2; it is lacking in appendix 1.

10. Appendix 1 has Karthago, i.e., Carthage, and it fits well, since the text is speaking about the Jews of North Africa. It appears that the one who added "and all the land of Spain" changed Karthago to Kartina in his assurance that Cartagena in Spain was meant.

11. This section to "captivity," which refers to the Jews of Apulia and North Africa and is, in Flusser's opinion, a later addition, is lacking in appendix 1. Ispalia is a transitional stage between the Latin Hispalis and modern Sevilla. [The introduction to *Sefer Hayashar* (ed. J. Dan, Jerusalem, 1986), 37, relates how the book was brought to Sevilla by an old man captured during the sack of Jerusalem, who, along with his substantial library, became an honored part of the entourage of his captor who resettled there. SB]

12. Spanish or Italian form for Baetis, modern Guadalquivir [from the Arabic *wadi al kabir*].

them.[13] Titus said to Joseph: "Choose from my entire kingdom a place to settle, and I will give it to you." Joseph chose the island in Roma[14] at the southern edge,[15] the sea[16] around it and on each side of it the Tibero, and he built houses there for all his family and a midrash for Torah[17] to pray there.

---

13. See *Yosippon,* chap 74, for similar phraseology.

14. This island in the Tiber is one of the oldest Jewish sites in Rome; see Hermann Vogelstein and Paul Rieger, *Geschichte der Juden in Rom* (Berlin, 1895–96), 1.36 [translated by Moses Hadas, *Rome* (Philadelphia, 1940), 18ff]. Note that the author of appendix 2 uses "Roma," whereas the author of appendix 1 follows *Yosippon*'s "Romi."

15. It is interesting that the author sites the island from the ancient center of Rome and not from the Jewish quarter Trastevere on the other side.

16. Perhaps read "water" here or "and the river Tiber surrounded it on every side."

17. This connects the Jewish settlement on the island and its synagogue to Joseph ben Gurion, who is Josephus.

ADDITIONS TO YOSIPPON

I. PHILO THE ALEXANDRIAN

Philo the Jew, an Alexandrian of the priestly class, wrote a book of wisdom [*sefer hahokhmah*] and lived during the days of Gaius and Claudius.[1] He was a boon companion of Shimon Caipha ben Yohanan.[2] This Philo wrote one book on the pronunciation of language [*mivta halashon*] in the Torah of Moses;[3] one book on the reality of things [*mezi'ut hadevarim*] that Ezra did not write, for the Torah scrolls had been burned in the days of the Kasdim, and he found them;[4] one book interpreting all twenty-four books of the Torah;[5] one book on change of names [*shinui shemot*];[6] one book on prohibition, oaths, and vows;[7] one book on the lives of sages;[8] one book on the Nephilim;[9] one book on the interpretation

---

1. Based on Jerome's *De viris illustribus*, chap. 11; he has for Yerahme'els "from the seed of priests" *de genere sacerdotum*.
2. Jerome writes that Philo was the friend of the Apostle Peter, who is so named in the following passage.
3. Jerome says in general that Philo wrote many excellent works on the five books of Moses and follows up with a detailed list of Philo's works. The Hebrew author misunderstood his source. The first book Jerome lists is *De confusione linguarum* (Concerning the confusion of tongues).
4. The second book listed by Jerome is *De natura et inventione nominum* (On the nature and invention of names). This imaginative and exaggerated explanation for the name of the book, which deals with the devising of names, was apparently added only by the Hebrew author, who understood the word *inventio* as the action of finding something lost.
5. Instead of this mistaken information, Jerome brings the names of certain books. Philo obviously did not write "a commentary on all twenty-four books," since it is apparent that he was not acquainted with all the books of the Bible.
6. This is the treatise called *De mutatione nominum*. Jerome calls this treatise "Why in Scripture the names are sometimes changed."
7. Jerome calls this treatise *De pactis libri duo* (Two books on the Covenants). The work is lost.
8. Jerome's *De vita sapientis* (Concerning the life of a sage).
9. *De gigantibus* (On the giants).

of dreams;[10] one book on questions and answers about the five books of Moses, its vessels, sacred vestments, thank-offerings, and holocausts;[11] one book on the cities of Judah and their destruction;[12] one book on Alexander the Makedonian, his valor and his deeds, who prowled the world and saw strange animals;[13] one book on agriculturalists;[14] one book on the Chariot.[15] Philo wrote many books in his wisdom, for he was a great sage in Torah and every matter.[16] And he was of the seed of Yehoshua ben Yehozedek, the high priest.[17]

---

10. These are the five books on dreams. In Jerome: *That Dreams Are Sent by God.*

11. Jerome lists these as three separate titles: *Quaestionum et solutionem in Exodum Libri quinque, De tabernaculo,* and *De victimis.* E. Richardson, *A Select Library of Nicene and Post-Nicene Fathers of the Christian Church,* Second Series, 3 (New York, 1892), 365, renders the title as *On Victims and Promises or Curses.*

12. Jerome recalls here the treatise *On the Jews* (*De Iudaeis*). The Hebrew author seems to recall the word *eversio* (destruction), and so wrote what he wrote.

13. Jerome has *De Alexandro et quod propriam rationem muta habeant* (On Alexander and that creatures have their own reason). This treatise is preserved only in Armenian translation and does not obviously deal with Alexander of Makedon. Based on the mention of creatures in Jerome, the Hebrew author conjectured that Philo wrote the famous book on Alexander of Makedonia (the Alexander Romance), where indeed it is related that Alexander "saw strange creatures." [An English version of the Hebrew translation of the book is in the final section of this book. SB]

14. Jerome's *De agricultura.*

15. So the Hebrew author apparently understood Jerome's words on Philo's book titled *On Contemplative Life.* Jerome says the book relates that the pious "contemplate divine things and ever pray to God" (quod videlicet caelestia contemplentur et semper orent Deum). From this, the author conjectures that the book dealt with mysticism. Philo's book actually deals with the life of a Jewish sect in Egypt called Therepeutae.

16. Finally, Jerome says that Philo wrote many books that did not reach us.

17. Source unknown for this genealogy. Manuscript has Yehozedok (*plene* spelling with additional *vav,* also in Yehoshua).

2. ON JOSEPHUS

Yosef ben Gurion the priest, his father's name was Matia [Matthias] and his surname Gurion.[1] He is Yosef ben Matia the priest [who] wrote many books in Judah [i.e., among the Jews]. One book[2] [is] on all the gentile kings from Adam until Titus and Vespasian and on all the kings of Judah and on the noblemen and satraps in the books of Media and Persia, Makedonia and Romi and the Hasmoneans. He also wrote from Genesis to Vespasian and until the fourteenth year of Domitian Caesar: in all twenty-four books.[3] He also wrote books about Apion and Philo and the Book of the Maccabees.[4] He also related[5] about Yoḥanan [John the Baptist][6] and Shimon ben Yoḥanan called Caipha, who was born in the village of Beth Tsaida,[7] and about Ya'akov [i.e., "James" SB], son of Yosef, brother

---

1. This is correct and also found in Hieronymus [Jerome] in his chap. 13. The addition of Gurion is the author's explanation to harmonize Josephus with the tradition of *Yosippon*.

2. Hieronymus writes that Josephus wrote twenty books of Antiquities from Creation to year twenty-four of Domitian.

3. The Hebrew author is mistaken based on the erroneous report of Hieronymus [see previous note]. He only wrote it in the twenty-fourth year of Domitian.

4. Reference to "Contra Apionum" divided into two books; the Hebrew author is inexact in following Hieronymus, who wrote that Apion was sent by the gentiles against Philo. This reference is apparently 4 Maccabees, which Hieronymus, according to custom, attaches to the other Maccabees. MS read "about the book of Maccabees."

5. Hieronymus writes about Josephus in chap. 13; the references to first-century individuals is based on other chapters of Hieronymus, but here the Hebrew author gives the erroneous impression that Josephus himself wrote about them.

6. This is Yoḥanan the Baptist about whom Josephus wrote in *AJ* 18.117.

7. Hieronymus, chap. 1: *Simon Petrus, filius Johannis, provinciae Galilaeae, e vico Bethsaida*. The author knew that Peter was called Cephas. He restored the Hebrew for Bethsaida, but in Hebrew MS Beth Ẓaida is mistakenly written Ẓadia.

of the crucified Jesus on his father's side,[8] for Yosef was the husband of Miriam [Mary], daughter of Ḥannah [Anna], daughter of Yehoyakim, mother of the crucified Jesus; before he betrothed Miriam, he had a wife named Miriam bat Ḥannah, and she was the sister of Miriam,[9] the mother of the crucified Jesus, and she bore Ya'akov to Yosef and died; then he betrothed Miriam, the sister of Miriam, and was stoned in Jerusalem by the Pharisees;[10] and also about Matia [i.e., Matthew] the Evangelist, whose name was Levi—he is Levi known as Matia[11] who wrote the gospel[12] in Hebrew for the Hebraists;[13] and also he wrote about Sha'ul called Pa'ul[14]—he is Paulus who was from the tribe of Benjamin; and he also wrote about Barnabas from Cyprus[15]—he is Yosef ha-Levi and about his[16] students Yoḥanan called Marcus the Evangelist[17] and about Yehudah [i.e., Jude][18] and about Lukus the Physician[19] and about Markus the pupil of Simon

---

8. Cf. Hieronymus, chap. 2, where he is called the brother of Jesus, and many opine that he was the son of Joseph: "but it seems to me that he was the son of Miriam sister of Jesus' mother." From the Hebrew text, it appears that the author used a Christian source that had a different tradition than that followed by Hieronymus, who established for successors the tradition that the mother of Ya'akov [i.e., James], whose name was Miriam [Mary], was the sister of Miriam [Mary], the mother of Jesus. Our text adds that Ya'akov was the son of Joseph from a previous marriage, a tradition among Christians since the second century, which the author used to supplement Hieronymus. On this, see W. Bauer, *Das Leben Jesu* (Darmstadt, 1967), 7–8. All these suppositions arose during the period when Christians began to believe that Mary gave birth to Jesus without the aid of a father and remained a virgin for the remainder of her life. The dilemma of the New Testament story arose from the mention of Jesus's brothers, among whom was James. The names of Jesus and Mary are erased in the MS.

9. Miriam is erased from MS, and "sister" has the pronoun "his" (rather than "her") suffixed.

10. See *AJ* 20.200–203, and Hieronymus, chap. 2, which both relate that James was stoned to death. But no source says that the Pharisees stoned James. Hieronymus does state in chap. 13 that Jesus was killed by the Pharisees and that Jerusalem was destroyed because of the death of James, contrary to Josephus, who does not mention these two contentions. Apparently either the Hebrew author or his source was confused by the contentions today found in Hieronymus.

11. From Hieronymus, chap. 3.

12. "*Euangelium*"; *Aven Gilion* [lit. "wicked folio"] is the spelling from b. *Shabbat* 116a (although here written with *ayin* rather than *aleph*, although both spellings are in Talmudic passage); the passage has been censored in modern editions; cf. *Dikdukei Sofrim, Shabbat*, 200.

13. No parallel in Hieronymus.

14. From Hieronymus, chap. 5: Saulus, Paulus.

15. See Hieronymus, chap. 6. Cyprus is written as Kipris in MS.

16. I.e., of Jesus. This statement does not fit the reality.

17. Mark is identified as Yoḥanan in Acts 12:12, but this datum is not found in Hieronymus.

18. I.e., Jude (cf. letter to him in New Testament and Hieronymus, chap. 4).

19. Cf. Hieronymus, chap. 7.

Caipha,[20] and Yoḥanan [i.e., John] ben Zebadiah the Evangelist who wrote a Book of Mysteries [*Sefer ha-Razim*][21] on the Isle of Padmos; and at age eighty-four he died in the days of Traianus.[22]

The following three additions to *Yosippon* are found in two MSS: Kaufmann MS and Rothschild MS. It is not known whether they existed independently and were interpolated or whether they were written on the basis of other sources by one of the scribes who copied *Yosippon*. It is clear, however, that they postdate *Yosippon*, since his stylistic influence is recognizable.

---

20. Mentioned above as Mark the Evangelist; see Hieronymus, chap. 8.
21. Cf. Hieronymus, chap. 8. MS has *Sefer Ḥarazim* and refers to John's Apocalypse [i.e., Revelations in the New Testament. SB].
22. MS has Ipadmos (written as one word, as is common in Mediterranean languages). Hieronymus writes that John died in Patmos in the reign of Trajan, sixty-eight years after the death of Jesus. The Hebrew author erred in the number of years as well as in his understanding of the source.

3. DEATH OF KLEOPATRA

When Kleopatra[1] saw that her husband was killed and that Augustus was coming to capture her and seize the country from her, she was terrified lest she be captured in her pride and in the wickedness of her deeds, for she had incited her husband to rebel against Augustus and fight him. So it came to pass when Augustus was about to invade Egypt that she put her golden crown on her head, adorned herself with royal garb and precious stones, sat down on a golden couch, took some kind of poisonous snake and placed it on her left side, and it bit her and she died. But she continued to sit as if she were still alive, for she had chosen death over life lest Augustus abuse her. When Augustus came, he paid heed to nothing beyond capturing her, for he had heard of her beauty, that there was no woman comparable to her in appearance, in looks, and in wisdom. So Augustus came to her house and found her sitting on her couch in her choicest garb, but she was dead. When Augustus saw her beauty, he was greatly saddened that he did not find her alive.

---

1. This addition is found in both MSS of *Yosippon* at the beginning of chap. 47 (after "Egypt"). It was also known to Abraham ibn Daud (*Sefer Hakabbalah*, section on the kings of the Second Temple period). The author used a source and gave it a literary adaptation, even adding a few details.

4. A SLEAZY AFFAIR IN THE DAYS OF TIBERIUS

Further,[1] in Aram, Amnostus[2] the Roman had a daughter, lovely in appearance and beautiful in form, and her name was Liza,[3] and she whored secretly in her father's house with a lad from among our bandits, for many Israelites cast off custom and left Jerusalem to sin with the gentiles. Now the girl loved the bandit and conceived by him, so she contacted him, saying: "Behold I am pregnant." And he said to her: "Tell your father: 'God came to me in a dream and said to me: "Say to your father—it is my will that you be my prophetess and bear me a son on earth."' And further tell him: 'Lo I have seen this vision many times—and you heed what he tells you.' And subsequently you say: 'I am pregnant.'" So she told these words to her father, and her father said to her: "And who can deny what god requests?[4] Do his will!" Subsequently she said to her father: "I am pregnant." And her father did not think ill of her, for they had guarded her there from the day that she spoke to him. When her time came, she gave birth to a son, and the people of Aram erred after this illusion.

---

1. This addition is found in both MSS after the story of Paulina, where the copyist wanted to illuminate "for throughout his realm there occurred in his days such scandals."
2. Perhaps we might read *amnestos* in Greek (the forgotten one), and if the assumption is correct, then it appears that this addition was written in a Greek environment. It is unlikely that there was a Greek source for this story since it is based on *Yosippon*, and his satire is strengthened by the identification of the father as a Roman.
3. Liza is a variation on Leda, who is mentioned in *Yosippon*, chap. 57. The author penned his imaginative story without realizing that Leda is drawn from Greek mythology.
4. This is precisely what Paulina's husband advises her in chap. 57.

5. ORIGIN OF CHRISTIANITY AND THE STORY OF SHOSHANA (SUSANNA)

CHAPTER I. ORIGIN OF CHRISTIANITY

1.[1] Then the outlaws[2] among our people bestirred themselves to do whatever was right in their eyes and behave wickedly and change their course. And when they were to appear in court before the judges in those days, the outlaws would go to the Roman officers in Judaea and say to them: "Since we rebelled against their Torah and entered the law of Caesar, they wish to kill us." And when sworn in [they would say]: "Hail Caesar!" The Roman leaders would [then] rescue them from the judge.

Many of our outlaws went forth and led astray many of the people of God, and they went to Edom,[3] where they changed their religion and so led them astray. They made signs and wonders for them with their magic, and the sages of Israel could do nothing against them for they were continually aided by Gaius Caesar.[4] The outlaws went to Nazareth of Edom and seduced many, and these outlaws were enriched from the wealth that the king gave them.

---

1. This story appears in both MSS and until "they changed the meaning of the Torah" also in MS Vatican 408. The later copyist added this from another MS after the story of Gaius's decree in chap. 58. An allusion to the story about the origins of Christianity can be found in the Mantua edition and also in Judah ibn Mosqoni's version. This chapter was edited with commentary by Israel Lévi, "Jésus, Caligula et Claude dans une interpolation du Josippon," *Revue des Etudes Juives* 91 (1931): 139–41, from the Rothschild MS. The story is rather confused and is full of the author's imaginative attempt to introduce his meager knowledge about the origins of Christianity alongside *Yosippon*'s relation about Gaius's decrees.
2. See Dan 11:14. Ultimately it is based on the Talmud, *Toldoth Yeshu*, and the author's lively imagination. The author calls them *perizim*, as in *Yosippon*.
3. The author refers to Edom in Israel, since to him Christianity, Rome, and Edom were all synonymous.
4. Caligula.

Sh'vy[5] and his cronies went to Gaius Caesar; they[6] told him that the angel of the Lord, his Son who had long been prophesied, came,[7] and he told the inhabitants of Jerusalem to accept your command and to mention your name as God,[8] but they did not listen to him and repulsed him and hounded him to kill him. "Where is he?" Gaius said. "Summon him!" His friends called him [i.e., Jesus], and he came before the king and said to him: "The Lord sent me to you to anoint you as god on Earth and to build an altar for you as a divinity and to mention your name as god." And Gaius blessed him and honored him.

Gaius sent an image of his body [*golem*] to Jerusalem, saying: "Here is the image of my picture. Bow down to it and bend your knee before it. Build an altar as God commanded you and keep your seasons and sabbaths." So he sent the image to Jerusalem.[9]

And it came to pass when the image arrived, the inhabitants of Jerusalem shut the city gate and did not allow the image to enter the city.

The king sent Yehoshua, Yehudah, and Marinus[10] from the sages of Israel to Caesar in Rome, and they came before Gaius Caesar. Caesar said to them: "Behold, [it is] your God's son[11] who sent me to be a divinity over the entire world. Accept me as a divinity over yourselves! And you, what do you think to do? Tell me your wish." Yehoshua and his colleagues replied:[12] "Let it be known to you, o king, that we shall not obey you in this matter or accept your counsel! Heaven forbid that we mention the name of other gods, save for our Lord; neither shall we swear, save in the name of our Lord, nor shall we build an altar, save for an altar to our Lord in the name of His holiness and to recall His majesty. And the outlaws of our people spoke words about the Lord our God that we cannot relate, and they have changed the meaning of the Torah."[13] Then Gaius

---

5. Author scrambles the name of Jesus.

6. Jesus, having apparently joined the outlaws in his native Nazareth, waited outside.

7. The angel was Jesus, about whom, the Christians claim, the biblical prophets foretold, but the whole story was a ruse.

8. Thus, the author blames Jesus and his disciples for Gaius's decrees.

9. *Yosippon* does not relate the story about the icon and the temple. The author of this story apparently developed the idea that he found in chap. 57 that mentions Pilatus, who brought the icon of Tiberius to Jerusalem. *Golem* refers to anything from an anthropoid lump of clay to a boor. In chap. 2, *Yosippon* uses it for a sarcophagus.

10. Yehuda is later identified as Yehudah Iscariote (see below). Marinus is a strange addition. Yehoshua ben Peraḥiah and his student Jesus are mentioned in the Talmud (*Sota* 47a and *Sanhedrin* 107b) and connected with Jesus of Nazareth in the Aramaic and Hebrew versions of *Toldoth Yeshu*; cf. Flusser, *Josippon*, 2.252n680.

11. I.e., Jesus.

12. These words are taken from Philo's reply to Gaius in chap. 58.

13. Thus, the sages accuse the Christians before Gaius.

waxed angry with Yehoshua and raged exceedingly against him, casting him out in contempt.[14]

He found his friends who waited in Gaius's courtyard and said to them: "A time of sorrow and rebuke is today"; "children have come to birth, and there is no strength to bring them forth,"[15] for Gaius has raged and commanded to array his troops to go against the king in Jerusalem to destroy the holy land, while the outlaws sit before him—Sh'vy sits to his right and many of our people who have gone astray after him. Claudius quarreled with him, before Caesar, for he was a prince, and Gaius raged against him.[16] "But there is a remedy for the matter: Let us return to the Primal Aid and to the ancestral hope, to the Lord our God who was always the aid of our fathers, and he shall help us and save us from his hand. Let us call for a fast and consecrate an assembly before God in the land of our enemies! There is no place at all for us to run to take refuge, save in the Tower of Strength, the Name of God, for unto it the righteous shall run and be exalted."[17]

So they consecrated a fast and called an assembly for three days and three nights. And God answered them in the land of their enemies and turned the evil back on Gaius Caesar.[18] On his way to the *ippodromio*—a place of entertainment where he amused himself—God aroused the strength of his troops, and thirty of his warriors leaped upon him with drawn swords, hacked him to pieces, and fed him to dogs, and the people assembled there to watch the horse race fled home.[19]

So the Lord avenged his servants[20] against Gaius Caesar, and Claudius Caesar succeeded him. He sent forth Yehoshua and his companions in great honor[21] after he made them a feast, where they sat before him and he honored them and gave over the outlaws into their hand. Claudius took the three outlaws[22] who

---

14. The author takes this from *Yosippon*, chap. 58, which he rewrites.

15. 2 Kings 19:3. [SB]

16. The author continues to adapt *Yosippon* chap. 58 and imagine this scene.

17. Cp. prayer book *ki nisgav shemo*.

18. The author follows *Yosippon*, chap. 58.

19. Not in *Yosippon*, although the author does mention the hippodrome in chaps. 49 and 55. This author understood the meaning of the hippodrome, or Roman *circus*, as a place for horse races and other entertainment, "all of which was done to gladden his spirit" (see *Yosippon*, chap. 40). His use of the term may indicate that this author also came from a Byzantine environment. The number thirty is not in *Yosippon*. The author may have taken it from David's "friends" [cf. 2 Sam 23:23] or from another source. The assembled crowd and the horse race are based on *Yosippon*, chap. 40.

20. *Yosippon*, chap. 58. Claudius is written as Kliodus.

21. So Claudius had treated Philo in chap. 58.

22. Unclear whom the author intends.

fled and killed them, then cast their corpses to dogs, lest the errant ones who followed them steal them during the night.[23]

Yehoshua and his colleagues came to Jerusalem, and the rest of the outlaws approached and stood before the Sanhedrin. Yehudah Iscariote,[24] at the command of the king, stood up from the ranks of the Sanhedrin, for the king had asked: "What is to be the fate of those men who stirred up Gaius Caesar against me?" He commanded to hang them on a tree.[25] So they hung them according to the king's command but against the will of the people, who were saying: "Those who were in your *havurah* [*collegium*] should return in repentance, for these men did not sin other than through the controversies among them." But the princes, the deputies, the elders, and the majority of the people rejoiced at their deaths, for they had sought to stir up Roman wars against them. And many went astray secretly following them, but they killed many of them from the city of Natzeret Edom[26] and stoned them.[27] But they could not eliminate them since they did this in secret. For who can know what is hidden in a man's guts except for the One who searches the mind and tries the heart—the Lord of Hosts is His Name.[28] So they were stirred up to commit many scandals such as these in Jerusalem, and wickedness continued to increase.

CHAPTER 2. SUSANNA'S AFFAIR

In those days, King Herod sent Ḥananel the priest and Naḥum ben Onkolius to Rome.[29] Now Ḥananel's wife, daughter of Eliakim, the high

---

23. Lest the Christians steal them and claim they resurrected.

24. Italian form of Iscariotes (Hebrew: Ish-Kiriyoth). Did the author identify him with the Yehudah sent to Rome?

25. I.e., crucifixion, apparently including Jesus.

26. See above text following note 9.

27. It seems that the author knew the circumstances of Stephan's death (Acts 7:54–60).

28. Jer 17:10. [SB]

29. Israel Lévi also published this chapter from the Rothschild MS, and Dov Heller commented on it briefly in his edition of the Pseudepigrapha [*Sepharim Ḥizoniim*, 1.558]. The story postdates *Yosippon* perhaps specifically as an addition to the book. It is apparent that the same author wrote this and the previous story. This version is a free adaptation of the apocryphal tale appended to the Greek translation of Daniel. There are two versions: one in the Septuagint and the other in Theodotion, a Latin rendition of which is in the Vulgate, and the latter perhaps is the version the author used. The adapter moved the story to the times of Herod and adjusted the names accordingly. See Flusser, *Josippon*, 2.55ff. So Daniel becomes the sage Naḥman, Shoshana becomes Ḥannah, Mariamme becomes the wife of Ḥananel, the high priest, daughter of Eliakim, a survivor of the Hasmonean House. Thus, he is able to date the life of Jesus to the times of Gaius Caesar and his death in the days of Claudius Caesar. Flusser argues [*Josippon*, 2.56] that this adaptor of *Yosippon* wrote these two stories and interpolated them into his text in order to supply more data on Jesus. It is unknown which Herod [Orodos in Hebrew text]. Perhaps he is

priest,[30] was beautiful in form and appearance, chaste and of attractive stature, and was in heart-felt awe of Shaddai; she was comparable in beauty to the chaste and saintly Maryami.[31]

When her husband, Ḥananel, went to Rome,[32] she sat in the house of her father, Eliakim, and he was a survivor of the Hasmonean family.[33] The elders of the people and their deputies used to attend court daily at his house,[34] and the deputies frequently saw his daughter Ḥannah[35] and went crazy over her beauty; their [evil] inclination burned within them, and they plotted cruel schemes against her in the orchard behind her father's house. And it came to pass when she went out to the orchard to pray for her husband, as was her daily wont,[36] one[37] of them rose, seized her, and said to her: "Hear me and do what I say!" But she was unwilling to heed him; he begged her, yet the woman refused; so he said to her: "If you do not heed me and fulfill my desire, I will surely bear witness against you that you whored with another man." She replied:[38] "We have learned that a man is not put to death on the testimony of one man." So he summoned two of his colleagues[39] and said: "Behold, we three will testify that you whored with another man, and you shall be burned, for you are the daughter of a priest." The woman screamed, and they too yelled out and seized her.[40]

The elders heard and came from Eliakim's house[41] and found the three deputies holding her. The elders said: "What's this?" And the three answered:

---

the Ḥananel whom Herod made priest [cf. *Yosippon*, chap. 45]. Naḥum ben Onkolius is totally unknown.

30. The apocryphal Susannah mentions only that she was wife to Yehoyakim and daughter of Ḥilkia, neither of whom identified as priests.

31. Herod's wife. The form of the name is from *Yosippon* and is a transliteration of the Greek Mariamme and should be pronounced Maryami, not Marimi, as Morvynne read it in the sixteenth century, whence it entered the English versions of *Yosippon*. [SB]

32. The author's assumption since his source does not mention it.

33. A creative touch: according to the source, her family was Sadducee, and Herod had massacred the Hasmoneans.

34. Chap. 4 of the source has the Jews meet at her husband's house because he was the most honored among them. The author adjusted the scene accordingly.

35. The source calls her Shoshanah.

36. Not in the author's source and a nice touch.

37. The source identifies two elders. Compare Susannah 14–16; and Theodotion's Latin 19–24. The following conversation appears only in the latter. Her response is not in sources. For biblical law, see Lev 21:9. This motif also appears in the parallel Samaritan story.

38. Not in sources.

39. Sources have only two elders.

40. Only in Theodotion 24 and not in Septuagint.

41. According to Theodotion 26, it is the husband's house, not the father's house.

"While the three of us were walking on the path, we heard a sound surreptitiously in the orchard, and we saw this woman, daughter of Eliakim,[42] was whoring; the boy struggled away from us[43] and fled; we could not identify him, but we seized this one." They brought her before the elders and the judges, and the wicked witnesses rose and testified against her,[44] saying: "We were walking on the path and saw a lad having intercourse on Ḥannah bat Eliakim under a certain tree, and lo, we seized her until the elders came, for we had shouted and they had heard our voices. The lad escaped from our hands, and we could not identify him."[45] And it came to pass when they had heard these words[46] that they condemned her to be burned,[47] and she was taken out. The women despised and reviled her, for they thought her guilty.[48] But Eliakim, her father,[49] went after her crying and shouting because he knew that she was chaste and that the witnesses were false witnesses.

As she passed the Temple,[50] she cried with bitter heart and yelled out, saying:[51] "O Lord God in whose Name this house is called, who searches the mind and tries the heart to give each one according to his ways and the fruit of his deeds,[52] reward me this day according to my ways. Do not make Your Torah false, for it is written there: 'The soul that sins shall die.'[53] These testified a lie against me,[54] and I was silent before the elders of Your people because I trusted in Your salvation, and You knew that I did not want to be unfaithful to my husband. And You Lord, Your deeds are pure, and all Your ways are Truth, make my judgment this day Truth!"[55]

---

42. Daughter of Eliakim is the author's addition.

43. Only in Theodotion 39.

44. According to the source, it was the elders who testified. The adapter adds the testimony.

45. Sources have two elders testify. Their words are added by the adapter.

46. See Susanna Septuagint 30 and Theodotion 41.

47. Not in sources.

48. Based on *Yosippon*, chap. 48, where they vilify Mariamme (Miriam), Herod's wife, in the same words.

49. Not in sources.

50. The author's assumption since he placed the scene in Jerusalem. Septuagint version has her prayer before the trial and Theodotion's after the death sentence.

51. In Theodotion, the woman's prayer follows the story of the death sentence, while in the Septuagint, the prayer precedes the trial.

52. Jer 17:10. [SB]

53. Ezek 18:4, 18:20. Not mentioned in sources.

54. Only in Theodotion 43.

55. Last sentence, "And You Lord," added by the author.

And it came to pass as she prayed to God that God heard her prayer,[56] and God stirred up the spirit of Naḥman the Sage[57] and the spirit of the king,[58] and the king ordered to bring the trial before him. The sage brought the woman, along with the elders, the people, and the witnesses,[59] to the king, and the king said to her: "How did these men seize you? Tell me!" And she told him all that befell her. The king said: "Remove everyone from us," and there remained Naḥman and the three witnesses. Naḥman took one witness and brought him into the room before the king. Naḥman said to the witness: "Tell what kind of tree under which you saw Ḥannah sinning?" He replied: "A walnut tree[60] planted in the corner of the orchard." And he put him in a room. The next witness came, and Naḥman said to him: "What tree did you see under which Ḥannah was sinning?" And he said: "An almond tree planted in the corner of the orchard." The third came, and he too differed and lied. Then the king said to Naḥman:[61] "Go with them to the house of Eliakim and see if the words are true." They entered the orchard, and Naḥman said to the first: "In which direction is the walnut planted?" And he [witness] said: "In the east corner." So they searched the orchard, and behold, there was no walnut tree in the entire orchard. They looked in the west corner for the almonds, as the second witness had said, and behold, there were no almonds in the orchard. Also, the third witness did not find a response. So God revealed the false testimony that the witnesses had testified against the innocent one, and God returned their fate upon their head; the king commanded, and they [his men] hung them [witnesses] on the tree.[62]

---

56. Only in Theodotion 44.

57. The source has "a young lad named Daniel."

58. No king is mentioned in the source. The adapter adds this following his mention of Herod at the beginning of the story.

59. The author adds "witnesses," who in the source are the elders themselves.

60. The source has "another tree" here; the second source has "oak" instead of almond and no third witness.

61. Not in the source and presumably the author's addition.

62. Septuagint has the two elders thrown into a valley, where an angel set fire to them. Their death is not treated in Theodotion. Presumably, the author intends crucifixion.

SELECTIONS FROM THE NORMATIVE VERSION OF *YOSIPPON*

I. BEGINNING OF THE SIEGE OF YODPHAT: THE ROMAN IRON RAM

167.[1] Vespasian commanded to build a siege dike near the city and upon it an iron ram that destroys and topples city walls. He brought the iron ram to the city and began to butt with the ram against the city wall of Yodphat in order to topple it.

This is the makeup of the iron ram with which they toppled city walls and destroyed them. First they took a huge beam, long and thick, and set at its tip a large and strong cap made of strong iron in the shape of a horned ram. The weight of the cap was half that of the beam, and it covered half of it. Then they would sink deep into the earth two large masts and hang the ramming beam between them with heavy ropes made from strong hemp and iron wire; and the spot where it hangs between the two masts is as near the wall as the fighters wish to butt the wall with its horns. At the rear of the beam, which is opposite the wall, strong iron rings are well nailed into it and ropes made of hemp and iron wire tied to them. When the fighters sought to topple the wall, they would strongly launch the ram's beam as if launching a small pike so that strong horns [i.e., hooks] would be stuck between the stones of the wall; then they would hang heavy weights in the rings at the end of the beam; at a distance, a large group, many men, would seize and gird themselves to pull the ropes passing

---

1. This description, taken from the Hominer edition, *Josiphon*, 252–54, is rather impressive given the Hebrew available to the author of this interpolation. I have tried to remain as close to his wording as possible, style permitting. Vetruvius, the Roman architect, has left us descriptions of these machines in his *De architectura*, book 10. Since the MS of Vetruvius was not discovered before the fifteenth century, the author's source is unknown. [Models of various rams described below are reproduced in Gaalya Cornfeld's edition of *Josephus: The Jewish War* (Grand Rapids, MI, 1982), 230, 231, 373, 442, 493, 504. SB]

through the rings at the end of the beam to lower the beam's rear end toward the ground. But no sooner is this done than the wall quakes and moves and the stones of her construction are detached from many places, and the wall falls to the ground.

Sometimes they would put the iron ram on a cart that goes on four huge wooden wheels covered with iron and with spikes nailed from the bottom. They make that ram with four legs like the ram's legs or more than four legs according to the size of the beam's ram; for the larger ram's beam, the cart's tongue is thirty cubits long, and for the smaller, ten cubits. But the number of wheels of the cart must correspond to the number of legs, for each leg of the ram is stabilized and inserted facing each wheel of the cart. When they want to topple a wall, men rush the cart, upon which is the ram, from a distance, with a huge crowd pushing it vigorously by the four tails of the wooden beams it has behind it, and with the ram upon it, they butt the city wall that they wish to topple. And the head of the iron ram that destroys walls, which is carried on the cart, has no horns; rather, it is huge and solid and made of very strong iron, and the neck of the headpiece is very thick. We shall speak about this matter further on. There is a wide wooden fence on both sides of the cart to protect those pushing it from behind when needed, lest they [defenders of the wall] cast arrows and stones upon them from the wall.

Most of the destroying iron rams used by Titus against Jerusalem were cart rams; he had no mast rams, except for two, as we shall relate further on. The ram's beam, which we described above, had the girth of ten linked men and a length of fifty cubits; inside it was hollow and filled with ox hide bound and woven after it was boiled somewhat. The wood has no use other than to erect and support the form. The wood of the beam is covered outside with thin iron. The reason for the skin inside is to prevent the beam breaking by the load of the weights that they hang in the rear rings when the men pull the end of the beam with ropes to lower it. The reason for the wood outside is to erect the form and support it. The reason for the iron over the wood is to protect the beam lest the defenders of the wall burn it from atop the wall. And the number of the horns on the ram's helmet at the end of the beam that butts the city wall is anyone's choice, only that there should not be less than ten horns. A beam of twenty cubits has no more than fifty horns, while a beam of one hundred cubits has as many as there are at a distance of one cubit from each other, and the thickness of each horn is as the thickness of one man's embrace, and its length is not less than a cubit and a half. A long wooden fence is opposite, covered with skins of oxen tanned with human urine, set up behind, flanking the beam to protect the men involved in the work of thrusting it, lest the archers atop the wall they were attacking smite them with arrows. The battering ram that Vespasian brought close to butt the city wall of Yodphat, in which we were besieged, was fifty cubits long, and twenty-five horns were on the ram's helmet; its girth was ten linked men; the thickness of each horn of the ram was the embrace of one man, and the space between each horn was one cubit. One thousand five hundred talents was the load of the weights hung at the rear when needed. One thousand five hundred strong soldiers were assigned to thrust it, for it was Vespasian's command to butt the wall with it. One hundred and fifty pair of oxen or three hundred pairs of horses and mules were needed to move the beam and all its equipment from place to place and from city to city by carts when they wanted to do so. The beam was not of one piece but rather joined from parts by iron chains and iron rings linked and joined when needed like one piece of marvelous work, joined as separate pieces, to lift it up section by section into mountain areas in order to fight against fortified cities atop the mountains, for they would set it up on a place proper for them to set it up there.

2. CROWNING OF VESPASIAN AND DEATH OF AGRIPAS

218.[1] In those days, Espasianus sent Antoninus and Manciminus, his two major generals and sage advisers, to invade Roma[2] and to do battle with Butalin [Vitellius] for some time and to kill him, and later he went there to become Caesar according to the customary law of the Caesarate in Roma and renew the crown of his imperium there. The two aforementioned generals went to Roma and assembled through their sagacity a very large force, and they fought with Butalin and killed him. In that fighting, eighty thousand men, the chosen of the Roman valiant, fell in the midst of the great city Roma.

219. Espasianus heard later that Butalin was smote in the fighting and was dead and that his generals whom he had sent governed there, so he hastened to go to Roma to become Caesar according to the law of the Caesarate, thus preserving the custom of Roma and renewing the crown of his imperium so that the imperium be rightly in his hand. He divided his whole army and force in two; half the army would go with him for aid and fighting, while half the army he left with his son Titus to besiege Jerusalem. When Espasianus went to the land of the Romans, as we related, he left his son Titus in Alexandria and commanded

---

1. From the longer version published by Hominer, *Josiphon*, 287–94. See Flusser, *Josippon*, 2.32ff; and for this passage, 38ff; Y. Baer, "Hebrew Sefer Yosifun," in *Sepher Dinaburg*, ed. Y. Baer, Y. Gutman, and M. Schwabe (Jerusalem, 1960), 186–89; and Percy E. Schramm, *Kaisar, Könige und Päpste*, vol. 3 (Stuttgart, 1969), 360–68, who argues that the description dates from the first half of the twelfth century, contemporary to Version C of *Yosippon*, in which it first appears, and its author was perhaps an eyewitness to it, if he did not talk to or read a contemporary account. The text describes a medieval coronation, not that of Vespasian.

2. This is the third spelling of Rome: here רומה, in *Yosippon*, it is רומי or רומא (Hominer, *Josiphon*, has רומא). [SB]

him, saying: "Don't you move from here until I send you a letter from Roma, advising you what to do, and do not besiege Jerusalem." And he said to him: "Yes, my father, I shall do according to your words. Command me, and I shall carry out your orders."

220. Espasianus the Caesar went to Roma. When he went to renew his imperium there, he took with him Agripas, the king, and Monbaz, his son, because he said: "Perhaps they will rebel against me." Therefore, he took with them and his army me, Yoseph the priest,[3] clapped in iron chains, for his advisers said to him: "True it is that you have not seen any sign of rebellion from Yoseph from the day he came to you, nor did his spirit don a cloak of betrayal, for he is a faithful man. Albeit who knows after we travel from here whether he might change and take pity on his people, flee to Jerusalem, and embolden the inhabitants with his bravery and wisdom and make peace between the people and the bandits within her, who by fighting prepare[4] the people of Jerusalem for destruction, and Jerusalem's denizens will enthrone him over them and he will be a foe to us. Also you, when you go to Roma, will need him, for he is wise and a trustworthy adviser. Anyone who hears his advice, in everything he attends, succeeds." Espasianus, hearing these words, found them to be appropriate and took me with him clapped in iron chains in the company of Agripas, the king, and his son, who went with me without being clapped in chains, neither hands nor feet; nonetheless, there were guards on duty lest they escape on the way.

221. When Espasianus arrived at Roma, all the denizens of the city went out to greet him, receiving him with great honor and joy and good heartedness. And they thanked him, saying that it was fitting for him to rule and become Caesar according to the law of the Caesarate. He commanded, and they put me in prison, but they left Agripas and his son on their own recognizance. On the following day, all the elders of Roma assembled to make Espasianus Caesar according to the law of the Caesarate, as was the custom of Roma, and Agripas and his son were with them. I implored the warden of the prison in Roma to appoint guards for me and escort me to the imperial palace of the Caesarate to see how they enthroned the Caesars in Roman custom. I found grace in his eyes, and he did according to my words. They brought me to the imperial palace of

---

3. Josephus never went to Rome to view Vespasian's crowning. Moreover, he was freed from his chains in Beirut. The adapter of Version B of *Yosippon* personalizes the description in Josephus's voice and in popular medieval fashion continually expands the text with contemporary allusions.

4. Hebrew has "understand"; suggested emendations in Hominer, *Josiphon*: "bring" or "prepare."

the Caesarate clapped in iron chains, and they stood us with him in a place from which I saw all that transpired.

222. This is the custom of the Caesarate according to the law in Roma.[5] All the Roman elders and the advisers from the temple of their gods bring the candidate for being Caesar, playing on cymbals and lyres and all sorts of instruments before him with laughter and blowing trumpets before him until they arrive with him about one thousand cubits from the palace, for the palace is on one side of the city near the sea, slightly distant from the city, albeit attached to it.[6] In the small campus in the first courtyard are one hundred thousand cavalry. When they bring him to that place, seven kings, chosen by the counsel of Roma, crowned by Caesar, approach him, and two of them bring him a white horse ready to mount a rider upon it, and both of them, one on the right and the other on the left, hold him by bridle and bit. Two others bring before it a ladder with seven steps all of gold, which he mounts to ride the horse.[7] Two of them, facing the rider, hold the horse behind them, one to the right and one to the left, until the rider mounts the horse via that ladder. Two of them, after he has mounted, stand on both sides of the horse, one on this side and one on the other, and the rider leans on each one of them with his hands and feet on each one. So he goes to the palace with the first two kings leading the horse step by step. The seventh king goes first of all on foot with drawn sword in hand, and before him are a thousand warriors on foot with drawn swords in their hands. There is no voice or speech or whisper, and the sounds of the players are silenced.

The seventh king who precedes calls in a loud voice and says these words: "Have you seen the man whom the God of the world has chosen to lead the inhabitants of his land and rule the world according to the law of the Caesarate? Here he is, honor him and magnify him, for he has the rule from God, and from him he receives the honor. And the Lord who fulfills his heart's request to magnify him to ascend to the height of the Caesarate on this day, He will direct him to lead the kings of the land and its inhabitants on the right path, to judge them

---

5. See Flusser, *Josippon*, 2.38. He refers to R. Elze, *Die Ordines für die Weihe und Krönung des Kaisers und der Kaiserin* (Hannover, 1960): *Incipit ordo Romanus ad benedicendum imperatorem, quando coronam accipit.* Perhaps the author of this section had one of these Ordines before him that has not survived, or he used his rich imagination to amplify what he was told by someone who observed the ceremony. Since the Ordines were ceremonial guides, it is not certain that all the material in them was implemented. Hence, it is difficult to relate this description to what actually happened, however it got to the author.

6. The author probably was never in Rome from this fanciful topography, although he may have been an Italian Jew.

7. This is attested; e.g., for the Ordines of Charles V, a ladder was brought for the pope (Elze, *Ordines*, 177, 183).

justly, to remove injustice and violence from the world, to lock up evildoers and the wicked, to capture them, to destroy them, to liquidate them, lest they prowl the land to destroy the realms and the inhabitants of the world and be encouraged to exploit and plunder.[8] He in his mercy and his sovereignty, which has been magnified above all so that no man can attain the wisdom of [his] speech in its majesty,[9] let him establish, support, strengthen, and uphold the sovereignty of Roma and the law of the Caesarate in her. And let him glorify, magnify, raise up, and sustain and guide in peace this one, our lord who is being made Caesar on his day, and say ye Amen."[10]

When the king finishes reading his speech, the six remaining kings, his colleagues behind him, say amen first, and after them all the people together with one voice answer amen. Following this, each of two riders standing each aside the candidate to become Caesar tosses seven times to each side pure gold coins to the poor people walking on both sides at a distance, lest the riders trample them. These collect them as best they can, and each of those tossing the coins throws them as far as he can, both many and few.[11] Those throwing them also are chosen by the counsel of Roma to be, after the ceremony of making the Caesar, the one on his right his deputy and the one on the left general of the entire army of the Romans; and the latter is to appoint the generals of the hosts at the head of the army when the Romans send a force whenever it should be sent.

Thus, the king is announced by the herald, who precedes on foot with drawn sword in hand,[12] heralding seven times what we have related, and when the candidate to become Caesar reaches the gate of the campus wherein is the palace, he heralds for the seventh time. When the candidate to become Caesar reaches the gate of this campus, he dismounts onto the shoulders of the seven kings, and there is a throne made totally of dried dirt. The seven kings seat him upon it and give him a thin wooden scepter. After this, the counselors of the city of Roma and the elders and the people bring before him a document of the bills of rights in Roma and request that he swear that he will not sully them or violate even one covenant of them after he becomes Caesar over them. He takes the

---

8. This represents the ideology of Roman rulers since Augustus; cf. Elze, *Ordines*, 55f, the prayer that begins, "*Prospice*" and has no hint to the Hebrew prayer, as Baer assumed (cf. Baer, "Hebrew Sefer Yosifun," 188n12a).

9. Cf. Ps 149:6.

10. This and other laudatory prayers are from the liturgy contained in the Ordines. The author has removed the Christian elements, however.

11. Cf. Elze, *Ordines*, 45, 105, 145, 167.

12. Cf. Elze, *Ordines*, 105, 145. The herald here is the *praefectus urbis*.

document and kisses each page and each side of it and places it on his head and swears that he will sustain all that is written in it and further that he will add good laws to the laws written in it, as appropriate in the eyes of the counselors of Roma. After this, he is requested to enter the campus, which is locked, and above on its towers stand the guards of the campus gates, and they request that he swear also to them that he will sustain the laws of the campus and the laws of the gatekeepers. So he swore and vowed he would do so.

Then the gatekeepers raised and set up his flag and his standard on the gate of the near tower, and they opened the gate.[13] The one being made Caesar entered the courtyard of the campus, and there all the kings present in Roma called out, saying: "May it be the will of the king of the kings of kings to make this Caesar from heaven and that he will accept His wisdom when we make him Caesar on earth." Then all the kings present there go on foot before him and he too on foot after them, and they bring him to the palace in which is the throne, seat of the Caesarate.

In this building are two thrones: one is the throne, seat of the Caesarate, and it is permanent, and the second is made for the occasion, where the candidate to become Caesar sits before being made Caesar. And when the candidate to become Caesar enters the building, he sits on the temporary throne. All the kings present there come, no less than seven, and two of them kiss his feet, and afterward they kiss the ground in front of him. Next come seven leaders[14] from the leaders of his kingdom, under each of whom are 24 leaders, and under each of the 24 secondary leaders, 120 tertiary leaders, and under each of the 120 tertiary leaders, 500 fourth-level leaders. The first seven leaders come with the chief leader, who rules over them, and he is the leader of Roma and the father of all the leaders ruling throughout the world, and he is called in Roma Pater and in Greek Patron.[15] The Patron puts in the right hand of the candidate to become Caesar a golden scepter of wood, partly not gilded, and on his head is hung

---

13. These are the two obligatory oaths: cf. Elze, *Ordines*, 32–33. The first entails the rights of the Romans and is attested in the twelfth century; the second is already attested from the period of Ludwig II; cf. Ludo Moritz Hartmann, *Geschichte Italiens im Mittelalter*, 3.2.259. The campus then would be the Church of Saint Peter in Rome. According to the Ordines, the candidate will be the "defensor huius sanctae romanae ecelesiae." Did the author err and think that this referred to the Church of Saint Peter and not to the entire Catholic Church?

14. The Hebrew is *hegemon*, which apparently means "bishop" here, as it does in *Megillat Aḥimaaz* and other contemporary Hebrew sources, an obvious anachronism based on the author's description of the ceremony, which he possibly witnessed. *Hegemon* will be consistently rendered as "leader" where it has the meaning of someone in the papal hierarchy. [SB]

15. I.e., the pope who was also bishop of Rome.

a small bag full of dust, and he placed on his [candidate's] small finger a ring made from the bone of a dead man.[16] In his [candidate's] left hand, he put a tall golden glass and upon it a gold apple round in the likeness of the whole Earth. After this he puts the crown of sovereignty on his head and crowns him king. After he crowned him king, the king kisses the hand of the aforementioned Patron.

At once the Patron takes the crown of the Caesarate and places it on his head above the crown of sovereignty and calls in a loud voice, saying: "Long live our lord the Caesar in peace and blessing and nobility over all the kings of the Earth." Then all the people present there answered together in one voice: Amen.

Next he kisses the Patron on the mouth and sits him on his right, and the chosen deputy sits on his left, and the chief military officer stands before him with drawn sword in hand. After this the Caesar orders to free every prisoner in jail for money, and he bears the burden from his treasures. And on that day, the Caesar goes to the palace of the Patron and there eats the morning meal on that day; also he eats the evening meal with the seven first kings who are involved with his Caesarate and with the first seven leaders who are involved with this one as well. In the evening, he goes to the palace and sleeps there, and there he sits in government to judge and decree as he wills, nor does he leave the palace save once a month on the day the moon is visible after the renewal of the moon.[17]

223. Some days after Espasianus became Caesar, he got angry with Agripas, for the wicked of Israel had maligned him, saying that he sought to betray him and had sent a letter to Jerusalem to this effect. He killed him and his son Monbaz by sword.[18] This was three and a half years before the destruction of Jerusalem; 1,290 days before this, the *tamid* ceased, and all this before the destruction

---

16. This is not in any of the Ordines and may be from the author's imagination, but there was a custom in Rome on July 1: *'quando coronam accipit et pulvis mortuorum cum ossibus ante eum ponebatur et stuppa ad figuram iuditii ante eum incendebatur* from *Graphia aureae urbis Romae* He claims too that it also occurred in Byzantium.

17. I.e., the first day after the new moon becomes visible. Flusser calls for a new commentary to this important passage that describes the crowning of the Caesar, which is based on a thorough comparison with extant medieval ceremonials. In his argument, he points up the inadequacies of previous commentators who did not pursue such research and so mislead the reader.

18. The historical Agripas, son of Agripas, did not die in Rome, nor did he have a son called Monbaz, who was actually the son of Queen Helen of Adiabene (*AJ* 20.32f; and later Talmudic sources). Medieval Jews, who did not know that Josephus identified Agripas as a convert, made him a born Jew and married his mother to Agripas (see Flusser, *Josippon*,

of the Temple, as it is written in Dan 12:11: "and from the time the *tamid* is removed" until the end of the story written there.

224. In that year, at that time during the month of the death of Agripas and his son, the Lord stirred the spirit of Espasianus the Caesar to remember me, Yosippon, in a spirit of compassion and love and peace. He ordered to bear me from prison and bring me before him. His servants did so and brought me before him, fettered and shackled in iron chains and fetters. Caesar greeted me in peace and spoke to me comforting and good words, saying: "You know that I have loved you from the day that I saw you. And if I have fettered you and shackled you in iron chains, I did not do this to you from bad feelings but rather so that the Roman generals would not envy you for your bravery and strength, understanding and wisdom, as they said: 'This one was our adversary during our battles, and he walks like one of us. Let's attack him and kill him.' Now be of good cheer, rejoice and be happy, for I now remove from you the fetters and iron chains, and you shall be before me just as one of my generals as long as you are in Roma. Indeed I am sending you to the land of Judaea to my son Titus, and you shall be for him as a father and a faithful adviser, for he it was who had compassion upon you and did not allow you to be killed, as you well know. Many times, too, he implored me to have mercy upon you and to release you from your imprisonment and to honor you, but from my fear of Roman jealousy against you, I did not honor his request."

So I said to him: "How can I act toward you and your son as an adviser when I see how you have killed Agripas and his son, two faithful allies of the kingdom of Roma with neither offense nor sin?" Caesar answered and said to me: "Silence, Yoseph! Do not mention either Agripas or his son to the good, for if you knew what they did to my crown and what they intended to do in revolt against my realm, you would burn their bones with your own hand. Do you know how I honored him and his son in the land of Judaea, and I honored him and raised him to be head in every part and corner? On his account, I diluted the strength of the Romans in his cities." I said: "Yes. I know that your words are true, Lord Caesar." Caesar responded again and said: "He rewarded me with evil, for when Roman generals in the land of Judaea, having heard that Butalin was made Caesar yet he was not fitting to the majesty of the Caesarate, they seized me to crown me and make me Caesar over the government of the Caesarate; he [Agripas], however, advised them not to make me Caesar. For he said: 'How could they do this?' How could they know me truly before sitting in judgment

---

2.36, for sources). Such supposition led to rather bizarre hypotheses by the author of Version C.

over me regarding the honor of the Caesarate to make me Caesar? Furthermore, when he came here, he and his son went from leader to leader until he reached the Patron to slander me and to tell things about me that I did not do. Therefore, I recognized that there was wickedness in the heart of Agripas, and I adjudged him a death sentence, for wherever is wickedness, there is judgment. And his son I judged likewise, for a traitor's son cannot be established in the land since his father's deed remains in his heart wherein was sown the seed of rebellion and betrayal. You, however, I always saw as righteous and loyal to me. Therefore, I entrust my son to your good advice."

Espasianus ordered to release and remove the fetters and the iron chains from me and to release Yoseph from Roman arrest and to conduct him in honor with the generals of the government of Roma and her counselors. Yoseph said: "Is it not a disgrace for me to open my iron chains while you do not open them from the Israelite prisoners with me in Roma? Now if I have found grace in your eyes, do hear me: unshackle all the prisoners of Israel who are with me in Roma, and I will be a faithful adviser forever. I shall hate your enemies and be hostile to your deadly foes." Espasianus did according to Yoseph's words and unshackled all the Israelite prisoners who were with Yoseph in Roma; and he cut off the fetters and the iron chains and sent him to his son Titus in Alexandria of Egypt.

225. Espasianus sent a letter to his son Titus, commanding him about Yoseph the priest, saying: "My dear son, behold, I am sending you Yoseph, general of the Jews, who is a war veteran with wisdom and counsel. Let him be a father and a trustworthy counsel, and do not swerve from his advice neither to the right nor left, for he is a wise man and his counsel correct. Be prepared always to honor him and bear him, for honor and majesty are his fate and the Lord his God is with him. Do not ever listen to the words of wicked ones who slander him before you about anything. And anyone who comes before you to relate some rebellious word about Yoseph, destroy him and liquidate him, for Yoseph is a trustworthy, reliable counselor, and anyone who trusts his counsel, his paths will be straightened. When Yoseph the general reaches you, after a rest of several days from the fatigue of the sea, prepare a route for yourself and go up to Jerusalem to besiege her. Should the Jews offer you peace and surrender to you and accept in name the rule of the Roman government there, be careful lest you harm them in any way. Rather repair the ruptures of the people and rebuild their cities destroyed through our battles and swear to them in kindness the good of the lands of the gentiles under our government and that they will be free from all tax for twenty years. Only that they raise the flag of the Roman government atop the citadel of Jerusalem three times a year during each pilgrimage when all Israel ascends to see the face of the Lord their God according to their

custom. In addition, let them offer a meal-offering sacrifice on our behalf on the holy altar that is in Jerusalem on every pilgrimage holiday. If they do not wish to make peace with you, destroy them and their cities by sword and by captivity. Further, if they desire Yoseph the general to rule over them, it is right in our eyes that he shall rule, but in all events rely on General Yoseph's counsel, and he shall be as a father and a patron, and you will be as a son to him."

226. After this, Yoseph sailed from Roma and arrived in Alexandria to Titus. When Titus heard that Yoseph had come, he rejoiced exceedingly, he and all the elders and sages with him, for Yoseph was full of the spirit of wisdom and under-standing, the spirit of counsel and courage, the spirit of knowledge and fear of God. He went forth to greet him with all the veterans of the Roman army, and they received him with great honor. Yoseph gave to Titus the document his father had sent him, and he read it. He replied to Yoseph, saying: "Everything that my father told me in his document I already intended to do for you, even though my father decrees this so; stay with me, be a father for me, and I will be a son for you, and in your counsel you will guide me."

3. ACTS OF BRAVERY OF THE JEWS

265. Titus ordered to array the two mast rams, the only remaining destroying equipment brought from Roma, and place them in siege positions and build dikes for them to butt again the wall of Jerusalem. The Roman woodworkers began to place the sieges at the sites that Titus had ordered them. The Jews left them alone to do this until they raised the ram beams between the masts. When they finished the work and there remained only to hang the rams between their masts and butt—and the Romans were cocksure about the Jews and spread the good word from one to the other that there no longer remained any bravery among the Jews, for they had not sallied to confront them for some time—one night shortly before dawn, the three leaders of the bandits, Elazar, Yoḥanan, and Shimon, took counsel what to do about this. Elazar said to them: "In another battle, the battle of the three cart rams where four of our valiant lads fought, you sallied and won a name for yourselves with your courage while I guarded the city gate for you; now you guard the gate for me and allow me to sally against them with the heroes that I choose from my warriors, and I too will gain[1] a name for valor." Yoḥanan and Shimon answered him: "Go out against them and gain a name for yourself for courage; the Lord of the Sanctuary and the Temple in Jerusalem will assist you; just be careful lest you enter the depth of fighting too much and be captured or killed; it will be a disgrace and an insult for us." Elazar answered, saying to them: "God will watch over me, for I rely on the righteousness of the worship of my father, Anani, the high priest, and my wickedness will not stand before me now, for there will be another place for God to be avenged on my spirit because of my wickedness."

Elazar chose 100 heroes from his warriors and he over them. He girded himself and went out to them before sunrise on that night. Around the masts

---

1. Read so as opposed to the text as written [p. 453, line 13], "I will be zealous."

were huge bonfires that the Romans stationed there had ignited and lit to drive off the night cold. There were 5,000 valiant Roman warriors and 150 experienced carpenters, masons, and blacksmiths. This was on the twenty-seventh day of the month Kislev in the ninth month of Titus's attack on Jerusalem. When Elazar went forth from Jerusalem with his 100 heroes, he and his heroes went forth leaping and jumping, and suddenly they leaped upon the Romans sitting in that place near the bonfires to warm themselves from the night cold. Some of the Romans were standing, others lying, and the Jews smote them at will with sword, cutting, killing, and destroying until not one of them was left. Many of them burned in the bonfires that were there, and they burned the ram beams with fire, they destroyed the iron of the rams and their horns until no structure of them remained, and the segments of the siege engines, the dikes, the masts, the weights, the rings, the ropes, the chains, and the cables they destroyed them in the fire and with stones until there remained nothing standing. They captured alive the skilled craftsmen who knew to build the weapons of destruction and burned them in the bonfires that were there: not one of them survived.

At morning light, Titus looked from a distance, and behold, smoke rises from the blaze of the trees, and the men burning and the stench of the smoke of those stinking and burning in the blaze emitted a vile stench that stank the camp.[2] He and all his camp ran to see what this was all about. Elazar, the bandit hero, with his 100 heroes carried away as many burned pieces as they could from the parts of the burned weapons of destruction, and each man carried a head of the artisans killed in the fire; they went with praise and thanks to God before them and ridicule, laughter, and derision against the Romans behind them; and they entered the gate of Jerusalem from which they sallied. Yoḥanan and Shimon received them in honor, and they too won there a reputation for valor.

266. At that time, many hordes assembled from all the nations, and they came to Jerusalem to aid the Romans from all the realm of the Caesarate of Roma, which was then at the height of its success, and the Caesar was Espasianus, father of Titus. Titus related to the leaders of the nations who came to assist him all that had happened to him in the war against Jerusalem, and he told them all the might of the courageous acts that the Jews had done against him: how they destroyed his warriors, wiped out his officers, ruined his men, and saddened his spirit in their battles, burning all the weapons of destruction and all his military equipment. Those men were astounded, and all the

---

2. Translation attempts to preserve the author's alliteration. [SB]

masses of gentiles were very much amazed at his words. He said to them: "The Jews still have courage and reputation and have had astounding battles with us; I can't tell even one of a thousand. Have you leaders of the gentile hordes seen in all your lives four men stand against 10,500 men, and all of them battle veterans; nor could the mass of 10,500 warriors capture those four men alive or kill them while they were in their midst smiting and killing, causing casualties around them just as one lops the tips of long gourds with sharp and heavy knives, as happened to us with four lads from Jerusalem's youth?" The gentile hordes and their leaders continued to be increasingly more and more amazed by the words of Titus about this. At that time, Titus said to the leaders of the gentile hordes who came to assist him, his officers, his warriors, and his army: "Do give us your council what we can do about this and not become disgraced, pilloried, and shamed when all the kingdoms on Earth hear about us, for those who hear from afar without knowing the Jews and their valorous acts will not believe this thing that is told them."

The leaders of the gentile hordes answered him, saying: "If it is good in the eyes of our lord, behold, the Romans are wearied and fatigued by the battles that encompass you from the Jews; now let them rest, and we who come now—and we are not fatigued—we shall try if we can to succeed in battle with them, for how can they withstand a great mass like our hordes?" Then the Roman generals said to Titus: "Thanks but no thanks to them for this [offer], for it will add grief to our gloom and pain to our suffering, for they too will fall as casualties before the Jews, and this too will be a disgrace upon us. If we who know their comings and doings[3] and their tactics cannot withstand them, when one of them puts to flight a thousand of us,[4] what can they do who have not tested them? Will not their value be before them like wall-hyssops before the cedars of Lebanon?"[5] The leaders of those hordes of gentiles said: "No! We shall go up against them and fight them[6] and win for ourselves a name for courage." And the leaders of those gentile hordes entreated the man Titus exceedingly, so he gave them leave to go up against the Jews and fight against them, saying: "Perhaps Jews will fall before these gentile masses who will do battle with them without fear, for they [Jews] do not know their [gentiles'] courage. Whereas when the Romans fight them, they fight with fear and trepidation."

----

3. See 2 Sam 3:25.
4. Josh 23:10.
5. 1 Kings 5:13.
6. Deut 1:41.

Eighty thousand men from those gentile hordes assembled: ten thousand Makedonians, twenty thousand from Britania, five thousand Armenians, ten thousand from Africa, ten thousand warriors from Burgonia, five thousand from the Bnei Kedar [Arabs], twenty thousand heroes from the warriors of Persia and Kasdim, and they were boisterous and bragged, and there was not a Roman among them. They went to the level place at the corner of the tomb of Yoḥanan, the high priest, and began to do battle with the Jews atop the wall and set ladders with wooden equipment protecting them to mount the wall against them. Yoḥanan, the bandit chieftain, said to Shimon and Elazar, his colleagues: "Do you agree that I go out and fight these uncircumcised and show them my valor?" Shimon said to him: "Two of us will go out, and one will stand at the gate, for there are many of them, and you will not prevail against them by yourself with only a few." Elazar said: "This advice is correct, and I will go out with Yoḥanan." Shimon said to them: "Both of you go out against them, and the Lord of the Sanctuary and the Temple in Jerusalem will put them in your hand and will not judge you at this time according to your paths and deeds."

Yoḥanan and Elazar sallied with 1,500 bandit warriors and smote sword cuts among the gentile hordes, killing and destroying from the morning of the battle until its evening. This occurred on the ninth of the month Tevet, the tenth since Titus came against Jerusalem. They destroyed from those gentile hordes 57,500 men and captured alive 3,000 officers and routed the remainder. Of the Jews, there fell on that day seven men, and the bandits brought their casualties into Jerusalem to bury them, lest the uncircumcised mistreat them. Yoḥanan and Elazar entered Jerusalem with their heroes amid laudation and thanks to God, while the fleeing remnants of those gentile hordes returned to Titus's camp in disgrace and reproach, shame and degradation. Titus said to them: "Your sentence is appropriate since you did not believe the Romans. Now your dead have won a reputation of shame and disgrace, and you, the remnant, are disgraced and degraded on this day." On the following day, the bandits took the 3,000 officers whom they captured alive, and they gouged one eye from each one and cut off a hand of everyone one of them, and they sent them to Titus's camp to be a shame and a disgrace for him.[7]

267. And it came to pass at that time that Titus took counsel with his officers, his warriors, and his Roman army and all the additional gentiles with them, saying: "What can be done against Israel and his valor, for all the warriors are fatigued from battling the bandits?" Each of his officers gave council to Titus

---

7. Compare Romanos II "Bulgaroctonos," about whose blinding of the Bulgarian army the author may have known. [SB]

according to his skill and wisdom to advise. All their council was contempt-ible to Titus, so he did not accept any of it, for it was not right in his eyes. Titus spoke to them in these words, saying: "This is my own council for Israel,[8] from which I will not swerve! Let us besiege this city without fighting, for their sustenance is finished and they have no food; perhaps famine will destroy them. Also, perhaps when they see that we do not engage in battle with them, they might fight against each other and do unto themselves what we desire to do unto them."

8. Isa 14:26.

4. AN INCIDENT BETWEEN YOSEPH BEN GURION AND THE BANDITS

274. Gurion the priest, father of Yoseph the priest, author of this book to Israel to be a witness and a memory for them, was at this time imprisoned in fetters and iron chains in one of the towers of Jerusalem, and he was aged, advanced in years, 103 years old, and no one came to him in the tower and no one left. During that time, his son Yoseph approached the wall at a distance opposite the tower in which his father, Gurion, was imprisoned, and he drew near a bit to know how his father was and what was done to him. Yoseph passed close to the wall of that tower, eyes fixed upon the tower where his father was imprisoned. Perhaps he could see the face of his father through the windows of the tower or via the slots in the tower that arrows are shot, and he could comfort him and speak to him personally and inform him that he was alive. Every time he passed that tower and he was looking up at it, the bandits would throw small rocks at him, and a large rock hit him in the head and smote him, and he fell off his chariot to the ground. The bandits hastened to descend to capture him. The Romans saw that Yoseph had fallen from his chariot and told this to Titus. Titus hastened and ordered his warriors to go to save him before the bandits reached him. The Romans did what Titus commanded, and they went to him, raised him, held him, and led him slowly, surrounding him with their shields from above and round about against the arrows and stones that the bandits threw at him from atop the wall; so the Romans saved him, and he did not die. The bandits in their haste to capture Yoseph because he had fallen raised a great cry.

275. Yoseph's mother was then eighty-five years old, and she was living in the house of Shimon the Cruel, which was near the tower, imprisoned without chains, but they did not let her leave the house. When the sound of the cry

containing Yoseph's name was heard, she asked those near her, saying: "What is this noise in my ears with the name Yoseph?"

They told her, saying: "The bandits raised a hue about her son Yoseph when they sallied to capture him, having struck him, and he had fallen from his chariot." Then the mother of Yoseph ben Gurion ran and went out of the house in which she had been imprisoned and mounted the wall as if she were fourteen years old. She placed her two hands on her head, disheveling her head, and her hair was white as snow from her curls to her girdle. She raised her voice in weeping and wailing and bitter voice, saying to all who heard her these words: "To this calamity has all my hope come, and to this has come my anticipation that I expected to live after the death of my son Yoseph, light of my eyes; now my great light is dead, and I will not be able to see him and bury him. And was not my hope and wish that he would bury me and in my old age feed me? In my sorrow and grief that I saw my family destroyed and wiped out by the bandits, I said, 'This one will comfort me.'[1] And now what will I do? There is no comfort for me from all the sons I bore, for the persecutors and the enemies of God among the bandits and the gentiles have destroyed eighteen sons. What else is there to do? Just to seek death, for I no longer lust for life. How can I be comforted when I see that my son is dead and I cannot bury him? Who would fill my request that I die this moment, for I do not desire to live after the death of my son Yoseph? Would that I die now with him and cover him with the clothes upon my flesh, as one cloak can cover two people and both he and I lie together as he is lying." Yoseph's mother ascended farther up the wall until she reached the tower; she stretched out her palms heavenward, spreading them, crying out in a loud and bitter voice, and her cry magnified, and her soul became more and more bitter. Crying bitterly and imploring, she says: "My son Yoseph, my son my son,[2] first born of my womb, my son, where are you? Speak to my heart; console me for I find no comfort."

The bandits listening to her laughed and made fun of her, and they were standing with her on the wall. The Romans below, outside the wall, when they heard her voice and Yoseph told them that she was his mother, they wept at her voice and grieved with the bitterness of her heart. The Jews too in Jerusalem, except for the bandits, wept at her voice exceedingly. They just hid their weeping, lest the men of Shimon the Cruel see them. Then the mother of Yoseph said to the bandits who were with her on the wall: "Why don't you kill me? Did I not bear Yoseph, my son, whom you killed? Did I not nurse him with these two

---

1. Gen 5:29.
2. 2 Sam 19:1.

breasts? Did I not raise him and bring him up and nourish him? And you, the enemies of God, you destroyed him with the rest of God's righteous. So now why do you let me live and not kill me? Let God judge between me and you who killed my son for no fault."[3] The bandits said to her: "Is it not in your hands now to drop yourself from the wall and die? Permission is given to you by us. Why don't you do so, and the Romans will receive you and bury you with honor, for we shall inform them that you are the mother of Yoseph the priest, well known to them and beloved by them."

She responded and said to them: "Woe, enemies of God, how can I do this great wickedness that I harm myself, that I bring about my own death with my hands, that I force my soul to leave my body ere my Lord requests it? Is it not known to everyone of intelligence that even if the soul is wiser than all the souls, if her master forces her to leave her nest without the permission of the elements for this, this soul is destroyed and lost and has no continuity and remainder? So how can I do this deed to myself, as my soul acknowledges the mishaps and happenstances of this world and [knows that] everything under heaven has its time and season?[4] And if you say: 'What advantage will I have if you kill me, for when you kill me, my soul shall be forced to leave her nest against the agreement of the elements of my body,' you have spoken in vain and uttered a total lie,[5] for there is a great difference between the two incidents even if both of them are equally bad.

"For if you kill me, I shall not hasten or hurry about this matter; rather, I shall strengthen my intellect to imagine my resting place and conceptualize for myself the passage of my soul's journey and engage in the task of parting with my corpse and leave off directing my body, putting it aside, nor will I prevent my physical nature from agreeing to death, and I will collect and assemble all my thoughts and ideas to cleave unto God our Lord. I will study intellectually the order of reality, and my soul will fly away from my corpse when I reach the study of the upper realm, and there my intellect will stay and rest, and I will be with God always, witnessing his loveliness along with the rest of the souls of the righteous each in his own place.

"But if I were to injure myself, once I imagine how I could injure myself enough to kill myself, my intellect would abandon its thought and hastily interrupt its study, and the physical nature of my corpse would not all agree to this since my intellect will not engage in the process of my soul parting from my

---

3. Only a mother could argue so under the circumstances. [SB]
4. Eccl 3:17.
5. Micah 2:11.

corpse; rather, it would continue to direct my body and will not agree to the action of the imagination that should serve it, and the elements of my nature will avoid agreeing on the parting of my soul, so I will die with my soul still in my body, and my soul will be frightened because of the action of my intellect when the great storm, which is of death, reaches my soul because of me. For this reason, there is a law among every people and nation not to bury anyone that injures himself or is a suicide, for there is nothing enduring to their soul and they do not have a share in the resurrection of the dead: for people bury the corpses of their dead, with the purpose [not only] that those corpses will not arouse grief in the relatives—for this the Indians burn all those who die among them who has stature in his family—but also they preserve them in a place that will remind the mourners to keen and wail lest they suddenly become lost to them, and this is the law among every people except for a few nations. Also to prevent the stench of those corpses from fouling the air inhaled by the living so that the living would die in it from the damaging factor that occurs among things that are naturally similar. And this is a general law among all the peoples under the heavens.

"In addition there is another reason[6] for burial such as the dust of the buried will be dispersed after some time to receive the spirit of life during the process of resurrection known to the divine spirits and known to all flesh; the spirit of life returns to it again, for it gathers and collects and shapes to the material prepared by those who implement the process who do this by the mouth of God. If a person will not be buried, and his corpse would be exposed to birds of the sky or animals of the earth[7] so that the dust of the body does not return to the earth as it was and its *ruaḥ* [spirit] returns to the God who gave it, behold, then the material of that corpse will not be collected and prepared for future resurrection, except after many permutations[8] pass over them in many periods; in every generation, there are innumerable causes that deny and prevent preparation for receiving resurrection, and this is God's secret among its worshipers. But you flock of bandits will not know it or understand it, for you are considered as animals, and the one who reveals his secret to you is a sinner in his soul."

When the bandits heard her words, again they mocked her, putting to derision and mockery the light of life, since they hated the sense of her words that sate the souls of sages with a plenitude of joy. She continued to weep until the

---

6. Literally "sign" or "letter"; the Hebrew *oth* perhaps reflecting a Latin *siglum*. My thanks to Alfred Ivry for his help with this Nec-Platonic speech by the mother. [SB]

7. Deut 28:26.

8. This seems to be a reference to metempsychosis. [SB]

whole Roman camp and many of the Hasidim Jews remaining in Jerusalem wept at her voice, for they heard her words and took to heart her utterances of wisdom. Yoseph, the priest son of Gurion the priest, heard the sound of his mother's words speaking to the bandits in a loud voice—he was below on the ground outside the wall opposite her. When he heard her voice, she was still on the wall; he took courage, girding himself, and neared closer to the wall; the Roman heroes surrounding him with their shields, hiding him to cover him lest a rock or arrow injure him from atop the wall, and Yoseph called out to his mother, saying: "Do not fear, mother, I escaped the hand of the bandits, and God did not give me into their hands. But would that I died on this day before I witnessed the burning of the Temple of God and the destruction of my people, for the *nephashot* [souls] within us are considered as prisoners in custody, and when they leave our corpses with the agreement of our nature and the desire of our intellect conceives of its resting place, the remaining *neshamah* [soul] goes forth free; so they go from darkness to light and light up with the light of life of our Lord God. The wicked advisers who were advising you, sainted mother, to injure yourself and to commit suicide by telling you: 'You have permission to drop yourself from the wall to the earth to your death,' I heard their words, and I heard your answer to them, and I knew before I heard that this would be your answer. Heaven forbid that the mother of Yoseph and the wife of Gurion follow the advice of the wicked; therefore, mother, suffer the bandits' yoke as best you can and submit to them and do not fight with happenstance that you cannot avoid, for they will perish and we shall survive."

GESTA ALEXANDROS

TRANSLATOR'S NOTE

The charismatic appeal of the conquering Alexander survives in the plethora of multilingual versions of Pseudo-Kallisthenes's early romance of Alexander.[1] It is also evidenced in the fulfillment of the promise made by the high priest in Jerusalem to magnify Alexander's name among newborn Jewish males, a practice followed through the millennia by myriads of Jews from the steppes of Asia to the plains of America.[2]

Many of the medieval Hebrew romances about Alexander were derived from vernacular versions of Pseudo-Kallisthenes. Some of these have been interpolated into different versions of *Sepher Yosippon*; others are extant as independent treatises.[3] One therefore might ask, Why translate this version?

Two factors, one historical and the other philological, justify the inclusion of this Alexander Romance in the present volume. As Flusser's introductory essay shows, the text presented here is based on an interpolation into *Sepher Yosippon* preserved in a fourteenth-century Italian manuscript. This interpolation, however, had already been inserted in *Sepher Yosippon* by the eleventh century

---

1. Cf. introductions to Albert Mugrdich Wolohojian, *The Romance of Alexander the Great by Pseudo-Callisthenes* (New York, 1979), Armenian; Israel J. Kazis, *The Book of the Gests of Alexander of Macedon* (Cambridge, MA, 1962), Hebrew; E. A. Wallis Budge, *The History of Alexander the Great* (Cambridge, MA, 1889), Syriac; Budge, *The Life and Exploits of Alexander the Great* (London, 1896), Ethiopic; E. H. Haight, *The Life of Alexander of Macedon by Pseudo-Callisthenes* (New York, 1955), Greek alpha text (ed. Wilhelm Kroll, *Historia Alexandri Magni* [Berlin, 1926]); Joseph Dan, *Aliloth Alexander Mukdon* (Jerusalem, 1969), Hebrew. *Yosippon*, chap. 10. See Joseph Dan, *The Hebrew Story in the Middle Ages* (Jerusalem, 1974), 100–108.

2. Discussed by Kazis, *Book of the Gests*, 28ff, chap. 2.

3. Conveniently summarized by Saskia Dönitz, "Alexander the Great in Medieval Hebrew Traditions," in *A Companion to Alexander Literature in the Middle Ages*, ed. Z. David Zuwiyya (Boston, 2011), 21–39.

in a more literary and altered fashion. Hence, it represents one of the earliest expansions (i.e., interpolations) of *Yosippon* and itself is the earliest Alexander Romance extant in Hebrew (chaps. 1–12).

In addition, this interpolation includes a lost Byzantine chronicle, ultimately derived from Eusebius yet preserving historical data that is unique (chap. 13). This latter contribution to our historical knowledge alone would justify the translation. Finally, this important interpolation includes a fragment from the end of Palladias's "On the Brahmans" and a variant version of the Talmudic story of Alexander located in Tractate *Tamid* 32b (chap. 14).[4]

As important as the historical contributions of this interpolation is its philological importance. A close examination of the Hebrew text reveals that the Hebrew author translated his text directly, even word for word and following the word order of the Greek original.[5] This literal dependence has been preserved in the following English translation for comparative purposes with other Greek versions. The names too have been transliterated rather than Anglicized in order to preserve the flavor of the original, in which they were difficult to decipher for the reader.[6] The lack of elegance in the translation is deliberate. It would have been easier to make texts reader friendly; however, that would not assist scholars to understand the translator's method or his relationship to the original text from which he worked. These points were pointed out by Flusser in his essay preceding the Alexander Romance. Now the reader and researcher can follow these points in more detail.[7]

More of value for deeper scholarly research is the contention of its modern editor that the Alexander Romance before us is a direct translation from a very early Greek copy of Pseudo-Kallisthenes, perhaps one as early as that used

---

4. Cf. David Flusser, "An 'Alexander Geste' in a Parma MS," *Tarbiz* 26 (1956–57): 165–84, English section, p. 5; this is summarized in Kazis, *Book of the Gests*, 35–37; Flusser, *Josippon*, 2.215–60.

5. See comments in my review of *A Hebrew Alexander Romance*, by Wout J. Van Bekkum, *Journal of Jewish Studies* 48 (1997): 166–67. There I suggested that those translations might possibly be student exercises. It is also a possibility to consider here.

6. Indeed, the popular editions of *Yosippon* have even further corrupted the names; e.g., in Hominer's edition, Boukephalon becomes Botsiphal (Hominer, *Josiphon*, 40), but beginning in chap. 6, one finds a more expanded interpolation of the Alexander romance that begins with his youth and the seduction of his mother. Our romance begins with Hominer's chap. 9 and the Byzantine chronicle in chap. 15, with further interpolations, among which a later author forces the identification of Joseph ben Gurion with Josephus (Hominer, *Josiphon*, 43).

7. This revised and corrected translation supersedes an earlier version that appeared as "Alexander and the Mysteries of India," *Journal of Indo-Judaic Studies* 2 (1999): 71–111.

by the Armenian translation (alpha version).[8] Thus, it preserves the structure and tone of the original. Moreover, since it is so literal (even to the detriment of Hebrew style and at times of comprehension), it is of immense importance in any scholarly attempt to restore the original text of Pseudo-Kallisthenes. The Parma interpolation, then, supersedes in value the later, more corrupted interpolations that appear in subsequent versions of *Yosippon*.[9]

Yet the Hebrew rendition is not merely a slavish translation of Pseudo-Kallisthenes. The anonymous author has attempted through omissions and additions to Judaize the text, that is, to make it acceptable to his Jewish intellectual and religious audience. Pseudo-Kallisthenes begins his Alexander Romance with the wonderful story of Nectanebus, Pharaoh of Egypt and master magician, who seduces Olympia, the wife of Phillip of Makedon, and thus sires Alexander the Great.[10] Given the author of *Yosippon*'s brilliant satirical pun on Paulina (see chap. 57), the absence of this story suggests that he did not know the entire text of Pseudo-Kallisthenes. The translator of Pseudo-Kallisthenes, on the other hand, does not see any historical value in this folk story, which itself is but an elaboration of Alexander's recognition as a god by the priesthood of the Siwa Oasis, who identified the conqueror of Egypt as the son of Ammon and Olympias. Therefore, he omitted it from his translation.[11] Such a story, in any case, bordered on the ridiculous to his more sophisticated and intellectually trained Jewish audience in Italy.[12]

The rest of the marvels related by Pseudo-Kallisthenes follow his summary of Alexander's successful wars. Finally, Alexander reaches the land of impenetrable darkness (chap. 6). There he meets inter alia the descendants of Yonadav ben Rechab, better known to posterity as the Rechabites. Later he encounters two fowl in that foul land, which predict Alexander's imminent conquest of India and his victory over its King Poros (in chap. 7). Whereupon Alexander decides to return to his camp and implements his sage and cautious preparation against losing his way, by following the dam that he took with him to her colt that was tethered at the entrance to that land of impenetrable darkness.[13]

---

8. See note 1 above.

9. See note 6 above. Since the Parma MS has never been translated, the literalness is justified for scholarly purposes.

10. A comparison of the Hebrew version in Kazis, *Book of the Gests*, with that of the Armenian in Wolohojian, *Romance of Alexander the Great*, shows the tendency of the Hebrew tradition to tone down the miraculous sensuality of this episode.

11. So Flusser argues (see note 5 above).

12. Cf. Flusser, *Josippon* 2.248–60.

13. This is not in the Armenian version (Wolohojian, *Romance of Alexander the Great*, 116), or the Hebrew version (*apud* Kazis, *Book of the Gests*) and differs from the legends in b. *Tamid* 32 a–b.

A text that sheds some light on this passage is the *History of the Rechabites*, which was in wide circulation during the Middle Ages in Greek, Ethiopic, and Syriac.[14] In retrospect, it seems difficult to assume that such a text was not known to our translator of Pseudo-Kallisthenes. On the other hand, it is not impossible that the translator had before him a Greek text in which the identification of the "Blessed Ones" had already been made by a previous editor. This question can only be resolved by further scholarly investigation based on a thorough edition of the Pseudo-Kallisthenes that was available to the editor or translator of the present edition.

Elements of the *History of the Rechabites* are relevant to a commentary on this interpolation into Pseudo-Kallisthenes. Chapters 8–10 of the Syriac version strongly suggest a lost Hebrew apocryphon that would predate both the undated *History of the Rechabites* (guesstimated to the first to fourth century) and very possibly the original of Pseudo-Kallisthenes (third to fourth century). Our Hebrew text, as we should recall here, is based on an early rendition of Pseudo-Kallisthenes's Alexander Romance.

The parallels between the *History of the Rechabites* and the History of the Brahmans should also be noted. While the Hebrew interpolation is clearly based on a Greek edition, the *History of the Rechabites* emphasizes the solitary intercourse between a man and his wife. Also, in chapter 8 of our Alexander Romance, the nude sages of India are called "Gymnosophists," while in the *History of the Rechabites*, the inhabitants are also naked.[15] There, however, the source is Pseudo-Kallisthenes, whose relation to the *History of the Rechabites* needs further study.

An area of research that needs to be explored is the tradition that attributes immortality to the descendants of Yonadav ben Rechab. While based on the passage in Jeremiah (35:19), the tradition is not extant in Hebrew literature until its appearance in the *Alphabet of Ben Sira*, a midrash that may be tentatively dated to the eighth–ninth century from unknown Jewish circles in Babylonia.[16] While

---

14. Most recently translated by James H. Charlesworth, *History of the Rechabites*, in his *The Old Testament Pseudepigrapha*, vol. 2 (Garden City, NY, 1985), 450–61. The core of this text (chaps. 8–10) has been assigned to the first century prior to the destruction of the Temple; cf. Elbert Garrett Martin, "The Account of the Blessed Ones: A Study of the Development of an Apocryphon on the Rechabites and Zosimus (The Abode of the Rechabites)" (PhD diss., Duke University, 1979), esp. 205ff.

15. See note 14 above.

16. Eli Yassif, *The Tales of Ben Sira in the Middle Ages: A Critical Text and Literary Studies* (Jerusalem, 1984), in Hebrew, suggests that the Rechabites in Christian sources parallel the descendants of Moses in the tradition of Eldad ha-Dani and Muslim legend. Cf. *Chronicles of Jerahmeel*, trans. Moses Gaster, with prolegomenon by Haim Schwarzbaum (New York,

the Christians had inserted this material into their traditions about Zosimus (or the *History of the Rechabites*), none of the early lists of Jewish immortals from the Talmudic period (second to fifth centuries) include the Rechabites. Therefore, one should ask why the tradition surfaces in the *Alphabet of Ben Sira*, whenever that midrash was finally edited.

This late list of immortals includes the following:[17]

> Enoch, servant of the Ethiopian king
> Seraḥ daughter of Asher
> Rabbi Judah's servant
> Batya, daughter of Pharaoh
> Yabetz
> Ḥiram, king of Tyre
> Rabbi Joshua ben Levi
> Eliezer, servant of Abraham
> Milḥom the bird and its seed
> Yonadav ben Rechab and his descendants

Of these, the final two are later additions, Milḥom and Yonadav ben Rechab.[18] The former, Milhom, seems to be the rabbinic equivalent of the Phoenix tradition, which had become a symbol of resurrection and immortality to the Christians.[19] The inclusion of Yonadav ben Rechab, on the other hand, in this list may be connected to his appearance in the Alexander Romance translated here, although the date of that translation has a *terminus post quem* of the eleventh-century manuscript within which it appears. Further studies of the Rechabites will have to clarify the relationship of these two texts, one from Arabic-speaking Babylonia and the other from the Greek-speaking environment of southern Italy. Since both the Rechabites and the Phoenix were already longtime symbols of immortality in Christian lands, it may be that the *Alphabet of Ben Sira* additions are indebted to Western sources (perhaps via Byzantine southern Italy).

1971), chap. 61 and p. 69. In a teasing aside, Cecil Roth, *The History of the Jews of Italy* (Philadelphia, 1946), 61, suggests an Italian provenance for the text.

17. Cf. text in J. D. Eisenstein, *Ozar Midrashim*, vol. 1 (New York, 1956), 50, and comments in Yassif, *Tales of Ben Sira*, 104; cf. *Yalkut Shimoni*, Ezek 28.

18. Cf. discussion in Yassif (n. 15), 109–10.

19. Cf. Ben Zion Wacholder and Steven Bowman, "Ezechielus the Dramatist and Ezechiel the Prophet: The Identification of the Mysterious *Zoon* in Ezechielus' *Exagoge*," *Harvard Theological Review* 78, nos. 3–4 (1985): 253–87.

It is not yet possible to unravel the connection between the popular Muslim and Jewish traditions about the descendants of Moses and their probable identification with the Rechabites.[20] What is certain is that so far as our extant sources indicate, the medieval traditions of the Rechabites have appeared (or reappeared) in the context of immortality by the ninth–tenth centuries; and it is not unlikely, then, that the translator of the Alexander Romance before us drew from this contemporary phenomenon. In that case, we should like to place him in the context of the renaissance of medieval Hebrew literature connected with Italian Jewry in the tenth to eleventh centuries.[21]

20. See chap. 6 below.
21. Cf. Flusser, *Josippon*, vol. 2.

I. DEATH OF PHILIPOS

I begin the romance of Alexandros:[1] Philipos, father of Alexandros, the Makedonian, ruled over Makedon and Yavan[2] for six years; and, through his great force and valor, he subdued and enslaved all the inhabitants surrounding his territory, and he subdued the Yevanim [Greeks] under his hand. Then Piltinos the king died,[3] and Philipos fought against the city of Byzantion,[4] and Philipos sent Alexandros, his son, against the city Thrakis[5] with a great force to fight against her. Then Pausanios Salonikon,[6] a valiant and rich man, desired and lusted to whore with Olympiada,[7] mother of Alexandros; he sent to her dolceurs to seduce her to leave her husband, but she did not accept. When Pausanios saw that Alexandros was off fighting, he took in hand his weapons, he and other veterans with him,[8]

---

1. This text is preserved in MS de Rossi 1087 in Parma, which contains three translations, most likely from the Greek: (a) the Greek romance on Alexander of Makedon; (b) an unknown Byzantine chronicle from Alexander to Augustus; (c) the end of Palladius's Book on the Brahmans. The later interpolations of the first two translations are somewhat confused; thus, this translation is from the original in the Parma MS, with occasional corrections from *Yosippon*. Also folio 5 of the Parma MS has been lost, and its translation has been supplied from *Yosippon*. Cf. Flusser, "Alexander Geste," English summary, p. 5. The original text occasionally has the form Alexandros (Greek), which seems to be a local tradition; the name has been standardized for this edition.
2. Makedonia and Greece are usually separate entities in Hebrew sources.
3. The Romance (1.23) speaks of Mothone (in the southwestern Peloponnesos), against which Alexander fought. The confusion perhaps stems from this name.
4. Medieval Constantinople, which Philip besieged in 340 BCE. This datum is not in the novel on Alexander.
5. Romance 1.23 has Philip send Alexander with a large force against a city of the Thracians.
6. Romance 1.24 has Pausanias the Thessalonikan.
7. Olympias.
8. Follows the Greek word order (μετὰ ἄλλων ἀνδρῶν γενναίων) rather than the Hebrew word order.

and he went to kill Philipos and take his wife; he smote Philipos a serious blow in his ribs,[9] but he did not die; and the land moaned.

On that day, Alexandros came from a victory of the war, and he beheld a great upheaval in the city and asked, "What is this?" When he heard the matter, he entered his father's palace and beheld his mother caught in Pausanios's hand; he longed to smite him with his sword, but he feared lest he kill his mother. His mother said to him: "Smite him!" So he smote him a great blow. Then Alexandros saw that his father still lived, so he took the sword and gave it to his father and said to him: "Take the sword and avenge your death!" Whereupon his father smote him, and Pausanios died. Then Philipos also died, and his son Alexandros buried him. Alexandros at age twenty succeeded his father, and he was wise[10] in every wisdom and constellations and in every matter; he was a warrior, and his teacher who taught him wisdom was Aristoteles the sage.[11] And this Alexandros, his image resembled neither his father nor his mother, Olympiada, for the form of his face was that of a lion, and his eyes were disfigured—his right eye was black and looked down,[12] while his left eye was white like a cat's eye;[13] his teeth were sharp like dog fangs,[14] and he was quick as a lion from his childhood.

---

9. So in source.

10. Follows Romance 1.13.

11. The source names additional teachers.

12. Renders Greek κατωφέρη.

13. Not found in other versions.

14. Comparison varies in other versions.

2. BEGINNING OF HIS WARS

His [Alexandros's] first battles[1] are recounted and considered as his father's wars: he found the Makedonians two myriads and 5,000 [25,000][2] and the fighting men 8,700 and Thrakes[3] 2,500, and the nation of Iskytos [Scythians] passing before him[4] 800, and the rest of the peoples constituting his army 60,600; all these he took out in the army. He took out five thousand talents of gold and gave this outlay for a fine fleet of one hundred ships. He took out another one thousand talents of gold and gave [them] to his army in Sikiliah [Sicily] and enslaved them under him.[5]

He crossed again into Italiah,[6] and the nobles of Romi [Rome] hearing [this] sent to him a crown made with pearls and gold,[7] and he accepted it with joy. From there he crossed by sea[8] and went against Afrikiyah, and the leaders of the army of the land went forth to greet him, and he set a tax over the land. He crossed from there into the land of Lybiah[9] and subdued it under him. Then he crossed into the land of Barbari[10] and went unto the river Okynus;[11] he beheld its waters pure and fresh[12] and craved to swim and bathe in the river, so he stripped off his clothes

---

1. Based on Romance 1.26.
2. Figures vary in different versions.
3. The source too mentions the Thracians.
4. Renders Greek προδρόμους.
5. So in Romance 1.29.
6. Based on Romance 1.29. In fact, Alexander never crossed into Italy.
7. Greek: στέφανον ἐκ χρυσοῦ καί μαργαρίτων κατασκευάσμενον.
8. Romance 1.30.
9. Transliterates Greek Λυβίη (Heb. Lub).
10. Romance 2.7 has Greeks going against the barbarians, which the translator understood as Berber Land in North Africa. Thus, he connects this story with the previous one on Libya.
11. Romance 2.8 has Okynos instead of Kydnos, which flows in Anatolian Cilicia.
12. Renders Greek οὗ τὸ ὕδωρ καθαρόν ἐστι καί διαυγέστατον.

and washed in the river. After he went out from the river, he felt ill, and his head pained, and he became very sick,[13] and Philipos the physician cured him with potions and ointments.[14] From there he crossed[15] into the land of Madai and the land of Paras [Persia][16] and the land of Great Ararat,[17] enslaving them under him. Then he crossed the river Phrat [Euphrates] and went into the land of Baktriani;[18] he stayed there and seized that place.

13. Renders Greek ἤλγησε τὴν κεφαλὴν καὶ χαλεπῶς διέκειτο.

14. Renders Greek τὸ πόσιμον φάρμακον (medicinal drink). The Hebrew formulation also appears in Shabbetai Donnolo, *Sepher ha-yakar*, ed. Sussmann Mŭntner (Jerusalem, 1949), 1.7.

15. Romance 2.9.

16. Added by the author.

17. On Great Armenia μεγάλη Ἀρμενία, cf. *Yosippon*, chap. 88, for identification of Armenia = Ararat.

18. Romance 2.10 has Βακτριανὴ χώρα; var. Βακτριανῶν χώρα (Land of the Baktrians).

3. WAR WITH DARIUS

When Darius,[1] king of Madai,[2] heard, he sent letters to him [Alexandros]: "I am Darius, king of kings and lord over all nations of the Earth. Know ye, Alexandros, my great name! Know ye not my name that even the God has honored me and established my throne?[3] How did you dare to cross the sea without my permission? And how were you enthroned over the nation of Makedon? Was this not enough for you, yet you took locales from my territory. Should you not have taken permission from me like a slave from his lord? Therefore, I have written to you that you should come to me and prostrate yourself before Darius, your god[4]—and if you disobey, I will imprison you unto death,[5] while if you come, I swear to you by the life of my father[6] that I will have compassion upon you for everything you have done."

Alexandros read[7] the letter but did not take the words seriously; rather, he trembled and filled with anger,[8] and he arrayed the army from his camp in the land of Arav to do battle with Darius. Darius too brought forth a great army, and a major battle ensued, and each side smote many from the other. The sun darkened on that day;[9] there was a great and powerful thunder, and the Persians fled from its noise. Darius left his chariot and mounted a horse and fled; Alexandros pursued him for sixty miles[10] and captured the mother of Darius, his wife, his

---

1. Romance 1.40.
2. The author adds on basis of Hebrew Dan 6:1, 11:1.
3. Greek: οἱ θεοὶ τετιμήκασιν καὶ σύνθρονον ἑαυτῶν ἔκριναν.
4. Renders Greek ἐλθεῖν καὶ προκυνεῖν θεῷ Δαρείῳ.
5. Renders Greek κολάσομαί σε θανάτω ἀνεκλατήτῳ.
6. Renders Greek ὄμνυμι δὲ σοι Δία μέγιστον πατέρα.
7. Romance 1.41.
8. Renders Greek παρωξύνθη.
9. Not in sources.
10. The source has sixty stades.

sons, and his chariot. Darius fled during the night, and Alexandros seized the house of Darius[11] and stayed there. He commanded to bury all the officers and veterans of the Persians;[12] the number of Makedonian dead was 500 infantry and 109 cavalry, and of the barbari,[13] 12 myriads [120,000] were killed, and 40,000 were captured alive, and of the Makedonians, 180 men were wounded.

After Darius fled,[14] he went and brought forth another army greater than the first, and Alexandros sent spies to reconnoiter the army.

---

11. Renders Greek τὴν Δαρείου σκηνήν (tent).
12. Renders Greek τοὺς ἀνδρωδεστάτους καί εὐγενεῖς τῶν Περσῶν.
13. τῶν δὲ βαρβάρων.
14. Romance 1.42.

4. ALEXANDROS IN YAVAN AND IN OTHER PLACES

Alexandros sent again[1] to Iskamandros,[2] general of his army, that he too assemble a great army and that the general of his army come to him with a great force and they go together into the land of Achaea.[3] From there[4] he passed into the land of Bottia and seized the land of Olynthon, all of it, and he crossed into the land of Canaan[5] and subdued all that land first. Then he crossed to the spring of Maiotin,[6] and he found that land starving; there was no food for the army of Makedonians, and many died from the hunger, until the king commanded them to eat from the horses. The king saw that they ate all the horses; and he passed[7] from place to place until he arrived at the city of Lokris,[8] which is Kiriakin;[9]

---

1. Romance 1.42.
2. Greek: Σκάμανδρος.
3. Greek: εἰς τὴν Ἀχαίαν (to Achaia).
4. Romance 1.44. Greek has Καὶ παρεγένετο ἐν δυσὶν ἡμέριαις εἰς τὴν Βοττίαν καὶ τὴν Ὄλυνθον καὶ ἐξεπόρθησεν ὅλην τὴν χώραν τῶν Χαλδαίων (and he arrived in two days at Bottia and Olynthon and destroyed all the land of the Chaldeans). Bottia and Olynthos are two cities in Greece.
5. The source has ἡ χώρα τῶν Χαλδαίων (land of the Chaldeans; Heb. *eretz ha-Kasdim*), but there it is a confusion for "land of the men of Chalkis," which is in Greece. The Hebrew translator rendered Kasdim as Canaan.
6. Greek has πρὸς Μαιωτίδα λίμνην (Maiotis harbor is the Sea of Azov today). The author's MS had Μαιῶτιν.
7. Romance 1.45.
8. Greek has εἰς Λόκρους (to the men of Lokris).
9. In one of the sources, the scribe must have written instead of ἡμέραν μίαν (one day) perhaps ἡμέραν ά (day one), which is Sunday in Hebrew or κυριακήν in Greek. The Hebrew author in turn saw κυριακήν and understood it to be another name for "Lokris," which is Kiriakin.

he entered into the temple of Apollonios[10] and stayed there with his army for one day.[11]

Then he crossed into the land of Agrakantos[12] in Sikiliah[13] to go into the land of Miẓrayim[14] with his army; he commanded his ships called "liverna"[15] to go by sea and cross unto the city of Tripoli and wait for him there, and he too crossed after them. He crossed to the city of Kartagini,[16] which is a large city[17] in the land of Afrikiah, and the measure of the city is 24 miles and 305 feet; he crossed from there to the river Tigris, which is Ḥidekel,[18] and he crossed into the land of Miẓrayim[19] with all his army.

---

10. Renders Greek εἰσελθὼν εἰς τὸ τοῦ Ἀπόλλωνος ἱερόν.

11. See note 9 above: ἡμέραν μίαν.

12. Renders Greek ἦλθε παρὰ τοὺς Ακραγανατίνους (to the men of Akragas); the latter is Agrigento in Sicily. Cf. Adolf Ausfeld, *Der griechische Alexanderroman* (Leipzig, 1907), 57.

13. Added by the author, who knew this perhaps because he came from southern Italy; see chap. 13 below, note 35.

14. Romance 1.34 has him go to Egypt at this point.

15. Greek has τὰ λίβερνα, a type of boat.

16. Source refers to Tripolis in Syria, but the author was thinking of Tripolis, εἰς Τρίπολιν, in North Africa and so added the data from his source (Romance 1.31) on Carthage.

17. See Romance 1.31; figures differ in various MSS.

18. The author follows Romance 1.39, where Alexander reaches Tyre. His MS mistakenly had εἰς Τιγρίν for εἰς Τύρον perhaps. [Afrikiah possibly from Arabic Ifriqiyah. SB]

19. Romance 1.39 has him in Syria. Ausfeld, *Der griechische Alexanderroman*, 57, suggests an error in the Greek version. Perhaps this had already been corrected in the MS that the author used, since Alexander passed from Tyre to Egypt at this point.

5. ALEXANDROS SPIES OUT DARIUS AND DARIUS'S DEATH

All the officers of Darius heard[1] and sent letters to Darius to inform him of the fact; he read the letters and worried much. And it came to pass when Alexandros[2] approached the land of Paras[3] and he saw the walls of the city exceedingly high, then he commanded, and they [his men] seized the sheep and cattle that were in that land and bound field shrubs and grasses to their carcasses and stampeded them, and the brush and grasses were dragged in the earth and threw up dust until the dust rose on high. The Persians saw the dust from afar and said that this dust is from the multitude of horses and from the abundance of his force, and they were terribly afraid.

When he [Alexandros] had approached to within five days'[4] march of Darius's city, he desired to send messengers to Darius to muster for battle, and he said to himself:[5] "If I were to send messengers, I should fear lest Darius might persuade them, and they would hand over my army and myself." He convinced himself to go alone. He took with him[6] one officer,[7] and his name was Eumilon,[8]

---

1. Cf. Romance 1.39 and 2.11–12.
2. Romance 2.13.
3. Variant MS for "city of Πέρσις."
4. So text, which reads ημέρας έ (for five days); see chap. 4, note 9, above.
5. The source has the god Amon give him this advice in a nocturnal dream.
6. Romance 2.14.
7. σατράπην.
8. Εὔμηλον, Greek accusative form of Εὔμηλος; the author uses the accusative form either through the influence of his source or through the Greek-speaking Jewish tradition of rendering names in the accusative; cf. D. Flusser, "Author of the Book *Josippon*," *Zion* 18 (1953): 109n3.

a battle veteran, and three horses with him and crossed the river Istrangan.[9] This river was frozen from the ice, and the frost was like stone;[10] wagons, horses, and cattle crossed over the ice, and after [some] days, it would melt. He [Alexandros] found it frozen;[11] he donned Makedonian garb[12] with a hat upon his head like the Makedonian hats[13] and crossed the river;[14] and the breadth of the river was about a mile.[15]

He came unto the gates of Paras,[16] and the gatekeeper asked him: "Who are you?" He said: "I am a messenger from Alexandros; bring me to him [Darius], and I shall speak with him." So he brought him to him. When he saw Darius dressed in royal clothing with precious stones and gold from his feet to the crown of his head and the golden scepter in his hand,[17] Alexandros was frightened before him. Darius asked him, saying to him: "Who are you?" He said: "I am a messenger from Alexandros, and he sent me to you so that you muster for battle with him—and if you tarry not to fight, know that you have a sickness of the heart[18] such that you cannot fight with my lord." Darius became angry and said to him: "Perhaps you are Alexandros because you speak to me in insult?"[19] He said: "No!" Darius took him for the night to eat and drink with him. And it happened when the chief butler[20] gave him to drink in a golden goblet, each time he put it in his bosom. Darius asked him: "What are you doing?" He said: "Thus do all those summoned to eat with my lord Alexandros." And so, when one of the lords of Darius who stand before him heard the voice of Alexandros, he recognized it and said to his comrade: "This one is Alexandros." Alexandros understood the whisper that they were murmuring in each other's ears that they were speaking about him, so he beguiled them with words and fled from them suddenly during the

---

9. Greek has ἐπὶ τὸν Στράγγαν ποταμὸν; the river was called Στράγγα. Here too the author uses the accusative form (see note 8). The author also adds the prefix "I," as was customary in the Talmud, which reflects demotic Greek usage.

10. Not found in any version of the Romance.

11. Following Romance 2.14.

12. Versions of the Romance do not identify provenance of clothes as Makedonian.

13. Following Romance 2.13.

14. Romance 2.14.80.

15. The source has one stade.

16. The source has πρὸς τὰς πύλας τῆς Περσίδος (i.e., Persians); possibly the error was already in the author's MS; see note 3 above.

17. Following the version in *Yosippon*.

18. Renders ἀσθενῆ ἔχειν τὴν ψυχήν.

19. Renders μετὰ θράσους.

20. Scene follows Romance 2.15.

night with the golden goblet in his bosom and rode upon his horse. He found the gatekeeper of the city sitting before the gate and in his hand a lit olive branch called "daida";[21] he killed him, exited, and left.

The Persians pursued him to capture him, but that night was dark, and they could not see him. He came to the river Istrangan,[22] and after he had crossed the river, the horse could not get its four legs out of the river, for the waters of the river were melting, so he jumped and dismounted from the horse onto the dry land, and the river took the horse. The Persians saw that the river had melted and Alexandros was saved, and they could not cross the river, for no man could cross that river, neither by ship nor by any kind of trick until it was frozen from ice, for it poured out from the mountains.[23] Alexandros went on foot for a bit[24] until he found his officer whom he had stationed there with two horses across the river, and he rode and went to his army.[25]

He mustered his army for battle,[26] counted them, and found them twelve myriads [120,000], and they came unto that river. Darius too came unto that river, and they found it frozen; Darius crossed it with his army. Alexandros rode on his horse, Boukaiphalon;[27] this was the horse that had a head of a bull,[28] and no other horse could draw near to him.

They waged a great battle, and many of the Persians fell. Darius fled with his men and crossed the river. And when the rest of his army, a remnant[29] [surviving] from the battle, came to cross after him, the waters of the river melted and engulfed[30] all of them.

Darius entered the palace of his kingdom, fell upon the ground, and wept in a loud voice. He rose[31] and wrote a letter to Alexandros, saying: "Pity me, pity me, and return my wife and my sons; do not destroy my palace;[32] and I will

---

21. The source has δαίδα (a torch). It is vocalized in the text, which means either the author or his Greek-speaking copyist vocalized this transliteration according to the medieval pronunciation, since neither could translate this word; hence, he added "olive branch," following Mishnah *Rosh ha-shanah* 2:3, even though he did not understand the Mishnaic usage.

22. See above: επì τòν Στράγγαν ποταμòν.

23. Not found in versions of Romance.

24. Greek has ὀλίγον.

25. Romance 2.16.

26. Romance 2.16.

27. Greek has Βουκέφαλον but is vocalized in Hebrew, which indicates that the author's MS had Βουκαίφαλον. The horse was called Boukephalos but written in the accusative case.

28. The author translates the name literally: *bous kephalos*; see chap. 7 below.

29. Greek has τò ἄλλο πλῆθος, which recalls the Hebrew *plitah*.

30. Greek ἥρπασε.

31. Romance 2.17.

32. Not in versions of the Romance.

give you gold aplenty and treasures and seventy of my concubines[33] who are in Shushan."[34]

Alexandros read out the letter unto the ears of all his army.

He laughed over the letter and said: "If he had been victorious over me, none of his gold would be worth anything to me—and if I am victorious over him, all of his gold will come into my hands." He remained in the land of Paras[35] all that flourishing autumn;[36] he sacrificed to other gods;[37] and he burned all the kingdoms of Kserksos.[38]

Darius thought in his heart[39] to muster for battle again with Alexandros and sent to Poros, king of Hodu,[40] to assist him. When Alexandros heard, he went to the land of Madai, for he had heard that Darius had gone to Batanin,[41] and pursued him. When Darius's lords heard[42] that Alexandros had arrived, they killed Darius. And so, when Alexandros arrived, those who murdered Darius fled until they could learn what Alexandros would do to them.[43] When Alexandros came, he found Darius between life and death,[44] and he wept over him in a loud voice,[45] and his spirit went forth in Alexandros's hands.[46] He commanded to bury him in the tombs[47] of kings;[48] Alexandros bore the corpse of Darius, he and his officers; they wept for him and lamented him. And he commanded that they kill the men who had murdered him.

---

33. Not in versions of the Romance, but Romance 2.19 has Darius promise eighty concubines to Poros if Poros were to assist Darius in battle.

34. Greek has ἐν Σούσοις.

35. I.e., Persians, as earlier.

36. Greek has τὸν ἀκμαιότατον χειμῶνα.

37. Greek has τοῖς ἐγχωρίοις θεοῖς.

38. Greek has τὰ Ξέρξου βασίλεια; the Hebrew translator understood βασίλεια as "kingdoms" and assumed the nominative of Ξέρξου to be Ξέρξος.

39. Romance 2.19.

40. Πῶρος; Hebrew for Hind, later India.

41. Greek has ἤκουσε γὰρ τὸν Δαρεῖον ειναι ἐν Ἐκβατάνοις. MS A of the Romance has ἐμβατάνοις; apparently the author's MS had ἐν βατάνοις, which resulted in the above BTNIN, which is vocalized in the Hebrew MS as Batanin by none other than the author.

42. ὁι τοῦ Δαρείου σατράπαι; Romance 2.20.

43. Greek has μέχρις οὗ μάθωσιν ποίαν γνώμην ἔχει παρ' αὐτῶν ὁ Ἀλέξανδρος.

44. Greek has ἡμίπνοον.

45. Greek has ἐπιστάς αὐτῷ πάνυ ἐδάκρυσεν.

46. Greek has ἔλειψε τὸ πνεῦμα ἐν χερσὶν Ἀλεξάνδρου.

47. Romance 2.21.

48. Greek has adverb βασιλικῶς.

6. ALEXANDROS'S TRAVELS IN THE LANDS OF MARVELS

And so when he [Alexandros] had subjected all that land under him,[1] Alexandros thought to cross from there to the land's end and through the desert;[2] he crossed through the land of Madai[3] with many inhabitants and went forth with a great army.

He came to one place and found a road through a really deep ravine:[4] he went through it for eight days and saw animals of every variety. He came to another place toward evening and found trees similar to apples;[5] he saw there men called *pithiki*;[6] their neck was long, and their hands and arms in the shape of a large saw. He commanded [his men] to catch them,[7] and they fled; they [Alexandros's men] killed 162,[8] while they [pithiki] killed of his men 163.[9] He rested the night there and ate of those fruits.

---

1. Romance 2.23.
2. Romance 2.32.
3. Also in the Armenian translation.
4. Greek has φάραγξ βαθυτάτη.
5. Greek has ευρεν ὕλην πόλλην δένδων . . . καρπὸν ἐχόντων μήλοις παρεμφερῆ.
6. μάκρους δὲ τραχήλους ἔχοντες τὰς χεῖρας, καὶ τοὺς πόδας πρίσι παρεμφερεῖς. Greek πίθηκοι not found by Flusser in the versions he was able to examine. It was certainly however in the translator's manuscript apparently as a later explanation for the strange men.
7. Greek has ἐκέλευσεν οὖν συλληφθῆναι ἐξ αὐτῶν.
8. Variants have 332 or 432.
9. Also in Version C of the Romance.

He went from there[10] to the land of klokin.[11] And there were men similar to giants,[12] hairy and red: their faces were like lions,[13] a girdle of skins around their loins, valiant men; and they came against him without weapons[14] and killed of his men 152;[15] he commanded to fire the forest, and the giants fled from the fire.

On the second day, Alexandros went to the caves of the giants and found huge animals[16] similar to dogs bound at the mouths of the caves: their height was four cubits; they were spotted and striped[17] with three eyes. And in the caves were fleas like "frascilona."[18]

From there he passed to another place and saw a hairy man, and he desired to catch him but could not. He commanded to disrobe one woman to send her out to him; perhaps he could be caught through lust; the man took her and led her away at a distance and ate her.[19] They went to catch him by force, and he spoke in his language.[20] Many men like him without number came out of the forest; Alexandros commanded: they [his men] fired the forest, and they [hairy men] fled from the fire. Alexandros captured five hundred[21] of them; they had no sense like other men and barked like dogs.

From there he crossed[22] to another place and found trees there. They sprouted from the ground from sunrise until the sixth hour of the day, and from the sixth hour of the day until sunset, the trees were hidden[23] and continued to diminish

---

10. Romance 2.33.

11. Greek has εἰς τὴν χλοικὴν χῶραν; Greek χλοικὴν (green) was confused in the author's MS as χλαυκὴν (= χλοακὴν of the Byzantine song).

12. Follows Greek literally: ἄνθρωποι γίγασι παρεμφερεῖς.

13. Follows Greek literally: πυρροί, ὄψεις ἔχοντες ὡς λέοντες (*pyrroi* for *adumim*—red).

14. Greek has ἄνευ λογχῶν καὶ βελῶν.

15. Variants have 120.

16. Greek has θηρία προσδεδεμένα ταῖς θύραις τῶν εἰσόδεν. ἦσαν δὲ ὡς κύνες μεγάλοι.

17. Source has ποικίλοι.

18. Source has: ὡς τοὺς παρ' ἡμῖν βατράχους πηδῶντας (as jumping frogs among us). Thus the word "frascilona" is the author's dialect, since all MS of *Yosippon* have *benei yonah* (pigeons). Only the Constantinople edition has "*silonia* and these are *benei yonah*." *Frasilona*, then, is apparently a diminutive of the word *frosc* (frog), i.e., *froscelin*. Maybe then we have a Lombard dialect, which the author learned from his contemporary Italian. This is not conclusive, however, since supporting evidence for this supposition has not been found.

19. Greek has ὁ δὲ ἁρπάσας αὐτήν καὶ δρομαίως ταύτην κατήσθιεν.

20. Greek has ἐταρτάρισε ἐν τῇ γλωττῃ αὐτοῦ.

21. Romance has three or four hundred.

22. Romance 2.36.

23. Greek has ἐξέλειπον ὥστε μὴ φανεῖσθαι ὅλως.

until nothing of them was seen. And the sap[24] of the trees was like "istaktin"[25] of Paras[26] that they burn as incense, and it had an exceedingly wonderful fragrance. He commanded to cut the trees and collect the sap—suddenly the men who were cutting the trees were struck with whips by devils.[27] The sound of the blows was audible and the blows were visible, but the beaters were not visible, though the voice was audible: "Don't cut the trees and don't collect from them!"[28] Crocodiles[29] and fish of many varieties[30] were there within the waters, and the fish could not be cooked, save in fresh and cold water.[31] Roosters[32] like our roosters were in that river; and everyone who went out to catch them the roosters would send forth fire from their body upon him, and the man would burn.

On the following day,[33] he walked for the whole day and found many beasts with five legs[34] and three eyes, and their height was six cubits.[35] He went to another place and found that entire land sand:[36] and he saw beasts like a wild ass,[37] this is an 'arod, and its length was five cubits,[38] and they had six eyes but could only see with two eyes. He went to another place and found men without heads; their eyes and mouth were in their chest,[39] and they spoke in the language of man[40] and ate fish;[41] they collected from the sand and from the earth itna,[42]

---

24. The word for sap (zi'ah) is a Hebrew medical term in Asaf harofe and Shabbetai Donnolo. Also, it appears in Syriac, but there it renders the Greek ἱδρώς. There is thus no indication whether the term ziah comes to the Hebrew via the Greek or Syriac.

25. Hebrew copy of Greek στακτήν in source.

26. Greek has δάκρυα δὲ ειχον ὡς Περσικὴν στακτήν.

27. Follows the Greek literally: ὑπό τινων δαιμόνων.

28. Follows the Greek μήτε εκκόπτειν μήτε συλλέγειν.

29. Greek has δράκοντες.

30. Literal translation of the Greek: καὶ ἰχθύων πολλὰ γένη.

31. Greek has ἐν ὕδατι ψυχρῷ πηγαίῳ.

32. Greek has ὄρνεα παρεμφερῆ τοῖς ὀρνέοις τοῖς παρ᾽ ἡμῖν ('birds similar to birds among us'); likewise, the Syriac has roosters and the Aramaic of the Talmud as well.

33. Romance 2.37.

34. The source has six legs.

35. The source has them at ten cubits.

36. Renders Greek εἰς ἀμμῶδι τινὰ τόπον.

37. Greek: θηρία ὅμοια ὀνάγροις; Hebrew 'arod from Job 39:5, which Septuagint renders ὄνος ἄγριος.

38. The source has twenty cubits.

39. Thus in the Armenian and Syriac translations.

40. Follows the Greek: λαλοῦντες δὲ ἀνθρωπίνως τῇ ἰδίᾳ γλώσσῃ.

41. Greek has ἰχθυοφάγοι.

42. Hebrew transliteration of Greek ὕδνα (truffles) and may reflect local dialect, as the translator indicates "which are eaten in our locales"; see chap. 1, note 1, reference to Alexandros.

which are eaten in our locales, the weight of each one was thirty lit.,[43] and they saw crabs as big as ships.[44]

He went from there[45] by way of the desert and came unto a sea and saw neither bird nor beast, only earth and sky alone. He went in a ship and came to an island, and the island was close to the land, and he heard them speaking in the language of man; they were Yevanim,[46] but he could not see the speakers. He sent some of his men swimming in the water to go to the island; a crab[47] went forth, jumped, and shook off[48] fifty-four[49] of his men; he became afraid and went from that place a journey of two days.

He arrived in a place of darkness[50] where the sun did not illuminate; he desired to enter there to see the generation called *makari*;[51] these are the generations of Yonadav ben Rechab.[52] And he took council with his friends to go there with thirteen hundred warriors. He took with him an ass nursing a foal and tied the foal at the entrance to the place; he set up his camp there and began to enter that place. He found the atmosphere of the place cloudy with darkness and vapor; a man could not see his comrade, and the land was filthy and full of mud.[53] Two huge fowl struck him:[54] their faces were the faces of man;[55] they were winged; and they spoke in the language of Yevanim and said to him: "Alexandros, why are you trespassing in the land of God? You cannot see the House of God and the house of his servants! Return, for you cannot walk among the islands where God's saints dwell![56] Do not vie to ascend to heaven's height!"

---

43. The source has twenty.
44. Also in the Armenian translation.
45. Romance 2.38.
46. Variation of the Greek: ἤκουον λαλίας ἀνθρώπων Ἑλληνικῇ διαλέκτῳ λαλούντων.
47. καρκίνοι is plural in Greek.
48. Cf. Ex 14:27.
49. Same number in Armenian translation.
50. Romance 2.39.
51. Transliterates Greek μάκαροι, meaning "blessed"; cf. translator's note. Flusser suggests that this means "spirits of the dead."
52. This identification is based on the medieval Jewish legend that the angel of death has no effect on the descendants of Yonadav ben Rechab, who are eternal; cf. Ginzberg, *Legends of the Jews*, 5.95, full reference and the source in Jer 35:19.
53. As with the Armenian translation, so the Hebrew skips over the end of this chapter and the beginning of the next. Each follows a similar Greek MS, which left out 2.39 from ἐπί σχοίνους δεκαπέντε to 2.40 σχοίνους τριάκοντα.
54. Romance 2.40.
55. Follows Greek: ἔχοντα ὄψεις ἀ νθρωπίνας.
56. I.e., the Isles of the Blessed of Greek legend; this phrase is not in the versions of the Romance.

Alexandros trembled[57] before the fowl. Then one bird spoke to him and said to him in the language of Yevanim: "Know ye, Alexandros, that you shall rule in the East and over the kingdom of Porus, king of Hodu." The fowl went their way, and the ass hastened to return to her son, the foal.

He went from there a full twenty days[58] and found his camp that he had set at the entrance to the place; he built gates[59] at the spot, closed up the entrance to the place, and wrote upon stones all that he saw.

---

57. Renders Greek Σύντρομος δὲ γενόμενος Ἀλέξανδρος.
58. The source has twenty-two.
59. Also in Armenian version.

7. THE WAR WITH POROS

He went from there[1] to the land of Hodu. When Poros, the king, heard, he sent him letters: "Get out of my land, lest I kill you by sword!" But Alexandros did not deign to heed him. Poros assembled a huge force[2] with ivory tuskers aplenty[3] and many beasts to fight with the Yevanim.[4] Alexandros was afraid of the beasts because he was not accustomed to war with beasts. Alexandros went by himself like a spy in the land of Prasiakin;[5] he disguised himself like an ex-soldier and as a merchant who buys food; they seized him and brought him to King Poros. He said to him: "Who are you?" And he said: "I am a former soldier in the army of Alexandros, and he sent me here." And he asked him further: "What will Alexandros do,[6] and why does he crave to fight with a great king like me?" And he permitted him to go on his way.

And so, when Alexandros went forth, he saw the beasts that Poros had prepared to fight against him. He gave it some thought and made images of copper[7] and commanded to light them with fire until they became like a burning flame, and he incited them skillfully with bronze instruments against the beasts. The beasts jumped upon the copper images to bite them and to seize them, and their mouths and bodies[8] were burned by the fire. Then the beasts rested; they

---

1. Romance 3.2.
2. Romance 3.3.
3. Renders καὶ πλείστους ἐλέφαντας; the Hebrew translator did not remember the Hebrew word for elephant (*pil*) and uses *shenhavim* (ivories).
4. Source has "who fought together with the Indians."
5. Source has εἰς τὴν Πρασιακὴν πόλιν.
6. Greek has πῶς ἔχει Ἀλέξανδρος; perhaps the writer's MS had πῶς πράττει Ἀλέξανδρος.
7. Renders Greek χαλκέους ἀνδρίαντας.
8. The translator or his MS unites two different versions: τὰ στόματα (mouths) and τὰ σώματα (bodies).

quieted from fighting with the Yevanim, and the Parsians defeated the Indians. During the battle, Alexandros's horse with the head of a bull[9] fell by a sly ruse of the king of Hodu; and Alexandros was sorely grieved over that horse.

The battle lasted[10] for twenty days, and Alexandros's men plotted to hand Alexandros over to the king of Hodu. Alexandros understood and sent to Poros, saying: "Come, you and I will fight while the entire army sits in peace." Poros was happy at this prospect, for Alexandros's height had no importance to him, since the height of Poros was five cubits tall, and Alexandros's height was three cubits. And the two of them arrayed for battle one against the other. And there was a great cry within the camp of Hodu, and Poros turned about to face his camp to understand what was the shout; Alexandros hastened and smote him in the navel[11] with his sword and killed him.

---

9. Hebrew translation of the Greek name Βουκέφαλος. See chap. 5, note 27.
10. Romance 3.4.
11. Renders Greek ὑπὸ τὸν βουβῶνα.

8. SAGES OF HODU

Alexandros[1] desired to go from there to Oksidrakas[2]—not to fight with the inhabitants but to see the sages living there; they were exceedingly wise and were naked, without clothes; for this reason, they were called in the language of the Yevanim Gymnosophists.[3] They lived in booths and in caves of dry earth.[4]

And so, when the inhabitants of the place heard, they sent sages with letters to him [Alexandros],[5] saying: "If you come to fight with us, you'll gain nothing,[6] for we have nothing for you to loot—and if you desire to enjoy of that which we have, don't come with force or in strength; rather, come among us with soft words and gentle language, and you will understand who we are, for to you, fighting is proper, while wisdom is proper to us."[7]

Alexandros went unto them[8] and saw all of them naked, without clothes, and the women and children in the open field like sheep.[9]

He asked one of them, saying to him: "Don't you have graves?"[10] He [the man] answered and said: "My dwelling[11] is my grave." He [Alexandros] asked one, saying to him: "Who number more, the living or the dead?" And he [the man] said to him [Alexandros]: "The dead are more numerous, for the poor[12]

---

1. Romance 3.5
2. Greek has προς Ὀξυδρακάς.
3. Greek accusative of γυμνοσοφιστάς (naked sages).
4. Greek has εἰς καλύβας καὶ εἰς κατάγαια καταμένοντες.
5. Greek has μετὰ γραμμάτων.
6. Greek has οὐδέν ὀνήσῃ.
7. Greek has σοὶ γὰρ ἔπεται πολεμεῖν, ἡμῖν δὲ φιλοσοφεῖν.
8. Romance 3.6.
9. Greek has ὡς ποίμνια προβάτων νεμόμενα.
10. Greek has Τάφους οὐκ ἔχετε.
11. Renders Greek χώρημα.
12. "Poor" is not in any variants.

and the dead are more numerous than the rich[13] and the living." He asked another, saying: "Between man and beast, who is wiser and more clever?"[14] He answered: "Man." He asked another, saying: "What is the kingdom?" He [the man] answered: "Extortion and robbery." He asked another, saying: "Which was first, night or day?" And he said: "Night, for the fetus in the mother's intestines is in darkness." He asked another, saying: "To whom can a man not lie?" He said: "To the god of truth who knows the truth."[15] He asked another: "Which is better, the right side or the left?" He answered: "The left, for the woman nurses her son first from the left breast,[16] and even kings take the scepter of royalty[17] in the left hand."

After he asked them many questions, he said to them: "Ask of me what I can give to you!" All of them shouted and said: "Eternal life!"[18] And he said to them: "I do not have authority."[19] They said to him: "If you do not have authority to give eternal life, why do you fight to pillage and loot and subdue the world under you?[20] And after your death, you do not know to whom you will leave it and all your honor!" Alexandros said to them: "This is from the authority of heaven[21] that we be as servants to those who come after us, for we have been created for this: for the sea will not move without wind, and the trees will not billow if the wind does not blow in them; and man will not succeed without the permission of heaven.[22]

"And I myself desired to be quiet, but the lord of all in whose hand is the soul of all the living did not permit me."[23] With these words, Alexandros went on his way.

---

13. "Rich" is not in any variants.

14. Greek has πανουργότερον.

15. Cf. *I Esdras* 4.40; *Yosippon*, chap. 6, last lines of Zerubavel's riddle.

16. Greek has θηλάξι δὲ γυνὴ πρῶτον δίδουσα τῷ παιδὶ τὸν εὐώμενον μαστόν.

17. Greek has τὸ τῆς ἀρχῆς σκῆπτρον.

18. Greek has ἀθανασίαν.

19. Greek has Ταύτην ἐγὼ οὐκ ἔχω ἐξουσίαν.

20. From here to the end of chap. 9, the text is from *Yosippon*, since one page is lacking in the Parma MS.

21. Greek has ταῦτα ἐκ τῆς ἄνωθεν προνοίας διοικοῦνται.

22. Permission and authority render the Hebrew *reshut*; Greek has here οὐκ ἐνεργεῖται ἄνθρωπος εἰ μὴ ἐκ τῆς ἄνωθεν προνοίας.

23. Greek has κ'ἀγὼ δὲ παύσασθαι θέλω τοῦ πολεμεῖν, ἀλλ' οὐκ ἐᾷ με ὁ τῆς γνώμης μου δεσπότες.

9. MARVELS OF HODU

He wrote a letter[1] to his teacher Aristoteles. He wrote to him all that had happened to him in the land of Hodu, saying: "When I arrived in the land of Prasiakin,[2] this is a city in the land of Hodu, I found the land strong and hard, and it is in the midst of the sea. I went there and beheld men similar to women, and they were eating fish,[3] speaking the Yevani language.[4] I asked them about the place, and they said to me: 'Look, this island in the midst of the sea is the burial of an ancestral king,[5] and there is much gold aplenty.' After they related this fact to me, they went and beached[6] their twelve boats. And I saw there huge beasts in the sea; we shouted at them, and they fled and drowned my men in the sea. And from much worry, I remained there for eight days.

"After I conquered Darius and subdued all the land, I marched about until I came to a city in the midst of the river; reeds[7] three hundred cubits long were there, and the city was established upon the reeds, and the waters of the river were bitter. Some of my men entered the river to go into the city, and beasts called *ippopotami*[8] went forth from the river and snatched forty-four[9] of my men. "I went from there and toward evening came unto a place and found there a spring of water, sweet as honey, and I spent that night there. My men kindled

---

1. Romance 3.17.

2. Greek has εἰς τὴν Πρασιακὴν πόλιν.

3. Greek has εὕρομεν . . . θηλυομόρφους ἰχθυοφάγους ἀνθρώπους.

4. The source actually has them speaking a barbarian language.

5. Greek has πάνυ ἀρχαίου βασίλεως τάφος.

6. Greek has καταλίποντες.

7. Hebrew *kanim*; Greek κάλαμοι.

8. Ἱπποπόταμοι, i.e., river horses; Hebrew drops the aspirate that is characteristic of spoken Greek. Greek Jews generally could not articulate *heh* or *ḥet*, and this is reflected in their transliterations of Greek.

9. Variants have other figures.

a fire, and all the beasts came from the forest to drink water. There were among them scorpions, about a cubit,[10] white and red and black and horned,[11] also crocodiles and lions and tigers and buffalo[12] and pigs and ivory tuskers[13] and men with six hands; they killed many of my men. And my men burned the forest with fire, and the creeping things[14] ran to the fire. There came against us one huge beast; the beast roared and killed twenty-six warriors of my men: others of my warriors killed the beast, and three hundred[15] of my men dragged and pulled the beast by force. And bats[16] were there, huge as doves, and possessing teeth like a man. We hunted and ate ravens[17] to sustain us.

"From there we went into the land of Kaspiaki,[18] and at the ninth[19] hour of the day, a great and very strong wind blew so that we could not stand on our feet; immediately we fell upon our faces to the ground until the wind abated.

"After this I conquered the city of Kaspiaki;[20] it is a city in the kingdom of Hodu. The inhabitants of the land said to me: 'We can show you wonder and wisdom befitting your honor;[21] come and we shall show you trees speaking like men.'[22] They led me to a certain garden, and there was sun and moon. I saw there trees like the trees of Miẓrayim called *mirobalanon*,[23] and their fruit was like *mirobalanon*, and they were male and female. The male tree had the sense[24] of a male, and the female tree had the sense of a female; and the name of the male was sun and the name of the female was moon, and the trees were saying: 'MUTU EMAN OUSAH.'[25] And at the time that the sun arrives, a voice in the language of

---

10. Greek has σκορπίοι πηχυαῖοι.

11. Greek has κερασταί, which the author took as an adjective.

12. Greek has ῥινοκέρατες.

13. Καὶ ἐλέφαντες, see chap. 7, note 13.

14. Hebrew *sheratzim* renders Greek τὰ ἕρπετα.

15. The source has one thousand.

16. Greek has νυκτερίδες.

17. Greek has νυκτικόρακες.

18. Greek has εἰς τὴν Πρασιακὴν γῆν; the author's MS was perhaps corrupt and contained Κασπιακήν.

19. The source has sixth hour.

20. See note 18 above.

21. Greek has ἔχομεν σοί δεῖξαί τι παράδοξαν ἀξίον σου.

22. Renders Greek ἀνθρωπιστί.

23. Greek accusative case of μυροβάλανος; Shabbatai Donnolo also speaks of this in his *Book of Remedies*.

24. Hebrew *da'at* renders Greek λογισμός.

25. *Yosippon* MSS have here *mut mut emah ḥoshekh*, מות מות אימה חושך. The text is corrupt in the Greek versions and their translations, including our author's. MS A has μουθοῦ ἐμαῦσαι; the Armenian translator's text had μουθουὰμ αὐοῦσα; our Hebrew translator's

Hodu went forth from the tree; and those who knew the language of Hodu did not wish to interpret for me, for they were afraid of me until I swore to them that I would not harm them. And they said: 'Know ye, Alexandros, that you will be quickly destroyed by your men and your relatives!' At the time that the moon rises, I prayed if I would hence see my mother, my brothers, and my loyal friends in the land of Makedonia. And with the setting of the sun, a voice in the Yevani language went forth from the tree: 'Know ye, Alexandros, that you will die in Bavel by the hand of your men and your relatives, and you shall not see your mother nor the land of Makedonia!' With the setting of the sun, I prayed again if I would hence see my wife and my mother in the land of Makedonia and if the days of my life would finish and end. And a voice went forth from the tree: 'Your years have finished, and the days of your life have ended, and finally you shall die in Bavel! And after your death, your mother will be destroyed[26] and your sister and brothers in a wicked and harsh destruction by the hand of their relatives. Do not question further, for you shall hear nothing.'"

---

text probably had μουθοῦ ἐμά οὖσα. Ausfeld, *Der griechische Alexanderroman*, chap. 4, 94n9, suggests that the Greek perhaps rendered "in the name of the gods of the sun and moon."

26. From this point, we return to the Parma MS (see chap. 8, note 20).

10. ALEXANDROS CHEZ KANDAKI THE QUEEN

"I went from there and left at evening time from the land of Prasiakin;[1] I went into the land of Paras and went into the kingdom of the land of Semiramis. A woman[2] of exceeding beauty was there:[3] she was a queen and her name was Kandaki; I sent letters to her, saying: 'Send me the god of Amon,[4] and I shall sacrifice before him, for I have heard that during the years that you subdued the land of Miẓrayim, you took the god of Amon from there—and if you do not send him to me, I will come against you to fight.'" She too sent a letter to him, saying: "We cannot send to you the god of Amon; rather, his priests[5] are sending to you one hundred bricks[6] of gold and five hundred Ethiopian youths without beard[7] and two hundred fine pearls and the crown of the god of Amon made of precious stones valued at one hundred liters of gold and four pierced pearls, eighty giant ones and eighty unpierced pearls, thirty boxes of ivory bone filled with elephants,[8] thirteen leopards[9] and buffalo,[10] fourteen panthers, which are

---

1. Greek has ἀπὸ τῆς Πρασιακῆς.
2. Romance 3.18.
3. Greek has γύνη ἔξουσα κάλλος ὑπερήφανον.
4. Greek Ἄμμων. The author writes "'Amon" (with *ayin*), rather than "Amon" (with *aleph*) since he was certain that there was a relationship between the Canaanite and the Egyptian god. [The term *elohim* in Hebrew is a plural noun used in the Bible as a singular collective noun. Hence, the translator uses the pronoun "him/it." SB]
5. Greek has πρεσβεῖς.
6. Greek has πλίνθους.
7. Greek has Αἰθίοπας ἀνήβους.
8. The source has ivory boxes.
9. Greek has παρδαλεῖς.
10. Greek has ρινοκέρατες.

beasts, ninety man-eating dogs,[11] forty bullocks who know to fight and strive,[12] four tusks of *pilim*, which are *elephantim*,[13] three hundred tiger skins, eight thousand branches of the tree *ebanos*,[14] which is a tree black like the horn of goats and bright.[15] Send messengers, and they will bring you this gift, for I too know that you have conquered every bit of the world."

Alexandros turned to go to her.[16] Whereas Kandaki had heard of his habit of acting in theft and deceit to capture kings, she sent forth to sketch and engrave[17] in secret the image of Alexandros so that it be in her hand; and she took the image and put it in the room.[18]

Kandavlis[19] ben Kandaki, the queen, went to Alexandros's camp; the guards took him and brought him to Iphtolomaios,[20] King Alexandros's second in command.[21] Iphtolomaios asked him: "Who are you?" He said: "Son of Kandaki, the queen, and I came with my wife and a small army, for I had an important secret[22] from the women called Amazones; a certain prince[23] seized me, took my wife, and killed many of my men."

Iphtolomaios went and reported to Alexandros all these things. Alexandros listened and said to Iphtolomaios: "Take the crown of my kingdom[24] and my clothes[25] and become king in my stead and act cleverly and call me by another name and say: 'Call to me Antigonos, a loyal messenger like me!'[26] When I come, pretend to tell me the words of the youth before you and say to me: 'What do you suggest to me that we do concerning the matter of this queen's son?'"

---

11. Greek has κύνες ἀνθρωποφάγοι.

12. Greek has ταῦροι μάχιμοι.

13. Greek has ὀδόντες ἐλεφάντων παρδαλεῖς; here the author remembers the Hebrew word *pil* for elephant.

14. Greek has ῥάβδοι ἐβένιναι.

15. The author's gloss.

16. Romance 3.19.

17. Greek has ζωγραφῆσαι.

18. Greek has ἐν ἀποκρύφῳ τόπῳ (in a hidden place).

19. Reflects the author's contemporary dialect for Κανδαύλης.

20. Renders Greek Πτολεμαῖος.

21. Renders Greek ἔχων τὰ δεύτερα τῆς βασιλείας.

22. Greek has τελέσαι μυστήριον παρὰ τὰς Ἀμαζόνας (to fulfill the holiday of the mystery with the Amazons); the author misunderstood μυστήριον as the Hebrew *sod* (secret), which resulted in his mistaken and unclear translation.

23. Greek has τύραννος (biblical *seren*).

24. Greek has διάδημα.

25. Greek has τὴν χλανίδα.

26. The source has παρασπίστης, which the author understood as πρεσβεὺς πιστός (loyal messenger; or possibly his MS was corrupt here).

Iphtolomaios donned garb in the image of Alexandros, and Kandavlis beheld him and feared lest he order him killed. Iphtolomaios said: "Summon to me Antigonos, my loyal messenger!" They summoned Alexandros in disguise to him, and Iphtolomaios related to him all the words that he [Alexandros] had put in his mouth. Alexandros answered, saying: "Give me an army, and I will go and rescue his wife from that prince."

When Kandavlis heard, he rejoiced over his words.[27] He went into the tent[28] and embraced Alexandros, saying to him: "If you trust me[29] and come with me to my mother, I will give you great gifts." Alexandros said to him: "Go and ask the king for me, for I too crave to see your mother." Kandavlis went to Iphtolomaios and asked him for him. Iphtolomaios said to him: "Look Kandavlis, I will send my messenger with you with a letter to your mother. See to it that you honor him and restore him to me whole just as he will restore you and your wife to your mother." Whereupon Kandavlis said: "I will take it upon myself to honor this man."[30]

They went together,[31] and he approached the queen;[32] his mother and brother met him and ran to kiss Kandavlis. Then Kandavlis said to them: "Don't kiss me! First kiss this man who delivered my wife and me, for this one is Antigonos; he is a loyal messenger[33] of King Alexandros." When they asked him how, he related to them all that had happened to him. Whereupon his mother and brother kissed him, and they led Alexandros to eat bread in the evening.

In the morning,[34] Kandaki donned royal garb, took Alexandros, and brought him to the room built of precious stones and gold, and its tiles were gold; and beds were there covered with Shin'ar spreads woven with gold and silken thread,[35] and the beds were of onyx and diamonds[36] with serpents of onyx[37] and intricately mounted with horses and weapons of war of precious

---

27. The author skips over the story of the rescue of Kandavlis's wife by Alexander either through his error or because it was lacking in his MS.

28. Romance 3.20.

29. Greek has πίστευσον σεαυτὸν ἐμοί.

30. Romance 3.21.

31. Romance 3.21.

32. Greek has εἰς τὰ βασίλεια (to the queen's palace); the author errs in his translation.

33. Here the source has ἄγγελος; see note 26 above.

34. Romance 3.22.

35. The source has σηρικὴ τέχνη.

36. Greek has κλιντῆρες δὲ οὐνιώνων καὶ βερύλλων τὰς βάσεις ἔχοντες; one version has onyx. See text following note 53.

37. Greek text was apparently quite corrupt.

stone—porphyry;[38] and at the foot of the chariot were horses—elephants[39] of precious stone; and facing them was a river of gold and golden trees with their fruit. And they ate there together with Kandavlis's brother.

On the following day, she [Kandaki] took Alexandros and showed him rooms built of chalk stone, which is "aeritos,"[40] and it appeared like the sun from the brightness of the stone within the room. Alexandros said to her: "All this glory is more fitting to Yevanim than to you." She replied and said in anger: "What's with you, Alexandros?" When Alexandros heard his name from her mouth, he answered her: "My name is not Alexandros but rather Antigonos, and I am a messenger sent from Alexandros."[41] Whereupon she said to him: "You are Alexandros!" Then she took him, brought him into the room, showed him his image, and said: "Do you not recognize the image of your face?[42] Why are you frightened and shaking? Are you not the subduer of the land of Paras and Hodu, the one who puts an end to the wars of Madai and Paras[43] and all the nations? And now by neither sword nor battle you are in the hand of a woman, so that you may know no matter how wise a man be, there is another like him wiser than he."

Alexandros got angry, gnashed his teeth,[44] and wanted to kill himself and her. And she said to him: "Don't gnash your teeth, for what can you do? Only because you rescued my son and daughter-in-law will I save you too from the hand of the *barbaron*,[45] and I will summon you before them by the name of Antigonos. Know that you killed Poros, king of Hodu, and this one, the wife of my youngest son, she is the daughter of Poros, and I will not expose you as Alexandros."

Kandaki went out[46] and said to her son Kandavlis and his wife: "If Alexandros had not saved you through his messenger, I would not be seeing your faces. Now we shall honor him and give him gifts." And her son, son-in-law to Poros, said to her: "It is true that Alexandros saved my brother and his wife; yet my wife wanted to make Alexandros worry[47] and be sad by killing this messenger of

---

38. Greek has ἐκ πορφυρίτου λίθου.

39. Greek has ἐλέφαντες, which is transliterated in the Hebrew.

40. Greek has κοιτῶνας διαυγεῖς ἐξ αερίτου λίθου; the author did not understand the Greek ἀερίτης (color of air) and transliterated the word.

41. Greek has ἄγγελος Ἀλεξάνδρου.

42. Greek has ἐπιγινώσκεις τὸν σεαυτοῦ χαρακτῆρα.

43. Greek has ὁ καθελὼν τρόπαια Μήδεν καὶ Πάρθων.

44. Greek has καὶ ἔτριξε τοὺς ὀδόντας.

45. Greek has κʼἀγώ σε φύλαξω πρὸς τοὺς βαρβάρους; "from the hand of" (*mi-yad*) added by the editor from *Yosippon*.

46. Romance 3.23.

47. Greek has λυπῆσαι θέλει τὸν Ἀλέξανδρον.

his in atonement for the blood of her father." Whereupon his mother answered: "For what benefit?[48] If this one were to die, she would not be victorious over Alexandros."

Then his brother Kandavlis said: "I will send forth his messenger whole in his body, and you and I will fight." And the two brothers began to strive and quarrel[49] with each other. Kandaki took Alexandros and brought him to the room and said to him in private: "Where indeed is your wisdom? It's up to you to give advice and speak suitably, for it is because of you that my sons desire to kill one another!"

Alexandros went forth and said to them: "If you should kill me, it will not grieve Alexandros,[50] for my lord has men greater and better than I. And if you desire to fight Alexandros, give me gifts, and I will go and bring him to you, and you may do unto him according to your will." And they heeded him and allowed him [to live].

When Kandaki heard, she said: "True it is that from an abundance of wisdom you did conquer all the lands!" They gave him a crown of emery worth many talents of gold[51] and a breastplate studded with onyx and diamond[52]—and onyx is called in the language of Yavan *ounion*, and diamond is called *berylon*—and a cloak of purple and gold;[53] and they sent him off in peace with her men. Alexandros went to his army;[54] they put the crown of his kingdom upon his head and dressed him in the garb of his royalty.

---

48. Greek has καὶ τί σοι ὄφελος.

49. See above text; also cf. *Yosippon*, chap. 57.

50. Greek has οὐδὲν μέλει Ἀλεξάνδρῳ; the Hebrew translation undoubtedly preserves a local expression.

51. Greek has στέφανον ἀδαμάντινον πολητάλαντον.

52. Greek has καὶ θώρακα δι᾽ οὐνιώναν καὶ βηρύλλων; see note 35 above.

53. Greek has χλαμύδα . . . ὁλοπόρφυρον διὰ χρυσοῦ.

54. Romance 3.25.

II. ALEXANDROS'S JOURNEYS OF MARVEL

He went to the Amazones,[1] the women, and sent them a letter, saying: "Have you not heard that I have conquered all the land? If you desire, give me a tax, and pray for me before the god,[2] and I shall let you stay in your place; but if not, I shall come and destroy you!"

They sent him a letter in return saying: "Don't you know that we too are trained in fighting? And we live on the river Amazonikon.[3] In the midst of the river is a large island, and a circumambulation of the island is a full year; and around the island is a great river surrounding [it] on every side, and the river has no source.[4] There is one pathway; twenty-seven myriads [270,000] of virgins bearing arms[5] garrison it. There are no males among us, for the males live across the river with the cattle and sheep they herd. And we sacrifice horses to our gods Zeus and Poseidon[6] annually for thirty days, and only once in every seven years the males come to us to lie with[7] his wife, and when the women conceive, the males go their way. And when they come against us to fight, twelve myriads [120,000] of us ride horses, and the rest stay to guard the island, and our males chase after us as infantry. If we win the battle, we get praise and a great reputation—but if our enemies defeat us, they get no praise for this at all, for the

---

1. Romance 3.25; Greek has ἐπὶ Ἀμαζόνας.
2. Heb. *Hamakom*, literally "the place." The translator uses this euphemism for god, which allows him to make a pun on leaving the Amazons in peace "in your place."
3. Greek has ἐσμέν γὰρ τοῦ Ἀμαζονικοῦ ποταμοῦ πέραν (across the river Amazonikon).
4. Follows Greek literally: ποταμὸς οὐκ ἔχων ἀρχέν.
5. Greek has παρθένοι ἔνοπλοι.
6. Greek has τῷ Διὶ καὶ Ποσιδῶνι; the author knew the term Zeus.
7. Cf. Deut 28:30.

one who defeats women, what praise does he get? You watch out, Alexandros, that such things do not happen to you! If you want peace, we shall give you a tax as you wish. Whatever you want, send us back a reply. If you do not wish peace, be informed that you will find us arrayed for battle in the mountains."

When Alexandros had read the letters,[8] he laughed a lot and then sent them another letter, saying: "If you desire that I destroy you and your country, stand in the mountains, drawn up in an army—and if you desire that I have mercy on you, cross the river and come to me, and I shall not destroy you. And send me some of you riding on horses; I will give to each one five pots full of gold."[9]

They sent him another letter, saying: "Come with our permission[10] and behold our country, and we shall give you one hundred talents of gold;[11] we have sent five hundred young girls bringing you gold and one hundred horses. And if the young girls take husbands for themselves from among your men, let them be with you; and we shall send you others in their stead."

Alexandros went to them[12] and beheld them very, very beautiful; their clothes were like the garb of Yevanim, like the daughters of Evyaines;[13] he took a tax from them[14] and went unto the Red Sea.[15] From there he went to the river Atlanta;[16] and many nations of many varieties live there; and he saw there *kynokephalous*, who have a head like a dog,[17] and others without a head, and their eyes and mouth are in their chest.

From there he went to another land, and that land was seven miles in the midst of the sea. He came there and found the city Ilios,[18] which is "city of the sun";[19] the size of the city was 120 miles,[20] and her citadels fourteen,

---

8. Romance 3.26.

9. Greek has χρυσοῦ μνᾶς εʹ.

10. Greek has διδόαμέν σοι ἐξουσίαν ἐλθεῖν.

11. Greek has χρυσοῦ τάλαντα ρʹ.

12. Romance 3.27.

13. Greek has ἐσθῆτα δὲ φοροῦσιν ἀνθινήν ('their clothes the clothing of flowers'); apparently the author's MS had εὐγενεῖς (nobles) instead of ἀνθινήν which he transliterated according to his local demotic dialect.

14. Romance 3.28.

15. Greek has ἐπὶ τὴν Ἐρυθράν θάλασσαν.

16. The author follows Greek literally: ἐπὶ τὸν Ἄτλαντα ποταμόν κυνοκέφαλους.

17. The author's gloss to the Greek word, which he translates.

18. Nominative case, whereas the Greek is in the genitive case: εὕρομεν πόλιν τοῦ Ἡλίου.

19. The author's gloss.

20. The source has 120 stades.

studded with gold and precious stone which are *ismargos*;[21] the priest of the temple was an Ethiopian,[22] and Alexandros sacrificed there to the sun.

He went from there a journey of three days; he found no light: he did not find light; therefore, he went on to the kingdom of Koresh and Kserkses,[23] kings of Paras; he seized there many houses full of gold and silver and precious things.[24]

---

21. Greek σμάραγδος (a precious stone of green color).
22. Greek Αἰθίοψ.
23. Cyrus and Ξέρξης-Xerxes, who is Ahasuerus of the biblical Esther.
24. Greek has καὶ ἄλλα σπουδαῖα.

12. DEATH OF ALEXANDROS

And after all these things[1] that Alexandros did and saw, then Antipatros,[2] general of his army, thought to himself to kill Alexandros with a drink of deadly poison. Antipatros concocted the poison in Bavel and put it in a lead vessel, for, from the poison's intensity of potency, he was not able to put it into a glass vessel or a copper vessel or bronze or clay—for all of them would split from the pungency of the poison, and outside the lead, he put a bronze vessel to protect it well. He sent the poison to his brother Ioulos,[3] who was Alexandros's chief butler.

The day came when Alexandros was angry at his chief butler and struck him on the head with his staff. The chief butler bore a grudge, a hatred in his heart toward Alexandros. After a few days, Alexandros made a feast for all his friends, and during the feast, the chief butler served him the poison in a cup of wine. After a long while, an intense pain seized him in the liver; suddenly he shouted a great cry like a man struck by a bow's centerpiece;[4] he made his will and died in Bavel.

Iphtolomaios, his second in command, took[5] the corpse of Alexandros and placed him in carts with mules and brought him there to the city of Alexandria, which he had built in Miẓrayim. The years of his life[6] were thirty-two years: at eighteen, he began to fight; and until he was twenty-five, he conquered

---

1. Romance 3.31.
2. Greek Ἀντίπατρος.
3. Greek Ἰούλλος.
4. Greek has ὡς τόξῳ πεπληγώς; Greek τόξον refers to an Oriental bow, which is two pieces of horn joined by a bow's cubit (πῆχυς); the image is of such a bow snapping the centerpiece back at the archer.
5. Romance 3.34; Iphtolomaios is postbiblical Hebrew version of Πτολεμαῖος (Ptolemy), biblical Talmi.
6. Romance 3.35.

twenty-two kings and subdued all the nations under him. The day of his birth was like the rising of the sun; and he died in the month called Pharmouthi in the language of Miẓrayim, which is the month Iyar,[7] on the fourth day with the setting of the sun. And the rest of the deeds of Alexandros and all the days of his kingdom were twelve years.[8]

Antipatros went[9] to Elada[10] in the land of Yevanim;[11] Patras is called after his name,[12] and he became their lord. Iphtolomaios, called Ologos,[13] became lord of Miẓrayim, and Seleukos Odikator[14] [ruled] from Aram unto Bavel. Roxanin,[15] daughter of Darius and wife of Alexandros, bore a son, and the Makedonim called his name Alexandros after his father's name.

---

7. Φαρμοῦθι. The source has month of April.

8. Flusser's conjecture.

9. From this point, the author uses unknown sources.

10. Ἑλλαδα is accusative form for Ἑλλας-Hellas.

11. The author's gloss translating previous words.

12. This is a unique etymology for the name Patras, which is also vocalized in the text. Benjamin of Tudela repeats this etymology from his text of *Yosippon*. On the Jewish community of Patras, see, for example, Samuel Krauss, *Studien zur byzantinisch-jüdische Geschichte* (Vienna, 1914), 79, 118. Benjamin of Tudela in his itinerary of the 1160s cites this, and probably his *Yosippon* contained a copy of this text.

13. Greek has ὁ Λάγου (son of Logos).

14. Greek has ὁ Νικατώρ; the author's text was corrupt.

15. Greek accusative form of Ρωξάνη.

13. FROM ALEXANDROS
TO AUGUSTOS

Iphtolomaios Ologos died,[1] and Demetrius Polioketes[2]—its meaning is "warrior"[3]—ruled, and he conquered the city of Shomron.[4] Demetrios died and was buried in his city Demetriah,[5] which he had built. Iphtolomaios, called Philadelphos,[6] son of Iphtolomaios Ologos, ruled for thirty-eight years, and he built Pharo,[7] which is in Alexandriah. This one[8] brought the books of the Jews into the land of Elada and put them in Alexandria;[9] and then Elazar, brother of Shimon, was made high priest. The Jews who were captives in the land of Miẓrayim went forth free. This king sent to Jerusalem and took Elazar the priest to translate and interpret for him all the books of the Jews into the language of the Yevanim.

---

1. The following is based on an unknown Byzantine chronicle that relies ultimately on Eusebius. [A fragment of a Romaniote chronicle from the Genizah now in London is in the process of being edited for publication. SB]
2. Greek for "conqueror of cities."
3. The author's gloss based on his understanding of the word πόλεμος.
4. Greek has τὴν πόλιν Σαμαρέων.
5. Not in extant sources.
6. Φιλάδελφος.
7. Φάρος-Pharos is the famous lighthouse in Alexandria.
8. The source has τὰς Ἰουδαίων γραφὰς ἐκ τῆς Ἑβραίων φωνῆς εἰς τὴν Ἑλλάδα μεταβληθῆναι ἐσπούδασε τὰς Ἰουδαίων γραφάς (*Chronicon Paschale* 173a); the author misunderstood the convoluted Greek and translated εἰς τὴν Ἑλλάδα μεταβληθῆναι as "brought to Greece."
9. The source has translation done in Alexandria; see *Yosippon*, chap. 12.

And 26 years of Olympiados,[10] the Romans subdued Kalabriah[11] and seized the city of Messene; this was the fourth exile [*galut*] of Messene.[12] In that year arose Ieron, the lord [*sar*] who was in Sikiliah,[13] and he seized Sarakusah.[14] At that time, Valerianos Ipato[15] acted to make Sikiliah subject to the Romans. In those days was Aratos the sage; then was made Phainomena;[16] and then they first counted silver coins[17] in Rome. In 129 of Ilympiados,[18] the Romans fought in Sarakusah, and Karkhedonins[19] came against the Romans in Sikiliah.[20] Iphtolomaios, called Evergetes, ruled in Miẓrayim for twenty-six years. King Nikodemon[21] built the city of Bithynin from the beginning and called its name Nikomediah. Then[22] the Romans fought in Sarakusah and conquered the city Karkhedoni[23] and returned[24] one hundred cities. Then[25] Antigonos set the sons of Athenes[26] free and built the city Kalamagnos, which is on the river Orontin.[27]

---

10. The source has 126th Olympiad; the author did not understand this reckoning.

11. Καλαβρία.

12. Μεσσήνη. Not in extant sources, author uses *galut* (exile) for conquest.

13. Syncellus 275d has Ἵερων τυράννος Σικελίας.

14. Greek has Συρακουσαί.

15. Synkellos has Οὐαλέριος ὑπατεύων Οὐαλεριάνος ὕπατος; the author's MS had Οὐαλεριάνος ὕπατος (consul).

16. The translator left a space in his MS; above word restored from Greek.

17. The source has ἀργυροῦν νόμισμα.

18. Eusebius has 124th Olympiad.

19. Men of Carthage.

20. MS has Silikiah, which is perhaps a *lapsus calami*. [See Flusser's PhD thesis, "תרגום מציאת עברי של הרומאן על אלכסנדרוס," at the Hebrew University of Jerusalem (1955), 15 (following note 17). SB]

21. Follows source based on Eusebius's source, perhaps from Anonymous Matr., 40.3. Νικομήδης ὁ Βιθυνῶν βασιλεὺς τὴν πόλιν ἐπικτίσας Νικομηδείαν ὠνόμασε; perhaps there is here a hint to the city Bithynion based on ὁ Βιθυνῶν, and the MS lacked the word βασιλεύς. Cf. A. H. M. Jones, *The Cities of the Eastern Roman Provinces* (New York, 1937), 151. The translator had difficulties with the concept "founding a city" until he found the phrase "built from the beginning," which he also uses at the very end of this chapter for the city of Shomron, although there it means "built anew."

22. The source has this in the 130th Olympiad.

23. Καρχηδονίοι is "men of Carthage."

24. Greek has ἔλαβον.

25. The source has 131st Olympiad.

26. Athens.

27. The Byzantine chronicle on which the author relied merged the previous data on Antigonos Gonatas with the information on the founding of the city Antigonia on the Orontes (Ἀντίγονος Ἀντιγονίαν τὴν πρὸς τῷ Ὀρόντῃ ποτάμῳ ἔκτισεν, ἣν Σέλευκος ἐπικτίσας Ἀντιοχείαν ὠνόμασε; cf. Synkellos 273c). The city mentioned in our translation may

In 134 of Olympiados[28] was Yosiphus the Jew, and he wrote the books.[29] Then Romans killed four myriads [forty thousand] of Galatiah.[30] In 135[31] of Olympiados was Yehoshua ben Sirakh,[32] the Jew among Jews. In 140 of Ilympiados ruled Iphtolomaios, called Philopator,[33] in Miẓrayim, and he ruled seventeen years. In 141 of Olympiados ruled Markilos, king[34] of the Romans; they captured Sarakusa and Kapuah, a large city[35] and subdued Sikiliah under them. Antiochus the Great,[36] King of Aram, conquered Philopator and captured him. In 144 of Olympiados,[37] Antiochus Epiphanes ruled thirty-six years.[38] This one instigated the Jews to lead them from their faith to believe in the faith of Yevanim, but the Jews did not want to obey him. Antiochus got angry at them and brought forth against them a great army; he killed many Jews and destroyed Jerusalem; this was the third *galut*.[39] He took the wealth of the Temple and defeated Jews, killing eighty thousand of its men.[40] He went from there to the land of Plishtim to enslave them under him.[41]

In 150 of Olympiados,[42] war was made by their [Romans'] slaves in Sikiliah; the Romans sent there Lukhkulos,[43] general of the army; he defeated and

---

represent the original name of the site and might be conjectured as a corruption of something like καλλίγονος?

28. The source has 133rd Olympiad.

29. Eusebius writes (in his Chronicle) of one Joseph ben Tubia. Either the Byzantine source or the author errs here by identifying this Joseph as Josephus Flavius. The version of *Yosippon* further emphasizes this identification: "Yosephus haYehudi is Yoseph ben Gurion haCohen haGadol who wrote *Sepher milḥamah.*"

30. In Asia Minor. The source has 138th Olympiad.

31. The source has 137th Olympiad.

32. This is Ben Sira; the author transliterates his Greek source.

33. Φιλοπάτωρ.

34. Μάρκελλος; Markellos was a consul and not a king.

35. Perhaps this, which is not found in the sources, is a hint to the author's southern Italian origin; see also chap. 4, note 13. [For this phraseology in a later Byzantine period, see Peter Charanis, "A Note on the Population and Cities of the Byzantine Empire in the Thirteenth Century," in *The Joshua Starr Memorial Volume* (New York, 1953), 135–48. SB]

36. Eusebius lists this under the 142nd Olympiad.

37. The source has 151st Olympiad.

38. This datum is the age of Antiochus the Great and not Epiphanes.

39. Not in sources.

40. Not in sources.

41. Antiochus Epiphanes's march to Paras (Persia). The author may possibly have read *ereẓ plishtim* (Philistia) for source's *ereẓ ha-Partim* (Parthia?), which he did not recognize; possibly the Byzantine source already included this error.

42. Eusebius gives two data: the slave war in Sicily began in the 161st Olympiad, and the slave revolt in Sicily was put down by Aquilius in the 165th Olympiad.

43. Who is this Lukhkulos? Eusebius mentions Aquilius; perhaps the Byzantine chronicle intends L. Licinius Lucullus, who was sent in 103 BCE to put down the slave revolt in

enslaved them under him, and the fighting quieted. In that year,[44] Horkanos, high priest, fought the city of Shomron,[45] called in the language of Yavan Sebastin,[46] and destroyed her to the foundation; afterward it was rebuilt by the hand of Herodos and called Sebastin; and then Kapitoleon in Roma was burned.[47] Then Digranes,[48] king of Armeniakin, took the daughter of Mithridates[49] as his wife; he brought forth a huge army and a heavy force and defeated Antiochus, the Great King of Aram,[50] removed him from his kingship, and subdued all the land as far as the land of Plishtim.[51] And from that year, Armeni[52] began to give tax to the Romans. In 177 of the Olympiados,[53] the city of Pompeia was built by Pompeios.

In that year,[54] Romans enslaved[55] Albania and Iberiah and Kolosos and the Bnei Arav [Arabians] under them. And Romans conquered Jerusalem through

---

Sicily, but he did not know how to take advantage of his victory. The author's spelling is interesting.

44. Eusebius has the 165th Olympiad.

45. Horkanos is ʻorkanos/Hyrcanus. Greek Σαμάρια.

46. Greek Σεβαστή in the accusative case Σεβαστήν.

47. Eusebius has the burning of Καπιτώλιον in 174th Olympiad, above Romi.

48. Digranes is King Τιγράνης-Tigranes of Armenia. [Heraclius in the sixth century had reorganized Byzantine Anatolia and created the Armeniakon theme (*pace* Theophanes the Confessor, but cf. "Armeniakon" in *The Oxford Dictionary of Byzantium*, 1.177). Perhaps the author is calling the kingdom by his contemporary name for the area. "Armeniakon" in British Library, London, in a Genizah fragment of the chronicle designated בכ by Flusser. SB]

49. This datum is not in Eusebius. Justinus (1.3.58) identifies her name as Cleopatra. *Bat* usually means daughter, and the text only identifies her as Bat Mithridates.

50. This is not Antiochus III, the Great, but rather Antiochus X Pius.

51. The Greek version of the chronicle had, no doubt, μέχρι Παλαιστίνης. The version in *Yosippon* glosses here: "called in Arabic Falastin." It is likely that these words were original to *Ma'ase Alexandros*, and the author (or copyist) of the Parma MS skipped them in error since the words end with Falastin and the previous word is Plishtim. Flusser suggests that this may shed light on the author's provenance in southern Italy, which neighbored on Arabophones. See note 59.

52. This is inexact; Eusebius lists Lucullus's conquest of Armenia in the 176th Olympiad. MS glosses after Armeni: "these are Amalek." This designation is still current among Turkish Sephardi Jews and the Jews of Georgia and eastern Galicia. [*Yosippon*'s hostility to the Armenians may reflect Jewish reaction to the ninth–tenth century Byzantine persecutions of the Jews. SB]

53. The datum that the author found in the Byzantine chronicle is not in Eusebius. Pompeiopolis (here called Pompeia) is the city Soloi in Cilicia, which was renamed after its conqueror, Pompey, who took it after his defeat of the pirates in 67 or 66, i.e., in the 176th Olympiad, not in the 177th.

54. Eusebius writes that Pompey subdued all Hiberia in the 177th Olympiad. The author adds further data from his Byzantine chronicle that corresponds to Eutropius 6.14. The latter says that "Pompeius initiated war with the Albani, . . . defeated Arsakis king of Hiberia, . . . gave Armenia to Deoterus, . . . and made Aristarchus king over the people of Colchis. Shortly thereafter he defeated the Ituraei and the Arabs."

55. Eusebius lists this under the 178th Olympiad; the Byzantine chronicle added a Roman perspective from an unknown source. This is not in Eusebius. Jerusalem was taken without

Pompeios, their king, without fighting, for he had compassion on the Jews,[56] and he took the king Aristobulos[57] alone[58] as captive because he had rebelled[59] against the Romans, for he had trusted in Mithridatos after the death of his father,[60] and because of this, the reign of Aristobulos came to an end; this was the fourth *galut* of Jerusalem.[61]

In the year 5470[62] from the creation of the world, in the calculation of the gentiles in 184 of Olympiados,[63] Kleopatra, daughter of Antiochus, king of Aram,[64] ruled for twenty-two years in Miẓrayim. In those days,[65] Kasios, king of Romans, destroyed the cities of Asiah,[66] fought the Jews, captured Jerusalem, and looted the Temple; this was the fifth *galut* of Jerusalem.[67] He also destroyed[68] the island called Rodos and many other islands and many cities.[69] When Iphtolomaios, who was king of Karenen, died,[70] he handed over his kingdom to the Romans.

---

a fight. Eutropius has twelve thousand Jews die in the fighting and the rest allowed to surrender on terms. As is well known, Hyrcanus's supporters opened the gates of the city. The Byzantine chronicle, based on a source that justifies the Roman conquest of Jerusalem, links the "pacific" conquest with the moderation of the conqueror.

56. These are the Albani, whom Eutropius also lists as conquered by Pompey during his eastern march toward Jerusalem. Kolosos may refer to Kolosai in Phrygia, or perhaps one should correct to Colchis, which is mentioned by Eutropius (6.14).

57. These words are lacking in the Parma MS but are preserved in *Yosippon*'s version; the translator/copyist skipped over them.

58. This word is not in Eusebius, nor is Pompey's alleged moderation; there is no reason to assume from this that the "moderate" Pompey did not also take Aristobulus's family.

59. Also not in Eusebius. This information clarifies his captivity to be a result of his alliance with Mithridates, king of Pontus.

60. This datum brings up the question of dating Aristobulus's alliance with Mithridates: (a) the latter's father died in 75–74 (BCE?), and there was no reason for any alliance; (b) in 68; however, Pompey threatened Pontus, which would impel Mithridates to seek alliances. Therefore, we should adjust the text to read "*after* the death of his mother," as Flusser argued, in "Alexander Geste," 18–19; see introduction.

61. The word *galut* here means "conquest"; the third *galut* was by Antiochus Epiphanes.

62. Synkellos dates this in the year 5446 of the Byzantine era.

63. Eusebius has this under the 182nd Olympiad.

64. She was the daughter of King Ptolemy of Egypt, and the Byzantine chronicle confused her with Kleopatra I, who was in fact the daughter of Antiochus, the Seleucid king of Syria.

65. According to Eusebius, Cassius looted the temple in the 184th Olympiad.

66. Not in Eusebius.

67. Not in Eusebius; see note 61 above.

68. Eusebius has this under the 184th Olympiad.

69. Not in Eusebius.

70. Eusebius has this under the 171st Olympiad.

In 185 of Olympiados,[71] Antonios loved Kleopatra, and Antonios ruled in the land of Paras. As he approached Kleopatra, Kleopatra heard and went out to greet him; they went to the land of Tarsos, and he married Kleopatra in Alexandriah; from there he took her to Romi; and he banished his first wife, Octaviah, sister of Kaisar, with her sons from his house. They made war between them, Agustos and this Antonios, because he was angry about his sister; Agustus Kaisar killed Antonios and Kleopatra and her sons Gaios and Kaisaros.[72] This Agustos set[73] Kornelios over Miẓrayim and sent Galos[74] to Romi.[75] Then occurred the battle of Kritim, that is, the island.[76] The kings of Miẓrayim 295 years.[77] In 190 of Olympiados,[78] Herodes ben Antipatros the Ashkeloni became king over the Jews; Agustos seized him,[79] imprisoned him, and sent him to Romi. Augustos went out and seized the land of Kantabres.[80] In 192 of Olympiados,[81] Tiberios, general of the army of Roma, built the city of Tavromeni and Tyndarin.

The first king[82] who ruled in Roma was Ioulios, and he was Gaios; from this one the Romans were strengthened in their kingdom to be mistress of kingdoms.[83] From this one all the kings of Romi were called Kaisaroi, for Romi was

---

71. Synkellos (588) has the same date, whereas Jerome has this in the 186th Olympiad. The story, however, follows the particulars in Synkellos.

72. Neither in Eusebius nor Synkellos; however, the information is substantially correct if we acknowledge that the author mistakenly read his source, which contained Γαίος Καίσαρος ὓιος. Augustus did order that Gaius, Caesar's son by Kleopatra, be killed.

73. According to Eusebius, 187th and 188th Olympiad.

74. The author's error. Cornelius Gallus (one man) was the first Roman governor over Egypt, who committed suicide (in 26 BCE) when Augustus exiled him.

75. No textual support in sources; perhaps the chronicle suggested that he was recalled to Rome to give an account of his tenure in Egypt.

76. Not supported in sources; perhaps this refers to an expedition against the pirates and the incorporation of Crete as a Roman province, which happened about this time.

77. Thus in Eusebius under the 187th Olympiad.

78. Eusebius has this in the 186th Olympiad.

79. Eusebius writes that Herod received his kingship from the Romans; the author was influenced by the exile of Archelous, son of Herod, to Vienna in Gaul.

80. The 190th Olympiad of Eusebius has "the rebelling Κάνταβροι were subdued."

81. This is not based on Eusebius and is a novel addition, to our knowledge. The Hebrew reflects possibly the following of the Byzantine chronicle: τῇ δὲ ρϙβ′ ὀλυμπιάδι Τιβέριος ὁ τῶν Ῥωμαίων στρατιγὸς Ταυρομένιον καὶ Τύνδαριν ᾠκοδόμησεν. This source informs us of the establishment of Colonia Augusta by Tiberius, the Roman general, in two Sicilian cities: Taurominion and Tyndaris. This occurred in the 192nd Olympiad, or 12–9 BCE. Cf. Flusser, "Alexander Geste," vol. 2, 247; see also introduction.

82. Based on Eusebius under the 183rd Olympiad.

83. Synkellos (305) has Επὶ τούτου τὰ Ῥωμαϊκὰ ἤκμασε; the Greek chronicle had apparently ἀπὸ τούτου.

a kingdom twice:[84] once in the days of Latinos and a second time[85] in the days of Ioulios, king of Romi; and Ioulios, the king, made the gentiles' intercalation of the year.[86] This one[87] called [the month] Ab [by] a new name, Ioulios, after his name, and he ruled four years and four months.[88] Agustos Kaisar ruled fifty-six years,[89] and Herodes ruled[90] at Agustos's command for thirty-seven years; he built the Temple[91] that was in Jerusalem, which Antiochos Epiphanes had destroyed; and Herodes built it twofold in its beauty, in width, length, and height. He also built the city of Shomron from the beginning[92] and called its name Sibastin,[93] and its meaning is Kaisaria.[94]

---

84. Not in Eusebius.

85. The Parma MS does not preserve the end of the chronicle and has, "here much is missing." It continues with the section from Palladius, which is in chap. 14. The remainder of the chronicle has been taken from the version in *Yosippon*.

86. This is correct; cf. *Chronicon Paschale* 187c.

87. Cf. Eusebius 184th Olympiad.

88. Eusebius, 183rd Olympiad, has four years and seven months.

89. Jerome, who translated Eusebius's chronicle into Latin, has fifty-six years and six months under the 184th Olympiad. Both Synkellos and Malalas have fifty-six years.

90. Eusebius, 186th Olympiad.

91. Cf. Synkellos 314c; Ἡρώδες τὸν Ἱεροσολύμων ναὸν διπλοῦν ἀνῳκοδόμησεν.

92. Eusebius, 109th Olympiad. See note 42 above.

93. Σεβαστήν, accusative for Σεβαστή-Sebaste, which is the Greek name for Σαμάρια-Samaria (Hebrew Shomron).

94. Eusebius speaks about the founding of Caesarea (which is not identified with Shomron-Sebaste) by Herod under the 192nd Olympiad. This mistake could have been made either by the Byzantine chronicle or by the Hebrew translator or even by the interpolator of this chronicle into *Yosippon*.

14. FRAGMENT FROM A TREATISE ON HODU AND A PASSAGE FROM THE TALMUD

. . . knows her[1] conjugally. And if a woman is barren, her husband crosses over to her for five years;[2] after five years, he divorces her out if she has not conceived. For this reason, the nation of Bragmanoi[3] is not numerous. When the time comes for them to cross over, they cross over in great fear and trembling, for they say that in the same river are creatures so huge that the elephant can enter their throats and also huge crocodiles[4] whose length is sixty cubits.[5] I saw one with my eyes and also ants as huge as a man's hand and scorpions almost a cubit. From fear of these animals, they tremble in their crossing, but in that place they are not seen but rather in other places. Many elephants are in it. This is the way of the Bragmanoi and their homeland and their creatures according to the words of Alexandros from Thebaios.[6]

Again, Alexandros said:[7] "As I was going, I arrived at a certain spring, ate bread and had with me salted *gildana* [fish]; and, as they were being washed, a

---

1. The author leaves a space before these words to indicate that his MS was missing a considerable amount, both the end of the Byzantine chronicle (see chap. 13, note 86) and the beginning of Palladius's little text titled, Περὶ τῶν τῆς Ἰνδίας ἔθνων καὶ τῶν Βραγμάνων. The translation was made either from the Greek or from one of the Latin translations (cf. Flusser, "Alexander Geste," 5–6).
2. Ambrose's and the Bamberg translations have *ad eam transit*.
3. Greek Βράγμανοι (Brahmans).
4. Greek δράκοντες; Latin *dracones*.
5. Both the Greek and Ambrose's translation have seventy cubits, but the Bamberg translation has sixty, as in our text.
6. Greek Θηβαῖος; Latin *Thebaeus*; i.e., a Theban.
7. Cf. b *Tamid* 32b in an interesting version.

sweet smell emanated from them. I said: 'This shows that this well comes from Eden.'" Some say he took some of the water and washed his face. Others say he went with that spring until he came to the opening of Gan Eden and raised his voice: "Open the gate for me." They said to him: "This is the gate of the lord; the righteous shall enter into it." He said: "I too am a king and am considered of some account." They gave him a skull [eyeball]. He went and weighed all his gold and silver against this, but it was not equal to it. He said to the rabbis: "How is this?" They said to him: "A skull of flesh and blood [a man] is never sated as long as it lives." He said to them: "And how do you know this?" They took a little dust and covered it [so it could not see], and immediately it was weighed down by this weight as it is written: "The Nether-world and Destruction are never satisfied, so the eyes of man are never satiated."[8]

DONE

Blessed is the One who gives strength to the weary, and to him without might he increases strength.[9]

COMPLETED

---

8. Cf. Prov 27:20.
9. Cf. Isa 40:29.

SELECT BIBLIOGRAPHY

Adam, Michael, trans. *Josippon*. Zürich, 1546.

Amelander, Menaḥem. *Keter Torah*. Amsterdam, 1743.

Asa, Avraham. *Sēfer Ben Guriōn = (Yosippon): First Ladino Translation*. Constantinople, 1743–44. Edited by Moshe Lazar. Culver City, CA: 2000.

Baer, Yitshak. "The Hebrew Sefer Yosifun." In *Sefer Dinaburg*, edited by Y. Baer, Y. Gutman, and M. Schwab, 178–205. Jerusalem, 1949.

Bell, Albert A. "Josephus and Pseudo-Hegesippus." In *Josephus, the Bible, and History*, edited by Louis H. Feldman and Gohei Hata, 334–39. Detroit, 1989.

Bonfil, Reuven. "Sepher Yosippon: Historia ke-Sifruth." Review of Flusser. *Davar*, September 28, 1981, 12, 13, 14.

Bonfil, Reuven, Oded Irshai, Guy G. Stroumsa, and Rina Talgam, eds. *Jews in Byzantium: Dialectics of Minority and Majority Cultures*. Leiden, 2012.

Börner-Klein, Dagmar, and Beat Zuber, trans. *Josippon*. Wiesbaden, 2010.

Bowman, Steven. "Dates in Sepher Yosippon." In *Pursuing the Text: Studies in Honor of Ben Zion Wacholder on the Occasion of His Seventieth Birthday*, edited by John C. Reeves and John Kampen, 349–59. Sheffield, UK, 1994.

———. "Josephus in Byzantium." In *Josephus, Judaism, and Christianity*, edited by Louis Feldman and Gohei Hata. Detroit, 1987.

———. "A Tenth-Century Byzantine Jewish Historian? A Review of David Flusser's Studies on the Josippon." *Byzantine Studies / Etudes Byzantines* 10 (1983): 133–36.

———. "Yosippon and Jewish Nationalism." *PAAJR* 61 (1995): 23–51.

Breithaupt, Johan Friedrich. *Josephus Hebraicus . . . Libri VI. Juxta editonem Venetam*. Gotha and Leipzig, 1710.

Cohen, Gershon. *The Book of Tradition: (Sefer ha-Qabbalah) by Abraham ibn Da'ud*. Philadelphia, 1967.

Conat, Abraham. *Sepher Josippon* Mantua. 1475–77.

Dönitz, Saskia. "Historiography among Byzantine Jews: The Case of Sefer Yosippon." In *Jews in Byzantium*, edited by Robert Bonfil, Oded Irshai, Guy G. Stroumsa, and Rina Talgam, 951–68. *Dialectics of Minority and Majority Cultures*. Leiden, 2012.

———. "Sefer Yosippon (Josippon)." In *A Companion to Josephus*, edited by Honora Howell Chapman and Zuleika Rodgers, 382–89. Oxford, 2016.

———. *Überlieferung und Rezeption des Sefer Yosippon*. Tübingen, 2013.

Feldman, Louis, and Gohei Hata. *Josephus and Modern Scholarship (1937–1980)*. New York, 1984.

Flusser, David. "The Author of *Sefer Josippon* as Historian." 1973. Reprinted in *Sefer Yosippon*, 28–51. *Hanusah Hamekori*. Jerusalem, 1979.

———. *The Josippon* [*Josephus Gorionides*]. 2 vols. Jerusalem, 1980–81.

———. "Josippon, a Medieval Version of Josephus." In *Josephus, Judaism, and Christianity*, edited by Louis Feldman and Gohei Hata. Detroit, 1987.

———, ed. *Sefer Yosippon*. Hanusah Hamekore. Photo of MS 8°41280 with additions. Jerusalem, 1979.

Gagnier, Johannes. *Yosippon = Josippon, sive Josephi Ben-Gorionis Historiæ Judaicæ libri sex*. Oxford, 1706.

Gaster, Moses. *The Chronicles of Jerahmeel*. Oxford, 1899.

Guenzburg, Baron David. *Yosifun: Kefi defus Mantovah* . . . Berdichev, 1913.

Hominer, Hayyim. *Josiphon of Joseph Ben Gorion ha-Cohen*. 4th ed. Jerusalem, 1978.

Ibn Khaldun. *Abir*. Vol. 2. Translation in progress.

"Josippon." In *The Jewish Encyclopedia*. New York, 1905.

Kamil, Murad. *Zēnā Aihūd (Geschichte der Juden) von Josef ben Gorion (Josippon) nach dem Handschriften herausgegeben*. Glückstadt, 1937.

Leeming, Henry, and Katherine Leeming, eds. *Josephus' "Jewish War" and Its Slavonic Version*. Leiden, 2003.

Morvyn, Peter. *A Compendious and Moste Marveylous History of the Latter Times of the Jewes Commune Weale*. London, 1558; reprinted in Boston, 1713; Vermont, 1819; Worcester, MA, 1805.

Muenster, Sebastian. *Josephus Hebraicus*. Basle, 1541.

Pollard, Richard M. "The De Excidio of 'Hegesippus' and the Reception of Josephus in the Early Middle Ages." *Viator* 46 (2015): 65–100.

Reiner, Jacob. "The Original Hebrew Yosippon in The Chronicles of Jerahmeel." *JQR* 60 (1969): 128–46.

Sela, Shulamit. *The Arabic Josippon*. 2 vols. Jerusalem, 2009.

———. "Josippon." In *Medieval Jewish Civilization. An Encyclopedia*, edited by Norman Roth, 377–80. London, 2013.

Tam ibn Yahya. *Sepher Yosippon*. Constantinople, 1510.

Vehlow, Katja. *Dorot Olam: A Critical Edition and Translation of Abraham Ibn Daud's Universal History*. New York, 2013.

Vollandt, Ronnie. "Ancient Jewish Historiography in Arabic Garb: Sepher Josippon between Southern Italy and Coptic Cairo." *Zutot* 11 (2014): 70–80.

Wellhausen, Julius. *Der arabische Josippus*. Berlin, 1897.

Yassif, Eli, ed. *Sefer ha-zikhronot hu divre ha-yamim le-yerahmi'el* [*The Book of Memory That Is the Chronicles of Jerahme'el*]. Tel Aviv, 2001.

SOURCES INDEX

HEBREW BIBLE

GENESIS

2:18 166	14:10 . . . . 127, 187n2, 272	27:33 . . . . 389n8
5:29 440	14:14 . . . . 14n45	30:30 . . . . 9n14
7:33 . . . . 376n2	14:15 . . . . .79, 95	30:34 25
8:4 . . . . 386n7	6:10 208	36:11 . . . . 8n10
9:25 5	19:3 187	37:11 46
10 . . . . .275n10	22 . . . . 239n4	40:10 . . . . 12, 55n19
10:4 5	25:3 . . . . 283n2	41:5 . . . . 245n7
11:8–9 . . . . 7n1	25:23 336	41:38 . . . . 26n2, 30
12:1 . . . . 173n2	25:31 283	50:17 52
14:5 79	26:14 . . . . 138n5	

EXODUS

4:24 . . . . 51n2	18:14–27 . . . . 19n2	19:6 . . . . 387n4
14:21 . . . . 129n2	18:16 19	19:11 92
14:26 338	18:18 19	23:5 163
14:27 . . . . .468n48	18:19 19	32:32 289
18:8 235	18:21 278	33:26 73
18:11 17	18:22 . . . . 19n3	

LEVITICUS

10:15 . . . . 30n2	19:18 318	26:37 338
12:7 123	21:9 . . . . .413n37	26:44 47
13:51 291	25:46 . . . . 51n1	

NUMBERS

1:51 . . . . .214n16	8:11 . . . . 30n2	17:23 328
3:10 . . . . .214n16	10:8–10 79	18:19 76
3:38 . . . . .214n16	16:21 341	22:4 . . . . 254n8
5:25 . . . . 30n2	16:22 205	22:34 52
6:4 213		

APOCRYPHA

NEW TESTAMENT

RABBINIC LITERATURE

BERAKHOTH

54a. 290n1

SHABBAT

116a. . . . . .402n12   200 . . . . .402n12

YOMA

23a. . . . . .213n11   69 . . . . .52nn4–5

TA'ANIT

52nn4–5, 52n7   4, 6. . . . . 396n6

SOTAH

8 . . . . .76n14, 278n6   33b . . . . 114n6   47a. 410n10

BABA BATRA

3b 180n8, 211n1

SANHEDRIN

97a. 208   107b. 410n10

TAMID

369nn4, 6   32a–b 449nn7, 13   32b 448

GENESIS RABBAH

65:27 . . . . 269n6

TARGUM YONATAN

389n8

PESIKTA RABBATI

67n1

ALPHABET OF BEN SIRA

450, 451

CHRONICLE OF JERAHMEEL

5n24, 41n1, 393n1, 450n16

DIKDUKE SOFRIM

402n12

RASHI

11n30, 17n3, 146n7, 211n1, 213n11

TOLDOTH YESHU

409n2, 410n10

GREEK AND LATIN LITERATURE

HIPPOLYTUS
22n7

JEROME
13n43, 63n2, 273n5, 274n6, 400nn15–16, 496n71, 496n89

MACROBIUS
294n8, 385n5

OROSIUS
41n4, 42n5

PHILO
De agricultura, 400n14; De Alexandro et quod propriam rationem muta habeant, 400n13; De confusione linguarum, 399n3; De gigantibus, 399n9; De mutatione nominum, 399n6; De natura et inventione nominum, 399n4; De pactis libri duo, 399n7; De tabernaculo, 400n11; De victimis, 400n11; De viris illustribus, 399n1; De vita sapientis, 399n8; Exordium, 275n10; On the Jews (De Iudaeis), 400n12; Quaestionum et solutionem in Exodum Libri quinque, 400n11; That Dreams Are Sent by God, 400n10

ROYAL FRANKISH ANNALS

MANUSCRIPTS

JERUSALEM MANUSCRIPT
55n18, 84n5, 388n6

KAUFMAN MANUSCRIPT
35n8, 54n13, 403

GENERAL INDEX